Connect *empowers* students.

Connect builds student confidence outside of class with adaptive technology that pinpoints exactly what a student knows and what she doesn't. With SmartBook, study time is as productive and efficient as possible. It identifies and closes knowledge gaps through a continually adapting reading experience that provides personalized learning resources at the precise moment of need. This ensures that every minute spent with SmartBook is returned to the student as the most value-added minute possible. The result? More confidence, better grades, and greater success.

Students are presented with learning resources when relevant to reinforce important concepts at the precise moment they need help.

When engaged with SmartBook's adaptive reading experience, students are guided toward textbook content that has the maximum learning impact every time they study.

Connect *simplifies* everyday life.

Put students first with Connect's new, intuitive mobile interface, which gives students and instructors flexible and convenient, anytime-anywhere access to all components of the Connect platform. It provides seamless integration of learning tools and places the most important priorities upfront in a new to-do list with a calendar view across all Connect courses. Enjoy on-the-go access with the new mobile interface designed for optimal use of tablet functionality.

Insight is Connect's new, one-of-a-kind visual analytics dashboard—now available for both instructors and students—that provides at-a-glance information regarding student performance, which is immediately actionable. Get an instant perspective on what's happening in class with the tap of a finger.

With **Connect**, the educational possibilities are **limitless**.

SOCIOLOGY

and Your Life
with
P.O.W.E.R. Learning

Richard T. Schaefer
DePaul University

Robert S. Feldman
University of Massachusetts, Amherst

McGraw Hill Education

SOCIOLOGY AND YOUR LIFE WITH P.O.W.E.R. LEARNING
Published by McGraw-Hill Education, 2 Penn Plaza, New York, NY 10121. Copyright © 2016 by McGraw-Hill Education. All rights reserved. Printed in the United States of America. No part of this publication may be reproduced or distributed in any form or by any means, or stored in a database or retrieval system, without the prior written consent of McGraw-Hill Education, including, but not limited to, in any network or other electronic storage or transmission, or broadcast for distance learning.

Some ancillaries, including electronic and print components, may not be available to customers outside the United States.

This book is printed on acid-free paper.

1 2 3 4 5 6 7 8 9 0 QVS/QVS 1 0 9 8 7 6 5

ISBN 978-1-25-9299568
MHID 1-25-9299562

Senior Vice President, Products & Markets: *Kurt L. Strand*
Vice President, General Manager, Products & Markets: *Michael Ryan*
Vice President, Content Design & Delivery: *Kimberly Meriwether David*
Managing Director: *Gina Boedeker*
Brand Manager: *Courtney Austermehle*
Director, Product Development: *Meghan Campbell*
Lead Product Developer: *Rhona Robbin*
Product Developer: *Briana Porco*
Director, Content Design & Delivery: *Terri Schiesl*
Digital Product Analyst: *John Brady*
Marketing Manager: *Kimberli Brownlee*
Program Manager: *Marianne Musni*
Content Project Managers: *Rick Hecker/Emily Kline*
Buyer: *Jennifer Pickel*
Design: *Debra Kubiak*
Content Licensing Specialists: *John Leland/Lorraine Buczek*
Cover Image: 1. (c) Hero Images Inc./ Alamy; 2. Ablestock.com/Getty Images; 3. George Doyle/Getty Images; 4. Photodisc/Superstock; 5. Getty Images; 6. Getty Images; 7. Pixtal/AGE Fotostock; 8. Steve Debenport/Getty Images; 9. (c)Hill Street Studios/Blend Images LLC; 10. Priscilla Gragg/Getty Images; 11. Getty Images; 12. Abel Mitja Varela/Getty Images; 13. Monkey Business Images Ltd/Getty Images; 14. (c)Dave and Lee Jacobs/Blend Images LLC; 15. AMV Photo/Getty Images; 16. (c)Image Source, all rights reserved.
Compositor: *Laserwords Private Limited*
Printer: *Quad/Graphics*

All credits appearing on page or at the end of the book are considered to be an extension of the copyright page.

Library of Congress Cataloging-in-Publication Data

Schaefer, Richard T.
    Sociology and your life with P.O.W.E.R. learning / Richard T. Schaefer.
        pages cm
    Summary: "Connect is the only integrated learning system that empowers students by continuously adapting to deliver precisely what they need, when they need it, and how they need it, so that your class time is more engaging and effective"— Provided by publisher.
    Summary: "*Sociology: A Brief Introduction* highlights the distinctive ways in which sociologists examine human social behavior, as well as the ways in which research findings contribute to our understanding of society. In doing so, it helps students to think like sociologists and to apply sociological theories and concepts to human interactions and institutions. In other words, *Sociology: A Brief Introduction* gives students the tools they need to take sociology with them when they graduate from college, begin to pursue careers, and become involved in their communities and the world at large"— Provided by publisher.
    ISBN 978-1-259-29956-8 (paperback)
    1. Sociology. I. Feldman, Robert. II. Title.
    HM586.S333 2015
    301—dc23
                                                                            2015005437

The Internet addresses listed in the text were accurate at the time of publication. The inclusion of a website does not indicate an endorsement by the authors or McGraw-Hill Education, and McGraw-Hill Education does not guarantee the accuracy of the information presented at these sites.

mheducation.com/highered

About the Authors

RICHARD T. SCHAEFER is Professor of Sociology at DePaul University. Growing up in Chicago, his early interest in social issues caused him to gravitate to sociology courses at Northwestern University, where he eventually received a B.A. in sociology, and at the University of Chicago, where he completed his M.A. and Ph.D. In 2004 he was named to the Vincent DePaul Professorship in recognition of his undergraduate teaching and scholarship. He has taught introductory sociology for over 35 years to students in colleges, adult education programs, nursing programs, and even a maximum-security prison.

Dr. Schaefer is the author of the thirteenth edition of *Sociology* (McGraw-Hill, 2012); *Sociology: A Brief Introduction,* eleventh edition (McGraw-Hill, 2015); and *Sociology in Modules,* third edition (McGraw-Hill, 2015). He is also the author of *Racial and Ethnic Groups,* now in its fourteenth edition (2014), *Racial and Ethnic Diversity in the USA* (first edition, 2014), and *Race and Ethnicity in the United States*, seventh edition (2013), all published by Pearson. Together with William Zellner, he coauthored the ninth edition of *Extraordinary Groups,* published by Worth in 2011. Dr. Schaefer served as the general editor of the three-volume *Encyclopedia of Race, Ethnicity, and Society,* published by Sage in 2008. These books have been translated into Chinese, Japanese, Portuguese, and Spanish, as well as adapted for use in Canadian colleges.

Dr. Schaefer's articles and book reviews have appeared in many journals, including *American Journal of Sociology; Phylon: A Review of Race and Culture; Contemporary Sociology; Sociology and Social Research; Sociological Quarterly;* and *Teaching Sociology.* He served as president of the Midwest Sociological Society in 1994–1995.

ROBERT S. FELDMAN is Professor of Psychological and Brain Science and Deputy Chancellor of the University of Massachusetts, Amherst. A recipient of the College Distinguished Teacher Award, he has taught classes ranging in size from 10 to nearly 500 students.

A Fellow of the American Psychological Association, the Association for Psychological Science, and the American Association for the Advancement of Science, Professor Feldman received a B.A. with high honors from Wesleyan University and an M.S. and Ph.D. from the University of Wisconsin–Madison. He is a winner of a Fulbright Senior Research Scholar and Lecturer Award and the Distinguished Alumnus Award from Wesleyan. He is president of the Federation of Associations in Behavioral and Brain Sciences (FABBS) Foundation, which advocates for the field of psychology.

He has written and edited more than 150 books, book chapters, and scientific articles. He has edited *Improving the First Year of College: Research and Practice*, and is author of *Understanding Psychology*, twelfth edition; *Psychology and Your Life*, second edition; and *P.O.W.E.R. Learning: Strategies for Success in College and Life*, sixth edition. His textbooks, which have been used by more than 2 million students around the world, have been translated into Spanish, French, Portuguese, Dutch, German, Italian, Chinese, Korean, and Japanese. His research interests include deception and honesty in everyday life, work that he described in *The Liar in Your Life*, a trade book published in 2009.

Professor Feldman loves music, is an enthusiastic pianist, and enjoys cooking and traveling. He serves on the Board of New England Public Radio. He has three children and two young grandsons. He and his wife, a psychologist, live in western Massachusetts in a home overlooking the Holyoke mountain range.

Brief Contents

Contents

1 Understanding Sociology   1

2 Sociological Research   30

10 Stratification by Gender   296

11 The Family and Human Sexuality   324

12 Health and the Environment   357

13 Education   393

14 Social Change in the Global Community 418

SUPPLEMENTAL E-BOOK CHAPTERS AVAILABLE IN CONNECT

15 Global Inequality 448

Boxed Features

Social Policy Sections

Maps

Tracking Sociological Perspectives Tables

Summing Up Tables

Taking Sociology with You . . . Wherever You Go!

Why Does Sociology Matter?

Whether you're a first-time student, returning to the classroom, or even an instructor leading a discussion, you've probably thought about that question. Sociologists examine what we think we know about society, from small-scale interactions to the broadest social change, which can be daunting for any student to take in. Living up to its name, *Sociology and Your Life with P.O.W.E.R. Learning* bridges the essential sociological theories, research, and concepts and the everyday realities we all experience. The program highlights the distinctive ways in which sociologists explore human social behavior—and how their research findings can be used to help us think critically about the broader principles that guide our lives. In doing so, it helps students to begin to think like sociologists, using what they have learned to evaluate human interactions and institutions independently. What do a police officer, a nurse, and a local business owner need to know about the community they serve? It turns out quite a lot. And *Sociology and Your Life* is poised to give students the tools they need to take sociology with them as they pursue careers and get involved in their communities and the world at large.

Why Students First?

Sociology and Your Life is designed to introduce readers to the field of sociology—no matter the reason for enrolling in the course—and to do so in a way that will nurture students' curiosity for a lifetime. The core content is oriented to students, with features and examples that apply sociology to their daily lives. The modular format, structured around learning objectives, allows students to study material in manageable chunks, with ample pedagogical support within the P.O.W.E.R. framework. The digital tools within Connect foster student preparedness before class for a more productive and engaging experience in class. These key elements of *Sociology and Your Life* add up to a program that promotes student success in college and beyond.

Why P.O.W.E.R. Learning?

A major challenge in introductory courses is that students at this level struggle with basic study skills and habits. It can be difficult to become a good student if you were never taught how to study effectively. And often, instructors don't have the time, the resources, or the expertise to teach success skills AND sociological concepts. The author team of Schaefer and Feldman offer a guided approach to meet this challenge. The P.O.W.E.R. Learning Framework was developed by Bob Feldman—psychologist, student success instructor, researcher, and author. It is a method for accomplishing any task using five simple and consistent steps: Prepare. Organize. Work. Evaluate. Rethink. This framework is integrated at every level of the text to help students learn sociological concepts while developing habits that will serve them well throughout their college careers and in their daily lives.

Key Features of *Sociology and Your Life with POWER Learning*

Help Your Students Succeed with Connect Sociology

Connect Sociology includes assignable and assessable quizzes, exercises, and interactive activities, all associated with learning objectives for *Sociology and Your Life*. Videos, interactive assessments, and scenario-based activities engage students and add real-world perspective to the introductory sociology course. In addition, printable, exportable reports show how well each student or section is performing on each course segment.

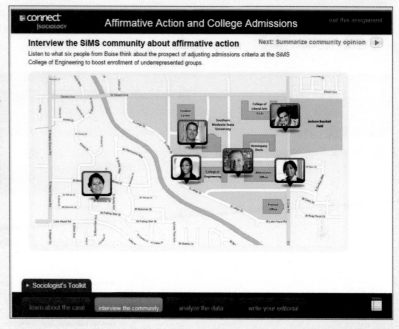

Provide a Smarter Text and Better Value with SmartBook

Boost student success with **SmartBook**—the first, and only, adaptive reading and study experience that highlights content based on what the individual student knows and doesn't know, and then provides focused help through targeted learning resources (including videos, animations, and other interactivities). SmartBook's intuitive technology optimizes student study time by creating a personalized learning path for improved course performance and overall student success.

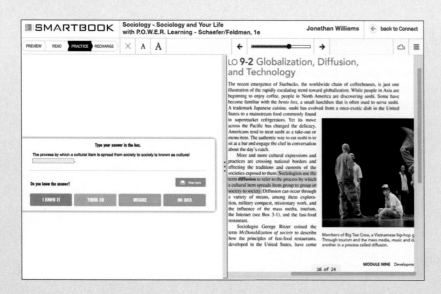

Access Performance Data Just in Time

Connect Insight is Connect's new one-of-a-kind visual analytics dashboard—now available for both instructors and students—that provides at-a-glance information regarding student performance, which is immediately actionable. By presenting assignment, assessment, and topical performance results together with a time metric that is easily visible for aggregate or individual results, Connect Insight gives the user the ability to take a just-in-time approach to teaching and learning, which was never before available. Connect Insight presents data that empowers students and helps instructors improve class performance in a way that is efficient and effective.

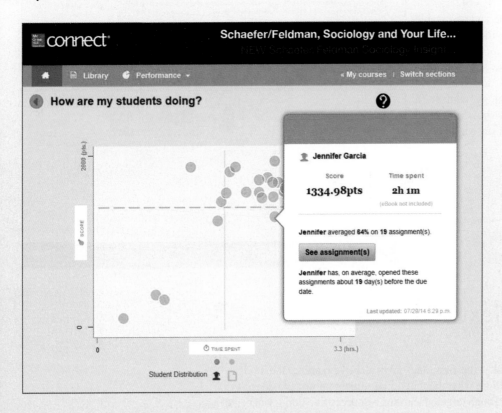

Make It Your Own

TM Design your own ideal course materials with McGraw-Hill's **Create** at www.mcgrawhillcreate.com. Rearrange or omit chapters, combine material from other sources, and upload your syllabus—or any other content you have written—to make the perfect resources for your students. Search thousands of leading McGraw-Hill textbooks to find the best content for your students, then arrange it to fit your teaching style. You can even personalize your book's appearance by selecting the cover and adding your name, school, and course information. When you order a Create book, you will receive a complimentary review copy (eComp) via email within about an hour. Register today at www.mcgrawhillcreate.com and craft your course resources to match the way you teach.

Modular format Each chapter is organized into modules that allow students to study material in smaller, more manageable chunks. Each module is self-contained with learning objectives and an outline at the start to help a student prepare for what's to come, and questions, summary points, and key terms to help them review.

E Evaluate

Read each question carefully and then select or provide the best answer.

1. The specialized language that subcultures employ as a way to create cohesion and a unique identity is called
   a. bilingualism.
   b. an argot.
   c. slang.
   d. an in-language.

2. Terrorist groups are examples of
   a. cultural universals.
   b. subcultures.

MODULE 10 Cultural Variation

P Prepare Learning Objectives

LO 10-1 Explain patterns of variation within cultures, including subcultures and countercultures.
LO 10-2 Describe the phenomenon of culture shock.
LO 10-3 Analyze through a sociological lens the implications of bilingualism on social policy.

O Organize Module Outline

Cultural Variation within Societies
    Subcultures
    Countercultures
    Culture Shock
Social Policy and Culture
    Studying Bilingualism

R Rethink

Consider these questions to get a deeper understanding of the material.

1. To what subcultures do you belong? How do they function in relation to the larger society?

2. Why do people experience culture shock? What does this reveal about the role of culture and of everyday customs?

RECAP

LO 10-1 **Explain patterns of variation within cultures, including subcultures and countercultures.**

- A subculture is a segment of society that shares customs, rules, and traditions that differ from those of the larger society. Members of a subculture even have a specialized language, called an argot, that distinguishes them from nonmembers.
- Countercultures are subcultures that deliberately oppose aspects of the larger culture.

LO 10-2 **Describe the phenomenon of culture shock.**

- The feeling of disorientation and dislocation experienced by people who are suddenly immersed in an unfamiliar culture is called culture shock.
- Culture shock can be a two-way street: the host culture may shock the individual, and the individual's cultural mannerisms may shock the host culture.

LO 10-3 **Analyze through a sociological lens the implications of bilingualism on social policy.**

- The social policy of bilingualism refers to the use of two languages in a setting, treating each as equally legitimate. It is supported by those who want to ease the transition of non-native-language speakers into a host society, but opposed by those who emphasize the importance of a single cultural tradition and language.
- Concern about immigrant families in the United States using their native languages instead of English is overblown. Immigrant populations generally follow the pattern by which younger family members quickly become fluent in English, and as time passes, a clear preference for using English emerges naturally.

KEY TERMS

Argot Specialized language used by members of a group or subculture.
Bilingualism The use of two languages in a particular setting, such as the workplace or schoolroom, treating each language as equally legitimate.
Counterculture A subculture that deliberately opposes certain aspects of the larger culture.
Culture shock The feeling of surprise and disorientation that people experience when they encounter cultural practices that are different from their own.
Subculture A segment of society that shares a distinctive pattern of customs, rules, and traditions that differs from the pattern of the larger society.

Sociology at **WORK** PEACE CORPS VOLUNTEER

JOHN EGAMI, a Peace Corps volunteer in Kampala, Uganda, works in elementary schools to develop literacy programs that will encourage students to read outside the classroom. "Ugandans, by tradition, are not readers," he explains. "It's rare for parents to read to their child, and the kids only learn to read enough to pass their exams."

His early efforts to get the children excited about reading met with polite disinterest. Then the holidays came and everyone went back to their native villages to celebrate with parents and grandparents. They returned with mountains of stories about their families and the holiday celebrations. Egami got an idea. He recorded all of the children's stories. The kids listened to them over and over. Listening with them, Egami clearly recognized the rich oral tradition of his students. They were skilled storytellers. If he wanted to get them to love reading, he was going to have to forge a link between their culture of oral expression and his reading goals for them. He transcribed the students' stories and printed them out. The kids loved these books, and they took delight in arguing over the shape and meaning of words. Egami's willingness to understand the Ugandans' culture had opened a window for his students to recognize the value of books and reading. ∎

Looking Ahead

IN THIS CHAPTER WE WILL SEE JUST HOW BASIC THE STUDY OF CULTURE is to sociology. Our discussion will focus both on general cultural practices found in all societies and on the wide variations that can distinguish one society from another. We will define and explore the major aspects of culture, including language, norms, sanctions, and values. We will see how cultures develop a dominant ideology, and how functionalist and conflict theorists view culture. And we'll study the development of culture around the world, including the cultural effects of the worldwide movement toward globalization. Finally, in the Social Policy section, we will look at the conflicts in cultural values that underlie current debates over bilingualism.

Sociology at Work The profiles offer short sketches of successful students who use the principles of sociology in their professional lives.

Looking Ahead These sections introduce the key concepts of each chapter, connecting the modules contained within it.

P.O.W.E.R. Study Strategies Using the P.O.W.E.R. framework, these boxes present steps for mastering the different skills students need to succeed in their introductory sociology course, such as notetaking, time management, and test-taking.

emPOWERme Sections at the end of each chapter revisit the P.O.W.E.R. Study Strategies, giving students a checklist to evaluate how well they have incorporated positive habits recommended to master that skill.

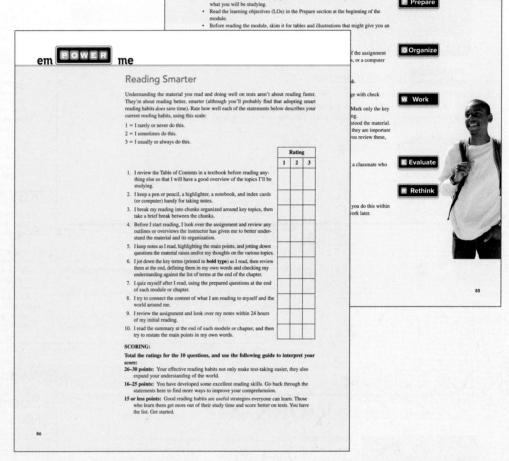

Additional Features

 Study Alert These marginal features offer advice and hints for students, signaling when critical concepts are presented and offering suggestions for learning those concepts effectively.

 Research Today These boxes present new sociological findings on topics such as sports, social networks, and transracial adoption.

 From the Perspective of . . . This feature highlights how sociology impacts a variety of professions. Whether students are in an allied health, nursing, criminal justice, technology, business, legal studies, or any other type of program, they can learn to make concrete connections between sociology and their chosen career.

 Sociology in the Global Community These boxes provide a global perspective on topics such as stratification, marriage, and the women's movement.

 Social Policy sections These end-of-chapter sections apply sociological concepts and theories to important social issues currently being debated by policymakers and the general public.

 Maps Mapping Life Nationwide and Mapping Life Worldwide maps show social trends in the United States as well as in the global community.

 Case Studies These scenarios at the end of each chapter allow students to apply sociological concepts and critical thought to a story or real-life situation.

Teaching Resources

Instructor's Manual. The instructor's manual incorporates tips for both new and experienced instructors and includes learning objectives, brief and detailed chapter outlines, chapter summaries, lecture outlines, lecture ideas, and topics for class discussion.

Test Bank. This resource offers multiple-choice, true/false, and essay questions for each chapter. McGraw-Hill's computerized EZ Test allows instructors to create customized exams using the publisher-supplied test items or instructors' own questions.

PowerPoint Slides. The PowerPoint slides include bulleted lecture points, figures, and maps. They can be used as is or modified to meet the needs of individual instructors.

These instructor resources can be accessed through the Library tab in Connect.

McGraw-Hill Campus is a first-of-its-kind institutional service that provides faculty with true, single sign-on access to all of McGraw-Hill's course content, digital tools, and other high-quality learning resources from any learning management system (LMS). This innovative offering allows secure, deep integration and seamless access to any of our course solutions, including Connect, LearnSmart, Create, and Tegrity. McGraw-Hill Campus covers our entire content library, including eBooks, assessment tools, presentation slides, and multimedia content, among other resources. This open and unlimited service allows faculty to quickly prepare for class, create tests or quizzes, develop lecture material, integrate interactive content, and much more.

Acknowledgments

From the Authors

The authors would like to thank many people at McGraw-Hill. We are grateful to Brand Manager Courtney Austermehle who was the driving force behind this book and making it come to fruition, along with strong support and encouragement from Managing Director, Gina Boedeker. We are both thrilled to be working again on a project with Lead Product Developer, Rhona Robbin. Rhona has taught us a considerable amount about good writing over the years, and both of us have benefited from her deft touch. In addition, working with Development Editor, Barbara Heinssen, has proven to be a pleasure. Her work ethic and expertise were considerable, and the team came to trust her instincts implicitly.

Finally, Briana Porco, Product Developer, Kimberli Brownlee, Marketing Manager, Stacy Ruel, Executive Market Development Manager, Marianne Musni, Program Manager, Rick Hecker, Lead Content Project Manager, Debra Kubiak, Senior Designer, John Brady, Senior Digital Product Analyst, and Diane Grayson, Brand Coordinator, also played significant roles in developing the project and bringing it to fruition. We are proud to be part of this world-class McGraw-Hill team.

From Richard Schaefer

As is evident from these acknowledgments, the preparation of a textbook is truly a collaborative effort. The most valuable member of this effort continues to be my wife, Sandy. She provides the support so necessary in my creative and scholarly activities.

I have had the good fortune to introduce students to sociology for many years. These students have been enormously helpful in spurring on my sociological imagination. In ways I can fully appreciate but cannot fully acknowledge, their questions in class and queries in the hallway have found their way into this work.

From Robert Feldman

I am thrilled to have worked with Rick Schaefer on this P.O.W.E.R. adaptation of Rick's seminal sociology title. I am glad to be able to collaborate with Rick in creating a book that incorporates the P.O.W.E.R. framework and study skills with the foundational content of the discipline of sociology. When I was training to be a social psychologist in graduate school, I took a number of sociology courses, and I am pleased to get back to my sociology roots with this book.

I would like to thank some of the senior folks in the company who made this book possible. Mike Ryan and Corey Reeves are both consummate strategic thinkers and good friends, and I thank them for helping to make it a reality.

At the end of the day, I would like to thank my terrific family. My wife, Kathy, sons, Jon and Josh, daughter, Sarah, daughters-in-law, Leigh and Julie, son-in-law, Jeff, and of course, my terrific grandkids, Alex and Miles, are the joy of my life. I thank them all with lots of love.

Academic Reviewers

This current edition has benefited from constructive and thorough evaluations provided by sociologists from both two-year and four-year institutions.

Dawn Aliberti, *Cleveland State University*

Angie Andrus, *Fullerton College*

Andrew J. Bark, *Mt. San Antonio College*

Georgia Bianchi, *University of Florida*

Annette Chamberlin, *Virginia Western Community College*

Tamu Chambers, *Hudson Valley Community College*

Margaret Choka, *Pellissippi State Community College*

Ronald Ferguson, *Ridgewater College*

Mark J. Guillette, *Valencia Community College*

Marta Henriksen, *Central New Mexico Community College*

Kathy Hipp, *Daniel Webster College*

John P. Hutchinson, *Community College of Baltimore County*

Robert Janiszewski, *Bryant & Stratton College, Albany*

Laura Johnson, *Southeast Missouri State University*

Nicole Jolly, *Delgado Community College*

Jason J. Leiker, *Utah State University*

Royal Loresco, *South Texas College*

Victor A. Martini, *Schenectady Community College*

Melinda Messineo, *Ball State University*

Daniel W. Milligan, *University of South Carolina, Salkehatchie*

Heidi Morehead, *New River Community College*

Kelly Mosel-Talavera, *Texas State University, San Marcos*

Wendy North-Ollendorf, *Northwestern Connecticut Community College*

James Peterson, *Tidewater Community College–Norfolk*

Robert Reed, *Tarrant County College*

Latasha Sarpy, *Bunker Hill Community College*

Paula J. Snyder, *Chaffey College*

Brooke Strahn-Koller, *Kirkwood Community College*

Vicki Tankersley, *Mercer University*

Kenrick Thompson, *Central New Mexico Community College*

Connect Consultants

The creation of *Connect Sociology* has been a highly collaborative effort. Thank you to the following for their guidance, insight, and innovative suggestions.

Douglas Adams, *University of Arkansas*

Paul Calarco, *Hudson Valley Community College*

Susan Ciriello, *Northern Virginia Community College*

Susan Cody-Rydzewski, *Georgia Perimeter College*

Lisa Coole, *Bridgewater College*

Gianna Durso Finley, *Mercer County Community College*

Ike Eberstein, *Florida State University*

Richard Ellefritz, *Oklahoma State University*

Carmon Hicks, *Ivy Tech Community College*

Curt Hosier, *Indiana University–Purdue University, Fort Wayne*

Erica Hunter, *University at Albany*

Jennifer Jacobson, *Yavapai College*

Marjorie Jolles, *Roosevelt University*

Jenny Kosinski, *Rock Valley College*

Terina Lathe, *Central Piedmont Community College*

Royal Loresco, *South Texas College*

Michael Loukinen, *Northern Michigan University*

Lori Maida, *Westchester Community College*

Melinda Messineo, *Ball State University*

Narayan Persaud, *Florida A&M University*

Sharon Placide, *Florida Atlantic University*

Matthew Reynolds, *College of Southern Idaho*

Olga Rowe, *Oregon State University*

Alan Rudy, *Central Michigan University*

Latasha Sarpy, *Bunker Hill Community College*

Megan Seely, *Sierra College*

Tomecia Sobers, *Fayetteville Tech Community College*

Karrie A. Snyder, *Northwestern University*

Rose Suggett, *Southeast Community College*

Margaret Taylor, *Greenville Technical College*

Lisa Weinberg, *Florida State University*

Connect Contributors

These instructors contributed their time, thought, and creativity to make our vision for *Connect Sociology* a reality. Thank you to the following content authors.

Russell Davis, *University of West Alabama*

Shelly Dutchin, *Western Technical College*

Lois Easterday, *Onondaga Community College*

Samuel Echevarria-Cruz, *Austin Community College*

Tammie Foltz, *Des Moines Area Community College*

Kimberly K. Hennessee, *Ball State University*

Curt Hosier, *Indiana University–Purdue University, Fort Wayne*

Marjorie Jolles, *Roosevelt University*

Thomas Kersen, *Jackson State University*

Jenny Kosinski, *Rock Valley College*

Laura Johnson, *Southeast Missouri State University*

David Locher, *Missouri Southern State University*

Linda Lombard, *Embry-Riddle Aeronautical University*

Kevin Parent, *Point Park University*

Tommy Sadler, *Union University*

Denise Shuster, *Owens Community College*

Rachel Stehle, *Cuyahoga Community College*

John C. Tenuto, *College of Lake County*

Marie Wallace, *Pima Community College*

Sally Vyain, *Ivy Tech Community College*

Symposium Attendees

Every year McGraw-Hill conducts several Introductory Sociology symposia for instructors from across the country. These events offer a forum for instructors to exchange ideas and experiences with colleagues they might not have the chance to meet otherwise. They also provide an opportunity for members of the McGraw-Hill team to learn about the needs and challenges of the Introductory Sociology course for both instructors and students. The feedback we have received has been invaluable and contributed—directly and indirectly—to this edition of *Sociology and Your Life:*

Linda Barker, *Coconino Community College*

Edward Brent, *University of Missouri, Columbia*

Mary Burbach-Cooper, *Metropolitan Community College*

Julio Caycedo, *Metropolitan Community College*

Margaret Choka, *Pellissippi State Community College*

Glynis Christine, *Austin Community College*

Margarita Decierdo, *Austin Community College*

Brian Donovan, *University of Kansas*

Richard Ellefritz, *Oklahoma State University*

Kellie Hagewen, *College of Southern Nevada*

Carmon Hicks, *Ivy Tech Community College*

Curt Hosier, *Indiana University–Purdue University, Fort Wayne*

Mark Kassop, *Bergen Community College*

Jenny Kosinski, *Rock Valley College*

Traci Minnick, *Triton College*

Irene Petten, *Columbus State Community College*

Paul Prew, *Minnesota State University, Mankato*

Matthew Reynolds, *College of Southern Idaho*

Paul Schnorr, *Northeast Wisconsin Technical College*

Tiffanye Sledge, *Tidewater Community College*

Erica Smith, *Northern Virginia Community College*

Rose Suggett, *Southeast Community College*

Dawn Tawwater, *Austin Community College*

Margaret Taylor, *Greenville Technical College*

Sharon Wiederstein, *Blinn College*

KC Williams, *Coastal Carolina Community College*

Mary Young-Marcks, *Southwestern Michigan College*

To the Students

Making the Grade: A Practical Guide to Studying Effectively

If you're reading this page, you're probably taking an introductory sociology course. Maybe you're studying sociology because you've always been interested in the interplay between individuals and society. Or maybe you have no idea what sociology is all about, but it's a required course. Whatever your reason for taking the course, it's a safe bet that you're interested in maximizing your understanding of the material and getting a good grade. And you want to do it as quickly and efficiently as possible.

Good news! You're taking the right course, and you're learning the right material. Researchers who study learning have identified a variety of guidelines and techniques that will help you learn and remember material. We'll apply these guidelines to your sociology class—but they apply to every other class you'll take in your college career. Good students are made, not born, and these suggestions will help you become an all-around better student.

Adopt the P.O.W.E.R. Learning Study Strategy

Let's begin with a brief consideration of a study strategy, applicable to all of your courses, including introductory sociology. Psychologists have created several excellent (and proven) techniques for improving study skills, one of which frames the content of this program: **P.O.W.E.R.—P**repare, **O**rganize, **W**ork, **E**valuate, **R**ethink. By employing the P.O.W.E.R. framework, you can increase your ability to learn and retain information and to think critically in all of your classes.

The P.O.W.E.R. learning strategy—which is built into this textbook—systematizes the acquisition of new material by providing a learning framework. It stresses the importance of learning outcomes and appropriate preparation before you begin to study, as well as the significance of self-evaluation and the incorporation of critical thinking into the learning process. Specifically, use of the P.O.W.E.R. learning system entails the following steps:

- *Prepare.* Before starting any journey, we need to know where we are headed. Academic journeys are no different; we need to know what our goals are. The *Prepare* stage consists of thinking about what we hope to gain from both the course as a whole (a long-term goal) and reading a specific section of the text by identifying specific goals that we seek to accomplish (a short-term goal). In *Sociology and Your Life,* these goals are listed as Learning Objectives at the beginning of every module and are indicated by a Prepare icon.

- *Organize.* Once we know what our goals are, we can develop a route to accomplish those goals. The *Organize* stage involves developing a mental road map of where we are headed. Read the outline at the beginning of each chapter and the start of each module, indicated by an Organize icon, to get an idea of what major topics and concepts are covered and how they are organized.

- *Work.* The key to the P.O.W.E.R. learning system is actually reading and studying the material presented in the book. Completing the *Work* will be more manageable because, if you have carried out the steps in the previous stages, you'll know where

you're headed and how you'll get there. Remember, the main text isn't the only material that you need to read and think about. It's also important to read the boxes and the marginal study alerts in order to gain a full understanding of the material. In the text, Work is indicated by a Work icon.

- *Evaluate.* The fourth step, *Evaluate,* provides the opportunity to determine how effectively you have mastered the material. In *Sociology and Your Life,* a series of questions at the end of each module permits a quick check of your understanding of the material and they are indicated by an Evaluate icon. Use the provided questions as additional opportunities to test yourself. Evaluating your progress is essential to assessing your degree of mastery of the material.

- *Rethink.* The final step in the P.O.W.E.R. learning system requires that you think critically about the content. Critical thinking entails reanalyzing, reviewing, questioning, and challenging assumptions. It affords you the opportunity to consider how the material fits with other information you have already learned. Every major section of *Sociology and Your Life* ends with a *Rethink* section, indicated by a Rethink icon. Answering its thought-provoking questions will help you understand the material more fully and at a deeper level.

Making use of the P.O.W.E.R. system embedded in this text will help you study, learn, and master the material more effectively. Moreover, it is a system that will be helpful in your other courses as well.

Manage Your Time

Without looking up from the page, answer this question: What time is it? Most of us are pretty accurate in our answer, whether it comes from an internal clock, a smartphone, or context clues—but *managing* our time often proves much more difficult. Nevertheless, it is a central aspect of any successful study plan. But remember, the goal of time management is not to schedule every waking moment of the day. Instead, we should aim to make informed choices about *how* we use our time, rather than letting the day slip by. The time management procedures that follow allow us to harness time for our own purposes.

Create a Time Log. A *time log,* or simply a record of how you actually have spent your time—including interruptions—is an essential tool to begin. You can keep track manually in a paper journal, electronically, or even with an app on your phone. It doesn't have to be a second-by-second record of every waking moment, but it should account for blocks of time in increments as short as 15 minutes. Now you can reflect on where your time goes. How do your perceptions of how you spend your time match up with reality? Be prepared to be surprised!

You should also identify the things that suck up your time. We all waste time on unimportant activities that keep us from doing the things we should be doing or want to do. Suppose you're studying, and your cell phone rings. Instead of speaking with a friend for a half hour, you might (a) let the phone ring but not answer it; (b) answer it, but tell your friend you are studying and will call her back; (c) speak with her for only a short while; or (d) send the call to voicemail and then turn the phone off. If you do any of these four things, you will have taken better control of your time.

Set Your Priorities. So now you know what's taking up your time, but you may not know what you *should* be doing instead. First, you need to determine your priorities. *Priorities* are the tasks and activities you need and want to do, rank-ordered from most important to least important. There are no right or wrong priorities; maybe spending time on your studies is most important to you, or maybe your top priority is spending time with your family. Only you can decide. Furthermore, what's important to you now may be less of a priority next month, next year, or in five years.

The best procedure is to start off by identifying priorities for an entire term. What do you need to accomplish? Don't just choose obvious, general goals, such as "passing all my classes." Instead, think in terms of specific, measurable activities, such as "spend one hour each day reading the textbook to prepare for upcoming sociology classes."

Identify Your Prime Time. Do you enthusiastically bound out of bed in the morning, ready to start the day and take on the world? Or are you zombielike before noon, only just beginning to rev up at 10:00 p.m.? We all have our own style based on some inborn body clock. Being aware of your best time of day will help you plan and schedule your time most effectively. Take on activities that require the greatest concentration when you're at your best, saving easier, less-involved activities during those trying parts of the day.

Master the Moment. You now know where you've lost time in the past, and your priority list is telling you where you need to head in the future. You've reached the point where you can organize yourself to take control of your time. Here's what you'll need:

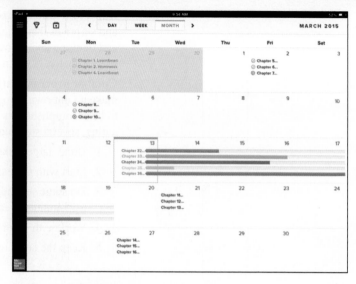

McGraw-Hill Connect offers calendar tools that keep track of assignments across all of your Connect courses, providing a high-level view of your coursework.

- *A master calendar* that shows every week (and all seven days of the week) of the term on one page. Using your class syllabi, input every assignment and test you will have on the master calendar, noting the date that it is due. Pencil in tentative assignments on the appropriate date. You should also include personal engagements and free time.

- *A weekly timetable,* a master grid with the days of the week across the top and the hours, from 6:00 a.m. to midnight, along the side. Fill in the times of all your fixed, prescheduled activities—the times that your classes meet, when you have to be at work, the times you have to pick up your child at day care, and any other recurring appointments. Add assignment due dates, tests, and any other activities on the appropriate days of the week. Then pencil in blocks of time necessary to prepare for those events.

- *A daily to-do list* can be written on a small, portable calendar that includes a separate page for each day of the week, or you can maintain a calendar electronically, if that is your preference. List all the things that you intend to do during the next day, and their priority. Start with the things you know you must do and that have fixed times, such as classes, work schedules, and appointments. Then add in the other things that you should accomplish, such as study an hour for an upcoming test; work on research for an upcoming paper; or finish up a lab report. Finally, be sure to list some things that may be of a lower priority from an academic standpoint but are enjoyable to you, like a run or a walk.

Controlling Time. Even with the best time management skills, our lives are filled with surprises. A crisis occurs; buses are late; computers break down; kids get sick. Tasks can take longer than we expect. The difference between effective and ineffective time management lies in how well you deal with the inevitable surprises. You can take control of your days and permit yourself to follow your intended schedule in several ways:

- **Just say no.** You don't have to agree to every request and every favor that others ask of you.

- **Get away from it all.** Go to the library. Lock yourself into your bedroom. Find an out-of-the-way unused classroom. Adopt a specific spot as your own, such as a corner desk in a secluded nook in the library. If you use it enough, your body and mind will automatically get into study mode as soon as you settle in.

- **Enjoy the sounds of silence.** Although many students insist they accomplish most while a television, radio, or CD is playing, scientific studies suggest otherwise—we are able to concentrate most when our environment is silent. Try working in silence for a few days. You may find that you get more done in less time than you would in a more distracting environment.

- **Take an e-break.** We may not control when communications arrive, but we can make the message wait until we are ready to receive it. Take an e-break and shut down your communication sources for a period of time—every device, turn them off. They'll wait.

Connect opens to a "To Do Today" list, providing your priorities for the day at a glance.

- **Expect the unexpected.** You'll never be able to escape from unexpected interruptions and surprises that require your attention. But by trying to anticipate them in advance, and thinking about how you'll react to them, you'll be positioning yourself to react more effectively when they do occur.

- **Combat procrastination.** Even when no one else is throwing interruptions at us, we make up our own. *Procrastination,* the habit of putting off and delaying tasks that are to be accomplished, is a problem that many of us face. If you find yourself procrastinating, several steps can help you:

    1. Break large tasks into small ones.

    2. Start with the easiest and simplest part of a task, and then do the harder parts.

    3. Do some self-negotiation—if I work on this assignment for one hour, I can take a 15-minute break to do whatever I want before I return to work.

    4. Work with others—for example, a study session with several of your classmates.

    5. Keep the costs of procrastination in mind.

Read Your Textbook Effectively

Reading a textbook is different from reading for pleasure. With textbooks, you have specific goals: understanding, learning, and ultimately recalling the information. You can take several steps to achieve these goals:

- **Read the frontmatter.** If you'll be using a text extensively throughout the term, start by reading the preface and/or introduction and scanning the table of contents—what publishers call the *frontmatter.* It is there that the author has a chance to explain, often more personally than elsewhere in the text, what he or she considers important. Knowing this will give you a sense of what to expect as you read. (Note: You're reading part of the frontmatter at this very moment!)

- **Identify your personal objectives.** Before you begin an assignment, think about what your specific objectives are. Will you be reading a textbook on which you'll be thoroughly tested? Or are you reading for background information? Is the material going to be useful to you personally? In your program? Your objectives for reading will help you determine which reading strategy to adopt and how much time you should devote to the reading assignment. You aren't expected to read everything with the same degree of intensity. You may feel comfortable skimming some material; other material may require your maximum effort.

- **Identify and use the advance organizers.** The next step in reading a textbook is to become familiar with the *advance organizers*—outlines, overviews, section objectives, or other clues to the meaning and organization of new material—provided in the material you are reading.

Sociology and Your Life includes Learning Objectives in every module. These direct you to the key points of every section in this textbook. If you can work through the concepts presented in the learning outcomes, you have gained an understanding of exactly what each module is designed to do!

- **Stay focused as you read.** There are a million and one possible distractions that can invade your thoughts as you read. Your job is to keep distracting thoughts at bay and focus on the material you are supposed to be reading. Here are some things you can do to help yourself stay focused:

- **Read in small bites.** If you think it is going to take you four hours to read an entire chapter, break up the four hours into more manageable time periods. Promise yourself that you'll read for one hour in the afternoon, another hour in

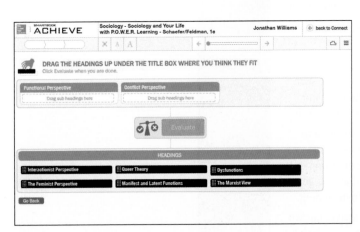

McGraw-Hill's adaptive reading experience, SmartBook, reinforces the chapter organization by building an outline of the material you're about to read in the "Preview" stage.

the evening, and the next two hours spaced out during the following day. Remember what you identified as your "prime time"—your best time of day for working—and schedule your reading for that time when possible.

- **Take a break.** Actually, plan to take several short breaks to reward yourself while you're reading. During your break, do something enjoyable—eat a snack, watch a bit of a ball game on television, play a video game, or the like. Just try not to get drawn into your break activity to the point that it takes over your reading time.

- **Highlight and take notes as you read.** Highlighting and taking notes as you read a textbook are essential activities. Good annotations can help you learn and review the information prior to tests, as well as helping you to stay focused as you read. You can do several things to maximize the effectiveness of your notes:

  - **Rephrase key points.** Make notes to yourself, in your own words, about what the author is trying to get across. Don't just copy what's been said. Think about the material, and rewrite it in words that are your own. The very act of writing engages an additional type of perception—involving the physical sense of moving a pen or pressing a keyboard.

  - **Highlight or underline key points.** Often the first or last sentence in a paragraph, or the first or last paragraph in a section, will present a key point. Before you highlight anything, though, read the whole paragraph through. Then you'll be sure that what you highlight is, in fact, the key information. You should find yourself highlighting only one or two sentences or phrases per page. In *highlighting and underlining, less is more.* One guideline: No more than 10% of the material should be highlighted or underlined. You may find it helpful to highlight only the information that helps you work through the concepts presented in the learning outcomes.

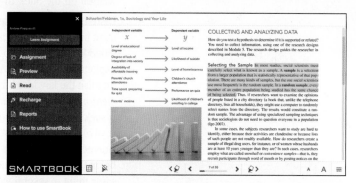

Your adaptive SmartBook does some of the work for you, highlighting content you should focus on, determined by the authors and student data. As you work through SmartBook assignments, the highlighting will adapt to show the content you need to focus on the most.

  - **Use arrows, diagrams, outlines, tables, timelines, charts, and other visuals to help you understand and later recall what you are reading.** If three examples are given for a specific point, number them. If a sequence of steps is presented, number each step. If a paragraph discusses a situation in which an earlier point does not hold, link the original point to the exception by an arrow. Representing the material graphically will get you thinking about it in new and different ways. The act of creating visual annotations will not only help you to understand the material better but will also ease its later recall.

- **Look up unfamiliar words.** Even though you may be able to figure out the meaning of an unfamiliar word from its context, look up unfamiliar words in a dictionary or online. You'll also find out what the word sounds like, which will be important if your instructor uses the word in class. *Sociology and Your Life* includes a glossary with definitions designed to help you gain a clear understanding of all the key terms in the text. Be sure to check it out if you need further clarification on any of the key terms within the modules.

Take Good Notes in Class

Perhaps you know students who manage to write down nearly everything their instructors say in class. And perhaps you have thought to yourself: "If only I took such painstaking notes, I'd do much better in my classes." Contrary to what many students think, however, good notetaking does not mean writing down every word that an instructor utters. With notetaking, less is often more. Let's consider some of the basic principles of notetaking:

- **Identify the instructor's—and your—goals for the course.** On the first day of class, most instructors talk about their objectives for the course. Most review the information on the class syllabus, the written document that explains the assignments for the semester. The information you get during that first session and through the syllabus is critical. In addition to the instructor's goals, you should have your own. What is it you want to learn from the course? How will the information from the course help you to enhance your knowledge, improve yourself as a person, and achieve your goals?

- **Complete assignments before coming to class.** Your instructor enthusiastically describes the characteristics of a bureaucracy, recounting the division of labor at your college or university. One problem: You have only the vaguest idea what a bureaucracy is. And the reason you don't know is that you haven't read the assignment. Chances are you have found yourself in this situation at least a few times, so you know first-hand that sinking feeling as you become more and more confused. The moral: Always go to class prepared. Instructors assume that their students have done what they've assigned, and their lectures are based upon that assumption. Don't forget to bring your textbook to class—during those times when you aren't as prepared, you will at least be able to use your text to follow along with your class discussions!

- **Use a notebook that assists in notetaking.** Loose-leaf notebooks are especially good for taking notes because they permit you to go back later and change the order of the pages or add additional material. Whatever kind of notebook you use, *use only one side of the page for writing; keep one side free of notes.* There may be times that you'll want to spread out your notes in front of you, and it's much easier if no material is written on the back of the pages.

- **Listen for the key ideas.** Not every sentence in a lecture is equally important. One of the most useful skills you can develop is separating the key ideas from supporting information. Good lecturers strive to make just a few main points. The rest of what they say consists of explanation, examples, and other supportive material that expand upon the key ideas. To distinguish the key ideas from their support, you need to be alert and always searching for the *meta-message* of your instructor's words—that is, the underlying main ideas that a speaker is seeking to convey. How can you discern the meta-message? One way is to *listen for keywords.* Phrases like "you need to know . . . ," "the most important thing that must be considered . . . ," "there are four problems with this approach . . . ," and—a big one—"this will be on the test . . ." should cause you to sit up and take notice. Also, if an instructor says the same thing in several ways, it's a clear sign that the material being discussed is important.

- **Use short, abbreviated phrases—not full sentences—when taking notes.** Forget everything you've ever heard about always writing in full sentences. In fact, it's often useful to take notes in the form of an outline. An outline summarizes ideas in short phrases and indicates the relationship among concepts through the use of indentations.

- **Pay attention to what your instructor provides during lecture, whether on the board, in overheads, in PowerPoint slides, or in lecture outlines.**

- **Listening is more important than seeing.** The information that your instructor projects on-screen, although important, ultimately is less critical than what he or she is saying. Pay primary attention to the spoken word and secondary attention to the screen.

- **Don't copy everything that is on every slide.** Instructors can present far more information on their slides than they would if they were writing on a blackboard. Oftentimes there is so much information that it's impossible to copy to it all down. Don't even try. Instead, concentrate on taking down the key points.

- **Remember that key points on slides are . . . key points.** The key points (often indicated by bullets) often relate to central concepts. Use these points to help organize your studying for tests, and don't be surprised if test questions directly assess the bulleted items on slides.

- **Check to see if the presentation slides are available online.** Some instructors make their class presentations available on the Web to their students, either before or after class time. If they do this before class, print them out and bring them to class. Then you can make notes on your copy, clarifying important points. If they are not available until after a class is over, you can still make good use of them when it comes time to study the material for tests.

- **Remember that presentation slides are not the same as good notes for a class.** If you miss a class, don't assume that getting a copy of the slides is sufficient. Studying the notes of a classmate who is a good note taker will be far more beneficial than studying only the slides.

Memorize Efficiently: Using Proven Strategies to Memorize New Material

Here's a key principle of effective memorization: Memorize what you need to memorize. *Forget about the rest.*

The average textbook chapter has something like 20,000 words. But, within those 20,000 words, there may be only 30 to 40 specific concepts that you need to learn. And perhaps there are only 25 keywords. *Those* are the pieces of information on which you should focus in your efforts to memorize. By extracting what is important from what is less crucial, you'll be able to limit the amount of the material that you need to recall. You'll be able to focus on what you need to remember. This book helps by defining specific Learning Objectives (LOs) that relate to the key concepts on which you need to focus.

You have your choice of dozens of techniques of memorization. As we discuss the options, keep in mind that no one strategy works by itself. Also, feel free to devise your own strategies or add those that have worked for you in the past.

Rehearsal. Say it aloud: rehearsal. Think of this word in terms of its three syllables: re–hear–sal. If you're scratching your head as to why you should do this, it's to illustrate the point of *rehearsal:* to transfer material that you encounter into long-term memory.

To test if you've succeeded in transferring the word *rehearsal* into your memory, put down this book and go off for a few minutes. Do something entirely unrelated to reading this book. Catch up on the latest sports scores on ESPN, check out Instagram, or read the front page of a newspaper. If the word *rehearsal* popped into your head when you picked up this book again, you've passed your first memory test—the word *rehearsal* has been transferred into your memory.

Rehearsal is the key strategy in remembering information. If you don't rehearse material, it will never make it into your memory. Repeating the information, summarizing it, associating it with other memories, and above all thinking about it when you first come across it will ensure that rehearsal will be effective in placing the material into your memory.

Mnemonics. This odd word (pronounced with the *m* silent—"neh-MON-ix") describes formal techniques used to make material more readily remembered. *Mnemonics* are the tricks of the trade that professional memory experts use, and you too can use them to nail down the information you will need to recall for tests.

Acronyms (e.g., Roy G. Biv to remember the colors of the rainbow), rhymes, and jingles are the most commonly used mnemonic devices.

Involve Multiple Senses. The more senses you can involve when you're trying to learn new material, the better you'll be able to remember. Here's why: Every time we encounter new information, all of our senses are potentially at work. Each piece of sensory information is stored in a separate location in the brain, and yet all the pieces are linked together in extraordinarily intricate ways.

What this means is that when we seek to remember the details of a specific event, recalling a memory of one of the sensory experiences can trigger recall of the other types of memories. You can make use of the fact that memories are stored in multiple ways by visualizing, drawing, and diagraming the material. You can also use your body (e.g., moving around, tracing figures with fingers, or thinking aloud). By doing so, you've increased the number of potential ways to trigger a relevant memory later, when you need to recall it. And when one memory is triggered, other related memories may come tumbling back.

Overlearning. Lasting learning doesn't come until you have overlearned the material. *Overlearning* consists of studying and rehearsing material past the point of initial mastery. Through overlearning, recall becomes automatic. Rather than searching for a fact, going through mental contortions until perhaps the information surfaces, overlearning permits us to recall the information without even thinking about it.

Use Test-Taking Strategies

Preparing for tests is a long-term proposition. It's not a matter of "giving your all" the night before the test. Instead, it's a matter of giving your all to every aspect of the course. Here are some guidelines that can help you do your best on tests.

Know What You Are Preparing For. Determine as much as you can about the test *before* you begin to study for it. The more you know about a test beforehand, the more efficient your studying will be. To find out about an upcoming test, first ask this question:

- Is the test called a "test," "exam," "quiz," or something else? The names imply different things:
  - *Essay:* Requires a fairly extended, on-the-spot composition about some topic. Examples include questions that call on you to describe a person, process, or event, or those that ask you to compare or contrast two separate sets of material.
  - *Multiple-choice:* Usually contains a question or statement, followed by a number of possible answers (usually four or five of them). You are supposed to choose the best response from the choices offered.
  - *True–false:* Presents statements about a topic that are either accurate or inaccurate. You are to indicate whether each statement is accurate (true) or inaccurate (false).
  - *Matching:* Presents two lists of related information, arranged in column form. Typically, you are asked to pair up the items that go together (e.g., a scientific term and its definition, or a writer and the title of a book he or she wrote).
  - *Short-answer:* Requires brief responses (usually a few sentences at most) in a kind of mini-essay.
  - *Fill-in:* Requires you to add one or more missing words to a sentence or series of sentences.

Match Test Preparation to Question Types. Each kind of test question requires a somewhat different style of preparation.

- **Essay questions.** Essay tests focus on the big picture—ways in which the various pieces of information being tested fit together. You'll need to know not just a series of facts, but also the connections between them, and you will have to be able to discuss these ideas in an organized and logical way.

  The best approach to studying for an essay test involves four steps:

1. Carefully reread your class notes and any notes you've made on assigned readings that will be covered on the upcoming exam. Also go through the readings themselves, reviewing underlined or highlighted material and marginal notes.

2. Think of likely exam questions. For example, use the keywords, phrases, concepts, and questions that come up in your class notes or in your text. Some instructors give out lists of possible essay topics; if yours does, focus on this list, but don't ignore other possibilities.

3. Without looking at your notes or your readings, answer each potential essay question—aloud. Don't feel embarrassed about doing this. Talking aloud is often more useful than answering the question in your head. You can also write down the main points that any answer should cover. (Don't write out *complete* answers to the questions unless your instructor tells you in advance exactly what is going to be on the test. Your time is probably better spent learning the material than rehearsing precisely formulated responses.)

4. After you've answered the questions, check yourself by looking at the notes and readings once again. If you feel confident that you've answered specific questions adequately, check them off. You can go back later for a quick review. But if there are questions that you had trouble with, review that material immediately. Then repeat the third step above, answering the questions again.

- **Multiple-choice, true–false, and matching questions.** Whereas the focus of review for essay questions should be on major issues and controversies, studying for multiple-choice, true–false, and matching questions requires more attention to the details. Almost anything is fair game for multiple-choice, true–false, and matching questions, so you can't afford to overlook anything when studying. It's a good idea to write down important facts on index cards: They're portable and available all the time, and the act of creating them helps drive the material into your memory. Furthermore, you can shuffle them and test yourself repeatedly until you've mastered the material.

- **Short-answer and fill-in questions.** Short-answer and fill-in questions are similar to essays in that they require you to recall key pieces of information rather than—as is the case with multiple-choice, true–false, and matching questions—finding it on the page in front of you. However, short-answer and fill-in questions typically don't demand that you integrate or compare different types of information. Consequently, the focus of your study should be on the recall of specific, detailed information.

Test Yourself. Once you feel you've mastered the material, test yourself on it. There are several ways to do this. *Sociology and Your Life* has dozens of activities available within Connect that can be used as practice quizzes, in addition to SmartBook assignments you can review to ensure retention of the material.

And you can also create a test for yourself, in writing, making its form as close as possible to what you expect the actual test to be. For instance, if your instructor has told you the classroom test will be primarily made up of short-answer questions, your test should reflect that. Again, use the learning outcomes within each module to guide you.

You might also construct a test and administer it to a classmate or a member of your study group. In turn, you could take a test that someone else has constructed. Constructing and taking practice tests are excellent ways of studying the material and cementing it into memory.

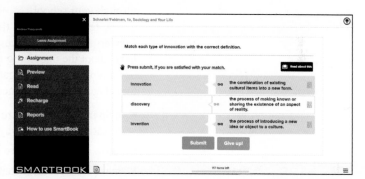

Above: As you answer questions, SmartBook is tracking your progress on key content in each module.

Below: Real-time reports quickly identify the concepts that require more of your attention.

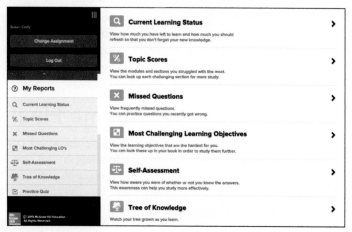

Deal with Test Anxiety. What does the anticipation of a test do to you? Do you feel shaky? Is there a knot in your stomach? Do you grit your teeth? *Test anxiety* is a temporary condition characterized by fears and concerns about test taking. Almost everyone experiences it to some degree, although for some people it's more of a problem than for others. You'll never eliminate test anxiety completely, nor do you want to. A little bit of nervousness can energize us, making us more attentive and vigilant. Like any competitive event, testing can motivate us to do our best.

On the other hand, for some students, anxiety can spiral into the kind of paralyzing fear that makes their mind go blank. There are several ways to keep this from happening to you:

1. **Prepare thoroughly.** The more you prepare, the less test anxiety you'll feel. Good preparation can give you a sense of control and mastery, and it will prevent test anxiety from overwhelming you.

2. **Take a realistic view of the test.** Remember that your future success does not hinge on your performance on any single exam. Think of the big picture: Put the task ahead in context, and remind yourself of all the hurdles you've passed so far.

3. **Visualize success.** Think of an image of your instructor handing back your test marked with a big "A." Or imagine your instructor congratulating you on your fine

performance the day after the test. Positive visualizations that highlight your potential success can help replace images of failure that may fuel test anxiety.

What if these strategies don't work? If your test anxiety is so great that it's getting in the way of your success, make use of your college's resources. Most provide a learning resource center or a counseling center that can provide you with personalized help.

Form a Study Group. *Study groups* are small, informal groups of students who work together to learn course material and study for a test. Forming such a group can be an excellent way to prepare for any kind of test. Some study groups are formed for particular tests, whereas others meet consistently throughout the term. The typical study group meets a week or two before a test and plans a strategy for studying. Members share their understanding of what will be on the test, based on what an instructor has said in class and on their review of notes and text material. Together, they develop a list of review questions to guide their individual study. The group then breaks up, and the members study on their own. If your class meets online, use e-mail or another means to have discussions with your classmates. Ask your instructor if there is a way for you to hold these online discussions through your school.

A few days before the test, members of the study group meet again. They discuss answers to the review questions, go over the material, and share any new insights they may have about the upcoming test. They may also quiz one another about the material to identify any weaknesses or gaps in their knowledge. Study groups can be extremely powerful tools because they help accomplish several things. They:

- help members organize and structure the material to approach their studying in a systematic and logical way.
- allow students to share different perspectives on the material.
- make it more likely that students will not overlook any potentially important information.
- force members to rethink the course material, explaining it in words that other group members will understand. This helps both understanding and recall of the information when it is needed on the test.
- help motivate members to do their best. When you're part of a study group, you're no longer working just for yourself; your studying also benefits the other study group members. Not wanting to let down your classmates in a study group may encourage you to put in your best effort.

Some Final Comments

We have discussed numerous techniques for increasing your study, classroom, and test effectiveness. But you need not feel tied to a specific strategy. You might want to combine other elements to create your own study system. Additional learning tips and strategies for critical thinking are presented throughout *Sociology and Your Life with P.O.W.E.R. Learning*.

Whatever learning strategies you use, you will maximize your understanding of the material in this book and master techniques that will help you learn and think critically in all of your academic endeavors. More important, you will optimize your understanding of the field of sociology. It is worth the effort: The excitement, challenges, and promise that sociology holds for you are significant.

Robert S. Feldman

Understanding Sociology

1

Sociology at **WORK** JOURNALIST

SHANE IRVING writes articles on sociological trends for magazines and newspapers. He also has a daily blog and an impressive following on Twitter. "I love writing about what's happening out there," he says. "We may be a divided society in many ways, but one thing that ties us together is the social changes we all experience, whatever our personal perspective on them may be."

Irving takes to the streets to find out what people are thinking and talking about. "When I find a topic that's gathering momentum, I start hunting for surveys and studies on the subject," he says. To stay current on research in the field, Irving keeps in touch with a half dozen sociologists at major universities around the country. "Sometimes they have something for me. Occasionally, I suggest a new area for possible study to them." While Irving enjoys mixing with all kinds of people and listening to them, it's the connections he's after. "The links between individuals and the larger society is what really fascinates me," he says. "How people influence the directions society takes, and how society in turn influences people's attitudes and behavior." ■

Looking Ahead

AS A FIELD OF STUDY, SOCIOLOGY IS EXTREMELY BROAD IN SCOPE. YOU will see throughout this book the range of topics sociologists investigate—from suicide to TV viewing habits, from Amish society to global economic patterns, from peer pressure to genetic engineering. Sociology looks at how others influence our behavior; how major social institutions like the government, religion, and the economy affect us; and how we ourselves affect other individuals, groups, and even organizations.

How did sociology develop? In what ways does it differ from other social sciences? This chapter will explore the nature of sociology as both a field of inquiry and a scientific discipline. We'll meet four pioneering thinkers—Émile Durkheim, Max Weber, Karl Marx, and W. E. B. DuBois—and examine the theoretical perspectives that grew out of their work. We'll note some of the practical applications for sociological theory and research, and consider how sociology helps us to develop a sociological imagination.

MODULE 1 What Is Sociology and How Did It Develop?

Use the P.O.W.E.R. Framework to prepare and organize your study of this module and every module in the book. Find a quiet place and read through the learning outcomes. Before reading each module, skim the content, including illustrations, and try to guess what will be discussed.

 Prepare **Learning Objectives** Use the Learning Objectives to understand the goals of the material in this Module.

LO 1-1 Explain the nature and characteristics of sociology as a discipline.
LO 1-2 Discuss the characteristics of sociological theory.
LO 1-3 Summarize the contributions of the major figures in the history of sociology.

 **Organize** **Module Outline** The Module Outline provides an overview of the module, permitting you to consider what the Module will be covering.

The Sociological Imagination
Sociology and the Social Sciences
Sociology and Common Sense
What Is Sociological Theory?
The Development of Sociology
 Early Thinkers
 Émile Durkheim
 Max Weber
 Karl Marx
 W. E. B. DuBois
 Twentieth-Century Developments

 **Work** Read this module, take notes, and jot down questions to raise about the study of sociology.

"What has sociology got to do with me or with my life?" As a student, you might well have asked this question when you signed up for your introductory sociology course. To answer it, consider these points: Are you influenced by what you see on television? Do you use the Internet? Did you vote in the last election? Are you familiar with binge drinking on campus? Do you use alternative medicine? These are just a few of the everyday life situations described in this book that sociology can shed light on. But as the opening excerpt indicates, sociology also looks at large social issues. We use sociology to investigate why thousands of jobs have moved from the United States to developing nations, what social forces promote prejudice, what leads someone to join a social movement and work for social change, how access to computer technology can reduce social inequality, and why relationships between men and women in Seattle differ from those in Singapore.

Sociology is, simply, the scientific study of social behavior and human groups. It focuses on social relationships; how those relationships influence people's behavior; and how societies, the sum total of those relationships, develop and change.

LO 1-1 The Sociological Imagination

In attempting to understand social behavior, sociologists rely on a particular type of critical thinking. A leading sociologist, C. Wright Mills, described such thinking as the **sociological imagination**—an awareness of the relationship between an individual and the wider society, both today and in the past (Mills [1959] 2000a). This awareness allows all of us (not just sociologists) to comprehend the links between our immediate, personal social settings and the remote, impersonal social world that surrounds and helps to shape us.

A key element in the sociological imagination is the ability to view one's own society as an outsider would, rather than only from the perspective of personal experiences and cultural biases. Consider something as simple as sporting events. On college campuses in the United States, thousands of students cheer well-trained football players. In Bali, Indonesia, dozens of spectators gather around a ring to cheer on roosters trained in cockfighting. In both instances, the spectators debate the merits of their favorites and bet on the outcome of the events. Yet what is considered a normal sporting event in one part of the world is considered unusual in another part.

The sociological imagination allows us to go beyond personal experiences and observations to understand broader public issues. Divorce, for example, is unquestionably a personal hardship for a husband and wife who split apart. However, C. Wright Mills advocated using the sociological imagination to view divorce not as simply an individual's personal problem but rather as a societal concern. Using this perspective, we can see that an increase in the divorce rate actually redefines a major social institution—the family. Today's households frequently include stepparents and half-siblings whose parents have divorced and remarried. Through the complexities of the blended family, this private concern becomes a public issue that affects schools, government agencies, businesses, and religious institutions.

Sociology and the Social Sciences

Is sociology a science? The term **science** refers to the body of knowledge obtained by methods based on systematic observation. Just like other scientific disciplines, sociology involves the organized, systematic study of phenomena (in this case, human behavior) in order to enhance understanding. All scientists, whether studying mushrooms or murderers, attempt to collect precise information through methods of study that are as objective as possible. They rely on careful recording of observations and accumulation of data.

Of course, there is a great difference between sociology and physics, between psychology and astronomy. For this reason, the sciences are commonly divided into natural and social sciences. **Natural science** is the study of the physical features of nature and the ways in which they interact and change. Astronomy, biology, chemistry, geology, and physics are all natural sciences. **Social science** is the study of the social features of humans and the ways in which they interact and change. The social sciences include sociology, anthropology, economics, history, psychology, and political science.

Sociology is the scientific study of social behavior and human groups.

These social science disciplines have a common focus on the social behavior of people, yet each has a particular orientation. Anthropologists usually study past cultures and preindustrial societies that continue today, as well as the origins of humans. Economists explore the ways in which people produce and exchange goods and services, along with money and other resources. Historians are concerned with the peoples and events of the past and their significance for us today. Political scientists study international relations, the workings of government, and the exercise of power and authority. Psychologists investigate personality and individual behavior. So what do *sociologists* focus on? They study the influence that society has on people's attitudes and behavior and the ways in which people interact and shape society. Because humans are social animals, sociologists examine our social relationships scientifically. The range of the relationships they investigate is vast, as the current list of sections in the American Sociological Association suggests (Table 1-1).

As the nation struggled to recover from a deep and lengthy recession, recently laid-off workers jostled the long-term unemployed at a crowded job fair in San Francisco. Sociologists use a variety of approaches to assess the full impact of economic change on society.

Let's consider how different social scientists might study the impact of the global recession that began in 2008. Historians would stress the pattern of long-term fluctuations in world markets. Economists would discuss the roles played by government, the private sector, and the world monetary system. Psychologists would study individual cases of emotional stress among workers, investors, and business owners. And political scientists would study the degree of cooperation among nations—or lack of it—in seeking economic solutions.

What approach would sociologists take? They might note a change in marital patterns in the United States. Since the recession began, the median age of first marriage has risen to 28.7 years for men and 26.7 years for women. Sociologists might also observe that today, fewer people are making that trip to the altar than in the past. If the U.S. marriage rate had remained the same as it was in 2006, about 4 million more Americans would have married by 2010.

Similarly, sociologists might evaluate the recession's impact on education. In the United States, private school enrollment from elementary through high school declined from 13.6 percent in 2006 to 12.8 percent in 2010 as families cut back on nonessential expenditures. Sociologists might even consider the recession's effect on environmental actions, such as carpooling. In all but 1 of the 50 largest metropolitan areas in the United States (New Orleans), the percentage of working people aged 16 to 64 dropped significantly during the recession. When friends and co-workers are laid off, carpools shrink and more people end up driving to work alone (El Nasser and Overberg 2011).

Besides doing research, sociologists have a long history of advising government agencies on how to respond to disasters. Certainly the poverty of the Gulf Coast region complicated the challenge of evacuating New Orleans in 2005. With Hurricane Katrina bearing down on the Gulf Coast, thousands of poor inner-city residents had no automobiles or other available means of escaping the storm. Added to that difficulty was the high incidence of disability in the area. New Orleans ranked second among the nation's 70 largest cities in the proportion of people over age 65 who are disabled—56 percent. Moving wheelchair-bound residents to safety requires specially equipped vehicles, to say nothing of handicap-accessible accommodations in public shelters. Clearly, officials must consider these factors in developing evacuation plans (Bureau of the Census 2005b).

Sociological analysis of the disaster did not end when the floodwaters receded. Long before residents of New Orleans staged a massive anticrime rally at City Hall in 2007,

TABLE 1-1 SECTIONS OF THE AMERICAN SOCIOLOGICAL ASSOCIATION

Aging and the Life Course	Emotions	Organizations, Occupations, and Work
Alcohol, Drugs, and Tobacco	Environment and Technology	Peace, War, and Social Conflict
Altruism, Morality, and Social Solidarity	Ethnomethodology and Conversation Analysis	Political Economy of the World-System
Animals and Society	Evolution, Biology, and Society	Political Sociology
Asia and Asian America	Family	Population
Body and Embodiment	Global and Transnational Sociology	Race, Gender, and Class
Children and Youth	History of Sociology	Racial and Ethnic Minorities
Collective Behavior and Social Movements	Human Rights	Rationality and Society
Communication and Information Technologies	International Migration	Religion
Community and Urban Sociology	Inequality, Poverty, and Mobility	Science, Knowledge, and Technology
Comparative and Historical Sociology	Labor and Labor Movements	Sex and Gender
Consumers and Consumption	Latino/a Sociology	Sexualities
Crime, Law, and Deviance	Law	Social Psychology
Culture	Marxist Sociology	Sociological Practice and Public Sociology
Development	Mathematical Sociology	Teaching and Learning
Disability and Society	Medical Sociology	Theory
Economic Sociology	Mental Health	
Education	Methodology	

Source: American Sociological Association 2014.

The range of sociological issues is very broad. For example, sociologists who belong to the Animals and Society section of the ASA may study the animal rights movement; those who belong to the Sexualities section may study global sex workers or the gay, bisexual, and transgendered movements. Economic sociologists may investigate globalization or consumerism, among many other topics.

researchers were analyzing resettlement patterns in the city. They noted that returning residents often faced bleak job prospects. Yet families who had stayed away for that reason often had trouble enrolling their children in schools unprepared for an influx of evacuees. Faced with a choice between the need to work and the need to return their children to school, some displaced families risked sending their older children home alone. Meanwhile, opportunists had arrived to victimize unsuspecting homeowners. And the city's overtaxed judicial and criminal justice systems, which had been understaffed before Katrina struck, had been only partially restored. All these social factors led sociologists and others to anticipate the unparalleled rise in reported crime the city experienced in 2006 and 2007 (Jervis 2008; Kaufman 2006).

Throughout this textbook, you will see how sociologists develop theories and conduct research to study and better understand societies. And you will be encouraged to use your sociological imagination to examine the United States (and other societies) from the viewpoint of a respectful but questioning outsider.

Sociology and Common Sense

Sociology focuses on the study of human behavior. Yet we all have experience with human behavior and at least some knowledge of it. All of us might well have theories about why people become homeless, for example. Our theories and opinions typically come from common sense—that is, from our experiences and conversations, from what we read, from what we see on television, and so forth.

In our daily lives, we rely on common sense to get us through many unfamiliar situations. However, this commonsense knowledge, while sometimes accurate, is not always reliable, because it rests on commonly held beliefs rather than on systematic analysis of facts. It was once considered common sense to accept that the earth was flat—a view rightly questioned by Pythagoras and Aristotle. Incorrect commonsense notions are not just a part of the distant past; they remain with us today.

Contrary to the common notion that women tend to be chatty compared to men, for instance, researchers have found little difference between the sexes in terms of their talkativeness. Over a five-year period they placed unobtrusive microphones on 396 college students in various fields, at campuses in Mexico as well as the United States. They found that both men and women spoke about 16,000 words per day (Mehl et al. 2007).

Like other social scientists, sociologists do not accept something as a fact because "everyone knows it." Instead, each piece of information must be tested and recorded, then analyzed in relation to other data. Sociologists rely on scientific studies in order to describe and understand a social environment. At times, the findings of sociologists may seem like common sense, because they deal with familiar facets of everyday life. The difference is that such findings have been *tested* by researchers. Common sense now tells us that the earth is round, but this particular commonsense notion is based on centuries of scientific work that began with the breakthroughs made by Pythagoras and Aristotle.

LO **1-2** What Is Sociological Theory?

Why do people commit suicide? One traditional commonsense answer is that people inherit the desire to kill themselves. Another view is that sunspots drive people to take their lives. These explanations may not seem especially convincing to contemporary researchers, but they represent beliefs widely held as recently as 1900.

Sociologists are not particularly interested in why any one individual commits suicide; they are more concerned with identifying the social forces that systematically cause some people to take their own lives. In order to undertake this research, sociologists develop a theory that offers a general explanation of suicidal behavior.

We can think of theories as attempts to explain events, forces, materials, ideas, or behavior in a comprehensive manner. In sociology, a **theory** is a set of statements that seeks to explain problems, actions, or behavior. An effective theory may have both explanatory and predictive power. That is, it can help us to see the relationships among seemingly isolated phenomena, as well as to understand how one type of change in an environment leads to other changes.

The World Health Organization (2010) estimates that almost a million people die from suicide every year. More than a hundred years ago, a sociologist tried to look at suicide data scientifically. Émile Durkheim ([1897] 1951) developed a highly original theory about the relationship between suicide and social factors. Durkheim was primarily concerned not with the personalities of individual suicide victims, but rather with suicide rates and how they varied from country to country. As a result, when he looked at the number of reported suicides in France, England, and Denmark in 1869, he also noted the total population of each country in order to determine the rate of suicide in each nation. He found that whereas England had only 67 reported suicides per million inhabitants, France had 135 per million and Denmark had 277 per million. The question then became "Why did Denmark have a comparatively high rate of reported suicide?"

Durkheim went much deeper into his investigation of suicide rates. The result was his landmark work *Suicide,* published in 1897. Durkheim refused to accept unproved explanations regarding suicide, including the beliefs that inherited tendencies or cosmic forces caused such deaths. Instead, he focused on social factors, such as the cohesiveness or lack of cohesiveness of religious, social, and occupational groups.

Durkheim's research suggested that suicide, although it is a solitary act, is related to group life. He found that people without religious affiliations had a higher suicide rate than those who were affiliated; the unmarried had much higher rates than married people;

Study Alert

Remember that a theory can both *explain* phenomena and *predict* how one change in an environment may create others.

and soldiers had a higher rate than civilians. In addition, there seemed to be higher rates of suicide in times of peace than in times of war and revolution, and in times of economic instability and recession rather than in times of prosperity. Durkheim concluded that the suicide rates of a society reflected the extent to which people were or were not integrated into the group life of the society.

Émile Durkheim, like many other social scientists, developed a theory to explain how individual behavior can be understood within a social context. He pointed out the influence of groups and societal forces on what had always been viewed as a highly personal act. Clearly, Durkheim offered a more *scientific* explanation for the causes of suicide than that of inherited tendencies or sunspots. His theory has predictive power, since it suggests that suicide rates will rise or fall in conjunction with certain social and economic changes.

Of course, a theory—even the best of theories—is not a final statement about human behavior. Durkheim's theory of suicide is no exception. Sociologists continue to examine factors that contribute to differences in suicide rates around the world and to a particular society's rate of suicide. In Las Vegas, for example, sociologists have observed that the chances of dying by suicide are strikingly high—twice as high as in the United States as a whole. Noting Durkheim's emphasis on the relationship between suicide and social isolation, researchers have suggested that Las Vegas's rapid growth and constant influx of tourists have undermined the community's sense of permanence, even among longtime residents. Although gambling—or more accurately, losing while gambling—may seem a likely precipitating factor in suicides there, careful study of the data has allowed researchers to dismiss that explanation. What happens in Vegas may stay in Vegas, but the sense of community cohesiveness that the rest of the country enjoys may be lacking (Wray et al. 2008, 2011).

LO **1-3** The Development of Sociology

People have always been curious about sociological matters—how we get along with others, what we do for a living, whom we select as our leaders. Philosophers and religious authorities of ancient and medieval societies made countless observations about human behavior. They did not test or verify those observations scientifically; nevertheless, their observations often became the foundation for moral codes. Several of these early social philosophers correctly predicted that a systematic study of human behavior would emerge one day. Beginning in the 19th century, European theorists made pioneering contributions to the development of a science of human behavior.

EARLY THINKERS

Auguste Comte The 19th century was an unsettling time in France. The French monarchy had been deposed in the revolution of 1789, and Napoleon had suffered defeat in his effort to conquer Europe. Amid this chaos, philosophers considered how society might be improved. Auguste Comte (1798–1857), credited with being the most influential of the philosophers of the early 1800s, believed that a theoretical science of society and a systematic investigation of behavior were needed to improve society. He coined the term *sociology* to apply to the science of human behavior.

Writing in the 1800s, Comte feared that the excesses of the French Revolution had permanently impaired France's stability. Yet he hoped that the systematic study of social behavior would eventually lead to more rational human interactions.

Harriet Martineau Scholars learned of Comte's works largely through translations by the English sociologist Harriet Martineau (1802–1876). But Martineau was a pathbreaker in her own right: she offered insightful observations of the customs and social practices of both her native Britain and the United States. Martineau's book *Society in America* ([1837] 1962) examined religion, politics, child rearing, and immigration in the young nation. It gave special attention to social class distinctions and to such factors as gender and race. Martineau ([1838] 1989) also wrote the first book on sociological methods.

Martineau's writings emphasized the impact that the economy, law, trade, health, and population could have on social problems. She spoke out in favor of the rights of women, the emancipation of slaves, and religious tolerance. Later in life, deafness did not keep her from being an activist. In Martineau's ([1837] 1962) view, intellectuals and scholars should not simply offer observations of social conditions; they should *act* on their convictions in a manner that will benefit society. That is why Martineau conducted research on the nature of female employment and pointed to the need for further investigation of the issue (Deegan 2003; Hill and Hoecker-Drysdale 2001).

Harriet Martineau, an early pioneer of sociology who studied social behavior both in her native England and in the United States. Martineau proposed some of the methods still used by sociologists, including systematic observation.

Herbert Spencer Another important early contributor to the discipline of sociology was Herbert Spencer (1820–1903). A relatively prosperous Victorian Englishman, Spencer (unlike Martineau) did not feel compelled to correct or improve society; instead, he merely hoped to understand it better. Drawing on Charles Darwin's study *On the Origin of Species,* Spencer applied the concept of evolution of the species to societies in order to explain how they change, or evolve, over time. Similarly, he adapted Darwin's evolutionary view of the "survival of the fittest" by arguing that it is "natural" that some people are rich while others are poor.

Spencer's approach to societal change was extremely popular in his lifetime. Unlike Comte, Spencer suggested that since societies are bound to change eventually, one need not be highly critical of present social arrangements or work actively for social change. This viewpoint appealed to many influential people in England and the United States who had a vested interest in the status quo and were suspicious of social thinkers who endorsed change.

ÉMILE DURKHEIM

Émile Durkheim made many pioneering contributions to sociology, including his important theoretical work on suicide. The son of a rabbi, Durkheim (1858–1917) was educated in both France and Germany. He established an impressive academic reputation and was appointed one of the first professors of sociology in France. Above all, Durkheim will be remembered for his insistence that behavior must be understood within a larger social context, not just in individualistic terms.

To give one example of this emphasis, Durkheim ([1912] 2001) developed a fundamental thesis to help explain all forms of society. Through intensive study of the Arunta, an Australian tribe, he focused on the functions that religion performed and underscored the role of group life in defining what we consider to be religion. Durkheim concluded that like other forms of group behavior, religion reinforces a group's solidarity.

Another of Durkheim's main interests was the consequences of work in modern societies. In his view, the growing division of labor in industrial societies, as workers became much more specialized in their tasks, led to what he called "anomie." **Anomie** refers to the loss of direction felt in a society when social control of individual behavior has become ineffective. Often, the state of anomie occurs during a time of profound social change, when people have lost their sense of purpose or direction. In a period of anomie, people are so confused and unable to cope with the new social environment that they may resort to suicide.

Like many other sociologists, Durkheim did not limit his interests to one aspect of social behavior. Later in this book we will consider his thinking on crime and punishment, religion, and the workplace. Few sociologists have had such a dramatic impact on so many different areas within the discipline.

MAX WEBER

Another important early theorist was Max Weber (pronounced VAY-ber). Born in Germany, Weber (1864–1920) studied legal and economic history, but gradually developed an interest in sociology. Eventually, he became a professor at various German universities. Weber taught his students that they should employ *verstehen* (pronounced fair-SHTAY-en), the German word for "understanding" or "insight," in their intellectual work. He pointed out that we cannot analyze our social behavior by the same type of objective criteria we use to measure weight or temperature. To fully comprehend behavior, we must learn the subjective meanings people attach to their actions—how they themselves view and explain their behavior.

For example, suppose that a sociologist was studying the social ranking of individuals in a fraternity. Weber would expect the researcher to employ *verstehen* to determine the significance of the fraternity's social hierarchy for its members. The researcher might examine the effects of athleticism or grades or social skills or seniority on standing within the fraternity. He or she would seek to learn how the fraternity members relate to other members of higher or lower status. While investigating these questions, the researcher would take into account people's emotions, thoughts, beliefs, and attitudes (Coser 1977).

We also owe credit to Weber for a key conceptual tool: the ideal type. An **ideal type** is a construct or model for evaluating specific cases. In his works, Weber identified various characteristics of bureaucracy as an ideal type. In presenting this model of bureaucracy, Weber was not describing any particular organization, nor was he using the term *ideal* in a way that suggested a positive evaluation. Instead, his purpose was to provide a useful standard for measuring how bureaucratic an actual organization is (Gerth and Mills 1958). Later in this book, we will use the concept of *ideal type* to study the family, religion, authority, and economic systems, as well as to analyze bureaucracy.

Although their professional careers coincided, Émile Durkheim and Max Weber never met and probably were unaware of each other's existence, let alone ideas. Such was not true of the work of Karl Marx. Durkheim's thinking about the impact of the division of labor in industrial societies was related to Marx's writings, while Weber's concern for a value-free, objective sociology was a direct response to Marx's deeply held convictions. Thus, it is not surprising that Karl Marx is viewed as a major figure in the development of sociology, as well as several other social sciences (Figure 1-1).

KARL MARX

Karl Marx (1818–1883) shared with Durkheim and Weber a dual interest in abstract philosophical issues and the concrete reality of everyday life. Unlike them, however, Marx was so critical of existing institutions that a conventional academic career was impossible. He spent most of his life in exile from his native Germany.

Marx's personal life was a difficult struggle. When a paper he had written was suppressed, he fled to France. In Paris, he met Friedrich Engels (1820–1895), with whom he formed a lifelong friendship. The two lived at a time when European and North American economic life was increasingly dominated by the factory rather than the farm.

While in London in 1847, Marx and Engels attended secret meetings of an illegal coalition of labor unions known as the Communist League. The following year they prepared a platform called *The Communist Manifesto,* in which they argued that the masses of people with no resources other than their labor (whom they referred to as the *proletariat*) should unite to fight for the overthrow of capitalist societies.

After completing *The Communist Manifesto,* Marx returned to Germany, only to be expelled. He then moved to England, where he continued to write books and essays. Marx lived there in extreme poverty; he pawned most of his possessions, and several of his children died of malnutrition and disease. Marx clearly was an outsider in British society, a fact that may well have influenced his view of Western cultures.

FIGURE 1-1 CONTRIBUTORS TO SOCIOLOGY

	Émile Durkheim 1858–1917	Max Weber 1864–1920	Karl Marx 1818–1883	W. E. B. DuBois 1868–1963
Academic training	Philosophy	Law, economics, history, philosophy	Philosophy, law	Sociology
Key works	1893—*The Division of Labor in Society* 1897—*Suicide: A Study in Sociology* 1912—*Elementary Forms of Religious Life*	1904–1905—*The Protestant Ethic and the Spirit of Capitalism* 1921—*Economy and Society*	1848—*The Communist Manifesto* 1867—*Das Kapital*	1899—*The Philadelphia Negro* 1903—*The Negro Church* 1903—*Souls of Black Folk*

Source: Developed by author.

In Marx's analysis, society was fundamentally divided between two classes that clashed in pursuit of their own interests. When he examined the industrial societies of his time, such as Germany, England, and the United States, he saw the factory as the center of conflict between the exploiters (the owners of the means of production) and the exploited (the workers). Marx viewed these relationships in systematic terms; that is, he believed that a system of economic, social, and political relationships maintained the power and dominance of the owners over the workers. Consequently, Marx and Engels argued that the working class should overthrow the existing class system. Marx's influence on contemporary thinking has been dramatic. His writings inspired those who would later lead communist revolutions in Russia, China, Cuba, Vietnam, and elsewhere.

Even apart from the political revolutions that his work fostered, Marx's significance is profound. Marx emphasized the *group* identifications and associations that influence an *individual's* place in society. This area of study is the major focus of contemporary sociology. Throughout this textbook, we will consider how membership in a particular gender classification, age group, racial group, or economic class affects a person's attitudes and behavior. In an important sense, we can trace this way of understanding society back to the pioneering work of Karl Marx.

W. E. B. DUBOIS

Marx's work encouraged sociologists to view society through the eyes of those segments of the population that rarely influence decision making. In the United States, some early Black sociologists, including W. E. B. DuBois (1868–1963), conducted research that they hoped would assist in the struggle for a racially egalitarian society. DuBois (pronounced doo-BOYSS) believed that knowledge was essential in combating prejudice and achieving tolerance and justice. Sociologists, he contended, needed to draw on scientific principles to study social problems such as those experienced by Blacks in the United States. To separate opinion from fact, he advocated research on the lives of Blacks. Through his in-depth studies of urban life, both White and Black, in cities such as Philadelphia and Atlanta, DuBois ([1899] 1995) made a major contribution to sociology.

Like Durkheim and Weber, DuBois saw the importance of religion to society. However, he tended to focus on religion at the community level and on the role of the church in the lives of its members ([1903] 2003). DuBois had little patience with theorists such as

Herbert Spencer, who seemed content with the status quo. He believed that the granting of full political rights to Blacks was essential to their social and economic progress.

Through what became known as the Atlanta Sociological Laboratory, DuBois also promoted groundbreaking research by other scholars. While investigating religion, crime, and race relations, these colleagues trained their students in sociological research. The extensive interviews conducted by students in Atlanta still enrich our understanding of human behavior (Earl Wright II 2012).

Because many of his ideas challenged the status quo, DuBois did not always find a receptive audience within either the government or the academic world. As a result, he became increasingly involved with organizations whose members questioned the established social order. In 1909 he helped to found the National Association for the Advancement of Colored People, better known today as the NAACP (Wortham 2008).

DuBois's insights have been lasting. In 1897 he coined the term **double consciousness** to refer to the division of an individual's identity into two or more social realities. He used the term to describe the experience of being Black in White America. Today, an African American holds the most powerful office in the nation, President of the United States. Yet for millions of African Americans, the reality of being Black in the United States typically is not one of power (DuBois [1903] 1961).

TWENTIETH-CENTURY DEVELOPMENTS

Sociology today builds on the firm foundation developed by Émile Durkheim, Max Weber, Karl Marx, and W. E. B. DuBois. However, the field certainly has not remained stagnant over the past hundred years. While Europeans have continued to make contributions to the discipline, sociologists from throughout the world and especially the United States have advanced sociological theory and research. Their new insights have helped us to better understand the workings of society.

Charles Horton Cooley Charles Horton Cooley (1864–1929) was typical of the sociologists who came to prominence in the early 1900s. Born in Ann Arbor, Michigan, Cooley received his graduate training in economics but later became a sociology professor at the University of Michigan. Like other early sociologists, he had become interested in this new discipline while pursuing a related area of study.

Cooley shared the desire of Durkheim, Weber, and Marx to learn more about society. But to do so effectively, he preferred to use the sociological perspective to look first at smaller units—intimate, face-to-face groups such as families, gangs, and friendship networks. He saw these groups as the seedbeds of society, in the sense that they shape people's ideals, beliefs, values, and social nature. Cooley's work increased our understanding of groups of relatively small size.

Jane Addams In the early 1900s, many leading sociologists in the United States saw themselves as social reformers dedicated to systematically studying and then improving a corrupt society. They were genuinely concerned about the lives of immigrants in the nation's growing cities, whether those immigrants came from Europe or from the rural American South. Early female sociologists, in particular, often took active roles in poor urban areas as leaders of community centers known as *settlement houses*. For example, Jane Addams (1860–1935), a member of the American Sociological Society, cofounded the famous Chicago settlement house called Hull House.

Jane Addams (right) was an early pioneer both in sociology and in the settlement house movement. She was also an activist for many causes, including the worldwide campaign for peace.

Addams and other pioneering female sociologists commonly combined intellectual inquiry, social service work, and political activism—all with the goal of assisting the underprivileged and creating a more egalitarian society. For example, working with the Black journalist and educator Ida Wells-Barnett, Addams successfully prevented racial segregation in the Chicago public schools. Addams's efforts to establish a juvenile court system and a women's trade union reveal the practical focus of her work (Addams 1910, 1930; Deegan 1991; Lengermann and Niebrugge-Brantley 1998).

Robert Merton Sociologist Robert Merton (1910–2003) made an important contribution to the discipline by successfully combining theory and research. Born to Slavic immigrant parents in Philadelphia, Merton won a scholarship to Temple University. He continued his studies at Harvard, where he acquired his lifelong interest in sociology. Merton's teaching career was based at Columbia University.

Merton (1968) produced a theory that is one of the most frequently cited explanations of deviant behavior. He noted different ways in which people attempt to achieve success in life. In his view, some may deviate from the socially approved goal of accumulating material goods or the socially accepted means of achieving that goal. For example, in Merton's classification scheme, *innovators* are people who accept the goal of pursuing material wealth but use illegal means to do so, including robbery, burglary, and extortion. Although Merton based his explanation of crime on individual behavior that has been influenced by society's approved goals and means, it has wider applications. His theory helps to account for the high crime rates among the nation's poor, who may see no hope of advancing themselves through traditional roads to success.

Merton also emphasized that sociology should strive to bring together the *macro-level* and *micro-level* approaches to the study of society. **Macrosociology** concentrates on large-scale phenomena or entire civilizations. Émile Durkheim's cross-cultural study of suicide is an example of macro-level research. More recently, macrosociologists have examined international crime rates and the stereotype of Asian Americans as a "model minority". In contrast, **microsociology** stresses the study of small groups, often through experimental means. Sociological research on the micro level has included studies of how divorced men and women disengage from significant social roles and of how a teacher's expectations can affect a student's academic performance.

Pierre Bourdieu Increasingly, scholars in the United States have been drawing on the insights of sociologists in other countries. The ideas of the French sociologist Pierre Bourdieu (1930–2002) have found a broad following in North America and elsewhere. As a young man, Bourdieu did fieldwork in Algeria during its struggle for independence from France. Today, scholars study Bourdieu's research techniques as well as his conclusions.

Bourdieu wrote about how capital in its many forms sustains individuals and families from one generation to the next. To Bourdieu, *capital* included not just material goods, but cultural and social assets. **Cultural capital** refers to noneconomic goods, such as family background and education, which are reflected in a knowledge of language and the arts. Not necessarily book knowledge, cultural capital refers to the kind of education that is valued by the socially elite. Though a knowledge of Chinese cuisine is culture, for example, it is not the prestigious kind of culture that is valued by the elite. In the United States, immigrants—especially those who arrived in large numbers and settled in ethnic enclaves—have generally taken two or three generations to develop the same level of cultural capital enjoyed by more established groups. In comparison, **social capital** refers to the collective benefit of social networks, which are built on reciprocal trust. Much has been written about the importance of family and friendship networks in providing people with an opportunity to advance. In his emphasis on cultural and social capital, Bourdieu's work extends the insights of early social thinkers such as Marx and Weber (Bourdieu and Passerson 1990; Poder 2011).

Today sociology reflects the diverse contributions of earlier theorists. As sociologists approach such topics as divorce, drug addiction, and religious cults, they can draw on the theoretical insights of the discipline's pioneers. A careful reader can hear Comte, Durkheim, Weber, Marx, DuBois, Cooley, Addams, and many others speaking through the pages of current research. Sociology has also broadened beyond the intellectual confines of North America and Europe. Contributions to the discipline now come from sociologists studying and researching human behavior in other parts of the world. In describing the work of these sociologists, it is helpful to examine a number of influential *theoretical perspectives,* also known as *approaches* or *views.*

E Evaluate Answer these questions to determine how much you have retained after reading the material.

Read each question carefully and then select or provide the best answer.

1. Émile Durkheim's groundbreaking research suggested that suicide rates in a society reflected
   a. the average education level of its members.
   b. the level of group integration felt by its members.
   c. the presence of a genetic disposition to suicide among its members.
   d. the mean age of members of the society.

2. Which sociologist made a major contribution to society through his in-depth studies of urban life, including both Blacks and Whites?
   a. W. E. B. DuBois
   b. Robert Merton
   c. Auguste Comte
   d. Charles Horton Cooley

3. Which sociologist cofounded the famous Chicago settlement house called Hull House and also worked to establish a juvenile court system?
   a. Robert Merton
   b. Harriet Martineau
   c. Pierre Bourdieu
   d. Jane Addams

4. In sociology and the other social sciences, a(n) _____ is a set of statements that seeks to explain problems, actions, or behavior.

5. Sociologist Max Weber coined the term _____ _____ in referring to a construct or model that serves as a measuring rod against which actual cases can be evaluated.

Answers
1 (b); 2 (a); 3 (d); 4 theory; 5 ideal type

R Rethink Use critical thinking to reflect on the material.

Consider these questions to get a deeper understanding of the material.

1. What aspects of the social and work environment of a fast-food restaurant would be of particular interest to a sociologist? How would the sociological imagination help in analyzing this topic?

2. What kinds of social and cultural capital do you possess? How did you acquire it? What keeps you from acquiring more?

RECAP

LO 1-1 Explain the nature and characteristics of sociology as a discipline.

- Sociology is the scientific study of social behavior and human groups.
- The sociological imagination is an awareness of the relationship between the individual and society, based on the ability to view society as an outsider might see it.
- Unlike other social sciences, sociology emphasizes the influence of groups on people's behavior and attitudes and the ways in which people shape society.

LO 1-2 Discuss the characteristics of sociological theory.

- Commonsense knowledge is not always reliable. Sociologists must rigorously test the information they use.
- Sociologists employ theories to examine relationships between seemingly unrelated observations or data.

LO 1-3 Summarize the contributions of the major figures in the history of sociology.

- Nineteenth-century thinkers who contributed sociological insights included Auguste Comte, a French philosopher; Harriet Martineau, an English sociologist; and Herbert Spencer, an English scholar.
- Other important figures in the development of sociology were Émile Durkheim, who pioneered work on suicide; Max Weber, who taught the need for insight in intellectual work; Karl Marx, who emphasized the importance of the economy and social conflict; and W. E. B. DuBois, who advocated the usefulness of both basic and applied research in combating prejudice and fostering racial tolerance and justice.
- In the 20th century, prominent sociologists included the U.S. sociologists Charles Horton Cooley and Robert Merton, and the French sociologist Pierre Bourdieu.
- Macrosociology concentrates on large-scale phenomena or entire civilizations; microsociology stresses the study of small groups.

KEY TERMS

Anomie The loss of direction felt in a society when social control of individual behavior has become ineffective.

Cultural capital Noneconomic goods, such as family background and education, which are reflected in a knowledge of language and the arts.

Double consciousness The division of an individual's identity into two or more social realities.

Ideal type A construct or model for evaluating specific cases.

Macrosociology Sociological investigation that concentrates on large-scale phenomena or entire civilizations.

Microsociology Sociological investigation that stresses the study of small groups, often through experimental means.

Natural science The study of the physical features of nature and the ways in which they interact and change.

Science The body of knowledge obtained by methods based on systematic observation.

Social capital The collective benefit of social networks, which are built on reciprocal trust.

Social science The study of the social features of humans and the ways in which they interact and change.

Sociological imagination An awareness of the relationship between an individual and the wider society, both today and in the past.

Sociology The scientific study of social behavior and human groups.

Theory In sociology, a set of statements that seeks to explain problems, actions, or behavior.

Verstehen The German word for "understanding" or "insight"; used to stress the need for sociologists to take into account the subjective meanings people attach to their actions.

MODULE 2 Major Theoretical Perspectives

 Prepare Learning Objectives

LO 2-1 Summarize the characteristics of the major theoretical perspectives in sociology.

LO 2-2 Determine why multiple perspectives can be used to explain sociological phenomena.

Organize Module Outline

Functionalist Perspective
    Manifest and Latent Functions
    Dysfunctions
Conflict Perspective
    The Marxist View
    The Feminist Perspective
    Queer Theory
Interactionist Perspective
The Sociological Approach

 **Work**

Sociologists view society in different ways. Some see the world basically as a stable and ongoing entity. They are impressed with the endurance of the family, organized religion, and other social institutions. Other sociologists see society as composed of many groups in conflict, competing for scarce resources. To still other sociologists, the most fascinating aspects of the social world are the everyday, routine interactions among individuals that we sometimes take for granted. These three views, the ones most widely used by sociologists, are the functionalist, conflict, and interactionist perspectives. Together, these approaches will provide an introductory look at the discipline.

LO 2-1 Functionalist Perspective

Think of society as a living organism in which each part of the organism contributes to its survival. This view is the **functionalist perspective**, which emphasizes the way in which the parts of a society are structured to maintain its stability. In examining any aspect of society, then, functionalists emphasize the contribution that it makes to overall social stability.

Talcott Parsons (1902–1979), a Harvard University sociologist, was a key figure in the development of functionalist theory. Parsons was greatly influenced by the work of Émile Durkheim, Max Weber, and other European sociologists. For more than four decades, he dominated sociology in the United States with his advocacy of functionalism. Parsons saw any society as a vast network of connected parts, each of which helps to maintain the system as a whole. His approach, carried forward by German sociologist Niklas Luhmann (1927–1998), holds that if an aspect of social life does not contribute to a society's stability or survival—if it does not serve some identifiably useful function or promote value consensus among members of society—it will not be passed on from one generation to the next (Joas and Knöbl 2009; Knudsen 2010).

Let's examine an example of the functionalist perspective. Many Americans have difficulty understanding the Hindu prohibition against slaughtering cows (specifically, zebu). Cattle browse unhindered through Indian street markets, helping themselves to oranges and mangoes while people bargain for the little food they can afford. What explains this devotion to the cow in the face of human deprivation—a devotion that appears to be dysfunctional?

The simple explanation is that cow worship is highly functional in Indian society, according to economists, agronomists, and social scientists who have studied the matter. Cows perform two essential tasks: plowing the fields and producing milk. If eating beef were permitted, hungry families might be tempted to slaughter their cows for immediate consumption, leaving themselves without a means of cultivation. Cows also produce dung, which doubles as a fertilizer and a fuel for cooking. Finally, cow meat sustains the neediest group in society, the *Dalit,* or untouchables, who sometimes resort to eating beef in secrecy. If eating beef were socially acceptable, higher-status Indians would no doubt bid up its price, placing it beyond the reach of the hungriest.

MANIFEST AND LATENT FUNCTIONS

A college catalog typically states various functions of the institution. It may inform you, for example, that the university intends to "offer each student a broad education in classical and contemporary thought, in the humanities, in the sciences, and in the arts." However, it would be quite a surprise to find a catalog that declared, "This university was founded in 1895 to assist people in finding a marriage partner." No college catalog will declare this as the purpose of the university. Yet societal institutions serve many functions, some of them quite subtle. The university, in fact, *does* facilitate mate selection.

Robert Merton (1968) made an important distinction between manifest and latent functions. **Manifest functions** of institutions are open, stated, and conscious functions. They involve the intended, recognized consequences of an aspect of society, such as the university's role in certifying academic competence and excellence. In contrast, **latent functions** are unconscious or unintended functions that may reflect hidden purposes of an institution. One latent function of universities is to hold down unemployment. Another is to serve as a meeting ground for people seeking marital partners.

Cows (zebu), traditionally considered sacred in India, wander freely through this city, respected by all who encounter them. The sanctity of the cow is still functional in India, where plowing, milking, and fertilizing are far more important to subsistence farmers than a diet that includes beef.

DYSFUNCTIONS

Functionalists acknowledge that not all parts of a society contribute to its stability all the time. A **dysfunction** refers to an element or process of a society that may actually disrupt the social system or reduce its stability.

We view many dysfunctional behavior patterns, such as homicide, as undesirable. Yet we should not automatically interpret them in this way. The evaluation of a dysfunction depends on one's own values, or as the saying goes, on "where you sit." For example, the official view in prisons in the United States is that inmate gangs should be eradicated because they are dysfunctional to smooth operations. Yet some guards have come to view prison gangs as a functional part of their jobs. The danger posed by gangs creates a "threat to security," requiring increased surveillance and more overtime work for guards, as well as requests for special staffing to address gang problems (G. Scott 2001).

LO **2-1** Conflict Perspective

Where functionalists see stability and consensus, conflict sociologists see a social world in continual struggle. The **conflict perspective** assumes that social behavior is best understood in terms of tension between groups over power or the allocation of resources, including housing, money, access to services, and political representation. The tension between competing groups need not be violent; it can take the form of labor negotiations, party politics, competition between religious groups for new members, or disputes over the federal budget.

Throughout most of the 1900s, the functionalist perspective had the upper hand in sociology in the United States. However, the conflict approach has become increasingly persuasive since the late 1960s. The widespread social unrest resulting from battles over civil rights, bitter divisions over the war in Vietnam, the rise of the feminist and gay liberation movements, the Watergate political scandal, urban riots, confrontations at abortion clinics, and shrinking economic prospects for the middle class have offered support for the conflict approach—the view that our social world is characterized by continual struggle between competing groups. Currently, the discipline of sociology accepts conflict theory as one valid way to gain insight into a society.

THE MARXIST VIEW

As we saw earlier, Karl Marx viewed struggle between social classes as inevitable, given the exploitation of workers that he perceived under capitalism. Expanding on Marx's work, sociologists and other social scientists have come to see conflict not merely as a class phenomenon but as a part of everyday life in all societies. In studying any culture, organization, or social group, sociologists want to know who benefits, who suffers, and who dominates at the expense of others. They are concerned with the conflicts between women and men, parents and children, cities and suburbs, Whites and Blacks, to name only a few. Conflict theorists are interested in how society's

Sociologists who take the Marxist view ask "Who benefits, who suffers, and who dominates?" What might these tattoos suggest to a Marxist theorist?

institutions—including the family, government, religion, education, and the media—may help to maintain the privileges of some groups and keep others in a subservient position. Their emphasis on social change and the redistribution of resources makes conflict theorists more radical and activist than functionalists (Dahrendorf 1959).

THE FEMINIST PERSPECTIVE

Sociologists began embracing the feminist perspective only in the 1970s, although it has a long tradition in many other disciplines. The **feminist perspective** sees inequity in gender as central to all behavior and organization. Because it focuses clearly on one aspect of inequality, it is often allied with the conflict perspective. Proponents of the feminist view tend to focus on the macro level, just as conflict theorists do. Drawing on the work of Marx and Engels, contemporary feminist theorists often view women's subordination as inherent in capitalist societies. Some radical feminist theorists, however, view the oppression of women as inevitable in *all* male-dominated societies, whether capitalist, socialist, or communist.

An early example of this perspective (long before the label came into use by sociologists) can be seen in the life and writings of Ida Wells-Barnett (1862–1931). Following her groundbreaking publications in the 1890s on the practice of lynching Black Americans, she became an advocate in the women's rights campaign, especially the struggle to win the vote for women. Like feminist theorists who succeeded her, Wells-Barnett used her analysis of society as a means of resisting oppression. In her case, she researched what it meant to be Black, a woman in the United States, and a Black woman in the United States (Giddings 2008; Wells-Barnett 1970).

QUEER THEORY

Traditionally, sociologists and other researchers have assumed that men and women are heterosexual. They either ignored other sexual identifications or treated them as abnormal. Yet as French social theorist Michel Foucault (1978) has pointed out, what is regarded as normal or even acceptable human sexuality varies dramatically from one culture to another, as well as from one time period to another. Today, in *queer theory,* sociologists have moved beyond narrow assumptions to study sexuality in all its forms.

Historically, the word *queer* was used in a derogatory manner, to stigmatize a person or behavior. Beginning in the early 1970s, however, gay and lesbian activists began to use the word as a term of empowerment. They dismissed the notion of heterosexuality as the only normal form of sexuality, along with the belief that people must be either heterosexual or homosexual. Instead, they recognized multiple sexual identities, including bisexuality. **Queer theory** is the study of society from the perspective of a broad spectrum of sexual identities, including heterosexuality, homosexuality, and bisexuality.

LO **2-1** Interactionist Perspective

Workers interacting on the job, encounters in public places like bus stops and parks, behavior in small groups—all these aspects of microsociology catch the attention of interactionists. Whereas functionalist and conflict theorists both analyze large-scale, society-wide patterns of behavior, theorists who take the **interactionist perspective** generalize about everyday forms of social interaction in order to explain society as a whole. Today, given rising concern over the cost and availability of gas, interactionists have begun to study a form of commuter behavior called "slugging." To avoid driving to work, commuters gather at certain preappointed places to seek rides from complete strangers. When a driver pulls into the parking area or vacant lot and announces his destination, the first slug in line who is headed for that destination jumps in. Rules of etiquette have emerged to smooth the social interaction between driver and passenger: neither the driver nor the passenger may eat or smoke; the slug may not adjust the windows or radio or talk on a cell phone. The presence of the slugs, who get a free ride, may allow the driver to use special lanes reserved for high-occupancy vehicles (Slug-Lines.com 2011).

Ida Wells-Barnett explored what it meant to be female and Black in the United States. Her work established her as one of the earliest feminist theorists.

Interactionism (also referred to as *symbolic interactionism*) is a sociological framework in which human beings are viewed as living in a world of meaningful objects. Those "objects" may include material things, actions, other people, relationships, and even symbols. Interactionists see symbols as an especially important part of human communication (thus the term *symbolic* interactionism). Symbols have a shared social meaning that is understood by all members of a society. In the United States, for example, a salute symbolizes respect, while a clenched fist signifies defiance. Another culture might use different gestures to convey a feeling of respect or defiance. These types of symbolic interaction are classified as forms of **nonverbal communication**, which can include many other gestures, facial expressions, and postures (Masuda et al. 2008).

Manipulation of symbols can be seen in dress codes. Schools frown on students who wear clothes displaying messages that appear to endorse violence or drug and alcohol consumption. Businesses stipulate the attire employees are allowed to wear on the job in order to impress their customers or clients. In 2005, the National Basketball Association (NBA) adopted a new dress code for the athletes who play professional basketball—one that involved not the uniforms they wear on court, but the clothes they wear off court on league business. The code requires "business casual attire" when players are representing the league. Indoor sunglasses, chains, and sleeveless shirts are specifically banned (Crowe and Herman 2005:A23).

While the functionalist and conflict approaches were initiated in Europe, interactionism developed first in the United States. George Herbert Mead (1863–1931) is widely regarded as the founder of the interactionist perspective. Mead taught at the University of Chicago from 1893 until his death. As his teachings have become better known, sociologists have expressed greater interest in the interactionist perspective. Many have moved away from what may have been an excessive preoccupation with the macro (large-scale) level of social behavior and have redirected their attention toward behavior that occurs on the micro (small-scale) level.

Erving Goffman (1922–1982) popularized a particular type of interactionist method known as the **dramaturgical approach**, in which people are seen as theatrical performers. The dramaturgist compares everyday life to the setting of the theater and stage. Just as actors project certain images, all of us seek to present particular features of our personalities while we hide other features. Thus, in a class, we may feel the need to project a serious image; at a party, we may want to look relaxed and friendly.

Study Alert

The differences between the main sociological perspectives—functionalist, conflict, and interactionist—can be confusing, so use the Tracking Sociological Perspectives Table to keep them straight.

LO 2-2 The Sociological Approach

Which perspective should a sociologist use in studying human behavior? Functionalist? Conflict? Interactionist? Feminist? Queer theorist? We simply cannot squeeze all sociological thinking into 4 or 5 theoretical categories—or even 10, if we include several other productive approaches. However, by studying the three major frameworks, we can better grasp how sociologists seek to explore social behavior. Table 1-2 summarizes these three broad approaches to sociological study.

Although no one approach is correct by itself, and sociologists draw on all of them for various purposes, many sociologists tend to favor one particular perspective over others. A sociologist's theoretical orientation influences his or her approach to a research problem in important ways—including the choice of what to study, how to study it, and what questions to pose (or not to pose). Box 1-1 (page 23) shows how researchers would study sports from different sociological perspectives.

From the perspective of . . .

A Police Officer How would having a conflict perspective of human behavior rather than a functionalist perspective affect the way you approach your duties in community policing?

	Functionalist	Conflict	Interactionist
View of Society	Stable, well integrated	Characterized by tension and struggle between groups	Active in influencing and affecting everyday social interaction
Level of Analysis Emphasized	Macro	Macro	Micro, as a way of understanding the larger macro phenomena
Key Concepts	Manifest functions Latent functions Dysfunctions	Inequality Capitalism Stratification	Symbols Nonverbal communication Face-to-face interaction
View of the Individual	People are socialized to perform societal functions	People are shaped by power, coercion, and authority	People manipulate symbols and create their social worlds through interaction
View of the Social Order	Maintained through cooperation and consensus	Maintained through force and coercion	Maintained by shared understanding of everyday behavior
View of Social Change	Predictable, reinforcing	Change takes place all the time and may have positive consequences	Reflected in people's social positions and their communications with others
Example	Public punishments reinforce the social order	Laws reinforce the positions of those in power	People respect laws or disobey them based on their own past experience
Proponents	Émile Durkheim Talcott Parsons Robert Merton	Karl Marx W. E. B. DuBois Ida Wells-Barnett	George Herbert Mead Charles Horton Cooley Erving Goffman

Whatever the purpose of sociologists' work, their research will always be guided by their theoretical viewpoints. For example, sociologist Elijah Anderson (1990) embraces both the interactionist perspective and the groundbreaking work of W. E. B. DuBois. For 14 years Anderson conducted fieldwork in Philadelphia, where he studied the interactions of Black and White residents who lived in adjoining neighborhoods. In particular, he was interested in their public behavior, including their eye contact—or lack of it—as they passed one another on the street. Anderson's research tells us much about the everyday social interactions of Blacks and Whites in the United States, but it does not explain the larger issues behind those interactions. Like theories, research results illuminate one part of the stage, leaving other parts in relative darkness.

 **E Evaluate**

Read each question carefully and then select or provide the best answer.

1. Thinking of society as a living organism in which each part of the organism contributes to its survival is a reflection of which theoretical perspective?
   a. the functionalist perspective
   b. the conflict perspective
   c. the feminist perspective
   d. the interactionist perspective

2. Karl Marx's view of the struggle between social classes inspired the contemporary
   a. functionalist perspective.
   b. conflict perspective.
   c. interactionist perspective.
   d. dramaturgical approach.

3. Erving Goffman's dramaturgical approach, which postulates that people present certain aspects of their personalities while obscuring other aspects, is a derivative of what major theoretical perspective?
   a. the functionalist perspective
   b. the conflict perspective
   c. the feminist perspective
   d. the interactionist perspective

4. The university's role in certifying academic competence and excellence is an example of a(n) _____ function.

5. The _____ view draws on the work of Karl Marx and Friedrich Engels in that it often views women's subordination as inherent in capitalist societies.

R Rethink

Consider these questions to get a deeper understanding of the material.

1. Consider the institution of a city police department from the functionalist perspective. What is a manifest function of this institution? What might be a latent function?

2. How might the conflict perspective consider party politics in the United States today? How are the Marxist, feminist, and queer perspectives relevant to this issue?

RECAP

LO 2-1 Summarize the characteristics of the major theoretical perspectives in sociology.

- The functionalist perspective emphasizes the way in which the parts of a society are structured to maintain its stability.
- The conflict perspective assumes that social behavior is best understood in terms of conflict or tension between competing groups.
- The feminist perspective, which is often allied with the conflict perspective, sees inequity in gender as central to all behavior and organization.
- Queer theory stresses that to fully understand society, scholars must study it from the perspective of a range of sexual identities, rather than exclusively from a "normal" heterosexual point of view.

- The interactionist perspective is concerned primarily with fundamental or everyday forms of interaction, including symbols and other types of nonverbal communication.

LO 2-2 Determine why multiple perspectives can be used to explain sociological phenomena.

- Sociologists make use of multiple perspectives, because each offers unique insights into the same issue.

KEY TERMS

Conflict perspective A sociological approach that assumes social behavior is best understood in terms of tension between groups over power or the allocation of resources, including housing, money, access to services, and political representation.

Dramaturgical approach A view of social interaction in which people are seen as theatrical performers.

Dysfunction An element or process of a society that may disrupt the social system or reduce its stability.

Feminist perspective A sociological approach that views inequity in gender as central to all behavior and organization.

Functionalist perspective A sociological approach that emphasizes the way in which the parts of a society are structured to maintain its stability.

Interactionist perspective A sociological approach that generalizes about everyday forms of social interaction in order to explain society as a whole.

Latent function An unconscious or unintended function that may reflect hidden purposes.

Manifest function An open, stated, and conscious function.

Nonverbal communication The sending of messages through the use of gestures, facial expressions, and postures.

Queer theory The study of society from the perspective of a broad spectrum of sexual identities, including heterosexuality, homosexuality, and bisexuality.

MODULE 3 Using Sociology

P Prepare Learning Objectives

LO 3-1 Describe the objectives of applied sociology.

LO 3-2 Explain applications of the sociological imagination to questions of globalization, social inequality, race, gender, and religion.

O Organize Module Outline

Applied and Clinical Sociology
Developing a Sociological Imagination
    Social Inequality
    Speaking across Race, Gender, and Religious Boundaries

You've seen how sociologists employ the major sociological perspectives in their research. How does sociology relate to *you,* your own studies, and your own career? In this module you'll learn about *applied* and *clinical sociology,* two growing fields that allow sociology majors and those with advanced degrees in sociology to apply what they have learned to real-world settings. You'll also see how to develop your sociological imagination, one of the keys to thinking like a sociologist.

LO **3-1** Applied and Clinical Sociology

Many early sociologists—notably, Jane Addams, W. E. B. DuBois, and George Herbert Mead—were strong advocates for social reform. They wanted their theories and findings to be relevant to policymakers and to people's lives in general. For instance, Mead was the treasurer of Hull House, where he applied his theory to improving the lives of those who were powerless (especially immigrants). He also served on committees dealing with Chicago's labor problems and public education. DuBois led the Atlanta Sociological Laboratory from 1895 to 1924, supporting scholars in their applied research on business, criminal justice, health care, and philanthropy (Earl Wright II 2012).

Today, **applied sociology** is the use of the discipline of sociology with the specific intent of yielding practical applications for human behavior and organizations. By extension, Michael Burawoy (2005), in his presidential address to the American Sociological Association, endorsed what he called *public sociology,* encouraging scholars to engage a broader audience in bringing about positive outcomes. In effect, the applied sociologist reaches out to others and joins them in their efforts to better society.

Often, the goal of applied or public sociology is to assist in resolving a social problem. For example, in the past 50 years, eight presidents of the United States have established commissions to delve into major societal concerns facing our nation. Sociologists are often asked to apply their expertise to studying such issues as violence, pornography, crime, immigration, and population. In Europe, both academic and government research departments are offering increasing financial support for applied studies.

One example of applied sociology is the growing interest in learning more about local communities. Since its founding in 1994, the Northeast Florida Center for Community Initiatives (CCI), based at the University of North Florida in Jacksonville, has conducted several community studies, including a homeless census and survey, an analysis of the economic impact of the arts in Jacksonville, and a long-term survey of the effects of Hurricane Katrina. Typical of applied sociology, these outreach efforts are collaborative, involving faculty, undergraduate and graduate students, volunteers, and community residents (Center for Community Initiatives 2012a).

Growing interest in applied sociology has led to such specializations as *medical sociology* and *environmental sociology.* The former includes research on how health care professionals and patients deal with disease. To give one example, medical sociologists have studied the social impact of the AIDS crisis on families, friends, and communities. Environmental sociologists examine the relationship between human societies and the physical environment. One focus of their work is the issue of "environmental justice", raised when researchers and community activists

The Center for Community Initiatives' Magnolia Project, an example of applied sociology, aims to decrease high rates of infant mortality.

Research Today

1-1 LOOKING AT SPORTS FROM FIVE SOCIOLOGICAL PERSPECTIVES

We watch sports. Talk sports. Spend money on sports. Some of us live and breathe sports. Because sports occupy much of our time and directly or indirectly consume and generate a great deal of money, it should not be surprising that sports have sociological components that can be analyzed from various theoretical perspectives. In this section we will look at sports from five major sociological perspectives.

Functionalist View

In examining any aspect of society, functionalists emphasize the contribution it makes to overall social stability. Functionalists regard sports as an almost religious institution that uses ritual and ceremony to reinforce the common values of a society. For example:

- Sports socialize young people into such values as competition and patriotism.
- Sports help to maintain people's physical well-being.
- Sports serve as a safety valve for both participants and spectators, who are allowed to shed tension and aggressive energy in a socially acceptable way.
- Sports bring together members of a community (who support local athletes and teams) or even a nation (during World Cup matches and the Olympics) and promote an overall feeling of unity and social solidarity.

Conflict View

Conflict theorists argue that the social order is based on coercion and exploitation. They emphasize that sports reflect and even exacerbate many of the divisions of society:

- Sports are a form of big business in which profits are more important than the health and safety of the workers (athletes).
- Sports perpetuate the false idea that success can be achieved simply through hard work, while failure should be blamed on the individual alone (rather than on injustices in the larger social system).

- Professional athletes' behavior can promote violence and the use of performance-enhancing drugs.
- Communities divert scarce resources to subsidize the construction of professional sports facilities.
- Sports maintain the subordinate role of Blacks and Latinos, who toil as athletes but are less visible in supervisory positions as coaches, managers, and owners.
- Team logos and mascots (like the Washington Redskins) disparage American Indians.

Feminist View

Feminist theorists consider how watching or participating in sports reinforces the roles that men and women play in the larger society:

- Although sports generally promote fitness and health, they may also have an adverse effect on participants' health. Men are more likely to resort to illegal steroid use (among bodybuilders and baseball players, for example); women, to excessive dieting (among gymnasts and figure skaters, for example).
- Gender expectations encourage female athletes to be passive and gentle, qualities that do not support the emphasis on competitiveness in sports. As a result, women find it difficult to enter sports traditionally dominated by men, such as Indy or NASCAR.
- Although professional women athletes' earnings are increasing, they typically trail those of male athletes.

Despite their differences, functionalists, conflict theorists, feminists, queer theorists, and interactionists would all agree that there is much more to sports than exercise or recreation.

Queer Theory

Proponents of queer theory emphasize the ways in which sports promote heterosexuality as the only acceptable sexual identity for athletes:

- Coaches and players routinely use slurs based on negative stereotypes of homosexuals to stigmatize athletes whose performance is inadequate.
- As a group, professional athletes are highly reluctant to display any sexual identity other than heterosexuality in public, for fear of damaging their careers and losing their fans and commercial sponsors.
- Parents who are not heterosexual encounter hostility when they try to register their children for sports or scouting programs, and are often rejected from coaching and other support roles.

Interactionist View

In studying the social order, interactionists are especially interested in shared understandings of everyday behavior. Interactionists examine sports on the micro level by focusing on how day-to-day social

(continued)

behavior is shaped by the distinctive norms, values, and demands of the world of sports:

- Sports often heighten parent–child involvement; they may lead to parental expectations for participation, and sometimes unrealistically, for success.
- Participation in sports builds the friendship networks that permeate everyday life.
- Despite class, racial, and religious differences, teammates may work together harmoniously and may even

abandon common stereotypes and prejudices.

- Relationships in the sports world are defined by people's social positions as players, coaches, and referees—as well as by the high or low status that individuals hold as a result of their performances and reputations.

Despite their differences, functionalists, conflict theorists, feminists, queer theorists, and interactionists would all agree that there is much more to sports than exercise or recreation. They would also agree that sports and

other popular forms of culture are worthy subjects of serious study by sociologists.

Let's Discuss

1. Have you experienced or witnessed discrimination in sports based on gender, race, or sexual identity? If so, how did you react? Has the representation of Blacks, women, or gays on teams been controversial on your campus? In what ways?
2. Which of the five sociological perspectives seems most useful to you in analyzing sports? Why?

Sources: Acosta and Carpenter 2001; Eitzen 2009; Fine 1987; Sefiha 2012; Sharp et al. 2013; Young 2004; Zirin 2008.

---

found that hazardous waste dumps are especially likely to be situated in poor and minority neighborhoods (M. Martin 1996).

The growing popularity of applied sociology has led to the rise of the specialty of clinical sociology. Louis Wirth (1931) wrote about clinical sociology more than 75 years ago, but the term itself has become popular only in recent years. While applied sociology may simply evaluate social issues, **clinical sociology** is dedicated to facilitating change by altering social relationships (as in family therapy) or restructuring social institutions (as in the reorganization of a medical center).

Applied sociologists generally leave it to policymakers to act on their evaluations. In contrast, clinical sociologists take direct responsibility for implementation and view those with whom they work as their clients. This specialty has become increasingly attractive to graduate students in sociology because it offers an opportunity to apply intellectual learning in a practical way. A shrinking job market in the academic world has made such alternative career routes appealing.

Applied and clinical sociology can be contrasted with **basic sociology** (also called *pure sociology*), which seeks a more profound knowledge of the fundamental aspects of social phenomena. This type of research is not necessarily meant to generate specific applications, although such ideas may result once findings are analyzed. When Durkheim studied suicide rates, he was not primarily interested in discovering a way to eliminate suicide. In this sense, his research was an example of basic rather than applied sociology.

LO **3-2** Developing a Sociological Imagination

In this book, we will be illustrating the sociological imagination in several different ways—by showing theory in practice and in current research; by noting the ways in which electronic devices and apps are changing our social behavior; by thinking globally; by exploring the significance of social inequality; by speaking across race, gender, and religious boundaries; and by highlighting social policy throughout the world.

Sociologists actively investigate a variety of issues and social behavior. We have already seen that research can shed light on the social factors that affect suicide rates. Sociological research often plays a direct role in improving people's lives, as in the case of increasing the participation of African Americans in diabetes testing. Throughout the rest of the book, the research performed by sociologists and other social scientists will shed light on group behavior of all types.

Furthermore, whatever their theoretical perspective or research techniques, sociologists recognize that social behavior must be viewed in a global context. **Globalization** is the worldwide integration of government policies, cultures, social movements, and financial markets through trade and the exchange of ideas. Although public discussion

---

> ## Study Alert
>
> It is important to understand the distinction between clinical and applied sociology, and how they contrast with basic sociology.

of globalization is relatively recent, intellectuals have been pondering both its negative and positive social consequences for a long time. Karl Marx and Friedrich Engels warned in *The Communist Manifesto* (written in 1848) of a world market that would lead to production in distant lands, sweeping away existing working relationships.

Today, developments outside a country are as likely to influence people's lives as changes at home. For example, though much of the world was already in recession by September 2001, the terrorist attacks on New York and Washington, D.C., caused an immediate economic decline, not just in the United States, but throughout the world. One example of the massive global impact was the downturn in international tourism, which lasted for at least two years. The effects have been felt by people far removed from the United States, including African game wardens and Asian taxi drivers. Some observers see globalization and its effects as the natural result of advances in communications technology, particularly the Internet and satellite transmission of the mass media. Others view it more critically, as a process that allows multinational corporations to expand unchecked.

Today, both the positive and negative aspects of globalization are receiving increased scrutiny from sociologists.

SOCIAL INEQUALITY

Who holds power? Who doesn't? Who has prestige? Who lacks it? Perhaps the major theme of analysis in sociology today is **social inequality**, a condition in which members of society have differing amounts of wealth, prestige, or power. For example, the disparity between what coffee bean pickers in developing nations are paid and the price you pay for a cup of coffee underscores global inequality. And the impact of Hurricane Katrina on residents of the Gulf Coast drew attention to social inequality in the United States. Predictably, the people who were hit the hardest by the massive storm were the poor, who had the greatest difficulty evacuating before the storm and have had the most difficulty recovering from it.

Some sociologists, in seeking to understand the effects of inequality, have made the case for social justice. W. E. B. DuBois ([1940] 1968:418) noted that the greatest power in the land is not "thought or ethics, but wealth." As we have seen, the contributions of Karl Marx, Jane Addams, and Ida Wells-Barnett also stressed this belief in the overarching significance of social inequality, and by extension, social justice. In this book, social inequality will be highlighted throughout.

SPEAKING ACROSS RACE, GENDER, AND RELIGIOUS BOUNDARIES

Sociologists include both men and women, who come from a variety of ethnic, national, and religious origins. In their work, sociologists seek to draw conclusions that speak to all people—not just the affluent or powerful. Doing so is not always easy. Insights into how a corporation can increase its profits tend to attract more attention and financial support than do, say, the merits of a needle exchange program for low-income inner-city residents. Yet today more than ever, sociology seeks to better understand the experiences of all people.

Sociologists have noted, for example, that the huge tsunami that hit South Asia in 2004 affected men and women differently. When the waves hit, mothers and grandmothers were at home with the children; men were outside working, where they were more likely to become aware of the impending disaster. Moreover, most of the men knew how to swim, a survival skill that women in these traditional societies usually do not learn. As a result, many more men than women survived the catastrophe—about 10 men for every 1 woman. In one Indonesian village typical of the disaster area, 97 of 1,300 people survived; only 4 were women. The impact of this gender imbalance will be felt for some time, given women's primary role as caregivers for children and the elderly (BBC News 2005).

E Evaluate

Read each question carefully and then select or provide the best answer.

1. A community organization that aims to provide free pre-school education for local families living below the poverty line is an example of
   a. clinical sociology.
   b. environmental sociology.
   c. applied sociology.
   d. basic sociology.

2. Unlike other applied sociologists, clinical sociologists assign responsibility for implementing change to
   a. state and federal agencies.
   b. themselves and their clients.
   c. sociological researchers.
   d. local policymakers.

3. The worldwide availability of high-speed satellite communications has enabled companies to set up help desks and customer support hotlines in distant countries. This is an example of which modern phenomenon?
   a. social mobility
   b. globalization
   c. social inequality
   d. economic cooperation.

4. The branch of sociology that focuses on research rather than on solving societal problems is called _____ sociology.

5. The situation in which different amounts of wealth, prestige, and power are possessed by different members of society is called _____.

Answers

1 (c); 2 (b); 3 (b); 4 basic (or pure); 5 social inequality

R Rethink

Consider these questions to get a deeper understanding of the material.

1. What issues facing your local community would you like to address with applied sociological research? Do you see any global connections to these issues?

2. In what specific ways does globalization affect your everyday life? Do you think the impact of globalization on our society is primarily positive or negative?

RECAP

LO 3-1 Describe the objectives of applied sociology.

- The goal of applied sociology is to use sociological methods and findings in the solution of practical problems in human behavior and organizations.
- Applied sociology is contrasted with basic (or pure) sociology, which focuses on using research to gain deeper knowledge of the fundamental aspects of social phenomena.
- The term *applied sociology* includes such practical applications of sociological methods as clinical sociology, medical sociology, and environmental sociology.
- Applied sociology has focused on social issues of interest to policymakers, labor advocates, immigrants, criminologists, and other segments of society.

LO 3-2 Explain applications of the sociological imagination to questions of globalization, social inequality, race, gender, and religion.

- The sociological imagination can be used to put sociological theory into practice in investigating issues such as the changes that electronic devices and applications are bringing to our social behavior, the effects of thinking and acting globally, the rising significance of social inequality, and the issues that stem from an increased emphasis on race, gender, and religious boundaries.

KEY TERMS

Applied sociology The use of the discipline of sociology with the specific intent of yielding practical applications for human behavior and organizations.

Basic sociology Sociological inquiry conducted with the objective of gaining a more profound knowledge of the fundamental aspects of social phenomena. Also known as *pure sociology.*

Clinical sociology Use of the discipline of sociology with the specific intent of altering social relationships or restructuring social institutions.

Globalization The worldwide integration of government policies, cultures, social movements, and financial markets through trade and the exchange of ideas.

Social inequality A condition in which members of society have differing amounts of wealth, prestige, or power.

The Case of . . . Parenting Options

Leslie Brown is a single parent of a two-year-old daughter. "I am still friends with her father, and he sees her whenever he likes, but I didn't want to get married," Leslie says. "I have a job and I like my independence." Leslie, a high school graduate, works for a fruit-canning company. "My mom and aunt take turns looking after my daughter while I'm working," she explains. "My whole family is wonderful about my choice. Everyone cleaned out their attics to help me set up my apartment— furniture, dishes, baby things." On weekends, Leslie and her daughter hang out with friends, many of whom are also single moms. "I live my life the way I want to," she says, "and that makes me feel strong."

Kara Lyndehurst is also a single parent by choice, but she has no ties to the father of her young son, nor has she ever revealed to him that he is the father. "I wanted a child, but not the bonds of marriage," Kara says. "I don't want to always be making compromises just to have it end in a messy divorce ten years down the road." Kara has a college degree in art history and, shortly before her son's birth, she left her hometown in the Northeast to take a job at a gallery in San Francisco. "I love my work," she says. "Setting up here on my own was a challenge, but I get a lot of satisfaction from building my life according to who I am and what I want."

1. Based on the information given in the case study, could you determine that single parenthood by choice is a sociological trend among women? Why or why not?

2. What cultural and/or social capital does Leslie appear to have? What about Kara?

3. What do you think will be the consequences for the two children of the different parenting styles of their mothers?

4. What do you think the functionalist perspective on the trend among women to opt for single parenthood might be? How about the feminist perspective?

5. How might a global trend toward women opting to be single parents affect government policies concerning children and families?

The P.O.W.E.R. Framework

The **P.O.W.E.R.** framework is based on an acronym—a word formed from the first letters of other words, in this case the steps in a proven approach to effective study and learning. **P.O.W.E.R.** stands for **P**repare, **O**rganize, **W**ork, **E**valuate, and **R**ethink—a simple but powerful framework that you can use in your studies and other aspects of your life. Once the **P.O.W.E.R.** framework becomes second nature, you will find it helpful for making both major and routine decisions, analyzing complex problems and tasks, and accomplishing all kinds of assignments.

Let's take a closer look at each of the steps.

- Read the Learning Objectives (LOs) for each module.
- Identify your long-term and short-term goals.
- Long-term goals are major accomplishments that will take some time to achieve. ("I plan to understand basic sociology and to get at least a B in this course.")
- Short-term goals are steps on the road to achieving long-term goals. ("I will understand the major concepts of the next module.")

- Read the outline provided under the "Organize" heading.
- Gather the tools you will need to meet your goals.
- Tools include physical tools (e.g., textbooks, a dictionary, your computer, a highlighter) and mental tools (e.g., concentration, determination, patience).
- To learn sociology, organizing includes thinking in advance about the major concepts and ideas you are likely to encounter.

W Work

- Using your preparation and organization, do the work needed to accomplish your task. This involves reading each module carefully.
- Stay motivated, think positively, and focus on taking control of the elements of your task that can be controlled.

E Evaluate

- As you proceed through your task, pause and consider from time to time how well the work you have accomplished matches your short-term goals.
- Take the "Evaluate" quizzes at the end of each module.
- Based on the quizzes and your own self-evaluation, adjust your work methods if they need improvement.

R Rethink

- Answer the Rethink questions at the end of each module.
- Think critically about what you have accomplished.
- Reconsider the outcome of your work and the goals and ideas that shaped it.
- Don't hesitate to repeat any step that you think could be done better.

Becoming an Effective Task Manager

Using the P.O.W.E.R. Framework will enable you to study and understand the material in this or any book more effectively. It can help you with many tasks, including those assigned to you by an employer. However, you have to develop the habits that will make this strategy work for you. For the following statements, choose **a** or **b** to describe your typical response to each situation, then check to see how you scored.

1. When I am faced with a difficult task, I usually:
   a. break it down into a series of smaller, manageable steps.
   b. just start in and hope to figure it out as I go.

2. When it comes to thinking about the future:
   a. I tend to take it one day at a time, doing whatever task is at hand.
   b. I keep a list of my goals, both long and short term, and plan my schedule to advance them.

3. Before I start a task:
   a. I give myself a "free day" so I won't feel all I do is work.
   b. I make a list of all the tools I will need and arrange them close at hand.

4. When I'm studying, I tend to:
   a. text my friends and keep an eye on my favorite sports team on TV.
   b. seek out a quiet spot away from distractions.

5. When I start to feel discouraged about the length of time a task is taking, I usually:
   a. remind myself why I started the task in the first place—what I hope to achieve.
   b. put everything away and do something I enjoy with friends.

6. If the next step in my project is to interview my instructor, and she calls to say she'll have to reschedule, I will probably:
   a. look for another part of the project that can be completed without the interview.
   b. take the day off. There's no point in pursuing the project until I get that interview.

7. Once I develop a goal:
   a. I like to stick to it exactly the way I planned it.
   b. I pause occasionally to evaluate the effectiveness of my work and make changes where needed.

8. When I finish a task, I:
   a. review it to see if I could improve any part of it.
   b. celebrate the end of a difficult job.

9. After a task is accomplished, I:
   a. move on to the next project.
   b. take time to reflect on the ideas that shaped it.

Give yourself 1 point for each of the following answers you selected: (1) a; (2) b; (3) b; (4) b; (5) a; (6) a; (7) b; (8) a; (9) b.

SCORE:

8–9 points: You have excellent habits for planning, managing, and evaluating your goals; the P.O.W.E.R. Framework will feel like an old friend as you use it to organize and understand the content of this book.

6–7 points: You have developed many good habits to help you achieve your goals. The P.O.W.E.R. Framework will introduce you to more ways to work effectively.

5 or less points: Don't be discouraged. Learning how to use the P.O.W.E.R. Framework is about to make your life a lot easier and help you achieve goals that eluded you before.

2 Sociological Research

Sociology at **WORK** MARKET RESEARCHER

LUISA BORGES enjoys her job as a market researcher for Bonnie & Delia Snacks. Recently, company executives asked her to investigate whether they were wasting their advertising dollars trying to be all things to all people. Should they push the butter cookies more? Drop oatmeal raisin altogether? Luisa used the scientific method to answer their questions. She defined the problem: Is the perception of our customers accurate? She then reviewed what was known about the snacking habits and preferences of Americans, and checked the customer data her company's researchers had collected over the past five years. She theorized that Bonnie & Delia Snacks had two distinct target customers, each with a different preference in cookies.

To test her theory, she designed and distributed surveys in the cookie aisles of selected grocery stores. She also conducted taste tests. Her hunch proved correct. Bonnie & Delia's customers fell into two groups: those who liked their cookies simple (shortbread, ginger) and those who preferred more exotic treats (coffee-toffee bites). As a result, the marketing team created two cookie lines—Bonnie's Basics and Delia's Decadence—and split its ad dollars to target each group separately. ■

Looking Ahead

IN THE THREE MODULES OF THIS CHAPTER, WE WILL EXAMINE THE research process used in sociological studies, starting with the scientific method sociologists employ to conduct research. We will first concentrate on researching the relationship of education to income as an example of using the scientific method. We'll then consider the different techniques sociologists use in their research design, such as surveys and experiments, and discuss the differences between quantitative and qualitative research. We'll look at how experiments can provide an understanding of cause-and-effect relationships between different variables. We'll also consider both the benefits and the drawbacks to the various methods, and we'll consider the efforts sociologists take to ensure that the results of their research are reliable and accurate, and we'll examine how they develop conclusions. We'll also explore the ways in which sociologists attempt to carry out research without violating the rights of those they study. We will pay particular attention to the ethical challenges sociologists face in studying human behavior, and to the debate raised by Max Weber's call for "value neutrality" in social science research.

In addition, we will review the American Sociological Association's (ASA) *Code of Ethics*, which all professional sociologists are expected to follow. We'll look at feminist and queer theorists' methodologies, and consider the role technology plays in research today. Finally, we'll discuss how sociologists approach research on sensitive topics such as human sexuality.

MODULE 4 What Is the Scientific Method?

LO 4-1 Explain how sociologists use the scientific method to answer questions of interest.

LO 4-2 Outline and describe the steps in the scientific method and how sociologists use it.

Conducting Effective Sociological Research
Outlining the Steps of the Scientific Method
    Defining the Problem
    Reviewing the Literature
    Formulating the Hypothesis
    Collecting and Analyzing Data
    Developing the Conclusion
    In Summary: The Scientific Method

Like all of us, sociologists are interested in the central questions of our time: Is the family falling apart? Why is there so much crime in the United States? Can the world feed a growing population? Such issues concern most people, whether or not they have academic training. However, unlike the typical citizen, the sociologist has a commitment to use the **scientific method** in studying society. The scientific method is a systematic, organized series of steps that ensures maximum objectivity and consistency in researching a problem.

LO 4-1 Conducting Effective Sociological Research

Whatever the area of sociological inquiry and whatever the perspective of the sociologist, there is one crucial requirement: imaginative, responsible research that meets the highest scientific and ethical standards.

Effective sociological research can be quite thought-provoking. It may suggest new questions that require further study, such as why we make assumptions about people who engage in atypical behaviors like self-injury. In some cases, rather than raising additional questions, a study will simply confirm previous beliefs and findings. Sociological research can also have practical applications. For instance, research results that disconfirm accepted beliefs about marriage and the family may lead to changes in public policy.

Many of us will never actually conduct scientific research. Why, then, is it important that we understand the scientific method? The answer is that it plays a major role in the workings of our society. Residents of the United States are constantly bombarded with "facts" or "data." A television news report informs us that "one in every two marriages in this country now ends in divorce," an assertion that is based on misleading statistics. Almost daily, advertisers cite supposedly scientific studies to prove that their products are superior. Such claims may be accurate or exaggerated. We can better evaluate such information—and will not be fooled so easily—if we are familiar with the standards of scientific research. These standards are quite stringent, and they demand as strict adherence as possible.

LO **4-2** Outlining the Steps of the Scientific Method

The scientific method requires precise preparation in developing research. Otherwise, the research data collected may not prove accurate. Sociologists and other researchers follow five basic steps in the scientific method: (1) defining the problem, (2) reviewing the literature, (3) formulating the hypothesis, (4) selecting the research design and then collecting and analyzing data, and (5) developing the conclusion (Figure 2-1). After reaching the conclusion, researchers write a report on their study. Often the report will begin with an *executive summary* of the method they followed and their conclusion. In this module, we'll use an actual example to illustrate the scientific method.

DEFINING THE PROBLEM

Does it "pay" to go to college? Some people make great sacrifices and work hard to get a college education. Parents borrow money for their children's tuition. Students work part-time jobs or even take full-time positions while attending evening or weekend classes. Does it pay off? Are there monetary returns for getting that degree?

The first step in any research project is to state as clearly as possible what you hope to investigate—that is, *define the problem*. In this instance, we are interested in knowing how schooling relates to income. We want to find out the earnings of people with different levels of formal schooling.

Early on, any social science researcher must develop an operational definition of each concept being studied. An **operational definition** is an explanation of an abstract concept that is specific enough to allow a researcher to assess the concept. For example, a sociologist interested in status might use membership in exclusive social clubs as an operational definition of status. Someone studying prejudice might consider a person's unwillingness to hire or work with members of minority groups as an operational definition of prejudice. In our example, we need to develop two operational definitions—education and earnings—in order to study whether it pays to get an advanced educational degree. We'll define *education* as the number of years of schooling a person has achieved and *earnings* as the income a person reports having received in the past year.

Initially, we will take a functionalist perspective (although we may end up incorporating other perspectives). We will argue that opportunities for more earning power are related to level of schooling, and that schools prepare students for employment.

REVIEWING THE LITERATURE

By conducting a *review of the literature*—relevant scholarly studies and information—researchers refine the problem under study, clarify possible techniques to be used in collecting data, and eliminate or reduce avoidable mistakes. In our example, we would

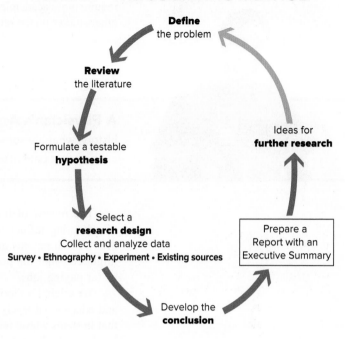

FIGURE 2-1 **THE SCIENTIFIC METHOD**

The scientific method allows sociologists to objectively and logically evaluate the data they collect. Their findings can suggest ideas for further sociological research.

examine information about the salaries for different occupations. We would see if jobs that require more academic training are better rewarded. It would also be appropriate to review other studies on the relationship between education and income.

From the perspective of . . .

A Physician's Assistant If you didn't have access to a patient's medical history, what are some of the risks you would face in making a preliminary diagnosis of that patient's illness?

The review of the literature would soon tell us that many factors besides years of schooling influence earning potential. For example, we would learn that the children of rich parents are more likely to go to college than those of poor parents, so we might consider the possibility that rich parents may later help their children to secure better-paying jobs.

We might also look at macro-level data, such as state-by-state comparisons of income and educational levels. In one macrolevel study based on census data, researchers found that in states whose residents have a relatively high level of education, household income levels are high as well (Figure 2-2). This finding suggests that schooling may well be related to income, though it does not speak to the micro-level relationship we are interested in. That is, we want to know whether *individuals* who are well educated are also well paid.

Study Alert

Be able to discuss the distinction between an independent variable and a dependent variable, and explain the role each plays in an experiment.

FORMULATING THE HYPOTHESIS

After reviewing earlier research and drawing on the contributions of sociological theorists, the researchers may then *formulate the hypothesis.* A **hypothesis** is a speculative statement about the relationship between two or more factors known as variables. Income, religion, occupation, and gender can all serve as variables in a study. We can define a **variable** as a measurable trait or characteristic that is subject to change under different conditions.

Researchers who formulate a hypothesis generally must suggest how one aspect of human behavior influences or affects another. The variable hypothesized to cause or influence another is called the **independent variable**. The other variable is termed the **dependent variable** because its action *depends* on the influence of the independent variable. In other words, the researcher believes that the independent variable predicts or causes change in the dependent variable. For example, a researcher in sociology might anticipate that the availability of affordable housing (the independent variable, x) affects the level of homelessness in a community (the dependent variable, y).

Our hypothesis is that the higher one's educational degree, the more money

It seems reasonable that these graduates of Fort Bethold Community College on the Fort Bethold Reservation, North Dakota, will earn more income than high school graduates. How would you go about testing that hypothesis?

FIGURE 2-2 EDUCATIONAL LEVEL AND HOUSEHOLD INCOME IN THE UNITED STATES

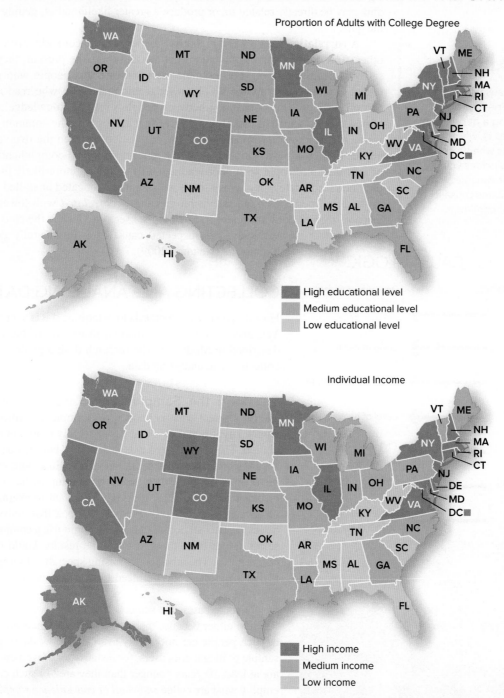

Proportion of Adults with College Degree

High educational level
Medium educational level
Low educational level

Individual Income

High income
Medium income
Low income

Notes: Cutoffs for high/medium and medium/low educational levels in 2012 were 31 percent and 25.7 percent of the population with a college degree, respectively; median for the entire nation was 29.1 percent. Cutoffs for high/medium and medium/low individual income levels in 2011 were $54,000 and $45,000, respectively; national median income was $51,371 in 2011.
Source: American Community Survey in Bureau of the Census 2013a:Table 80201.

one will earn. The independent variable that is to be measured is the level of education. The variable that is thought to depend on it—income—must also be measured.

Identifying independent and dependent variables is a critical step in clarifying cause-and-effect relationships. As shown in Figure 2-3 **causal logic** involves the relationship between a condition or variable and a particular consequence, with one leading to the other. For instance, being less integrated into society may be directly related to, or produce a greater likelihood of, suicide. Similarly, the time students spend reviewing material for a quiz may be directly related to, or produce a greater likelihood of, getting a high score on the quiz.

A **correlation** exists when a change in one variable coincides with a change in the other. Correlations are an indication that causality *may* be present; they do not necessarily indicate causation. For example, data indicate that people who prefer to watch televised news programs are less knowledgeable than those who read newspapers and newsmagazines. This correlation between people's relative knowledge and their choice of news media seems to make sense, because it agrees with the common belief that television dumbs down information. But the correlation between the two variables is actually caused by a third variable, people's relative ability to comprehend large amounts of information. People with poor reading skills are much more likely than others to get their news from television, while those who are more educated or skilled turn more often to the print media. Though television viewing is *correlated* with lower news comprehension, then, it does not *cause* it. Sociologists seek to identify the *causal* link between variables; the suspected causal link is generally described in the hypothesis (Neuman 2009).

Study Alert

Remember that causal logic describes an independent variable influencing a dependent variable (*x* leads to *y*), whereas a **correlation** occurs when a change in one variable *coincides* with a change in another variable. A correlation indicates causality may exist but does not confirm it.

FIGURE 2-3 **CAUSAL LOGIC**

Independent variable

x

Dependent variable

y

Level of educational degree → Level of income

Degree of lack of integration into society → Likelihood of suicide

Availability of affordable housing → Level of homelessness

Parents' church attendance → Children's church attendance

Time spent preparing for quiz → Performance on quiz

Parents' income → Likelihood of children's enrolling in college

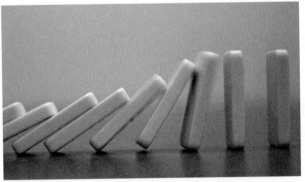

In *causal logic*, an independent variable (often designated by the symbol *x*) influences a dependent variable (often designated as *y*); thus, *x* leads to *y*. For example, parents who attend church regularly (*x*) are more likely to have children who are churchgoers (*y*). Notice that the first two pairs of variables are taken from studies already described in this textbook.

Source: Developed by author.

COLLECTING AND ANALYZING DATA

How do you test a hypothesis to determine if it is supported or refuted? You need to collect information, using one of the research designs described in Module 5. The research design guides the researcher in collecting and analyzing data.

Selecting the Sample In most studies, social scientists must carefully select what is known as a sample. A **sample** is a selection from a larger population that is statistically representative of that population. There are many kinds of samples, but the one social scientists use most frequently is the random sample. In a **random sample**, every member of an entire population being studied has the same chance of being selected. Thus, if researchers want to examine the opinions of people listed in a city directory (a book that, unlike the telephone directory, lists all households), they might use a computer to randomly select names from the directory. The results would constitute a random sample. The advantage of using specialized sampling techniques is that sociologists do not need to question everyone in a population (Igo 2007).

In some cases, the subjects researchers want to study are hard to identify, either because their activities are clandestine or because lists of such people are not readily available. How do researchers create a sample of illegal drug users, for instance, or of women whose husbands are at least 10 years younger than they are? In such cases, researchers employ what are called *snowball* or *convenience samples*—that is, they recruit participants through word of mouth or by posting notices on the Internet. With the help of special statistical techniques, researchers can draw conclusions from such nonrandom samples.

It is all too easy to confuse the careful scientific techniques used in representative sampling with the many *nonscientific* polls that receive much more media attention. For example, website viewers are often encouraged to register their views on headline news or political contests. Such polls reflect nothing more than the views of those who happened to visit the website and took the time, perhaps at some cost, to register their opinions. These data do not necessarily reflect (and indeed may distort) the views of the broader population. Not everyone has access to a computer on a regular basis, or the means and/or inclination to register their opinions. Even when these techniques include answers from tens of thousands of people, they will be far less accurate than a carefully selected representative sample of 1,500 respondents.

For the purposes of our research example, we will use information collected in the American Community Survey conducted by the Bureau of the Census. Each year, the Census Bureau surveys approximately 77,000 households across the United States. Technicians at the bureau then use the data to estimate the nation's entire population.

Ensuring Validity and Reliability The scientific method requires that research results be both valid and reliable. **Validity** refers to the degree to which a measure or scale truly reflects the phenomenon under study. A valid measure of income depends on the gathering of accurate data. Various studies show that people are reasonably accurate in reporting how much money they earned in the most recent year. If a question is written unclearly, however, the resulting data might not be accurate. For example, respondents to an unclear question about income might report their parents' or spouse's income instead of their own.

Reliability refers to the extent to which a measure produces consistent results. Some people may not disclose accurate information, but most do. In the American Community Survey, about 98 percent of the households that researchers approach participate in the survey. The Census Bureau checks their responses against those of similar households, to ensure that the data do not differ significantly from other known responses. The Bureau also checks their responses for reliability, since more and more data are being collected online (American Community Survey 2013b).

From the perspective of . . .

A Legislative Aide What might happen if you were to give your congressperson faulty research on which to base a critical decision about the best way to handle toxic waste in your state?

DEVELOPING THE CONCLUSION

Scientific studies, including those conducted by sociologists, do not aim to answer all the questions that can be raised about a particular subject. Therefore, the conclusion of a research study represents both an end and a beginning. Although it terminates a specific phase of the investigation, it should also generate ideas for future study.

Supporting Hypotheses In our example, we find that the data support our hypothesis: people with more formal schooling *do* earn more money than others. Those with a high school diploma earn more than those who failed to complete high school, but those with an associate's degree earn more than high school graduates. The relationship continues through more advanced levels of schooling, so that those with graduate degrees earn the most.

The relationship is not perfect, however. Some people who drop out of high school end up with high incomes, and some with advanced degrees earn modest incomes, as shown in Figure 2-4. A successful entrepreneur, for example, might not have much formal schooling, while the holder of a doctorate may choose to work for a low-paying nonprofit

FIGURE 2-4 IMPACT OF A COLLEGE EDUCATION ON INCOME

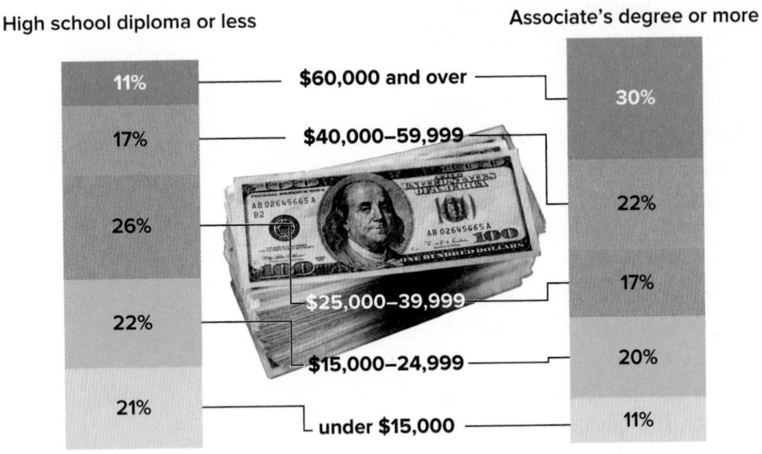

High school diploma or less   Associate's degree or more

11%	$60,000 and over	30%
17%	$40,000–59,999	22%
26%		22%
	$25,000–39,999	17%
22%	$15,000–24,999	20%
21%	under $15,000	11%

Forty-three percent of people with a high school diploma or less (left) earn under $25,000 a year, while only 28 percent earn $40,000 or more. In contrast, only 31 percent of those with an associate's degree or higher (right) earn less than $25,000, while 52 percent earn $40,000 or more.

Source: Author's analysis of DeNavas-Walt et al. 2013, Detailed Table PINC-03. Only people with earnings included.

How would researchers study our attitudes toward people who smoke cigarettes in public? They would likely use respondents' past smoking behavior as a control variable. In that case, they might hypothesize that respondents who smoke may be more tolerant of smoking in public than respondents who don't smoke. Another interesting question would be whether people who have quit smoking feel differently about lighting up in public than other nonsmokers. What do you think?

institution. Sociologists are interested in both the general pattern that emerges from their data and exceptions to the pattern.

Sociological studies do not always generate data that support the original hypothesis. Many times, a hypothesis is refuted, and researchers must reformulate their conclusions. Unexpected results may also lead sociologists to reexamine their methodology and make changes in the research design.

Controlling for Other Factors A **control variable** is a factor that is held constant to test the relative impact of an independent variable. For example, if researchers wanted to know how adults in the United States feel about restrictions on smoking in public places, they would probably attempt to use a respondent's smoking behavior as a control variable. That is, how do smokers versus nonsmokers feel about smoking in public places? The researchers would compile separate statistics on how smokers and nonsmokers feel about anti-smoking regulations.

Our study of the influence of education on income suggests that not everyone enjoys equal educational opportunities, a disparity that is one of the causes of social inequality. Since education affects a person's income, we may wish to call on the conflict perspective to explore this topic further. What impact does a person's race or gender have? Is a woman with a college degree likely to earn as much as a man with similar schooling? Later in this textbook we will consider these other factors and variables. That is, we will examine the impact that education has on income while controlling for variables such as gender and race.

IN SUMMARY: THE SCIENTIFIC METHOD

Let us briefly summarize the process of the scientific method through a review of the example. We *defined a problem* (the question of whether it pays to get a higher educational degree). We *reviewed the literature* (other studies of the relationship between education and income) and *formulated a hypothesis* (the higher one's educational degree, the more money one will earn). We *collected and analyzed the data,* making sure the sample was representative and the data were valid and reliable. Finally, we *developed the conclusion:* the data do support our hypothesis about the influence of education on income.

Read each question carefully and then select or provide the best answer.

1. The first step in any sociological research project is to
   a. collect data.
   b. define the problem.
   c. review previous research.
   d. formulate a hypothesis.

2. The variable that the researcher believes may be causing or influencing another is called the
   a. dependent variable.
   b. hypothetical variable.
   c. correlation variable.
   d. independent variable.

3. A correlation exists when
   a. one variable causes something to occur in another variable.
   b. two or more variables are causally related.
   c. a change in one variable coincides with a change in another variable.
   d. a positive or negative relationship exists between two variables.

4. A(n) _____ is a speculative statement about the relationship between two or more factors known as variables.

5. _____ refers to the degree to which a measure or scale truly reflects the phenomenon under study.

Answers

1 (b); 2 (a); 3 (d); 4 hypothesis; 5 Validity

Consider these questions to get a deeper understanding of the material.

1. Suppose you wanted to examine whether videogames that involve driving skills can help people learn to drive well. How would you begin to set up an experiment? What would be your hypothesis and your variables?

2. Suppose that two researchers use different operational definitions for the same term. Can both researchers' results be reliable and valid? Explain.

RECAP

LO 4-1 Explain how sociologists use the scientific method to answer questions of interest.

- Sociologists are committed to the use of the scientific method in their research efforts.

LO 4-2 Outline and describe the steps in the scientific method and how sociologists use it.

- There are five basic steps in the scientific method: defining the problem, reviewing the literature, formulating the hypothesis, collecting and analyzing the data, and developing the conclusion.
- Whenever researchers wish to study abstract concepts, such as intelligence or prejudice, they must develop workable operational definitions.
- A hypothesis states a possible relationship between two or more variables.
- By using a sample, sociologists avoid having to test everyone in a population.
- According to the scientific method, research results must possess both validity and reliability.

KEY TERMS

Causal logic The relationship between a condition or variable and a particular consequence, with one leading to the other.

Control variable A factor that is held constant to test the relative impact of an independent variable.

Correlation A relationship between two variables in which a change in one coincides with a change in the other.

Dependent variable The variable in a causal relationship that is subject to the influence of another variable.

Hypothesis A speculative statement about the relationship between two or more variables.

Independent variable The variable in a causal relationship that causes or influences a change in another variable.

Operational definition An explanation of an abstract concept that is specific enough to allow a researcher to assess the concept.

Random sample A sample for which every member of an entire population has the same chance of being selected.

Reliability The extent to which a measure produces consistent results.

Sample A selection from a larger population that is statistically representative of that population.

Scientific method A systematic, organized series of steps that ensures maximum objectivity and consistency in researching a problem.

Validity The degree to which a measure or scale truly reflects the phenomenon under study.

Variable A measurable trait or characteristic that is subject to change under different conditions.

Major Research
Designs and Development

W Work

An important aspect of sociological research is deciding *how* to collect the data. A **research design** is a detailed plan or method for obtaining data scientifically. Selection of a research design is often based on the theories and hypotheses the researcher starts with (Merton 1948). The choice requires creativity and ingenuity, because it directly influences both the cost of the project and the amount of time needed to collect the data.

LO 5-1 Elements of Design

The elements of research designs that sociologists regularly use to generate data include surveys, ethnography, experiments, and existing sources.

SURVEYS

Almost all of us have responded to surveys of one kind or another. We may have been asked what kind of detergent we use, which presidential candidate we intend to vote for, or what our favorite television program is. A **survey** is a study, generally in the form of an interview or questionnaire, that provides researchers with information about how people think and act. As anyone who watches the news during presidential campaigns knows, surveys have become a staple of political life.

When you think of surveys, you may recall seeing online polls that offer instant results. Although such polls can be highly interesting, they reflect only the opinions of those who visit the website and choose to respond online. As we have seen, a survey must be based on precise, representative sampling if it is to genuinely reflect a broad range of the population. In our wired world, more and more people can be reached only through their cell phones.

In preparing to conduct a survey, sociologists must not only develop representative samples; they must also exercise great care in the wording of questions. An effective survey question must be simple and clear enough for people to understand. It must also be specific enough so that there are no problems in interpreting the results. Open-ended questions ("What do you think of the programming on educational television?") must be carefully phrased to solicit the type of information desired. Surveys can be indispensable sources of information, but only if the sampling is done properly and the questions are worded accurately and without bias.

In wording questions, researchers must also pay careful attention to changes in society. In December 2010, officials at the Bureau of Labor Statistics recognized the effects of an extended recession by changing a decades-old practice. In the past, multiple-choice questions about how long a respondent had been unemployed had ended with a maximum of "99 weeks or over." By the end of 2010, joblessness had become so chronic that the bureau increased the number of choices, ending with "290 weeks or longer."

There are two main forms of the survey: the **interview**, in which a researcher obtains information through face-to-face, phone, or online questioning, and the **questionnaire**, in which the researcher uses a printed or written form to obtain information from a respondent. Each of these has its own advantages. An interviewer can obtain a higher response rate, because people find it more difficult to turn down a personal request for an interview than to throw away a written questionnaire. In addition, a skillful interviewer can go beyond written questions and probe for a subject's underlying feelings and reasons. Patricia and Peter Adler (2011) conducted 139 in-depth interviews for their book on the sensitive subject of self-injury. On the other hand, questionnaires have the advantage of being cheaper, especially in large samples.

Why do people have sex? A straightforward question, but until recently it was rarely investigated scientifically, despite its significance to public health, marital counseling, and criminology. To find the answer, researchers interviewed nearly 2,000 undergraduates at the University of Texas at Austin. In developing the question for the interview, they first asked a random sample of 400 students to list all the reasons why they had ever had sex. The explanations were highly diverse, ranging from "I was drunk" to "I wanted to feel closer to God." The team then asked another sample of 1,500 students to rate the importance of each of the 287 reasons given by the first group. Table 2-1 ranks the results. Nearly every reason was rated most important by at least some respondents. Though there were some gender differences in the replies, there was significant consensus between men and women on the top 10 reasons (Meston and Buss 2007).

The survey is an example of **quantitative research**, which collects and reports data primarily in numerical form. Most of the survey research discussed so far in this book has been quantitative. While this type of research can make use of large samples, it can't offer great depth and detail on a topic. That is why researchers also make use of **qualitative research**, which relies on what is seen in field and naturalistic settings, and often focuses on small groups and communities rather than on large groups or whole nations. The most common form of qualitative research is ethnography, or observation, which we consider next.

TABLE 2-1 **TOP REASONS WHY MEN AND WOMEN HAD SEX**

Reason	Men	Women
I was attracted to the person	1	1
It feels good	2	3
I wanted to experience the physical pleasure	3	2
It's fun	4	8
I wanted to show my affection to the person	5	4
I was sexually aroused and wanted the release	6	6
I was "horny"	7	7
I wanted to express my love for the person	8	5
I wanted to achieve an orgasm	9	14
I wanted to please my partner	10	11
I realized I was in love	17	9
I was "in the heat of the moment"	13	10

Source: Meston and Buss 2007:506.

Throughout this book you will find examples of both quantitative and qualitative research, since both are used widely. Some sociologists prefer one type of research to the other, but we learn most when we draw on many different research designs and do not limit ourselves to a particular type of research.

ETHNOGRAPHY

Investigators often collect information or test hypotheses through firsthand studies. **Ethnography** is the study of an entire social setting through extended systematic field-work. **Observation**, or direct participation in closely watching a group or organization, is the basic technique of ethnography. However, ethnographic research also includes the collection of historical information and the conduct of in-person interviews. Although ethnography may seem a relatively informal method compared to surveys or experiments, ethnographic researchers are careful to take detailed notes while observing their subjects.

In some cases, the sociologist actually joins a group for a period, to get an accurate sense of how it operates. This approach is called *participant observation.* In Barbara Ehrenreich's widely read book *Nickel and Dimed: On (Not) Getting By in America,* the author was a participant observer. Disguising herself as a divorced, middle-aged housewife without a college degree, Ehrenreich set out to see what life was like for low-wage workers. Her book chronicles her own and others' experiences trying to make ends meet on a minimum wage (Ehrenreich 2001).

During the late 1930s, in a classic example of participant-observation research, William F. Whyte moved into a low-income Italian neighborhood in Boston. For nearly four years he was a member of the social circle of "corner boys" that he describes in *Street Corner Society.* Whyte revealed his identity to these men and joined in their conversations, bowling, and other leisure-time activities. His goal was to gain greater insight into the community that these men had established. As Whyte (1981:303) listened to Doc, the leader of the group, he "learned the answers to questions I would not even have had the sense to ask if I had been getting my information solely on an interviewing basis." Whyte's work was especially valuable, since at the time the academic world had little direct knowledge of the poor, and tended to rely for information on the records of social service agencies, hospitals, and courts (P. Adler et al. 1992).

Carnegie Mellon University's Data Truck lets researchers go where their subjects are—from nightclubs to marathon races. Equipped with the latest technology, the truck allows social scientists to enter the responses to their community surveys into their databases on-site. It also gives them access to online social networks in the area, and even lets them videotape street activity.

The initial challenge that Whyte faced—and that every participant observer encounters—was to gain acceptance into an unfamiliar group. It is no simple matter for a college-trained sociologist to win the trust of a religious cult, a youth gang, a poor Appalachian community, or a circle of skid row residents. It requires a great deal of patience and an accepting, non-threatening type of personality on the part of the observer.

Ethnographic research poses other complex challenges for the investigator. Sociologists must be able to fully understand what they are observing. In a sense, then, researchers must learn to see the world as the group sees it in order to fully comprehend the events taking place around them. This raises a delicate issue. If the research is to be successful, the observer cannot allow the close associations or even friendships that inevitably develop to influence the subjects' behavior or the conclusions of the study. Even while working hard to gain acceptance from the group being studied, the participant observer *must* maintain some degree of detachment.

EXPERIMENTS

When sociologists want to study a possible cause-and-effect relationship, they may conduct experiments. An **experiment** is an artificially created situation that allows a researcher to manipulate variables.

In the classic method of conducting an experiment, two groups of people are selected and matched for similar characteristics, such as age or education. The researchers then assign the subjects to one of two groups: the experimental or the control group. The **experimental group** is exposed to an independent variable; the **control group** is not. Thus, if scientists were testing a new type of antibiotic, they would administer the drug to an experimental group but not to a control group.

In some experiments, just as in observation research, the presence of a social scientist or other observer may affect the behavior of the people being studied. Sociologists have used the term **Hawthorne effect** to refer to the unintended influence that observers of experiments can have on their subjects. The term originated as the result of an experiment conducted at the Hawthorne plant of the Western Electric Company during the 1920s and 1930s. Researchers found that *every* change they made in working conditions—even reduced lighting—seemed to have a positive effect on workers' productivity. They concluded that workers had made a special effort to impress their observers. Though the carefully constructed study did identify some causes for changes in the workers' behavior that did not have to do with their being observed, the term *Hawthorne effect* has become synonymous with a placebo or guinea pig effect (Franke and Kaul 1978).

USE OF EXISTING SOURCES

Sociologists do not necessarily need to collect new data in order to conduct research and test hypotheses. The term **secondary analysis** refers to a variety of research techniques that make use of previously collected and publicly accessible information and data. Generally, in conducting secondary analysis, researchers use data in ways that were unintended by the initial collectors of information. For example, census data are compiled for specific uses by the federal government but are also valuable to marketing specialists in locating everything from bicycle stores to nursing homes.

Sociologists consider secondary analysis to be *nonreactive*—that is, it does not influence people's behavior. For example, Émile Durkheim's statistical analysis of suicide neither increased nor decreased human self-destruction. Researchers, then, can avoid the Hawthorne effect by using secondary analysis.

There is one inherent problem, however: the researcher who relies on data collected by someone else may not find exactly what is needed. Social scientists who are studying family violence can use statistics from police and social service agencies on *reported* cases of spouse abuse and child abuse, but how many cases are not reported? Government bodies have no precise data on *all* cases of abuse.

Many social scientists find it useful to study cultural, economic, and political documents, including newspapers, periodicals, radio and television tapes, the Internet, scripts, diaries, songs, folklore, and legal papers (Table 2-2). In examining these sources, researchers employ a technique known as **content analysis**, which is the systematic coding and objective recording of data, guided by some rationale. Box 2-1 describes a recent content study of gender differences in the way Boy Scouts and Girl Scouts earn merit badges.

Content analysis can be revealing. Following a recent increase in devastating hurricanes, floods, and prolonged droughts, many people have expressed the need to educate

TABLE 2-2 **EXISTING SOURCES USED IN SOCIOLOGICAL RESEARCH**

Most Frequently Used Sources

Census data

Crime statistics

Birth, death, marriage, divorce, and health statistics

Other Sources

Newspapers and periodicals

Personal journals, diaries, e-mail, and letters

Records and archival material of religious organizations, corporations, and other organizations

Transcripts of radio programs

Motion pictures and television programs

Web pages, blogs, and chat rooms

Song lyrics

Scientific records (such as patent applications)

Speeches of public figures (such as politicians)

Votes cast in elections or by elected officials on specific legislative proposals

Attendance records for public events

Videos of social protests and rallies

Literature, including folklore

Source: Developed by author.

Research Today

2-1 GENDER MESSAGES IN SCOUTING

Nearly 5 million children in the United States participate in scouting. What gender messages do these young people receive during their time as Scouts?

A key form of guidance not just for Scouts but for their leaders is the Scouts' handbook. Sociologist Kathleen Denny did a content analysis of the Boy Scouts' *Webelos Handbook* and the *Junior Girl Scout Handbook*. Focusing specifically on material for Scouts in the fourth and fifth grades, she found that both

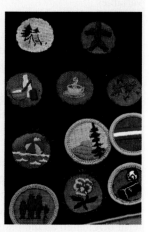

Merit badges for boys (left) and girls (right)

handbooks delivered traditional gender messages. Girl Scout activities were more likely than Boy Scout activities to be communal or other-oriented; Boy Scout activities were more likely to be solo undertakings.

> *The most gender-specific aspect of the Girl Scout handbook is the subjects of the badges themselves.*

Denny found that the names of merit badges also conveyed traditional gender messages. Girl Scout badge names often include puns or other forms of word play; Boy Scout badges do not. For example, the Boy Scout badge for studying rocks and geology is called simply the Geologist badge; the comparable Girl Scout badge is called the Rocks Rock badge. Boy Scout badges more often have career-oriented names—Engineer, Craftsman, Scientist; Girl Scout badge names have less of a career orientation—Sky Search instead of Astronomer, Car Care instead of Mechanic.

The most gender-specific aspect of the Girl Scout handbook is the subjects of the badges themselves. Many refer to stereotypically feminine activities: Caring for Children, Looking Your Best, Sew Simple. Besides personal hygiene and healthy eating, the Looking Your Best badge includes an "Accessory Party," which requires Scouts to "experiment to see how accessories highlight your features and your outfit." Needless to say, such badges are not offered in the Boy Scouts. The most nearly comparable one in the Boy Scout handbook is the Fitness badge, which includes activities such as keeping a food diary and warning a relative about the dangers of drugs and alcohol.

Denny acknowledges that Scout handbooks are not the only influence on gender roles in scouting. How are gender messages communicated in person during troop or pack meetings and ceremonies, for example? How do parents reinforce or mediate the gender themes in scouting? And how do children adjust to, accept, or rebel against the gender messages they receive as Scouts? Denny's research suggests the need for further research on gender socialization in the Boy Scouts and Girl Scouts.

Let's Discuss

1. Did you participate in scouting as a child? If so, were you aware of the gender messages you were receiving as part of the scouting experience? How did you react?
2. If you were a Scout leader yourself, what kind of gender model would you attempt to be? How would you become that kind of model?

Sources: Boy Scouts of America 2010; K. Denny 2011; Girl Scouts of the USA 2001:39; World Association of Girl Guides and Girl Scouts 2011.

TABLE 2-3 MAJOR RESEARCH DESIGNS

Method	Examples	Advantages	Limitations
Survey	Questionnaires Interviews	Yields information about specific issues	Can be expensive and time-consuming
Ethnography	Observation	Yields detailed information about specific groups or organizations	Involves months if not years of labor-intensive data
Experiment	Deliberate manipulation of people's social behavior	Yields direct measures of people's behavior	Ethical limitations on the degree to which subjects' behavior can be manipulated
Existing sources/ Secondary analysis	Analysis of census or health data Analysis of films or TV commercials	Cost-efficiency	Limited to data collected for some other purpose

future generations about climate change. To assess children's awareness of the environment, sociologists conducted a content analysis of award-winning picture books over the last 70 years. Their work revealed a noticeable *decline* in depictions of the natural environment and animals. Today, when children's books do address environmental events, they are more likely to portray volcanic eruptions than floods or bad weather. Even when books about urban areas show smokestacks emitting huge quantities of black smoke, the story line does not identify air pollution as a problem (J. Williams et al. 2012).

Table 2-3 summarizes the major research designs, along with their advantages and limitations.

LO 5-2 Developments of Methodology

Sociologists have developed several new methodological approaches. These contemporary methods have helped produce significant advances in the field of sociology.

FEMINIST METHODOLOGY

The feminist perspective has had a great impact on the current generation of social researchers. How might this perspective influence research? Although researchers must be objective, their theoretical orientation may influence the questions they ask—or just as important, the questions they fail to ask. Until recently, for example, researchers frequently studied work and the family separately. Yet feminist theorists see the two spheres of activity as being closely integrated. Similarly, work and leisure, paid and unpaid domestic work may be seen not as two separate spheres, but as two sides of the same coin.

Recently, feminist scholars have become interested in self-injury. Research shows that 85 percent of self-injurers are female; feminist researchers seek to explain why women predominate in this population. Rather than treat the behavior as a medical disorder, they note that society encourages women much more than men to attend to their bodies through hair removal, skin treatments, and depigmentation. Given this heightened attention to the female body, feminists suggest that specific instances of victimization can lead women to self-injure. They also seek to better understand male self-injurers, and are testing the hypothesis that among men, self-injury is a manifestation of hypermasculinity in the tolerance of pain (P. Adler and Adler 2011:25–27, 35–36).

Feminist researchers tend to involve and consult their subjects more than other researchers, and they are more oriented toward seeking change, raising the public consciousness, and influencing policy. They are particularly open to a multidisciplinary approach, such as making use of historical evidence or legal studies (T. Baker 1999; Lofland 1975; Reinharz 1992).

QUEER THEORY AND METHODOLOGY

If researchers wish to generalize about society, their findings must be representative of all people. Over the last generation, feminist theorists have insisted that women deserve as much attention from researchers as men. Similarly, exponents of queer theory ask whether researchers consider gays and lesbians in their studies, or simply assume that the generalizations they make apply to everyone, whether heterosexual or gay?

According to the National Bureau of Economic Research, most research significantly underreports the proportion of gays and lesbians in the population; it also underestimates the percentage of people who hold anti-gay views. The bureau suggests using a "veiled reporting" technique, in which respondents are asked whether they consider themselves to be heterosexual in the context of other much less sensitive questions, such as "Did you spend a lot of time playing video games as a child?" In one study, when respondents were asked about their sexual orientation within a group of such questions, 19 percent reported they were nonheterosexual; when the question was asked more directly, the proportion was 11 percent (Coffman et al. 2013).

This study suggests that if researchers want to generalize about *both* heterosexuals and homosexuals, they should be extremely careful in wording questions about respondents' sexual orientation—compared even to other sensitive topics, such as political and religious affiliations.

LO **5-3** The Data-Rich Future

Advances in technology have affected all aspects of our lives, and sociological research is no exception. Massive increases in available data have allowed sociologists to undertake research that was virtually impossible just a decade ago. In the recent past, only people with grants or major institutional support could work easily with large amounts of data. Now anyone with a computer can access huge amounts of data and learn more about social behavior.

Across the United States, cities and towns of all sizes receive and record citizens' complaints. Sometimes those complaints are acted upon; sometimes, for a variety of reasons, they are merely recorded into a database. In Boston, researchers found a treasure trove of data on housing complaints, covering everything from poor heating and chronic dampness to the presence of pests, such as bedbugs. Hundreds of thousands of calls had been recorded along with specific addresses, allowing researchers to compare housing conditions from one neighborhood to another.

Researchers soon realized that the data could be mapped to show the relative seriousness of the city's housing problems at a glance. As the team noted, the data are not an exact indication of "problem housing areas," because homeowners are much more likely than renters to call for government assistance, regardless of their income. Conversely, problems often go unreported in neighborhoods where renters dominate, whether tenants are rich or poor (O'Brien et al. 2013; Scharfenberg 2013).

In foreign countries, data are sometimes as available as they are in the United States. From 2009 through fall 2013, countries around the world experienced intense bursts of influenza. How did medical researchers track the virus's spread across a nation, much less the world? Epidemiologists typically rely on reports that originate in doctors' offices and are funneled through government agencies. Data collection is a time-consuming process, with many days passing between the detection of symptoms and the publication of official statistics. However, public health researchers may have found a way to track contagious diseases using Google. By monitoring the topics people search for and compensating for the relative access to computers in different countries (high in Sweden and low in Nigeria, for example), they can monitor the spread of disease almost in real time. Although their first efforts at online data tracking overestimated the outbreak, their accuracy improves with each passing year (Dukić et al. 2011; D. Lazer et al. 2014).

Similarly, in the past sociologists had to rely on victims' complaints or police reports to understand crime patterns. Now they are beginning to access real-time, geocoded (that is, location-specific) incident reports. These new data will offer sociologists much more information, which they can interpret and relate to other aspects of the social environment (G. King 2011). One ethical concern raised by all these data involves individual privacy. Sociologists now have access to information about people's real estate transactions, campaign contributions, online product purchases, and even travel along tollways. What steps should they take to protect the privacy of the individuals whose data they are using? This is not an academic question. Today, 87 percent of the people in the United States can be personally identified given only their gender, date of birth, and ZIP code (G. King 2011).

E Evaluate

Read each question carefully and then select or provide the best answer.

1. Through which type of research technique does a sociologist ensure that data are statistically representative of the population being studied?
   a. sampling
   b. experiments
   c. ethnography
   d. control variables

2. In the 1930s, William F. Whyte moved into a low-income Italian neighborhood in Boston to gain insight into that community. For nearly four years, he was a member of a social circle that he describes in *Street Corner Society*. What type of research technique did Whyte use?
   a. experiment
   b. survey
   c. secondary analysis
   d. participant observation

3. Émile Durkheim's statistical analysis of suicide was an example of what kind of research technique?
   a. ethnography
   b. observation research
   c. secondary analysis
   d. experimental research

4. If scientists were testing a new type of toothpaste in an experimental setting, they would administer the toothpaste to a(n) _____ group, but not to a(n) _____ group.

5. The term _____ _____ refers to the unintended influence that observers of experiments can have on their subjects.

Answers

1 (a); 2 (d); 3 (c); 4 experimental, control; 5 Hawthorne effect

R Rethink

Consider these questions to get a deeper understanding of the material.

1. How could you set up an experiment to study the effects of TV watching on schoolchildren's grades?

2. Suppose you were part of a group assigned to study homelessness in your community. Which research technique would you find most useful? How would you use that technique?

RECAP

LO 5-1 Summarize the characteristics, advantages, and limitations of the major research designs.

- An important component of scientific research is devising a plan for collecting data, called a research design.
- The two principal forms of survey research are the interview and the questionnaire.
- Ethnography allows sociologists to study certain behaviors and communities that cannot be investigated through other research methods.
- When sociologists wish to study a cause-and-effect relationship, they may conduct an experiment.
- Sociologists also make use of existing sources in secondary analysis and content analysis.

LO 5-2 Describe the impact of feminist theory and queer theory on sociological research practices.

- The participation of increasing numbers of women in sociological research has influenced the topics chosen for study, the ways in which topics are handled and viewed, and the ways in which research questions are posed.
- Researchers using the feminist perspective have focused research on the integration of family and work studies; the study of phenomena such as self-injury and sex trafficking; and the supposed divide between industrial and developing nations.
- In a similar fashion, exponents of queer studies insist that gay and lesbian issues and gay and lesbian participants be included in the sociological research agenda.

LO 5-3 Discuss the benefits and challenges of conducting research online.

- Technology plays an important role in sociological research, whether through a computer database or information obtained from the Internet.
- Databases retained for particular uses have proven to be rich resource for many types of content analysis, providing surprisingly rich analytical material for sociological and medical studies.

- The ethical issue of privacy presents a challenge for researchers wishing to tap into databases collected for entirely different reasons.

KEY TERMS

Content analysis The systematic coding and objective recording of data, guided by some rationale.

Control group The subjects in an experiment who are not introduced to the independent variable by the researcher.

Ethnography The study of an entire social setting through extended systematic fieldwork.

Experiment An artificially created situation that allows a researcher to manipulate variables.

Experimental group The subjects in an experiment who are exposed to an independent variable introduced by a researcher.

Hawthorne effect The unintended influence that observers of experiments can have on their subjects.

Interview A face-to-face, phone, or online questioning of a respondent to obtain desired information.

Observation A research technique in which an investigator collects information through direct participation, by closely watching a group or community.

Qualitative research Research that relies on what is seen in field or naturalistic settings more than on statistical data.

Quantitative research Research that collects and reports data primarily in numerical form.

Questionnaire A printed or written form used to obtain information from a respondent.

Research design A detailed plan or method for obtaining data scientifically.

Secondary analysis A variety of research techniques that make use of previously collected and publicly accessible information and data.

Survey A study, generally in the form of an interview or questionnaire, that provides researchers with information about how people think and act.

MODULE 6 Ethics of Research

P Prepare | Learning Objectives

LO 6-1 List the basic principles of the American Sociological Association's *Code of Ethics*.

LO 6-2 Apply ethical principles—including conflict of interest and value neutrality—to the challenges that researchers encounter in conducting research.

LO 6-3 Analyze through a sociological lens the challenges in conducting research on human sexuality and the potential impact of such research on social policy.

O Organize | Module Outline

The ASA Code of Ethics
    Confidentiality
    Conflict of Interest
    Value Neutrality
Social Policy and Sociological Research
    Studying Human Sexuality

W Work

A biochemist cannot inject a drug into a human being unless it has been thoroughly tested and the subject agrees to the shot. To do otherwise would be both unethical and illegal. Sociologists, too, must abide by certain specific standards in conducting research, called a **code of ethics**.

LO **6-1** The ASA Code of Ethics

The professional society of the discipline, the American Sociological Association (ASA), first published the society's *Code of Ethics* in 1971 and reviewed it most recently in 1997. It puts forth the following basic principles:

1. Maintain objectivity and integrity in research.
2. Respect the subject's right to privacy and dignity.
3. Protect subjects from personal harm.
4. Preserve confidentiality.
5. Seek informed consent when data are collected from research participants or when behavior occurs in a private context.
6. Acknowledge research collaboration and assistance.
7. Disclose all sources of financial support (American Sociological Association 1999).

These basic principles probably seem clear-cut. How could they lead to any disagreement or controversy? Yet many delicate ethical questions cannot be resolved simply by reading these seven principles. For example, should a sociologist who is engaged in participant-observation research always protect the confidentiality of subjects? What if the subjects are members of a religious cult allegedly involved in unethical and possibly illegal activities? What if the sociologist is interviewing political activists and is questioned by government authorities about the research?

Because most sociological research uses *people* as sources of information—as respondents to survey questions, subjects of ethnography, or participants in experiments—these sorts of questions are important. In all cases, sociologists need to be certain they are not invading their subjects' privacy. Generally, they do so by assuring subjects of anonymity and by guaranteeing the confidentiality of personal information. In addition, research proposals that involve human subjects must now be overseen by a review board, whose members seek to ensure that subjects are not placed at an unreasonable level of risk. If necessary, the board may ask researchers to revise their research designs to conform to the code of ethics.

We can appreciate the seriousness of the ethical problems researchers confront by considering the experience of sociologist Rik Scarce, described in the next section. Scarce's vow to protect his subjects' confidentiality got him into considerable trouble with the law.

> ## Study Alert
>
> You can use a mnemonic (a memory trick) to remember these principles. The sentence "Ordering personal hamburgers can cause a delay" stands for **O**bjectivity, **P**rivacy, **H**arm, **C**onfidentiality, **C**onsent, **A**ssistance, **D**isclose.

CONFIDENTIALITY

Like journalists, sociologists occasionally find themselves subject to questions from law enforcement authorities because of knowledge they have gained in the course of their work. This uncomfortable situation raises profound ethical questions.

In May 1993, Rik Scarce, a doctoral candidate in sociology at Washington State University, was jailed for contempt of court. Scarce had declined to tell a federal grand jury what he knew—or even whether he knew anything—about a 1991 raid on a university research laboratory by animal rights activists. At the time, Scarce was conducting research for a book about environmental protesters and knew at least one suspect in the break-in. Curiously, although he was chastised by a federal judge, Scarce won respect from fellow prison inmates, who regarded him as a man who "wouldn't snitch" (Monaghan 1993:A8).

The American Sociological Association supported Scarce's position when he appealed his sentence. Scarce maintained his silence. Ultimately the judge ruled that nothing would be gained by further incarceration, and Scarce was released after serving 159 days in jail. In January 1994, the U.S. Supreme Court declined to hear Scarce's case on appeal. The Court's failure to consider his case led Scarce (2005) to argue that federal legislation is needed to clarify the right of scholars and members of the press to preserve the confidentiality of those they interview.

LO 6-2 CONFLICT OF INTEREST

Sometimes disclosing all the sources of funding for a study, as required in principle 7 of the ASA's *Code of Ethics,* is not a sufficient guarantee of ethical conduct. Especially in the case of both corporate and government funding, money given ostensibly for the support of basic research may come with strings attached. Accepting funds from a private organization or even a government agency that stands to benefit from a study's results can call into question a researcher's objectivity and integrity (principle 1).

From the perspective of . . .

A Pharmaceutical Technician What could be the consequences to your company and its consumers if someone doctored the data to fit a desired outcome while developing a new medicine?

LO 6-2 VALUE NEUTRALITY

The ethical considerations of sociologists lie not only in the methods they use and the funding they accept, but also in the way they interpret their results. Max Weber ([1904] 1949) recognized that personal values would influence the questions that sociologists select for research. In his view, that was perfectly acceptable, but under no conditions could a researcher allow his or her personal feelings to influence the *interpretation* of data. In Weber's phrase, sociologists must practice **value neutrality** in their research.

As part of this neutrality, investigators have an ethical obligation to accept research findings even when the data run counter to their personal views, to theoretically based explanations, or to widely accepted beliefs. For example, Émile Durkheim challenged popular conceptions when he reported that social (rather than supernatural) forces were an important factor in suicide.

Although some sociologists believe that neutrality is impossible, ignoring the issue would be irresponsible. Let's consider what might happen if researchers brought their own biases to the investigation. A person investigating the impact of intercollegiate sports on alumni contributions, for example, might focus only on the highly visible revenue-generating sports of football and basketball and neglect the so-called minor sports, such as tennis or soccer, which are more likely to involve women athletes. Despite the early work of W. E. B. DuBois and Jane Addams, sociologists still need to be reminded that the discipline often fails to adequately consider all people's social behavior.

In her book *The Death of White Sociology* (1973), Joyce Ladner called attention to the tendency of mainstream sociology to treat the lives of African Americans as a social problem. More recently, feminist sociologist Shulamit Reinharz (1992) has argued that sociological research should be not only inclusive but also open to bringing about social change and to drawing on relevant research by nonsociologists. Both Ladner and Reinharz maintain that researchers should always analyze whether women's unequal social status has affected their studies in any way. For example, one might broaden the study of the

A floating containment barrier (or boom) encircles the Exxon oil tanker *Valdez* after it was grounded on a reef off the coast of Alaska. Exxon was found negligent in the environmental disaster and was ordered to pay $5.3 billion for the cleanup. On appeal, the company managed to reduce the damages to $500 million based on academic research that it had funded—research that some scholars believe involved a conflict of interest.

impact of education on income to consider the implications of the unequal pay status of men and women. The issue of value neutrality does not mean that sociologists can't have opinions, but it does mean that they must work to overcome any biases, however unintentional, that they may bring to their analysis of research.

Sociologist Peter Rossi (1987) admits to having liberal inclinations that direct him to certain fields of study. Yet in line with Weber's view of value neutrality, Rossi's commitment to rigorous research methods and objective interpretation of data has sometimes led him to controversial findings that are not necessarily supportive of his liberal values. For example, his measure of the extent of homelessness in Chicago in the mid-1980s fell far below the estimates of the Chicago Coalition for the Homeless. Coalition members bitterly attacked Rossi for hampering their social reform efforts by minimizing the extent of homelessness. Rossi (1987:79) concluded that "in the short term, good social research will often be greeted as a betrayal of one or another side to a particular controversy."

LO 6-3 SOCIAL POLICY and Sociological Research

We have seen that researchers rely on a number of tools, from simple observational research to the latest in computer technologies. Because in the real world sociological research can have far-reaching consequences for public policy and public welfare, we'll consider its impact on the study of human sexuality.

STUDYING HUMAN SEXUALITY

How can researchers study human sexual behavior? Neuroscientists Ogi Ogas and Sai Gaddam (2011) studied millions of web searches, websites, and videos related to sex. They found that women and men differ decidedly in their preferences, but very little (if any) distinction between heterosexuals and homosexuals, other than their sexual orientation. This type of research has significant limitations, however. Ogas and Gaddam could not distinguish between online fantasies and rational desires, or between a single search and one of many repeated searches by the same person. Nevertheless, this cyber study is a step forward in the effort to understand human sexual behavior (Bartlett 2011).

In this age of devastating sexually transmitted diseases, there is no time more important to increase our scientific understanding of human sexuality. As we will see, however, this is a difficult topic to research, not only because of privacy concerns but because of all the preconceptions, myths, and beliefs people bring to the subject of sexuality. Many people actively oppose research on human sexuality. How does one carry out scientific research on such a controversial and personal topic?

Applying Sociology Sociologists have little reliable national data on patterns of sexual behavior in the United States. Until the 1990s, the only comprehensive study of sexual behavior was the famous two-volume *Kinsey Report,* prepared in the 1940s (Kinsey et al. 1948, 1953; see also Igo 2007). Although the *Kinsey Report* is still widely quoted, the volunteers interviewed for the report were not representative of the nation's adult population.

In part, we lack reliable data on patterns of sexual behavior because it is difficult for researchers to obtain accurate information about this sensitive subject. Moreover, until AIDS emerged in the 1980s, there was little scientific demand for data on sexual behavior, except for specific concerns such as contraception. And even though the AIDS crisis has reached dramatic proportions, government funding for studies of sexual behavior is still controversial and therefore difficult to obtain.

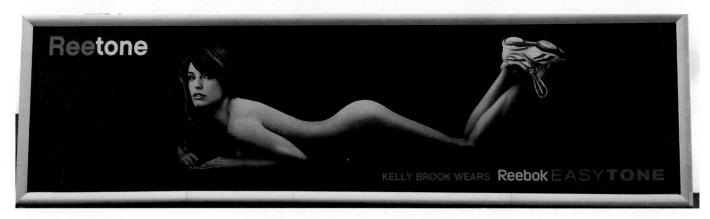

Sex may sell, but persuading legislators to fund research on human sexual behavior is still a challenge.

FIGURE 2-5 MEDIAN AGE OF FIRST SEX

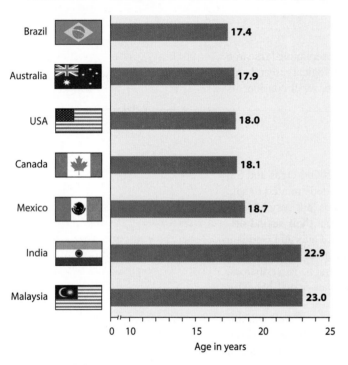

Source: Durex 2007.

The controversy surrounding research on human sexual behavior raises the issue of value neutrality, which becomes especially delicate when one considers the relationship of sociology to the government. The federal government has become the major source of funding for sociological research. Yet Max Weber urged that sociology remain an autonomous discipline and not become unduly influenced by any one segment of society. According to Weber's ideal of value neutrality, sociologists must remain free to reveal information that is embarrassing to the government, or for that matter, supportive of government institutions.

Initiating Policy In 1987 the National Institute of Child Health and Human Development sought proposals for a national survey of sexual behavior. Sociologists responded with various plans that a review panel of scientists approved for funding. However, in 1991, the U.S. Senate voted to forbid funding any survey of adult sexual practices. Despite the vote, sociologists developed the National Health and Social Life Survey (NHSLS) to better understand the sexual practices of adults in the United States. The researchers raised $1.6 million of *private* funding to make their study possible (Laumann et al. 1994a, 1994b).

The authors of the NHSLS believe that their research is important. They argue that data from their survey allow interest groups to more easily address public policy issues such as AIDS, sexual harassment, welfare reform, sex discrimination, abortion, teenage pregnancy, and family planning. Moreover, the research findings help to counter some commonsense notions. For instance, contrary to the popular beliefs that women regularly use abortion for birth control and that poor teens are the most likely socioeconomic group to have abortions, researchers found that three-fourths of all abortions are the first for the woman, and that well-educated and affluent women are more likely to have abortions than poor teens (Sweet 2001).

The usefulness of the NHSLS in addressing public policy issues has proved influential. As Figure 2-5 shows, scholars around the world are now studying human sexual behavior, in an effort to reduce the occurrence of HIV/AIDS.

Read each question carefully and then select or provide the best answer.

1. A researcher who is a committed atheist must take particular care to make sure that her research study of religious practices on her college campus is designed and conducted in accordance with which principle from the ASA's *Code of Ethics?*
   a. preserving confidentiality
   b. obtaining informed consent
   c. maintaining objectivity
   d. protecting subjects from harm

2. What is the most effective way to ensure subjects' right to privacy in a sociological research study?
   a. guaranteeing anonymity
   b. respecting subjects' dignity
   c. obtaining a signed consent form
   d. using randomization in selecting a sample

3. Medical schools that accept funds from pharmaceutical companies to support university research must be particularly careful to avoid violating which ethical principle?
   a. preservation of privacy
   b. conflict of interest
   c. value neutrality
   d. obtaining informed consent

4. The American Sociological Association's *Code of Ethics* requires sociologists to reveal the nature and potential risks of a research study and to obtain participants' agreement to take part. This is called _____ _____.

5. As part of their commitment to _____ neutrality, investigators have an ethical obligation to accept research findings even when the data run counter to their personal views or to widely accepted beliefs.

Answers
1 (c); 2 (a); 3 (b); 4 informed consent; 5 value

Consider these questions to get a deeper understanding of the material.

1. If you were planning a study of human sexuality, which of the principles of the ASA's *Code of Ethics* would particularly concern you? What ethical problems might arise in such a study, and how would you attempt to prevent them?

2. Why did Max Weber specify the need for neutrality in the interpretation of data? Is complete value neutrality possible in sociological research? To what extent should researchers try to overcome their own biases?

RECAP

LO 6-1 List the basic principles of the American Sociological Association's *Code of Ethics*.

- The *Code of Ethics* of the American Sociological Association calls for objectivity, protection of privacy, protection from harm, confidentiality, informed consent, acknowledgment of assistance, and disclosure of sources of financial support.

LO 6-2 Apply ethical principles—including conflict of interest and value neutrality—to the challenges that researchers encounter in conducting research.

- The issue of conflict of interest is especially relevant to privately funded research that may affect public policy. If a company funds research that can affect its profits, the conflict of interest issue almost always arises.
- Max Weber urged sociologists to practice value neutrality in their research by ensuring that their personal feelings do not influence their interpretation of data.

LO 6-3 Analyze through a sociological lens the challenges in conducting research on human sexuality and the potential impact of such research on social policy.

- In an age of diseases related to human sexual practices, it is important to increase understanding of sexuality, but the ability to perform research is hampered by concerns about privacy, issues of personal morality, and preconceptions and myths about sexuality.
- Despite failure to obtain government funding, researchers privately developed the National Health and Social Life Survey (NHSLS) to better understand the sexual practices of adults in the United States.

KEY TERMS

Code of ethics The standards of acceptable behavior developed by and for members of a profession.

Value neutrality Max Weber's term for objectivity of sociologists in the interpretation of data.

The Case of . . . the Foregone Conclusion

Kyle Larsen's program of study required him to take a basic science course. He chose Introduction to Ecoscience because he cared about the environment. For a midterm project, students had to investigate energy use by comparing similar products. Kyle decided to look at fuel efficiency in cars. Were some cars more "green" than others? The instructor reviewed the scientific method for research, but Kyle didn't bother to take notes. He already had a plan.

Kyle knew that small cars often got better mileage than large vehicles. He also knew that city driving could eat up more gas than highway trips. He designated his two-door compact with a V-4 engine, Car A. His sister's gas-guzzling SUV with its monster V-8 engine would be Car B. She lived far away, in the mountains, but all she had to do was keep a log of the number of miles she drove for a week and the amount of gas she used in that time. "Just local driving," he told her. "No big highway trips." His sister agreed. Kyle was happy. It was an easy project, and the hypothesis he was testing—small cars were more "green" than big cars—would be proved right.

Three weeks later, the instructor returned Kyle's project. He was shocked to receive a failing grade. The instructor's written remarks included: "Fuel efficiency isn't just about engine size" and "Poor use of scientific method."

1. Which steps of the scientific method of research does Kyle appear to have followed? Which steps did he ignore? How do you think the steps he skipped affected his conclusion?

2. Kyle's instructor commented, "Fuel efficiency isn't just about engine size." How could a review of the literature have helped Kyle to avoid this mistake? What sources could he have used?

3. What problems do you see with Kyle's research design? How could it have been improved?

4. How did Kyle's lack of value neutrality impact each of the five basic steps of the scientific method?

  **Study Strategies**

Setting Effective Goals

All of us have hopes and dreams—but these are only vague wishes unless we take the time and make the effort to make them real. Through effective goal setting, you can turn your dreams into goals, your goals into actions, and your actions into achievements.

Here is a framework for setting goals that can make a difference in your life.

- Think about which aspects of your life you want to set goals for, such as school, work, and family. Focus on one set at a time.
- Identify long-term goals that are genuinely important to you.
- Write down your long-term goals on a chart. Writing is the first step toward making a commitment.
- Share your goals with others in your family or study group. This is another step in committing yourself.

- Prioritize your goals, choosing only the most important ones to work on.
- Be realistic about your ability to focus. The fewer the goals the better. There will be time for additional goals later.

- Turn each goal into an action plan by breaking down large goals into sub-goals, or steps that will lead to the ultimate goal.
- Be specific. Goals and sub-goals should be particular and measurable so you'll know when you achieve them. Instead of "I will do well in my sociology class," write "I will get a B or better as my final sociology grade this semester," and then set sub-goals such as, "I will complete all my sociology homework on time this month" and "I will get no grade less than a B on tests and quizzes this month."
- Include a specific time in your sub-goals (e.g., "by the end of the month").
- Be realistic. Only you know if a sub-goal of "completing all homework on time this semester" is practical. If not, perhaps "completing at least 80% of homework on time this month" is a more realistic start. If you write goals that are unachievable, you'll abandon the whole goal-setting framework in a hurry.

- Track your progress on a written chart. Mark areas of success and areas where improvement is needed.
- Share your progress with others. They will help to keep you on track.

- Revisit your progress toward your ultimate goal after a reasonable amount of time has passed (e.g., a semester).
- Celebrate your sub-goal successes and accept your failures. No one succeeds 100% of the time.
- At the same time, persist and recommit to your goals. Adjust your sub-goals or work methods to make your next progress report better.

Are You Getting What You Want Out of Life?

Going through life without goals is a lot like driving a car without any clue about where you're headed. It may be fun at first, but time passes quickly and you wind up getting nowhere with nothing to show for it. Learning to set goals is learning to get what you want. To see how your goal-setting habits stack up, mark each of the following items "That's Me" or "Not Me," then use the scale below to find your score:

That's Me = 1

Not Me = 0

	That's Me	Not Me
1. Rather than just saying "I want to do better on tests," I form specific, measurable goals such as "I want to raise my test average this semester from a C to a B."		
2. I put my goals in writing and document my progress at regular intervals.		
3. I make my goals challenging but attainable within a stated time frame.		
4. With a larger goal, I break the process into smaller steps or sub-goals.		
5. I prioritize my goals according to what is most important and/or must be accomplished within a certain time frame.		
6. Once I've formulated a goal, I list all the actions I will need to take to achieve it.		
7. I state my goals in positive language: "I will read assignments nightly" rather than "I won't waste time after dinner."		
8. I tell others about my goals to keep myself from backsliding as well as to gain support for my efforts.		
9. When I'm struggling or feel like giving up, I take time to visualize having achieved my goal and imagine the satisfaction I will feel.		
10. I regularly monitor my progress toward my goals and make adjustments when necessary.		

SCORE:

8–10 You have your priorities straight. You set clear goals, define the steps needed to achieve them, and monitor your progress regularly.

5–7 You understand the value of goals but may not be defining them clearly or monitoring them effectively. Check over items 1–10 above to see where you can improve.

Below 5 Perhaps you have worried that setting goals will make you less of a free spirit, but remember: You're only as free as your ability to direct your own course and achieve your dreams. Get started with the goal-setting tips listed above. For more inspiration, check out this chapter's P.O.W.E.R. Study Strategies: Setting Effective Goals.

Culture

Sociology at **WORK** PEACE CORPS VOLUNTEER

JOHN EGAMI, a Peace Corps volunteer in Kampala, Uganda, works in elementary schools to develop literacy programs that will encourage students to read outside the classroom. "Ugandans, by tradition, are not readers," he explains. "It's rare for parents to read to their child, and the kids only learn to read enough to pass their exams."

His early efforts to get the children excited about reading met with polite disinterest. Then the holidays came and everyone went back to their native villages to celebrate with parents and grandparents. They returned with mountains of stories about their families and the holiday celebrations. Egami got an idea. He recorded all of the children's stories. The kids listened to them over and over. Listening with them, Egami clearly recognized the rich oral tradition of his students. They were skilled storytellers. If he wanted to get them to love reading, he was going to have to forge a link between their culture of oral expression and his reading goals for them. He transcribed the students' stories and printed them out. The kids loved these books, and they took delight in arguing over the shape and meaning of words. Egami's willingness to understand the Ugandans' culture had opened a window for his students to recognize the value of books and reading. ■

Looking Ahead

IN THIS CHAPTER WE WILL SEE JUST HOW BASIC THE STUDY OF CULTURE is to sociology. Our discussion will focus both on general cultural practices found in all societies and on the wide variations that can distinguish one society from another. We will define and explore the major aspects of culture, including language, norms, sanctions, and values. We will see how cultures develop a dominant ideology, and how functionalist and conflict theorists view culture. And we'll study the development of culture around the world, including the cultural effects of the worldwide movement toward globalization. Finally, in the Social Policy section, we will look at the conflicts in cultural values that underlie current debates over bilingualism.

MODULE 7 The Study of Culture

P Prepare Learning Objectives

LO 7-1 Explain the sociological meaning of culture and society.

LO 7-2 Compare and contrast ethnocentrism and cultural relativism.

LO 7-3 Illustrate the differences between sociobiological and sociological cultural explanations of human social behavior.

What Is Culture?
    Cultural Universals
    Ethnocentrism
    Cultural Relativism
    Sociobiology and Culture

 **Work**

LO 7-1 What Is Culture?

Culture is the totality of learned, socially transmitted customs, knowledge, material objects, and behavior. It includes the ideas, values, and artifacts (for example, DVDs, comic books, and birth control devices) of groups of people. Patriotic attachment to the flag of the United States is an aspect of culture, as is a national passion for the tango in Argentina.

Sometimes people refer to a particular person as "very cultured" or to a city as having "lots of culture." That use of the term *culture* is different from our use in this textbook. In sociological terms, culture does not refer solely to the fine arts and refined intellectual taste. It consists of *all* objects and ideas within a society, including slang words, ice-cream cones, and rock music. Sociologists consider both a portrait by Rembrandt and the work of graffiti spray painters to be aspects of culture. A tribe that cultivates soil by hand has just as much culture as a people that relies on computer-operated machinery. Each people has a distinctive culture with its own characteristic ways of gathering and preparing food, constructing homes, structuring the family, and promoting standards of right and wrong.

The fact that you share a similar culture with others helps to define the group or society to which you belong. A fairly large number of people are said to constitute a **society** when they live in the same territory, are relatively independent of people outside their area, and participate in a common culture. Metropolitan Los Angeles is more populous than at least 150 nations, yet sociologists do not consider it a society in its own right. Rather, they see it as part of—and dependent on—the larger society of the United States.

A society is the largest form of human group. It consists of people who share a common heritage and culture. Members of the society learn this culture and transmit it from one generation to the next. They even preserve their distinctive culture through literature, art, video recordings, and other means of expression.

Cultural practices vary across societies. In China, married couples rarely wear wedding rings. To signify their commitment, couples who appear in public often sport matching or complementary outfits.

Sociologists have long recognized the many ways in which culture influences human behavior. Through what has been termed a tool kit of habits, skills, and styles, people of a common culture construct their acquisition of knowledge, their interactions with kinfolk, their entrance into the job market—in short, the way in which they live. If it were not for the social transmission of culture, each generation would have to reinvent television, not to mention the wheel (Swidler 1986).

Having a common culture also simplifies many day-to-day interactions. For example, when you buy an airline ticket, you know you don't have to bring along hundreds of dollars in cash. You can pay with a credit card. When you are part of a society, you take for granted many small (as well as more important) cultural patterns. You assume that theaters will provide seats for the audience, that physicians will not disclose confidential information, and that parents will be careful when crossing the street with young children. All these assumptions reflect basic values, beliefs, and customs of the culture of the United States.

Today, when text, sound, and video can be transmitted around the world instantaneously, some aspects of culture transcend national borders. The German philosopher Theodor Adorno and others have spoken of the worldwide **culture industry** that standardizes the goods and services demanded by consumers. Adorno contends that globally, the primary effect of popular culture is to limit people's choices. Yet others have shown that the culture industry's influence does not always permeate international borders. Sometimes the culture industry is embraced; at other times, soundly rejected (Adorno [1971] 1991:98–106; Horkheimer and Adorno [1944] 2002).

CULTURAL UNIVERSALS

All societies have developed certain common practices and beliefs, known as **cultural universals**. Many cultural universals are, in fact, adaptations to meet essential human needs, such as the need for food, shelter, and clothing. Anthropologist George Murdock (1945:124) compiled a list of cultural universals, including athletic sports, cooking, dancing, visiting, personal names, marriage, medicine, religious ritual, funeral ceremonies, sexual restrictions, and trade.

The cultural practices Murdock listed may be universal, but the manner in which they are expressed varies from culture to culture. For example, one society may let its members choose their marriage partners; another may encourage marriages arranged by the parents.

Not only does the expression of cultural universals vary from one society to another; within a society, it may also change dramatically over time. Each generation, and each year for that matter, most human cultures change and expand.

LO 7-2 ETHNOCENTRISM

Many everyday statements reflect our attitude that our culture is best. We use terms such as *underdeveloped, backward,* and *primitive* to refer to other societies. What "we" believe is a religion; what "they" believe is superstition and mythology.

It is tempting to evaluate the practices of other cultures on the basis of our perspectives. Sociologist William Graham Sumner (1906) coined the term **ethnocentrism** to refer to the tendency to assume that one's own culture and way of life represent the norm or are superior to all others. The ethnocentric person sees his or her group as the center or defining point of culture and views all other cultures as deviations from what is "normal." Westerners who think cattle are to be used for food might look down on India's Hindu religion and culture, which view the cow as sacred. Or people in one culture may dismiss as unthinkable the mate selection or child-rearing practices of another culture. In sum, our view of the world is dramatically influenced by the society in which we were raised.

Ethnocentrism is hardly limited to citizens of the United States. Visitors from many African cultures are surprised at the disrespect that children in the United States show their parents. People from India may be repelled by our practice of living in the same household with dogs and cats. Many Islamic fundamentalists in the Arab world and Asia view the United States as corrupt, decadent, and doomed to destruction. All these people may feel comforted by membership in cultures that in their view are superior to ours.

From the perspective of . . .

A Classroom Paraprofessional   How would it benefit the students of a multiethnic, multiracial urban school if the teaching staff evaluated student behaviors from the viewpoint of cultural relativism rather than ethnocentrism?

LO 7-2 CULTURAL RELATIVISM

While ethnocentrism means evaluating foreign cultures using the familiar culture of the observer as a standard of correct behavior, **cultural relativism** means viewing people's behavior from the perspective of their own culture. It places a priority on understanding other cultures, rather than dismissing them as "strange" or "exotic." Unlike ethnocentrists, cultural relativists employ the kind of value neutrality in scientific study that Max Weber saw as so important.

Cultural relativism stresses that different social contexts give rise to different norms and values. Thus, we must examine practices such as polygamy, bullfighting, and monarchy within the particular contexts of the cultures in which they are found. Although cultural relativism does not suggest that we must unquestionably accept every cultural variation, it does require a serious and unbiased effort to evaluate norms, values, and customs in light of their distinctive culture.

Consider the practice of children marrying adults. Most people in North America cannot fathom the idea of a 12-year-old girl marrying. The custom, which is illegal in the United States, is common in West Africa and South Asia. Should the United States respect such marriages? The apparent answer is no. In 2006 the U.S. government spent $623 million to discourage the practice in many of the countries with the highest child-marriage rates (Figure 3-1).

From the perspective of cultural relativism, we might ask whether one society should spend its resources to dictate the norms of another. However, federal officials have defended the government's actions. They contend that child marriage deprives girls of education, threatens their health, and weakens public health efforts to combat HIV/AIDS (Jain and Kurz 2007; B. Slavin 2007).

LO 7-3 SOCIOBIOLOGY AND CULTURE

While sociology emphasizes diversity and change in the expression of culture, another school of thought, sociobiology, stresses the universal aspects of culture. **Sociobiology** is the systematic study of how biology affects human social behavior. Sociobiologists assert that many of the cultural traits humans display, such as the almost universal expectation that women will be nurturers and men will be providers, are not learned but are rooted in our genetic makeup.

Sociobiology is founded on the naturalist Charles Darwin's (1859) theory of evolution. In traveling the world, Darwin had noted small variations in species—in the shape of a bird's beak, for example—from one location to another. He theorized that over hundreds of generations, random variations in genetic makeup had helped certain members of a species to survive in a particular environment. A bird with a differently shaped beak might have been better at gathering seeds than other birds, for instance. In reproducing, these lucky individuals had passed on their advantageous genes to succeeding generations.

FIGURE 3-1 COUNTRIES WITH HIGH CHILD MARRIAGE RATES

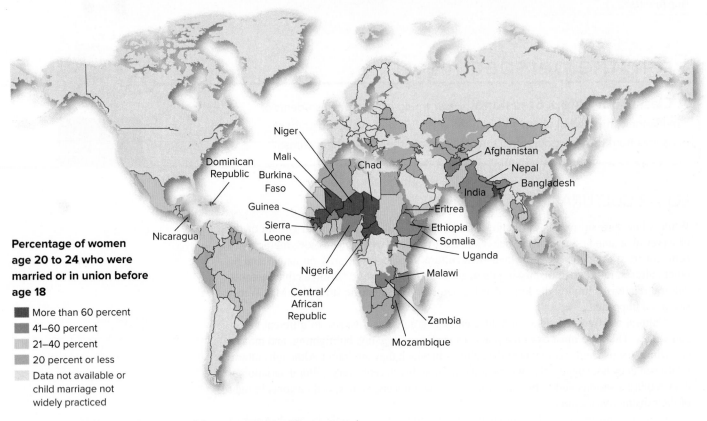

Percentage of women age 20 to 24 who were married or in union before age 18

- More than 60 percent
- 41–60 percent
- 21–40 percent
- 20 percent or less
- Data not available or child marriage not widely practiced

In 21 countries, 40 percent or more of the women under 18 are married.

Note: Data are the most recent available, ranging from 1987 to 2006.
Source: UNICEF 2010.

Eventually, given their advantage in survival, individuals with the variation began to out-number other members of the species. The species was slowly adapting to its environment. Darwin called this process of adaptation to the environment through random genetic variation *natural selection.*

Sociobiologists apply Darwin's principle of natural selection to the study of social behavior. They assume that particular forms of behavior become genetically linked to a species if they contribute to its fitness to survive (van den Berghe 1978). In its extreme form, sociobiology suggests that *all* behavior is the result of genetic or biological factors, and that social interactions play no role in shaping people's conduct.

Sociobiologists do not seek to describe individual behavior on the level of "Why is Fred more aggressive than Jim?" Rather, they focus on how human nature is affected by the genetic composition of a *group* of people who share certain characteristics (such as men or women, or members of isolated tribal bands). In general, sociobiologists have stressed the basic genetic heritage that *all* humans share and have shown little interest in speculating about alleged differences between racial groups or nationalities. A few researchers have tried to trace specific behaviors, like criminal activity, to certain genetic markers, but those markers are not deterministic. Family cohesiveness, peer group behavior, and other social factors can override genetic influences on behavior (Guo et al. 2008; E. Wilson 1975, 1978).

Certainly most social scientists would agree that there is a biological basis for social behavior. Like interactionists, however, conflict theorists and functionalists believe that people's behavior rather than their genetic structure defines social reality. Conflict theorists fear that the sociobiological approach could be used as an argument against efforts to assist disadvantaged people, such as schoolchildren who are not competing successfully (Freese 2008; Machalek and Martin 2010; E. Wilson 2000).

E Evaluate

Read each question carefully and then select or provide the best answer.

1. Which of the following is an aspect of culture?
   a. a comic book
   b. patriotic attachment to the flag of the United States
   c. slang words
   d. all of the above

2. People's adaptations to meet the needs for food, shelter, and clothing are examples of what George Murdock referred to as
   a. norms.
   b. folkways.
   c. cultural universals.
   d. cultural practices.

3. What is the term used when one places a priority on understanding other cultures, rather than dismissing them as "strange" or "exotic"?
   a. cultural relativism
   b. culture shock
   c. ethnocentrism
   d. cultural value

4. In contrast to ethnocentrists, cultural relativists employ what Max Weber called _____ neutrality.

Answers
1 (d); 2 (c); 3 (a); 4 value

R Rethink

Consider these questions to get a deeper understanding of the material.

1. Select two cultural universals from George Murdock's list and analyze them from a functionalist perspective. Why are these practices found in every culture? What functions do they serve?

2. What are some of the problems with looking at social behavior from a sociobiological point of view? What are some benefits? How useful do you find this perspective?

RECAP

LO 7-1 Explain the sociological meaning of culture and society.

- Culture is the totality of learned, socially transmitted customs, knowledge, material objects, and behavior shared by a particular group of people.

- A shared culture helps to define the group or society to which individuals belong.
- Cultural universals, or common practices found in every culture, include marriage, sports, cooking, medicine, and sexual restrictions. Although such practices are universal, their expression varies from culture to culture.

LO 7-2 Compare and contrast ethnocentrism and cultural relativism.

- People who assume that their culture is superior to others engage in ethnocentrism. In contrast, cultural relativism is the practice of viewing the behavior of other people from the perspective of their culture.
- Cultural relativists demonstrate the application of value neutrality, as defined by Max Weber.

LO 7-3 Illustrate the differences between sociobiological and sociological explanations of human social behavior.

- Sociobiology explains aspects of culture from the point of view of biology, especially natural selection. In this view, many cultural traits and behaviors exist today because they have contributed to a culture's survival.
- Many sociological theorists, including conflict theorists and other interactionists, reject the more extreme versions of sociobiology.

KEY TERMS

Cultural relativism The viewing of people's behavior from the perspective of their own culture.

Cultural universals A common practice or belief found in every culture.

Culture The totality of learned, socially transmitted customs, knowledge, material objects, and behavior.

Culture industry The worldwide media industry that standardizes the goods and services demanded by consumers.

Ethnocentrism The tendency to assume that one's own culture and way of life represent the norm or are superior to all others.

Society A fairly large number of people who live in the same territory, are relatively independent of people outside their area, and participate in a common culture.

Sociobiology The systematic study of how biology affects human social behavior.

Elements of Culture

Learning Objectives

LO 8-1 Define language and describe its influence on culture.

LO 8-2 Distinguish between norms and values and identify examples of sanctions for formal and informal norms.

LO 8-3 Discuss the differences in values concepts for global cultural war and clash of civilizations.

LO 8-4 Analyze culture and the dominant ideology using the major sociological perspectives.

Module Outline

Role of Language
    Language: Written and Spoken
    Nonverbal Communication
Norms and Values
    Norms
    Values
Global Culture War
Sociological Perspectives on Culture

LO **8-1** Role of Language

Language is one of the major elements of culture. It is also an important component of cultural capital. Recall from Chapter 1 that Pierre Bourdieu used the term *cultural capital* to describe noneconomic assets, such as family background and past educational investments, which are reflected in a person's knowledge of language and the arts.

Members of a society generally share a common language, which facilitates day-to-day exchanges with others. When you ask a hardware store clerk for a flashlight, you don't need to draw a picture of the instrument. You share the same cultural term for a small, portable, battery-operated light. However, if you were in England and needed this item, you would have to ask for an electric torch. Of course, even within the same society, a term can have a number of different meanings. In the United States, *pot* signifies both a container that is used for cooking and an intoxicating drug. In this section we will examine the cultural influence of language, which includes both the written and spoken word and nonverbal communication.

LANGUAGE: WRITTEN AND SPOKEN

Seven thousand languages are spoken in the world today—many more than the number of countries. For the speakers of each one, whether they number 2,000 or 200 million, language is fundamental to their shared culture.

The English language, for example, makes extensive use of words dealing with war. We speak of "conquering" space, "fighting" the "battle" of the budget, "waging war" on drugs, making a "killing" on the stock market, and "bombing" an examination; something monumental or great is "the bomb." An observer from an entirely different and warless culture could gauge the importance that war and the military have had in our lives simply by recognizing the prominence that militaristic terms have in our language. Similarly, the Sami people of northern Norway and Sweden have a rich diversity of terms for snow, ice, and reindeer (Haviland et al. 2008; Magga 2006).

Language is, in fact, the foundation of every culture. **Language** is an abstract system of word meanings and symbols for all aspects of culture. It includes speech, written characters, numerals, symbols, and nonverbal gestures and expressions. Because language is the foundation of every culture, the ability to speak other languages is crucial to intercultural relations. Throughout the Cold War era, beginning in the 1950s and continuing well into the 1970s, the U.S. government encouraged the study of Russian by developing special language schools for diplomats and military advisers who dealt with the Soviet Union. And following September 11, 2001, the nation recognized how few skilled translators it had for Arabic and other languages spoken in Muslim countries. Language quickly became a key not only to tracking potential terrorists, but also to building diplomatic bridges with Muslim countries willing to help in the war against terrorism.

Language does more than simply describe reality; it also serves to *shape* the reality of a culture. For example, most people in the United States cannot easily make the verbal distinctions concerning snow and ice that are possible in the Sami culture. As a result, they are less likely to notice such differences.

The **Sapir-Whorf hypothesis**, named for two linguists, describes the role of language in shaping our interpretation of reality. According to Sapir and Whorf, because people can conceptualize the world only through language, language *precedes* thought. Thus, the word symbols and grammar of a language organize the world for us. The Sapir-Whorf hypothesis also holds that language is not a given. Rather, it is culturally determined, and it encourages a distinctive interpretation of reality by focusing our attention on certain phenomena (Sapir 1929).

For decades, the Navajo have referred to cancer as *lood doo na'dziihii*. Now, through a project funded by the National Cancer Institute, the tribal college is seeking to change the phrase. Why? Literally, the phrase means "the sore that does not heal," and health educators are concerned that tribal members who have been diagnosed with cancer view it as a death sentence. Their effort to change the Navajo language, not easy in itself, is complicated by the Navajo belief that to talk about the disease is to bring it on one's people (Fonseca 2008).

Similarly, feminist theorists have noted that gender-related language can reflect—although in itself it does not determine—the traditional acceptance of men and women in certain occupations. Each time we use a term such as *mailman, policeman,* or *fireman,* we are implying (especially to young children) that these occupations can be filled only by males. Yet many women work as *mail carriers, police officers,* and *firefighters*—a fact that is being increasingly recognized and legitimized through the use of such nonsexist language.

Language can shape how we see, taste, smell, feel, and hear. It also influences the way we think about the people, ideas, and objects around us. Language communicates a culture's most important norms, values, and sanctions. That's why the decline of an old language or the introduction of a new one is such a sensitive issue in many parts of the world (see the Social Policy section at the end of this chapter).

A native speaker trains instructors from the Oneida Nation of New York in the Berlitz method of language teaching. As of 2012, there were 527 speakers of the Oneida language. Many Native American tribes are taking similar steps to recover their seldom used languages, realizing that language is the essential foundation of any culture.

Study Alert

Language, the foundation of every culture, does more than describe reality. It also helps *shape* the reality of a culture. The Sapir-Whorf hypothesis describes how language does this.

NONVERBAL COMMUNICATION

If you don't like the way a meeting is going, you might suddenly sit back, fold your arms, and turn down the corners of your mouth. When you see a friend in tears, you may give a quick hug. After winning a big game, you probably high-five your teammates. These are all examples of *nonverbal communication,* the use of gestures, facial expressions, and other visual images to communicate.

We are not born with these expressions. We learn them, just as we learn other forms of language, from people who share our same culture. This statement is as true for the basic expressions of happiness and sadness as it is for more complex emotions, such as shame or distress (Fridlund et al. 1987).

Using American Sign Language, a form of nonverbal communication, a football coach discusses a play with his team. The Silent Warriors, four-time national champions and the pride of the Alabama School for the Deaf, have defeated both hearing and nonhearing teams.

Like other forms of language, nonverbal communication is not the same in all cultures. For example, sociological research done at the micro level documents that people from various cultures differ in the degree to which they touch others during the course of normal social interactions. Even experienced travelers are sometimes caught off guard by these differences. In Saudi Arabia, a middle-aged man may want to hold hands with a partner after closing a business deal. In Egypt, men walk hand in hand in the street; in cafés, they fall asleep while lounging in each other's arms. These gestures, which would shock an American businessman, are considered compliments in those cultures. The meaning of hand signals is another form of nonverbal communication that can differ from one culture to the next. In Australia, the thumbs-up sign is considered rude (Passero 2002; Vaughan 2007).

A related form of communication is the use of symbols to convey meaning to others. **Symbols** are the gestures, objects, and words that form the basis of human communication. The thumbs-up gesture, a gold star sticker, and the smiley face in an e-mail are all symbols. Often deceptively simple, many symbols are rich in meaning and may not convey the same meaning in all social contexts. Around someone's neck, for example, a cross can symbolize religious reverence; over a grave site, a belief in everlasting life; or set in flames, racial hatred.

LO 8-2 Norms and Values

"Wash your hands before dinner." "Thou shalt not kill." "Respect your elders." All societies have ways of encouraging and enforcing what they view as appropriate behavior while discouraging and punishing what they consider to be inappropriate behavior. They also have a collective idea of what is good and desirable in life—or not. In this section we will learn to distinguish between the closely related concepts of norms and values.

NORMS

Norms are the established standards of behavior maintained by a society. For a norm to become significant, it must be widely shared and understood. For example, in movie theaters in the United States, we typically expect that people will be quiet while the film is shown.

Of course, the application of this norm can vary, depending on the particular film and type of audience. People who are viewing a serious artistic film will be more likely to insist on the norm of silence than those who are watching a slapstick comedy or horror movie.

One persistent social norm in contemporary society is that of heterosexuality. As sociologists, and queer theorists especially, note, children are socialized to accept this norm from a very young age. Overwhelmingly, parents describe adult romantic relationships to their children exclusively as heterosexual relationships. That is not necessarily because they consider same-sex relationships unacceptable, but more likely because they see heterosexuality as the norm in marital partnerships. According to a national survey of mothers of three- to six-year-olds, one in five mothers teaches her young children that homosexuality is wrong. The same survey showed that parenting reflects the dominant ideology, in which homosexuality is treated as a rare exception. Most parents assume that their children are heterosexual; only one in four has even considered whether his or her child might grow up to be gay or lesbian (K. Martin 2009).

Types of Norms Sociologists distinguish between norms in two ways. First, norms are classified as either formal or informal. **Formal norms** generally have been written down and specify strict punishments for violators. In the United States, we often formalize norms into laws, which are very precise in defining proper and improper behavior. Sociologist Donald Black (1995) has termed **law** "governmental social control," meaning that laws are formal norms enforced by the state. Laws are just one example of formal norms. Parking restrictions and the rules of a football or basketball game are also considered formal norms.

In contrast, **informal norms** are generally understood but not precisely recorded. Standards of proper dress are a common example of informal norms. Our society has no specific punishment, or *sanction,* for a person who shows up at school or work wearing inappropriate clothing. Laughter is usually the most likely response.

Norms are also classified by their relative importance to society. When classified in this way, they are known as *mores* and *folkways.* **Mores** (pronounced "*MOR*-ays") are norms deemed highly necessary to the welfare of a society, often because they embody the most cherished principles of a people. Each society demands obedience to its mores; violation can lead to severe penalties. Thus, the United States has strong mores against murder, treason, and child abuse, which have been institutionalized into formal norms.

Folkways are norms governing everyday behavior. Folkways play an important role in shaping the daily behavior of members of a culture. Society is less likely to formalize folkways than mores, and their violation raises comparatively little concern. For example, walking up a down escalator in a department store challenges our standards of appropriate behavior, but it will not result in a fine or a jail sentence.

Norms and Sanctions Suppose a football coach sends 12 players instead of 11 onto the field. Imagine a college graduate showing up in shorts for a job interview at a large bank. Or consider a driver who doesn't put money in a parking meter. These people have violated widely shared and understood norms. So what happens? In each of these situations, the person will receive sanctions if his or her behavior is detected.

Sanctions are penalties and rewards for conduct concerning a social norm. Note that the concept of *reward* is included in this definition. Conformity to a norm can lead to positive sanctions such as a pay raise, a medal, a word of gratitude, or a pat on the back. Negative sanctions include fines, threats, imprisonment, and stares of contempt.

Table 3-1 summarizes the relationship between norms and sanctions. As you can see, the sanctions that are associated with formal norms (which are written down and codified) tend to be formal as well. If a college football coach sends too many players onto the field, the team will be penalized 15 yards. The driver who fails to put money in the parking meter will receive a ticket and have to pay a fine. But sanctions for violations of informal norms can vary. The college graduate who goes to the bank interview in shorts will probably lose any chance of getting the job; on the other hand, he or she might be so brilliant that bank officials will overlook the unconventional attire.

TABLE 3-1 NORMS AND SANCTIONS

	Sanctions	
Norms	Positive	Negative
Formal	Salary bonus	Demotion
	Testimonial dinner	Firing from a job
	Medal	Jail sentence
	Diploma	Expulsion
Informal	Smile	Frown
	Compliment	Humiliation
	Cheers	Bullying

The entire fabric of norms and sanctions in a culture reflects that culture's values and priorities. The most cherished values will be most heavily sanctioned; matters regarded as less critical will carry light and informal sanctions.

Acceptance of Norms People do not follow norms, whether formal or informal, in all situations. In some cases, they can evade a norm because they know it is weakly enforced. It is illegal for U.S. teenagers to drink alcoholic beverages, yet drinking by minors is common throughout the nation. (In fact, teenage alcoholism is a serious social problem.)

In some instances, behavior that appears to violate society's norms may actually represent adherence to the norms of a particular group. Teenage drinkers are conforming to the standards of their peer group when they violate norms that condemn underage drinking. Similarly, business executives who use shady accounting techniques may be responding to a corporate culture that demands the maximization of profits at any cost, including the deception of investors and government regulatory agencies.

Norms are violated in some instances because one norm conflicts with another. For example, suppose that you live in an apartment building and one night hear the screams of the woman next door, who is being beaten by her husband. If you decide to intervene by ringing their doorbell or calling the police, you are violating the norm of minding your own business, while following the norm of assisting a victim of violence.

Acceptance of norms is subject to change as the political, economic, and social conditions of a culture are transformed. Until the 1960s, for example, formal norms throughout much of the United States prohibited the marriage of people from different racial groups. Over the past half century, however, such legal prohibitions have been cast aside. The process of change can be seen today in the increasing acceptance of single parents and growing support for the legalization of same-sex marriage.

When circumstances require the sudden violation of long-standing cultural norms, the change can upset an entire population. In Iraq, where Muslim custom strictly forbids touching by strangers for men and especially for women, the war that began in 2003 brought numerous daily violations of the norm. Outside important mosques, government offices, and other facilities likely to be targeted by terrorists, visitors had to be patted down and have their bags searched by Iraqi security guards. To reduce the discomfort caused by the procedure, women were searched by female guards and men by male guards. Despite that concession, and the fact that many Iraqis admitted or even insisted on the need for such measures, people still winced at the invasion of their personal privacy. In reaction to the searches, Iraqi women began to limit the contents of the bags they carried or simply left them at home (Rubin 2003).

VALUES

Though we each have a personal set of values—which may include caring or fitness or success in business—we also share a general set of values as members of a society. Cultural **values** are these collective conceptions of what is considered good, desirable, and proper—or bad, undesirable, and improper—in a culture. They indicate what people in a given culture prefer as well as what they find important and morally right (or wrong). Values may be specific, such as honoring one's parents and owning a home, or they may be more general, such as health, love, and democracy. Of course, the members of a society do not uniformly share its values. Angry political debates and billboards promoting conflicting causes tell us that much.

Values influence people's behavior and serve as criteria for evaluating the actions of others. The values, norms, and sanctions of a culture are often directly related. For example, if a culture places a high value on the institution of marriage, it may have norms (and strict sanctions) that prohibit the act of adultery or make divorce difficult. If a culture views private property as a basic value, it will probably have stiff laws against theft and vandalism.

The values of a culture may change, but most remain relatively stable during any one person's lifetime. Socially shared, intensely felt values are a fundamental part of our lives in the United States. Sociologist Robin Williams (1970) has offered a list of basic values. It includes achievement, efficiency, material comfort, nationalism, equality, and the supremacy of science and reason over faith. Obviously, not all 320 million people in this country agree on all these values, but such a list serves as a starting point in defining the national character.

Each year more than 200,000 entering college students at nearly 300 of the nation's four-year colleges fill out a questionnaire about their values. Because this survey focuses on an array of issues, beliefs, and life goals, it is commonly cited as a barometer of the nation's values. The respondents are asked what values are personally important to them. Over the past half century, the value of "being very well-off financially" has shown the strongest gain in popularity; the proportion of first-year college students who endorse this value as "essential" or "very important" rose from 42 percent in 1966 to 81 percent in 2012 (Figure 3-2).

During the 1980s and 1990s, support for values having to do with money, power, and status grew. At the same time, support for certain values having to do with social awareness and altruism, such as "helping others," declined. According to the 2011 nationwide survey, only 42 percent of first-year college students stated that "influencing social values" was an "essential" or "very important" goal. The proportion of students for whom "helping to promote racial understanding" was an essential or very important goal reached a record high of 46 percent in 1992, then fell to 35.3 percent in 2012. Like other aspects of culture, such as language and norms, a nation's values are not necessarily fixed.

Whether the slogan is "Think Green" or "Reduce Your Carbon Footprint," students have been exposed to values associated with environmentalism. How many of them accept those values? Poll results over the past 40 years show fluctuations, with a high of nearly 46 percent of students indicating a desire to become involved in cleaning up the environment. By the 1980s, however, student support for embracing this objective had dropped to around 20 percent or even lower (see Figure 3-2). Even with recent attention to global warming, the proportion remains level at only 26.5 percent of first-year students in 2012.

Values can also differ in subtle ways not just among individuals and groups, but from one culture to another. For example, in Japan, young children spend long hours working with tutors, preparing for entrance exams required for admission to selective schools. No stigma is attached to these services, known as "cram schools"; in fact, they are highly valued. Yet in South Korea, people have begun to complain that cram schools give affluent students an unfair advantage. Since 2008, the South Korean government has regulated the after-school tutoring industry, limiting its hours and imposing fees on the schools. Some think this policy has lowered their society's expectations of students, describing it as an attempt to make South Koreans "more American" (Ramstad 2011; Ripley 2011).

Another example of cultural differences in values is public opinion regarding the treatment of different racial and ethnic groups. As Figure 3-3 shows, opinion on the need for equal treatment of different racial and ethnic groups varies dramatically from one country to another.

Study Alert

Remember that norms are society's established expectations for typical behavior in varying situations, whereas values are the commonly held beliefs about what is considered proper or moral and improper or immoral behavior in a culture.

FIGURE 3-2 LIFE GOALS OF FIRST-YEAR COLLEGE STUDENTS IN THE UNITED STATES, 1966–2012

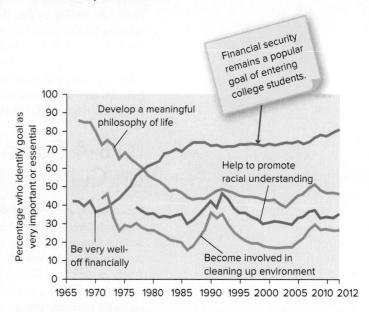

Sources: Pryor et al. 2007, 2013.

FIGURE 3-3 VALUING ETHNICITY BY COUNTRY

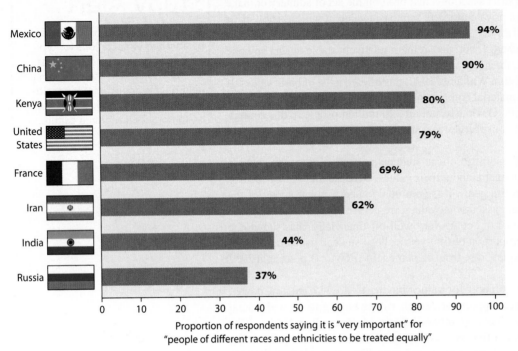

Mexico 94%
China 90%
Kenya 80%
United States 79%
France 69%
Iran 62%
India 44%
Russia 37%

0 10 20 30 40 50 60 70 80 90 100

Proportion of respondents saying it is "very important" for
"people of different races and ethnicities to be treated equally"

Source: Council on Foreign Relations 2009.

LO **8-3** Global Culture War

For almost a generation, public attention in the United States has focused on **culture war**, or the polarization of society over controversial cultural elements. Originally, in the 1990s, the term referred to political debates over heated issues such as abortion, religious expression, gun control, and sexual orientation. Soon, however, it took on a global meaning—especially after 9/11, as Americans wondered, "Why do they hate us?" Through 2000, global studies of public opinion had reported favorable views of the United States in countries as diverse as Morocco and Germany. But after the United States established a military presence in Iraq and Afghanistan, foreign opinion of the United States became quite negative (J. Hunter 1991; Kohut et al. 2005, 2007).

In the past 30 years, extensive efforts have been made to compare values in different nations, recognizing the challenges in interpreting value concepts in a similar manner across cultures. Psychologist Shalom Schwartz has measured values in more than 60 countries. Around the world, certain values are widely shared, including benevolence, which is defined as "forgiveness and loyalty." In contrast, power, defined as "control or dominance over people and resources," is a value that is endorsed much less often (Hitlin and Piliavin 2004; S. Schwartz and Bardi 2001).

Despite this evidence of shared values, some scholars have interpreted the terrorism, genocide, wars, and military occupations of the early 21st century as a "clash of civilizations." According to this thesis, cultural and religious identities, rather than national or political loyalties, are becoming the prime source of international conflict. Critics of this thesis point out that conflict over values is nothing new; only our ability to create havoc and violence has grown. Furthermore, speaking of a clash of "civilizations" disguises the sharp divisions that exist within large groups. Christianity, for example, runs the gamut from Quaker-style pacifism to certain elements of the Ku Klux Klan's ideology (Berman 2003; Huntington 1993; Said 2001).

LO **8-4** Sociological Perspectives on Culture

Functionalist and conflict theorists agree that culture and society are mutually supportive, but for different reasons. Functionalists maintain that social stability requires a consensus and the support of society's members; strong central values and common norms provide that support. This view of culture became popular in sociology beginning in the 1950s. It was borrowed from British anthropologists who saw cultural traits as a stabilizing element in a culture. From a functionalist perspective, a cultural trait or practice will persist if it performs functions that society seems to need or contributes to overall social stability and consensus.

Conflict theorists agree that a common culture may exist, but they argue that it serves to maintain the privileges of certain groups. Moreover, while protecting their self-interest, powerful groups may keep others in a subservient position. The term **dominant ideology** describes the set of cultural beliefs and practices that helps to maintain powerful social, economic, and political interests. This concept was first used by Hungarian Marxist Georg Lukacs (1923) and Italian Marxist Antonio Gramsci (1929), but it did not gain an audience in the United States until the early 1970s. In Karl Marx's view, a capitalist society has a dominant ideology that serves the interests of the ruling class.

From a conflict perspective, the dominant ideology has major social significance. Not only do a society's most powerful groups and institutions control wealth and property; even more important, they control the means of producing beliefs about reality through religion, education, and the media. Feminists would also argue that if all a society's most important institutions tell women they should be subservient to men, that dominant ideology will help to control women and keep them in a subordinate position.

A growing number of social scientists believe that it is not easy to identify a core culture in the United States. For support, they point to the lack of consensus on national values, the diffusion of cultural traits, the diversity within our culture, and the changing views of young people (look again at Figure 3-2). Instead, they suggest that the core culture provides the tools that people of all persuasions need to develop strategies for social change. Still, there is no denying that certain expressions of values have greater influence than others, even in as complex a society as the United States (Swidler 1986).

E Evaluate

Read each question carefully and then select or provide the best answer.

1. Which of the following statements is true according to the Sapir-Whorf hypothesis?
   a. Language simply describes reality.
   b. Language does not transmit stereotypes related to race.
   c. Language precedes thought.
   d. Language is not an example of a cultural universal.

2. Which of the following statements about norms is correct?
   a. People do not follow norms in all situations. In some cases, they evade a norm because they know it is weakly enforced.
   b. In some instances, behavior that appears to violate society's norms may actually represent adherence to the norms of a particular group.
   c. Norms are violated in some instances because one norm conflicts with another.
   d. All of the above are correct.

3. Which of the following statements about values is correct?
   a. Values never change.
   b. The values of a culture may change, but most remain relatively stable during any one person's lifetime.
   c. Values are constantly changing; sociologists view them as being very unstable.
   d. The values of a culture may change, but only after periods of intense social conflict.

4. "Put on some clean clothes for dinner" and "Thou shalt not kill" are both examples of _____ found in U.S. culture.

5. From a(n) _____ perspective, the dominant ideology has major social significance. Not only do a society's most powerful groups and institutions control wealth and property, but more importantly, they control the means of production.

Answers

1 (c); 2 (d); 3 (b); 4 norms; 5 conflict

R Rethink

Consider these questions to get a deeper understanding of the material.

1. In the United States, is the norm of heterosexuality formal or informal? Would you categorize it with mores or folkways? Explain.

2. Do you think the United States has a dominant ideology? If so, how would you describe it? Whose interests does it serve?

RECAP

LO 8-1 Define language and describe its influence on culture.

- Language includes speech, written characters, numerals, and symbols, as well as gestures and other forms of nonverbal communication.
- Language both describes culture and shapes it. According to the Sapir-Whorf hypothesis, language precedes thought and shapes our interpretation of reality.
- Nonverbal communication is the use of gestures, facial expressions, and other visual signs to communicate.

LO 8-2 Distinguish between norms and values and identify examples of sanctions for formal and informal norms.

- Sociologists distinguish between norms in two ways, classifying them as formal or informal and as mores or folkways.
- The formal (defined) norms of a culture will carry the heaviest sanctions; informal (generally understood) norms will carry light sanctions.
- Mores are norms that embody cherished principles of a society, and folkways are informal norms that govern everyday behavior.
- Values are comparatively stable and influence behavior, serving as criteria for evaluating the actions of others.

LO 8-3 Discuss the differences in values concepts for global cultural war and clash of civilizations.

- The notion of global cultural war holds that societies today are engaged in serious disputes that focus on controversial elements of culture, an idea that generally disregards evidence of widely shared human values.
- Some scholars and politicians have interpreted terrorism, genocide, and other forms of military struggle as evidence of a clash of civilizations, involving cultural and religious issues rather than strictly national or political concerns.

LO 8-4 Analyze culture and the dominant ideology using the major sociological perspectives.

- The dominant ideology of a culture is the set of cultural beliefs and practices that helps to maintain powerful social, economic, and political interests.
- Identifying a dominant, or core, culture in the United States is difficult, and perhaps undesirable, because of the extensive cultural variation within U.S. society.

KEY TERMS

Culture war The polarization of society over controversial cultural elements.

Dominant ideology A set of cultural beliefs and practices that helps to maintain powerful social, economic, and political interests.

Folkway A norm governing everyday behavior whose violation raises comparatively little concern.

Formal norm A norm that has been written down and that specifies strict punishments for violators.

Informal norm A norm that is generally understood but not precisely recorded.

Language An abstract system of word meanings and symbols for all aspects of culture; includes gestures and other nonverbal communication.

Law Governmental social control.

Mores Norms deemed highly necessary to the welfare of a society.

Norm An established standard of behavior maintained by a society.

Sanction A penalty or reward for conduct concerning a social norm.

Sapir-Whorf hypothesis A hypothesis concerning the role of language in shaping our interpretation of reality. It holds that language is culturally determined.

Symbol A gesture, object, or word that forms the basis of human communication.

Value A collective conception of what is considered good, desirable, and proper—or bad, undesirable, and improper—in a culture.

MODULE 9 Development of Culture around the World

 **Prepare** Learning Objectives

LO 9-1 Explain the processes by which culture develops and spreads.

LO 9-2 Demonstrate the ways in which technology has affected the speed of cultural diffusion.

 **Organize** Module Outline

Innovation

Globalization, Diffusion, and Technology

Today, despite the preference most of us have for our own way of life, powerful forces link us to others around the world. Thus, students in the United States may study the novels of Leo Tolstoy, the art of Pablo Picasso, or the films of Ang Lee. They may listen to pop music from Nigeria or South Korea, or follow the progress of social movements in Iran, Egypt, or Syria via satellite TV and social media. In this section we will examine two of the social processes that make these global links possible: innovation and the diffusion of culture through globalization and technology.

LO **9-1** Innovation

The process of introducing a new idea or object to a culture is known as **innovation**. Innovation interests sociologists because of the social consequences of introducing something new. There are two forms of innovation: discovery and invention. **Discovery** involves making known or sharing the existence of an aspect of reality. The finding of the structure of the DNA molecule and the identification of a new moon of Saturn are both acts of discovery. A significant factor in the process of discovery is the sharing of newfound knowledge with others. In contrast, an **invention** results when existing cultural items are combined into a form that did not exist before. The bow and arrow, the automobile, and the television are all examples of inventions, as are Protestantism and democracy.

LO **9-2** Globalization, Diffusion, and Technology

The recent emergence of Starbucks, the worldwide chain of coffeehouses, is just one illustration of the rapidly escalating trend toward globalization. While people in Asia are beginning to enjoy coffee, people in North America are discovering sushi. Some have become familiar with the *bento box,* a small lunchbox that is often used to serve sushi. A trademark Japanese cuisine, sushi has evolved from a once-exotic dish in the United States to a mainstream food commonly found in supermarket refrigerators. Yet its move across the Pacific has changed the delicacy. Americans tend to treat sushi as a take-out or menu item. The authentic way to eat sushi is to sit at a bar and engage the chef in conversation about the day's catch.

More and more cultural expressions and practices are crossing national borders and affecting the traditions and customs of the societies exposed to them. Sociologists use the term **diffusion** to refer to the process by which a cultural item spreads from group to group or society to society. Diffusion can occur through a variety of means, among them exploration, military conquest, missionary work, and the influence of the mass media, tourism, the Internet (see Box 3-1), and the fast-food restaurant.

Sociologist George Ritzer coined the term *McDonaldization of society* to describe how the principles of fast-food restaurants, developed in the United States, have come

Members of Big Toe Crew, a Vietnamese hip-hop group, rehearse for a performance. Through tourism and the mass media, music and dance spread from one culture to another in a process called diffusion.

to dominate more and more sectors of societies throughout the world. For example, hair salons and medical clinics now take walk-ins. In Hong Kong, sex selection clinics offer a menu of items, from fertility enhancement to methods of increasing the likelihood of having a child of the desired sex. And religious groups—from evangelical preachers on local stations or websites to priests at the Vatican Television Center—use marketing techniques similar to those that are used to sell Happy Meals.

McDonaldization is associated with the melding of cultures, through which we see more and more similarities in cultural expression. In Japan, for example, African entrepreneurs have found a thriving market for hip-hop fashions popularized by teens in the United States. Similarly, the familiar Golden Arches of McDonald's can be seen around the world. Yet corporations like McDonald's have had to make some adjustments of their own. Until 2001, McDonald's ran its *overseas* operations from corporate headquarters in suburban Chicago. After a few false starts, executives recognized the need to develop the restaurant's menus and marketing strategies overseas, relying on advice from local people. Now, at over 3,700 restaurants in Japan, customers can enjoy the Mega Tamago Burger—beef, bacon, and fried egg with special sauces. In India, patrons who don't eat beef can order a vegetarian McAloo Tikki potato burger. Because some strict vegetarians in India refuse to eat among nonvegetarians, in 2013 McDonald's began opening vegetarian-only restaurants there (Gasparro and Jargon 2012; Ritzer 2010, 2013).

From the perspective of . . .

A Small-Deli Owner What challenges does the "McDonaldization of society" pose for owners of small restaurants and retail shops trying to establish a market presence?

Study Alert

Material culture concerns the physical or technological features of our lives (food, houses, the Internet) while nonmaterial culture describes the way we use these objects, as well as our customs, beliefs, communication patterns, and type of government. Culture lag occurs when material culture makes a rapid advance to which the nonmaterial culture then struggles to adapt.

Technology in its many forms has increased the speed of cultural diffusion and broadened the distribution of cultural elements. Sociologist Gerhard Lenski has defined **technology** as "cultural information about the ways in which the material resources of the environment may be used to satisfy human needs and desires" (Nolan and Lenski 2009:357). Today's technological developments no longer await publication in journals with limited circulation. Press conferences, often carried simultaneously on the Internet, trumpet the new developments.

Technology not only accelerates the diffusion of scientific innovations but also transmits culture. The English language and North American culture dominate the Internet and World Wide Web. Such control, or at least dominance, of technology influences the direction of cultural diffusion. For example, websites cover even the most superficial aspects of U.S. culture but offer little information about the pressing issues faced by citizens of other nations. People all over the world find it easier to visit electronic chat rooms about the latest reality TV shows than to learn about their own governments' policies on day care or infant nutrition.

Sociologist William F. Ogburn (1922) made a useful distinction between the elements of *material* and *nonmaterial culture*. **Material culture** refers to the physical or technological aspects of our daily lives, including food, houses, factories, and raw materials. **Nonmaterial culture** refers to ways of using material objects, as well as to customs, beliefs, philosophies, governments, and patterns of communication. Generally, the nonmaterial culture is more resistant to change than the material culture. Consequently, Ogburn introduced the term **culture lag** to refer to the period of maladjustment when the nonmaterial culture is still struggling to adapt to new material conditions. For example, in 2010, manufacturers introduced electronic cigarettes, battery-powered tubes that turn nicotine-laced liquid into a vapor mist. The innovation soon had officials at airlines (which ban smoking) and the Food and Drug Administration scrambling to respond to the latest technology (Kesmodel and Yadron 2010; Swidler 1986).

Sociology in the Global Community

3-1 LIFE IN THE GLOBAL VILLAGE

Imagine a "borderless world" in which culture, trade, commerce, money, and even people move freely from one place to another. Popular culture is widely shared, whether it be Japanese sushi or U.S. running shoes, and the English speaker who answers questions over the telephone about your credit card account is as likely to be in India or Ireland as in the United States. In this world, even the sovereignty of nations is at risk, challenged by political movements and ideologies that span nations.

What caused this great wave of cultural diffusion? First, sociologists take note of advances in communications technology. Satellite TV, cell phones, the Internet, and the like allow information to flow freely across the world, linking global markets. In 2008, this process reached the point where consumers could view videos on handheld devices and surf the Internet on their wireless cell phones, shopping online at Amazon.com, eBay, and other commercial websites from cars, airports, and cafeterias. Second, corporations in the industrial nations have become multinational, with both factories and markets in developing countries. Business leaders welcome the opportunity to sell consumer goods in populous countries such as China. Third, these multinational firms have cooperated with global financial institutions, organizations, and governments to promote free trade—unrestricted or lightly restricted commerce across national borders.

Globalization is not universally welcomed. Many critics see the dominance of "businesses without borders" as benefiting the rich, particularly the very wealthy in industrial countries, at the expense of the poor in less developed nations. They consider globalization to be a successor to the imperialism and colonialism that oppressed Third World nations for centuries.

Even **Pirates of the Caribbean** *movies and Lady Gaga may be seen as threats to native cultures.*

Another criticism of globalization comes from people who feel overwhelmed by global culture. Embedded in the concept of globalization is the notion of the cultural domination of developing nations by more affluent nations. Simply put, people lose their traditional values and begin to identify with the culture of dominant nations. They may discard or neglect their native languages and dress as they attempt to copy the icons of mass-market entertainment and fashion. Even *Pirates of the Caribbean* movies and Lady Gaga may be seen as threats to native cultures, if they dominate the media at the expense of local art forms. As Sembene Ousmane, one of Africa's most prominent writers and filmmakers, noted, "[Today] we are more familiar with European fairy tales than with our own traditional stories" (World Development Forum 1990:4).

Globalization has its positive side, too. Many developing nations are taking their place in the world of commerce and bringing in much needed income. The communications revolution helps people to stay connected and gives them access to knowledge that can improve living standards and even save lives.

Let's Discuss

1. How are you affected by globalization? Which aspects of globalization do you find advantageous and which objectionable?
2. How would you feel if the customs and traditions you grew up with were replaced by the culture or values of another country? How might you try to protect your culture?

Sources: Dodds 2000; Giddens 1991; Hirst and Thompson 1996; D. Martin et al. 2006; Ritzer 2007; Sernau 2001; Tedeschi 2006.

Read each question carefully and then select or provide the best answer.

1. What term do sociologists use to refer to the process by which a cultural item spreads from group to group or society to society?
   a. diffusion
   b. globalization
   c. innovation
   d. cultural relativism

2. The appearance of Starbucks coffeehouses in China is a sign of what aspect of culture?
   a. innovation
   b. globalization
   c. diffusion
   d. cultural relativism

3. A person experiences _____ _____ when he or she feels disoriented, uncertain, out of place, even fearful when immersed in an unfamiliar culture.

4. The term _____ _____ refers to the fact that the material culture changes more rapidly than the nonmaterial culture.

Answers

1 (a); 2 (b); 3 culture shock; 4 culture lag

R Rethink

Consider these questions to get a deeper understanding of the material.

1. Name one culturally significant discovery and one culturally significant invention that occurred in your lifetime. How did these innovations change your culture?

2. Describe one positive and one negative example of McDonaldization that you have experienced.

RECAP

LO 9-1 Explain the processes by which culture develops and spreads.

- Culture expands through the process of innovation, which includes both discovery and invention.

- Discovery involves learning and sharing newly acquired knowledge with others, while invention involves combining existing cultural items into something that did not exist before.
- Diffusion—the spread of cultural items from one place to another—has fostered globalization. Some people resist ideas that seem too foreign, as well as those they perceive as threatening to their values and beliefs.

LO 9-2 Demonstrate ways in which technology has affected the speed of cultural diffusion.

- Technology greatly accelerates the global spread of culture, especially the cultures of the more developed countries. In a phenomenon called cultural lag, the material culture—physical or technological aspects of daily life—spreads more quickly and effectively than the nonmaterial culture—customs, beliefs, and philosophies.
- The influence of technology has been magnified by the Internet, which makes technological discovery and invention available almost instantaneously around the world.
- There is some concern that the Internet has had the effect of forcing the spread of U.S. culture and the English language around the globe.

KEY TERMS

Culture lag A period of maladjustment when the nonmaterial culture is still struggling to adapt to new material conditions.

Diffusion The process by which a cultural item spreads from group to group or society to society.

Discovery The process of making known or sharing the existence of an aspect of reality.

Innovation The process of introducing a new idea or object to a culture through discovery or invention.

Invention The combination of existing cultural items into a form that did not exist before.

Material culture The physical or technological aspects of our daily lives.

Nonmaterial culture Ways of using material objects, as well as customs, beliefs, philosophies, governments, and patterns of communication.

Technology Cultural information about the ways in which the material resources of the environment may be used to satisfy human needs and desires.

MODULE 10 Cultural Variation

W Work

LO 10-1 Cultural Variation within Societies

Despite the presence of cultural universals such as courtship and religion, great diversity exists among the world's many cultures. Inuit tribes in northern Canada, dressed in fur for the hunt, share little with farmers in southeast Asia, who dress lightly for work in their hot, humid rice paddies. Cultures adapt to meet specific circumstances, such as climate, level of technology, population, and geography.

Even *within* a single nation, certain segments of the populace develop cultural patterns that differ from the patterns of the dominant society—thus the difficulty of identifying a core culture in the United States, where regional differences fuel culture wars between conservatives and liberals. Moreover, in every region, specific communities tend to band together to form their own culture within a culture, called a *subculture*.

SUBCULTURES

Rodeo riders, residents of a retirement community, workers on an offshore oil rig—all are examples of what sociologists refer to as *subcultures*. A **subculture** is a segment of society that shares a distinctive pattern of customs, rules, and traditions that differs from the pattern of the larger society. The existence of many subcultures is characteristic of complex societies such as the United States.

Members of a subculture participate in the dominant culture while engaging in unique and distinctive forms of behavior. Frequently, a subculture will develop an **argot**, or specialized language that distinguishes it from the wider society. Athletes who play *parkour,* an extreme sport that combines forward running with fence leaping and the vaulting of walls, water barriers, and even moving cars, speak an argot they devised especially to

Employees of an international call center in India socialize after their shift has ended. Call center employees, whose odd working hours isolate them from others, tend to form tight-knit subcultures.

describe their feats. Parkour runners talk about doing *King Kong vaults*—diving arms first over a wall or grocery cart and landing in a standing position. They may follow this maneuver with a *tic tac*—kicking off a wall to overcome some kind of obstacle (Kidder 2012).

Such argot allows insiders—the members of the subculture—to understand words with special meanings. It also establishes patterns of communication that outsiders can't understand. Sociologists associated with the interactionist perspective emphasize that language and symbols offer a powerful way for a subculture to feel cohesive and maintain its identity.

In India, a new subculture has developed among employees at the international call centers established by multinational corporations. To serve customers in the United States and Europe, the young men and women who work there must be fluent speakers of English. But the corporations that employ them demand more than proficiency in a foreign language; they expect their Indian employees to adopt Western values and work habits, including the grueling pace U.S. workers take for granted.

In effect, workers at these call centers live in a state of virtual migration—not quite in India, but not in the United States, either. Significantly, call centers allow employees to take the day off only on U.S. holidays, like Labor Day and Thanksgiving—not on Indian holidays like Diwali, the Hindu festival of lights. While most Indian families are home celebrating, call center employees see only each other; when they have the day off, no one else is free to socialize with them. As a result, these employees have formed a tight-knit subculture based on hard work and a taste for Western luxury goods and leisure-time pursuits (Rowe et al. 2013).

Another shared characteristic among some employees at Indian call centers is their contempt for the callers they serve. In performing their monotonous, repetitive job day after day, hundreds of thousands of these workers have come to see the faceless Americans they deal with as slow, often rude customers. Such shared understandings underpin this emerging subculture (Bhagat 2007; Gentleman 2006; Patel 2010).

Functionalist and conflict theorists agree that variation exists within cultures. Functionalists view subcultures as variations of particular social environments and as evidence that differences can exist within a common culture. However, conflict theorists suggest that variations often reflect the inequality of social arrangements within a society. A conflict theorist would view the challenges to dominant social norms by African American activists, the feminist movement, and the gay rights movement as reflections of inequity based on race, gender, and sexual orientation. Conflict theorists also argue that subcultures sometimes emerge when the dominant society unsuccessfully tries to suppress a practice, such as the use of illegal drugs.

Table 3-2 summarizes the major sociological perspectives on culture.

COUNTERCULTURES

By the end of the 1960s, an extensive subculture had emerged in the United States, composed of young people turned off by a society they believed was too materialistic and technological. The group included primarily political radicals and hippies who had dropped out of mainstream social institutions. These young men and women rejected the pressure to accumulate cars, homes, and an endless array of material goods. Instead, they expressed

TABLE 3-2

SOCIOLOGICAL PERSPECTIVES ON CULTURE

	Functionalist Perspective	Conflict Perspective	Feminist Perspective	Interactionist Perspective
Norms	Reinforce societal standards	Reinforce patterns of dominance	Reinforce roles of men and women	Are maintained through face-to-face interaction
Values	Are collective conceptions of what is good	May perpetuate social inequality	May perpetuate men's dominance	Are defined and redefined through social interaction
Culture and Society	Culture reflects a society's strong central values	Culture reflects a society's dominant ideology	Culture reflects society's view of men and women	A society's core culture is perpetuated through daily social interactions
Cultural Variation	Subcultures serve the interests of subgroups	Countercultures question the dominant social order; ethnocentrism devalues groups	Cultural relativism respects variations in the way men and women are viewed in different societies	Customs and traditions are transmitted through intergroup contact and through the media

a desire to live in a culture based on more humanistic values, such as sharing, love, and coexistence with the environment. As a political force, this subculture opposed the United States' involvement in the war in Vietnam and encouraged draft resistance (Flacks 1971; Roszak 1969).

When a subculture conspicuously and deliberately opposes certain aspects of the larger culture, it is known as a **counterculture**. Countercultures typically thrive among the young, who have the least investment in the existing culture. In most cases, a 20-year-old can adjust to new cultural standards more easily than someone who has spent 60 years following the patterns of the dominant culture (Zellner 1995).

In the last decade, counterterrorism experts have become concerned about the growth of ultraconservative militia groups in the United States. Secretive and well armed, members of these countercultural groups tend to be antigovernment, and they often tolerate racism in their midst. Watchdogs estimate that 334 militias are operating in the United States today (Southern Poverty Law Center 2013).

LO 10-2 CULTURE SHOCK

Ever stepped out the door on your first day in a foreign country and felt weak in the knees? Anyone who feels disoriented, uncertain, out of place, or even fearful when immersed in an unfamiliar culture may be experiencing **culture shock**. This unsettling experience may even be mutual—the visitor's cultural habits may shock members of the host culture. Imagine, for example, that you are traveling in Japan. You know that you should remove your shoes and leave them at the door when you visit someone's home. However, there are many more customs that you are unfamiliar with. During a visit with one family, as you

Members of the militia group Ohio Defense Force engage in paramilitary exercises, imagining they are destroying a threatening Muslim stronghold in the United States. Ultraconservative militia groups are a form of counterculture.

enter the bathroom, you see several pairs of identical slippers. Thinking they are for guests, you put on a pair and rejoin your host, who reacts with horror. Unwittingly, you have worn a pair of toilet slippers into the living room (McLane 2013).

From the perspective of . . .

A Social Worker How would you expect culture shock to affect your clients who are recent immigrants from the Middle East? What steps could you take to help ease the transition for these new Americans?

All of us, to some extent, take for granted the cultural practices of our society. As a result, it can be surprising and even disturbing to realize that other cultures do not follow our way of life. The fact is, customs that seem strange to us may be considered normal and proper in other cultures, which may see our social practices as odd.

Resistance to technological change can lead not only to culture lag, but to some real questions of cultural survival.

LO 10-3 SOCIAL POLICY and Culture

We have seen that researchers rely on a number of tools, from simple observational research to the latest in computer technologies. Because in the real world sociological research can have far-reaching consequences for public policy and public welfare, let's consider its impact on bilingualism.

STUDYING BILINGUALISM

The staff in the emergency room is unprepared. Although the issue is not a medical one, the doctors and nurses do not understand the patient's complaints, nor can they communicate effectively with her companion. This type of incident, which occurs frequently, can have serious consequences. According to a study of two large pediatric emergency departments in Massachusetts, even when the second language is a common one like Spanish, interpreting errors can lead to clinically significant mistakes in 22 percent of such cases. In other words, language errors put patients at risk (Flores et al. 2012).

How can we learn to work and live effectively when Americans speak so many different languages? Throughout the world, not just emergency rooms but schools and other institutions must deal with people who speak many languages. **Bilingualism** refers to the use of two languages in a particular setting, such as the workplace or schoolroom, treating each language as equally legitimate. Thus, a teacher of bilingual education may instruct children in their native language while gradually introducing them to the language of the host society. If the curriculum is also bicultural, children will learn about the mores and folkways of both the dominant culture and the subculture.

To what degree should schools in the United States present the curriculum in a language other than English? This issue has prompted a great deal of debate among educators and policymakers. According to the Bureau of the Census, 61 million U.S. residents over age five—that's about 21 percent of the population—spoke a language other than English as their primary language at home in 2011 (Figure 3-4). Indeed, 29 other languages are each spoken by at least 200,000 U.S. residents (C. Ryan 2013).

This segment of the population is expected to increase modestly by 2020. For example, the proportion of older Hispanics who speak Spanish is expected to hold steady or increase slightly. However, younger Hispanics—those under 45—will be less likely than their elders to speak Spanish. A similar trend is expected for speakers of European and Asian languages: many elders will continue to speak a second language, while the younger generation will tend to favor English.

This trend toward linguistic diversity is expected to continue into the foreseeable future. Even as the children and grandchildren of immigrants adopt English as their first language, a significant proportion of the U.S. population will continue to speak a language other than English (Ortman and Shin 2011).

Do bilingual programs help the children of these families to learn English? It is difficult to reach firm conclusions, because bilingual programs in general vary so widely in their quality and approach. They differ in the length of the transition to English and in how long they allow students to remain in bilingual classrooms. Moreover, results have been mixed. In the years since California effectively dismantled its bilingual education program, reading and math scores of students with limited English proficiency rose dramatically, especially in the lower grades. Yet a major overview of 17 studies, done at Johns Hopkins University, found that students who are offered lessons in both English and their home languages make better progress than similar students who are taught only in English (R. Slavin and Cheung 2003).

FIGURE 3-4   PERCENTAGE OF PEOPLE WHO SPEAK A LANGUAGE OTHER THAN ENGLISH AT HOME, BY STATE

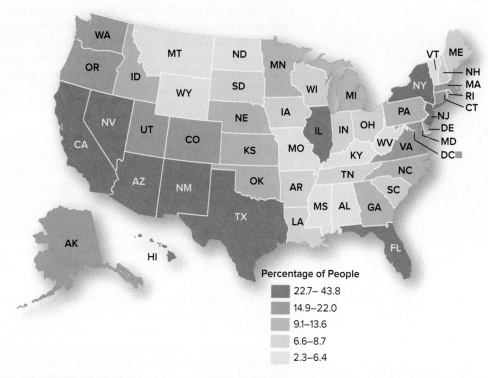

Percentage of People
- 22.7– 43.8
- 14.9–22.0
- 9.1–13.6
- 6.6–8.7
- 2.3–6.4

Note: Data drawn from the 2011 American Community Survey of people five years and over. National average was 20.8 percent.
Source: C. Ryan 2013.

Applying Sociology to Bilingualism For a long time, people in the United States demanded conformity to a single language. This demand coincided with the functionalist view that language serves to unify members of a society. Little respect was granted to immigrants' cultural traditions; a young person would often be teased about his or her "funny" name, accent, or style of dress.

Recent decades have seen challenges to this pattern of forced obedience to the dominant ideology. Beginning in the 1960s, active movements for Black pride and ethnic pride insisted that people regard the traditions of all racial and ethnic subcultures as legitimate and important. Conflict theorists explain this development as a case of subordinated language minorities seeking opportunities for self-expression. Partly as a result of these challenges, people began to view bilingualism as an asset. It seemed to provide a sensitive way of assisting millions of non-English-speaking people in the United States to *learn* English in order to function more effectively within the society.

The perspective of conflict theory also helps us to understand some of the attacks on bilingual programs. Many of them stem from an ethnocentric point of view, which holds that any deviation from the majority is bad. This attitude tends to be expressed by those who wish to stamp out foreign influence wherever it occurs, especially in our schools. It does not take into account that success in bilingual education may actually have beneficial results, such as decreasing the number of high school dropouts and increasing the number of Hispanics in colleges and universities.

Initiating Bilingual Policy Bilingualism has policy implications largely in two areas: efforts to maintain language purity and programs to enhance bilingual education. Nations vary dramatically in their tolerance for a variety of languages. China continues to tighten its cultural control over Tibet by extending instruction of Mandarin, a Chinese dialect, from high school into the elementary schools there, which will now be bilingual along with Tibetan. In contrast, nearby Singapore establishes English as the medium of instruction but allows students to take their mother tongue as a second language, be it Chinese, Malay, or Tamil.

One bilingual hot spot is Québec, the French-speaking province of Canada. The Québécois, as they are known, represent 83 percent of the province's population, but only 25 percent of Canada's total population. A law implemented in 1978 mandated education in French for all Québec's children except those whose parents or siblings had learned English elsewhere in Canada. While special laws like this one have advanced French in the province, dissatisfied Québécois have tried to form their own separate country. In 1995, the people of Québec indicated their preference of remaining united with Canada by only the narrowest of margins (50.5 percent). Language and language-related cultural areas both unify and divide this nation of 33 million people (*The Economist* 2005b; R. Schaefer 2014).

Policymakers in the United States have been somewhat ambivalent in dealing with the issue of bilingualism. In 1965, the Elementary and Secondary Education Act (ESEA) provided for bilingual, bicultural education. In the 1970s, the federal government took an active role in establishing the proper form for bilingual programs. However, more recently, federal policy has been less supportive of bilingualism, and local school districts have been forced to provide an increased share of funding for their bilingual programs. Yet bilingual programs are an expense that many communities and states are unwilling to pay for and are quick to cut back. In 1998, voters in California approved a proposition that all but eliminated bilingual education: it requires instruction in English for 1.4 million children who are not fluent in the language.

In the United States, repeated efforts have been made to introduce a constitutional amendment declaring English as the nation's official language. As of 2012, 31 states had declared English their official language—an action that is now more symbolic than legislative in its significance.

Public concern over a potential decline in the use of English appears to be overblown. In reality, most immigrants and their offspring quickly become fluent in English and abandon their mother tongue. Nevertheless, many people are impatient with those immigrants who continue to use their mother tongue. The release in 2006 of *"Nuestro Himno,"* the Spanish-language version of the "Star-Spangled Banner," produced a strong public reaction: 69 percent of those who were surveyed on the topic said the anthem should be sung only in English. In reaction against the Spanish version, at least one congressman defiantly sang the national anthem in English—with incorrect lyrics. And the proprietor of a restaurant in Philadelphia posted signs advising patrons that he would accept orders for his famous steak sandwiches only in English. Throughout the year, passions ran high as policymakers debated how much support to afford people who speak other languages (J. Carroll 2006; U.S. English 2012).

In the end, the immigrant's experience is not only about learning a new language. It is about learning a whole new culture—a new totality of socially transmitted customs, knowledge, material objects, and behavior (Viramontes 2007).

Read each question carefully and then select or provide the best answer.

1. The specialized language that subcultures employ as a way to create cohesion and a unique identity is called
   a. bilingualism.
   b. an argot.
   c. slang.
   d. an in-language.

2. Terrorist groups are examples of
   a. cultural universals.
   b. subcultures.
   c. countercultures.
   d. dominant ideologies.

3. Which of the following is a typical language pattern within immigrant families in the United States?
   a. The younger family members quickly learn English but prefer to speak their native language.
   b. The older family members speak their native language only until they learn to speak English without accent.
   c. The younger family members experience language confusion, speaking both their home language and English haltingly.
   d. The older family members learn a bit of English but speak their native language almost exclusively.

4. _____ are subcultures that openly oppose aspects of the larger culture, often including the central government.

5. A person experiences _____ when he or she feels disoriented, uncertain, out of place, even fearful when immersed in an unfamiliar culture.

Answers

1 (b); 2 (c); 3 (d); 4 Countercultures; 5 culture shock

R Rethink

Consider these questions to get a deeper understanding of the material.

1. To what subcultures do you belong? How do they function in relation to the larger society?

2. Why do people experience culture shock? What does this reveal about the role of culture and of everyday customs?

RECAP

LO 10-1 Explain patterns of variation within cultures, including subcultures and countercultures.

- A subculture is a segment of society that shares customs, rules, and traditions that differ from those of the larger society. Members of a subculture even have a specialized language, called an argot, that distinguishes them from nonmembers.
- Countercultures are subcultures that deliberately oppose aspects of the larger culture.

LO 10-2 Describe the phenomenon of culture shock.

- The feeling of disorientation and dislocation experienced by people who are suddenly immersed in an unfamiliar culture is called culture shock.
- Culture shock can be a two-way street: the host culture may shock the individual, and the individual's cultural mannerisms may shock the host culture.

LO 10-3 Analyze through a sociological lens the implications of bilingualism on social policy.

- The social policy of bilingualism refers to the use of two languages in a setting, treating each as equally legitimate. It is supported by those who want to ease the transition of non-native-language speakers into a host society, but opposed by those who emphasize the importance of a single cultural tradition and language.
- Concern about immigrant families in the United States using their native languages instead of English is overblown. Immigrant populations generally follow the pattern by which younger family members quickly become fluent in English, and as time passes, a clear preference for using English emerges naturally.

KEY TERMS

Argot Specialized language used by members of a group or subculture.

Bilingualism The use of two languages in a particular setting, such as the workplace or schoolroom, treating each language as equally legitimate.

Counterculture A subculture that deliberately opposes certain aspects of the larger culture.

Culture shock The feeling of surprise and disorientation that people experience when they encounter cultural practices that are different from their own.

Subculture A segment of society that shares a distinctive pattern of customs, rules, and traditions that differs from the pattern of the larger society.

The Case of . . . the Culture Clash

The student population at a New Jersey high school is composed of Latinos, Whites, and Cambodians whose families have recently immigrated. "We share a building, but we might as well be three separate schools," says Cheryl Lymon, a guidance counselor. "Check out the lunchroom any day of the week. The Cambodian kids sit on the right, the White kids on the left, and the Latino kids are out on the patio." The school has tried a variety of ideas to break up these segregated communities. "The principal outlawed any club or sport whose membership was not integrated. That shut down the Latina dance troupe, the all-White lacrosse team, and the computer animation club the Cambodian boys started, but the new rule only made things worse. The kids blamed each other," Lymon says. The Latino girls complained that "the White girls just don't have the moves" to join their dance troupe, and the lacrosse team members said "the Cambodians and the Latinos just don't have the hustle to win the game."

Several of the teachers tried to organize a "Festival of Cultures" event where everyone would bring food common to their culture and dress in native costume. But, as one of the kids said to Lymon, "This culture festival thing, what's that about? I'm White. I'm American. So, I'm supposed to bring hotdogs and wear a John Deere cap?" Lymon shakes her head. "There's something we need to do to unite these kids, or at least get them talking to each other more," she says, "but none of us knows quite what that something is." Lymon pauses. "It's a shame, really. The sum of what these kids have in common is so much greater than their differences."

1. What do you think of the principal's decision to ban all clubs whose membership did not reflect the school's diverse population? What value might maintaining their subcultures have to students? What might be the negative effects?

2. Do you see examples in this story of ethnocentrism? Explain. Do you think ethnocentrism is ever based on reality? List any instances where you believe it is justified by the facts.

3. Do you think the proposed "Festival of Cultures" will be useful in bringing students from diverse groups together? Why or why not? If you were a guidance counselor at this high school, what kind of event would you suggest to help students interact in a positive way?

4. The student who said he was White and American suggests he believes he has no particular culture. Do you think this is possible? What do you know about dominant cultures that might explain his words?

5. Do you agree with Lymon's view that what the students have in common is greater than their differences? Why or why not?

 **Study Strategies**

Strategies for Reading Sociology (and Other) Textbooks

Like all others, sociology textbooks can be frightening. They are often long, with technical words and ideas that may seem complicated. Here are some strategies for reading and studying sociology texts (this one included) that can help you understand more of what you read and perform better on quizzes and tests.

- Look at the Table of Contents pages in the front of the book to get an overview of what you will be studying.
- Read the learning objectives (LOs) in the Prepare section at the beginning of the module.
- Before reading the module, skim it for tables and illustrations that might give you an idea of its content and organization.

- Read the outline in the Organize section at the start of the module.
- Gather your tools, including a pen or pencil, highlighters, a copy of the assignment (so you'll be sure to read the right material), and paper, index cards, or a computer for taking notes.
- Give yourself enough time—and a quiet space—to do the reading.
- Set a goal for how much you are going to read before taking a break.

- Write while you read, jotting notes to yourself and marking the page with check marks, arrows, and diagrams.
- Highlight and underline important points—but do this selectively. Mark only the key material. Highlighting everything is the same as highlighting nothing.
- Stop and think after you read a section. Check that you have understood the material.
- Pay attention to key terms. These are printed in **bold type** because they are important for understanding major ideas and concepts in sociology. To help you review these, they are gathered together at the end of each module.

- Answer the Evaluate questions at the end of the module.
- Pretend you are explaining the material you have read (e.g., telling a classmate who didn't read the assignment about the material).

- Answer the Rethink questions at the end of the module.
- Read Recap at the end of the module.
- Consult Key Terms at the end of each module as needed.
- Look over the assignment again, along with any notes you took. If you do this within 24 hours of first reading the assignment, it can save you hours of work later.

Reading Smarter

Understanding the material you read and doing well on tests aren't about reading faster. They're about reading better, smarter (although you'll probably find that adopting smart reading habits *does* save time). Rate how well each of the statements below describes your current reading habits, using this scale:

1 = I rarely or never do this.

2 = I sometimes do this.

3 = I usually or always do this.

	Rating		
	1	2	3
1. I review the Table of Contents in a textbook before reading anything else so that I will have a good overview of the topics I'll be studying.			
2. I keep a pen or pencil, a highlighter, a notebook, and index cards (or computer) handy for taking notes.			
3. I break my reading into chunks organized around key topics, then take a brief break between the chunks.			
4. Before I start reading, I look over the assignment and review any outlines or overviews the instructor has given me to better understand the material and its organization.			
5. I keep notes as I read, highlighting the main points, and jotting down questions the material raises and/or my thoughts on the various topics.			
6. I jot down the key terms (printed in **bold type**) as I read, then review them at the end, defining them in my own words and checking my understanding against the list of terms at the end of the chapter.			
7. I quiz myself after I read, using the prepared questions at the end of each module or chapter.			
8. I try to connect the content of what I am reading to myself and the world around me.			
9. I review the assignment and look over my notes within 24 hours of my initial reading.			
10. I read the summary at the end of each module or chapter, and then try to restate the main points in my own words.			

SCORING:

Total the ratings for the 10 questions, and use the following guide to interpret your score:

26–30 points: Your effective reading habits not only make test-taking easier, they also expand your understanding of the world.

16–25 points: You have developed some excellent reading skills. Go back through the statements here to find more ways to improve your comprehension.

15 or less points: Good reading habits are useful strategies everyone can learn. Those who learn them get more out of their study time and score better on tests. You have the list. Get started.

Socialization and the Life Course

4

Sociology at WORK CORRECTIONAL COUNSELOR

JOAN HARRIS works with women inmates at a small prison facility outside Los Angeles. As a correctional counselor, Harris helps inmates create relapse-prevention plans that usually include further education and learning new job skills. But the most important thing, she believes, is the opportunities she provides for the women to practice normal social relationships. "I started the Chill Out club," Harris says. "We get together twice a week, leave our issues behind, and just enjoy sharing a pizza and watching a movie or dancing to music."

Harris understands how critical the role of socialization is to the development of self. "So many of these women have suffered physical and emotional abuse. The mirrors their world has held up to them reflect something ugly and worthless," she says. "I help them to find a better, truer mirror. One that shows their strengths. A lot of the women have a wonderful, arch humor and a keen nose for what is practical. Those are great traits to have in the real world." ■

Looking Ahead

IN THIS CHAPTER WE WILL EXAMINE THE ROLE OF SOCIALIZATION IN human development. We will begin by analyzing the interaction of heredity with environmental factors. Then we will explore how people develop perceptions, feelings, and beliefs about themselves. We will pay particular attention to important agents of socialization, including the family, schools, peers, the media and technology, the workplace, and religion. As we will see, socialization is a process that spans the entire life course. In the Social Policy section that closes the chapter, we will focus on the socialization experience of group child care for young children.

MODULE 11 The Role of Socialization

P Prepare | Learning Objectives

LO 11-1 Explain the role of socialization in shaping human behavior and attitudes.

LO 11-2 Describe the effects of isolation and neglect on the social development of young children.

LO 11-3 Explain what twin studies suggest about the effects of heredity and environment on social development.

O Organize | Module Outline

Socialization
Social Environment: The Impact of Isolation
    Extreme Isolation: Isabelle
    Extreme Neglect: Romanian Orphans
    Primate Studies
The Influence of Heredity

Sociologists are interested in the lifelong process of **socialization**, through which people learn the attitudes, values, and behaviors appropriate for members of their culture. Socialization occurs through human interactions that begin in infancy and continue through retirement. We learn a great deal from those people most important in our lives—immediate family members, best friends, and teachers. But we also learn from people we see on the street, on television, on the Internet, and in films and magazines. From a microsociological perspective, socialization helps us to discover how to behave "properly" and what to expect from others if we follow (or challenge) society's norms and values. From a macrosociological perspective, socialization provides for the transmission of a culture from one generation to the next, to ensure the long-term continuity of a society.

Socialization also shapes our self-images. For example, in the United States, a person is viewed as "too heavy" or "too short" because he or she does not conform to the ideal cultural standard of physical attractiveness. Such an unfavorable evaluation is an aspect of socialization that can significantly influence self-esteem and shape one's personality. In everyday speech, the term **personality** refers to a person's typical patterns of attitudes, needs, characteristics, and behavior.

How much of the personality is shaped by culture, as opposed to inborn traits? In what ways does socialization continue into adulthood? Who are the most powerful agents of socialization? These are some of the issues that we will consider in this chapter.

LO **11-1** Socialization

What makes us who we are? Is it the genes we are born with, or the environment in which we grow up? Researchers have traditionally clashed over the relative importance of biological inheritance and environmental factors in human development—a conflict called the *nature versus nurture* (or *heredity versus environment*) debate. Today, most social scientists have moved beyond this debate, acknowledging instead the *interaction* of these variables in shaping human development. However, we can better appreciate how heredity and environmental factors interact and influence the socialization process if we first examine situations in which one factor operates almost entirely without the other (Homans 1979).

LO **11-2** Social Environment: the Impact of Isolation

In the 1994 movie *Nell,* Jodie Foster played a young woman hidden from birth by her mother in a backwoods cabin. Raised without normal human contact, Nell crouches like an animal, screams wildly, and speaks or sings in a language all her own. This movie was drawn from the actual account of an emaciated 16-year-old boy who appeared mysteriously in 1828 in the town square of Nuremberg, Germany (Lipson 1994).

Some viewers may have found the story of Nell difficult to believe, but social scientists have encountered similar cases. The two cases that follow describe the documented effects of extreme social isolation and neglect.

EXTREME ISOLATION: ISABELLE

The dramatic story of a child called Isabelle was all too real. For the first six years of her life, Isabelle lived in almost total seclusion in a darkened room. She had little contact with other people, with the exception of her mother, who could neither speak nor hear. Isabelle's mother's parents had been so deeply ashamed of Isabelle's illegitimate birth that they kept her hidden away from the world. Ohio authorities finally discovered the child in 1938, when Isabelle's mother escaped from her parents' home, taking her daughter with her.

When she was discovered at age six, Isabelle could not speak; she could merely make various croaking sounds. Her only communications with her mother were simple gestures. Isabelle had been largely deprived of the typical interactions and socialization experiences of childhood. Since she had seen few people, she showed a strong fear of strangers and reacted almost like a wild animal when confronted with an unfamiliar person. As she became accustomed to seeing certain individuals, her reaction changed to one of extreme apathy. At first, observers believed that Isabelle was deaf, but she soon began to react to nearby sounds. On tests of maturity, she scored at the level of an infant rather than a six-year-old.

Specialists developed a systematic training program to help Isabelle adapt to human relationships and socialization. After a few days of training, she made her first attempt to verbalize. Although she started slowly, Isabelle quickly passed through six years of development. In a little over two months she was speaking in complete sentences. Nine months later she could identify both words and sentences. Before Isabelle reached age nine, she was ready to attend school with other children. By age 14 she was in sixth grade, doing well in school, and emotionally well adjusted.

Yet without an opportunity to experience socialization in her first six years, Isabelle had been hardly human in the social sense when she was first discovered. Her inability to communicate at the time of her discovery—despite her physical and cognitive potential to learn—and her remarkable progress over the next few years underscore the impact of socialization on human development (K. Davis 1947:435/1/en/437).

The scientists involved with Isabelle's case concluded that all children need socialization in the form of love, care, and affection. Absent that kind of attention, humans cannot learn to speak and interact with others as expected. This need for positive social interaction does not end with childhood; it continues throughout the life span.

Unfortunately, other children who have been locked away or severely neglected have not fared so well as Isabelle. In many instances, the consequences of their social isolation have proved much more damaging.

EXTREME NEGLECT: ROMANIAN ORPHANS

Isabelle's experience is important to researchers because there are only a few cases of children who were reared in total isolation. However, there are many cases of children raised in extremely neglectful social circumstances. In the 1990s, public attention focused on infants and young children who grew up in orphanages in the formerly communist countries of Eastern Europe. In Romanian orphanages, babies once lay in their cribs for 18 to 20 hours a day, curled against their feeding bottles, receiving little care from adults. This minimal attention continued for the first five years of their lives. Many of them grew up fearful of human contact, and prone to unpredictable antisocial behavior. As recently as 2004, some 32,000 Romanian children were institutionalized in this manner.

In Romania, special programs emphasizing social interaction have helped orphans to overcome years of social isolation.

This situation came to light as families in North America and Europe began to adopt thousands of the orphans. For about 20 percent of those adopted, adjustment problems were so dramatic that the adopting families suffered guilty fears of being ill-fit parents. Many of them asked for assistance in dealing with the children. Slowly, efforts were made to introduce the deprived youngsters to feelings of attachment and socialization that they had never experienced before (Groza et al. 1999; Craig Smith 2006).

In 2001, Romania bowed to pressure and placed a moratorium on international adoptions. The state took steps to reunite orphans with their birth families, place them with adoptive families in Romania, or settle them in small group homes. With supervision from attentive caregivers and specialists, the once-abandoned children have made remarkable progress. UNICEF is now using the program as a model for other nations that are dealing with such children. Worldwide, an estimated 2 million children are living in institutional care (Aslanian 2006; *The Economist* 2013a; Ironside 2011; UNICEF 2009).

As with Isabelle, the Romanian orphans underscored the significance of the social environment in a child's development. Increasingly, researchers are emphasizing the importance of the earliest socialization experiences for all children, including those who grow up in more normal environments. We know now that it is not enough to care for an infant's physical needs; parents must also concern themselves with their children's social development. If, for example, children are discouraged from having friends even as toddlers, they will miss out on experiences with peers that are critical to their socialization and emotional growth.

PRIMATE STUDIES

Studies of animals raised in isolation also support the importance of socialization in development. Harry Harlow (1971), a researcher at the primate laboratory of the University of Wisconsin, conducted tests with rhesus monkeys that had been raised away from their mothers and away from contact with other monkeys. As was the case with Isabelle, the rhesus monkeys raised in isolation were fearful and easily frightened. They did not mate, and the females who were artificially inseminated became abusive mothers. Apparently, isolation had had a damaging effect on the monkeys.

A creative aspect of Harlow's experimentation was his use of "artificial mothers." In one such experiment, Harlow presented monkeys raised in isolation with two substitute mothers—one cloth-covered replica and one covered with wire that had the ability to offer milk. Monkey after monkey went to the wire mother for the life-giving milk, yet spent much more time clinging to the more motherlike cloth model. It appears that the infant monkeys developed greater social attachments from their need for warmth, comfort, and intimacy than from their need for milk.

While these studies may seem to suggest that heredity can be dismissed as a factor in the social development of humans and animals, studies of twins reveal a fascinating interplay between heredity and environment.

LO 11-3 The Influence of Heredity

Identical twins Oskar Stohr and Jack Yufe were separated soon after their birth and raised on different continents, in very different cultural settings. Oskar was reared as a strict Catholic by his maternal grandmother in the Sudetenland of Czechoslovakia. As a member of the Hitler Youth movement in Nazi Germany, he learned to hate Jews. In contrast, his brother Jack was reared in Trinidad by the twins' Jewish father. Jack joined an Israeli

kibbutz (a collective settlement) at age 17 and later served in the Israeli army. When the twins were reunited in middle age, however, some startling similarities emerged: They both wore wire-rimmed glasses and mustaches. They both liked spicy foods and sweet liqueurs, were absentminded, flushed the toilet before using it, stored rubber bands on their wrists, and dipped buttered toast in their coffee (Holden 1980).

The twins also differed in many important respects: Jack was a workaholic; Oskar enjoyed leisure-time activities. Oskar was a traditionalist who was domineering toward women; Jack was a political liberal who was much more accepting of feminism. Finally, Jack was extremely proud of being Jewish, whereas Oskar never mentioned his Jewish heritage (Holden 1987).

Oskar and Jack are prime examples of the interplay of heredity and environment. For a number of years, the Minnesota Twin Family Study has been following 137 sets of identical twins reared apart to determine what similarities, if any, they show in personality traits, behavior, and intelligence. Preliminary results from the available twin studies indicate that *both* genetic factors *and* socialization experiences are influential in human development. Certain characteristics, such as temperaments, voice patterns, and nervous habits, appear to be strikingly similar even in twins reared apart, suggesting that these qualities may be linked to hereditary causes. However, identical twins reared apart differ far more in their attitudes, values, chosen mates, and even drinking habits; these qualities, it would seem, are influenced by environmental factors. In examining clusters of personality traits among such twins, researchers have found marked similarities in their tendency toward leadership or dominance, but significant differences in their need for intimacy, comfort, and assistance.

Researchers have also been impressed with the similar scores on intelligence tests of twins reared apart in *roughly similar* social settings. Most of the identical twins register scores even closer than those that would be expected if the same person took a test twice. At the same time, however, identical twins brought up in *dramatically different* social environments score quite differently on intelligence tests—a finding that supports the impact of socialization on human development (Segal 2012).

We need to be cautious in reviewing studies of twin pairs and other relevant research. Widely broadcast findings have often been based on preliminary analysis of extremely small samples. For example, one study (not involving twin pairs) was frequently cited as confirming genetic links with behavior. Yet the researchers had to retract their conclusions after they increased the sample and reclassified two of the original cases. After those changes, the initial findings were no longer valid.

Critics add that studies of twin pairs have not provided satisfactory information concerning the extent to which separated identical twins may have had contact with each other, even though they were raised apart. Such interactions—especially if they were extensive—could call into question the validity of the twin studies. As this debate continues, we can certainly anticipate numerous efforts to replicate the research and clarify the interplay between heredity and environmental factors in human development (Horgan 1993; Plomin 1989).

E Evaluate

Read each question carefully and then select or provide the best answer.

1. The term used in everyday speech to refer to a person's typical patterns of attitudes, needs, characteristics, and behaviors is
   a. socialization.
   b. personality.
   c. nurture.
   d. nature.

2. _____ is the term used by sociologists to refer to the lifelong process whereby people learn the attitudes, values, and behaviors appropriate for members of their culture.

3. Studies of twins raised apart suggest that both _____ and _____ influence human development.

Answers

1 (b); 2 Socialization; 3 heredity, environment

R Rethink

Consider these questions to get a deeper understanding of the material.

1. What might be some ethical concerns regarding research on environmental influences on people's behavior?

2. What are some social policy implications of research on the effects of early socialization experiences?

RECAP

LO 11-1 Explain the role of socialization in shaping human behavior and attitudes.

- Socialization is the process through which people learn the attitudes, values, and actions appropriate for members of their culture.
- Socialization affects the overall cultural practices of a society; it also shapes self-image and self-esteem.

LO 11-2 Describe the effects of isolation and neglect on the social development of young children.

- Extreme isolation brings fear of strangers and the inability to communicate or to interact with others. A child raised in isolation retains the physical and cognitive potential to learn and, with continuous love, care, and affection, can achieve developmental gains.
- Infants and young children deprived of human attention in dysfunctional orphanages can become fearful of human contact and quite antisocial. With the help of attentive caregivers and specialists, such children can make substantial progress.
- Studies of primates also support the importance of socialization in development.

LO 11-3 Explain what twin studies suggest about the effects of heredity and environment on social development.

- Studies of identical twins raised separately reveal that such twins share many surprising characteristics and behaviors, but also differ in many significant respects.
- Twin studies have been taken as a demonstration that both genetic factors and socialization experiences influence human development.

KEY TERMS

Personality A person's typical patterns of attitudes, needs, characteristics, and behavior.

Socialization The lifelong process in which people learn the attitudes, values, and behaviors appropriate for members of a particular culture.

MODULE 12 The Self and Socialization

P Prepare Learning Objectives

LO 12-1 Summarize the contributions of Cooley, Mead, and Goffman regarding the role of social interaction in the development of the sense of self.

LO 12-2 Explain how major psychologists, including Freud and Piaget, have interpreted the development of the self.

O Organize Module Outline

Sociological Approaches to the Self
  Cooley: Looking-Glass Self
  Mead: Stages of the Self
  Mead: Theory of the Self
  Goffman: Presentation of the Self
Psychological Approaches to the Self

W Work

We all have various perceptions, feelings, and beliefs about who we are and what we are like. How do we come to develop them? Do they change as we age?

We were not born with these understandings. Building on the work of George Herbert Mead (1964b), sociologists recognize that our concept of who we are, the *self,* emerges as we interact with others. The **self** is a distinct identity that sets us apart from others. It is not a static phenomenon, but continues to develop and change throughout our lives.

LO 12-1 Sociological Approaches to the Self

Sociologists and psychologists alike have expressed interest in how the individual develops and modifies the sense of self as a result of social interaction. The work of sociologists Charles Horton Cooley and George Herbert Mead, pioneers of the interactionist approach, has been especially useful in furthering our understanding of these important issues.

COOLEY: LOOKING-GLASS SELF

In the early 1900s, Charles Horton Cooley advanced the belief that we learn who we are by interacting with others. Our view of ourselves, then, comes not only from direct contemplation of our personal qualities but also from our impressions of how others perceive us. Cooley used the phrase **looking-glass self** to emphasize that the self is the product of our social interactions.

The process of developing a self-identity or self-concept has three phases. First, we imagine how we present ourselves to others—to relatives, friends, even strangers on the street. Then we imagine how others evaluate us (attractive, intelligent, shy, or strange). Finally, we develop some sort of feeling about ourselves, such as respect or shame, as a result of these impressions (Cooley 1902; Michael C. Howard 1989).

A subtle but critical aspect of Cooley's looking-glass self is that the self results from an individual's "imagination" of how others view him or her. As a result, we can develop self-identities based on *incorrect* perceptions of how others see us. A student may react strongly to a teacher's criticism and decide (wrongly) that the instructor views the student as stupid. This misperception may be converted into a negative self-identity through the following process: (1) the teacher criticized me, (2) the teacher must think that I'm stupid, (3) I *am* stupid. Yet self-identities are also subject to change. If the student receives an A at the end of the course, he or she will probably no longer feel stupid.

MEAD: STAGES OF THE SELF

George Herbert Mead continued Cooley's exploration of interactionist theory. Mead (1934, 1964a) developed a useful model of a three-stage process by which the self emerges: the preparatory stage, the play stage, and the game stage.

The Preparatory Stage During the *preparatory stage,* children merely imitate the people around them, especially family members with whom they continually interact. Thus, a small child will bang on a piece of wood while a parent is engaged in carpentry work, or will try to throw a ball if an older sibling is doing so nearby.

As they grow older, children become more adept at using symbols, including the gestures and words that form the basis of human communication. By interacting with relatives and friends, as well as by watching cartoons on television and looking at picture books, children in the preparatory stage begin to understand symbols. They will continue to use this form of communication throughout their lives.

The Play Stage Mead was among the first to analyze the relationship of symbols to socialization. As children develop skill in communicating through symbols, they gradually become more aware of social relationships. As a result, during the *play stage,* they begin to pretend to be other people. Just as an actor "becomes" a character, a child becomes a doctor, parent, superhero, or ship captain.

Mead, in fact, noted that an important aspect of the play stage is role-playing. **Role taking** is the process of mentally assuming the perspective of another and responding from that imagined viewpoint. For example, through this process a young child will gradually learn when it is best to ask a parent for favors. If the parent usually comes home from work in a bad mood, the child will wait until after dinner, when the parent is more relaxed and approachable.

The Game Stage In Mead's third stage, the *game stage,* the child of about age eight or nine no longer just plays roles but begins to consider several tasks and relationships simultaneously. At this point in development, children grasp not only their own social positions but also those of others around them—just as in a basketball game the players must understand their own and everyone else's positions. Consider a girl or boy who is part of a Scout troop out on a weekend hike in the mountains. The child must understand what he or she is expected to do but must also recognize the responsibilities of other Scouts as well as the leaders. This is the final stage of development under Mead's model; the child can now respond to numerous members of the social environment.

Mead uses the term **generalized other** to refer to the attitudes, viewpoints, and expectations of society as a whole that a child takes into account in his or her behavior. Simply put, this concept suggests that when an individual acts, he or she takes into account an entire group of people. For example, a child will not act courteously merely to please a particular parent. Rather, the child comes to understand that courtesy is a widespread social value endorsed by parents, teachers, and religious leaders.

Table 4-1 summarizes the three stages of the self outlined by George Herbert Mead.

MEAD: THEORY OF THE SELF

Mead is best known for his theory of the self. According to Mead (1964b), the self begins at a privileged, central position in a person's world. Young children picture themselves as the focus of everything around them and find it difficult to consider the perspectives of others. For example, when shown a mountain scene and asked to describe what an observer on the opposite side of the mountain might see (such as a lake or hikers), young children describe only objects visible from their vantage point. This childhood tendency to place ourselves at the center of events never entirely disappears. Many people with a fear of flying automatically assume that if any plane goes down, it will be the one they are on. And who reads the horoscope section in the paper without looking at their own horoscope first? Why else do we buy lottery tickets, if we do not imagine ourselves winning?

Nonetheless, as people mature, the self changes and begins to reflect greater concern about the reactions of others. Parents, friends, co-workers, coaches, and teachers are often among those who play a major role in shaping a person's self. The term **significant others** is used to refer to those individuals who are most important in the development of the self. Many young people, for example, find themselves drawn to the same kind of work their parents engage in (H. Sullivan [1953] 1968).

TABLE 4-1 **MEAD'S STAGES OF THE SELF** Summing Up

Stage	Self Present?	Definition	Example
Preparation	No	Child imitates the actions of others.	When adults laugh and smile, child laughs and smiles.
Play	Developing	Child takes the role of a single other, as if he or she were the other.	Child first takes the role of doctor, then the role of patient.
Game	Yes	Child considers the roles of two or more others simultaneously.	In game of hide-and-seek, child takes into account the roles of both hider and seeker.

How do we manage our "self"? How do we display to others who we are? Erving Goffman, a sociologist associated with the interactionist perspective, suggested that many of our daily activities involve attempts to convey impressions of who we are. His observations help us to understand the sometimes subtle yet critical ways in which we learn to present ourselves socially. They also offer concrete examples of this aspect of socialization.

Early in life, the individual learns to slant his or her presentation of the self in order to create distinctive appearances and satisfy particular audiences. Goffman (1959) referred to this altering of the presentation of the self as **impression management**.

From the perspective of . . .

An Employment Specialist   How could *impression management* be useful to your clients who are seeking work after a long period of unemployment? What would you advise them to do and say at a job interview to avoid being tagged as a "loser"?

In analyzing such everyday social interactions, Goffman makes so many explicit parallels to the theater that his view has been termed the **dramaturgical approach**. According to this perspective, people resemble performers in action. For example, a clerk may try to appear busier than he or she actually is if a supervisor happens to be watching. A customer in a singles' bar may try to look as if he or she is waiting for a particular person to arrive.

Goffman (1959) also drew attention to another aspect of the self, **face-work**. How often do you initiate some kind of face-saving behavior when you feel embarrassed or rejected? In response to a rejection at the singles' bar, a person may engage in face-work by saying, "There really isn't an interesting person in this entire crowd." We feel the need to maintain a proper image of the self if we are to continue social interaction.

Face-work is a necessity for those who are unemployed. In an economic downturn like the recent recession, unemployment affects people of all social classes, many of whom are unaccustomed to being jobless. A recent ethnographic study found the newly unemployed redefining what it means to be out of work. They were focusing more than in the past on what they were accomplishing, and had begun to value volunteer work more since they had become volunteers themselves. Participants in this study engaged in both impression management and face-work (Garrett-Peters 2009).

Goffman's work on the self represents a logical progression of sociological studies begun by Cooley and Mead on how personality is acquired through socialization and how we manage the presentation of the self to others. Cooley stressed the process by which we create a self; Mead focused on how the self develops as we learn to interact with others; Goffman emphasized the ways in which we consciously create images of ourselves for others.

LO **12-2** Psychological Approaches to the Self

Psychologists have shared the interest of Cooley, Mead, and other sociologists in the development of the self. Early work in psychology, such as that of Sigmund Freud (1856–1939), stressed the role of inborn drives—among them the drive for sexual gratification—in channeling human behavior. More recently, psychologists such as Jean Piaget have emphasized the stages through which human development progresses.

People judge us by our appearance, attire, body language, demeanor, and mannerisms. Knowing that they do, most of us alter the way we present ourselves to others, a strategy that Goffman called impression management.

Like Charles Horton Cooley and George Herbert Mead, Freud believed that the self is a social product, and that aspects of one's personality are influenced by other people (especially one's parents). However, unlike Cooley and Mead, he suggested that the self has components that work in opposition to each other. According to Freud, our natural impulsive instincts are in constant conflict with societal constraints. Part of us seeks limitless pleasure, while another part favors rational behavior. By interacting with others, we learn the expectations of society and then select behavior most appropriate to our culture. (Of course, as Freud was well aware, we sometimes distort reality and behave irrationally.)

Research on newborn babies by the Swiss child psychologist Jean Piaget (1896–1980) has underscored the importance of social interactions in developing a sense of self. Piaget found that newborns have no self in the sense of a looking-glass image. Ironically, though, they are quite self-centered; they demand that all attention be directed toward them. Newborns have not yet separated themselves from the universe of which they are a part. For these babies, the phrase "you and me" has no meaning; they understand only "me." However, as they mature, children are gradually socialized into social relationships, even within their rather self-centered world.

In his well-known **cognitive theory of development**, Piaget (1954) identified four stages in the development of children's thought processes. In the first, or *sensorimotor,* stage, young children use their senses to make discoveries. For example, through touching they discover that their hands are actually a part of themselves. During the second, or *preoperational,* stage, children begin to use words and symbols to distinguish objects and ideas. The milestone in the third, or *concrete operational,* stage is that children engage in more logical thinking. They learn that even when a formless lump of clay is shaped into a snake, it is still the same clay. In the fourth, or *formal operational,* stage, adolescents become capable of sophisticated abstract thought and can deal logically with ideas and values.

According to Piaget, social interaction is the key to development. As children grow older, they pay increasing attention to how other people think and why they act in particular ways. In order to develop a distinct personality, each of us needs opportunities to interact with others. As we saw earlier, Isabelle was deprived of the chance for normal social interactions, and the consequences were severe (Kitchener 1991).

We have seen that a number of thinkers considered social interaction the key to the development of an individual's sense of self. As is generally true, we can best understand this topic by drawing on a variety of theory and research. Table 4-2 summarizes the rich literature, both sociological and psychological, on the development of the self.

TABLE 4-2   THEORETICAL APPROACHES TO
DEVELOPMENT OF THE SELF

Tracking Sociological Perspectives

Scholar	Key Concepts and Contributions	Major Points of Theory
Charles Horton Cooley 1864–1929 sociologist (USA)	Looking-glass self	Stages of development not distinct; feelings toward ourselves developed through interaction with others
George Herbert Mead 1863–1931 sociologist (USA)	The self Generalized other	Three distinct stages of development; self develops as children grasp the roles of others in their lives
Erving Goffman 1922–1982 sociologist (USA)	Impression management Dramaturgical approach Face-work	Self developed through the impressions we convey to others and to groups
Sigmund Freud 1856–1939 psychotherapist (Austria)	Psychoanalysis	Self influenced by parents and by inborn drives, such as the drive for sexual gratification
Jean Piaget 1896–1980 child psychologist (Switzerland)	Cognitive theory of development	Four stages of cognitive development

E Evaluate

Read each question carefully and then select or provide the best answer.

1. Which of the following social scientists used the phrase *looking-glass self* to emphasize that the self is the product of our social interactions with other people?
   a. George Herbert Mead
   b. Charles Horton Cooley
   c. Erving Goffman
   d. Jean Piaget

2. In what he called the *play stage* of socialization, George Herbert Mead asserted that people mentally assume the perspectives of others, thereby enabling them to respond from that imagined viewpoint. This process is referred to as
   a. role taking.
   b. the generalized other.
   c. the significant other.
   d. impression management.

3. George Herbert Mead is best known for his theory of what?
   a. presentation of the self
   b. cognitive development
   c. the self
   d. impression management

4. According to child psychologist Jean Piaget's cognitive theory of development, children begin to use words and symbols to distinguish objects and ideas during which stage in the development of the thought process?
   a. the sensorimotor stage
   b. the preoperational stage
   c. the concrete operational stage
   d. the formal operational stage

5. A _____ _____ is an individual such as a parent, friend, or teacher who is most important in the development of the self.

Answers

1 (b); 2 (a); 3 (c); 4 (b); 5 significant other

R Rethink

Consider these questions to get a deeper understanding of the material.

1. How would Erving Goffman's dramaturgical approach describe impression management among members of one of the following groups: athletes, college instructors, parents, physicians, or politicians?

2. What are some similarities between Mead's stages of the self and Piaget's cognitive development stages? What are some differences?

RECAP

LO 12-1 Summarize the contributions of Cooley, Mead, and Goffman regarding the role of social interaction in the development of the sense of self.

- In the early 1900s, Charles Horton Cooley advanced the belief that we learn who we are by interacting with others, a phenomenon he called the looking-glass self.
- George Herbert Mead, best known for his theory of the self, proposed that as people mature, their selves begin to reflect their concern about reactions from others—both generalized others and significant others.
- Erving Goffman has shown that in many of our daily activities, we try to convey distinct impressions of who we are, a process he called impression management.

LO 12-2 Explain how major psychologists, including Freud and Piaget, have interpreted the development of the self.

- Sigmund Freud emphasized the role of inborn drives in channeling human behavior. He viewed the development of self as a social process influenced heavily by parents in which a person's impulsive instincts conflict with societal constraints.
- Jean Piaget developed a cognitive theory of development, consisting of four distinct stages through which children pass: the sensorimotor, the preoperational, the concrete operational, and the formal operational. He regarded social interaction as the key to development.

KEY TERMS

Cognitive theory of development The theory that children's thought progresses through four stages of development.

Dramaturgical approach A view of social interaction in which people are seen as theatrical performers.

Face-work The efforts people make to maintain the proper image and avoid public embarrassment.

Generalized other The attitudes, viewpoints, and expectations of society as a whole that a child takes into account in his or her behavior.

Impression management The altering of the presentation of the self in order to create distinctive appearances and satisfy particular audiences.

Looking-glass self A concept that emphasizes the self as the product of our social interactions.

Role taking The process of mentally assuming the perspective of another and responding from that imagined viewpoint.

Self A distinct identity that sets us apart from others.

Significant other An individual who is most important in the development of the self, such as a parent, friend, or teacher.

MODULE 13 Agents of Socialization

P Prepare <u>Learning Objectives</u>

LO 13-1 Explain how the family, the school, and peer groups affect socialization from the early years into young adulthood.

LO 13-2 Analyze the ways in which technology and the institutions of work, religion, and the state contribute to the socialization process during the life course.

O Organize <u>Module Outline</u>

Family
School
Peer Group
Mass Media and Technology
Workplace
Religion and the State

As we have seen, the culture of the United States is defined by rather gradual movements from one stage of socialization to the next. The continuing and lifelong socialization process involves many different social forces that influence our lives and alter our self-images.

The family is the most important agent of socialization in the United States, especially for children. In this chapter, we'll also discuss six other agents of socialization: the school, the peer group, the mass media and technology, the workplace, religion, and the state.

LO **13-1** Family

The lifelong process of learning begins shortly after birth. Since newborns can hear, see, smell, taste, and feel heat, cold, and pain, they are constantly orienting themselves to the surrounding world. Human beings, especially family members, constitute an important part of their social environment. People minister to the baby's needs by feeding, cleaning, carrying, and comforting the baby.

In the United States, social development also includes exposure to cultural assumptions regarding gender and race. Black parents, for example, have learned that children as young as age two can absorb negative messages about Blacks in children's books, toys, and television shows—all of which are designed primarily for White consumers. At the same time, Black children are exposed more often than others to the inner-city youth gang culture. Because most Blacks, even those who are middle class, live near very poor neighborhoods, their children are susceptible to these influences, despite their parents' strong family values (Linn and Poussaint 1999; Pattillo-McCoy 1999).

The term **gender role** refers to expectations regarding the proper behavior, attitudes, and activities of males and females. For example, we traditionally think of "toughness" as masculine—and desirable only in men—while we view "tenderness" as feminine. Other cultures do not necessarily assign these qualities to each gender in the way that our culture does. The existence of gender roles does not imply that inevitably, males and females will

assume certain roles, nor does it imply that those roles are quite distinct from one another. Rather, gender roles emphasize the fact that males and females are not genetically predetermined to occupy certain roles.

From the perspective of . . .

A Preschool Teacher Knowing that children as young as age two absorb negative messages about race and gender in books, TV shows, and toys, what resources and activities would you select to use in your classroom? What are some books, toys, and activities you would choose to avoid?

As the primary agents of childhood socialization, parents play a critical role in guiding children into those gender roles deemed appropriate in a society. Other adults, older siblings, the mass media, and religious and educational institutions also have a noticeable impact on a child's socialization into feminine and masculine norms. A culture or subculture may require that one sex or the other take primary responsibility for the socialization of children, economic support of the family, or religious or intellectual leadership. In some societies, girls are socialized mainly by their mothers and boys by their fathers—an arrangement that may prevent girls from learning critical survival skills. In South Asia, fathers teach their sons to swim to prepare them for a life as fishermen; girls typically do not learn to swim. When a deadly tsunami hit the coast of South Asia in 2004, many more men survived than women.

LO 13-1 School

Like the family, schools have an explicit mandate to socialize people in the United States—especially children—into the norms and values of our culture.

As conflict theorists Samuel Bowles and Herbert Gintis (1976) have observed, schools in this country foster competition through built-in systems of reward and punishment, such as grades and evaluations by teachers. Consequently, a child who is experiencing difficulty trying to learn a new skill can sometimes come to feel stupid and unsuccessful. However, as the self matures, children become capable of increasingly realistic assessments of their intellectual, physical, and social abilities.

Functionalists point out that schools, as agents of socialization, fulfill the function of teaching children the values and customs of the larger society. Conflict theorists agree, but add that schools can reinforce the divisive aspects of society, especially those of social class. For example, higher education in the United States is costly despite the existence of financial aid programs. Students from affluent backgrounds therefore have an advantage in gaining access to universities and professional training. At the same time, less affluent young people may never receive the preparation that would qualify them for the best-paying and most prestigious jobs.

A daughter learns how to weave fabric from her mother in Guatemala. The family is the most important agent of socialization.

4-1 *RUM SPRINGA*: RAISING CHILDREN AMISH STYLE

All families face challenges raising their children, but what if your parents expected you not to dance, listen to music, watch television, or access the Internet? This is the challenge faced by Amish teens and their parents, who embrace a lifestyle of the mid-1800s. Amish youths—boys in particular—often rebel against their parents' strict morals by getting drunk, behaving disrespectfully, and indulging in "worldly" activities, such as buying a car. At times even the girls may become involved, to their families' dismay. As one scholar puts it, "The rowdiness of Amish youth is an embarrassment to church leaders and a stigma in the larger community" (Kraybill 2001:138).

Yet the strong pull of mainstream American culture has led Amish parents to routinize, almost to accept, some of their

All families face challenges raising their children, but what if your parents expected you not to dance, listen to music, watch television, or access the Internet?

children's worldly activities. They expect adolescents to test their subculture's boundaries during a period of discovery called *rum springa*, a German term meaning "running around." A common occurrence during which young people attend barn dances and break social norms that forbid drinking, smoking, and driving cars, *rum springa* is definitely not supported by the Amish religion.

Parents often react to these escapades by looking the other way, sometimes literally. If they hear radio music coming from the barn, or a motorcycle driving onto their property in the middle of the night, they don't retaliate by punishing their offspring. Instead, they pretend not to notice, secure in the knowledge that Amish children almost always return to the community's traditional

values. Indeed, despite the flirtation with popular culture and modern technology that is common during the *rum springa*, the vast majority of Amish youths do return to the Amish community and become baptized. Scholars report that 85 to 90 percent of Amish children accept the faith as young adults.

To mainstream Americans, this little known and understood subculture became a source of entertainment when in 2004, UPN aired a 10-week reality program called *Amish in the City*. In the series, five Amish youths allegedly on *rum springa* moved in with six worldly wise young adults in Los Angeles. On behalf of the Amish community, some critics called the series exploitative, a sign of how vulnerable the Amish are. No similar series would be developed on the rebellion of Muslim or Orthodox Jewish youths, they charged.

Let's Discuss

1. Do you or anyone you know come from a subculture that rejects mainstream American culture? If so, describe the community's norms and values. How do they resemble and how do they differ from Amish norms and values?
2. Why do you think so many Amish youths return to their families' way of life after rebelling against it?

Sources: Kraybill 2001; R. Schaefer and Zellner 2011; Shachtman 2006; Stevick 2007; Weinraub 2004.

LO **13-1** Peer Group

As a child grows older, the family becomes somewhat less important in social development. Instead, peer groups increasingly assume the role of Mead's significant others. Within the peer group, young people associate with others who are approximately their age, and who often enjoy a similar social status (Giordano 2003).

We can see how important peer groups are to young people when their social lives are strained by war or disaster. In Baghdad, the overthrow of Saddam Hussein has profoundly changed teenagers' worlds, casting doubt on their future. Some young people have lost relatives or friends; others have become involved with fundamentalist groups or fled with their families to safer countries. Those youths who are left behind can suffer intense loneliness and boredom. Confined to their homes by crime and terrorism, those fortunate enough to have computers turn to Internet chat rooms or immerse themselves in their studies. Through e-mail, they struggle to maintain old friendships interrupted by wartime dislocation (Sanders 2004).

Gender differences are noteworthy among adolescents. Boys and girls are socialized by their parents, peers, and the media to identify many of the same paths to popularity, but

TABLE 4-3 HIGH SCHOOL POPULARITY

What Makes High School Girls Popular?		What Makes Gigh School Boys Popular?	
According to College Men:	According to College Women:	According to College Men:	According to College Women:
1. Physical attractiveness	1. Grades/intelligence	1. Participation in sports	1. Participation in sports
2. Grades/intelligence	2. Participation in sports	2. Grades/intelligence	2. Grades/intelligence
3. Participation in sports	3. General sociability	3. Popularity with girls	3. General sociability
4. General sociability	4. Physical attractiveness	4. General sociability	4. Physical attractiveness
5. Popularity with boys	5. Clothes	5. Car	5. School clubs/government

Note: Students at the following universities were asked in which ways adolescents in their high schools had gained prestige with their peers: Cornell University, Louisiana State University, Southeastern Louisiana University, State University of New York at Albany, State University of New York at Stony Brook, University of Georgia, and University of New Hampshire.
Source: Suitor et al. 2001:445.

to different degrees. Table 4-3 compares male and female college students' reports of how girls and boys they knew became popular in high school. The two groups named many of the same paths to popularity but gave them a different order of importance. While neither men nor women named sexual activity, drug use, or alcohol use as one of the top five paths, college men were much more likely than women to mention those behaviors as a means to becoming popular, for both boys and girls.

LO 13-2 Mass Media and Technology

In the past century, media innovations—radio, motion pictures, recorded music, television, and the Internet—have become important agents of socialization. The question is no longer whether young people are plugged in, but how they use these resources. Today, 95 percent of those aged 12 to 17 are on the Internet. No surprise there, but 91 percent of them post photos identifying themselves by name. Ninety-two percent use their real names, and 82 percent post their birth dates on social media. Increasingly, then, socialization occurs online. The age at which young people go online has also been dropping, prompting concern about the potential for media abuse at an earlier and earlier age. Over the last decade, the American Academy of Pediatrics began by publishing concerns about teen use of the Internet. Recently, the organization published guidelines for the 90 percent of *infants* who use the Internet—via their parents, of course (American Academy of Pediatrics 2011, 2013; Madden et al. 2013).

The media, however, are not always a negative socializing influence. Television programs and even commercials can introduce young people to unfamiliar lifestyles and cultures. Not only do children in the United States learn about life in "faraway lands," but inner-city children learn about the lives of farm children, and vice versa. The same thing happens in other countries.

Sociologists and other social scientists have begun to consider the impact of technology on socialization. They are particularly interested in the online friendship networks, like Facebook and Twitter. To assess the importance of social media in our daily lives, they typically begin by studying how we use them. In a novel approach, some researchers have asked what would happen if we stopped using social media.

Not just in industrial nations, but in Africa and other developing areas, people have been socialized into relying on new communications technologies. Not long ago, if Zadhe Iyombe wanted to talk to his mother, he had to make an eight-day trip from the capital city of Kinshasa up the Congo River by boat to the rural town where he was born. Now both he and his mother have access to a cell phone, and they send text messages to each other daily. Iyombe and his mother

In Soroti, Uganda, a woman makes a quick telephone call. Cell phones play a critical role in communications and commerce in developing countries, where other ways of connecting are less available or more expensive.

are not atypical. Although cell phones aren't cheap, 1.4 billion owners in developing countries have come to consider them a necessity. Today, there are more cell phones in developing nations than in industrial nations—the first time in history that developing nations have outpaced the developed world in the adoption of a telecommunications technology (K. Sullivan 2006).

That said, not all new communications technologies are widely available in developing nations. For example, many people in these countries cannot afford broadband Internet service. In terms of their relative income, broadband service is 40 times more expensive to people in developing countries than it is to the typical person in an industrialized nation (International Telecommunication Union 2012).

LO 13-2 Workplace

Learning to behave appropriately in an occupation is a fundamental aspect of human socialization. It used to be that going to work began with the end of our formal schooling, but that is no longer the case, at least not in the United States. More and more young people work today, and not just for a parent or relative. Adolescents generally seek jobs in order to make spending money; 80 percent of high school seniors say that little or none of what they earn goes to family expenses. These teens rarely look on their employment as a means of exploring vocational interests or getting on-the-job training.

Some observers feel that the increasing number of teenagers who are working earlier in life and for longer hours are finding the workplace almost as important an agent of socialization as school. In fact, a number of educators complain that student time at work is adversely affecting schoolwork. The level of teenage employment in the United States is the highest among industrial countries, which may provide one explanation for why U.S. high school students lag behind those in other countries on international achievement tests.

Socialization in the workplace changes when it involves a more permanent shift from an after-school job to full-time employment. Occupational socialization can be most intense during the transition from school to job, but it continues throughout one's work history. Technological advances may alter the requirements of the position and necessitate some degree of resocialization. Today, men and women change occupations, employers, or places of work many times during their adult years. For example, the typical worker spends about four years with an employer. Occupational socialization continues, then, throughout a person's years in the labor market (Bialik 2010).

From the perspective of . . .

A Human Resources Manager How would you minimize isolation and increase occupational socialization for employees who largely work from home?

College students today recognize that occupational socialization is not socialization into one lifetime occupation. They anticipate going through a number of jobs. The Bureau of Labor Statistics (2010) has found that from ages 18 to 42, the typical person has held 11 jobs. This high rate of turnover in employment applies to both men and women, and to those with a college degree as well as those with a high school diploma.

LO 13-2 Religion and the State

Increasingly, social scientists are recognizing the importance of both religion and government ("the state") as agents of socialization, because of their impact on the life course. Traditionally, family members have served as the primary caregivers in our culture, but in the 20th century, the family's protective function was steadily transferred to outside agencies such as hospitals, mental health clinics, and child care centers. Many of these agencies are run by groups affiliated with certain religions or by the state.

Both organized religion and government have impacted the life course by reinstituting some of the rites of passage once observed in agricultural communities and early industrial societies. For example, religious organizations stipulate certain traditional rites that may bring together all the members of an extended family, even if they never meet for any other reason. And government regulations stipulate the ages at which a person may drive a car, drink alcohol, vote in elections, marry without parental permission, work overtime, and retire. These regulations do not constitute strict rites of passage: most 18-year-olds choose not to vote, and most people choose their age of retirement without reference to government dictates.

In the Social Policy section at the end of this chapter, we will see that government is under pressure to become a provider of child care, which would give it a new and direct role in the socialization of infants and young children.

E Evaluate

Read each question carefully and then select or provide the best answer.

1. Which social institution is considered to be the most important agent of socialization in the United States, especially for children?
   a. the family
   b. the school
   c. the peer group
   d. the mass media

2. The term *gender role* refers to
   a. physical abilities and limitations imposed on people because they are male or female.
   b. careers and occupations devoted to dealing primarily with either men or women.
   c. mental abilities and personality traits largely determined by a person's gender.
   d. expectations regarding the proper behavior, attitudes, and activities of males and females.

3. Which sociological perspective emphasizes that schools in the United States foster competition through built-in systems of reward and punishment?
   a. the functionalist perspective
   b. the conflict perspective
   c. the interactionist perspective
   d. the psychological perspective

4. The _____ perspective emphasizes the role of schools in teaching the values and customs of the larger society.

5. As children grow older, the family becomes less important in social development, while _____ groups become more important.

Answers
1 (a); 2 (d); 3 (b); 4 functionalist; 5 peer

R Rethink

Consider these questions to get a deeper understanding of the material.

1. How would functionalists and conflict theorists differ in their analysis of socialization by the mass media?

2. What sanctions or rules have you observed that limit the ways in which people access and use online social networks? What are the purposes of such sanctions?

RECAP

LO 13-1 Explain how the family, the school, and peer groups affect socialization from the early years into young adulthood.

- As the primary agents of socialization, parents play a critical role in guiding children into those gender roles deemed appropriate in a society.
- Schools in the United States also have an explicit mandate to socialize people—especially children—into the norms and values of our culture.
- Peer groups become more important than the family as children grow older and associate with persons of their own age and social status. Peers remain important agents of socialization through adolescence.
- Gender differences are especially important during adolescence as popularity becomes a central objective.

LO 13-2 Analyze the ways in which technology and the institutions of work, religion, and the state contribute to the socialization process during the life course.

- The mass media have both a positive and negative socializing influence. Television and the Internet can interfere with schoolwork and contribute to young people's preconceptions and stereotypes, but it can also introduce them to unfamiliar lifestyles and cultures.
- The Internet and cell phones have had a powerful influence, mostly for the better, on otherwise isolated populations by enhancing their communication opportunities.
- Socialization in the workplace begins with part-time employment while we are in school and continues as we work full time and change jobs throughout our lives.
- Religion and the state shape the socialization process by regulating the life course and influencing our views of appropriate behavior at particular ages.

KEY TERMS

Gender role Expectations regarding the proper behavior, attitudes, and activities of males and females.

MODULE 14 Socialization throughout the Life Course

Work

LO 14-1 The Life Course

Among the Kota people of the Congo in Africa, adolescents paint themselves blue. Mexican American girls go on a daylong religious retreat before dancing the night away. Egyptian mothers step over their newborn infants seven times, and graduating students at the Naval Academy throw their hats in the air. These are all ways of celebrating **rites of passage**, a ritual that marks the symbolic transition from one social position to another.

Rites of passage are a worldwide social phenomenon. The Kota rite marks the passage to adulthood. The color blue, viewed as the color of death, symbolizes the death of childhood. Hispanic girls celebrate reaching womanhood with a *quinceañera* ceremony at age 15. In the Cuban American community of Miami, the popularity of the *quinceañera* supports a network of party planners, caterers, dress designers, and the Miss Quinceañera Latina pageant. For thousands of years, Egyptian mothers have welcomed their newborns to the world in the Soboa ceremony by stepping over the seven-day-old infant seven times.

These specific ceremonies mark stages of development in the life course. They indicate that the process of socialization continues through all stages of the life cycle. In fact, some researchers have chosen to concentrate on socialization as a lifelong process. Sociologists and other social scientists who take such a **life course approach** look closely at the social factors that influence people throughout their lives, from birth to death, including gender and income. They recognize that biological changes mold but do not dictate human behavior.

Several life events mark the passage to adulthood, including marriage and the birth of a first child. Of course, these turning points vary from one society or even one generation

A young Apache woman undergoes a mudding ceremony traditionally used in rites of passage, such as puberty and in some cases weddings.

to the next. In the United States, the key event seems to be the completion of formal schooling. However, educational completion is not as clearly defined today as it was a generation or two ago. More and more people are taking full-time jobs while finishing their schooling, or returning to school to obtain a professional certificate or advanced degree. Similarly, the milestones associated with leaving home, finding a stable job, and establishing a long-term personal relationship do not now occur at specific ages (Silva 2012; T. Smith 2003).

One result of these overlapping steps to independence is that in the United States, unlike some other societies, there is no clear dividing line between adolescence and adulthood. Nowadays, few young people finish school, get married, and leave home at about the same age, clearly establishing their transition to adulthood. The terms *youthhood, emerging adulthood,* and *not quite adult* have been coined to describe the prolonged ambiguous status that young people in their 20s experience (Côté 2000; Settersten and Ray 2011; Christian Smith 2007).

LO 14-1 Anticipatory Socialization and Resocialization

The development of a social self is literally a lifelong transformation that begins in the crib and continues as one prepares for death. Two types of socialization occur at many points throughout the life course: anticipatory socialization and resocialization.

Anticipatory socialization refers to processes of socialization in which a person rehearses for future positions, occupations, and social relationships. A culture can function more efficiently and smoothly if members become acquainted with the norms, values, and behavior associated with a social position before actually assuming that status. Preparation for many aspects of adult life begins with anticipatory socialization during childhood and adolescence, and continues throughout our lives as we prepare for new responsibilities.

You can see the process of anticipatory socialization take place when high school students start to consider what colleges they may attend. Traditionally, this task meant looking at publications received in the mail or making campus visits. However, with new technology, more and more students are using the web to begin their college experience. Colleges are investing more time and money in developing attractive websites through which students can take virtual campus tours and hear audio clips of everything from the college anthem to a sample zoology lecture.

Occasionally, assuming a new social or occupational position requires us to *unlearn* an established orientation. **Resocialization** refers to the process of discarding former behavior patterns and accepting new ones as part of a transition in one's life. Often resocialization occurs during an explicit effort to transform an individual, as happens in reform schools, therapy groups, prisons, religious conversion settings, and political indoctrination camps. The process of resocialization typically involves considerable stress for the individual—much more so than socialization in general, or even anticipatory socialization (Gecas 2004).

Resocialization is particularly effective when it occurs within a total institution. Erving Goffman (1961) coined the term **total institution** to refer to an institution that regulates all aspects of a person's life under a single authority, such as a prison, the military, a mental hospital, or a convent. Because the total institution is generally cut off from the rest of society, it provides for all the needs of its members. Quite literally, the crew of a merchant vessel at sea becomes part of a total institution. So elaborate are its requirements, so all-encompassing its activities, a total institution often represents a miniature society.

Goffman (1961) identified four common traits of total institutions:

- All aspects of life are conducted in the same place under the control of a single authority.
- Any activities within the institution are conducted in the company of others in the same circumstances—for example, army recruits or novices in a convent.
- The authorities devise rules and schedule activities without consulting the participants.
- All aspects of life within a total institution are designed to fulfill the purpose of the organization. Thus, all activities in a monastery might be centered on prayer and communion with God (Davies 1989; P. Rose et al. 1979).

People often lose their individuality within total institutions. For example, a person entering prison may experience the humiliation of a **degradation ceremony** as he or she is stripped of clothing, jewelry, and other personal possessions. From this point on, scheduled daily routines allow for little or no personal initiative. The individual becomes secondary and rather invisible in the overbearing social environment (Garfinkel 1956).

LO 14-1 Role Transitions throughout the Life Course

We have seen that socialization is a lifelong process. We simply do not experience things the same way at different points in the life course. For example, one study found that even falling in love differs according to where we are in the life course. Young unmarried adults tend to treat love as a noncommittal game or an obsession characterized by possessiveness and dependency. People over age 50 are much more likely to see love as involving commitment, and they tend to take a practical approach to finding a partner who meets a set of rational criteria. That does not mean that romance is dead among the older generation, however. Among those age 65 and over, 39 percent are "head over heels in love," compared to only 25 percent of those ages 18 to 34. The life course, then, affects the manner in which we relate to one another (G. Anderson 2009; Montgomery and Sorell 1997).

How we move through the life course varies dramatically, depending on our personal preferences and circumstances. Some of us marry early, others late; some have children and some don't. These individual patterns are influenced by social factors such as class, race, and gender. Only in the most general terms, then, can we speak of stages or periods in the life course.

One transitional stage, identified by psychologist Daniel Levinson, begins at the time at which an individual

This sandwich-generation mom cares for both her aging parent and her children. Increasingly, members of the baby boom generation find themselves caring for two generations at once.

gradually enters the adult world, perhaps by moving out of the parental home, beginning a career, or marrying. The next transitional period, the midlife transition, typically begins at about age 40. Men and women often experience a stressful period of self-evaluation, commonly known as the **midlife crisis**, in which they realize that they have not achieved basic goals and ambitions and have little time left to do so. Thus, Levinson (1978, 1996) found that most adults surveyed experienced tumultuous midlife conflicts within the self and with the external world.

THE SANDWICH GENERATION

During the late 1990s social scientists focused on the **sandwich generation**—adults who simultaneously try to meet the competing needs of their parents and their children. That is, caregiving goes in two directions: (1) to children, who even as young adults may still require significant direction, and (2) to aging parents, whose health and economic problems may demand intervention by their adult children. By 2010, 13 million Americans were caring for both their children *and* their parents.

Like the role of caring for children, the role of caring for aging parents falls disproportionately on women. Overall, women provide 66 percent of the care their parents receive, and even more as the demands of the role grow more intense and time-consuming. Increasingly, middle-aged women and younger are finding themselves on the "daughter track," as their time and attention are diverted by the needs of their aging mothers and fathers (National Alliance for Caregiving 2009).

The last major transition identified by Levinson occurs after age 60—sometimes well after that age, given advances in health care, greater longevity, and gradual acceptance within society of older people. This point, when people transition to a different lifestyle, is a time of dramatic changes in everyday life.

ADJUSTING TO RETIREMENT

Retirement is a rite of passage that marks a critical transition. Typically, symbolic events are associated with this rite of passage, such as retirement gifts, a retirement party, and special moments on the last day on the job. The preretirement period itself can be emotionally charged, especially if the retiree is expected to train his or her successor (Atchley 1976).

Today, the retirement stage is complicated by economic deterioration. From 1950 to 1990, the average age at retirement in the United States declined; since then, however, it has risen. In 1990, 11.8 percent of those over age 64 were in the labor force. By 2010, the proportion had increased to 17.4 percent, and is projected to hit 22.6 percent by 2020. In that year, the proportion of people still working in their upper 70s will match the proportion of those who were working in their upper 60s in 1990. Indeed, as recently as 2011, 5 percent of women and 10 percent of men over age 75 were still working.

A variety of factors explains this reversal in the trend toward earlier retirement. Changes in Social Security benefits, the recent economic recession, and workers' concern about maintaining their health insurance and pension benefits have all contributed. At the same time, life expectancy has increased and the quality of people's health has improved (Toossi 2012).

Phases of Retirement Gerontologist Robert Atchley (1976) has identified several phases of the retirement experience:

- *Preretirement,* a period of anticipatory socialization as the person prepares for retirement

- *The near phase,* when the person establishes a specific departure date from his or her job

- *The honeymoon phase,* an often euphoric period in which the person pursues activities that he or she never had time for before

- *The disenchantment phase,* in which retirees feel a sense of letdown or even depression as they cope with their new lives, which may include illness or poverty
- *The reorientation phase,* which involves the development of a more realistic view of retirement alternatives
- *The stability phase,* a period in which the person has learned to deal with life after retirement in a reasonable and comfortable fashion
- *The termination phase,* which begins when the person can no longer engage in basic, day-to-day activities such as self-care and housework

Retirement is not a single transition, then, but rather a series of adjustments that varies from one person to another. The length and timing of each phase will differ for each individual, depending on such factors as financial status and health. A particular person will not necessarily go through all the phases identified by Atchley (Reitzes and Mutran 2006).

Some factors, such as being forced into retirement or being burdened with financial difficulties, can further complicate the retirement process. People who enter retirement involuntarily or without the necessary means may never experience the honeymoon phase. In the United States, many retirees continue in the paid labor force, often taking part-time jobs to supplement their pensions. The impact of the prolonged economic downturn that began in 2008 on this pattern remains to be seen.

Like other aspects of life in the United States, the experience of retirement varies according to gender, race, and ethnicity. White males are most likely to benefit from retirement wages, as well as to have participated in a formal retirement preparation program. As a result, anticipatory socialization for retirement is most complete for White men. In contrast, members of racial and ethnic minority groups—especially African Americans—are more likely to exit the paid labor force through disability than through retirement. Because of their comparatively lower incomes and smaller savings, men and women from racial and ethnic minority groups work intermittently after retirement more often than older Whites (National Institute on Aging 1999; Quadagno 2011).

"Have you given much thought to what kind of job you want after you retire?"

Naturally Occurring Retirement Communities (NORCs) With recent improvements in health care, older Americans have gained new choices in where to live. Today, rather than residing in nursing homes or planned retirement communities, many of them congregate in areas that have gradually become informal centers for senior citizens. Social scientists have dubbed such areas **naturally occurring retirement communities (NORCs)**.

Using observation research, census data, and interviews, sociologists have developed some interesting conclusions about NORCs in the United States, which account for an estimated 17 to 25 percent of people age 65 or older. These communities can be as small as a single apartment building or as large as a neighborhood in a big city. Often, they emerge as singles and young couples move out and older people move in. Sometimes couples simply remain where they are; as they grow older, the community becomes noticeably grayer. Such has been the case in the Fort Hamilton neighborhood in Brooklyn, New York, where a third of residents are now over 55. In time, business establishments that cater to the elderly—pharmacies, medical supply outlets, small restaurants, senior citizen centers—relocate to NORCs, making them even more attractive to older citizens.

Unfortunately, residents of some of these communities are threatened by gentrification, or the takeover of low-income neighborhoods by higher-income residents. In Chicago, a high-rise building known as Ontario Place is converting to a condominium, at prices that current residents cannot afford. About half the building's occupants are Russian immigrants; most of the others are elderly or disabled people living on fixed incomes. These people are distressed not just because they will need to move, but because their community is being destroyed (Gregor 2013; Piturro 2012; Sheehan 2005).

LO 14-2 SOCIAL POLICY and Socialization

We have seen that researchers rely on a number of tools, from simple observational research to the latest in computer technologies. Because in the real world sociological research can have far-reaching consequences for public policy and public welfare, let's consider its impact on child care around the world.

CHILD CARE AROUND THE WORLD

Child care programs are not just babysitting services; they have an enormous influence on the development of young children—an influence that has been growing with the movement of more and more women into the paid labor force. The rise in single-parent families, increased job opportunities for women, and the need for additional family income have all propelled mothers of young children into the working world. Who should care for the children of working mothers during working hours?

Preschoolers typically are not cared for by their parents. Seventy-three percent of employed mothers depend on others to care for their children, and 30 percent of mothers who aren't employed have regular care arrangements. In fact, children under age five are more likely to be cared for on a daily basis by their grandparents than by their parents. Over a third of them are cared for by nonrelatives in nursery schools, Head Start programs, day care centers, family day care, and other arrangements (Bureau of the Census 2008c).

Researchers have found that high-quality child care centers do not adversely affect the socialization of children; in fact, good day care benefits children. The value of preschool programs was documented in a series of studies conducted in the United States. Researchers found no significant differences in infants who had received extensive nonmaternal care compared with those who had been cared for solely by their mothers. They also reported that more and more infants in the United States are being placed in child care outside the home, and that overall, the quality of those arrangements is better than has been found in previous studies. It is difficult, however, to generalize about child care, since there is so much variability among day care providers, and even among government policies from one state to another (Loeb et al. 2004; Ludwig and Sawhill 2007; NICHD 2007).

Few people in the United States or elsewhere can afford the luxury of having a parent stay at home, or of paying for high-quality live-in child care. For millions of mothers and fathers, finding the right

Children play at the Communicare day care center in Perth, Australia. The Australian government subsidizes children's attendance at day care and afterschool programs from birth to age 12.

kind of child care is a challenge both to parenting and to the pocketbook. At present, the federal government supports child care through subsidized programs, which target low-income families, and income tax credits, which benefit families with moderate incomes. The annual expenditure to assist low-income parents is about $12 billion; the expenditure to support parents with moderate incomes is $58 billion (Cushing-Daniels and Zedlewski 2008).

Applying Sociology to Child Care Studies that assess the quality of child care outside the home reflect the micro level of analysis and the interest of interactionists in the impact of face-to-face interaction. These studies also explore macro-level implications for the functioning of social institutions like the family. Some of the issues surrounding day care have also been of interest to those who take the conflict perspective.

In the United States, high-quality day care is not equally available to all families. Parents in affluent communities have an easier time finding day care than those in poor or working-class communities. Finding *affordable* child care is also a problem. Viewed from a conflict perspective, child care costs are an especially serious burden for lower-class families. The poorest families spend 25 percent of their income for preschool child care, whereas families who are *not* poor pay only 6 percent or less of their income. Despite these problems, subsidized child care has steadily declined over the last decade.

Feminist theorists echo the concern of conflict theorists that high-quality child care receives little government support because it is regarded as "merely a way to let women work." Nearly all child care workers (97 percent) are women; many find themselves in low-status, minimum-wage jobs. Typically, food servers, messengers, and gas station attendants make more money than the 23 million child care workers in the United States, whose average annual salary of $19,605 puts them right at the poverty level for a family of three (Barnett et al. 2013; Bureau of the Census 2011a; Ruiz 2010).

Initiating Child Care Policy Policies regarding child care outside the home vary throughout the world. Most developing nations do not have the economic base to provide subsidized child care. Thus, working mothers rely largely on relatives or take their children to work. In the comparatively wealthy industrialized countries of western Europe, government provides child care as a basic service, at little or no expense to parents. But even those countries with tax-subsidized programs occasionally fall short of the need for high-quality child care.

When policymakers decide that child care is desirable, they must determine the degree to which taxpayers should subsidize it. In Sweden and Denmark, one-half to two-thirds of preschoolers were in government-subsidized child care full-time in 2003. In the United States, annual fees for full-time child care of a four-year-old range from an average of $3,900 in Mississippi to an average of $11,678 in Massachusetts (Immervoll and Barber 2005; NACCRRA 2010).

Japan is facing a special dilemma. Traditionally, married women and certainly married mothers did not remain in the labor force. Although this social pattern is slowly changing, the availability of day care has not kept pace. Many Japanese policymakers have difficulty recognizing the need for day care. "Is your work so important that you must put your baby in childcare?" they ask. "Why are you being so self-centered?" Little wonder that a single private day care center in Japan recently had a waiting list of 25,000 children (Tabuchi 2013:A9).

We have a long way to go in making high-quality child care more affordable and accessible, not just in the United States but throughout the world as well. In an attempt to reduce government spending, France is considering cutting back the budgets of subsidized nurseries, even though waiting lists exist and the French public heartily disapproves of cutbacks. In Germany, reunification has reduced the options previously open to East German mothers, who had become accustomed to government-supported child care. Experts in child development view such reports as a vivid reminder of the need for greater government and private-sector support for child care. From a public policy point of view, the case for expanded child care is especially persuasive. According to recent research, reductions in public assistance, together with increased tax revenue from parents' earnings, would outweigh the cost of government subsidies to child care programs (Domeij and Klein 2013; L. King 1998).

E Evaluate

Read each question carefully and then select or provide the best answer.

1. On the first day of basic training in the army, a recruit's civilian clothes are replaced by army "greens" and all privacy is lost, even to the point of using communal bathrooms. All these humiliating activities are part of
   a. becoming a significant other.
   b. impression management.
   c. a degradation ceremony.
   d. face-work.

2. In recent days, many older Americans are choosing to congregate in areas that have become informal centers of senior life. Social scientists refer to such centers as
   a. semi-independent settlement houses.
   b. naturally occurring retirement communities.
   c. modified nursing care facilities.
   d. planned retirement communities.

3. Viewed from a _____ perspective, the fact that child care costs are more burdensome for working-class families than for affluent families is highly problematic.

4. Preparation for many aspects of adult life begins with _____ socialization during childhood and adolescence and continues throughout our lives as we prepare for new responsibilities.

5. Resocialization is most effective when it occurs within a(n) _____ institution.

Answers
1 (c); 2 (b); 3 conflict; 4 anticipatory; 5 total

R Rethink

Consider these questions to get a deeper understanding of the material.

1. Have you had personal experience of anticipatory socialization in your lifetime? Of resocialization? Explain.

2. What rite of passage has become less important today than it was in your parents' generation? Which one has become more important? Explain.

RECAP

LO 14-1 Explain the role of socialization throughout the life course.

- Socialization proceeds throughout the life course. Some societies mark stages of development with formal rites of passage. In U.S. culture, significant events such as the end of formal schooling serve to change a person's status.
- In recent years, economic and cultural changes have led to the disappearance of any clear dividing line between adolescence and adulthood.
- Anticipatory socialization, a process of rehearsal for future positions, and resocialization, the abandonment of older behavior patterns and the adoption of new ones, occur at several points in the life course.
- Since the 1990s, the "sandwich generation" has arisen in the United States—adults providing care simultaneously to parents and children—a role assumed disproportionately by women.
- The final rite of passage during the life course is retirement, a significant enough transition that Robert Atchley has identified seven distinct phases within it.

LO 14-2 Analyze through a sociological lens the impact of child care on socialization.

- As more and more mothers of young children have entered the labor market, the demand for child care has increased dramatically, posing policy questions for many nations around the world.

KEY TERMS

Anticipatory socialization Processes of socialization in which a person rehearses for future positions, occupations, and social relationships.

Degradation ceremony An aspect of the socialization process within some total institutions, in which people are subjected to humiliating rituals.

Life course approach A research orientation in which sociologists and other social scientists look closely at the social factors that influence people throughout their lives, from birth to death.

Midlife crisis A stressful period of self-evaluation that begins at about age 40.

Naturally occurring retirement community (NORC) An area that has gradually become an informal center for senior citizens.

Resocialization The process of discarding former behavior patterns and accepting new ones as part of a transition in one's life.

Rite of passage A ritual marking the symbolic transition from one social position to another.

Sandwich generation The generation of adults who simultaneously try to meet the competing needs of their parents and their children.

Total institution An institution that regulates all aspects of a person's life under a single authority, such as a prison, the military, a mental hospital, or a convent.

The Case of . . . Rolling with the Punches

Olivia Jordan has always been ambitious. "I get that from my father," she says. "He grew up poor, on the south side of Chicago, but he studied hard and became a teacher." Jordan studied law and became a corporate lawyer. "I had strong writing skills and I was good at logic. Everyone I knew in college was planning to study law," she notes.

At 30, Jordan married a banker. "Marriage didn't really change anything," she says. "We still worked hundred-hour weeks." Then, Jordan had a child, a daughter born with cerebral palsy. "My life did a one-eighty right there," she says. "I had this child I adored, and she needed a lot." At first, Jordan tried to work half-time, "but that's impossible in the sort of law I practiced," she says. When her firm asked her to step down, she devoted her life to raising her daughter. "I read tons of research on cerebral palsy, joined support groups, took my daughter to the Special Olympics. It was a whole new culture and I just dove in."

Last year, Jordan's husband died suddenly. "I thought, okay, I need to go back to work. My daughter's 14 now. She's doing well." Jordan decided she'd like to work as an advocate for families with autistic children. "I know what it's like to be on your own, dealing with a challenged child," she says. With her legal skills, she was hired by the first organization she applied to. "It's funny," she says. "Now, I'm fighting all those bigwig lawmakers, trying to get a fair deal for people instead of corporations. But I'm learning the ropes and I'm loving the fight."

1. If our sense of self is largely derived from our perceptions of how others see us, what do you think Jordan believed others saw in her?

2. Jordan had to "start over" not once, but twice. In her examples of resocialization, do you see examples of anticipatory socialization? Describe them.

3. How might Jordan's life have turned out differently if she had remained a full-time lawyer?

4. How has Jordan been an agent of socialization for her daughter?

5. What do you think her daughter has learned from Jordan's behavior and choices?

Study Strategies

Improving Your Memory

Sociology, like any academic field, requires you to recall a lot of information. Work on your memory to help you recall sociological concepts, terms, steps, lists, and other items. Luckily, we all have the ability to store huge amounts of information—the trick is to find it when you need it. The following strategies—if you practice them—will help you strengthen your memory.

 **Prepare**

- Identify what you need to remember: a list of definitions, an ordered set of steps, the contributions of major sociologists, etc.

 **Organize**

- Gather some "memory tools": paper, index (flash) cards, computer (for the Internet, where you can find out about *mnemonics*—tricks to help you recall information).
- Relate what you need to remember to what you already know. For instance, relate concepts about culture, values, or ethnicity to your personal experiences or knowledge.

 **Work**

- Rehearse new material, going over it repeatedly (aloud, if possible).
- Create *acronyms* (words composed of the first letters of things on your list), like HOMES for the Great Lakes (Huron, Ontario, Michigan, Erie, Superior).
- It may be easier to create an *acrostic* (a sentence whose first letters are the first letters of the things on your list) like "**D**on't **L**et **H**arry **D**rink **C**ocoa" for Define, Literature, Hypothesis, Data, and Conclusion—the steps in the scientific process).
- Use your other senses: Draw pictures, say things aloud, or create a rhyme or a song and recite or sing it to help you remember.
- For lists, use rhymes for the numbers from 1 to 10 (e.g., sun, zoo, tree, door, hive, sticks, heaven, gate, mine, den), and picture in your head funny images linking your list to the "numbers."
- Use any kinds of wordplay and puns that may help—the crazier the better. ("I've GOTTO remember that *gato* is 'cat' in Spanish.")

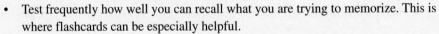 **Evaluate**

- Test frequently how well you can recall what you are trying to memorize. This is where flashcards can be especially helpful.
- Form a study group and work together to test your memories.

Rethink

- Your mind needs time to create lasting memories. Don't leave memorization to the last minute.
- In a few days, go back to the material you tried to memorize and see how well you do. This helps to solidify memories and find gaps.

em **POWER** me

You Must Remember This

Read each statement and circle the items that reflect things you regularly do to help you remember information.

1. I identify what I need to remember, then repeat that material aloud.

2. I draw pictures and diagrams to help me visualize features and relationships of concepts I need to memorize.

3. I quiz myself on key concepts or terms using flashcards I make.

4. When I need to memorize lists or a series of steps, I use acronyms, for example, P.O.W.E.R. to remember Prepare, Organize, Work, Evaluate, Rethink.

5. I join study groups because it's useful to test what I can recall with others.

6. I make personal links to information I need to recall, relating key concepts to my everyday life and experiences.

7. I revisit material I've studied within a day or two to see how well I can remember key ideas and terms.

8. When I need to memorize a list in order or a key phrase, I sometimes use acrostics. For example, Multiply and Divide before Adding and Subtracting—the order of operations in mathematics—becomes My Dad Adores Salami.

Give yourself 1 point for each of the items circled.

SCORE:

7–8 points: Congratulations! You have a wealth of mnemonics (memory tricks) to help you retain any new material you're learning.

5–6 points: You have developed many useful memory aids. Pick up some more from the items listed.

4 or less points: Try out the ideas suggested in the items. They make memorization easy and fun.

5 Social Interaction, Groups, and Social Structure

Sociology at WORK   LABOR RELATIONS ARBITRATOR

LEON FERRARA is a labor relations arbitrator. "When a company's union and management can't settle a disagreement, I get called in to hear all the facts of the dispute and decide on a fair outcome," Ferrara explains. "Basically, I'm like a judge." Ferrara is well suited for the job. He used to work in management for the Ford Motor Company, but his father was a union member and worked the assembly line for 38 years. "I've seen both sides," he says, "and I've never forgotten my roots."

Ferrara has a favorite saying: *We're all in this together.* "I try to frame the discussion that way when I attend a hearing," he says. "I listen to both sides' arguments and then I remind them that they are working together to produce a product. In modern industry, there's such a division of labor, people forget that every individual's contribution is valuable. Management can't take the attitude that labor is expendable, and labor can't turn a deaf ear to the people in suits just because they're in suits. The product suffers then and the whole enterprise sours. My final decisions always stress the interdependent nature of the workplace. People at all levels must respect each other and be allowed to participate in decision making." ■

Looking Ahead

IN THIS CHAPTER WE WILL STUDY SOCIAL STRUCTURE AND ITS EFFECT ON our social interactions. What determines a person's status in society? How do our social roles affect our social interactions? What is the place of social institutions such as the family, religion, and government in our social structure? How can we better understand and manage large organizations such as multinational corporations? We'll begin by considering how social interactions shape the way we view the world around us. Next, we'll focus on the five basic elements of social structure: statuses, social roles, groups, social networks, and social institutions such as the family, religion, government, and the mass media. We'll see that functionalists, conflict theorists, and interactionists approach social institutions quite differently. Finally, we'll compare our modern social structure with simpler forms, using typologies developed by Émile Durkheim, Ferdinand Tönnies, and Gerhard Lenski. The Social Policy section at the end of the chapter focuses on the changing role of labor unions.

MODULE 15 Social Interaction and Reality

 Prepare <u>Learning Objectives</u>

LO 15-1 Define the terms social interaction, social structure, and social reality, and describe how they are related to one another.

LO 15-2 Explain ascribed status and achieved status, and describe how master status can constrain achieved status.

LO 15-3 Illustrate the social role expectations of role conflict, role strain, and role exit.

 **Organize** Module Outline

Social Reality
Elements of Social Structure
    Statuses
    Social Roles

 W **Work**

LO **15-1** Social Reality

Sociologists use the term **social interaction** to refer to the ways in which people respond to one another, whether face-to-face or over the telephone or on the computer. The term **social structure** refers to the way in which a society is organized into predictable relationships. The two concepts of social interaction and social structure are central to sociological study. They are closely related to socialization, the process through which people learn the attitudes, values, and behaviors appropriate to their culture.

When someone in a crowd shoves you, do you automatically push back? Or do you consider the circumstances of the incident and the attitude of the instigator before you react? Chances are you do the latter. According to sociologist Herbert Blumer (1969:79), the distinctive characteristic of social interaction among people is that "human beings interpret or 'define' each other's actions instead of merely reacting to each other's actions." In other words, our response to someone's behavior is based on the *meaning* we attach to his or her actions. Reality is shaped by our perceptions, evaluations, and definitions.

These meanings typically reflect the norms and values of the dominant culture and our socialization experiences within that culture. As interactionists emphasize, the meanings that we attach to people's behavior are shaped by our interactions with them and with the larger society. Social reality is literally constructed from our social interactions (Berger and Luckmann 1966).

How do we define our social reality? Consider something as simple as how we regard tattoos. At one time, most of us in the United States considered tattoos weird or kooky. We associated them with fringe countercultural groups, such as punk rockers, biker gangs, and skinheads. Among many people, a tattoo elicited an automatic negative response. Now, however, so many people have tattoos—including society's trendsetters and major sports figures—and the ritual of getting a tattoo has become so legitimized, that mainstream culture regards tattoos differently. At this point, as a result of increased social interaction with tattooed people, tattoos look perfectly at home to us in a number of settings.

The nature of social interaction and what constitutes reality varies across cultures. In Western societies, with their emphasis on romantic love, couples see marriage as a relationship as well as a social status. From Valentine's Day flowers to more informal, everyday gestures, professions of love are an expected part of marriage. In Japan, however, marriage is considered more a social status than a relationship. Although many or most Japanese couples undoubtedly do love each other, saying "I love you" does not come easily to them, especially not to husbands. Nor do most husbands call their wives by name (they prefer "Mother") or look them in the eyes. In 2006, in an effort to change these restrictive customs, some Japanese men formed the Devoted Husband Organization, which has been sponsoring a new holiday, Beloved Wives Day. In 2008, this group organized an event called Shout Your Love from the Middle of a Cabbage Patch Day. Dozens of men stood in a cabbage patch north of Tokyo and shouted, "I love you!" to their wives, some of whom had never heard their husbands say those words. In another rare gesture, husbands pledged to be home by 8 p.m. that day (Japan Aisaika Organization 2012; Kambayashi 2008).

The ability to define social reality reflects a group's power within a society. In fact, one of the most crucial aspects of the relationship between dominant and subordinate groups is the ability of the dominant or majority group to define a society's values. Sociologist William I. Thomas (1923), an early critic of theories of racial and gender differences, recognized that the "definition of the situation" could mold the thinking and personality of the individual. Writing from an interactionist perspective, Thomas observed that people respond not only to the objective features of a person or situation but also to the *meaning* that person or situation has for them.

As we have seen throughout the past 60 years—first in the civil rights movement of the 1950s and 1960s and since then among such groups as women, the elderly, gays and lesbians, and people with disabilities—an important aspect of the process of social change involves redefining or reconstructing social reality. Members of subordinate groups challenge traditional definitions and begin to perceive and experience reality in a new way.

LO 15-2 Elements of Social Structure

All social interaction takes place within a social structure, including those interactions that redefine social reality. For purposes of study, we can break down any social structure into five elements: statuses, social roles, groups, social networks, and social institutions. These elements make up social structure just as a foundation, walls, and ceilings make up a building's structure. We will discuss statuses and roles in this module, and groups, social networks, and social institutions in the next module.

STATUSES

We normally think of a person's *status* as having to do with influence, wealth, and fame. However, sociologists use the term **status** to refer to any of the full range of socially defined positions within a large group or society, from the lowest to the highest. Within our society, a person can occupy the status of president of the United States, fruit picker, son or daughter, violinist, teenager, resident of Minneapolis, dental technician, or neighbor. A person can hold a number of statuses at the same time.

Ascribed and Achieved Status Sociologists view some statuses as *ascribed* and others as *achieved* (Figure 5-1). An **ascribed status** is assigned to a person by society without regard for the person's unique talents or characteristics. Generally, the assignment takes place at birth; thus, a person's racial background, gender, and age are all considered ascribed statuses. Though these characteristics are biological in origin, they are significant mainly because of the *social* meanings they have in our culture. Conflict theorists are especially interested in ascribed statuses, since they often confer privileges or reflect a person's membership in a subordinate group.

In most cases, we can do little to change an ascribed status, but we can attempt to change the traditional constraints associated with it. For example, the Gray Panthers—an activist political group founded in 1971 to work for the rights of older people—have tried to modify society's negative and confining stereotypes of the elderly. As a result of their work and that of other groups supporting older citizens, the ascribed status of "senior citizen" is no longer as difficult for millions of older people.

An ascribed status does not necessarily have the same social meaning in every society. In a cross-cultural study, sociologist Gary Huang (1988) confirmed the long-held view that respect for the elderly is an important cultural norm in China. In many cases, the prefix "old" is used respectfully: calling someone "old

FIGURE 5-1 SOCIAL STATUSES

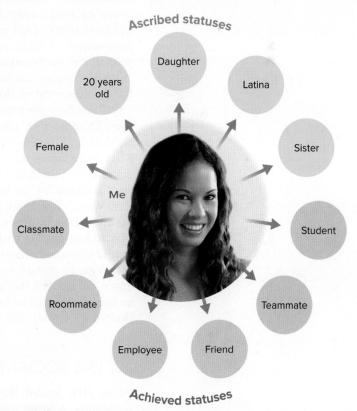

Ascribed statuses

Daughter · Latina · 20 years old · Sister · Female · Me · Student · Classmate · Teammate · Roommate · Employee · Friend

Achieved statuses

Source: Developed by author.

Ascribed status may intersect with a person's achieved status. This man's achieved status as a low-income worker, combined with his minority ethnic status, contrast sharply with the high status of his customer.

teacher" or "old person" is like calling a judge in the United States "your honor." Huang points out that positive age-seniority language distinctions are uncommon in the United States; consequently, we view the term *old man* as more of an insult than a celebration of seniority and wisdom.

Unlike ascribed statuses, an **achieved status** comes to us largely through our own efforts. Both "computer programmer" and "prison guard" are achieved statuses, as are "lawyer," "pianist," "sorority member," "convict," and "social worker." We must do something to acquire an achieved status—go to school, learn a skill, establish a friendship, invent a new product. But as we will see in the next section, our ascribed status heavily influences our achieved status. Being male, for example, would decrease the likelihood that we would consider child care as a career.

Master Status Each person holds many different and sometimes conflicting statuses; some may connote higher social position and some, lower position. How, then, do others view one's overall social position? According to sociologist Everett Hughes (1945), societies deal with inconsistencies by agreeing that certain statuses are more important than others. A **master status** is a status that dominates others and thereby determines a person's general position in society. For example, Arthur Ashe, who died of AIDS in 1993, had a remarkable career as a tennis star, but at the end of his life, his status as a well-known personality with AIDS may have outweighed his statuses as a retired athlete, author, and political activist. Throughout the world, many people with disabilities find that their status as disabled receives undue weight, overshadowing their actual ability to perform successfully in meaningful employment.

Our society gives such importance to race and gender that they often dominate our lives. These ascribed statuses frequently influence our achieved status. The Black activist Malcolm X (1925–1965), an eloquent and controversial advocate of Black power and Black pride during the early 1960s, recalled that his feelings and perspectives changed dramatically in middle school. Elected class president and finishing near the top of his class academically, he had developed a positive outlook. However, his teachers, all of them White, discouraged him from taking more challenging courses, which they felt were not appropriate for Black students. When his eighth-grade English teacher, a White man, advised him that his goal of becoming a lawyer was not realistic, and encouraged him instead to become a carpenter, Malcolm X concluded that his being a Black man (ascribed status) was an obstacle to his dream of becoming a lawyer (achieved status). In the United States, the ascribed statuses of race and gender can function as master statuses that have an important impact on one's potential to achieve a desired professional and social status (Malcolm X [1964] 1999:37; Marable 2011:36–38).

LO 15-3 SOCIAL ROLES

What Are Social Roles? Throughout our lives, we acquire what sociologists call social roles. A **social role** is a set of expectations for people who occupy a given social position or status. Thus, in the United States, we expect that cab drivers will know how to get around a city, that receptionists will be reliable in handling phone messages, and that police officers will take action if they see a citizen being threatened. With each distinctive social status—whether ascribed or achieved—come particular role expectations. However, actual performance varies from individual to individual. One secretary may assume extensive administrative responsibilities, while another may focus on clerical duties.

Roles are a significant component of social structure. Viewed from a functionalist perspective, roles contribute to a society's stability by enabling members to anticipate the behavior of others and to pattern their actions accordingly. Yet social roles can also be dysfunctional if they restrict people's interactions and relationships. If we view a person *only* as a "police officer" or "supervisor," it will be difficult to relate to him or her as a friend or neighbor.

Role Conflict Imagine the delicate situation of a woman who has worked for a decade on an assembly line in an electrical plant, and has recently been named supervisor of her unit. How is this woman expected to relate to her longtime friends and co-workers? Should she still go out to lunch with them, as she has done almost daily for years? Is it her responsibility to recommend the firing of an old friend who cannot keep up with the demands of the assembly line?

Role conflict occurs when incompatible expectations arise from two or more social positions held by the same person. Fulfillment of the roles associated with one status may directly violate the roles linked to a second status. In the example just given, the newly promoted supervisor will most likely experience a sharp conflict between her social and occupational roles. Such role conflicts call for important ethical choices. The new supervisor will have to make a difficult decision about how much allegiance she owes her friend and how much she owes her employers, who have given her supervisory responsibilities.

Another type of role conflict occurs when individuals move into occupations that are not common among people with their ascribed status. Male preschool teachers and female police officers experience this type of role conflict. In the latter case, female officers must strive to reconcile their workplace role in law enforcement with the societal view of a woman's role, which does not embrace many skills needed in police work. And while female police officers encounter sexual harassment, as women do throughout the labor force, they must also deal with the "code of silence," an informal norm that precludes their implicating fellow officers in wrongdoing (Fletcher 1995; S. Martin 1994).

Role Strain Role conflict describes the situation of a person dealing with the challenge of occupying two social positions simultaneously. However, even a single position can cause problems. Sociologists use the term **role strain** to describe the difficulty that arises when the same social position imposes conflicting demands and expectations.

People who belong to minority cultures may experience role strain while working in the mainstream culture. Criminologist Larry Gould (2002) interviewed officers of the Navajo Nation Police Department about their relations with conventional law enforcement officials, such as sheriffs and FBI agents. Besides enforcing the law, Navajo Nation officers practice an alternative form of justice known as Peacemaking, in which they seek reconciliation between the parties to a crime. The officers expressed great confidence in Peacemaking, but worried that if they did not make arrests, other law enforcement officials would think they were too soft, or "just taking care of their own." Regardless of the strength of their ties to traditional Navajo ways, all felt the strain of being considered "too Navajo" or "not Navajo enough."

From the perspective of . . .

An Environmental Activist   How do you handle the role strain you experience when the company you work for opts to use coal-powered plants instead of wind-powered plants, and there are no other jobs readily available in your community?

Role Exit Often, when we think of assuming a social role, we focus on the preparation and anticipatory socialization a person undergoes for that role. Such is true if a person is about to become an attorney, a chef, a spouse, or a parent. Yet until recently, social

According to sociologist Helen Rose Fuchs Ebaugh, role exit is a four-stage process. Is this transgendered person in the first or the fourth stage of changing genders?

scientists have given little attention to the adjustments involved in *leaving* social roles.

Sociologist Helen Rose Fuchs Ebaugh (1988) developed the term **role exit** to describe the process of disengagement from a role that is central to one's self-identity in order to establish a new role and identity. Drawing on interviews with 185 people—among them ex-convicts, divorced men and women, recovering alcoholics, ex-nuns, former doctors, retirees, and transsexuals—Ebaugh (herself an ex-nun) studied the process of voluntarily exiting from significant social roles.

Ebaugh has offered a four-stage model of role exit. The first stage begins with *doubt.* The person experiences frustration, burnout, or simply unhappiness with an accustomed status and the roles associated with the social position. The second stage involves a *search for alternatives.* A person who is unhappy with his or her career may take a leave of absence; an unhappily married couple may begin what they see as a temporary separation.

The third stage of role exit is the *action stage* or *departure.* Ebaugh found that the vast majority of her respondents could identify a clear turning point that made them feel it was essential to take final action and leave their jobs, end their marriages, or engage in another type of role exit. Twenty percent of respondents saw their role exit as a gradual, evolutionary process that had no single turning point.

The fourth stage of role exit involves the *creation of a new identity.* Many of you participated in a role exit when you made the transition from high school to college. You left behind the role of offspring living at home and took on the role of a somewhat independent college student living with peers in a dorm. Sociologist Ira Silver (1996) has studied the central role that material objects play in this transition. The objects students choose to leave at home (like stuffed animals and dolls) are associated with their prior identities. They may remain deeply attached to those objects, but do not want them to be seen as part of their new identities at college. The objects they bring with them symbolize how they now see themselves and how they wish to be perceived. iPods and wall posters, for example, are calculated to say, "This is me."

E Evaluate

Read each question carefully and then select or provide the best answer.

1. In the U.S., cab drivers are expected to know how to get around a city. This expectation is an example of
   a. role conflict.
   b. role strain.
   c. social role.
   d. master status.

2. What occurs when incompatible expectations arise from two or more social positions held by the same person?
   a. role conflict
   b. role strain
   c. role exit
   d. role reversal

3. The term _____ _____ refers to the way in which a society is organized into predictable relationships.

4. The African American activist Malcolm X wrote in his autobiography that his position as a Black man, a(n) _____ status, was an obstacle to his dream of becoming a lawyer, a(n) _____ status.

5. Sociologist Helen Rose Fuchs Ebaugh developed the term _____ _____ to describe the process of disengagement from a role that is central to one's self-identity in order to establish a new role and identity.

Answers

1 (c); 2 (a); 3 social structure; 4 ascribed, achieved; 5 role exit

Rethink

Consider these questions to get a deeper understanding of the material.

1. Identify instances in your own recent experience when two or more people defined the same social reality differently, and describe what you observed.

2. Think of a positive achieved status (e.g., prison guard) and a negative one (e.g., convict). Is it possible for a person to lose an achieved status? Is it easier to lose a positive or a negative achieved status? Why?

RECAP

LO 15-1 Define the terms social interaction, social structure, and social reality, and describe how they are related to one another.

- Social interaction refers to the ways in which people respond to one another. Social structure refers to the way in which a society is organized into predictable relationships.
- People shape their social reality based on what they learn through their social interactions. Social change comes from redefining or reconstructing social reality.

LO 15-2 Explain ascribed status and achieved status, and describe how master status can constrain achieved status.

- An ascribed status is generally assigned to a person at birth, whereas an achieved status is attained largely through one's own effort.
- Some ascribed statuses, such as race and gender, can function as master statuses that affect a person's potential to achieve a certain professional or social status.

LO 15-3 Illustrate the social role expectations of role conflict, role strain, and role exit.

- A social role is a set of expectations for people who occupy a particular social position or status.

- With each distinctive status—whether ascribed or achieved—come particular social roles.
- Role conflict occurs when one person holds two or more social positions with contradictory expectations, or when people take on an occupation that is uncommon for people of their ascribed status.
- Role strain occurs when a person simultaneously occupies two social positions with conflicting demands and expectation, and role exit occurs when a person leaves a role that is central to his or her self-identity and must establish a new role and identity.

KEY TERMS

Achieved status A social position that a person attains largely through his or her own efforts.

Ascribed status A social position assigned to a person by society without regard for the person's unique talents or characteristics.

Master status A status that dominates others and thereby determines a person's general position in society.

Role conflict The situation that occurs when incompatible expectations arise from two or more social positions held by the same person.

Role exit The process of disengagement from a role that is central to one's self-identity in order to establish a new role and identity.

Role strain The difficulty that arises when the same social position imposes conflicting demands and expectations.

Social interaction The ways in which people respond to one another.

Social role A set of expectations for people who occupy a given social position or status.

Social structure The way in which a society is organized into predictable relationships.

Status A term used by sociologists to refer to any of the full range of socially defined positions within a large group or society.

MODULE 16 Understanding Groups

Prepare Learning Objectives

LO 16-1 Differentiate among the different types of groups, and explain how they influence thought and behavior.

LO 16-2 Define social networks and explain their functions.

LO 16-3 Analyze social institutions from a functionalist, conflict, and interactionist perspective.

LO **16-1** Groups

In sociological terms, a **group** is any number of people with similar norms, values, and expectations who interact with one another on a regular basis. The members of a women's basketball team, a hospital's business office, a synagogue, or a symphony orchestra constitute a group. However, the residents of a suburb would not be considered a group, since they rarely interact with one another at one time.

Groups play a vital part in a society's social structure. Much of our social interaction takes place within groups and is influenced by their norms and sanctions. Being a teenager or a retired person takes on special meanings when we interact within groups designed for people with that particular status. The expectations associated with many social roles, including those accompanying the statuses of brother, sister, and student, become more clearly defined in the context of a group.

The groups we interact with also play an important role in our daily lives, sometimes in unexpected ways. Émile Durkheim ([1893] 1933) noted how a heinous crime can shock us, eliciting a communal response that serves to protect us in the future. In April 2007, a senior at Virginia Tech fired nearly 300 rounds of ammunition at two locations on campus, killing 32 people and wounding 17 others. Sociologists James Hawdon and John Ryan (2011) of Virginia Tech conducted three web-based surveys of the students and faculty, the first of them nine days after the shooting and the last of them 10 months later. They found that people who joined in with established, ongoing group activities that were specific to the tragedy did not necessarily find relief or a sense of solidarity with other members of the community. More critical to people's recovery was continued participation in clubs and friendship groups in the weeks following the tragedy. Group solidarity does make a difference.

PRIMARY AND SECONDARY GROUPS

Charles Horton Cooley (1902) coined the term **primary group** to refer to a small group characterized by intimate, face-to-face association and cooperation. The members of a street gang constitute a primary group; so do members of a family living in the same household, as do a group of "sisters" in a college sorority.

Primary groups play a pivotal role both in the socialization process and in the development of roles and statuses. Indeed, primary groups can be instrumental in a person's day-to-day existence. When we find ourselves identifying closely with a group, it is probably a primary group.

We also participate in many groups that are not characterized by close bonds of friendship, such as large college classes and business associations. The term **secondary group** refers to a formal, impersonal group in which there is little social intimacy or mutual understanding (Table 5-1). Secondary groups often emerge in the workplace among those who share special understandings about their occupation. The distinction between primary and secondary groups is not always clear-cut, however. Some social clubs may become so large and impersonal that they no longer function as primary groups.

IN-GROUPS AND OUT-GROUPS

A group can hold special meaning for members because of its relationship to other groups. For example, people in one group sometimes feel antagonistic toward or threatened by another group, especially if that group is perceived as being different, either culturally or racially. To identify these "we" and "they" feelings, sociologists use two terms first employed by William Graham Sumner (1906): *in-group* and *out-group*.

An **in-group** can be defined as any group or category to which people feel they belong. Simply put, it comprises everyone who is regarded as "we" or "us." The in-group may be as narrow as a teenage clique or as broad as an entire society. The very existence of an in-group implies that there is an out-group that is viewed as "they" or "them." An **out-group** is a group or category to which people feel they do *not* belong.

In-group members typically feel distinct and superior, seeing themselves as better than people in the out-group. Proper behavior for the in-group is simultaneously viewed as unacceptable behavior for the out-group. This double standard enhances the sense of superiority. Sociologist Robert Merton (1968) described this process as the conversion of "in-group virtues" into "out-group vices." We can see this differential standard operating in worldwide discussions of terrorism. When a group or a nation takes aggressive actions, it usually justifies them as necessary, even if civilians are hurt or killed. Opponents are quick to label such actions with the emotion-laden term of *terrorist* and appeal to the world community for condemnation. Yet these same people may themselves retaliate with actions that hurt civilians, which the first group will then condemn.

Conflict between in-groups and out-groups can turn violent on a personal as well as a political level. In 1999 two disaffected students at Columbine High School in Littleton, Colorado, launched an attack on the school that left 15 students and teachers dead, including themselves. The gunmen, members of an out-group that other students referred to as the Trenchcoat Mafia, apparently resented taunting by an in-group referred to as the Jocks. Similar episodes have occurred in schools across the nation, where rejected adolescents, overwhelmed by personal and family problems, peer group pressure, academic responsibilities, or media images of violence, have struck out against more popular classmates.

REFERENCE GROUPS

Both primary groups and in-groups can dramatically influence the way an individual thinks and behaves. Sociologists call any group that individuals use as a standard for evaluating

TABLE 5-1 COMPARISON OF PRIMARY AND SECONDARY GROUPS

Primary Group	Secondary Group
Generally small	Usually large
Relatively long period of interaction	Relatively short duration, often temporary
Intimate, face-to-face association	Little social intimacy or mutual understanding
Some emotional depth to relationships	Relationships generally superficial
Cooperative, friendly	More formal and impersonal

A pizza delivery crew is an example of a *secondary group*—a formal, impersonal group in which there is little social intimacy or mutual understanding. While waiting for the next delivery, members of this crew in Surrey, England, will become well enough acquainted to distinguish those who see the job as temporary from those who view it as permanent. They will learn who looks forward to deliveries in perceived high-risk areas and who does not. They may even spend time together after work, joking or boasting about their exploits on the job, but their friendships typically will not develop beyond that point.

At a powwow, a drum circle breathes spirit into an ancient tribal tradition. These accomplished ceremonial musicians may serve as a reference group for onlookers who want to know more about drumming.

themselves and their own behavior a **reference group**. For example, a high school student who aspires to join a social circle of hip-hop music devotees will pattern his or her behavior after that of the group. The student will begin dressing like these peers, listening to the same downloads and DVDs, and hanging out at the same stores and clubs.

Reference groups have two basic purposes. They serve a normative function by setting and enforcing standards of conduct and belief. The high school student who wants the approval of the hip-hop crowd will have to follow the group's dictates, at least to some extent. Reference groups also perform a comparison function by serving as a standard against which people can measure themselves and others. An actor will evaluate himself or herself against a reference group composed of others in the acting profession (Merton and Kitt 1950).

Reference groups may help the process of anticipatory socialization. For example, a college student majoring in finance may read the *Wall Street Journal,* study the annual reports of corporations, and listen to midday stock market news on the radio. Such a student is using financial experts as a reference group to which he or she aspires.

Often, two or more reference groups influence us at the same time. Our family members, neighbors, and co-workers all shape different aspects of our self-evaluation. In addition, reference group attachments change during the life cycle. A corporate executive who quits the rat race at age 45 to become a social worker will find new reference groups to use as standards for evaluation. We shift reference groups as we take on different statuses during our lives.

Study Alert

Reference groups set and enforce standards of conduct and belief and can function as a standard against which people can measure themselves and others.

Can you outwit, outplay, outlast your competition? Maybe a coalition can help. In *Survivor: Blood vs. Water,* filmed on Palaui Island in the Philippines, coalition building continued to be a key to success in the long-running television series, now in its 17th season.

COALITIONS

As groups grow larger, coalitions begin to develop. A **coalition** is a temporary or permanent alliance geared toward a common goal. Coalitions can be broad-based or narrow and can take on many different objectives. Sociologist William Julius Wilson (1999) has described community-based organizations in Texas that include Whites and Latinos, working class and affluent, who have banded together to work for improved sidewalks, better drainage systems, and comprehensive street paving. Out of this type of coalition building, Wilson hopes, will emerge better interracial understanding.

Some coalitions are intentionally short-lived. For example, short-term coalition building is a key to success in popular TV programs like *Survivor.* In the program's first season, *Survivor: Borneo,* broadcast in 2000, the four members of the "Tagi alliance" banded together to vote fellow castaways off the island. The political world is also the scene of many temporary coalitions. For example, in 1997 big tobacco companies joined with antismoking groups to draw up a settlement for reimbursing states for tobacco-related medical costs. Soon after the settlement was announced the coalition members returned to their decades-long fight against each other (Pear 1997).

LO **16-2** Social Networks

Groups do not merely serve to define other elements of the social structure, such as roles and statuses; they also link the individual with the larger society. We all belong to a number of different groups, and through our acquaintances make connections with people in different social circles. These connections are known as a **social network**—a series of social relationships that links a person directly to others, and through them indirectly to still more people. Social networks are one of the five basic elements of social structure.

Broadly speaking, social networks encompass all the routine social interaction we have with other individuals. Traditionally, researchers have limited their network studies to face-to-face contacts and phone conversations, although recently they have begun to study interaction through all types of new media. We should be careful, however, not to equate social media like Facebook and Twitter with social networks, which include a much broader spectrum of social interaction.

Social networks can center on virtually any activity, from sharing job information to exchanging news and gossip, or even sharing sex. In the mid-1990s, sociologists studied romantic relationships at a high school with about 1,000 students. They found that about 61 percent of the girls had been sexually active over the past 18 months. Among the sexually active respondents, the researchers counted only 63 steady couples, or pairs with no other partners. A much larger group of 288 students—almost a third of the sample—was involved in a free-flowing network of relationships (Bearman et al. 2004). This research on high schoolers' sexual activity, an example of applied sociology, has clear implications for public health.

Involvement in social networks—commonly known as *networking*—is especially valuable in finding employment. Albert Einstein was successful in finding a job only when a classmate's father put him in touch with his future employer. These kinds of contacts— even those that are weak and distant—can be crucial in establishing social networks and facilitating the transmission of information.

During the recent economic downturn, electronic social networks have served a new purpose, encouraging the jobless. Websites and chat rooms that cannot locate jobs for those who have been thrown out of work concentrate instead on helping them to stick together, support one another, and maintain a positive attitude. For the unemployed, online conversations with friends or even strangers in the same predicament can be an invaluable morale booster (R. Scherer 2010b).

Research indicates, however, that both in person and online, not everyone participates equally in social networks. Women and racial and ethnic minorities are at a disadvantage when seeking new and better job opportunities or social contacts (Trimble and Kmec 2011).

LO **16-3** Social Institutions

The mass media, the government, the economy, the family, and the health care system are all examples of social institutions found in our society. **Social institutions** are organized patterns of beliefs and behavior centered on basic social needs, such as replacing personnel (the family) and preserving order (the government).

A close look at social institutions gives sociologists insight into the structure of a society. Consider religion, for example. The institution of religion adapts to the segment of society that it serves. Church work has very different meanings for ministers who serve a skid row area and those who serve a suburban middle-class community. Religious leaders assigned to a skid row mission will focus on tending to the ill and providing food and shelter. In contrast, clergy in affluent suburbs will be occupied with counseling those considering marriage and divorce, arranging youth activities, and overseeing cultural events.

FUNCTIONALIST PERSPECTIVE

One way to understand social institutions is to see how they fulfill essential functions. Anthropologists and sociologists have identified five major tasks, or functional prerequisites, that a society or relatively permanent group must accomplish if it is to survive:

1. *Replacing personnel.* Any group or society must replace personnel when they die, leave, or become incapacitated. This task is accomplished through such means as immigration, annexation of neighboring groups, acquisition of slaves, or sexual reproduction. The Shakers, a religious sect that came to the United States in 1774, are a conspicuous example of a group that has *failed* to replace personnel. Their religious beliefs commit the Shakers to celibacy; to survive, the group must recruit new members. At first, the Shakers proved quite successful in attracting members, reaching a peak of about 6,000 members in the United States during the 1840s. As of 2011, however, the only Shaker community left in this country was a farm in Maine with three members—one man and two women (R. Schaefer and Zellner 2011).

2. *Teaching new recruits.* No group or society can survive if many of its members reject the group's established behavior and responsibilities. Thus, finding or producing new members is not sufficient; the group or society must also encourage recruits to learn and accept its values and customs. Such learning can take place formally, within schools (where learning is a manifest function), or informally, through interaction in peer groups (where learning is a latent function).

3. *Producing and distributing goods and services.* Any relatively permanent group or society must provide and distribute desired goods and services to its members. Each society establishes a set of rules for the allocation of financial and other resources. The group must satisfy the needs of most members to some extent, or it will risk the possibility of discontent and ultimately disorder.

4. *Preserving order.* Throughout the world, indigenous and aboriginal peoples have struggled to protect themselves from outside invaders, with varying degrees of success. Failure to preserve order and defend against conquest leads to the death not only of a people, but of a culture as well.

5. *Providing and maintaining a sense of purpose.* In order to fulfill the first four requirements, people must feel motivated to continue as members of a group or society. Patriotism, tribal identities, religious values, or personal moral codes can help people to develop and maintain such a sense of purpose. Whatever the motivator, in any society there remains one common and critical reality: if an individual does not have a sense of purpose, he or she has little reason to contribute to a society's survival.

This list of functional prerequisites does not specify *how* a society and its corresponding social institutions will perform each task. For example, one society may protect itself from external attack by amassing a frightening arsenal of weaponry, while another may make determined efforts to remain neutral in world politics and to promote cooperative relationships with its neighbors. No matter what its particular strategy, any society or relatively permanent group must attempt to satisfy all these functional prerequisites for survival. If it fails on even one condition, the society runs the risk of extinction (Aberle et al. 1950; R. Mack and Bradford 1979).

CONFLICT PERSPECTIVE

Conflict theorists do not agree with the functionalist approach to social institutions. Although proponents of both perspectives agree that social institutions are organized to meet basic social needs, conflict theorists object to the idea that the outcome is necessarily efficient and desirable.

From a conflict perspective, the present organization of social institutions is no accident. Major institutions, such as education, help to maintain the privileges of the most powerful individuals and groups within a society, while contributing to the powerlessness

> ## Study Alert
>
> Be prepared to describe the similarities and differences in how social institutions are viewed by each of the three major sociological perspectives: functionalist, conflict, and interactionist.

of others. To give one example, public schools in the United States are financed largely through property taxes. This arrangement allows more affluent areas to provide their children with better-equipped schools and better-paid teachers than low-income areas can afford. As a result, children from prosperous communities are better prepared to compete academically than children from impoverished communities. The structure of the nation's educational system permits and even promotes such unequal treatment of schoolchildren.

Conflict theorists argue that social institutions such as education have an inherently conservative nature. Without question, it has been difficult to implement educational reforms that promote equal opportunity—whether bilingual education, school desegregation, or mainstreaming of students with disabilities. From a functionalist perspective, social change can be dysfunctional, since it often leads to instability. However, from a conflict view, why should we preserve the existing social structure if it is unfair and discriminatory?

Social institutions also operate in gendered and racist environments, as conflict theorists, as well as feminists and interactionists, have pointed out. In schools, offices, and government institutions, assumptions about what people can do reflect the sexism and racism of the larger society. For instance, many people assume that women cannot make tough decisions—even those in the top echelons of corporate management. Others assume that all Black students at elite colleges represent affirmative action admissions. Inequality based on gender, economic status, race, and ethnicity thrives in such an environment—to which we might add discrimination based on age, physical disability, and sexual orientation. The truth of this assertion can be seen in routine decisions by employers on how to advertise jobs, as well as whether to provide fringe benefits such as child care and parental leave.

INTERACTIONIST PERSPECTIVE

Social institutions affect our everyday behavior, whether we are driving down the street or waiting in a long shopping line. Sociologist Mitchell Duneier (1994a, 1994b) studied the social behavior of the word processors, all women, who work in the service center of a large Chicago law firm. Duneier was interested in the informal social norms that emerged in this work environment and the rich social network these female employees created.

The Network Center, as it is called, is a single, windowless room in a large office building where the law firm occupies seven floors. The center is staffed by two shifts of word processors, who work either from 4:00 p.m. to midnight or from midnight to 8:00 a.m. Each word processor works in a cubicle with just enough room for her keyboard, terminal, printer, and telephone. Work assignments for the word processors are placed in a central basket and then completed according to precise procedures.

At first glance, we might think that these women labor with little social contact, apart from limited breaks and occasional conversations with their supervisor. However, drawing on the interactionist perspective, Duneier learned that despite working in a large office, these women find private moments to talk (often in the halls or outside the washroom) and share a critical view of the law firm's attorneys and day-shift secretaries. Indeed, the word processors routinely suggest that their assignments represent work that the "lazy" secretaries should have completed during the normal workday. Duneier (1994b) tells of one word processor who resented the lawyers' superior attitude and pointedly refused to recognize or speak with any attorney who would not address her by name.

Interactionist theorists emphasize that our social behavior is conditioned by the roles and statuses we accept, the groups to which we belong, and the institutions within which we function. For example, the social roles associated with being a judge occur within the larger context of the criminal justice system. The status of judge stands in relation to other statuses, such as attorney, plaintiff, defendant, and witness, as well as to the social institution of government. Although courts and jails have great symbolic importance, the judicial system derives its continued significance from the roles people carry out in social interactions (Berger and Luckmann 1966).

Table 5-2 summarizes the three major sociological perspectives on social institutions.

TABLE 5-2 SOCIOLOGICAL PERSPECTIVES ON SOCIAL INSTITUTIONS

Perspective	Role of Social Institutions	Focus
Functionalist	Meeting basic social needs	Essential functions
Conflict	Meeting basic social needs	Maintenance of privileges and inequality
Interactionist	Fostering everyday behavior	Influence of the roles and statuses we accept

E Evaluate

Read each question carefully and then select or provide the best answer.

1. The Shakers, a religious sect that came to the United States in 1774, has seen their group's membership diminish significantly due to their inability to
   a. teach new recruits.
   b. preserve order.
   c. replace personnel.
   d. provide and maintain a sense of purpose.

2. Which sociological perspective argues that the present organization of social institutions is no accident?
   a. the functionalist perspective
   b. the conflict perspective
   c. the interactionist perspective
   d. the global perspective

3. _____ groups often emerge in the workplace among those who share special understandings about their occupation.

4. In many cases, people model their behavior after groups to which they may not belong. These groups are called _____ groups.

5. In studying the social behavior of word processors in a Chicago law firm, sociologist Mitchell Duneier drew on the _____ perspective.

Answers

1 (c); 2 (b); 3 Secondary; 4 reference; 5 interactionist

R Rethink

Consider these questions to get a deeper understanding of the material.

1. What are some primary and secondary groups that you belong to or have belonged to? Explain the differences in terms of social interactions.

2. Think of a social institution with which you have personal familiarity. How would you analyze the functions and purposes of that institution from a functionalist and a conflict perspective?

RECAP

LO 16-1 Differentiate among the different types of groups, and explain how they influence thought and behavior.

- A primary group is characterized by close, face-to-face association and cooperation, while a secondary group is more formal and impersonal. Primary groups play a significant role in socialization and in the development of roles and statuses.
- People tend to see the world in terms of in-groups ("us") and out-groups ("them"), a perception often fostered by the groups themselves.
- Reference groups set and enforce standards of conduct and serve as a source of comparison for people's evaluations of themselves and others.
- Large groups allow coalitions to form and serve as links to social networks and their resources.

LO 16-2 Define social networks and explain their functions.

- Social networks consist of both direct links to persons we know and indirect links through those persons to others.
- Social networks can serve many purposes, including job searching and the exchange of news and ideas. Networking, the use of extended social networks for particular purposes, has been enhanced by the emergence of Internet-based social media.

LO 16-3 Analyze social institutions from a functionalist, conflict, and interactionist perspective.

- Social institutions are organized patterns of beliefs and behavior, such as the government, the economy, the family, the media, and the health care system.
- From a functionalist perspective, social institutions fulfill essential functions, such as replacing personnel, training new recruits, and preserving order.
- Conflict theorists charge that social institutions help to maintain the privileges of the powerful while contributing to the powerlessness of others.
- Interactionist theorists stress that our social behavior is conditioned by the roles and statuses we accept, the groups to which we belong, and the institutions within which we function.

KEY TERMS

Coalition A temporary or permanent alliance geared toward a common goal.

Group Any number of people with similar norms, values, and expectations who interact with one another on a regular basis.

In-group Any group or category to which people feel they belong.

Out-group A group or category to which people feel they do not belong.

Primary group A small group characterized by intimate, face-to-face association and cooperation.

Reference group Any group that individuals use as a standard for evaluating themselves and their own behavior.

Secondary group A formal, impersonal group in which there is little social intimacy or mutual understanding.

Social institution An organized pattern of beliefs and behavior centered on basic social needs.

Social network A series of social relationships that links a person directly to others, and through them indirectly to still more people.

MODULE 17 Understanding Organizations

P Prepare Learning Objectives

LO 17-1 Describe the characteristics and functions of formal organizations.

LO 17-2 Demonstrate how the characteristics of Weber's construct of an ideal bureaucracy are applied to organizations.

LO 17-3 Explain the process of bureaucratization and its effects in organizations.

O Organize Module Outline

Formal Organizations and Bureaucracies
Characteristics of a Bureaucracy
    Bureaucratization as a Process
    Oligarchy: Rule by a Few
Bureaucracy and Organizational Culture

W Work

LO **17-1** Formal Organizations and Bureaucracies

As contemporary societies have shifted to more advanced forms of technology and their social structures have become more complex, our lives have become increasingly dominated by large secondary groups referred to as *formal organizations*. A **formal organization** is a group designed for a special purpose and structured for maximum efficiency.

Being an accountant in a large corporation may be a relatively high-paying occupation. In Marxist terms, however, accountants are vulnerable to alienation, since they are far removed from the product or service that the corporation creates.

The U.S. Postal Service, McDonald's, and the Boston Pops orchestra are examples of formal organizations. Though organizations vary in their size, specificity of goals, and degree of efficiency, they are all structured to facilitate the management of large-scale operations. They also have a bureaucratic form of organization, described later in the module.

In our society, formal organizations fulfill an enormous variety of personal and societal needs, shaping the lives of every one of us. In fact, formal organizations have become such a dominant force that we must create organizations to supervise other organizations, such as the Securities and Exchange Commission (SEC) to regulate brokerage companies. Although it sounds more exciting to say that we live in the "computer age" than to say that we live in the "age of formal organization," the latter is probably a more accurate description (Azumi and Hage 1972; Etzioni 1964).

Ascribed statuses such as gender, race, and ethnicity can influence how we see ourselves within formal organizations. For example, a study of female lawyers in the nation's largest law firms found significant differences in the women's self-images, depending on the relative presence or absence of women in positions of power. In firms in which less than 15 percent of partners were women, the female lawyers were likely to believe that "feminine" traits were strongly devalued and that "masculine" traits were equated with success. As one female attorney put it, "Let's face it: this is a man's environment, and it's sort of Jock City, especially at my firm." Women in firms where female lawyers were better represented in positions of power had a stronger desire for and higher expectations of promotion (Ely 1995:619).

LO 17-2 Characteristics of a Bureaucracy

A **bureaucracy** is a component of formal organization that uses rules and hierarchical ranking to achieve efficiency. Rows of desks staffed by seemingly faceless people, endless lines and forms, impossibly complex language, and frustrating encounters with red tape—all these unpleasant images have combined to make *bureaucracy* a dirty word and an easy target in political campaigns. As a result, few people want to identify their occupation as "bureaucrat," despite the fact that all of us perform various bureaucratic tasks. In an industrial society, elements of bureaucracy enter into almost every occupation.

Max Weber ([1913–1922] 1947) first directed researchers to the significance of bureaucratic structure. In an important sociological advance, Weber emphasized the basic similarity of structure and process found in the otherwise dissimilar enterprises of religion, government, education, and business. Weber saw bureaucracy as a form of organization quite different from the family-run business. For analytical purposes, he developed an ideal type of bureaucracy that would reflect the most characteristic aspects of all human organizations. By **ideal type** Weber meant a construct or model for evaluating specific cases. In actuality, perfect bureaucracies do not exist; no real-world organization corresponds exactly to Weber's ideal type.

Weber proposed that whether the purpose is to run a church, a corporation, or an army, the ideal bureaucracy displays five basic characteristics. A discussion of those characteristics, as well as the dysfunctions of a bureaucracy, follows.

1. **Division of labor.** Specialized experts perform specific tasks. In your college bureaucracy, the admissions officer does not do the job of registrar; the guidance counselor does not see to the maintenance of buildings. By working at a specific task, people are more likely to become highly skilled and carry out a job with maximum efficiency. This emphasis on specialization is so basic a part of our lives that we may not realize it is a fairly recent development in Western culture.

The downside of division of labor is that the fragmentation of work into smaller and smaller tasks can divide workers and remove any connection they might feel to the overall objective of the bureaucracy. In *The Communist Manifesto* (written in 1848), Karl Marx and Friedrich Engels charged that the capitalist system reduces workers to a mere "appendage of the machine" (Tucker 1978). Such a work arrangement, they wrote, produces extreme **alienation**—a condition of estrangement or dissociation from the surrounding society. According to both Marx and conflict theorists, restricting workers to very small tasks also weakens their job security, since new employees can easily be trained to replace them.

Although division of labor has certainly enhanced the performance of many complex bureaucracies, in some cases it can lead to **trained incapacity**; that is, workers become so specialized that they develop blind spots and fail to notice obvious problems. Even worse, they may not care about what is happening in the next department. Some observers believe that such developments have caused workers in the United States to become less productive on the job.

In some cases, the bureaucratic division of labor can have tragic results. In the wake of the coordinated attacks on the World Trade Center and the Pentagon on September 11, 2001, Americans wondered aloud how the FBI and CIA could have failed to detect the terrorists' elaborately planned operation. The problem, in part, turned out to be the division of labor between the FBI, which focuses on domestic matters, and the CIA, which operates overseas. Officials at these intelligence-gathering organizations, both of which are huge bureaucracies, are well known for jealously guarding information from one another. Subsequent investigations revealed that they knew about Osama bin Laden and his Al-Qaeda terrorist network in the early 1990s. Unfortunately, five federal agencies—the CIA, FBI, National Security Agency, Defense Intelligence Agency, and National Reconnaissance Office—failed to share their leads on the network. Although the hijacking of the four commercial airliners used in the massive attacks may not have been preventable, the bureaucratic division of labor definitely hindered efforts to defend against terrorism, undermining U.S. national security.

2. **Hierarchy of authority.**   Bureaucracies follow the principle of hierarchy; that is, each position is under the supervision of a higher authority. A president heads a college bureaucracy; he or she selects members of the administration, who in turn hire their own staff. In the Roman Catholic Church, the pope is the supreme authority; under him are cardinals, bishops, and so forth.

3. **Written rules and regulations.**   What if your sociology professor gave your classmate an A for having such a friendly smile? You might think that wasn't fair, that it was against the rules. Through written rules and regulations, bureaucracies generally offer employees clear standards for an adequate (or exceptional) performance. In addition, procedures provide a valuable sense of continuity in a bureaucracy. Individual workers will come and go, but the structure and past records of the organization give it a life of its own that outlives the services of any one bureaucrat.

Of course, rules and regulations can overshadow the larger goals of an organization to the point that they become dysfunctional. What if a domestic abuse counselor failed to listen to an injured woman because she had no valid proof of U.S. citizenship? If blindly applied, rules no longer serve as a means to achieving an objective, but instead become important (and perhaps too important) in their own right. Robert Merton (1968) used the term **goal displacement** to refer to overzealous conformity to official regulations.

4. **Impersonality.**   Max Weber wrote that in a bureaucracy, work is carried out *sine ira et studio*, "without hatred or passion." Bureaucratic norms dictate that officials perform their duties without giving personal consideration to people as individuals. Although this norm is intended to guarantee equal treatment for each person, it also contributes to the often cold and uncaring feeling associated with modern organizations. We typically think of big government and big business when we think of impersonal bureaucracies. In some cases, the impersonality that is associated with a bureaucracy can have tragic results. More frequently, bureaucratic impersonality produces frustration and disaffection. Today, even small firms filter callers with electronic menus.

> # Study Alert
>
> Keep in mind the definitions of each of Weber's five basic characteristics of the ideal bureaucracy: division of labor, hierarchy of authority, written rules and regulations, impersonality, and employment based on technical qualifications.

5. **Employment based on technical qualifications.**   Within the ideal bureaucracy, hiring is based on technical qualifications rather than on favoritism, and performance is measured against specific standards. Written personnel policies dictate who gets promoted, and people often have a right to appeal if they believe that particular rules have been violated. Such procedures protect bureaucrats against arbitrary dismissal, provide a measure of security, and encourage loyalty to the organization.

Although ideally, any bureaucracy will value technical and professional competence, personnel decisions do not always follow that ideal pattern. Dysfunctions within bureaucracy have become well publicized, particularly because of the work of Laurence J. Peter. According to the **Peter principle**, every employee within a hierarchy tends to rise to his or her level of incompetence (Peter and Hull 1969). This hypothesis, which has not been directly or systematically tested, reflects a possible dysfunctional outcome of advancement on the basis of merit. Talented people receive promotion after promotion, until sadly, some of them finally achieve positions that they cannot handle with their usual competence.

Table 5-3 summarizes the five characteristics of bureaucracy. These characteristics, developed by Max Weber a century ago, describe an ideal type rather than an actual bureaucracy. Not every formal organization will possess all five of Weber's characteristics. In fact, wide variation exists among actual bureaucratic organizations.

BUREAUCRATIZATION AS A PROCESS

Have you ever had to speak to 10 or 12 individuals in a corporation or government agency just to find out which official has jurisdiction over a particular problem? Ever been transferred from one department to another until you finally hung up in disgust? Sociologists have used the term **bureaucratization** to refer to the process by which a group, organization, or social movement becomes increasingly bureaucratic.

Normally, we think of bureaucratization in terms of large organizations. But bureaucratization also takes place within small-group settings. Sociologist Jennifer Bickman Mendez (1998) studied domestic houseworkers employed in central California by a nationwide franchise. She found that housekeeping tasks were minutely defined, to the point that employees had to follow 22 written steps for cleaning a bathroom. Complaints and special requests went not to the workers, but to an office-based manager.

Bureaucratization is not limited to Western industrial societies. In 2012, Xi Jinping became general secretary of China's Communist Party, the nation's highest office. In his

TABLE 5-3 CHARACTERISTICS OF A BUREAUCRACY		Summing Up	
		Negative Consequence	
	Positive Consequence	**For the Individual**	**For the Organization**
Division of labor	Produces efficiency in a large-scale corporation	Produces trained incapacity	Produces a narrow perspective
Hierarchy of authority	Clarifies who is in command	Deprives employees of a voice in decision making	Permits concealment of mistakes
Written rules and regulations	Let workers know what is expected of them	Stifle initiative and imagination	Lead to goal displacement
Impersonality	Reduces bias	Contributes to feelings of alienation	Discourages loyalty to company
Employment based on technical qualifications	Discourages favoritism and reduces petty rivalries	Discourages ambition to improve oneself elsewhere	Fosters Peter principle

first public address, Jinping pledged to end the party's "undue emphasis on formalities and bureaucracy" in order to deliver a "better life" for the Chinese people (I. Johnson 2012:A19; Malcolm Moore 2012).

OLIGARCHY: RULE BY A FEW

Conflict theorists have examined the bureaucratization of social movements. The German sociologist Robert Michels (1915) studied socialist parties and labor unions in Europe before World War I and found that such organizations were becoming increasingly bureaucratic. The emerging leaders of the organizations—even some of the most radical—had a vested interest in clinging to power. If they lost their leadership posts, they would have to return to full-time work as manual laborers.

Through his research, Michels originated the idea of the **iron law of oligarchy**, which describes how even a democratic organization will eventually develop into a bureaucracy ruled by a few, called an oligarchy. Why do oligarchies emerge? People who achieve leadership roles usually have the skills, knowledge, or charismatic appeal (as Weber noted) to direct, if not control, others. Michels argued that the rank and file of a movement or organization look to leaders for direction and thereby reinforce the process of rule by a few. In addition, members of an oligarchy are strongly motivated to maintain their leadership roles, privileges, and power.

LO 17-3 Bureaucracy and Organizational Culture

How does bureaucratization affect the average individual who works in an organization? The early theorists of formal organizations tended to neglect this question. Max Weber, for example, focused on the management personnel in bureaucracies, but had little to say about workers in industry or clerks in government agencies.

According to the **classical theory** of formal organizations, or **scientific management approach**, workers are motivated almost entirely by economic rewards. This theory stresses that only the physical constraints on workers limit their productivity. Therefore, workers may be treated as a resource, much like the machines that began to replace them in the 20th century. Under the scientific management approach, management attempts to achieve maximum work efficiency through scientific planning, established performance standards, and careful supervision of workers and production. Planning involves efficiency studies but not studies of workers' attitudes or job satisfaction.

Not until workers organized unions—and forced management to recognize that they were not objects—did theorists of formal organizations begin to revise the classical approach. Social scientists became aware that along with management and administrators, informal groups of workers have an important impact on organizations. An alternative way of considering bureaucratic dynamics, the **human relations approach**, emphasizes the role of people, communication, and participation in a bureaucracy. This type of analysis reflects the interest of interactionist theorists in small-group behavior. Unlike planning under the scientific management approach, planning based on the human relations approach focuses on workers' feelings, frustrations, and emotional need for job satisfaction.

The gradual move away from a sole focus on the physical aspects of getting the job done—and toward the concerns and needs of workers—led advocates of the human relations approach to stress the less formal aspects of bureaucratic structure. Informal groups and social networks within organizations develop partly as a result of people's ability to create more direct forms of communication than under the formal structure. Charles Page (1946) used the term *bureaucracy's other face* to refer to the unofficial activities and interactions that are such a basic part of daily organizational life.

Today, research on formal organizations is following new avenues. Among them are

- the recent arrival of a small number of women and minority group members in high-level management;
- in large corporations, the decision-making role of groups that lie outside the top ranks of leadership;
- the loss of fixed boundaries in organizations that have outsourced key functions;
- and the role of the Internet in influencing business and consumer preferences.

Though research on organizations still embraces Max Weber's insights, then, it has gone well beyond them (Hamm 2007; Kleiner 2003; W. Scott and Davis 2007).

E Evaluate

Read each question carefully and then select or provide the best answer.

1. The U.S. Postal Service, the Boston Pops orchestra, and the college or university in which you are currently enrolled as a student are all examples of
   a. primary groups.
   b. reference groups.
   c. formal organizations.
   d. triads.

2. According to Weber, one positive consequence of bureaucracy is that it reduces bias because of which characteristic?
   a. impersonality
   b. hierarchy of authority
   c. written rules and regulations
   d. employment based on technical qualifications

3. According to the Peter principle,
   a. all bureaucracies are notoriously inefficient.
   b. if something *can* go wrong, it *will.*
   c. every employee within a hierarchy tends to rise to his or her level of incompetence.
   d. all line workers get burned in the end.

4. Max Weber developed a(n) _____ _____ of bureaucracy, which reflects the most characteristic aspects of all human organizations.

Answers

1 (c); 2 (a); 3 (c); 4 ideal type

R Rethink

Consider these questions to get a deeper understanding of the material.

1. Choose a large organization with which you are familiar (e.g., your college, workplace, or religious institution) and apply Weber's ideal type of bureaucracy to it. How well does it correspond to Weber's ideal type?

2. What are some benefits and drawbacks of large formal organizations?

RECAP

LO 17-1 Describe the characteristics and functions of formal organizations.

- A formal organization is a group designed for a special purpose and structured for maximum efficiency.
- As societies have become more complex, formal organizations have become more powerful and widespread by filling a wide range of personal and societal needs.

LO 17-2 Demonstrate how the characteristics of Weber's construct of an ideal bureaucracy are applied to organizations.

- A bureaucracy is a type of formal organization that uses rules and hierarchical ranking to achieve efficiency.
- Max Weber identified five basic characteristics of an ideal type of bureaucracy: division of labor, hierarchical authority, written rules and regulations, impersonality, and employment based on technical qualifications.

- A bureaucracy is a type of formal organization that uses rules and hierarchical ranking to achieve efficiency.
- The term *bureaucratization* refers to the process by which groups, organizations, and social movements grow increasingly bureaucratic.
- Robert Michels formulated the iron law of oligarchy, stating that even a democratic organization will develop into a bureaucracy ruled by a few people—an oligarchy.
- Under bureaucracies, workers tend to be regarded as economic resources rather than people. The human relations approach, espoused by labor unions, emphasizes the importance of people, communication, and participation in organizations.

KEY TERMS

Alienation A condition of estrangement or dissociation from the surrounding society.

Bureaucracy A component of formal organization that uses rules and hierarchical ranking to achieve efficiency.

Bureaucratization The process by which a group, organization, or social movement becomes increasingly bureaucratic.

Classical theory An approach to the study of formal organizations that views workers as being motivated almost entirely by economic rewards.

Formal organization A group designed for a special purpose and structured for maximum efficiency.

Goal displacement Overzealous conformity to official regulations of a bureaucracy.

Human relations approach An approach to the study of formal organizations that emphasizes the role of people, communication, and participation in a bureaucracy and tends to focus on the informal structure of the organization.

Ideal type A construct or model for evaluating specific cases.

Iron law of oligarchy A principle of organizational life under which even a democratic organization will eventually develop into a bureaucracy ruled by a few individuals.

Peter principle A principle of organizational life according to which every employee within a hierarchy tends to rise to his or her level of incompetence.

Scientific management approach Another name for the classical theory of formal organizations.

Trained incapacity The tendency of workers in a bureaucracy to become so specialized that they develop blind spots and fail to notice obvious problems.

MODULE 18 Social Structure in Global Perspective

P Prepare Learning Objectives

LO 18-1 Describe Durkheim's, Tönnies's, and Lenski's approaches to classifying forms of social structure.

LO 18-2 Analyze from the perspective of social structure the characteristics and condition of labor unions, especially in the United States.

O Organize Module Outline

Durkheim's Mechanical and Organic Solidarity

Tönnies's *Gemeinschaft* and *Gesellschaft*

Lenski's Sociocultural Evolution Approach
    Preindustrial Societies
    Industrial Societies
    Postindustrial and Postmodern Societies

Social Policy and Organizations
    The State of the Unions Worldwide

Modern societies are complex, especially compared to earlier social arrangements. Sociologists Émile Durkheim, Ferdinand Tönnies, and Gerhard Lenski developed ways to contrast modern societies with simpler forms of social structure.

LO **18-1** Durkheim's Mechanical and Organic Solidarity

In his *Division of Labor* ([1893] 1933), Durkheim argued that social structure depends on the division of labor in a society—in other words, on the manner in which tasks are performed. Thus, a task such as providing food can be carried out almost totally by one individual, or it can be divided among many people. The latter pattern is typical of modern societies, in which the cultivation, processing, distribution, and retailing of a single food item are performed by literally hundreds of people.

In societies in which there is minimal division of labor, a collective consciousness develops that emphasizes group solidarity. Durkheim termed this collective frame of mind **mechanical solidarity**, implying that all individuals perform the same tasks. In this type of society, no one needs to ask, "What do your parents do?" since all are engaged in similar work. Each person prepares food, hunts, makes clothing, builds homes, and so forth. Because people have few options regarding what to do with their lives, there is little concern for individual needs. Instead, the group is the dominating force in society. Both social interaction and negotiation are based on close, intimate, face-to-face social contacts. Since there is little specialization, there are few social roles.

As societies become more advanced technologically, they rely on greater division of labor, so that no individual can go it alone. Dependence on others becomes essential for group survival. In Durkheim's terms, mechanical solidarity is replaced by **organic solidarity**, a collective consciousness resting on the need a society's members have for one another. Durkheim chose the term *organic solidarity* because in his view, individuals become interdependent in much the same way as organs of the human body.

LO **18-1** Tönnies's *Gemeinschaft* and *Gesellschaft*

"I'd like to think of you as a person, David, but it's my job to think of you as personnel."

In a *Gesellschaft*, people are likely to relate to one another in terms of their roles rather than their relationships.

Ferdinand Tönnies (1855–1936) was appalled by the rise of an industrial city in his native Germany during the late 1800s. In his view, the city marked a dramatic change from the ideal of a close-knit community, which Tönnies termed a *Gemeinschaft,* to that of an impersonal mass society, known as a *Gesellschaft* (Tönnies [1887] 1988).

The **Gemeinschaft** (pronounced guh-mine-shoft) is typical of rural life. It is a small community in which people have similar backgrounds and life experiences. Virtually everyone knows one another, and social interactions are intimate and familiar, almost as among kinfolk. In this community there is a commitment to the larger social group and a sense of togetherness among members. People relate to others in a personal way, not just as "clerk" or "manager." With this personal interaction comes little privacy, however: we know too much about everyone.

Social control in the *Gemeinschaft* is maintained through informal means such as moral persuasion, gossip, and even gestures. These techniques work effectively because people genuinely care how others feel about them. Social change is relatively limited in the *Gemeinschaft;* the lives of members of one generation may be quite similar to those of their grandparents.

In contrast, the **Gesellschaft** (pronounced guh-zell-shoft) is an ideal community that is characteristic of modern urban life. In this community most people are strangers who feel little in common with other residents. Relationships are governed by social roles that grow out of immediate tasks, such as purchasing a product or arranging a business meeting. Self-interest dominates, and there is little consensus concerning values or commitment to the group. As a result, social control must rest on more formal techniques, such as laws and legally defined punishments. Social change is an important aspect of life in the *Gesellschaft;* it can be strikingly evident even within a single generation.

From the perspective of . . .

A Community Organizer Given that most people are strangers in modern urban life, what steps could you take to increase commitment to the larger social group among people with a similar background or status, and draw their attention to the values they do share?

Table 5-4 summarizes the differences between the *Gemeinschaft* and the *Gesellschaft.* Sociologists have used these terms to compare social structures that stress close relationships with those that emphasize less personal ties. It is easy to view the *Gemeinschaft* with nostalgia, as a far better way of life than the rat race of contemporary existence. However, the more intimate relationships of the *Gemeinschaft* come at a price. The prejudice and discrimination found there can be quite confining; ascribed statuses such as family background often outweigh a person's unique talents and achievements. In addition, the *Gemeinschaft* tends to distrust individuals who seek to be creative or just to be different.

TABLE 5-4 COMPARISON OF THE *GEMEINSCHAFT* AND *GESELLSCHAFT*   Summing Up

Gemeinschaft	Gesellschaft
Rural life typifies this form.	Urban life typifies this form.
People share a feeling of community that results from their similar backgrounds and life experiences.	People have little sense of commonality. Their differences appear more striking than their similarities.
Social interactions are intimate and familiar.	Social interactions are likely to be impersonal and task-specific.
People maintain a spirit of cooperation and unity of will.	Self-interest dominates.
Tasks and personal relationships cannot be separated.	The task being performed is paramount; relationships are subordinate.
People place little emphasis on individual privacy.	Privacy is valued.
Informal social control predominates.	Formal social control is evident.
People are not very tolerant of deviance.	People are more tolerant of deviance.
Emphasis is on ascribed statuses.	Emphasis is on achieved statuses.
Social change is relatively limited.	Social change is very evident, even within a generation.

LO **18-1** Lenski's Sociocultural Evolution Approach

Sociologist Gerhard Lenski takes a very different view of society and social structure. Rather than distinguishing between two opposite types of society, as Tönnies did, Lenski sees human societies as undergoing a process of change characterized by a dominant pattern known as **sociocultural evolution**. This term refers to long-term social trends resulting from the interplay of continuity, innovation, and selection (Nolan and Lenski 2009:361).

In Lenski's view, a society's level of technology is critical to the way it is organized. Lenski defines **technology** as "cultural information about the ways in which the material resources of the environment may be used to satisfy human needs and desires" (Nolan and Lenski 2009:357). The available technology does not completely define the form that a particular society and its social structure take. Nevertheless, a low level of technology may limit the degree to which a society can depend on such things as irrigation or complex machinery. As technology advances, Lenski writes, a community evolves from a preindustrial to an industrial and finally a postindustrial society.

PREINDUSTRIAL SOCIETIES

How does a preindustrial society organize its economy? If we know that, we can categorize the society. The first type of preindustrial society to emerge in human history was the **hunting-and-gathering society**, in which people simply rely on whatever foods and fibers are readily available. Technology in such societies is minimal. Organized into groups, people move constantly in search of food. There is little division of labor into specialized tasks.

Hunting-and-gathering societies are composed of small, widely dispersed groups. Each group consists almost entirely of people who are related to one another. As a result, kinship ties are the source of authority and influence, and the social institution of the family takes on a particularly important role. Tönnies would certainly view such societies as examples of the *Gemeinschaft*.

Social differentiation within the hunting-and-gathering society is based on ascribed statuses such as gender, age, and family background. Since resources are scarce, there is relatively little inequality in terms of material goods. By the close of the 20th century, hunting-and-gathering societies had virtually disappeared (Nolan and Lenski 2009).

Horticultural societies, in which people plant seeds and crops rather than merely subsist on available foods, emerged about 12,000 years ago. Members of horticultural societies are much less nomadic than hunters and gatherers. They place greater emphasis on the production of tools and household objects. Yet technology remains rather limited in these societies, whose members cultivate crops with the aid of digging sticks or hoes (Wilford 1997).

The last stage of preindustrial development is the **agrarian society**, which emerged about 5,000 years ago. As in horticultural societies, members of agrarian societies engage primarily in the production of food. However, technological innovations such as the plow allow farmers to dramatically increase their crop yields. They can cultivate the same fields over generations, allowing the emergence of larger settlements.

The agrarian society continues to rely on the physical power of humans and animals (as opposed to mechanical power). Nevertheless, its social structure has more carefully defined roles than that of horticultural societies. Individuals focus on specialized tasks, such as the repair of fishing nets or blacksmithing. As human settlements become more established and stable, social institutions become more elaborate and property

Preindustrial societies still exist in some remote areas. These indigenous people are from the Envira region of the Amazon rain forest, in Brazil.

TABLE 5-5 STAGES OF SOCIOCULTURAL EVOLUTION   Summing Up

Societal Type	First Appearance	Characteristics
Hunting-and-gathering	Beginning of human life	Nomadic; reliance on readily available food and fibers
Horticultural	About 12,000 years ago	More settled; development of agriculture and limited technology
Agrarian	About 5,000 years ago	Larger, more stable settlements; improved technology and increased crop yields
Industrial	1760–1850	Reliance on mechanical power and new sources of energy; centralized workplaces; economic interdependence; formal education
Postindustrial	1960s	Reliance on services, especially the processing and control of information; expanded middle class
Postmodern	Latter 1970s	High technology; mass consumption of consumer goods and media images; cross-cultural integration

rights more important. The comparative permanence and greater surpluses of an agrarian society allow members to create artifacts such as statues, public monuments, and art objects and to pass them on from one generation to the next.

Table 5-5 summarizes Lenski's three stages of sociocultural evolution, as well as the stages that follow, described next.

INDUSTRIAL SOCIETIES

Although the Industrial Revolution did not topple monarchs, it produced changes every bit as significant as those resulting from political revolutions. The Industrial Revolution, which took place largely in England during the period 1760 to 1830, was a scientific revolution focused on the application of nonanimal (mechanical) sources of power to labor tasks. An **industrial society** is a society that depends on mechanization to produce its goods and services. Industrial societies rely on new inventions that facilitate agricultural and industrial production, and on new sources of energy, such as steam.

As the Industrial Revolution proceeded, a new form of social structure emerged. Many societies underwent an irrevocable shift from an agrarian-oriented economy to an industrial base. No longer did an individual or a family typically make an entire product. Instead, specialization of tasks and manufacturing of goods became increasingly common. Workers, generally men but also women and even children, left their family homesteads to work in central locations such as factories.

POSTINDUSTRIAL AND POSTMODERN SOCIETIES

When Lenski first proposed the sociocultural evolutionary approach in the 1960s, he paid relatively little attention to how maturing industrialized societies may change with the emergence of even more advanced forms of technology. More recently, he and other sociologists have studied the significant changes in the occupational structure of industrial societies as they shift from manufacturing to service economies. In the 1970s, sociologist Daniel Bell wrote about the technologically advanced **postindustrial society**, whose economic system is engaged primarily in the processing and control of information. The main output of a postindustrial society is services rather than manufactured goods. Large numbers of people become involved in occupations devoted to the teaching, generation, or dissemination of ideas. Jobs in fields such as advertising, public relations, human resources, and computer information systems would be typical of a postindustrial society (D. Bell [1973] 1999).

Bell views the transition from industrial to postindustrial society as a positive development. He sees a general decline in organized working-class groups and a rise in interest

Sociology in the Global Community

5-1 DISNEY WORLD: A POSTMODERN THEME PARK

In the late 1970s, scholars began writing about the postmodern society and its preoccupation with consumer goods and media images. Walt Disney World is a living example of this type of society. Over 120 million people visit a Disney theme park each year. In fact, Disney operates the eight most-visited amusement parks in the world. On three different continents, the Magic Kingdom funnels newly arrived visitors through a quaint-looking Main Street, where Cinderella's Castle beckons to children of all ages.

Behind the Main Street façade, one finds endless opportunities to shop. In heavily air-conditioned stores, visitors can indulge in buying sprees that typify the postmodern preoccupation with consumer goods. Later, at the exits from popular attractions, visitors encounter more shopping opportunities, tailored to what they have just seen. This practice of piggy-backing shops on exhibits is now duplicated in prestigious museums throughout the world, where shops are located just outside special exhibitions of real art and authentic treasures.

In the postmodern world, time-space is often compressed. Clutching a toy version of a fictional bear from the 1920s (Winnie-the-Pooh), a young visitor to Disney World reserves a ticket for a trip to New Orleans in the 1850s (the Pirates of the Caribbean attraction). In the meantime, she will travel through the 1930s in one continuous boat ride on the Congo, Zambezi, Amazon, and Irrawaddy rivers (the Jungle Cruise attraction).

The French sociologist Jean Baudrillard (1929–2007) coined the term **hyperconsumerism** to refer to the practice of buying more than we need or want, and often more than we can afford, under such circumstances. Of course, one need not walk down Main Street in Orlando to engage in hyperconsumerism. Advertising permeates the modern world, whether we are on foot or online, tempting us to engage in unnecessary purchases out of a desire that approaches greed. Consumption is so important in the postmodern world that it has become a means of self-identification. Today, conversations are more likely to start with "Where did you get that stroller?" or "Who are you wearing?" than with any reference to the social issues that plague the postmodern world.

Behind the Main Street façade, one finds endless opportunities to shop.

Another essential element of postmodernism, *globalism*, is on display at Disney World, where cultural elements have been stripped of any foreign trappings. Here, Cinderella and Snow White are not figures taken from German folklore, but "Disney characters." Similarly, Belle from *Beauty and the Beast* has largely lost her 18th-century French roots, and Pinocchio is no longer recognizable as an Italian.

Nearby, Epcot's World Showcase takes the opposite approach, offering museum-like re-creations of specific cultures. Here one finds no evidence of cultural diffusion or globalization—no Starbucks in Epcot's China, no Dunkin' Donuts in Great Britain, no hip-hop in Japan. Instead, a representation of a Mayan temple is flanked by a replica of a medieval Norwegian wooden-stave church and a re-creation of the Temple of Heaven in Beijing. Visitors stroll through a managed reality that is both an ideal and a simplified rendering of 10 different cultures, compressed in time-space.

Postmodernism is on display everywhere, not just in the theme park. It can be seen in the information-driven, consumer-oriented global society we all inhabit. Whether we like it or not, new technologies and the digital transmission of culture are constantly disengaging us from a particular time or place, facilitating our hyperconsumerism.

Let's Discuss

1. In just the last 24 hours, what evidence of hyperconsumerism have you witnessed?
2. How often do you find yourself moving seamlessly across time or space, in one way or another?

Sources: Baudrillard [1970] 1998; Boje 1995; Brannigan 1992; Bryman 1995; Fjellman 1992; L. Klein 1994; Kratz and Karp 1993; Scoville 2010; Themed Entertainment Association 2012.

groups concerned with national issues such as health, education, and the environment. Bell's outlook is functionalist, because he portrays the postindustrial society as basically consensual. As organizations and interest groups engage in an open and competitive process of decision making, Bell believes, the level of conflict between diverse groups will diminish, strengthening social stability.

Conflict theorists take issue with Bell's functionalist analysis of the postindustrial society. For example, Michael Harrington (1980), who alerted the nation to the problems of the poor in his book *The Other America,* questioned the significance that Bell attached to the growing class of white-collar workers. Harrington conceded that scientists, engineers, and economists are involved in important political and economic decisions, but he disagreed with Bell's claim that they have a free hand in decision making, independent of the interests of the rich. Harrington followed in the tradition of Marx by arguing that conflict between social classes will continue in the postindustrial society.

Sociologists have gone beyond discussion of the postindustrial society to the ideal of the postmodern society. A **postmodern society** is a technologically sophisticated society that is preoccupied with consumer goods and media images (Brannigan 1992). Such societies consume goods and information on a mass scale. Postmodern theorists take a global perspective, noting the ways that culture crosses national boundaries. For example, residents of the United States may listen to reggae music from Jamaica, eat sushi and other Japanese foods, and wear clogs from Sweden. And online social networks know no national boundaries. Box 5-1 describes one of the fixtures of the postmodern society, the theme park.

The emphasis of postmodern theorists is on observing and describing newly emerging cultural forms and patterns of social interaction. Within sociology, the postmodern view offers support for integrating the insights of various theoretical perspectives—functionalism, conflict theory, feminist theory, and interactionism—while incorporating other contemporary approaches. Feminist sociologists argue optimistically that with its indifference to hierarchies and distinctions, the postmodern society will discard traditional values of male dominance in favor of gender equality. Yet others contend that despite new technologies, postindustrial and postmodern societies can be expected to display the same problems of inequality that plague industrial societies (Denzin 2004; Smart 1990; B. Turner 1990; van Vucht Tijssen 1990).

Durkheim, Tönnies, and Lenski present three visions of society's social structure. While they differ, each is useful, and this textbook will draw on all three. The sociocultural evolutionary approach emphasizes a historical perspective. It does not picture different types of social structure coexisting within the same society. Consequently, one would not expect a single society to include hunters and gatherers along with a postmodern culture. In contrast, Durkheim's and Tönnies's theories allow for the existence of different types of community—such as a *Gemeinschaft* and a *Gesellschaft*—in the same society. Thus, a rural New Hampshire community located 100 miles from Boston can be linked to the city by modern information technology. The main difference between these two theories is a matter of emphasis. While Tönnies emphasized the overriding concern in each type of community—one's own self-interest or the well-being of the larger society—Durkheim emphasized the division (or lack of division) of labor.

The work of these three thinkers reminds us that a major focus of sociology has been to identify changes in social structure and the consequences for human behavior. At the macro level, we see society shifting to more advanced forms of technology. The social structure becomes increasingly complex, and new social institutions emerge to assume some functions that once were performed by the family. On the micro level, these changes affect the nature of social interactions. Each individual takes on multiple social roles, and people come to rely more on social networks and less on kinship ties. As the social structure becomes more complex, people's relationships become more impersonal, transient, and fragmented.

LO 18-2 SOCIAL POLICY and Organizations

We have seen that researchers rely on a number of tools, from simple observational research to the latest in computer technologies. Because in the real world sociological research can have far-reaching consequences for public policy and public welfare, let's consider its impact on labor unions.

FIGURE 5-2 **LABOR UNION MEMBERSHIP WORLDWIDE**

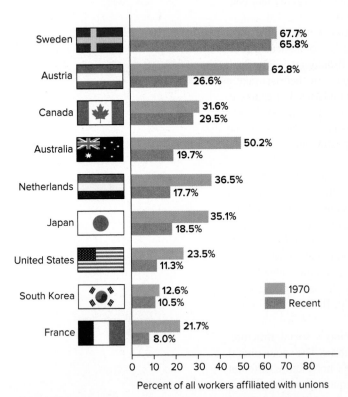

Percent of all workers affiliated with unions

Note: Recent data from 2008–2010, except for Sweden and the United States (2012) and the Netherlands (2007).
Sources: New Unionism Network 2011; Trottman and Maher 2013; Visser 2006:45.

THE STATE OF THE UNIONS WORLDWIDE

How many people do you know who belong to a labor union? Chances are you can name a lot fewer people than someone could 50 years ago. In 1954 unions represented 39 percent of workers in the private sector of the U.S. economy; in 2012 they represented only 11.3 percent—the lowest share in more than 70 years. As Figure 5-2 shows, the decline in unionization is common to virtually all industrial nations. What has happened to diminish the importance of organized labor? Can workers be represented adequately without strong unions?

Labor unions consist of organized workers who share either the same skill (as in electronics) or the same employer (as in the case of postal employees). Unions began to emerge during the Industrial Revolution in England, in the 1700s. Groups of workers banded together to extract concessions from employers (for example, safer working conditions, a shorter workweek) and to protect their positions.

Historically, labor unions have engaged in restrictive practices that are regarded today as discriminatory. They frequently tried to protect their jobs by limiting entry to their occupation based on gender, race, ethnicity, citizenship, age, and sometimes rather arbitrary measures of skill levels. Today we see less of this protection of special interests. In selected industries, unions now play a vital role in keeping Blacks' wages competitive with those of Whites (Rosenfeld and Klegkamp 2012).

The power of labor unions varies widely from country to country. In some countries, such as Britain and Mexico, unions play a key role in the foundation of governments. In others, such as Japan and Korea, their role in politics is very limited, and their ability to influence even the private sector is relatively weak. In the United States, unions can sometimes have a significant influence on employers and elected officials, but their effect varies dramatically by type of industry and even region of the country (S. Zimmerman 2008b).

Few people today would dispute the fact that union membership is declining. Among the reasons for the decline are the following:

1. **Changes in the type of industry.** Manufacturing jobs, the traditional heart of the labor union, have declined, giving way to postindustrial service jobs.

2. **Growth in part-time jobs.** Between 1982 and 1998 the number of temporary jobs in the United States rose 577 percent, while total employment increased only 41 percent. Only in 2000 did laws governing collective bargaining allow temporary workers to join a union.

3. **The legal system.** The United States has not made it particularly easy for unions to organize and bargain, and some government measures have made it more difficult. A dramatic example was President Ronald Reagan's firing of 11,000 air traffic controllers in 1981, when their union threatened they would walk off the job while seeking a new contract.

4. **Globalization.** The threat of jobs leaving the country has undercut the ability of union leaders to organize workers at home. Some say that labor union demands for wage increases and additional benefits have themselves spurred the exodus of jobs to developing nations, where wages are significantly lower and unions are virtually nonexistent.

5. **Employer offensives.** Increasingly hostile employers have taken court action to block unions' efforts to represent their members.

Around the world, the economic downturn that began in 2008 has had special consequences for labor unions. Like nonunion workers, many union members lost their jobs in the recession; others saw their contracts renegotiated. As part of the $17.4 billion auto bailout legislation passed by the U.S. Congress in 2008, the United Auto Workers (UAW) accepted a nearly 20 percent pay cut. This and other rollbacks of benefits were largely accepted by U.S. unions, but in Europe, thousands of workers turned out in protest. Although some union leaders in the United States expect the hardship caused by the economic slowdown to raise union membership, how well unions will be able to represent their members through tough times remains to be seen (S. Greenhouse 2008a, 2009).

Applying Sociology to Unionism Both Marxists and functionalists would view unions as a logical response to the emergence of impersonal, large-scale, formal, and often alienating organizations. This view certainly characterized the growth of unions in major manufacturing industries with a sharp division of labor. However, as manufacturing has declined, unions have had to look elsewhere for growth.

Worldwide, today's labor unions bear little resemblance to those early unions organized spontaneously by exploited workers. In line with Robert Michels's iron law of oligarchy, unions have become increasingly bureaucratized under a sometimes self-serving leadership. Conflict theorists would point out that the longer union leaders are in office, the less responsive they are to the needs and demands of the rank and file, and the more concerned with maintaining their own positions and power. Yet research shows that under certain circumstances, union leadership can change significantly. Smaller unions are vulnerable to changes in leadership, as are unions whose membership shifts in composition from predominantly White to African American or Latino.

Sociologists have linked the recent decline in private-sector union membership to a widening gap between hourly workers' wages and managerial and executive compensation. As union membership declined—and with it the unions' bargaining power—employers began to offer union workers less attractive pay packages. Eventually, the trend spread to nonunionized companies in the same industries, which typically strive to match union compensation in order to be competitive. In these businesses, employers no longer feel a need to raise wages to attract employees (Western and Rosenfeld 2011).

Initiating Labor Policy U.S. law grants workers the right to self-organize via unions. However, the United States is unique among industrial democracies in allowing employers to actively oppose their employees' decision to organize. The recent economic recession has compounded employers' opposition to unions and is even threatening workers' rights in established unions. Today, state and local governments across the United States are facing significant budget deficits. In an effort to cut costs, many elected officials are moving to shrink the pensions that government workers gained through collective bargaining. In some states, officials want not only to reduce retirees' benefits, but also to curtail union workers' collective bargaining rights.

In Europe, labor unions tend to play a major role in political elections. The ruling party in Great Britain, in fact, is called the Labour Party. Unions play a lesser role in U.S. politics, although they have recently been attacked for their large financial contributions to political campaigns. In addition to the role of unions in national politics, international trade unions sometimes speak out on common issues. In 2009 one of them condemned "corporate grand theft"—a reference to corporate executives who spend lavishly on themselves while laying off workers. Despite efforts dating back to Karl Marx and Friedrich Engels's call for the workers of all countries to unite (1847), no global union has emerged (International Trade Union Confederation 2009).

Though unions are a global force, their form and substance varies from country to country. In China, where there is only one political party, the government ordered Walmart's 31,000 workers to unionize, over the corporation's objections. Chinese unions are controlled by the Communist Party, whose membership has declined as the party's pervasive control has weakened. Nevertheless, these unions are more likely to listen to the government than independent unions, which listen to the workers who are their members (E. Wang 2013; Zhang 2009).

E Evaluate

Read each question carefully and then select or provide the best answer.

1. Social control in what Ferdinand Tönnies termed a *Gemeinschaft* community is maintained through all but which of the following means?
   a. moral persuasion
   b. gossip
   c. legally defined punishment
   d. gestures

2. Sociologist Daniel Bell uses which of the following terms to refer to a society whose economic system is engaged primarily in the processing and control of information?
   a. postmodern
   b. horticultural
   c. industrial
   d. postindustrial

3. One effect of globalization on the U.S. workforce has been
   a. the movement of U.S. jobs to countries where costs are lower.
   b. increased training of U.S. workers in foreign languages.
   c. the relocation of U.S. workers to overseas plants.
   d. increased immigration of overseas workers to work in U.S. companies.

4. According to Émile Durkheim, societies with a minimal division of labor are characterized by _____ solidarity, while societies with a complex division of labor are characterized by _____ solidarity.

5. A(n) _____ society is a technologically sophisticated society that is preoccupied with consumer goods and media images.

Answers

1 (c); 2 (d); 3 (a); 4 mechanical, organic; 5 postmodern

R Rethink

Consider these questions to get a deeper understanding of the material.

1. What are some social factors that might determine whether a society's culture moves to a new stage of sociocultural development?

2. Discuss labor unions from a functionalist perspective and from a conflict perspective. What do you think is the future of U.S. labor unions?

RECAP

LO 18-1 Describe Durkheim's, Tönnies's, and Lenski's approaches to classifying forms of social structure.

- In Émile Durkheim's view, social structure depends on the division of labor in a society. According to Durkheim, societies with minimal division of labor have a collective consciousness called mechanical solidarity; those with greater division of labor show an interdependence called organic solidarity.

- Ferdinand Tönnies distinguished the close-knit community of *Gemeinschaft* from the impersonal mass society of *Gesellschaft*.

- According to Gerhard Lenski, a society's social structure changes as its culture and technology become more sophisticated, a process called sociocultural evolution. Historically, many societies have moved from preindustrial status, through the industrial stage, and into postindustrial and postmodern status.

LO 18-2 Analyze from the perspective of social structure the characteristics and condition of labor unions, especially in the United States.

- Although the origins of labor unions can be viewed from a Marxist and functionalist perspective, as a logical response to the size, impersonality, and alienation of large industrial organizations, unions themselves have grown increasingly bureaucratic and have become victims of the iron law of oligarchy.

- Over the past half century, major shifts in the U.S. economy have caused labor union membership to decline and the power of unions to decrease. As power shifts to employers, workers' rights are often threatened.

KEY TERMS

Agrarian society The most technologically advanced form of preindustrial society. Members engage primarily in the production of food, but increase their crop yields through technological innovations such as the plow.

Gemeinschaft A close-knit community, often found in rural areas, in which strong personal bonds unite members.

Gesellschaft A community, often urban, that is large and impersonal, with little commitment to the group or consensus on values.

Horticultural society A preindustrial society in which people plant seeds and crops rather than merely subsist on available foods.

Hunting-and-gathering society A preindustrial society in which people rely on whatever foods and fibers are readily available in order to survive.

Hyperconsumerism The practice of buying more than we need or want, and often more than we can afford; a preoccupation of postmodern consumers.

Industrial society A society that depends on mechanization to produce its goods and services.

Labor union Organized workers who share either the same skill or the same employer.

Mechanical solidarity A collective consciousness that emphasizes group solidarity, characteristic of societies with minimal division of labor.

Organic solidarity A collective consciousness that rests on mutual interdependence, characteristic of societies with a complex division of labor.

Postindustrial society A society whose economic system is engaged primarily in the processing and control of information.

Postmodern society A technologically sophisticated society that is preoccupied with consumer goods and media images.

Sociocultural evolution Long-term social trends resulting from the interplay of continuity, innovation, and selection.

Technology Cultural information about the ways in which the material resources of the environment may be used to satisfy human needs and desires.

The Case of . . . Awkward First Impressions

Jerome Smith remembers the day he met Marcos Vega. "We were sitting on the sidelines of a pick-up basketball game," Smith recalls. "The silence was awkward, so I made this stupid joke. I said, 'What do you think the odds are we'll make it into the game before the half?' Vega stared pointedly at my wheelchair and said, 'For you, buddy, not so good.' I could have returned the insult. Marcos was a short kid, the shortest boy in our grade, and a super-nerd to boot. But I thought it was probably these things that were making life hard for him, making him mean, so I just laughed and asked if he thought we'd do better running a three-legged race. 'You're crazy, dude,' he said, but he was laughing too, and that eased the tension. We started talking and discovered we had a lot in common. Chess. Classic horror films. Math puzzles. We became best friends. We even started a math club at school. Joked about how it was our 'sport.'"

When Vega and Smith went to different colleges, they kept in touch. "Now, Marcos is a lawyer with the ACLU and I'm a psychologist," Smith says. "Not bad for a runty Hispanic kid and a disabled Black boy from the slums of North Philly."

1. What similarities in their ascribed status do Jerome and Marcos share? Does any aspect of either man's ascribed status predict his achieved status? How powerful a predictor of achieved status are social expectations, in your opinion?

2. A master status is said to dominate other statuses and determine a person's general position in society. Do you think this was true for Jerome in childhood? Do you think it is true now that he is an adult with a profession? Why or why not?

3. If an out-group is defined as a group or category to which people feel they do not belong, what would be some of the characteristics of the out-group for Jerome and Marco?

What's Your Learning Style?

People have different learning styles—ways in which they take in and process information for later use. Use this P.O.W.E.R. plan to identify your preferred learning style so you can optimize classwork, homework, and test preparation by playing to your strengths and compensating for your weaknesses (e.g., by studying with others with different learning styles). (The emPOWERme exercise in this chapter will help you work out your preferred learning style.)

- Think about how you learn in school and outside school.
- Be sure to think of both good learning experiences and bad ones.

- If possible, explore your learning style with others by forming a study group specifically to discuss learning styles and experiences.
- If you have to go it alone, find a quiet place and some paper, set aside a block of time, and prepare to do some soul-searching.

- Think how you learn most effectively:
  - Do you primarily learn by reading written materials in books, magazines, or online? If so you're a **reader**.
  - Do you learn best by listening to lectures, hearing people explain things, asking someone to tell you how to do things? If so, you're a **listener**.
  - Do you learn best by seeing or making pictures—drawings, diagrams, charts, photos, or films? If so, you're a visual learner, a **viewer**.
  - Do you learn best by manipulating objects or performing hands-on activities? If so, you're a **toucher**.
- Most people have a preferred, general-purpose learning style, although they also use other styles depending on what they have to learn (for example, even a **reader** might want to view a YouTube video to see how to tie a bowtie).

- Evaluate what you found out about how you learn most effectively.
- Discuss what you learned with your study group.
- Think how to align your coursework with your learning style, which can affect how you study, attend classes, take notes, do homework, review your classwork, and prepare for tests.
- For instance, if you're a **listener**, maybe your instructors will permit you to record their lectures. If you're a **toucher**, maybe you can make cardboard models of what you're studying or move salt shakers and sugar packets on the tabletop to represent concepts. *Have fun with your learning style!*

- In a few months, reevaluate whether your understanding of your learning style has affected your schoolwork. Make any necessary adjustments.

What's Your Receptive Learning Style?

We all learn in a variety of ways, but each of us has a *preferred* receptive learning style—Reader, Viewer, Toucher, Listener—the primary way we take in new material. Use the following scale to rate each of the statements as to how useful the strategy is to you in learning new information:

1 = Not very or not at all useful
2 = Somewhat useful
3 = Very useful

	1	2	3
1. Watching a film or video presentation			
2. Taking part in group discussions			
3. Learning a complex procedure or game by reading written directions			
4. Making flash cards to use as a study and review tool			
5. Doing lab work or taking part in hands-on demonstrations			
6. Using pictures and diagrams to master complex material			
7. Listening to a recorded lecture or book			
8. Recalling how to spell a word by seeing it in my head			
9. Performing a procedure myself rather than reading or hearing about it			
10. Repeating important terms and key ideas aloud when studying			
11. Writing down key facts and major points as a tool for recalling them			
12. Studying instructors' handouts and lecture notes			

SCORING:

Circle the number of every statement you rate as a **3**. Now, check below to see which receptive learning style you most often rated as a **3**. Don't worry—it's common to have a "mixed" style (in which two or more styles receive preference). Just use what you have discovered here to help you learn more effectively.

Learning Style Items:

Reader (items 3, 8, 12)
Listener (items 2, 7, 10)
Viewer (items 1, 4, 6)
Toucher (items 5, 9, 11)

The **Mass Media**

6

Sociology at WORK PRODUCT DEVELOPER

AANIYA BAHRI works as a product developer for a breakfast foods company. "We're not as big as, say, Kellogg's but we have a young, forward-looking staff," Bahri says, "and we know how to use social media to foster growth." A case in point: Bahri was recently assigned to develop breakfast alternatives for the under-35 age group, a group research shows often skips breakfast, but also values healthy eating. Bahri connected with the company's Twitter followers to pose the question: What is the number one reason you skip breakfast? The response was rapid and to the point: No time. As followers tweeted to one another, Bahri inserted herself in the conversation and confirmed that the under-35s would like a healthy breakfast product, *but* it had to be mobile. That meant single-serving units. To find out more, Bahri set up a Facebook fan page to which she directed her Twitter followers. "It's a way to collect data," Bahri explains. "I also used it to run a contest to develop specific product flavors." Over the course of a month, two new on-the-go breakfast options were born: Cranberry Nut yogurt bars and Morning Crunch muffins. "The winners each received $1,000," Bahri says, "and we got our products." ■

Looking Ahead

FEW ASPECTS OF SOCIETY ARE AS CENTRAL AS THE MASS MEDIA. Through the media we expand our understanding of people and events beyond what we experience in person. The media inform us about different cultures and lifestyles and about the latest forms of technology. For sociologists, the key questions are how the mass media affect our social institutions and how they influence our social behavior.

Why are the media so influential? Who benefits from media influence and why? How do we maintain cultural and ethical standards in the face of negative media images? In this chapter we will consider the ways sociology helps us to answer these questions. First we will look at how proponents of the various sociological perspectives view the media. Then we will examine who makes up the media's audience, not just at home but around the world. The chapter closes with a Social Policy section on the right to privacy in a digital age.

MODULE 19 Sociological Perspectives on the Media

P Prepare <u>Learning Objectives</u>

LO 19-1 Describe the social effects of the rapid spread of mass media.

LO 19-2 Interpret recent media trends from the point of view of the major sociological perspectives (functionalist, conflict, feminist, and interactionist).

W Work

LO **19-1** Mass Media

Once the only media available to us—radio, television, the Internet—were a one-way experience, from the producer to the audience. Today, anyone can become a producer and distribute content to others. This rapid transition from old-fashioned technologies to new interactive technologies has profoundly changed the ways people use media.

And that's not all; the lines between various media are blurring. Today we use the telephone not just to talk with others, but to watch television and movies. Both television and the Internet are examples of the **mass media**, which embrace print and electronic means of communication that carry messages to widespread audiences. Print media include newspapers, magazines, and books; electronic media include radio, satellite radio, television, motion pictures, and the Internet. Advertising, which falls into both categories, is also a form of mass media.

The social impact of the mass media is obvious. Consider a few examples. TV dinners were invented to accommodate the millions of couch potatoes who can't bear to miss their favorite television programs. Today, screen time has gone well beyond television viewing to include time spent on smartphones. Candidates for political office rely on their media consultants to project a winning image both in print and in the electronic media. World leaders use all forms of media for political advantage, whether to gain territory or to bid on hosting the Olympics. And in parts of Africa and Asia, AIDS education projects owe much of their success to media campaigns.

The social impact of the mass media has become so huge, in fact, that scholars have begun to speak of *cultural convergence*. The term **cultural convergence** refers to the flow of content across multiple media, and the accompanying migration of media audiences. As you watch a television program, for example, you wonder what the star of the show is doing at the moment, and turn to the Internet. Later, while texting your best friend, you tell her what you learned, accompanied by a Google Earth map showing the celebrity's location. Using Photoshop, you may even include the star's image next to your own, post the photo on your Facebook page, and then tweet your friends (send them a mini-blog) to create a caption. Media convergence is not orchestrated by the media, sophisticated though they may be. You initiate it, using techniques you likely learned by interacting with others, either face-to-face or through the media (Jenkins 2006).

Over the past decade especially, new technologies have made new forms of mass media available to U.S. households. These new technologies have changed people's viewing and listening habits. People spend a lot of time with the media, more and more of it on the Internet. Media consumers have moved away from television and toward digital images downloaded to their computers and portable devices. Increasingly, they learn not just about the famous but about ordinary people by viewing their Facebook pages or by keeping in touch with their friends via Twitter.

How do people's viewing and listening habits affect their social behavior? In the following sections we'll use the four major sociological perspectives to examine the impact of the mass media and changes in their usage patterns (Nelson 2004).

LO **19-2** Functionalist Perspective

One obvious function of the mass media is to entertain. Except for clearly identified news or educational programming, we often think the explicit purpose of the mass media is to occupy our leisure time—from newspaper comics and crossword puzzles to the latest music releases on the Internet. While that is true, the media have other important functions. They also socialize us, enforce social norms, confer status, and promote consumption. An important dysfunction of the mass media is that they may act as a narcotic, desensitizing us to distressing events (Lazarsfeld and Merton 1948; C. Wright 1986).

AGENT OF SOCIALIZATION

The media increase social cohesion by presenting a common, more or less standardized view of culture through mass communication. Sociologist Robert Park (1922) studied how newspapers helped immigrants to the United States adjust to their environment by changing their customary habits and teaching them the opinions of people in their new home country. Unquestionably, the mass media play a significant role in providing a collective experience for members of society. Think about how the mass media bring together members of a community or even a nation by broadcasting important events and ceremonies (such as inaugurations, press conferences, parades, state funerals, and the Olympics) and by covering disasters.

Which media outlets did people turn to in the aftermath of the September 11, 2001, tragedy? Television, radio, and the telephone were the primary means by which people in the United States bonded. But the Internet also played a prominent role. About half of all Internet users—more than 5 million people—received some kind of news about the attacks online (D. Miller and Darlington 2002).

Today, the news media have moved further online. Afghans of all political persuasions now connect with the Muslim community overseas to gain both social and financial support. In the realm of popular culture, a spontaneous global sharing of reactions to Michael Jackson's sudden death in 2009 crashed the websites for Google, the *Los Angeles Times*, TMZ celebrity news, Perez Hilton's blog, and Twitter (Rawlinson and Hunt 2009; Shane 2010).

Time to Tweet! In 2012, after struggling briefly with an iPad touch screen, former Pope Benedict XVI dispatched his first Twitter message, which read in part, "I bless all you from my heart." Using the handle @Pontifex, the pope posts in eight of the many languages used by members of the worldwide Roman Catholic community (Donadio 2012:A8).

Some are concerned about the media's socialization function, however. For instance, many people worry about the effect of using television as a babysitter and the impact of violent programming on viewer behavior. Some people adopt a blame-the-media mentality, holding the media accountable for anything that goes wrong, especially with young people. Yet the media also have positive effects on young people. For young and even not-so-young adults, for example, a new sort of tribalism is emerging online, in which communities develop around common interests or shared identities (Tyrene Adams and Smith 2008).

From the perspective of . . .

An Educator What are some ways you could use the Internet and smartphones to foster the social norm that cyberbullying is unacceptable among your students?

ENFORCER OF SOCIAL NORMS

The media often reaffirm proper behavior by showing what happens to people who act in a way that violates societal expectations. These messages are conveyed when the bad guy gets clobbered in cartoons or is thrown in jail on *CSI*. Yet the media also sometimes glorify disapproved behavior, whether it is physical violence, disrespect to a teacher, or drug use.

The media also play a critical role in human sexuality. For example, programs have been created to persuade teens not to send nude images of themselves to selected friends. Such images often go viral (that is, spread across the Internet) and may be used to harass teens and their parents. To define normative behavior regarding these images, one organization has launched a "That's not cool" campaign, complete with stalker messages that can be e-mailed to those who misuse such images. The widespread dissemination of compromising images that were meant to be shared only among close friends is just one aspect of the social phenomenon called *cyberbullying* (Chan 2009; Clifford 2009a; Gentile 2009).

CONFERRAL OF STATUS

The mass media confer status on people, organizations, and public issues. Whether it is an issue like the homeless or a celebrity like Kim Kardashian, they single out one from thousands of other similarly placed issues or people to become significant. Table 6-1 shows how often certain public figures are prominently featured on magazine covers and the online source for celebrity information, IMDb. Obviously, *People* magazine alone was not responsible for making Princess Diana into a worldwide figure, but collectively, all the media outlets created a notoriety that Princess Victoria of Sweden, for one, did not enjoy.

Another way the media confer celebrity status on individuals is by publishing information about the frequency of Internet searches. Some newspapers and websites carry regularly updated lists of the most heavily researched individuals and topics of the

Product placement ("brand casting") is an increasingly important source of revenue for motion picture studios. The movie *Men in Black 3* (2012) featured many brands, including Cadillac, Cracker Jack, Dunkin' Donuts, John Deere, Rolaids, and Viagra (Brandchannel.com 2013).

TABLE 6-1 STATUS CONFERRED BY THE MEDIA

Time Rank/Person/Times on Cover	*People* Rank/Person/Times on Cover	*Ebony* Rank/Person/Times on Cover	*Rolling Stone* Rank/Person/Times on Cover	*IMDb* Rank/Person
1. Richard Nixon (55)	1. Princess Diana (54)	1. Janet Jackson (18)	1. Paul McCartney (28)	1. Johnny Depp
2. Ronald Reagan (38)	2. Jennifer Aniston (41)	2. Halle Berry (17)	2. John Lennon (26)	2. Brad Pitt
3. Bill Clinton (35)	3. Julia Roberts (35)	2. Michael Jackson (17)	3. Bono (22)	3. Angelina Jolie
4. Barack Obama (31)	4. Brad Pitt (33)	4. Muhammad Ali (16)	3. Bob Dylan (22)	4. Tom Cruise
4. Hillary Clinton (31)	5. Prince William (24)	4. Whitney Houston (16)	5. Mick Jagger (21)	5. Natalie Portman
4. George W. Bush (31)	5. Demi Moore (24)	6. Denzel Washington (11)	5. Bruce Springsteen (21)	6. Christian Bale
7. George H. W. Bush (25)	7. Angelina Jolie (21)	6. Diahann Carroll (11)	7. Madonna (19)	7. Scarlett Johansson
8. Dwight Eisenhower (22)	8. Britney Spears (18)	6. Lena Horne (11)	8. Jimi Hendrix (18)	8. Jennifer Aniston
8. Lyndon Johnson (22)	9. Michael Jackson (17)	6. Sidney Poitier (11)	8. Keith Richards (18)	9. Keira Knightley
8. Gerald Ford (22)	9. Elizabeth Taylor (17)	10. Beyoncé (10)	10. George Harrison (17)	10. Emma Watson
		10. Vanessa Williams (10)		
		10. Bill Cosby (10)		

Source: Author's content analysis of primary cover subject for full run of the periodicals beginning with *Time,* March 3, 1923; *People,* March 4, 1974; *Ebony,* November 1945; and *Rolling Stone,* September 1967 through September 1, 2013. When a periodical runs multiple covers, each version is counted. In case of ties, the more recent cover person is listed first. IMDb rank based on cumulative 2003–2012 p age views by the more than 110 million unique viewers per month at IMDb.com.

week. The means may have changed since the first issue of *Time* magazine hit the stands in 1923, but the media still confer status—often electronically.

PROMOTION OF CONSUMPTION

Postmodern societies are characterized by **hyperconsumerism**, a term coined by the French sociologist Jean Baudrillard (1929–2007) to refer to the practice of buying more than we need or want, and often more than we can afford. The media certainly promote this behavior pattern. Twenty thousand commercials a year—that is the number the average child in the United States watches on television alone, not to mention other media platforms.

Young people cannot escape commercial messages. They show up on high school scoreboards, at rock concerts, and as banners on web pages. They also surface in the form of *product placement*—for example, the Coca-Cola glasses that sit in front of the judges on *American Idol.* Product placement is nothing new. In 1951 *The African Queen* prominently displayed Gordon's Gin aboard the boat carrying Katharine Hepburn and Humphrey Bogart. However, commercial promotion has become far more common today: *American Idol* alone features over 4,600 product appearances each season. Moreover, advertisers are attempting to develop brand or logo loyalty at younger and younger ages (Buckingham 2007; Rodman 2011:395).

FIGURE 6-1 BRANDING THE GLOBE

Canada
47 Thomson-Reuters

Great Britain
32 HSBC
82 Johnnie Walker
89 Smirnoff
95 Burberry

Netherlands
40 Philips
73 Shell
92 Heineken

Switzerland
37 Nescafé
56 Nestlé

Sweden
21 H&M
26 Ikea

Finland
57 Nokia

South Korea
8 Samsung
43 Hyundai
83 Kia

Mexico
93 Corona

United States
1 Apple
2 Google
3 Coca-Cola
4 IBM
5 Microsoft
6 GE
7 McDonald's
9 Intel
13 Cisco
14 Disney
15 HP
16 Gillette
18 Oracle
19 Amazon
20 Pepsi

Spain
36 Zara
84 Santander

France
17 Luis Vuitton
39 L'Oréal
49 Danone
54 Hermès
59 AXA
60 Cartier
99 Moët & Chandon

Germany
11 Mercedes-Benz
12 BMW
25 SAP
34 Volkswagen
45 Siemens
51 Audi
55 Adidas
63 Allianz
64 Porsche

Italy
38 Gucci
72 Prada
98 Ferrari

Japan
10 Toyota
20 Honda
35 Canon
40 Sony
65 Nissan
67 Nintendo
68 Panasonic

Homes of Top 100 Brands
- USA
- Germany
- France, Japan
- Great Britain, Finland
- Italy, Netherlands, South Korea
- Canada, Mexico, Spain, Sweden, Switzerland

Note: Map shows the top 100 brands in the world in 2013 by country of ownership, except for the United States, for which only brands in the top 20 are shown. The United States has a total of 55 of the 100 leading brands.
Source: Based on Interbrand 2013.

Based on revenue and name recognition, these are the brands that dominate the global marketplace. Just 14 nations account for all the top 100 brands.

Using advertising to develop a brand name with global appeal is an especially powerful way to encourage consumption. U.S. corporations have been particularly successful in creating global brands. An analysis of the 100 most successful brands worldwide, each of which derives at least a third of its earnings outside the home country, shows that 55 of them originated in the United States; 45 others come from 13 different countries (Figure 6-1).

Media advertising has several clear functions: it supports the economy, provides information about products, and underwrites the cost of media. In some cases, advertising becomes part of the entertainment. A national survey showed that 51 percent of viewers watch the Super Bowl primarily for the commercials, and one-third of online conversations about the Super Bowl the day of and the day after the event are driven by Super Bowl advertising. Yet advertising's functions are related to dysfunctions. Media advertising contributes to a consumer culture that creates needs and raises unrealistic expectations of what is required to be happy or satisfied. Moreover, because the media depend heavily on advertising revenue, advertisers can influence media content (Carey and Gelles 2010; Nielsen Company 2010).

DYSFUNCTION: THE NARCOTIZING EFFECT

In addition to the functions just noted, the media perform a *dysfunction*. Sociologists Paul Lazarsfeld and Robert Merton (1948) created the term **narcotizing dysfunction** to refer to the phenomenon in which the media provide such massive amounts of coverage that the audience becomes numb and fails to act on the information, regardless of how compelling the issue. Interested citizens may take in the information but make no decision or take no action.

Consider how often the media initiate a great outpouring of philanthropic support in response to natural disasters or family crises. But then what happens? Research shows that as time passes, viewer fatigue sets in. The mass media audience becomes numb, desensitized to the suffering, and may even conclude that a solution to the crisis has been found (S. Moeller 1999).

The media's narcotizing dysfunction was identified 70 years ago, when just a few homes had television—well before the advent of electronic media. At that time, the dysfunction went largely unnoticed, but today commentators often point out the ill effects of addiction to television or the Internet, especially among young people. Street crime, explicit sex, war, and HIV/AIDS apparently are such overwhelming topics that some in the audience may feel they have acted—or at the very least learned all they need to know—simply by watching the news.

LO 19-2 Conflict Perspective

Conflict theorists emphasize that the media reflect and even exacerbate many of the divisions in our society and world, including those based on gender, race, ethnicity, and social class. They point in particular to the media's ability to decide what is transmitted, through a process called *gatekeeping*. Conflict theorists also stress the way interest groups monitor media content; the way powerful groups transmit society's dominant ideology through the mass media; and the technological gap between the haves and have-nots, which limits people's access to the Internet.

GATEKEEPING

What story pops up when you check your favorite news outlet? What motion picture plays on three screens rather than one at the local cineplex? What picture isn't released at all? Behind these decisions are powerful figures—publishers, editors, and other media moguls.

The mass media constitute a form of big business in which profits are generally more important than the quality of the programming. Within the mass media, a relatively small number of people control what eventually reaches the audience through **gatekeeping**. This term describes how material must travel through a series of gates (or checkpoints) before reaching the public. Thus, a select few decide what images to bring to a broad audience. In many countries the government plays a gatekeeping role. Even the champions of Internet freedom, who pride themselves on allowing people to pass freely through the gate, may quickly channel them in certain directions.

Gatekeeping, which prevails in all kinds of media, is not a new concept. The term was coined by a journalism scholar in the 1940s to refer to the way that small-town newspaper editors control which events receive public attention. As sociologist C. Wright Mills ([1956] 2000b) observed, the real power of the media is that they can control what is being presented. In the recording industry, gatekeepers may reject a popular local band because it competes with a group already on their label. Even if the band is recorded, radio programmers may reject the music because it does not fit the station's sound. Television programmers may keep a pilot for a new TV series off the air because they believe it does not appeal to the target audience (which is sometimes determined by advertising sponsors). Similar decisions are made by gatekeepers in the publishing industry.

Gatekeeping is not as dominant in at least one form of mass media, the Internet. You can send virtually any message to an electronic bulletin board, and create a web page or web log (blog) to advance any argument, including one that insists the earth is flat. The Internet is a means of quickly disseminating information (or misinformation) without going through any significant gatekeeping process.

Nevertheless, the Internet is not totally without restrictions. In many nations, laws regulate content on issues such as gambling, pornography, and even politics. And popular Internet service providers will terminate accounts for offensive behavior. After the terrorist attacks in 2001, eBay did not allow people to sell parts of the World Trade Center via its online auction. Despite such interference, growing numbers of people are actively involved in online communities.

Today, many countries try to control political dissent by restricting citizens' access to online comments unfavorable to the government. Beginning in 2011, online criticism fueled dissent in Arab countries like Egypt, Tunisia, Libya, Bahrain, and Syria. Using social media, activists in these countries encouraged their followers to demonstrate against the government at predetermined locales. To further encourage citizen engagement, activists posted cell phone videos of the protests on the Internet. In China, however, government officials marshaled the state's vast resources to mobilize an army of cyber-police, software developers, web monitors, and paid online propagandists. These cyber-soldiers watch, filter, censor, and guide Chinese Internet users in an effort to minimize online dissent (Castells 2012; *The Economist* 2013b; Preston and Stelter 2011).

MEDIA MONITORING

The term *media monitoring* is used most often to refer to interest groups' monitoring of media content. The public reaction to the shootings at Virginia Tech in April 2007 provides one example. People did not need to be constant news monitors to learn of the rampage. Ever since the mass shootings at Columbine High School near Littleton, Colorado, in 1999, news outlets of every type have descended on the sites of such school shootings, offering insight into the perpetrators and their families, covering the mass expressions of grief, and following the communities' efforts to recover. Once again, though media outlets provided valuable information and quickly reassured viewers, listeners, and readers that the shooters posed no further danger, many people criticized the reality that they constructed through their coverage.

The term *media monitoring* can also be applied to government monitoring of individuals' phone calls without their knowledge. For example, the federal government has been criticized for authorizing wiretaps of U.S. citizens' telephone conversations without judicial approval. Government officials argue that the wiretaps were undertaken in the interest of national security, to monitor contacts between U.S. citizens and known terrorist groups following the terrorist attacks of September 11, 2001. But critics who take the conflict perspective, among others, are concerned by the apparent invasion of people's privacy (Gertner 2005). We will examine the right to privacy in greater detail in the Social Policy section at the end of this chapter.

From the perspective of . . .

A Health Care Worker How would you handle people who post racial or gender slurs on an online health forum that you monitor?

What are the practical and ethical limits of media monitoring? In daily life, parents often oversee their children's online activities and scan the blogs they read—which are, of course, available for anyone to see. Most parents see such monitoring of children's media use and communications as an appropriate part of adult supervision. Yet their snooping sets an example for their children, who may use the technique for their own ends. Some media analysts have noted a growing trend among adolescents: the use of new media to learn not-so-public information about their parents (Delaney 2005).

One unanticipated benefit of government monitoring of private communications has been expedited disaster relief. As in the aftermath of Hurricane Katrina in 2005, the U.S. government turned to media monitoring following the 2010 earthquake in Haiti. At the Department of Homeland Security, employees at the National Operations Center monitored 31 social media sites for information regarding the disaster. The intelligence they gathered helped responders to locate people in need of rescue and identify areas outside Port-au-Prince where relief was necessary (Department of Homeland Security 2010).

DOMINANT IDEOLOGY: CONSTRUCTING REALITY

Conflict theorists argue that the mass media maintain the privileges of certain groups. Moreover, powerful groups may limit the media's representation of others to protect their own interests. The term **dominant ideology** describes a set of cultural beliefs and practices that helps to maintain powerful social, economic, and political interests. The media transmit messages that essentially define what we regard as the real world, even though those images frequently vary from the ones that the larger society experiences.

Mass media decision makers are overwhelmingly White, male, and wealthy. It may come as no surprise, then, that the media tend to ignore the lives and ambitions of subordinate groups, among them working-class people, African Americans, Hispanics, gays and lesbians, people with disabilities, overweight people, and older people. Worse yet, media content may create false images or stereotypes of these groups that then become accepted as accurate portrayals of reality. **Stereotypes** are unreliable generalizations about all members of a group that do not recognize individual differences within the group. Some broadcasters use stereotypes deliberately in a desperate bid for attention, with the winking approval of media executives.

Queer theorists have long studied the way the media present homosexuality. They have analyzed the frequent invisibility of homosexual characters, as well as the problematic ways in which they are made visible. From the perspective of queer theorists, significant strides have been made in the portrayal of nonheterosexuality as a normal and possible alternative to heterosexuality. Still, stigmatization of gays and lesbians persists, in the media as well as in society (Sloop 2009).

Television offers many examples of this tendency to ignore reality. How many overweight TV characters can you name? Even though in real life 1 out of every 4 women is obese (30 or more pounds over a healthy body weight), only 3 out of 100 TV characters are portrayed as obese. Heavyset television characters have fewer romances, talk less about sex, eat more often, and are more often the object of ridicule than their thin counterparts (Hellmich 2001).

On the other hand, television news and other media outlets do alert people to the health implications of obesity. As with constructions of reality, whether some of this coverage is truly educational is debatable. Increasingly, the media have framed the problem not merely as an individual or personal one, but as a broad structural problem involving, for example, the manner in which food is processed and sold (Saguy and Almeling 2008).

Similarly, about 45 percent of all youths in the United States are children of color, yet few of the faces they see on television reflect their race or cultural heritage. Using content analysis, sociologists have found that only 2 of the nearly 60 prime-time series aired in recent years—*Ugly Betty* and *George Lopez*—focused on minority performers. What is more, programs that are shown earlier in the evening, when young people are most likely to watch television, are the least diverse (Grazian 2010:129; NAACP 2008; Wyatt 2009).

Another concern about the media, from the conflict perspective, is that television distorts the political process. Until the U.S. campaign finance system is truly reformed, the candidates with the most money (often backed by powerful lobbying groups) will be able to buy exposure to voters and saturate the air with commercials attacking their opponents.

DOMINANT IDEOLOGY: WHOSE CULTURE?

CSI: Crime Scene Investigation (Les Experts) is a big hit in France, despite that nation's pride in its *"exception culturelle,"* which protects French film, television, and music producers from foreign competition. In Japan, *Glee* is must-watch TV, and *Columbo* reruns still garner viewers. Those are only the legally viewed hit shows. In Latin America, where illicit downloading of TV programs is common, the most popular shows include *Breaking Bad, Homeland,* and

Despite the popularity of Hollywood entertainment, media that are produced abroad for local consumption also do well. The animated series *Freej* features Muslim grandmothers who stumble on a cursed book while tackling their culture's wedding traditions. Produced in Dubai, the United Arab Emirates, for adult viewers, the series was launched in 2006.

Modern Family. In North Korea, *Desperate Housewives* is a cult hit. Although government officials and cultural purists may decry these shows' popularity, U.S. media are still widely watched and imitated. As sociologist Todd Gitlin puts it, American popular culture is something that "people love, and love to hate" (2002:177; Agence France-Presse 2013).

We risk being ethnocentric if we overstress U.S. dominance, however. For example, *Survivor, Who Wants to Be a Millionaire, Big Brother,* and *Iron Chef*—immensely popular TV programs in the United States—came from Sweden, Britain, the Netherlands, and Japan, respectively. Even *American Idol* originated in Britain as *Pop Idol,* featuring Simon Cowell. And the steamy telenovelas of Mexico and other Spanish-speaking countries owe very little of their origin to the soap operas on U.S. television. Unlike motion pictures, television is gradually moving away from U.S. domination and is now more likely to be locally produced (Bielby and Harrington 2008; Colucci 2008).

A related trend, the most novel one to date in this century, is the growth of **hyper-local media**, which refers to reporting that is highly local. What has been going on in that vacant lot down the street? Which Chinese takeout food is popular in your neighborhood? Why did all those police cars converge on Main Street the night before last? Hyper-local media answer these questions. The term was coined in 1991, to refer to the inclusion of local news on 24-hour cable news channels.

Today, with the development of online websites and blogs, hyper-local media have become even more localized and oriented toward special interests. As a result, cultural values and media profiles are no longer defined only by nation, but by community and even by neighborhood. During the Arab Spring, for example, residents of Cairo, armed with cell phones and personal computers, provided hyper-local media coverage of street incidents in their neighborhoods—incidents that had national and international implications (Pavlik 2013).

Nations that feel a loss of identity may try to defend against the cultural invasion from foreign countries, especially the economically dominant United States. Yet as sociologists know, audiences are not necessarily passive recipients of foreign cultural messages, either in developing nations or in industrial nations. Thus, research on consumers of cultural products like television, music, and film must be placed in social context. Although people may watch and even enjoy media content, that does not mean that they will accept values that are alien to their own (Bielby and Harrington 2008).

Many developing nations have long argued for a greatly improved two-way flow of news and information between industrial nations and developing nations. They complain that news from the Third World is scant, and what news there is reflects unfavorably on the developing nations. For example, what do you know about South America? Most people in the United States will mention the two topics that dominate the news from countries south of the border: revolution and drugs. Most know little else about the continent.

To remedy this imbalance, a resolution to monitor the news and content that cross the borders of developing nations was passed by the United Nations Educational, Scientific, and Cultural Organization (UNESCO) in the 1980s. The United States disagreed with the proposal, which became one factor in the U.S. decision to withdraw from UNESCO in the mid-1980s. In 2005, the United States opposed another UNESCO plan, meant to reduce the diminishment of cultural differences. Hailed as an important step toward protecting threatened cultures, particularly the media markets in developing nations, the measure passed the UN's General Assembly by a vote of 148–2. The United States, one of the two dissenters, objected officially to the measure's vague wording, but the real concern was clearly the measure's potential impact on a major U.S. export (Dominick 2009; Riding 2005).

THE DIGITAL DIVIDE

Finally, as numerous studies have shown, advances in communications technology are not evenly distributed. Worldwide, low-income groups, racial and ethnic minorities, rural residents, and the citizens of developing countries have far less access than others to the latest technologies—a gap that is called the **digital divide**. People in low-income households, rural areas, and developing countries, for example, are less likely than others to have Internet access. When marginalized people do gain Internet access, they are still likely to trail the privileged. They may have dial-up service instead of broadband, or broadband instead of wireless Internet. The issue is not merely access to the Internet, but the cost and availability of broadband service. High-speed Internet connections are becoming increasingly essential for everything from completing school assignments to consulting with medical personnel and conducting business through routine financial transactions.

The digital divide is most evident in developing countries. In Africa, 4 percent of the population has Internet access. These fortunate few typically pay the highest rates in the world—$250 to $300 a month—for the slowest connection speeds. Box 6-1 examines the global disconnect between the haves and have-nots of the information age (Robinson and Crenshaw 2010; P. Schaefer 2008).

LO **19-2** Feminist Perspective

Feminists share the view of conflict theorists that the mass media stereotype and misrepresent social reality. According to this view, the media powerfully influence how we look at men and women, communicating unrealistic, stereotypical, and limiting images of the sexes.

Educators and social scientists have long noted the stereotypical portrayal of women and men in the mass media. Women are often shown as being shallow and obsessed with beauty. They are more likely than men to be presented unclothed, in danger, or even physically victimized. When women achieve newsworthy feats in fields traditionally dominated by men, such as professional sports, the media are often slow to recognize their accomplishments.

Even when they are covered by the press, female athletes are not treated equally by television commentators. Communications researchers conducted a content analysis of over 200 hours of nationally televised coverage of professional golf events. The study showed that when female golfers are successful, they are more likely than male golfers to be called strong and intelligent. When they are not successful, they are more likely than

Sociology in the Global Community

6-1 THE GLOBAL DISCONNECT

Bogdan Ghirda, a Romanian, is paid 50 cents an hour to participate in multiplayer Internet games like City of Heroes and Star Wars. He is sitting in for someone in an industrialized country who does not want to spend days ascending to the highest levels of competition in order to compete with players who are already "well armed." This arrangement is not unusual. U.S.-based services can earn hundreds of dollars for recruiting someone in a less developed country, like Ghirda, to represent a single player in an affluent industrial country.

Meanwhile, in Africa, the resource-poor nation of Rwanda is developing its economy by encouraging investments in information and communications technologies. In 2011, through a combination of public investment and private competition among telecommunications companies, mobile phone and data transmission service in the country reached 96 percent. The challenges Rwanda faces remain immense: energy needs that are expensive to meet, a shortage of skilled computer specialists, and weak finances, to name a few. However, this nation of 11 million, with a per capita income of just $605 a year, may be able to create a stable economy based on new telecommunications technologies.

These two situations illustrate the technological disconnect between the developing and industrial nations. Around the world, developing nations lag far behind industrial nations in their access to and use of new technologies. The World Economic Forum's Networked Readiness Index (NRI), a ranking of 144 nations, shows the relative preparedness of individuals, businesses, and governments to benefit from information technologies. As the accompanying table shows, the haves of the world—countries like Singapore, Switzerland, and the United States—are network ready; the have-nots—countries like Swaziland, Yemen, and Haiti—are not.

For developing nations, the consequences of the global disconnect are far more serious than an inability to surf the Net.

For developing nations, the consequences of the global disconnect are far more serious than an inability to surf the Net. Thanks to the Internet, multinational organizations can now function as a single global unit, responding instantly in real time, 24 hours a day. This new capability has fostered the emergence of what sociologist Manuel Castells calls a "global economy." But if large numbers of people—indeed, entire nations—are disconnected from the new global economy, their economic growth will remain slow and the well-being of their people will remain retarded. Those citizens who are educated and skilled will immigrate to other labor markets, deepening the impoverishment of nations on the periphery.

Let's Discuss

1. For nations on the periphery, what might be some specific social and economic consequences of the global disconnect?
2. What factors might complicate efforts to remedy the global disconnect in developing nations?

NETWORKED READINESS INDEX

Top 10 Countries	Bottom 10 Countries
1. Finland	135. Mauritania
2. Singapore	136. Swaziland
3. Sweden	137. Madagascar
4. Netherlands	138. Lesotho
5. Norway	139. Yemen
6. Switzerland	140. Guinea
7. Great Britain	141. Haiti
8. Denmark	142. Chad
9. United States	143. Sierra Leone
10. Taiwan	144. Burundi

Sources: Anatale et al. 2013; Bilbao-Osorio et al. 2013; Castells 2010a; T. Thompson 2005.

men to be described as lacking in athletic ability. In contrast, male golfers receive more comments on their concentration and commitment. These findings suggest a subtle sexism, with women being portrayed as innately talented and men being portrayed as superior in mental or emotional makeup (T. Jacobs 2009).

Another aim of feminist research is to determine whether the media have a different impact on women than on men. Recently, researchers found that adolescent boys are almost three times as likely as adolescent girls to participate in online gaming. Young females who do participate are more likely than boy gamers to get into serious fights and report obesity. Clearly, this topic deserves further study (Desai et al. 2010).

A continuing, troubling issue for feminists and society as a whole is pornography. Feminists tend to be very supportive of freedom of expression and self-determination, rights that are denied to women more often than to men. Yet pornography presents women as sex objects and seems to make viewing women that way acceptable. Nor are concerns about pornography limited to this type of objectification and imagery, as well as their implicit endorsement of violence against women. The industry that creates risqué adult images for videos, DVDs, and the Internet is largely unregulated, even putting its performers at risk.

Feminist scholars are cautiously optimistic about new media. Although women are represented among bloggers, by some measures they are responsible for only about 10 percent of the most popular blogs. Still, in conservative cultures like Saudi Arabia, online media offer women the opportunity to explore lifestyles that traditional media outlets largely ignore (Jesella 2008; Worth 2008).

As in other areas of sociology, feminist researchers caution against assuming that what holds true for men's media use is true for everyone. Researchers, for example, have studied the different ways that women and men approach the Internet. Though men are only slightly more likely than women ever to have used the Internet, they are much more likely to use it daily. Yet according to a 2009 study, more women than men use the Internet. Not surprisingly, men account for 91 percent of the players in online sports fantasy leagues. Perhaps more socially significant, however, is the finding that women are more likely than men to maintain friendship networks through e-mail (Boase et al. 2006; Fallows 2006; Pew Internet Project 2009; Rainie 2005).

LO 19-2 Interactionist Perspective

Interactionists are especially interested in shared understandings of everyday behavior. These scholars examine the media on the micro level to see how they shape day-to-day social behavior. Increasingly, researchers talk about mass media in the context of *social capital,* as described by sociologist Pierre Bourdieu. **Social capital** is the collective benefit of social networks, which are built on reciprocal trust. The Internet generally, and social media in particular, offer us almost constant connectivity with others. These media increase our contact with family members, friends, and acquaintances, both those who live nearby and those who are far away. They also facilitate the development of new ties and new social networks (Bourdieu and Passerson 1990; Neves 2013).

Online social networks, in fact, have become a new way of promoting consumption. As Figure 6-2 shows, advertisers have traditionally marketed products and services through one-way spot ads, mass mailings, or billboards, whether they are promoting flat-screen televisions or public service messages like "Don't drink and drive." Now, using social networks, they can find consumers online and attempt to develop a two-way relationship with them there. Through Facebook, for example, Burger King awarded a free Whopper to anyone who would delete 10 friends. Facebook's staff was not happy with Burger King's promotion, which notified 239,906 Facebook users that they had been dropped for a burger—an action that violated the network's policy. Nevertheless, Burger King created a vast network of consumers who enjoy Whoppers. Similarly, Kraft Foods encouraged people to post images of the Wiener-mobile on the photo site Flickr (Bacon Lovers' Talk 2009; Burger King 2009; Gaudin 2009).

FIGURE 6-2 MARKETING ONLINE THROUGH SOCIAL NETWORKS

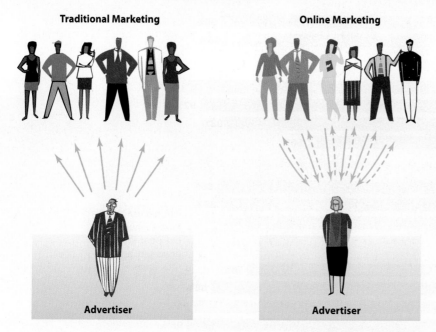

Traditional Marketing   Online Marketing

Advertiser   Advertiser

Traditional forms of advertising (left) allow only one-way communication, from the advertiser to the consumer. Online social networks (right) offer two-way communication, allowing advertisers to develop a relationship with consumers.

Relationship marketing is not the only new use for online social networks. In 2010, texting became a new source of philanthropy in the aftermath of the massive earthquake in Haiti.

Interactionists note, too, that friendship networks can emerge from shared viewing habits or from recollection of a cherished television series from the past. Family members and friends often gather for parties centered on the broadcasting of popular events such as the Super Bowl or the Academy Awards. And as we've seen, television often serves as a babysitter or playmate for children and even infants.

The rise of the Internet has also facilitated new forms of communication and social interaction. Grandparents can now keep up with their grandchildren via e-mail, or even watch them on their laptops via Skype. Gay and lesbian teens have online resources for support and information. People can even find their lifetime partners through computer dating services.

Some troubling issues have been raised about day-to-day life on the Internet, however. What, if anything, should be done about terrorists and other extremist groups who use the Internet to exchange messages of hatred and even bomb-making recipes? What, if anything, should be done about the issue of sexual expression on the Internet? How can children be protected from it? Should "hot chat" and X-rated film clips be censored? Or should expression be completely free?

Though the Internet has created a new platform for extremists, hate groups, and pornographers, it has also given people greater control over what they see and hear. That is, the Internet allows people to manage their media exposure so as to avoid sounds, images, and ideas they do not enjoy or approve of. The legal scholar Cass Sunstein (2002) has referred to this personalized approach to news information gathering as *egocasting*. One social consequence of this trend may be a less tolerant society. If we read, see, and hear only what we know and agree with, we may be much less prepared to meet people from different backgrounds or converse with those who express new viewpoints.

Study Alert

Be sure you are able to distinguish the differences between the functionalist, feminist, conflict, and interactionist perspectives on the mass media.

FIGURE 6-3 WHO'S ON THE INTERNET

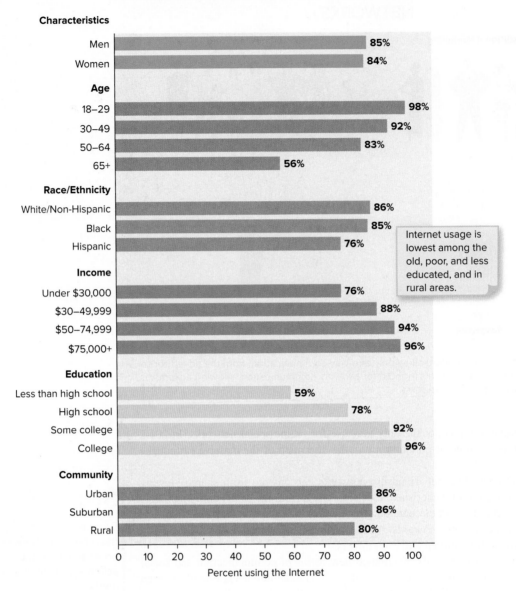

Characteristics

Men 85%
Women 84%

Age
18–29 98%
30–49 92%
50–64 83%
65+ 56%

Race/Ethnicity
White/Non-Hispanic 86%
Black 85%
Hispanic 76%

Income
Under $30,000 76%
$30–49,999 88%
$50–74,999 94%
$75,000+ 96%

Education
Less than high school 59%
High school 78%
Some college 92%
College 96%

Community
Urban 86%
Suburban 86%
Rural 80%

Internet usage is lowest among the old, poor, and less educated, and in rural areas.

Percent using the Internet

Note: Based on a national survey taken April–May 2013.
Source: Pew Internet and American Life Project 2013.

Furthermore, while many people in the United States embrace the Internet, we should note that information is not evenly distributed throughout the population. The same people, by and large, who experience poor health and have few job opportunities have been left off the information highway. Figure 6-3 breaks down Internet usage by gender, age, race, income, education, and community type. Note the large disparities in usage between those with high and low incomes, and between those with more and less education. The data also show a significant racial disparity. Though educators and politicians have touted the potential benefits to the disadvantaged, Internet usage may be reinforcing existing social-class and racial barriers.

The interactionist perspective helps us to understand one important aspect of the entire mass media system—the audience. How do we actively participate in media events? How do we construct with others the meaning of media messages? We will explore these questions in the section that follows. (Table 6-2 summarizes the various sociological perspectives on the media.)

TABLE 6-2 SOCIOLOGICAL PERSPECTIVES ON THE MASS MEDIA

Theoretical Perspective	Emphasis
Functionalist	Socialization
	Enforcement of social norms
	Conferral of status
	Promotion of consumption
	Narcotizing effect (dysfunction)
Conflict	Gatekeeping
	Media monitoring
	Construction of reality
	Digital divide
Feminist	Misrepresentation of women
	Differential impact on women
Interactionist	Impact on social behavior
	Source of friendship networks
	Social capital

E Evaluate

Read each question carefully and then select or provide the best answer.

1. The flow of content across multiple media and the coordinated use of different media simultaneously is called
   a. the digital divide.
   b. cultural convergence.
   c. role strain.
   d. hyperconsumerism.

2. Sociologist Robert Park studied how newspapers helped immigrants to the United States adjust to their environment by changing their customary habits and by teaching them the opinions held by people in their new home country. His study was conducted from which sociological perspective?
   a. the functionalist perspective
   b. the conflict perspective
   c. the interactionist perspective
   d. the dramaturgical perspective

3. Paul Lazarsfeld and Robert Merton created the term
   _____ _____ to refer to the phenomenon in which the media provide such massive amounts of information that the audience becomes numb and generally fails to act on the information, regardless of how compelling the issue.

4. Sociologists blame the mass media for the creation and perpetuation of _____, or generalizations about all members of a group that do not recognize individual differences within the group.

5. Both _____ and _____ theorists are troubled that the victims depicted in violent imagery are often those who are given less respect in real life: women, children, the poor, racial minorities, citizens of foreign countries, and even the physically disabled.

Answers

1 (b); 2 (a); 3 narcotizing dysfunction; 4 stereotypes; 5 conflict, feminist

R Rethink

Consider these questions to get a deeper understanding of the material.

1. What do you think is the most important function of the mass media in present-day U.S. society? Why?

2. People in the United States can now get their news from many different news sources rather than from just a few national TV networks. What effect has this had on the ability of the media to promote a dominant ideology?

RECAP

LO 19-1 Describe the social effects of the rapid spread of mass media.

- The mass media are print and electronic instruments of communication that carry messages to widespread audiences. They pervade all social institutions, from entertainment to education to politics.
- The media have grown so pervasive that the flow of content and the use of media by audiences can easily cross media devices in a phenomenon called cultural convergence.

LO 19-2 Interpret recent media trends from the point of view of the major sociological perspectives (functionalist, conflict, feminist, and interactionist).

- From the functionalist perspective, the media entertain, socialize, enforce social norms, confer status, and promote consumption. They can be dysfunctional to the extent that they desensitize us to serious events and issues, a phenomenon called the narcotizing dysfunction.
- Conflict theorists think the media reflect and even deepen the divisions in society through gatekeeping, or control over which material reaches the public; media monitoring, the covert observation of people's media usage and choices; and support of the dominant ideology, which defines reality, overwhelming local cultures.
- Feminist theorists point out that media images of the sexes communicate unrealistic, stereotypical, limiting, and sometimes violent perceptions of women.
- Interactionists examine the media on the micro level to see how they shape day-to-day social behavior. Interactionists have studied shared TV viewing and intergenerational use of e-mail and social media.

KEY TERMS

Cultural convergence The flow of content across multiple media, and the accompanying migration of media audiences.

Digital divide The relative lack of access to the latest technologies among low-income groups, racial and ethnic minorities, rural residents, and the citizens of developing countries.

Dominant ideology A set of cultural beliefs and practices that helps to maintain powerful social, economic, and political interests.

Gatekeeping The process by which a relatively small number of people in the media industry control what material eventually reaches the audience.

Hyperconsumerism The practice of buying more than we need or want, and often more than we can afford; a preoccupation of postmodern consumers.

Hyper-local media Reporting that is highly local and typically Internet-based.

Mass media Print and electronic means of communication that carry messages to widespread audiences.

Narcotizing dysfunction The phenomenon in which the media provide such massive amounts of coverage that the audience becomes numb and fails to act on the information, regardless of how compelling the issue.

Social capital The collective benefit of social networks, which are built on reciprocal trust.

Stereotype An unreliable generalization about all members of a group that does not recognize individual differences within the group.

MODULE 20 The Audience

 **Prepare** Learning Objective

LO 20-1 Summarize the aspects of an audience from the level of both microsociology and macrosociology.

Organize Module Outline

Who Is in the Audience?
  The Segmented Audience
  Audience Behavior

Ever feel like text-messaging everyone you know, to encourage them to vote for your favorite performer on a certain reality program? Ever looked over someone's shoulder as he watched last week's episode of *American Idol* on his iPhone—and been tempted to reveal the ending to him? Ever come across an old CD and tried to remember the last time you or a friend listened to one, or heard the songs in the order in which they were recorded? In this and many other ways, we are reminded that we are all part of a larger audience.

LO **20-1** Who Is in the Audience?

The mass media are distinguished from other social institutions by the necessary presence of an audience. It can be an identifiable, finite group, such as an audience at a jazz club or a Broadway musical, or a much larger and undefined group, such as *Dancing with the Stars* viewers or readers of the same issue of *USA Today*. The audience may be a secondary group gathered in a large auditorium or a primary group, such as a family watching the latest Disney video at home.

We can look at the audience from the level of both *microsociology* and *macrosociology*. At the micro level, we might consider how audience members, interacting among themselves, respond to the media, or in the case of live performances, actually influence the performers. At the macro level, we might examine broader societal consequences of the media, such as the early childhood education delivered through programming like *Sesame Street*.

Even if an audience is spread out over a wide geographic area and members don't know one another, it is still distinctive in terms of age, gender, income, political party, formal schooling, race, and ethnicity. The audience for a ballet, for example, would likely differ substantially from the audience for alternative music.

THE SEGMENTED AUDIENCE

Increasingly, the media are marketing themselves to a *particular* audience. Once a media outlet, such as a radio station or a magazine, has identified its audience, it targets that group. To some degree, this specialization is driven by advertising. Media specialists have sharpened their ability, through survey research, to identify particular target audiences. Thus, during the midterm elections in 2010, the two major political parties placed TV advertisements in markets where surveys indicated they would find support. For example, the Republican Party placed ads on college football games and *America's Funniest Home Videos*. The Democratic Party bought time on *Dr. Phil* (Parker 2010).

The specialized targeting of audiences has led some scholars to question the "mass" in mass media. For example, the British social psychologist Sonia Livingstone (2004) has written that the media have become so segmented, they have taken on the appearance almost of individualization. Are viewing audiences so segmented that large collective audiences are a thing of the past? That is not yet clear. Even though we seem to be living in an age of *personal* computers, large formal organizations still do transmit public messages that reach a sizable, heterogeneous, and scattered audience.

AUDIENCE BEHAVIOR

Sociologists have long researched how audiences interact with one another and how they share information after a media event. The role of audience members as opinion leaders particularly intrigues social researchers. An **opinion leader** is someone who influences the opinions and decisions of others through day-to-day personal contact and communication. For example, a movie or theater critic functions as an opinion leader. Sociologist Paul Lazarsfeld and his colleagues (1948) pioneered the study of opinion leaders in their

> **Study Alert**
>
> It is important to be able to distinguish a microsociological view of an audience from a macrosociological view in order to differentiate between individual and broader societal impacts.

research on voting behavior in the 1940s. They found that opinion leaders encourage their relatives, friends, and co-workers to think positively about a particular candidate, perhaps pushing them to listen to the politician's speeches or read the campaign literature.

Despite the role of opinion leaders, members of an audience do not all interpret media in the same way. Often their response is influenced by their social characteristics, such as occupation, race, education, and income. Take the example of the televised news coverage of the riots in Los Angeles in 1992. The riots were an angry response to the acquittal of two White police officers accused of severely beating a Black motorist. Sociologist Darnell Hunt (1997) wondered how the social composition of audience members would affect the way they interpreted the news coverage. Hunt gathered 15 groups from the Los Angeles area, whose members were equally divided among Whites, Blacks, and Latinos. He showed each group a 17-minute clip from the televised coverage of the riots and asked members to discuss how they would describe what they had just seen to a 12-year-old. In analyzing the discussions, Hunt found that although gender and class did not cause respondents to vary their answers much, race did.

Hunt went beyond noting simple racial differences in perceptions; he analyzed how the differences were manifested. For example, Black viewers were much more likely than Latinos or Whites to refer to the events in terms of "us" versus "them." Another difference was that Black and Latino viewers were more animated and critical than White viewers as they watched the film clip. White viewers tended to sit quietly, still and unquestioning, suggesting that they were more comfortable with the news coverage than the Blacks or Latinos.

E Evaluate

Read each question carefully and then select or provide the best answer.

1. Sociologist Paul Lazarsfeld and his colleagues pioneered the study of
   a. the audience.
   b. opinion leaders.
   c. the media's global reach.
   d. media violence.

2. In his study of how the social composition of audience members affected how they interpreted the news coverage of riots in Los Angeles in 1992, sociologist Darnell Hunt found what kind of differences in perception?
   a. racial
   b. gender
   c. class
   d. religious

3. The division of audiences into target groups based on such characteristics as age, gender, income, political party, education, race, and ethnicity is called audience _____.

Answers

1 (b); 2 (a); 3 segmentation

R Rethink

Consider these questions to get a deeper understanding of the material.

1. What type of audience is targeted by the producers of professional wrestling on TV? *American Idol*? A family comedy? What factors determine the makeup of a particular audience?

2. Who do you consider to be personal opinion leaders? Why are those people influential to you? Would your parents, teachers, or friends choose the same opinion leaders? Why or why not?

RECAP

LO 20-1 Summarize the aspects of an audience from the level of both microsociology and macrosociology.

- The mass media require the presence of an audience, whether it is small and well defined or large and amorphous.
- We can analyze the audience from the micro level, considering the reactions of audience members to the media, or from the macro level, examining the broad effects of the media on society.
- As media outlets have increased in number, media marketers have increasingly targeted more segmented (or specialized) audiences.
- Social researchers have studied the role of opinion leaders in influencing audiences.
- Despite the influence of opinion leaders, audience members do not all interpret media the same way. Other factors, such as occupation, race, gender, education, and income, influence audience response.

KEY TERMS

Opinion leader Someone who influences the opinions and decisions of others through day-to-day personal contact and communication.

MODULE 21 The Media's Global Reach

P Prepare | Learning Objectives

LO 21-1 Describe the global nature of the media and the societal effects of media spread.
LO 21-2 Analyze the pros and cons of creating social policy to regulate the media.

O Organize | Module Outline

The Global Nature of the Media
Social Policy and the Mass Media
    The Right to Privacy

W Work

LO 21-1 The Global Nature of the Media

Has the rise of the electronic media created a *global village*? Canadian media theorist Marshall McLuhan predicted it would nearly 50 years ago. Today, physical distance is no longer a barrier, and instant messaging is possible across the world. The mass media have indeed created a global village. Not all countries are equally connected, as Figure 6-4

FIGURE 6-4 MEDIA PENETRATION IN SELECTED COUNTRIES

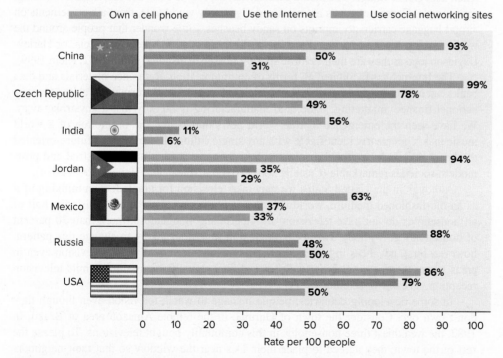

Legend: Own a cell phone | Use the Internet | Use social networking sites

- China: 93%, 50%, 31%
- Czech Republic: 99%, 78%, 49%
- India: 56%, 11%, 6%
- Jordan: 94%, 35%, 29%
- Mexico: 63%, 37%, 33%
- Russia: 88%, 48%, 50%
- USA: 86%, 79%, 50%

Rate per 100 people (0 – 100)

Note: Data from multinational interviews of 26,210 adults, March–April 2012.
Source: Pew Research Center Global Attitudes Project 2012:1, 5.

Cell phone ownership is high around the world, but in some countries outside the United States, texting is more common than calling.

In 2012 "Sexy and I Know It," by the LMFAO duo of SkyBlu and Redfoo, was the most frequently downloaded cell phone ringtone. Because today's media provide multiple services, music fans can use the Internet to access recorded music and listen to it on their cell phones (Billboard 2012).

shows, but the progress has been staggering, considering that voice transmission was just beginning 100 years ago (McLuhan 1964, 1967).

Sociologist Todd Gitlin considers *global torrent* a more apt metaphor for the media's reach than *global village*. The media permeate all aspects of everyday life. Take advertising, for example. Consumer goods are marketed vigorously worldwide, from advertisements on airport baggage carriers to imprints on sandy beaches. Little wonder that people around the world develop loyalty to a brand and are as likely to sport a Nike, Coca-Cola, or Harley-Davidson logo as they are their favorite soccer or baseball insignia (Gitlin 2002; Klein 1999).

The Internet has facilitated all forms of communication. Reference materials and data banks can now be made accessible across national boundaries. Information related to international finance, marketing, trade, and manufacturing is literally just a keystroke away. We have seen the emergence of true world news outlets and the promotion of a world music that is not clearly identifiable with any single culture. Even the most future-oriented thinker would find the growth in the reach of the mass media in postindustrial and post-modern societies remarkable (Castells 2001, 2010b; Croteau and Haynes 2006, 2014).

Although in the United States we may take television for granted, even thinking of it as an old-fashioned medium, worldwide that is not necessarily the case. In India, half of all households do not have television; in Nigeria and Bangladesh, more than 70 percent of households go without. Two technological advances are likely to change this pattern, however. First, advances in battery power now allow viewers to watch television even in areas where there is no electricity. Second, digital signal transmission permits television reception via cable or satellite.

In some developing countries, people manage to watch television even though they don't own one. Consider the town of Gurupá, in the remote Amazon area of Brazil. In 1982, the wealthiest three households in this community bought televisions. To please the rest of the town, they agreed to place their TVs near the window so that their neighbors could watch them as well. As the TV owners proudly displayed their new status symbol, TV watching became a community social activity. The introduction of a new technology had created a new social norm (Kenny 2009; Pace 1993, 1998).

Media use can take on added importance in developing nations. Consider Kenya, a nation the size of Texas. During a recent malaria outbreak, public health researchers monitored the text messages Kenyans sent on their 15 million cell phones and used the content to map the spread of the dreaded disease. Surprisingly, they found that travelers were carrying the disease along less-traveled regional routes rather than the heavily traveled roads to and from the capital city, Nairobi. The information they gleaned proved vital to them in concentrating malaria control efforts (Wesolowski et al. 2012).

Around the world, people rely increasingly on digital media, from cell phones to the Internet. This trend has raised new concerns about the right to privacy. Should government officials have the right to monitor people's text messages, even if they are protecting the public's health? The Social Policy section that follows examines the social implications of digital media, from censorship to criminal activity.

LO 21-2 **SOCIAL POLICY** and the Mass Media

New technologies can create new social norms. In Gurupá, Brazil, television watching became a community social activity when three new TV owners agreed to share their sets with the community of 3,000.

We have seen that researchers rely on a number of tools, from simple observational research to the latest in computer technologies. Because in the real world sociological research can have far-reaching consequences for public policy and public welfare, let's consider its impact on the right to privacy.

THE RIGHT TO PRIVACY

"You have no privacy anyway. Get over it," the CEO of Sun Microsystems stated bluntly in 1999. A little more than a decade later, speaking at an awards ceremony, Facebook founder Mark Zuckerberg claimed that people no longer expect to have privacy, given the rise of social media. In his view, privacy is no longer a "social norm" (Carr 2010:W2, Bobbie Johnson 2010).

If there was any doubt about the effect of the new mass media on people's privacy, it disappeared in 2013 when Edward Snowden, an IT specialist working as a contractor to the U.S. government, began leaking information about the National Security Agency's data-gathering activities. The NSA is charged with gathering intelligence on foreign security threats, both within the United States and abroad. However, Snowden revealed that in an operation code-named PRISM, agency sleuths had been secretly gathering huge amounts of information on ordinary citizens by infiltrating their accounts at some of the nation's largest technology companies—Google, Apple, Microsoft, Facebook, AOL, YouTube, and Yahoo. In light of such revelations, we might ask whether any of us can expect to keep our private information private in the postmodern digital age.

This sweeping challenge to privacy comes from **big data**, a term coined by sociologist Charles Tilly (1980) to refer to the rapid collection and analysis of enormous amounts of information by supercomputers. The accumulation of digital data has made it increasingly easy for business firms, government agencies, and even criminals to retrieve and store information about private individuals. In public places, at work, and on the Internet, surveillance devices track our every move, whether it is a keystroke or an ATM withdrawal. The information they accumulate includes everything from our buying habits to our web-surfing patterns.

As these technologies increase the power to monitor our behavior, they raise fears of their misuse for criminal or even undemocratic purposes. In short, they threaten not

just our privacy, but our freedom from crime and censorship as well. Some obvious violations of privacy, such as identity theft—the misuse of credit card and Social Security numbers to masquerade as another person—have been well documented. Other violations involve online surveillance of dissident political groups by authoritarian regimes and the unauthorized release of classified government documents. In 2010, WikiLeaks released thousands of classified U.S. foreign policy documents on its website, causing some people to condemn the action as treasonous and others to praise it as a blow against government censorship (O'Harrow Jr. 2005).

From the perspective of . . .

An Airport Security Officer What types of surveillance do you think should be allowable to monitor passengers?

Other privacy violations are subtler, and not strictly illegal. For example, many commercial websites use "cookies" and tracking technology to monitor visitors' websurfing. Using that information, marketers can estimate a visitor's age, gender, and zip code, and from that data, the person's income. They can then select advertisements that will appeal specifically to that person. So depending on who we are, or at least appear to be, one of us might see ads about weight-loss products and another, ads about travel to exotic locations.

Is this approach to online marketing just effective advertising, or is it an invasion of privacy? Because the information that marketers gather in this way can be tied to other devices a person uses, such as a cell phone or computer, some critics see online tracking as a form of fingerprinting (Angwin 2010; Angwin and Valentino-DeVries 2010a).

Applying Sociology to the Media From a sociological point of view, the complex issues of privacy and censorship can be considered illustrations of **culture lag**, a period of maladjustment when the nonmaterial culture is still struggling to adapt to new material conditions. As usual, the material culture (technology) is changing faster than the nonmaterial culture (norms for controlling the use of technology). Too often, the result is an anything-goes approach to the use of new technologies.

Sociologists' views on the use and abuse of new technologies differ depending on their theoretical perspective. Functionalists take a generally positive view of the Internet, pointing to its manifest function of facilitating communication. From their perspective, the Internet performs the latent function of empowering people with few resources—from hate groups to special-interest organizations—to communicate with the masses.

Functionalists also note that digital surveillance can assist law enforcement agencies in preventing or detecting crimes in progress. For example, facial recognition technology can be used to identify stalkers, find lost children, or even track terrorists. Yet they admit that warrantless surveillance of people who lead mostly normal lives is dysfunctional.

In contrast, conflict theorists stress the danger that the most powerful groups in a society will use technology to violate the privacy of the less powerful.

A Google Street View car drives through an English town, photographing it for use with Google's online map service. Even though Google's activities occur largely on public property, people have objected to them as an invasion of privacy. Some of the images Google captures include bystanders who happen to be in the area, as well as people's backyards and even the interior of their homes, as seen through open windows and doors.

Interactionists observe that making our web profiles and other information about ourselves publicly available may affect our future social interactions, and not necessarily for the good. One out of four college and university admissions officers reports Googling or checking out applicants' social media pages. Over a third of those gatekeepers have found something online that can hurt applicants (Belkin and Porter 2012).

Initiating Media Policy Legislation regarding the surveillance of electronic communications has not always upheld citizens' right to privacy. In 1986, the federal government passed the Electronic Communications Privacy Act, which outlawed the surveillance of telephone calls except with the permission of both the U.S. attorney general and a federal judge. Telegrams, faxes, and e-mails did not receive the same degree of protection, however. In 2001, one month after the terrorist attacks of September 11, Congress passed the Patriot Act, which relaxed existing legal checks on surveillance by law enforcement officers. Federal agencies are now freer to gather data electronically, including people's credit card receipts and banking records (Gertner 2005).

Today, most other types of online monitoring have yet to be tested in court, including the use of tracking technologies and the compilation and sale of personal profiles to merchandisers. Consistent with the concept of culture lag, privacy advocates complain that the 1986 law, which was enacted before the Internet as we know it even existed, has not kept pace with advancing technology. For example, in 2011 federal and state courts approved a total of 2,732 wiretaps using Supreme Court–approved methods that date back to 1928. However, in the same year government agencies made well over a million requests of mobile-phone companies for information on cell phone users—requests that require only a subpoena, not court approval. Many of those requests included "tower dumps," which reveal the whereabouts of every-one in the area with a cell phone, suspects or not. Such sweeps resemble the NSA's PRISM operation in their indiscriminate nature. To date, proposed legislation has focused mainly on the consumer side of privacy. For example, in 2012 the Federal Trade Commission issued a strong call for legislation that would require companies like Google to respect Internet users' privacy by adding a "Do Not Track" button to their browsers (Angwin 2012; *The Economist* 2013c).

If anything, however, people seem to be less vigilant about maintaining their privacy today than they were before the information age. Young people who have grown up browsing the Internet seem to accept the existence of the "cookies" and "spyware" they may pick up while surfing. They have become accustomed to adult surveillance of their conversation in electronic chat rooms. And many see no risk in providing personal information about themselves to strangers they meet online. Little wonder that college professors find their students do not appreciate the political significance of their right to privacy (Turkle 2004, 2011).

The need for online privacy seems only to be increasing, however. In a new practice called *weblining,* data-gathering companies are monitoring people's online activities not so much for merchandising purposes, but to collect negative personal information. Based on this information, collected from the websites people search or the products and people they friend, a person may be denied a job opportunity or assigned a low credit rating. Data-gathering companies also offer information on searches having to do with mental issues like bipolar disorder and anxiety, which can make it difficult for a person to secure affordable health insurance. Although weblining has not yet drawn policymakers' attention, it is sure to do so in the future (Andrews 2012).

George Orwell's novel *Nineteen Eighty-Four* describes a future in which all citizens suffer intensive surveillance by the government ("Big Brother"). In this poster for the 1956 motion picture version, Big Brother hovers over editor Winston Smith, played by Edmund O'Brien.

In the near future, new technological innovations will again redefine the limits of surveillance. Sensors are being installed in more and more objects, from appliances to electronic readers, to facilitate their use. It is only a matter of time before manufacturers begin compiling big data on how we use our refrigerators and microwaves, on what we read or scan down to the sentence level. Some corporations are installing sensors on security badges, to record employees' movements and conversations.

To many people, there is a fine line between this use of big data and Big Brother, a fictional character in George Orwell's *Nineteen Eighty-Four.* Published in 1949, the novel describes a future in which the government, directed by the quasi-divine leader Big Brother, secretly scrutinizes people's every move, then manipulates their view of society and even themselves. Little wonder that in 2013, sales of *Nineteen Eighty-Four* increased 7,000 percent within a week of news about Edward Snowden's leaks (Orwell 1949; Price 2013; Silverman 2013).

E Evaluate

Read each question carefully and then select or provide the best answer.

1. In the 1960s, a Canadian media theorist predicted that the rise of electronic media would lead to the emergence of a "global village." The name of this theorist is
   a. George Orwell.
   b. Mark Zuckerberg.
   c. Charles Tilly.
   d. Marshall McLuhan.

2. From a sociological point of view, the current controversy over privacy and media censorship illustrates the concept of
   _____ _____.

Answers

1 (d); 2 culture lag

R Rethink

Consider these questions to get a deeper understanding of the material.

1. Use the functionalist, conflict, and interactionist perspectives to assess the effects of global TV programming on developing countries.

2. Discuss how the values of freedom of speech, right to privacy, and national security conflict in considerations of regulating the media. Which of the three values do you think is most important? Why?

RECAP

LO 21-1 Describe the global nature of the media and the societal effects of media spread.

- The media have a global reach thanks to new communications technologies, especially the Internet.
- In the postmodern digital age, new technologies that facilitate the collection and sharing of personal information are threatening people's right to privacy.
- Similarly, new communication technologies threaten the security of individuals and nations.

LO 21-2 Analyze the pros and cons of creating social policy to regulate the media.

- Efforts to design social policy to regulate the media must deal with a confusing array of social values, including the right to privacy, the need for security, and the sanctity of freedom of speech.
- Each value—a pro—has at least one corresponding counter-value—a con. No universally acceptable solutions to abuses of the media have yet been fashioned by policy leaders.

KEY TERMS

Big data The rapid collection and analysis of enormous amounts of information by supercomputers.

Culture lag A period of maladjustment when the nonmaterial culture is still struggling to adapt to new material conditions.

The Case of . . . Tweeting Her Life Away?

Daria Harper spins fantasies about the good life and hopes we'll buy her visions, or more accurately, the products she pushes. Harper is an account executive at a large New York City advertising firm. Her greatest tool? The explosion of available media options. "It's not just *where* we place our ads," Harper says. "It's also about mining the trends and capturing the data." She feels she literally could not do the job clients expect without the Internet—especially social networking sites—and her smartphone, both of which keep her in touch with trends in other media like film and television. "Better and faster than any assistant I could hire," she says.

On a typical day, Harper tracks over 50 Twitter feeds to map consumer feedback, preferences, and needs related to whatever products her firm is advertising. "I have to follow the competition, too," she says. Harper also subscribes to a service that streams the newest television ads in categories she preselects to her via the Internet. "That's my lunchtime viewing," she admits. In the evenings, Harper surfs the Internet looking for global trends in categories like cars, food, clothing, liquor, entertainment, furniture, and politics. "My job is all about lifestyle—creating and promoting a certain lifestyle based on what products my clients need to sell," she says. "But that fantasy lifestyle has to be connected to what's happening, everywhere, out there. I have to know what's hot and then try to jump one step ahead of that. It's my whole life, really."

1. Is Harper a "gatekeeper"? Reflect on the decisions she makes in developing an ad campaign as you give reasons for your answer.

2. In what ways is advertising used to confer status? Give some examples.

3. Harper refers to the "fantasy lifestyle" that is the world she creates for her clients' products. Do you think advertising, in part, constructs reality? Why or why not?

4. Could Harper's ad firm and others like it be considered "opinion leaders"? Why or why not?

What's Your Personality Type?

In addition to learning styles, people have personalities that can also affect success in school and life. Introverted people, for instance, tend to avoid speaking up in class, and teachers may mark them down for nonparticipation. On the other hand, rational thinkers may be favored by the U.S. education system, compared with more intuitive people. Use the accompanying P.O.W.E.R. plan to get a sense of your personality—and to figure out how to make it work for you.

- Think about your personality by considering your personal experiences in different situations.

- Use a study group, if possible, to explore your personality style.

- Think of your experiences in school, extracurricular activities, work, or other settings.
- While most people fall between the end points described next, you should be able to place yourself on these four dimensions.
  Are you more:
    - an **extravert** or an **introvert**? **Extraverts** like working with others and considering their thoughts and actions. **Introverts** prefer to work independently and are less affected by others' ideas.
    - an **intuitor** or a **sensor**? **Intuitors** are "big-picture people," solving problems creatively by making leaps of judgment, but showing little patience for details. **Sensors** are "detail people," preferring a concrete, logical approach and carefully analyzing facts, but sometimes missing the big picture.
    - a **thinker** or a **feeler**? **Thinkers** prefer logic over emotion, making decisions systematically. **Feelers** rely on emotional responses and are influenced by personal values and attachments to others.
    - a **judger** or a **perceiver**? **Judgers** are quick to decide and like to set goals, accomplish them, and move on. **Perceivers** try to gather as much information as possible and look at all sides of an issue—which sometimes interferes with task completion.

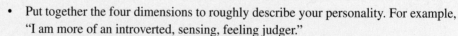

- Put together the four dimensions to roughly describe your personality. For example, "I am more of an introverted, sensing, feeling judger."
- Discuss the consequences of your personality with your study group.

- Apply what you know about your personality to your education, work, family life, and other aspects of your life.

You've Got Personality

Use the following checklist to identify four aspects of your personality: extravert/introvert, intuitor/sensor, thinker/feeler, and judger/perceiver. Every aspect of your personality has a strength you can exploit to be more successful in school, and in life.

	That's Me	Not Me
1. I enjoy completing a project on my own.		
2. I rarely follow recipes. It's more fun cooking with what's at hand.		
3. I try to never let my emotions affect my judgment.		
4. I like to mull things over. A compelling argument can change my mind.		
5. A perfect holiday for me would be renting a cabin with friends.		
6. I like to have all the facts at hand before I analyze a situation.		
7. I believe our emotions give us vital clues as to what's really right for us.		
8. I keep a to-do list and enjoy crossing off each task as I finish it.		
9. I like to work in groups so we can share ideas and problem-solve together.		
10. In a new situation, I follow my hunches to decide what action to take.		
11. I like to develop a system for everything. It makes life easier.		
12. I pride myself on considering all points of view in an important issue.		
13. I prefer to travel alone so that I can see and do the things that interest me.		
14. Before starting a project, I make a plan or outline so I don't miss steps.		
15. I rely on my personal values to guide my decisions.		
16. Shopping is easy for me. I know what I like and I make decisions quickly.		

Tick off the item numbers below that you rated **That's Me** to find your personality type and tips for making use of your individual style:

Extravert: _____ 5, _____ 9 Study in groups and develop projects with others.

Introvert: _____ 1, _____ 13 Seek tasks you can complete independently.

Intuitor: _____ 2, _____ 10 Seek tasks that allow for creative solutions.

Sensor: _____ 6, _____ 14 Choose concrete tasks where you can apply logical principles.

Thinker: _____ 3, _____ 11 Analyze situations systematically and look for patterns.

Feeler: _____ 7, _____ 15 Use your emotional responses to enrich your understanding of material.

Perceiver: _____ 4, _____ 12 Seek projects where you can explore and analyze multiple viewpoints.

Judger: _____ 8, _____ 16 Use goal-setting to facilitate learning.

7 Deviance, Crime, and Social Control

Sociology at **WORK** ELEMENTARY TEACHER

CALEB LEWIS teaches second grade at a school in the Bronx. While he emphasizes the traditional three Rs, he's also strong on what he calls the Social Rs: rules, rights, respect. "Most of my kids come from struggling families," Lewis says. "The adults in their lives have not had many breaks. They are doing their best, but often it's all they can do to feed the kids. Many of my students have experienced homelessness. It's a tough life that doesn't give you much in the way of what the dominant culture calls 'normal.'" That's where Lewis's Social Rs come in. "To succeed in school or the world, you need to know the rules. What behavior is expected of you," he says. Each year, Lewis and his students draw up a list of classroom rules. "We talk about what behaviors help everyone in the room, and what behaviors hurt or interfere with others' education." This leads naturally into the second R: rights. "I tell them, 'You got a right to learn. A right to feel safe in this school. A right to be heard. But others have the same rights. That's when we start talking about the third R, respect." How do students react to Lewis's Social Rs? "They calm to them," he says. "It gives the kids a sense of self-control and safety to know what is expected of them, what they can expect from others, a way to live together." ■

Looking Ahead

THIS CHAPTER EXAMINES THE RELATIONSHIPS AMONG DEVIANCE AND conformity, crime and social control. We will begin by defining deviance and describing the stigma that is associated with it. Then we will distinguish between conformity and obedience, and examine a surprising experiment on obedience to authority. We will study the mechanisms societies use, both formal and informal, to encourage conformity and discourage deviance, paying particular attention to the law and how it reflects our social values.

Next, we will focus on theoretical explanations for deviance, including the functionalist approach; interactionist-based theories; labeling theory, which draws on both the interactionist and the conflict perspectives; and conflict theory. In the last part of the chapter we will focus on crime, a specific type of deviant behavior. We will look at various types of crime found in the United States, the ways crime is measured, and international crime rates. Finally, the Social Policy section considers the controversial topic of gun control.

MODULE 22 Deviance

 **Prepare** | Learning Objectives

LO 22-1 Explain the concept of deviance as it is understood by sociologists.

LO 22-2 Compare and contrast the understanding of deviance offered by the three major perspectives, labeling theory, and the feminist perspective.

W Work

LO **22-1** What Is Deviance?

For sociologists, the term *deviance* does not mean perversion or depravity. **Deviance** is behavior that violates the standards of conduct or expectations of a group or society. In the United States, alcoholics, compulsive gamblers, and people with mental illness would all be classified as deviants. Being late for class is categorized as a deviant act; the same is true of wearing jeans to a formal wedding. On the basis of the sociological definition, we are all deviant from time to time. Each of us violates common social norms in certain situations (Best 2004).

Is being overweight an example of deviance? In the United States and many other cultures, unrealistic standards of appearance and body image place a huge strain on people—especially women and girls—based on how they look. Journalist Naomi Wolf (1992) has used the term *beauty myth* to refer to an exaggerated ideal of beauty, beyond the reach of all but a few females, which has unfortunate consequences. In order to shed their "deviant" image and conform to unrealistic societal norms, many women and girls become consumed with adjusting their appearances. Yet what is deviant in one culture may be celebrated in another.

Deviance involves the violation of group norms, which may or may not be formalized into law. It is a comprehensive concept that includes not only criminal behavior but also many actions that are not subject to prosecution. The public official who takes a bribe has defied social norms, but so has the high school student who refuses to sit in an assigned seat or cuts class. Of course, deviation from norms is not always negative. A member of an exclusive social club who speaks out against a traditional policy of not admitting women, Blacks, and Jews is deviating from the club's norms. So is a police officer who blows the whistle on corruption or brutality within the department.

What is considered deviant can shift from one social era to another. In most instances, those with the greatest status and power define what is acceptable and what is deviant. For example, despite serious medical warnings against the dangers of tobacco, made since 1964, cigarette smoking continued to be accepted for decades—in good part because of the power of tobacco farmers and cigarette manufacturers. Only after a long campaign led by public health and anticancer activists did cigarette smoking become more of a deviant activity. Today, many state and local laws limit where people can smoke.

In 2009, baseball fans were shocked by the revelation that like several other baseball greats, superstar Alex Rodriguez had used banned substances and lied about it. In 2013, he was suspended for 211 games, including the entire 2014 season.

LO **22-1** Deviance and Social Stigma

A person can acquire a deviant identity in many ways. Because of physical or behavioral characteristics, some people are unwillingly cast in negative social roles. Once assigned a deviant role, they have trouble presenting a positive image to others and may even experience lowered self-esteem. Whole groups of people—for instance, "short people" or "redheads"—may be labeled in this way. The interactionist Erving Goffman coined the term **stigma** to describe the labels society uses to devalue members of certain social groups (Goffman 1963; Heckert and Best 1997).

In the aftermath of the 2012 school shooting in Newtown, Connecticut, the issue of mental illness surfaced almost immediately, amid rumors that the shooter suffered from an untreated mental disorder. In many people's eyes, such assumptions stigmatize all people with mental illness, whatever the definition of the term, as potentially violent criminals. Overwhelming evidence shows that the opposite is true, however: the vast majority of people with psychiatric disorders do *not* commit violent acts. Only 4 percent of violent crimes in the United States can be attributed to people with mental illness. Gun violence is discussed further in the Social Policy section at the end of this chapter, on gun control (R. Friedman 2012; Nocera 2012).

Stigmatization also affects people who look different from others in the eyes of their peers. Prevailing expectations about beauty and body shape may prevent people who are regarded as ugly or obese from advancing as rapidly as their abilities permit. Both overweight and anorexic people are assumed to be weak in character, slaves to their appetites or to media images. Because they do not conform to the beauty myth, they may be viewed as "disfigured" or "strange" in appearance, bearers of what Goffman calls a "spoiled identity." However, what constitutes disfigurement is a matter of interpretation. Of the 17 million cosmetic procedures done every year in the United States alone, many are performed on women who would be defined objectively as having a normal appearance. And while feminist sociologists have accurately noted that the beauty myth makes many women feel uncomfortable with themselves, men too lack confidence in their appearance. The number of males who choose to undergo cosmetic procedures has risen sharply in recent years (American Academy of Cosmetic Surgery 2010).

Often people are stigmatized for deviant behaviors they may no longer engage in. The labels "compulsive gambler," "ex-convict," "recovering alcoholic," and "ex–mental patient" can stick to a person for life. Goffman draws a useful distinction between a prestige symbol that draws attention to a positive aspect of one's identity, such as a wedding band or a badge, and a stigma symbol that discredits or debases one's identity, such as a conviction for child molestation. While stigma symbols may not always be obvious, they can become a matter of public knowledge. Starting in 1994, many states required convicted sex offenders to register with local police departments. Some communities publish the names and addresses, and in some instances even the pictures, of convicted sex offenders on the web.

While some types of deviance will stigmatize a person, other types do not carry a significant penalty. Examples of socially tolerated forms of deviance can be found in the world of high technology.

Deviant or normal? Television personality and recording artist Heidi Montag shocked fans in 2010 by revealing that she had undergone 10 plastic surgery procedures in a single day. Montag had already undergone breast augmentation, collagen lip injections, and rhinoplasty. Would you consider her behavior deviant?

Study Alert

Deviance involves the violation of group or societal norms, including not only criminal behavior but also many actions that are not subject to prosecution, whereas *stigma* describes the labels society uses to devalue members of certain social groups who they feel are deviant in some way.

In Finland (left), a young man relaxes in his prison cell, which resembles a college dorm room. In the United States (right), prisoners at a super-maximum-security prison watch television in cages that prevent them from making physical contact with guards or other prisoners. The rate of imprisonment in Finland is less than one-half that of England and one-fourth that of the United States.

LO 22-1 Deviance and Technology

Technological innovations such as pagers and voice mail can redefine social interactions and the standards of behavior related to them. When the Internet was first made available to the general public, no norms or regulations governed its use. Because online communication offers a high degree of anonymity, uncivil behavior—speaking harshly of others or monopolizing chat room space—quickly became common. Online bulletin boards designed to carry items of community interest became littered with commercial advertisements. Such deviant acts are beginning to provoke calls for the establishment of formal rules for online behavior. For example, policymakers have debated whether to regulate the content of websites featuring hate speech and pornography.

Some deviant uses of technology are criminal, though not all participants see it that way. On the street, the for-profit pirating of software, motion pictures, and music has become a big business. On the Internet, the downloading of music by individual listeners, which is typically forbidden by copyright, is widely accepted. The music and motion picture industries have waged much publicized campaigns to stop these illegal uses of their products, yet among many people, no social stigma attaches to them. Deviance, then, is a complex concept. Sometimes it is trivial, sometimes profoundly harmful. Sometimes it is accepted by society and sometimes soundly rejected.

LO 22-2 Sociological Perspectives on Deviance

Social control refers to the techniques and strategies for preventing deviant behavior in any society. Deviant acts are subject to both informal and formal social controls. **Informal social control** is used to casually enforce norms. **Formal social control** is carried out by authorized agents, such as police officers, employers, military offices, and managers of movie theaters. The nonconforming or disobedient person may face disapproval, loss of friends, fines, or even imprisonment. Why, then, does deviance occur?

Early explanations for behavior that deviated from societal expectations blamed supernatural causes or genetic factors (such as "bad blood" or evolutionary throwbacks to primitive ancestors). By the 1800s, substantial research efforts were made to identify biological factors that lead to deviance, and especially to criminal activity. Though such research was discredited in the 20th century, contemporary studies, primarily by biochemists, have sought

In Singapore, a custodian removes a bit of litter from an otherwise spotless floor. Strict social controls prevail in the city-state, where the careless disposal of a cigarette butt or candy wrapper carries a $200 fine.

to isolate genetic factors that suggest a likelihood of certain personality traits. Although criminality (much less deviance) is hardly a personality characteristic, researchers have focused on traits that might lead to crime, such as aggression. Of course, aggression can also lead to success in the corporate world, in professional sports, or in other walks of life.

The contemporary study of the possible biological roots of criminality is but one aspect of the larger debate over sociobiology. In general, sociologists have been critical of any emphasis on the genetic roots of crime and deviance. The limitations of current knowledge about the link between genetics and antisocial behavior have led them to draw largely on other approaches to explain deviance (Walsh 2000).

FUNCTIONALIST PERSPECTIVE

According to functionalists, deviance is a common part of human existence, with positive as well as negative consequences for social stability. Deviance helps to define the limits of proper behavior. Children who see one parent scold the other for belching at the dinner table learn about approved conduct. The same is true of the driver who receives a speeding ticket, the department store cashier who is fired for yelling at a customer, and the college student who is penalized for handing in papers weeks overdue.

Durkheim's Legacy Émile Durkheim ([1895] 1964) focused his sociological investigations mainly on criminal acts, yet his conclusions have implications for all types of deviant behavior. In Durkheim's view, the punishments established within a culture (including both formal and informal mechanisms of social control) help to define acceptable behavior and thus contribute to stability. If improper acts were not sanctioned, people might stretch their standards of what constitutes appropriate conduct.

Sociologist Kai Erikson (1966) illustrated the boundary-maintenance function of deviance in his study of the Puritans of 17th-century New England. By today's standards, the Puritans placed tremendous emphasis on conventional morals. Their persecution and execution of women as witches represented a continuing attempt to define and redefine the boundaries of their community. In effect, their changing social norms created crime waves, as people whose behavior was previously acceptable suddenly faced punishment for being deviant (R. Schaefer and Zellner 2011).

Durkheim ([1897] 1951) introduced the term **anomie** into sociological literature to describe the loss of direction felt in a society when social control of individual behavior has become ineffective. Anomie is a state of normlessness that typically occurs during a period of profound social change and disorder, such as a time of economic collapse. People become more aggressive or depressed, which results in higher rates of violent crime and suicide. Since there is much less agreement on what constitutes proper behavior during times of revolution, sudden prosperity, or economic depression, **conformity**, a going along with peers, and **obedience**, compliance with higher authorities in a hierarchical structure, become less significant as social forces. It also becomes much more difficult to state exactly what constitutes deviance.

Merton's Theory of Deviance What do a mugger and a teacher have in common? Each is "working" to obtain money that can then be exchanged for desired goods. As this example illustrates, behavior that violates accepted norms (such as mugging) may be based on the same basic objectives as the behavior of people who pursue more conventional lifestyles.

On the basis of this kind of analysis, sociologist Robert Merton (1968) adapted Durkheim's notion of anomie to explain why people accept or reject the goals of a society, the socially approved means of fulfilling their aspirations, or both. Merton maintained that one important cultural goal in the United States is success, measured largely in terms of money. In addition to providing this goal for people, our society offers specific instructions on how to pursue success—go to school, work hard, do not quit, take advantage of opportunities, and so forth.

What happens to individuals in a society with a heavy emphasis on wealth as a basic symbol of success? Merton reasoned that people adapt in certain ways, either by conforming to or by deviating from such cultural expectations. His **anomie theory of deviance** posits five types of behavior or basic forms of adaptation (Table 7-1).

TABLE 7-1 MERTON'S DEVIANCE THEORY

Summing Up

Does the individual accept:	Nondeviant	Deviant			
	Conformity	Retreatism	Innovation	Ritualism	Rebellion
the goals of society, such as acquisition of wealth?	👍	👎	👍	👎	👎 👍
the use of acceptable means, such as hard work?	👍	👎	👎	👍	👎 👍

Source: Adapted by author, Richard Schaefer, from Chapter VI, "Social Structure and Anomie," in Merton 1968.

Conformity to social norms, the most common adaptation in Merton's typology, is the opposite of deviance. It involves acceptance of both the overall societal goal ("acquisition of wealth") and the approved means ("hard work"). In Merton's view, there must be some consensus regarding accepted cultural goals and the legitimate means for attaining them. Without such a consensus, societies could exist only as collectives of people rather than as unified cultures, and might experience continual chaos.

The other four types of behavior represented in Table 7-1 all involve some departure from conformity. The *retreatist* has basically retreated (or withdrawn) from both the goals and the means of society. In the United States, drug addicts and vagrants are typically portrayed as retreatists. Concern has been growing that adolescents who are addicted to alcohol will become retreatists at an early age.

In Merton's typology, the *innovator* accepts the goals of society but pursues them with means that are regarded as improper. For instance, a safecracker may steal money to buy consumer goods and expensive vacations.

The *ritualist* has abandoned the goal of material success and become compulsively committed to the institutional means. Work becomes simply a way of life rather than a means to the goal of success. An example would be the bureaucratic official who blindly applies rules and regulations without remembering the larger goals of the organization. Certainly that would be true of a welfare caseworker who refuses to assist a homeless family because the family's last apartment was in another district.

The final type of behavior or adaptation identified by Merton reflects people's attempts to create a *new* social structure. The *rebel* feels alienated from the dominant means and goals and may seek a dramatically different social order. Members of a revolutionary political organization, such as a militia group, can be categorized as rebels according to Merton's model.

Merton made a key contribution to the sociological understanding of deviance by pointing out that deviants such as innovators and ritualists share a great deal with conforming people. The convicted felon may hold many of the same aspirations as people with no criminal background. The theory helps us to understand deviance as a socially created behavior rather than as the result of momentary pathological impulses. However, this theory of deviance has not been applied systematically to real-world crime. Box 7-1 examines scholars' efforts to confirm the theory's validity.

INTERACTIONIST PERSPECTIVE

The functionalist approach to deviance explains why people violate rules or laws despite pressure to conform and obey. A **law** may be defined as governmental social control (Black 1995). However, functionalists do not indicate how a given person comes to commit a deviant act or why on some occasions crimes do or do not occur. The emphasis on everyday behavior that is the focus of the interactionist perspective offers such an explanation: cultural transmission theory.

Cultural Transmission In the course of studying graffiti writing by gangs in Los Angeles, sociologist Susan A. Phillips (1999) discovered that the writers learned from one another. In fact, Phillips was surprised by how stable their focus was over time. She also noted how other ethnic groups built on the models of the African American and Chicano gangs, superimposing Cambodian, Chinese, or Vietnamese symbols.

Humans *learn* how to behave in social situations, whether properly or improperly. There is no natural, innate manner in which people interact with one another. These simple ideas are not disputed today, but such was not the case when sociologist Edwin Sutherland (1883–1950) first advanced the idea that an individual undergoes the same basic socialization process in learning conforming and deviant acts.

Sutherland's ideas have been the dominating force in criminology. He drew on the **cultural transmission** school, which emphasizes that one learns criminal behavior by interacting with others. Such learning includes not only the techniques of lawbreaking (for example, how to break into a car quickly and quietly) but also the motives, drives, and rationalizations of the criminal. The cultural transmission approach can also

Research Today

7-1 DOES CRIME PAY?

A driver violates the speed limit to get to a job interview on time. A financially strapped parent shoplifts goods that her family needs. These people may feel justified in violating the law because they do so to meet a reasonable objective. In Robert Merton's terms, they are *innovators*—people who violate social norms to achieve a commonly shared societal goal. Although their actions are criminal and potentially hurtful to others, from their own short-term perspective, their actions are functional.

Carried to its logical conclusion, innovation can and does become a career for some people. Yet from a purely economic point of view, even considering the fact that crime may pay is controversial, because doing so may seem to tolerate or encourage rule violation. Nothing is more controversial than the suggestion that gang-run drug deals are profitable and produce "good jobs." Although some people may see drug dealers as a cross between MBA-educated professionals and streetwise entrepreneurs, society in general does not admire these innovators.

Sociologist Sudhir Venkatesh collected detailed data on the illegal drug trade during his observation research on a Chicago street gang. Working with economist Steven Levitt, coauthor of the best seller *Freakonomics,* to analyze the business of selling crack cocaine, he found that less than 5 percent of even the gang leaders earned $100,000 per year. The rest of the leaders and virtually all the rank and file earned less than the minimum wage. In fact, most were unpaid workers seeking to move up in the gang hierarchy. (Thus the title of a chapter in Levitt's book, "Why Do Drug Dealers Still Live with Their Moms?") As Levitt notes, the drug gang is like most corporations: the top 2 percent of workers take home most of the money.

Less than 5 percent of even the gang leaders earned $100,000 per year. The rest of the leaders and virtually all the rank and file earned less than the minimum wage.

Why, from a sociological *and* an economic perspective, do these nonprofitable practices persist, especially considering that one in every four members of drug-oriented street gangs is eventually killed? One reason, of course, is the public's almost insatiable demand for illegal drugs. And from the drug peddler's perspective, few legitimate jobs are available to young adults in poverty-stricken areas, urban or rural. Functionally, these youths are contributing to their household incomes by dealing drugs.

Scholars see a need for further research on Merton's concept of innovation. Why, for example, do some disadvantaged groups have lower rates of reported crime than others? Why do many people who are caught in adverse circumstances reject criminal activity as a viable alternative? Merton's theory of deviance does not easily answer such questions.

Let's Discuss

1. Do you know anyone who has stolen out of need? If so, did the person feel justified in stealing, or did he or she feel guilty? How long did the theft continue?
2. Economically, profit is the difference between revenues and costs. What are the costs of the illegal drug trade, both economic and social? Is this economic activity profitable for society?

Sources: Clinard and Miller 1998; Kingsbury 2008; S. Levitt and Dubner 2006; S. Levitt and Venkatesh 2000; Rosen and Venkatesh 2008; Venkatesh 2008.

be used to explain the behavior of those who habitually abuse alcohol or drugs.

Sutherland maintained that through interactions with a primary group and significant others, people acquire definitions of proper and improper behavior. He used the term **differential association** to describe the process through which exposure to attitudes *favorable* to criminal acts leads to the violation of rules. Research suggests that this view of differential association also applies to noncriminal deviant acts, such as smoking, truancy, and early sexual behavior.

Sutherland offers the example of a boy who is sociable, outgoing, and athletic and who lives in an area with a high rate of delinquency. The youth is very likely to come into contact with peers who commit acts of vandalism, fail to attend school, and so forth, and may come to adopt such behavior. However, an introverted boy who lives in the same neighborhood may stay away from his peers and avoid delinquency. In another community, an outgoing and athletic boy may join a Little League baseball team or a scout troop because of his interactions with peers. Thus, Sutherland views improper behavior as the result of the types of groups to which one belongs and the kinds of friendships one has.

According to social disorganization theory, strong communal bonds can enhance neighborhood ties, reducing the likelihood of criminal behavior.

According to critics, the cultural transmission approach may explain the deviant behavior of juvenile delinquents or graffiti artists, but it fails to explain the conduct of the first-time impulsive shoplifter or the impoverished person who steals out of necessity. While it is not a precise statement of the process through which one becomes a criminal, differential association theory does direct our attention to the paramount role of social interaction in increasing a person's motivation to engage in deviant behavior (Loughran et al. 2013; Sutherland et al. 1992).

Social Disorganization Theory The social relationships that exist in a community or neighborhood affect people's behavior. Philip Zimbardo (2007a:24–25) once did an experiment that demonstrated the power of communal relationships. He abandoned a car in each of two different neighborhoods, leaving its hood up and removing its hub caps. In one neighborhood, people started to strip the car for parts before Zimbardo had finished setting up a remote video camera to record their behavior. In the other neighborhood, weeks passed without the car being touched, except for a pedestrian who stopped to close the hood during a rainstorm.

What accounts for the strikingly different outcomes of Zimbardo's experiment in the two communities? According to **social disorganization theory**, increases in crime and deviance can be attributed to the absence or breakdown of communal relationships and social institutions, such as the family, school, church, and local government. This theory was developed at the University of Chicago in the early 1900s to describe the apparent disorganization that occurred as cities expanded with rapid immigration and migration from rural areas. Using the latest survey techniques, Clifford Shaw and Henry McKay literally mapped the distribution of social problems in Chicago. They found high rates of social problems in neighborhoods where buildings had deteriorated and the population had declined. Interestingly, the patterns persisted over time, despite changes in the neighborhoods' ethnic and racial composition.

From the perspective of . . .

A Government Worker What would you predict might occur when a municipality ceases its collection of trash to hundreds of suburban homes (as a response to residents being behind in their tax payments)?

According to social disorganization theory, strong communal bonds can enhance neighborhood ties, reducing the likelihood of criminal behavior.

This theory is not without its critics. To some, social disorganization theory seems to "blame the victim," leaving larger societal forces, such as the lack of jobs or high-quality schools, unaccountable. Critics also argue that even troubled neighborhoods have viable, healthy organizations, which persist despite the problems that surround them.

More recently, social disorganization theorists have taken to emphasizing the effect of social networks on communal bonds. These researchers acknowledge that communities are not isolated islands. Residents' bonds may be enhanced or weakened by their ties to groups outside the immediate community (Jensen 2005; Sampson and Graves 1989; Shaw and McKay 1942).

LABELING PERSPECTIVE

The Saints and the Roughnecks were groups of high school males who were continually engaged in excessive drinking, reckless driving, truancy, petty theft, and vandalism. There the similarity ended. None of the Saints was ever arrested, but every Roughneck was frequently in trouble with police and townspeople. Why the disparity in their treatment? On the basis of observation research in their high school, sociologist William Chambliss (1973) concluded that social class played an important role in the varying fortunes of the two groups.

The Saints hid behind a facade of respectability. They came from "good families," were active in school organizations, planned on attending college, and received good grades. People generally viewed their delinquent acts as a few isolated cases of sowing wild oats. The Roughnecks had no such aura of respectability. They drove around town in beat-up cars, were generally unsuccessful in school, and aroused suspicion no matter what they did.

We can understand such discrepancies by using an approach to deviance known as **labeling theory**. Unlike Sutherland's work, labeling theory does not focus on why some individuals come to commit deviant acts. Instead, it attempts to explain why certain people (such as the Roughnecks) are *viewed* as deviants, delinquents, bad kids, losers, and criminals, whereas others whose behavior is similar (such as the Saints) are not seen in such harsh terms. Reflecting the contribution of interactionist theorists, labeling theory emphasizes how a person comes to be labeled as deviant or to accept that label. Sociologist Howard Becker (1963:9; 1964), who popularized this approach, summed it up with this statement: "Deviant behavior is behavior that people so label."

Labeling theory is also called the **societal-reaction approach**, reminding us that it is the *response* to an act, not the behavior itself, that determines deviance. For example, studies have shown that some school personnel and therapists expand educational programs designed for learning-disabled students to include those with behavioral problems. Consequently, a "troublemaker" can be improperly labeled as "learning-disabled," and vice versa (Grattet 2011).

Labeling and Agents of Social Control Traditionally, research on deviance has focused on people who violate social norms. In contrast, labeling theory focuses on police, probation officers, psychiatrists, judges, teachers, employers, school officials, and other regulators of social control. These agents, it is argued, play a significant role in creating the deviant identity by designating certain people (and not others) as deviant. An important aspect of labeling theory is the recognition that some individuals or groups have the power to *define* labels and *apply* them to others. This view ties into the conflict perspective's emphasis on the social significance of power.

In recent years the practice of *racial profiling,* in which people are identified as criminal suspects purely on the basis of their race, has come under public scrutiny. Studies confirm the public's suspicions that in some jurisdictions, police officers are much more likely to stop Black males than White males for routine traffic violations, in the expectation of finding drugs or guns in their cars. Civil rights activists refer to these cases sarcastically as DWB (Driving While Black) violations. Beginning in 2001, profiling took a new turn as people who appeared to be Arab or Muslim came under special scrutiny. (Racial profiling will be examined in more detail in Chapter 8.)

The popularity of labeling theory is reflected in the emergence of a related perspective, called social constructionism. According to the **social constructionist perspective**, deviance is the product of the culture we live in. Social constructionists focus specifically on the decision-making process that creates the deviant identity. They point out that "child abductors," "deadbeat dads," "spree killers," and "date rapists" have always been with us, but at times have become *the* major social concern of policy-makers because of intensive media coverage (Liska and Messner 1999; E. R. Wright et al. 2000).

How do certain behaviors come to be viewed as a problem? Cigarette smoking, which was once regarded as a polite, gentlemanly activity, is now considered a serious health hazard, not only to the smoker but also to others nearby who don't smoke. Recently, people have become concerned about the danger, especially to children, posed by *thirdhand smoke*—smoke-related chemicals that cling to clothes and linger in rooms, cars, even elevators (Winickoff et al. 2009).

CONFLICT PERSPECTIVE

Conflict theorists point out that people with power protect their interests and define deviance to suit their needs. Sociologist Richard Quinney (1974, 1979, 1980) was a leading exponent of the view that the criminal justice system serves the interests of the powerful. Crime, according to Quinney (1970), is a definition of conduct created by authorized agents of social control—such as legislators and law enforcement officers—in a politically organized society. He and other conflict theorists argue that law-making is often an attempt by the powerful to coerce others into their morality (see also Spitzer 1975).

In the 1930s, the Federal Bureau of Narcotics launched a campaign to portray marijuana as a dangerous drug rather than a pleasure-inducing substance. From a conflict perspective, those in power often use such tactics to coerce others into adopting a different point of view.

This theory helps to explain why our society has laws against gambling, drug use, and prostitution, many of which are violated on a massive scale. (We will examine these "victimless crimes" later in the chapter.) According to conflict theorists, criminal law does not represent a consistent application of societal values, but instead reflects competing values and interests. Thus, the U.S. criminal code outlaws marijuana because of its alleged harm to users, yet cigarettes and alcohol—both of which can be harmful to users—are sold legally almost everywhere.

In fact, conflict theorists contend that the entire criminal justice system in the United States treats suspects differently based on their racial, ethnic, or social-class background. In many cases, officials in the system use their own discretion to make biased decisions about whether to press charges or drop them, whether to set bail and how much, whether to offer parole or deny it. Researchers have found that this kind of **differential justice**—differences in the way social control is exercised over different groups—puts African Americans and Latinos at a disadvantage in the justice system, both as juveniles and as adults. On average, White offenders receive shorter sentences than comparable Latino and African American offenders, even when prior arrest records and the relative severity of the crime are taken into consideration (Brewer and Heitzeg 2008; Sandefur 2008; Schlesinger 2011).

The perspective advanced by conflict and labeling theorists forms quite a contrast to the functionalist approach to deviance. Functionalists see standards of deviant behavior as merely reflecting cultural norms; conflict and labeling theorists point out that the most powerful groups in a society can shape laws and standards and determine who is (or is not) prosecuted as a criminal. These groups would be unlikely to apply the label "deviant" to the corporate executive whose decisions lead to large-scale environmental pollution. In the opinion of conflict theorists, agents of social control and other powerful groups can impose their own self-serving definitions of deviance on the general public.

FEMINIST PERSPECTIVE

Feminist criminologists such as Freda Adler and Meda Chesney-Lind have suggested that many of the existing approaches to deviance and crime were developed with only men in mind. For example, in the United States, for many years any husband who forced his wife to have sexual intercourse—without her consent and against her will—was not legally considered to have committed rape. The law defined rape as pertaining only to sexual relations between people who were not married to each other, reflecting the overwhelmingly male composition of state legislatures at the time.

It took repeated protests by feminist organizations to get changes in the criminal law defining rape. Beginning in 1993, husbands in all 50 states could be prosecuted under most circumstances for the rape of their wives. There remain alarming exceptions in no fewer than 30 states, however. For example, the husband is exempt when he does not need to use force because his wife is asleep, unconscious, or mentally or physically impaired. These interpretations still rest on the notion that the marriage contract entitles a husband to sex (Bergen 2006).

In the future, feminist scholarship can be expected to grow dramatically. Particularly on topics such as white-collar crime, drinking behavior, drug abuse, and differential sentencing rates between the genders, as well as on the fundamental question of how to define deviance, feminist scholars will have much to say.

We have seen that over the past century, sociologists have taken many different approaches in studying deviance, arousing some controversy in the process. Table 7-2 summarizes the various theoretical approaches to this topic.

Study Alert

It is important to understand and be able to differentiate the five perspectives on deviance: functionalist, interactionist, labeling, conflict, and feminist perspectives.

TABLE 7-2 **SOCIOLOGICAL PERSPECTIVES ON DEVIANCE**

Tracking Sociological Perspectives

Approach	Theoretical Perspective	Proponents	Emphasis
Anomie	Functionalist	Émile Durkheim Robert Merton	Adaptation to societal norms
Cultural transmission/ Differential association	Interactionist	Edwin Sutherland	Patterns learned through others
Social disorganization	Interactionist	Clifford Shaw Henry McKay	Communal relationships
Labeling/Social constructionist	Interactionist	Howard Becker William Chambliss	Societal response to acts
Conflict	Conflict	Richard Quinney	Dominance by authorized agents Discretionary justice
Feminist	Conflict/ Feminist	Freda Adler Meda Chesney-Lind	Role of gender Women as victims and perpetrators

Read each question carefully and then select or provide the best answer.

1. Which of the following is an example of innovation as defined in Robert Merton's anomie theory of deviance?
   a. An advocate for a new form of government initiates a blog.
   b. A bureaucrat demands higher wages.
   c. A prison guard agitates for a labor union.
   d. A student copies an assigned essay from the Internet.

2. Which of the following theories contends that criminal victimization increases when communal relationships and social institutions break down?
   a. labeling theory
   b. conflict theory
   c. social disorganization theory
   d. differential association theory

3. Which of the following conducted observation research on two groups of high school males (the Saints and the Roughnecks) and concluded that social class played an important role in the varying fortunes of the two groups?
   a. Richard Quinney
   b. Edwin Sutherland
   c. Émile Durkheim
   d. William Chambliss

4. _____ is a state of normlessness that typically occurs during a period of profound social change and disorder, such as a time of economic collapse.

5. _____ theorists view standards of deviant behavior as merely reflecting cultural norms, whereas _____ and _____ theorists point out that the most powerful groups in a society can shape laws and standards and determine who is (or is not) prosecuted as a criminal.

Answers
1 (d); 2 (c); 3 (d); 4 Anomie; 5 Functionalist, conflict, labeling

R Rethink

Consider these questions to get a deeper understanding of the material.

1. Using examples drawn from work or college life, illustrate each of Merton's five modes of individual adaptation.

2. Explain the presence of both criminals and law-abiding citizens in an inner-city neighborhood in terms of the interactionist perspective.

RECAP

LO 22-1 Explain the concept of deviance as it is understood by sociologists.

- Deviant behavior violates social norms, some informal and some formalized as laws.

- Some forms of deviance, such as alcoholism, carry a negative social stigma, while other forms are more or less accepted. A social stigma (such as *compulsive gambler*), once gained, is very hard to lose.
- What is considered socially deviant can change over time, influenced typically by those with power and status.

LO 22-2 Compare and contrast the understanding of deviance offered by the three major perspectives, labeling theory, and the feminist perspective.

- From a functionalist point of view, deviance and its consequences help to define the limits of proper behavior.
- Some interactionists maintain that people learn criminal behavior by interacting with others (cultural transmission). To them, deviance results from exposure to attitudes that are favorable to criminal acts (differential association).
- Other interactionists attribute increases in crime and deviance to the absence or breakdown of communal relationships and social institutions, such as the family, school, church, and local government (social disorganization theory).
- An important aspect of labeling theory is the recognition that some people are viewed as deviant, while others who engage in the same behavior are not.
- From the conflict perspective, laws and punishments are a reflection of the interests of the powerful.
- The feminist perspective emphasizes that cultural attitudes and differential economic relationships help to explain gender differences in deviance and crime.

KEY TERMS

Anomie Durkheim's term for the loss of direction felt in a society when social control of individual behavior has become ineffective.

Anomie theory of deviance Robert Merton's theory of deviance as an adaptation of socially prescribed goals or of the means governing their attainment, or both.

Conformity Going along with peers—individuals of our own status who have no special right to direct our behavior.

Cultural transmission A school of criminology that argues that criminal behavior is learned through social interactions.

Deviance Behavior that violates the standards of conduct or expectations of a group or society.

Differential association A theory of deviance that holds that violation of rules results from exposure to attitudes favorable to criminal acts.

Differential justice Differences in the way social control is exercised over different groups.

Formal social control Social control that is carried out by authorized agents, such as police officers, judges, school administrators, and employers.

Informal social control Social control that is carried out casually by ordinary people through such means as laughter, smiles, and ridicule.

Labeling theory An approach to deviance that attempts to explain why certain people are viewed as deviants while others engaged in the same behavior are not.

Law Governmental social control.

Obedience Compliance with higher authorities in a hierarchical structure.

Social constructionist perspective An approach to deviance that emphasizes the role of culture in the creation of the deviant identity.

Social control The techniques and strategies for preventing deviant human behavior in any society.

Social disorganization theory The theory that crime and deviance are caused by the absence or breakdown of communal relationships and social institutions.

Societal-reaction approach Another name for *labeling theory*.

Stigma A label used to devalue members of certain social groups.

MODULE 23 Social Control

P Prepare Learning Objectives

LO 23-1 Explain the role of norms and sanctions in establishing social control.

LO 23-2 Illustrate the ways in which conformity and obedience differ.

LO 23-3 Compare and contrast formal and informal social control.

LO 23-4 Discuss why sociologists see the creation of laws as a social process.

O Organize Module Outline

Norms and Social Control
    Conformity and Obedience
    Informal and Formal Social Control
Law and Society

W Work

LO 23-1 Norms and Social Control

As we saw in Chapter 3, each culture, subculture, and group has distinctive norms governing appropriate behavior. Laws, dress codes, organizational bylaws, course requirements, and the rules of sports and games all express social norms.

Social control occurs on all levels of society. In the family, we are socialized to obey our parents simply because they are our parents. Peer groups introduce us to informal norms, such as dress codes, that govern the behavior of their members. Colleges establish standards they expect of students. In bureaucratic organizations, workers encounter a formal system of rules and regulations. Finally, the government of every society legislates and enforces social norms.

Most of us respect and accept basic social norms and assume that others will do the same. Even without thinking, we obey the instructions of police officers, follow the day-to-day rules at our jobs, and move to the rear of elevators when people enter. Such behavior reflects an effective process of socialization to the dominant standards of a culture. At the same time, we are well aware that individuals, groups, and institutions *expect* us to act "properly." This expectation carries with it **sanctions**, or penalties and rewards for conduct concerning a social norm. If we fail to live up to the norm, we may face punishment through informal sanctions such as fear and ridicule or formal sanctions such as jail sentences or fines.

The challenge to effective social control is that people often receive competing messages about how to behave. While the state or government may clearly define acceptable behavior, friends or fellow employees may encourage quite different behavior patterns. Historically, legal measures aimed at blocking discrimination based on race, religion, gender, age, and sexual orientation have been difficult to implement, because many people tacitly encourage the violation of such measures.

Functionalists maintain that people must respect social norms if any group or society is to survive. In their view, societies literally could not function if massive numbers of people defied standards of appropriate conduct. In contrast, conflict theorists contend that the successful functioning of a society will consistently benefit the powerful and work to the disadvantage of other groups. They point out that in the United States, widespread resistance to social norms was necessary to win our independence from Great Britain, to overturn the institution of slavery, to allow women to vote, to secure civil rights, and to force an end to the war in Vietnam.

LO 23-2 CONFORMITY AND OBEDIENCE

Techniques for social control operate on both the group level and the societal level. People we think of as peers or equals influence us to act in particular ways; the same is true of people who hold authority over us or occupy awe-inspiring positions. Social psychologist Stanley Milgram (1975) made a useful distinction between these two levels of social control.

The Milgram Experiment Milgram used the term conformity to mean going along with peers—individuals of our own status who have no special right to direct our behavior. In contrast, obedience is compliance with higher authorities in a hierarchical structure. Thus, a recruit entering military service will typically *conform* to the habits and language of other recruits and *obey* the orders of superior officers. Students will *conform* to the drinking behavior of their peers and *obey* the requests of campus security officers.

If ordered to do so, would you comply with an experimenter's instruction to administer increasingly painful electric shocks to a subject? Most people would say no; yet Milgram's research (1963, 1975) suggests that most of us *would* obey such orders. In his words (1975:xi), "Behavior that is unthinkable in an individual . . . acting on his own may be executed without hesitation when carried out under orders."

Milgram placed advertisements in New Haven, Connecticut, newspapers to recruit subjects for a learning experiment at Yale University. Participants included postal clerks, engineers, high school teachers, and laborers. They were told that the purpose of the research was to investigate the effects of punishment on learning. The experimenter, dressed in a gray technician's coat, explained that in each test, one subject would be randomly selected as the "learner," while another would function as the "teacher." However, the experiment was rigged so that the real subject would always be the teacher, while an associate of Milgram's served as the learner.

At this point, the learner's hand was strapped to an electric apparatus. The teacher was taken to an electronic "shock generator" with 30 levered switches labeled from 15 to 450 volts. Before beginning the experiment, all subjects received sample shocks of 45 volts, to convince them of the authenticity of the experiment. The experimenter then instructed the teacher to apply shocks of increasing voltage each time the learner gave an incorrect answer on a memory test. Teachers were told that "although the shocks can be extremely painful, they cause no permanent tissue damage." In reality, the learner did not receive any shocks.

[Study Alert

Remember that conformity is a voluntary following of one's peers, whereas obedience is compliance with higher authorities in a hierarchical structure.]

In a prearranged script, the learner deliberately gave incorrect answers and expressed pain when "shocked." For example, at 150 volts, the learner would cry out, "Get me out of here!" At 270 volts, the learner would scream in agony. When the shock reached 350 volts, the learner would fall silent. If the teacher wanted to stop the experiment, the experimenter would insist that the teacher continue, using such statements as "The experiment requires that you continue" and "You have no other choice; you *must* go on" (Milgram 1975:19–23).

Reflecting on the Milgram Experiment

The results of this unusual experiment stunned and dismayed Milgram and other social scientists. A sample of psychiatrists had predicted that virtually all subjects would refuse to shock innocent victims. In their view, only a "pathological fringe" of less than 2 percent would continue administering shocks up to the maximum level. Yet almost *two-thirds* of participants fell into the category of "obedient subjects."

Why did these subjects obey? Why were they willing to inflict seemingly painful shocks on innocent victims who had never done them any harm? There is no evidence that these subjects were unusually sadistic; few seemed to enjoy administering the shocks. Instead, in Milgram's view, the key to obedience was the experimenter's social role as a "scientist" and "seeker of knowledge."

Milgram pointed out that in the modern industrial world, we are accustomed to submitting to impersonal authority figures whose status is indicated by a title (professor, lieutenant, doctor) or by a uniform (the technician's coat). Because we view the authority as larger and more important than the individual, we shift responsibility for our behavior to the authority figure. Milgram's subjects frequently stated, "If it were up to me, I would not have administered shocks." They saw themselves as merely doing their duty (Milgram 1975).

From a conflict perspective, our obedience may be affected by the value we place on those whom our behavior affects. While Milgram's experiment shows that in general, people are willing to obey authority figures, other studies show that they are even more willing to obey if they feel the "victim" is deserving of punishment. Sociologist Gary Schulman (1974) re-created Milgram's experiment and found that White students were significantly more likely to shock Black learners than White learners. By a margin of 70 percent to 48 percent, they imposed more shocks on the Black learners than on the White learners.

From an interactionist perspective, one important aspect of Milgram's findings is the fact that subjects in follow-up studies were less likely to inflict the supposed shocks as they were moved physically closer to their victims. Moreover, interactionists emphasize the effect of *incrementally* administering additional dosages of 15 volts. In effect, the experimenter negotiated with the teacher and convinced the teacher to continue inflicting higher levels of punishment. It is doubtful that anywhere near the two-thirds rate of obedience would have been reached had the experimenter told the teachers to administer 450 volts immediately (Allen 1978; Katovich 1987).

Milgram launched his experimental study of obedience to better understand the involvement of Germans in the annihilation of 6 million Jews and millions of other people during World War II. In an interview conducted long after the publication of his study, he suggested that "if a system of death camps were set up in the United States of the sort we had seen in Nazi Germany, one would be able to find sufficient personnel for those camps in any medium-sized American town." Though many people questioned his remark, the revealing photos taken at Iraq's Abu Ghraib prison in 2004, showing U.S. military guards humiliating if not torturing Iraqi prisoners, recalled the experiment Milgram had done two generations earlier. Under conducive circumstances, otherwise

In one of Stanley Milgram's experiments, the learner supposedly received an electric shock from a shock plate when he answered a question incorrectly. At the 150-volt level, the learner would demand to be released and would refuse to place his hand on the shock plate. The experimenter would then order the actual subject, the teacher, to force the hand onto the plate, as shown in the photo. Though 40 percent of the true subjects stopped complying with Milgram at this point, 30 percent did force the learner's hand onto the shock plate, despite his pretended agony.

normal people can and often do treat one another inhumanely (CBS News 1979:7–8; Hayden 2004; Zimbardo 2007a).

How willing would participants in this experiment be to shock learners today? Although many people may be skeptical of the high levels of conformity Milgram found, recent replications of his experiment confirm his findings. In 2006, using additional safeguards to protect participants' welfare, psychologist Jerry Burger (2009) repeated part of Milgram's experiment with college undergraduates. To avoid biasing the participants, Burger was careful to screen out students who had heard of Milgram's study. The results of the replication were startlingly similar to Milgram's: participants showed a high level of willingness to shock the learner, just as the participants in Milgram's experiment had almost half a century earlier. At the most comparable point in the two studies, Burger measured a rate of 70 percent full obedience—lower, but not significantly so, than the rate of 82.5 percent measured two generations earlier.

LO 23-3 INFORMAL AND FORMAL SOCIAL CONTROL

The sanctions that are used to encourage conformity and obedience—and to discourage violation of social norms—are carried out through both informal and formal social control. People use informal social control casually to enforce norms. Examples include smiles, laughter, a raised eyebrow, and ridicule.

In the United States and many other cultures, adults often view spanking, slapping, or kicking children as a proper and necessary means of informal social control. Child development specialists counter that such corporal punishment is inappropriate because it teaches children to solve problems through violence. They warn that slapping and spanking can escalate into more serious forms of abuse. Yet, despite a policy statement by the American Academy of Pediatrics that corporal punishment is not effective and can indeed be harmful, 59 percent of pediatricians support the use of corporal punishment, at least in certain situations. Our culture widely accepts this form of informal social control (Chung et al. 2009).

Formal social control is carried out by authorized agents and can serve as a last resort when socialization and informal sanctions do not bring about desired behavior. Sometimes, informal social control can actually undermine formal social control, encouraging people to violate social norms.

From the perspective of . . .

A High School Counselor If you want to avoid resorting to formal social controls to prevent violent behavior among students, what informal social controls could you use instead?

Historically, the death penalty has been intended as a significant form of social control. The threat of execution was meant as much to discourage others from committing capital crimes as it was to punish those who did. However, researchers have been unable to establish what if any deterrence effect executions may have, leading many people to question the effectiveness of the death penalty. As Figure 7-1 shows, the death penalty is still on the books in 35 states, where it is used to a greater or lesser extent.

In 2007, in the wake of the mass shootings at Virginia Tech, many college officials reviewed security measures on their campuses. Administrators were reluctant to end or even limit the relative freedom of movement students on their campuses enjoyed. Instead, they concentrated on improving emergency communications between campus police and students, faculty, and staff. Reflecting a reliance on technology to maintain social control, college leaders called for replacement of the "old" technology of e-mail with instant alerts that could be sent to people's cell phones via instant messaging.

FIGURE 7-1   EXECUTIONS BY STATE SINCE 1976

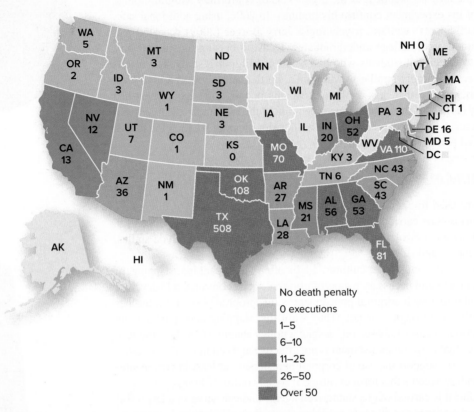

No death penalty
0 executions
1–5
6–10
11–25
26–50
Over 50

Note: Number of executions carried out from January 17, 1977, to December 18, 2013, not including three federal executions. Illinois carried out 12 executions before abolishing the death penalty. Maryland and New Mexico, which still have people on death row, have abolished the death penalty for future cases.
Source: Death Penalty Information Center 2014.

In the aftermath of September 11, 2001, new measures of social control became the norm in the United States. Some of them, such as stepped-up security and surveillance at airports and high-rise buildings, were highly visible to the public. The federal government has also publicly urged citizens to engage in informal social control by watching for and reporting people whose actions seem suspicious (Monahan 2011).

Many people think this kind of social control goes too far. Civil rights advocates worry that the government's request for information on suspicious activities may encourage negative stereotyping of Muslims and Arab Americans. Clearly, there is a trade-off between the benefits of surveillance and the right to privacy.

LO 23-4 Law and Society

Some norms are so important to a society that they are formalized into laws regarding people's behavior. Law may be defined as governmental social control (Black 1995). Some laws, such as the prohibition against murder, are directed at all members of society. Others, such as fishing and hunting regulations, affect particular categories of people. Still others govern the behavior of social institutions (for instance, corporate law and laws regarding the taxing of nonprofit enterprises).

Sociologists see the creation of laws as a social process. Because laws are passed in response to a perceived need for formal social control, sociologists have sought to explain how and why such a perception arises. In their view, law is not merely a static body of rules handed down from generation to generation. Rather, it reflects continually changing standards of what is right and wrong, of how violations are to be determined, and of what sanctions are to be applied (Schur 1968).

Sociologists representing varying theoretical perspectives agree that the legal order reflects the values of those in a position to exercise authority. Therefore, the creation of civil and criminal law can be a most controversial matter. Should it be against the law to employ illegal immigrants, to have an abortion, to allow prayer in public schools, or to smoke on an airplane? Such issues have been bitterly debated, because they require a choice among competing values. Not surprisingly, laws that are unpopular—such as the one-time prohibition of alcohol under the Eighteenth Amendment and the widespread establishment of a 55-mile-per-hour speed limit on highways—become difficult to enforce when there is no consensus supporting the norms.

One current and controversial debate over laws governing behavior is whether people should be allowed to use marijuana legally, for medical purposes. Although the majority of adults polled in national surveys support such a use, the federal government continues to regard all uses of marijuana as illegal. In 2005 the Supreme Court upheld the federal government's position. Nevertheless, 19 states and the District of Columbia have granted citizens the right to use marijuana for medical purposes—even if that privilege rests on dubious legal grounds (Figure 7-2).

MAPPING LIFE NATIONWIDE

FIGURE 7-2 THE STATUS OF MEDICAL MARIJUANA

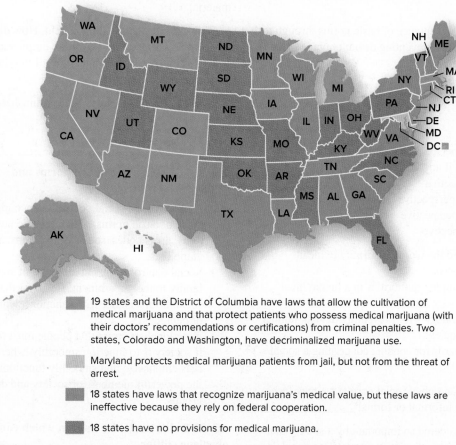

19 states and the District of Columbia have laws that allow the cultivation of medical marijuana and that protect patients who possess medical marijuana (with their doctors' recommendations or certifications) from criminal penalties. Two states, Colorado and Washington, have decriminalized marijuana use.

Maryland protects medical marijuana patients from jail, but not from the threat of arrest.

18 states have laws that recognize marijuana's medical value, but these laws are ineffective because they rely on federal cooperation.

18 states have no provisions for medical marijuana.

The actions some states have taken to legalize marijuana are largely symbolic. Federal law still prohibits doctors from writing prescriptions for marijuana, and pharmacies from distributing the substance. Although patients can still be prosecuted by the federal government for possessing or using marijuana, the Obama administration has decided not to prosecute medical marijuana users who comply with state laws.

Source: NORML 2013.

Socialization is the primary source of conforming and obedient behavior, including obedience to law. Generally, it is not external pressure from a peer group or authority figure that makes us go along with social norms. Rather, we have internalized such norms as valid and desirable and are committed to observing them. In a profound sense, we want to see ourselves (and to be seen) as loyal, cooperative, responsible, and respectful of others. In the United States and other societies around the world, people are socialized both to want to belong and to fear being viewed as different or deviant.

Control theory suggests that our connection to members of society leads us to systematically conform to society's norms. According to sociologist Travis Hirschi and other control theorists, our bonds to family members, friends, and peers induce us to follow the mores and folkways of our society. We give little conscious thought to whether we will be sanctioned if we fail to conform. Socialization develops our self-control so well that we don't need further pressure to obey social norms. Although control theory does not effectively explain the rationale for every conforming act, it nevertheless reminds us that while the media may focus on crime and disorder, most members of most societies conform to and obey basic norms (Brewis et al. 2011; Gottfredson and Hirschi 1990; Hirschi 1969).

E Evaluate

Read each question carefully and then select or provide the best answer.

1. Society brings about acceptance of basic norms through techniques and strategies for preventing deviant human behavior. This process is termed
   a. stigmatization.
   b. labeling.
   c. law.
   d. social control.

2. Which sociological perspective argues that people must respect social norms if any group or society is to survive?
   a. the conflict perspective
   b. the interactionist perspective
   c. the functionalist perspective
   d. the feminist perspective

3. Stanley Milgram used the word *conformity* to mean
   a. going along with peers.
   b. compliance with higher authorities in a hierarchical structure.
   c. techniques and strategies for preventing deviant human behavior in any society.
   d. penalties and rewards for conduct concerning a social norm.

4. If we fail to respect and obey social norms, we may face punishment through informal or formal _____.

5. Some norms are considered so important by a society that they are formalized into _____ controlling people's behavior.

Answers

1 (d); 2 (c); 3 (a); 4 sanctions; 5 laws

R Rethink

Consider these questions to get a deeper understanding of the material.

1. Think about a job you once held. How did your employer exercise social control over the employees? How did you, as an employee, use social control in relating to those around you?

2. Should some illegal drugs be decriminalized? Why or why not?

RECAP

LO 23-1 Explain the role of norms and sanctions in establishing social control.

- A society uses social control to encourage the acceptance of basic norms, which include laws, rules, regulations, dress codes, social conventions, and similar social guidelines.
- Social control occurs at all levels of society, from the family to the government. Behavior that supports or defies social norms is met with sanctions, which may be rewards or penalties.
- Functionalists stress that people must respect social norms if society is to function smoothly, whereas conflict theorists emphasize that smoothly functioning societies benefit the powerful members of society and disadvantage other groups.

LO 23-2 Illustrate the ways in which conformity and obedience differ.

- Stanley Milgram defined conformity as going along with one's peers, whereas obedience is compliance with higher authorities in a hierarchical structure. In a formal organization, members *conform* to the behavior they observe in other members, but *obey* the orders and directives of individuals in authority.

- Rather than *conforming* to societal norms regarding the administration of punishment to experimental subjects, a significant number of people in Milgram's shock experiment showed *obedience* to authority.

LO 23-3 Compare and contrast formal and informal social control.

- The sanctions that encourage conformity and obedience are imposed through formal and informal social control.
- Informal social control refers to casual signs of approval or disapproval imposed by other members of society.
- Formal social control is carried out by officially authorized agents. Often, means of formal social control become controversial, such as the death penalty, laws against marijuana use, and heightened security and surveillance measures.

LO 23-4 Discuss why sociologists see the creation of laws as a social process.

- Some norms are so important to a society, they are formalized into laws. Because laws are passed in response to needs perceived by members of society at particular times, law-making is a social process that can be highly controversial.
- Laws are not unchanging decrees; instead, they reflect continually changing standards of right and wrong and judgments about appropriate sanctions. What is illegal at one time may be legal at another, and unpopular laws may be ignored.

KEY TERMS

Control theory A view of conformity and deviance that suggests our connection to members of society leads us to systematically conform to society's norms.

Sanction A penalty or reward for conduct concerning a social norm.

MODULE 24 Crime

P Prepare Learning Objectives

LO 24-1 Differentiate between deviance and crime and describe the six types of crime.

LO 24-2 Explain methods of gathering crime statistics and describe their limitations.

LO 24-3 Summarize crime trends in the United States and internationally.

O Organize Module Outline

Types of Crime
    Victimless Crimes
    Professional Crime
    Organized Crime
    White-Collar and Technology-Based Crime
    Hate Crimes
    Transnational Crime
Crime Statistics
    Index Crimes and Victimization Surveys
    Crime Trends
    International Crime Rates
Social Policy and Social Control
    Gun Control

Crime is on everyone's mind. Until recently, college campuses were viewed as havens from crime. But at today's colleges and universities, crime goes well beyond cheating and senior class pranks.

Crime is a violation of criminal law for which some governmental authority applies formal penalties. It represents a deviation from formal social norms administered by the state. Laws divide crimes into various categories, depending on the severity of the offense, the age of the offender, the potential punishment, and the court that holds jurisdiction over the case.

LO **24-1** Types of Crime

Rather than relying solely on legal categories, however, sociologists classify crimes in terms of how they are committed and how society views the offenses. In this section we will examine six types of crime differentiated by sociologists: victimless crimes, professional crime, organized crime, white-collar and technology-based crime, hate crimes, and transnational crime.

VICTIMLESS CRIMES

When we think of crime, we tend to think of acts that endanger people's economic or personal well-being against their will (or without their direct knowledge). In contrast, sociologists use the term **victimless crime** to describe the willing exchange among adults of widely desired but illegal goods and services, such as prostitution (Schur 1965, 1985).

Some activists are working to decriminalize many of these illegal practices. Supporters of decriminalization are troubled by the attempt to legislate a moral code for adults. In their view, prostitution, drug abuse, gambling, and other victimless crimes are impossible to prevent. The already overburdened criminal justice system should instead devote its resources to street crimes and other offenses with obvious victims.

From the perspective of . . .

A Health Worker How would you argue that selling marijuana is not a victimless crime?

Despite widespread use of the term *victimless crime,* however, many people object to the notion that there is no victim other than the offender in such crimes. Excessive drinking, compulsive gambling, and illegal drug use contribute to an enormous amount of personal and property damage. A person with a drinking problem may become abusive to a spouse or children; a compulsive gambler or drug user may steal to pursue his or her obsession. And feminist sociologists contend that prostitution, as well as the more disturbing aspects of pornography, reinforce the misconception that women are "toys" who can be treated as objects rather than people. According to critics of decriminalization, society must not give tacit approval to conduct that has such harmful consequences (Melissa Farley and Malarek 2008).

The controversy over decriminalization reminds us of the important insights of labeling that conflict theorists presented earlier. Underlying this debate are two questions: Who has the power to label gambling, prostitution, and public drunkenness as "crimes"? and Who has the power to label such behaviors as "victimless"? The answer is generally the state legislatures, and in some cases, the police and the courts.

PROFESSIONAL CRIME

Although the adage "Crime doesn't pay" is familiar, many people do make a career of illegal activities. A **professional criminal**, or *career criminal,* is a person who pursues crime as a day-to-day occupation, developing skilled techniques and enjoying a certain degree of status among other criminals. Some professional criminals specialize in burglary, safecracking, hijacking of cargo, pickpocketing, and shoplifting. Such people have acquired skills that reduce the likelihood of arrest, conviction, and imprisonment. As a result, they may have long careers in their chosen professions.

Edwin Sutherland (1937) offered pioneering insights into the behavior of professional criminals by publishing an annotated account written by a professional thief. Unlike the person who engages in crime only once or twice, professional thieves make a business of stealing. They devote their entire working time to planning and executing crimes, and sometimes travel across the nation to pursue their "professional duties." Like people in regular occupations, professional thieves consult with their colleagues concerning the demands of work, becoming part of a subculture of similarly occupied individuals. They exchange information on places to burglarize, on outlets for unloading stolen goods, and on ways of securing bail bonds if arrested.

ORGANIZED CRIME

A 1976 government report devotes three pages to defining the term *organized crime.* For our purposes, we will consider **organized crime** to be the work of a group that regulates relations among criminal enterprises involved in illegal activities, including prostitution, gambling, and the smuggling and sale of illegal drugs. Organized crime dominates the world of illegal business just as large corporations dominate the conventional business world. It allocates territory, sets prices for goods and services, and acts as an arbitrator in internal disputes. A secret, conspiratorial activity, it generally evades law enforcement. It takes over legitimate businesses, gains influence over labor unions, corrupts public officials, intimidates witnesses in criminal trials, and even "taxes" merchants in exchange for "protection" (National Advisory Commission on Criminal Justice 1976).

Organized crime serves as a means of upward mobility for groups of people struggling to escape poverty. Sociologist Daniel Bell (1953) used the term *ethnic succession* to describe the sequential passage of leadership from Irish Americans in the early part of the 20th century to Jewish Americans in the 1920s and then to Italian Americans in the early 1930s. Ethnic succession has become more complex, reflecting the diversity of the nation's latest immigrants. Colombian, Mexican, Russian, Chinese, Pakistani, and Nigerian immigrants are among those who have begun to play a significant role in organized crime activities (Chin 1996; Kleinknecht 1996).

WHITE-COLLAR AND TECHNOLOGY-BASED CRIME

Income tax evasion, stock manipulation, consumer fraud, bribery and extraction of kickbacks, embezzlement, and misrepresentation in advertising—these are all examples of **white-collar crime**, illegal acts committed in the course of business activities,

"KICKBACKS, EMBEZZLEMENT, PRICE-FIXING, BRIBERY... THIS IS AN EXTREMELY HIGH-CRIME AREA."

often by affluent, "respectable" people. In his 1939 presidential address to the American Sociological Association, Edwin Sutherland (1949, 1983) likened these crimes to organized crime because they are often perpetrated through occupational roles.

A new type of white-collar crime has emerged in recent decades: computer crime. The use of high technology allows criminals to carry out embezzlement or electronic fraud, often leaving few traces, or to gain access to a company's inventory without leaving home. According to a study by the FBI and the National White Collar Crime Center, over 300,000 Internet crimes are reported every year, ranging from scams on online auction sites to identity theft (Internet Crime Complaint Center 2012).

When Charles Horton Cooley spoke of the self and Erving Goffman of impression management, surely neither scholar could have envisioned the insidious crime of identity theft. Each year about 14 percent of all adults find that their personal information has been misused for criminal purposes. Unfortunately, with our society's growing reliance on electronic financial transactions, assuming someone else's identity has become increasingly easy (Vamosi et al. 2010).

Identity theft does not necessarily require technology. A criminal can obtain someone's personal information by pickpocketing or by intercepting mail. However, the widespread exchange of information online has allowed criminals to access large amounts of personal information. Public awareness of the potential harm from identity theft took a giant leap in the aftermath of September 11, 2001, when investigations revealed that several hijackers had used fraudulent IDs to open bank accounts, rent apartments, and board planes. A law enacted in 2004 makes identity theft punishable by a mandatory prison sentence if it is linked to other crimes. Still, unauthorized disclosures of information, even if accidental, persist (Brubaker 2008).

Sutherland (1940) coined the term *white-collar crime* in 1939 to refer to acts by individuals, but the term has been broadened more recently to include offenses by businesses and corporations as well. *Corporate crime,* or any act by a corporation that is punishable by the government, takes many forms and includes individuals, organizations, and institutions among its victims. Corporations may engage in anticompetitive behavior, environmental pollution, medical fraud, tax fraud, stock fraud and manipulation, accounting fraud, the production of unsafe goods, bribery and corruption, and health and safety violations (J. Coleman 2006).

For many years, corporate wrongdoers got off lightly in court by documenting their long history of charitable contributions and agreeing to help law enforcement officials find other white-collar criminals. Unfortunately, that is still the case. The highly visible jailing of multimedia personality Martha Stewart in 2004, as well as recent disclosures of "Wall Street greed," may lead the casual observer to think that government is cracking down on white-collar crime. However, an independent analysis found that from 2000 through 2009, the number of white-collar crimes that were prosecuted increased only modestly (Transactional Records Access Clearinghouse 2009).

The leniency shown to white-collar criminals is not limited to the United States. Japan did not level a fine for insider trading on a major financial corporation until 2012. The profit from the crime was about $119,000; the penalty was $600 (Fukase and Inagaki 2012).

Even when a person is convicted of corporate crime, the verdict generally does not harm his or her reputation and career aspirations nearly so much as conviction for street crime would. Apparently, the label "white-collar criminal" does not carry the stigma of the label "felon convicted of a violent crime." Conflict theorists don't find such differential treatment surprising. They argue that the criminal justice system largely disregards the crimes of the affluent, focusing on crimes committed by the poor. Generally, if an offender holds a position of status and influence, his or her crime is treated as less serious, and the sanction is much more lenient (Simpson 2013).

HATE CRIMES

In contrast to other crimes, hate crimes are defined not only by the perpetrators' actions, but by the purpose of their conduct. The government considers an ordinary crime to be a **hate crime** when the offender is motivated to choose a victim based on race, religion, ethnic group, national origin, or sexual orientation, and when evidence shows that hatred prompted the offender to commit the crime. Hate crimes are sometimes referred to as *bias crimes* (Department of Justice 2008).

In 1990, Congress passed the Hate Crimes Statistics Act, which created a national mandate to identify crimes based on race, religion, ethnic group, and national origin. (Before that time, only 12 states had monitored such crimes.) Since then the act has been broadened to include disabilities, both physical and mental, and sexual orientation. In addition, some jurisdictions impose harsher sanctions (jail time or fines) for hate crimes than for other crimes. For example, if the penalty for assault is a year in jail, the penalty for an assault identified as a hate crime might be two years.

In 2013, law enforcement agencies submitted data on hate crimes to the federal government. The statistics included official reports of almost 7,200 hate crimes and bias-motivated offenses. As Figure 7-3 shows, race was the apparent motivation in approximately 48 percent of the reports. Although vandalism and intimidation were the most common crimes, 40 percent of the incidents involved assault, rape, or murder.

The vast majority of hate crimes, although not all of them, are committed by members of the dominant group against those who are relatively powerless. One in every six racially based hate crimes is an anti-White incident. Except for the most horrific hate crimes, these offenses receive little media attention; anti-White incidents probably receive even less. Clearly, hostility based on race knows no boundaries.

TRANSNATIONAL CRIME

More and more, scholars and police officials are turning their attention to **transnational crime**, or crime that occurs across multiple national borders. In the past, international crime was often limited to the clandestine shipment of goods across the border between two countries. But increasingly, crime is no more restricted by such borders than is legal commerce. Rather than concentrating on specific countries, international crime now spans the globe.

Historically, probably the most dreadful example of transnational crime has been slavery. At first, governments did not regard slavery as a crime, but merely regulated it as they would the trade in goods. In the 20th century, transnational crime grew to embrace trafficking in endangered species, drugs, and stolen art and antiquities.

Transnational crime is not exclusive of some of the other types of crime we have discussed. For example, organized criminal networks are increasingly global. Technology definitely facilitates their illegal activities, such as trafficking in child pornography. Beginning in the 1990s, the United Nations began to categorize transnational crimes; Table 7-3 lists some of the more common types.

Bilateral cooperation in the pursuit of border criminals such as smugglers has been common for many years. The first global effort to control international crime was the International Criminal Police Organization (Interpol), a cooperative network of European police forces founded to stem the movement

FIGURE 7-3   CATEGORIZATION OF REPORTED HATE CRIMES

Source: Incidents reported for 2012 in 2013. Federal Bureau of Investigation 2013.

TABLE 7-3   TYPES OF TRANSNATIONAL CRIME

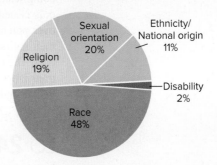

Bankruptcy and insurance fraud

Computer crime (treating computers as both a tool and a target of crime)

Corruption and bribery of public officials

Environmental crime

Hijacking of airplanes (skyjacking)

Illegal drug trade

Illegal money transfers (money laundering)

Illegal sales of firearms and ammunition

Infiltration of legal businesses

Intellectual property crime

Networking of criminal organizations

Sea piracy

Terrorism

Theft of art and cultural objects

Trafficking in body parts (includes illegal organ transplants)

Trafficking in human beings (includes sex trade)

Source: Compiled and updated by the author based on Mueller 2001 and United Nations Office on Drugs and Crime 2010.

of political revolutionaries across borders. While such efforts to fight transnational crime may seem lofty—an activity with which any government should cooperate—they are complicated by sensitive legal and security issues. Most nations that have signed protocols issued by the United Nations, including the United States, have expressed concern over potential encroachments on their national judicial systems, as well as concern over their national security. Thus, they have been reluctant to share certain types of intelligence data. The terrorist attacks of September 11, 2001, increased both the interest in combating transnational crime and sensitivity to the risks of sharing intelligence data (Deflem 2005; Felson and Kalaitzidis 2005).

LO **24-2** Crime Statistics

Crime statistics are not as accurate as social scientists would like, especially since they deal with an issue of grave concern to the people of the United States. Unfortunately, they are frequently cited as if they were completely reliable. Such data do serve as an indicator of police activity, as well as an approximate indication of the level of certain crimes. Yet it would be a mistake to interpret these data as an exact representation of the incidence of crime.

INDEX CRIMES AND VICTIMIZATION SURVEYS

Typically, the crime data reported in the United States are based on **index crimes**, or the eight types of crime tabulated each year by the Federal Bureau of Investigation (FBI). This category of criminal behavior generally consists of those serious offenses that people think of when they express concern about the nation's crime problem. Index crimes include murder, rape, robbery, and assault—all of which are violent crimes committed against people—as well as the property crimes of burglary, larceny-theft, motor vehicle theft, and arson (Table 7-4). The crime index is published annually by the FBI as part of the *Uniform Crime Reports*.

Obviously, many serious offenses, such as white-collar crimes, are not included in this index (although they are recorded elsewhere). In addition, the crime index is disproportionately devoted to property crimes, whereas most citizens are more worried about

TABLE 7-4 NATIONAL CRIME RATES AND PERCENTAGE CHANGE

Crime Index Offenses in 2012	Number Reported	Rate per 100,000 Inhabitants	Percentage Change in Rate Since 2003
Violent crime			
Murder	14,827	5	−17
Forcible rape	84,376	27	−17
Robbery	354,520	113	−21
Aggravated assault	760,739	242	−18
Total	1,214,462	387	−19
Property crime			
Burglary	2,103,787	670	−10
Larceny-theft	6,150,598	1,959	−19
Motor vehicle theft	721,053	230	−47
Total	8,975,438	2,859	−20

Notes: Arson was designated an index offense beginning in 1979; data on arson were still incomplete as of 2012. Because of rounding, the offenses may not add to totals.
Source: Department of Justice 2013: Tables 1, 1a.

violent crimes. Thus, a significant decrease in the number of rapes and robberies could be overshadowed by a slightly larger increase in the number of automobiles stolen, leading to the mistaken impression that *personal* safety is more at risk than before.

The most serious limitation of official crime statistics is that they include only those crimes actually *reported* to law enforcement agencies. Because members of racial and ethnic minority groups often distrust law enforcement agencies, they may not contact the police. Feminist sociologists and others have noted that many women do not report rape or spousal abuse out of fear they will be blamed for the crime.

Partly because of these deficiencies in official statistics, the National Crime Victimization Survey was initiated in 1972. The Bureau of Justice Statistics, in compiling this annual report, seeks information from law enforcement agencies, but also interviews households across the nation and asks if they were victims of a specific set of crimes during the preceding year. In general, those who administer **victimization surveys** question ordinary people, not police officers, to determine whether they have been victims of crime.

Unfortunately, like other crime data, victimization surveys have particular limitations. They require that victims understand what has happened to them and are willing to disclose such information to interviewers. Fraud, income tax evasion, and blackmail are examples of crimes that are unlikely to be reported in victimization studies.

LO 24-3 CRIME TRENDS

Crime fills the news reports on television, over the Internet, and in the newspaper. As a result, the public regards crime as a major social problem. Yet there has been a significant decline in violent crime in the United States in recent years, after many years of increases.

How much has crime declined? Consider this: the rate of crime being reported in 2012 was comparable to what it was back when gasoline cost 29 cents a gallon and the average person earned less than $6,000 a year. That was 1963.

Dramatic declines have occurred within the last decade. As Table 7-4 shows, both violent crime and property crime dropped about 20 percent in the last 10 years. Although a tragic 14,827 people were murdered in 2012, in 1991 that number was a staggering 24,700. Declines have also been registered in victimization surveys (Figure 7-4).

What explains these declines in both index crimes and victimization rates? Possible explanations include the following:

- Community-oriented policing and crime prevention programs
- New gun control laws
- A massive increase in the prison population, which at least prevents inmates from committing crimes outside prison
- New surveillance technologies
- Better residential and business security
- The decline of the crack cocaine epidemic, which soared in the late 1980s
- The aging of the population, as the number of people in their 50s increased and the number in their 20s decreased

No single explanation could account for such a marked change in crime rates. Taken together, however, these changes in public policy, public health, technology, and demographics may well explain it (Florida 2011; Uggen 2012; James Q. Wilson 2011; Wood 2012).

Feminist scholars draw our attention to one significant countertrend: the proportion of major crimes committed by women has increased. However, violent crimes committed by women, which have never been common, have declined. Despite the

FIGURE 7-4 **VICTIMIZATION RATES, 1993–2012**

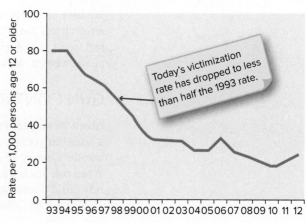

Source: Truman et al. 2013.

"mean girls" headlines in the tabloid magazines, every reliable measure shows that among women, fights, weapons possession, assaults, and violent injuries have plunged over the last decade (Males and Lind 2010).

LO 24-3 INTERNATIONAL CRIME RATES

If developing reliable crime data is difficult in the United States, making useful cross-national comparisons is even more difficult. Nevertheless, with some care, we can offer preliminary conclusions about how crime rates differ around the world.

During the 1980s and 1990s, violent crimes were much more common in the United States than in western Europe. Murders, rapes, and robberies were reported to the police at much higher rates in the United States. Yet the incidence of certain other types of crime appears to be higher elsewhere. For example, England, Ireland, Denmark, and New Zealand all have higher rates of car theft than the United States. Developing nations have significant rates of reported homicide due to civil unrest and political conflict among civilians (van Dijk et al. 2007).

A particularly worrisome development has been the rapid escalation in homicide rates in developing countries that supply drugs to industrialized countries, especially the United States. The huge profits generated by cocaine exports to North America and Europe have allowed drug gangs to arm themselves to the point of becoming illegal armies. Homicide rates in Mexico are now about twice as high as those in the United States. Honduras, Guatemala, Venezuela, and El Salvador's homicide rates are three to five times those of Mexico (*The Economist* 2010c).

Why are rates of violent crime generally so much higher in the United States than in western Europe? Sociologist Elliot Currie (1985, 1998) has suggested that our society places greater emphasis on individual economic achievement than other societies. At the same time, many observers have noted that the culture of the United States has long tolerated, if not condoned, many forms of violence. Coupled with sharp disparities between poor and affluent citizens, significant unemployment, and substantial alcohol and drug abuse, these factors combine to produce a climate conducive to crime.

Another contributor to violent crime in the United States is the prevalence of guns in our society. Although gun rights activists claim that access to guns does not contribute to violent behavior, the United States has a far higher rate of gun violence than other countries where gun ownership is more tightly controlled. In the Social Policy section that follows, we'll consider the pros and cons in the heated debate over gun control.

SOCIAL POLICY and Social Control

We have seen that researchers rely on a number of tools, from time-tested observational research and use of existing sources to the latest in computer technologies. Because in the real world, sociological research can have far-reaching consequences for public policy and public welfare, we will evaluate its impact on gun control.

GUN CONTROL

About 20 minutes into the midnight screening of *The Dark Knight Rises,* James Holmes, a disturbed young man armed with a handgun, a shotgun, and a semiautomatic rifle, burst into the Century 16 movie theater in Aurora, Colorado, and began firing indiscriminately. When the attack was over, 12 people lay dead and 58 others were injured. On that day in July 2012, journalists noted that the crime marked the 125th fatal mass shooting since the 1999 attack on Columbine High, also in Colorado.

Before the year's end, another mass shooting took place in Newtown, Connecticut. Twenty-six people, most of them children, were killed at the Sandy Hook Elementary School. Unlike other mass killings, the event in Newtown galvanized the public, raising calls for stricter gun controls. Yet as gun ownership advocates were quick to point out, Connecticut already had the fifth most restrictive gun laws of any state in the nation (Brady Campaign 2013; Hopper and Ortiz 2012).

Guns and ammunition are big business in the United States, where the Second Amendment to the Constitution guarantees the "right of the people to keep and bear arms." Currently, about 35 percent of U.S. households have some type of firearm on the premises. Informal gun clubs of both a primary- and secondary-group nature flourish across the country. On a national basis, powerful formal organizations promote gun ownership. Clearly, owning a gun is not a deviant act in our society (Federal Bureau of Investigation 2012).

Those U.S. households that own guns possess a lot of them. To put the statistics into perspective, the United States has more guns per person than any other country in the world—888 firearms per 100 people. Yemen holds second place with 55 firearms per 100 people; Switzerland has 46 and Finland, 45 guns per 100 residents (Zakaria 2012).

Over the last two decades, the demand for stricter gun controls has declined rather than grown. At its highest point of support, 66 percent of Americans felt that controlling gun ownership was more important than protecting the right to own a gun. By 2012, even in the aftermath of the shootings in Newtown, that measure had dropped to 49 percent. During this time, the National Rifle Association (NRA) used its impressive power to block or dilute gun control efforts.

Although reported crime has declined in recent years, the role of firearms in crime has remained fairly consistent. Over the past five years, two-thirds of all murders were committed with firearms. Although gun owners frequently insist that they need to own firearms to protect themselves and their loved ones from violent criminals, high-profile assassinations of public figures such as President John F. Kennedy, Senator Robert Kennedy, Dr. Martin Luther King Jr., and Beatle John Lennon have forced legislators to consider stricter gun control measures.

Gun control legislation began with the Brady Handgun Violence Prevention Act, named after White House press secretary Jim Brady, who was seriously wounded in the 1981 assassination attempt against President Ronald Reagan. John Hinckley, the would-be assassin, had given false information about himself at the pawnshop where he bought the gun that he used to shoot Reagan and Brady. The Brady Act, which took effect in 1994, mandates that firearms dealers must run criminal history background checks on people who wish to purchase guns. About 2 percent of all gun purchases are denied as a result of such background checks. Denials are most commonly made because the prospective purchaser is a convicted felon or has had a restraining order filed against him because of domestic violence (Federal Bureau of Investigation 2012; Frandsen et al. 2013).

Not satisfied with the restrictions in the Brady Act, gun control advocates claim that even stricter legislation is needed. Opponents respond that the Brady Act hampers only honest people; those with criminal intent can turn to other sources for guns. Instead of passing further legislation, they suggest strengthening and enforcing existing penalties for the illegal use of guns.

In 2008, in the landmark case *District of Columbia v. Heller,* the Supreme Court struck down a near-total ban on firearms in the nation's capitol by a 5-4 ruling. Two years later, by a 5-4 vote in *McDonald v. City of Chicago,* the Court overturned a firearms ban that had stood in Chicago for 28 years. The two verdicts were lauded by those who favor gun rights, but denounced by advocates of gun control. Gun rights groups

A gun owner engages in target practice with her bolt-action rifle. Many gun enthusiasts enjoy competing in marksmanship contests.

continue to test the constitutionality of other restrictions on gun ownership, even as gun control advocates work to craft legislation that will be acceptable to the justices (Pilkington 2010; Winkler 2009).

Applying Sociology to Gun Control As we have noted before, sociologists and other researchers often have difficulty securing funding for research on controversial issues. In 1993, a study commissioned by the Centers for Disease Control (CDC) concluded that statistically, a firearm that is kept in the home is far more likely to be involved in the death of a family member than to be used in self-defense. In response, gun supporters charged that the CDC's study was politically motivated. Three years later, under pressure from lobbyists, Congress prohibited all federal agencies from collecting data and from funding or conducting research on firearms ownership and gun violence. The ban has stood since 1996. Although privately funded research continues, donors' willingness and financial ability to support it varies over time (Kellerman et al. 1993; S. Lee 2013).

Particularly alarming to sociologists has been the virtual cutoff of federal funding for research into the causes of gun violence. Studies of the links between video games, media images, and gun violence have effectively been blocked by those who suspect that such research would support gun controls. Lobbyists have even blocked funds that would help the CDC to better understand how and when the use of firearms results in violent death (Hillsman 2013).

Conflict theorists contend that powerful groups like the NRA can dominate the legislative process in this way because of their ability to mobilize resources in opposition to the will of the majority. Founded in 1871, the NRA has over 4 million members; state rifle associations, with 4 to 5 million members, support many of the NRA's goals. In contrast, the Brady Campaign to Prevent Gun Violence, a key organization in the gun control battle, has only 400,000 members. Compared to the NRA's formidable war chest, the Brady Campaign's resources are limited.

Interactionists note that both opponents and proponents of gun control use symbols to their advantage. Opponents typically point to the Constitution and the tradition of gun ownership. Proponents point to spectacular episodes of violence, such as spree shootings on college campuses, as proof of the need to restrict firearms sales. Yet gun rights supporters see the same events as proof that students need guns to defend themselves (Lio et al. 2008).

Interactionists have also studied how gun rights organizations like the NRA present their argument to their own members. Among sympathizers, they frame the issue not so much as one of safety or crime, but of civil rights. Gun rights advocates see the Constitution as the basis for their campaign to facilitate gun ownership (Gregory 2007).

Initiating Gun Control Policy Advocates for stricter gun control laws recommend a series of measures that they would like to see enacted:

- Strengthen the tools that law enforcement officers need to crack down on corrupt gun dealers and curb illegal gun trafficking.
- Extend Brady background checks to all gun sales.
- Seek to regulate assault weapons and large-capacity ammunition magazines.
- Stop large-volume gun sales that supply gun traffickers.

Towns, states, and the federal government all have the authority to regulate the possession and sale of firearms, and gun control advocates have attempted to pass these measures at all levels of government.

These proposed legal restrictions on gun ownership have met strong opposition from both the NRA and firearms manufacturers. The NRA—which spent $20 million in the 2012 election cycle alone—has been particularly successful in defeating political candidates who favor stricter gun controls, and in backing those who seek to weaken such restrictions. Except in a handful of states, office seekers rarely risk taking an antigun position. Alarmed by the NRA's rhetoric, many voters fear that gun controls will restrict their ability to protect themselves, independent of law enforcement. Thus, in the year after the

Newtown shootings, state legislatures enacted 109 new gun laws, 70 of which *loosened* firearms restrictions (M. Scherer 2013; Yourish and Buchanan 2013).

Public health advocates have weighed in on the issue, noting the 30,000 people in the United States who die every year through gun violence, whether by suicide, homicide, or accidental discharge. This group advocates making guns safer—for example, by adding an indicator that the gun is loaded and/or a latch that prevents a magazine from being removed with a bullet still in the firing chamber. A more sophisticated approach to increasing safety would be to "personalize" firearms by requiring the owner/user to activate a code before the gun can be used. Public safety officials have also weighed in, observing that in 10 states firearms deaths exceed motor vehicle deaths (G. Brown 2008a, 2008b; Violence Policy Center 2012).

E Evaluate

Read each question carefully and then select or provide the best answer.

1. Compared with other types of crime, white-collar crime
   a. receives harsher social sanctions and criminal penalties.
   b. is more concerned with secrecy, deception, and evasion.
   c. does less damage to the criminal's reputation and future career.
   d. is more often committed spontaneously, without planning or conspiracy.

2. The term *bias crime* is another name for
   a. hate crime.
   b. professional crime.
   c. technology-based crime.
   d. organized crime.

3. From the feminist perspective, prostitution and some forms of pornography are not _____ crimes.

4. Daniel Bell used the term _____ to describe the process during which leadership of organized crime was transferred from Irish Americans to Jewish Americans and later to Italian Americans and others.

5. Consumer fraud, bribery, and income tax evasion are considered _____ crimes.

Answers

1 (c); 2 (a); 3 victimless; 4 ethnic succession; 5 white-collar

R Rethink

Consider these questions to get a deeper understanding of the material.

1. Why is it useful for sociologists to have victimization surveys in addition to reported crime data?

2. What role does labeling theory play in the fact that people who commit white-collar crimes are penalized less both socially and formally than those who commit other types of crimes?

RECAP

LO 24-1 Differentiate between deviance and crime and describe the six types of crime.

- Crime, a violation of criminal law that bears official penalties, represents a deviation from formal (not informal) social norms administered by the state.
- Sociologists differentiate among so-called victimless crimes (such as drug use and prostitution), professional crime, organized crime, white-collar crime, hate crimes, and transnational crime.
- Explain how crime statistics are gathered, and explain limitations of current methods of reporting crime statistics.

LO 24-2 Explain methods of gathering crime statistics and describe their limitations.

- Crime statistics are based on what the FBI terms *index crimes,* which focus more on crimes against property than on crimes against persons. Many serious crimes, such as white-collar crimes, are not included in this index.
- The most serious limitation of official crime statistics is that they include only reported crimes. Many crimes are "invisible"—not reported because of distrust of the police, fear of revenge, or shame.

LO 24-3 Summarize crime trends in the United States and internationally.

- Rates of violent crime in the United States have been dropping in recent decades, but they are higher than the rates in other Western societies. Rates of other types of crime vary from nation to nation.
- Gun violence has become a major problem not just in the United States, but around the world. Yet gun control legislation in the United States is extremely controversial, opposed by powerful interest groups whose members see it as an abridgment of their constitutional right to bear arms.

KEY TERMS

Crime A violation of criminal law for which some governmental authority applies formal penalties.

Hate crime A criminal offense committed because of the offender's bias against a race, religion, ethnic group, national origin, or sexual orientation. Also referred to as *bias crime.*

Index crimes The eight types of crime tabulated each year by the FBI in the *Uniform Crime Reports:* murder, rape, robbery, assault, burglary, theft, motor vehicle theft, and arson.

Organized crime The work of a group that regulates relations among criminal enterprises involved in illegal activities, including prostitution, gambling, and the smuggling and sale of illegal drugs.

Professional criminal A person who pursues crime as a day-to-day occupation, developing skilled techniques and enjoying a certain degree of status among other criminals.

Transnational crime Crime that occurs across multiple national borders.

Victimization survey A questionnaire or interview given to a sample of the population to determine whether people have been victims of crime.

Victimless crime A term used by sociologists to describe the willing exchange among adults of widely desired but illegal goods and services.

White-collar crime Illegal acts committed by affluent, "respectable" individuals in the course of business activities.

The Case of . . . Doing Their Own Thing

Erin Martin and her partner Raoul Davis are part of a loose-knit community in New Mexico. "What binds us to the other dozen families living nearby is that we've all made some sort of personal commitment to finding a new, greener, more *human* way of living," Martin explains. Like their friends, Martin and Davis grow most of their own food, wear secondhand clothes, and use bicycles instead of cars. "We don't do TV," Martin says. "We don't want to fill our heads with those values. You know, 'Buy this and you'll be happy. Have more stuff and you'll be loved.' It's just so cynical." For many of their day-to-day needs, Martin and Davis barter goods and services with their friends. "We helped our neighbors dig a root cellar last week," Martin says. "This week, they're coming to help us reroof the back part of the house."

Martin and Davis aren't blind to the world around them. "We go into town about once every two weeks," Martin says, "and people stare at us with the same kind of looks they'd give a bunch of motorcycle thugs." Suspicion has even dogged them to their doorstep. "The sheriff showed up here once," Martin says. "He said someone in town told him we were messing with dangerous drugs out here, doing weird 'sex things.' We let him look over our place even though he had no warrant. In the end, he sort of apologized for barging in." Martin shakes her head, "People think if you're doing something different from them, you must be doing something wrong."

1. Do you think Martin and Davis are deviants? If so, how do they violate the standards of conduct or expectations of their society?

2. What evidence do you see that Martin and Davis are being stigmatized by the townspeople?

3. What do Martin's attitudes about TV suggest she understands about social control?

4. Why do you think one of the townspeople went to the sheriff with the story about drugs and "weird" sexual practices?

5. Do you think the lifestyle Martin, Davis, and their friends have chosen is a result of social disorganization? Why or why not?

Taking Notes in Class

Taking good notes in class isn't easy, especially in sociology, a subject with many technical terms and new concepts. Still, notetaking is a critical skill that you should work to develop. What instructors say in class is usually the content that they believe to be most important. The following proven techniques should help you improve your sociology notetaking.

 **Prepare**

- Do your homework from the previous class: Come to class with your textbook read and your assignments complete.
- Pick a seat that will enable you to see and hear clearly.
- Do some quick prep work before class: Skim your notes from the previous class and then find the blank page on which you will take notes.

 **Organize**

- Have a good writing tool (pen, pencil, or computer) and a backup.
- Tip: Write on only one side of your note paper, leaving the other side for later additions or clarifications.

Work

- Listen actively and try to make sense of the instructor's words. Don't just mechanically write down every word—it won't make sense.
- Boil it down! Don't write complete sentences. Use abbreviations.
- Remember your learning style: If you're a *visual learner,* use diagrams and drawings—even silly cartoons. If you have a *reading* learning style, ask the instructor to write key words or phrases on the board.
- If you don't understand something, ask the instructor to clarify. You're probably not alone in being confused. (Follow your personality style: If you have an *introverted* personality, ask privately, after class.)

 **Evaluate**

- Look over your notes. If you missed something, ask the instructor or a classmate for help.
- Take a few minutes to expand on your notes so they aren't completely mysterious later.

Rethink

- Use mnemonics (memory tricks) to memorize key concepts and important lists.
- Read over your notes soon after class, and then again a day later. This procedure will help you to transfer the information you have learned from short-term memory to long-term memory. A few minutes of memorization now will save literally hours later.
- If you have a study group, get together with them to discuss the content of the class.

Rate Your Notetaking Skills

The ability to take good notes is key to recalling the essential content of any course. Good notes are also a lifesaver as you review for exams. But how do you know if you are taking the kind of notes that will best serve your needs? Read through the following statements, then place a check mark in the column to the right that best describes how often the statement applies to you.

	Frequently	Sometimes	Rarely
1. I can read my notes from last week and still make sense of them.			
2. My notes only contain important points. There is no extra material.			
3. If I discover a "hole" when reviewing my notes, I go back to the book, handout, or instructor to fill in the missing information.			
4. I can review my notes three months later and reconstruct the essential content of the class.			
5. My notes interpret and summarize the ideas behind the instructor's words.			
6. I listen for clues such as "you need to know" and "don't forget" to determine what I should note.			
7. I use abbreviations in my notes, such as "i.e." for "that is" or "meaning," and "e.g." for "for example."			
8. I take notes in outline form or draw diagrams to show relationships of concepts.			
9. I notice what the instructor is most enthusiastic about and include that in my notes.			
10. I note definitions, quotations, and formulas the instructor writes on the board or uses in PowerPoint slides.			

SCORE:

Count up the number of times you checked "frequently."

9-10: Your notetaking skills are topnotch. Review at exam time should be easy.

6-8: You have a number of excellent notetaking skills, but you can add more from the list here. Your goal is to answer "frequently" to item 4.

Less than 6: Starting with your next class, begin incorporating the notetaking skills listed here. You will find taking notes and reviewing material a lot easier once you stop trying to write down everything the instructor says.

8 Stratification and Social Mobility in the United States

MODULE 25 Social Stratification

MODULE 26 Stratification by Social Class

MODULE 27 Poverty

Sociology at **WORK** DIRECTOR OF COMMUNITY SOUP KITCHEN

LEE GREENBAUM runs a soup kitchen in Pittsburgh. On any given evening from 5 to 8 p.m., he and his staff of volunteers serve meals to over 3,000 people. It's a major effort that requires starting the day at first light and working cleanup until midnight. It also requires Greenbaum, as director of the soup kitchen, to solicit and coordinate food donations. "It's a little easier now to get some generosity from the community. The media has recently made people aware of the sharp divide in wealth in this country," Greenbaum says. "But we had 2,000 people a day back in the boom-time of the 1990s, and no one wanted to know. The attitude was 'Don't spoil my party.'" Greenbaum says people from a wide variety of situations come to his door. "I get the unemployed whose jobs were shipped overseas and their pensions stolen. I get minimum-wage workers who eat here and sleep God knows where. The ones with kids are really heartbreaking." Greenbaum even gets some college students. They're hardly freeloading, he says. "There's an awful lot of students working 20- to 30-hour weeks, and taking out loans, who still can't pay the rent *and* eat." One in five households can't meet basic needs. That means *food*," Greenbaum says. "Be honest, no one would choose to come here if they had another option." ■

Looking Ahead

EVER SINCE PEOPLE FIRST BEGAN TO SPECULATE ABOUT THE NATURE of human society, their attention has been drawn to the differences between individuals and groups within society. The term **social inequality**, which has been much in the headlines recently, describes a condition in which members of society have differing amounts of wealth, prestige, or power. Some degree of social inequality characterizes every society.

When a system of social inequality is based on a hierarchy of groups, sociologists refer to it as **stratification**: a structured ranking of entire groups of people that perpetuates unequal economic rewards and power in a society. These unequal rewards are evident not only in the distribution of wealth and income, but even in the distressing mortality rates of impoverished communities. Stratification involves the ways in which one generation passes on social inequalities to the next, producing groups of people arranged in rank order, from low to high.

Stratification is a crucial subject of sociological investigation because of its pervasive influence on human interactions and institutions. It results inevitably in social inequality, because certain groups of people stand higher in social rankings, control scarce resources, wield power, and receive special treatment. As we will see in this chapter, the consequences of stratification are evident in the unequal distribution of both income and wealth in industrial societies. The term **income** refers to salaries and wages. In contrast, **wealth** is an inclusive term encompassing all a person's material assets, including land, stocks, and other types of property.

Is social inequality an inescapable part of society? How does government policy affect the life chances of the working poor? Is this country still a place where a hardworking person can move up the social ladder? This chapter focuses on the unequal distribution of socially valued rewards and its consequences. We will begin by examining four general systems of stratification, including the one most familiar to us, the social class system. We will examine three sociological perspectives on stratification, paying particular attention to the theories of Karl Marx and Max Weber. We'll also ask whether stratification is universal and see what sociologists, including functionalist and conflict theorists, have to say about that question.

We will see too how sociologists define social class, and examine the consequences of stratification for people's wealth and income, safety, and educational opportunities. Then we will take a close look at poverty, particularly the question of who belongs to the underclass and why. And we will confront the question of social mobility, both upward and downward. Finally, in the Social Policy section, we will examine the issue of minimum wage laws.

P Prepare Learning Objectives

LO 25-1 Define stratification and describe the four general systems of stratification.

LO 25-2 Describe Rossides's five-class model as applied to the United States.

LO 25-3 Analyze stratification using the views of Marx and Weber and the major sociological perspectives.

O Organize Module Outline

W Work

LO **25-1** Systems of Stratification

Sociologists consider stratification on many levels, ranging from its impact on the individual to worldwide patterns of inequality. No matter where we look, however, disparities in wealth and income are substantial. Take income and poverty patterns in the United States, for example. As the top part of Figure 8-1 shows, in some states the median household income is 25 percent higher than that in other states. And as the bottom part of the figure shows, the poverty rate in many states is 200 percent that of other states.

Look at the four general systems of stratification examined here—slavery, castes, estates, and social classes—as ideal types useful for purposes of analysis. Any stratification system may include elements of more than one type. For example, prior to the Civil War, you could find in the southern states of the United States both social classes dividing Whites from Whites and the institutionalized enslavement of Blacks.

To understand these systems better, it may be helpful to review the distinction between *achieved status* and *ascribed status,* explained in Chapter 5. **Ascribed status** is a social position assigned to a person by society without regard for the person's unique talents or characteristics. In contrast, **achieved status** is a social position that a person attains largely

FIGURE 8-1   THE 50 STATES: CONTRASTS IN INCOME AND POVERTY LEVELS

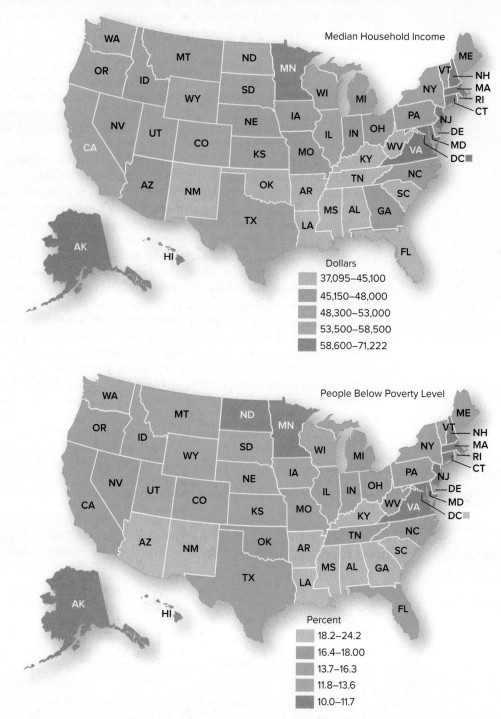

Median Household Income

Dollars
- 37,095–45,100
- 45,150–48,000
- 48,300–53,000
- 53,500–58,500
- 58,600–71,222

People Below Poverty Level

Percent
- 18.2–24.2
- 16.4–18.00
- 13.7–16.3
- 11.8–13.6
- 10.0–11.7

Note: National median household income was $51,371; national poverty rate, 15.9 percent.
Source: 2012 census data presented in Bureau of the Census 2013a: Tables R1701, R1901.

through his or her own efforts. The two are closely linked. The nation's most affluent families generally inherit wealth and status, while many members of racial and ethnic minorities inherit disadvantaged status. Age and gender, as well, are ascribed statuses that influence a person's wealth and social position.

SLAVERY

The most extreme form of legalized social inequality for both individuals and groups is **slavery**. What distinguishes this oppressive system of stratification is that enslaved individuals are *owned* by other people, who treat these human beings as property, just as if they were household pets or appliances.

Slavery has varied in the way it has been practiced. In ancient Greece, the main source of slaves was piracy and captives of war. Although succeeding generations could inherit slave status, it was not necessarily permanent. A person's status might change, depending on which city-state happened to triumph in a military conflict. In effect, all citizens had the potential to become slaves or receive freedom, depending on the circumstances of history. In contrast, in the United States and Latin America, where slavery was an ascribed status, racial and legal barriers prevented the freeing of slaves.

Today, the Universal Declaration of Human Rights, which is binding on all members of the United Nations, prohibits slavery in all its forms. Yet more people are enslaved today than at any point in world history. In many developing countries, bonded laborers are imprisoned in virtual lifetime employment; in some countries, human beings are owned outright. But a form of slavery also exists in Europe and the United States, where guest workers and illegal immigrants have been forced to labor for years under terrible conditions, either to pay off debts or to avoid being turned over to immigration authorities.

Both these situations are likely to involve the transnational crime of trafficking in humans. Each year an estimated 600,000 to 800,000 men, women, and children are transported across international borders for slavery or sexual exploitation. In 2000, the U.S. Congress passed the Trafficking Victims Protection Act, which established minimum standards for the elimination of human trafficking. The act requires the State Department to monitor other countries' efforts to vigorously investigate, prosecute, and convict individuals who participate in trafficking—including government officials. Each year, the department reports its findings, some of which are shown in Table 8-1. Tier 1 and Tier 2 countries are thought to be largely in compliance with the act. Tier 2 Watch countries are making efforts to comply, though trafficking remains a significant concern. Tier 3 countries are not compliant and are not making significant efforts to comply.

TABLE 8-1   HUMAN TRAFFICKING REPORT

Tier 1 Full Compliance	Tier 2 Significant Effort	Tier 2 Watch List Some Effort, But Trafficking Remains a Concern	Tier 3 Noncompliant, No Effort
Australia	Bolivia	Afghanistan	China
Canada	Brazil	Burma	Congo (Dem. Rep.)
Colombia	Chile	Haiti	Cuba
Denmark	Greece	Iraq	Iran
France	India	Kenya	Kuwait
Germany	Japan	Lebanon	North Korea
Great Britain	Mexico	Malaysia	Russia
Norway	Philippines	Panama	Saudi Arabia
Poland	South Africa	Thailand	Sudan
South Korea	Turkey	Ukraine	Syria
Spain	Vietnam	Venezuela	Zimbabwe

Note: Each tier lists only a sample of all nations classified. Since the *Human Trafficking Report* is created by the State Department, in the report the level of compliance by the United States is considered to be "full compliance."
Source: Department of State 2013.

CASTES

Castes are hereditary ranks that are usually religiously dictated and that tend to be fixed and immobile. Caste membership is an ascribed status (at birth, children automatically assume the same position as their parents). Each caste is quite sharply defined, and members are expected to marry within that caste.

The caste system is generally associated with Hinduism in India and other countries. In India there are four major castes, called *varnas.* A fifth category of outcastes, referred to as the *untouchables,* represents 16 percent of the population; its members are considered so lowly and unclean as to have no place within this stratification system. In an effort to avoid perpetuating the historical stigma these people bear, the government now refers to the untouchables as *scheduled castes.* The untouchables themselves prefer *Dalit* ("the repressed"), a term that communicates their desire to overcome their disadvantaged status.

In 1950, after gaining independence from Great Britain, India adopted a new constitution that formally outlawed the caste system. Over the past decade or two, however, urbanization and technological advances have brought more change to India's caste system than government or politics has in more than half a century. The anonymity of city life tends to blur caste boundaries, allowing the *Dalit* to pass unrecognized in temples, schools, and places of employment. And the globalization of high technology has opened up India's social order, bringing new opportunities to those who possess the skills and ability to capitalize on them.

The term *caste* can also be applied in recent historical contexts outside India. For example, the system of stratification that characterized the southern United States from the end of the Civil War through the 1960s resembled a caste system. So did the rigid system of segregation that prevailed in the Republic of South Africa under apartheid, from 1948 through the 1990s. In both cases, race was the defining factor that placed a person in the social hierarchy.

ESTATES

A third type of stratification system, called *estates,* was associated with feudal societies during the Middle Ages. The **estate system**, or *feudalism,* required peasants to work land leased to them by nobles in exchange for military protection and other services. The basis for the system was the nobles' ownership of land, which was critical to their superior and privileged status. As in systems based on slavery and caste, inheritance of one's position largely defined the estate system. The nobles inherited their titles and property; the peasants were born into a subservient position within an agrarian society.

As the estate system developed, it became more differentiated. Nobles began to achieve varying degrees of authority. By the 12th century, a priesthood had emerged in most of Europe, along with classes of merchants and artisans. For the first time there were groups of people whose wealth did not depend on land ownership or agriculture. This economic change had profound social consequences as the estate system ended and a class system of stratification came into existence.

LO 25-2 SOCIAL CLASSES

A **class system** is a social ranking based primarily on economic position in which achieved characteristics can influence social mobility. In contrast to slavery and caste systems, the boundaries between classes are imprecisely defined, and one can move from one stratum, or level, of society to another. Even so, class systems maintain stable stratification hierarchies and patterns of class division, and they, too, are marked by unequal distribution of wealth and power. Class standing, although it is achieved, is heavily dependent on family and ascribed factors, such as race and ethnicity.

Sociologist Daniel Rossides (1997) uses a five-class model to describe the class system of the United States: the upper class, the upper-middle class, the lower-middle class,

Worried about home foreclosures? Not the wealthy. The rich now spend $50,000 to $250,000 on their children's playhouses and tree houses.

the working class, and the lower class. Although the lines separating social classes in his model are not so sharp as the divisions between castes, members of the five classes differ significantly in ways other than just income level.

Upper and Lower Classes Rossides characterizes about 1 to 2 percent of the people of the United States as *upper class*. This group is limited to the very wealthy, who associate in exclusive clubs and social circles. In contrast, the *lower class,* consisting of approximately 20 to 25 percent of the population, disproportionately consists of Blacks, Hispanics, single mothers with dependent children, and people who cannot find regular work or must make do with low-paying work. This class lacks both wealth and income and is too weak politically to exercise significant power.

Both these classes, at opposite ends of the nation's social hierarchy, reflect the importance of ascribed status and achieved status. Ascribed statuses such as race and disability clearly influence a person's wealth and social position. People with disabilities are particularly vulnerable to unemployment, are often poorly paid, and tend to occupy the lower rungs of the occupational ladder. Regardless of their actual performance on the job, the disabled are stigmatized as not earning their keep. We will look again at the plight of the lower class when we consider poverty and welfare policies.

The economist John Kenneth Galbraith (1977:44) observed that "of all classes the rich are the most noticed and the least studied." The poor receive a good deal of attention from reporters, social activists, and policymakers seeking to alleviate their poverty, but the very affluent, who live apart from the rest of the population, are largely a mystery. Since Galbraith's comment, moreover, the residential separation of the rich has grown. The newspaper's society page may give us a peek at members of this class, but we know very little about their everyday lives. Statistically, over 2 million households in the United States are worth more than $10 million each. Less than 10 percent of these people inherited their money, and very few of them are celebrities (Massey 2007).

Middle Class Sandwiched between the upper and lower classes in this model are the upper-middle class, the lower-middle class, and the working class. The *upper-middle class,* about 10 to 15 percent of the population, includes professionals such as doctors, lawyers, and architects. They participate extensively in politics and take leadership roles in voluntary associations. The *lower-middle class,* about 30 to 35 percent of the population, includes less affluent professionals (such as elementary school teachers and nurses), owners of small businesses, and a sizable number of clerical workers. While not all members of the middle class hold degrees from a college, they share the goal of sending their children there.

The middle class is currently under a great deal of economic pressure. Close analysis indicates that of those who lost their middle-class standing during the latter 20th century, about half rose to a higher ranking in the social class system, while half dropped to a lower position. These data mean that the United States is moving toward a "bipolar income distribution." That is, a broadly based middle class is slowly being replaced by two growing groups of rich and poor.

Sociologists and other scholars have identified several factors that have contributed to the shrinking size of the middle class:

- *Disappearing opportunities for those with little education.* Today, most jobs require formal schooling, yet less than a third of adults between ages 35 and 44 have prepared themselves with a college degree.

- *Global competition and rapid advances in technology.* These two trends, which began several decades ago, mean that workers are more easily replaced now than they were in the past. Increasingly, globalization and technological advances are affecting the more complex jobs that were once the bread and butter of middle-class workers.

- *Growing dependence on the temporary workforce.* For those workers who have no other job, temporary positions are tenuous at best, because they rarely offer health care coverage or retirement benefits.

- *The rise of new growth industries and non-union workplaces, like fast-food restaurants.* Industries may have added employment opportunities, but they are at the lower end of the wage scale.

Today, the once broadly based middle class is on the defensive and is slowly being squeezed by two growing groups, the rich and the poor.

Middle-class families want comfortable homes, college degrees for their children, occasional family vacations, affordable health care—the cost of which has been growing faster than inflation—and retirement security. The answer, for many people, is either to go without or to work longer hours at multiple jobs (Blank 2010, 2011; Khan 2013; Massey 2007; Thurow 1984).

Working Class Rossides describes the *working class*—about 40 to 45 percent of the population—as people who hold regular manual or blue-collar jobs. Certain members of this class, such as electricians, may have higher incomes than people in the lower-middle class. Yet even if they have achieved some degree of economic security, they tend to identify with manual workers and their long history of involvement in the labor movement of the United States.

Of the five classes, the working class is declining noticeably in size. In the economy of the United States, service and technical jobs are replacing those involved in the actual manufacturing or transportation of goods.

Class Warfare On September 17, 2011, two thousand protesters assembled in New York City, claiming to represent the vast majority of Americans. In their own words, these members of what soon became known as the Occupy Wall Street movement were "the 99 percent"—those Americans who had suffered as the wealthiest 1 percent flourished. In the next few weeks the movement, which had begun in Canada, spread across the United States to Honolulu and then throughout the world (Peralta 2011; M. Scherer 2011).

With Occupy Wall Street in the headlines, political leaders began to speak of class conflict. To some, the Occupy movement's call for a reduction in social inequality seemed a reply to the federal government's favorable tax treatment of the affluent. Before the recession began, the Bush administration had lowered the income tax rate paid by high-income filers. In 2009, the Tea Party pushed Congress to maintain that tax cut, despite a growing deficit. Others insisted that the affluent actually paid less in taxes than the average citizen, given the many loopholes—offshore bank accounts, and so on—available to them. In Congress, the suggestion that the rich should pay the same effective tax rate as other citizens was met with an angry charge of class warfare.

As we will see shortly, by any statistical measure, the gulf between the rich and everyone else in the United States has grown over the last decade—indeed, over the last 50 years. Yet people do not tend to identify with or see themselves as members of a specific social class. Still, as the rhetoric heated up during the 2012 presidential campaign, and the

Study Alert

Be sure to understand the factors that contribute to the shrinking size of the middle class: fewer opportunities for those with little education, global competition and rapid changes in technology, growing reliance on a temporary workforce, and the rise of nonunion workplaces and new growth industries.

Reactions to the Occupy Wall Street movement varied with people's socioeconomic status. "How about you occupy a job?" former New York City mayor Rudy Giuliani (left) retorted. At the other extreme, Native American leaders observed that their lands have been occupied for five centuries.

Occupy Wall Street movement remained visible, a growing share of the population thought they saw evidence of class conflict. In December 2011, 66 percent of the public (compared to 47 percent in 2009) said they perceived "strong" conflict between the rich and the poor. Younger adults, women, and African Americans were most likely to hold this view. Interestingly, personal income had little to do with such perceptions: the rich were just as likely as the poor to agree with the existence of class conflict (Archer and Orr 2011; Morin and Motel 2013; Skocpol and Williamson 2012).

Indeed, the growing perception that the rich have been flourishing at the expense of everyone else is supported by the facts. Between 2002 and 2012, family incomes of the top hundredth of 1 percent of Americans increased 76 percent, to an average of $21.6 million a year. That figure does not include income from stocks, bonds, and real estate holdings, which was considerable. During the same period, family incomes of the bottom 90 percent of Americans *dropped* 11 percent, to $34,000 a year (Saez 2013).

LO 25-3 Sociological Perspectives on Stratification

Sociologists have hotly debated stratification and social inequality and have reached varying conclusions. No theorist stressed the significance of class for society—and for social change—more strongly than Karl Marx. Marx viewed class differentiation as the crucial determinant of social, economic, and political inequality. In contrast, Max Weber questioned Marx's emphasis on the overriding importance of the economic sector, arguing that stratification should be viewed as having many dimensions.

KARL MARX'S VIEW OF CLASS DIFFERENTIATION

Karl Marx was concerned with stratification in all types of human society, beginning with primitive agricultural tribes and continuing into feudalism. However, his main focus was on the effects of economic inequality on all aspects of 19th-century Europe. The plight of the working class made him feel that it was imperative to strive for changes in the class structure of society.

In Marx's view, social relations during any period of history depend on who controls the primary mode of economic production, such as land or factories. Differential access to scarce resources shapes the relationship between groups. Thus, under the feudal estate system, most production was agricultural, and the land was owned by the nobility. Peasants had little choice but to work according to terms dictated by those who owned the land.

Using this type of analysis, Marx examined social relations within **capitalism**—an economic system in which the means of production are held largely in private hands and the main incentive for economic activity is the accumulation of profits. Marx focused on the two classes that began to emerge as the feudal estate system declined, the bourgeoisie and the proletariat. The **bourgeoisie**, or capitalist class, owns the means of production, such as factories and machinery; the **proletariat** is the working class. In capitalist societies, the members of the bourgeoisie maximize profit in competition with other firms. In the process, they exploit workers, who must exchange their labor for subsistence wages. In Marx's view, members of each class share a distinctive culture. Marx was most interested in the culture of the proletariat, but he also examined the ideology of the bourgeoisie, through which that class justifies its dominance over workers.

According to Marx, exploitation of the proletariat will inevitably lead to the destruction of the capitalist system, because the workers will revolt. But first, the working class must develop **class consciousness**—a subjective awareness of common vested interests and the need for collective political action to bring about social change. Often, workers must overcome what Marx termed **false consciousness**, or an attitude held by members of a class that does not accurately reflect their objective position. A worker with false consciousness may adopt an individualistic viewpoint toward capitalist exploitation ("*I* am being exploited by *my* boss").

A miner peers into the dark at Peabody Energy's Gateway Mine near Coulterville, Illinois. Karl Marx would identify coal miners as members of the proletariat, or working class. Even today, miners are poorly compensated for the considerable dangers they face. Such exploitation of the working class is a core principle of Marxist theory.

In contrast, the class-conscious worker realizes that all workers are being exploited by the bourgeoisie and have a common stake in revolution.

For Marx, class consciousness was part of a collective process in which the proletariat comes to identify the bourgeoisie as the source of its oppression. Revolutionary leaders will guide the working class in its struggle. Ultimately, the proletariat will overthrow the rule of both the bourgeoisie and the government (which Marx saw as representing the interests of capitalists) and will eliminate private ownership of the means of production. In Marx's rather utopian view, classes and oppression will cease to exist in the postrevolutionary workers' state.

How accurate were Marx's predictions? He failed to anticipate the emergence of labor unions, whose power in collective bargaining weakens the stranglehold that capitalists maintain over workers. Moreover, as contemporary conflict theorists note, he did not foresee the extent to which political liberties and relative prosperity could contribute to false consciousness. Many workers came to view themselves as individuals striving for improvement within free societies that offer substantial mobility, rather than as downtrodden members of a social class who face a collective fate. Even today, "class warfare" seems to refer more to diminished individual expectations than to a collective identity. Finally, Marx did not predict that Communist Party rule would be established and later overthrown in the former Soviet Union and throughout Eastern Europe. Still, the Marxist approach to the study of class is useful in stressing the importance of stratification as a determinant of social behavior and the fundamental separation in many societies between two distinct groups, the rich and the poor.

MAX WEBER'S VIEW OF STRATIFICATION

Unlike Karl Marx, Max Weber ([1913–1922] 1947) insisted that no single characteristic (such as class) totally defines a person's position within the stratification system. Instead, writing in 1916, he identified three distinct components of stratification: class, status, and power.

Weber used the term **class** to refer to a group of people who have a similar level of wealth and income. For example, certain workers in the United States try to support

their families through minimum-wage jobs. According to Weber's definition, these wage earners constitute a class because they share the same economic position and fate. Although Weber agreed with Marx on the importance of this economic dimension of stratification, he argued that the actions of individuals and groups cannot be understood *solely* in economic terms.

Weber used the term **status group** to refer to people who have the same prestige or lifestyle. An individual gains status through membership in a desirable group, such as the medical profession. But status is not the same as economic class standing. In our culture, a successful pickpocket may belong to the same income class as a college professor. Yet the thief is widely regarded as holding low status, whereas the professor holds high status.

For Weber, the third major component of stratification has a political dimension. **Power** is the ability to exercise one's will over others. In the United States, power stems from membership in particularly influential groups, such as corporate boards of directors, government bodies, and interest groups. Conflict theorists generally agree that two major sources of power—big business and government—are closely interrelated. For instance, many of the heads of major corporations also hold powerful positions in the government or military.

With Mt. Everest in the background, a wealthy golfer plays a shot in a remote location, which he reached by helicopter. Traveling to exotic places to indulge in sports that most people play at home is an example of Thorstein Veblen's concept of conspicuous consumption, a spending pattern common to those at the very top of the social ladder.

To summarize, in Weber's view, each of us has not one rank in society but three. Our position in a stratification system reflects some combination of class, status, and power. Each factor influences the other two, and in fact the rankings on these three dimensions often tend to coincide. John F. Kennedy came from an extremely wealthy family, attended exclusive preparatory schools, graduated from Harvard University, and went on to become president of the United States. Like Kennedy, many people from affluent backgrounds achieve impressive status and power.

INTERACTIONIST PERSPECTIVE

Both Karl Marx and Max Weber looked at inequality primarily from a macrosociological perspective, considering the entire society or even the global economy. Marx did suggest the importance of a more microsociological analysis, however, when he stressed the ways in which individuals develop a true class consciousness.

Interactionists, as well as economists, have long been interested in the importance of social class in shaping a person's lifestyle. The theorist Thorstein Veblen (1857–1929) noted that those at the top of the social hierarchy typically convert part of their wealth into

From the perspective of . . .

A Classroom Teacher How would you handle the school drive to collect holiday gifts for poor children when some of your students are the children these gifts are intended for?

conspicuous consumption—that is, they purchase goods not to survive but to flaunt their superior wealth and social standing. For example, they may purchase more automobiles than they can reasonably use, or build homes with more rooms than they can possibly occupy. In an element of conspicuous consumption called *conspicuous leisure,* they may jet to a remote destination, staying just long enough to have dinner or view a sunset over some historic locale (Veblen [1899] 1964).

Today, conspicuous consumption has found a new outlet in the cyberworld. Users of social media can now see their friends' vacations and snazzy new cars online—an experience that can provoke what researchers call *Facebook envy.* Studies done in the United States and Germany show that even otherwise happy people can suffer envy and distress over this kind of digitally shared conspicuous consumption (Shea 2013).

At the other end of the spectrum, behavior that is judged to be typical of the lower class is subject not only to ridicule but even to legal action. Communities have, from time to time, banned trailers from people's front yards and sofas from their front porches. In some communities, it is illegal to leave a pickup truck in front of the house overnight. In others, street vendors who sell fruit, flowers, and water face restrictions meant not to serve the general public, but to protect their storefront competitors (Campo-Flores 2013).

Is Stratification Universal?

Must some members of society receive greater rewards than others? Do people need to feel socially and economically superior to others? Can social life be organized without structured inequality? These questions have been debated for centuries, especially among political activists. Utopian socialists, religious minorities, and members of recent counter-cultures have all attempted to establish communities that to some extent or other would abolish inequality in social relationships.

Social scientists have found that inequality exists in all societies—even the simplest. For example, when anthropologist Gunnar Landtman ([1938] 1968) studied the Kiwai Papuans of New Guinea, at first he noticed little differentiation among them. Every man in the village did the same work and lived in similar housing. However, on closer inspection, Landtman observed that certain Papuans—men who were warriors, harpooners, and sorcerers—were described as "a little more high" than others. In contrast, villagers who were female, unemployed, or unmarried were considered "down a little bit" and were barred from owning land.

Stratification is universal in that all societies maintain some form of social inequality among members. Depending on its values, a society may assign people to distinctive ranks based on their religious knowledge, skill in hunting, physical attractiveness, trading expertise, or ability to provide health care. But why has such inequality developed in human societies? And how much differentiation among people, if any, is actually essential?

Functionalist and conflict theorists offer contrasting explanations for the existence and necessity of social stratification. Functionalists maintain that a differential system of rewards and punishments is necessary for the efficient operation of society. Conflict theorists argue that competition for scarce resources results in significant political, economic, and social inequality.

FUNCTIONALIST PERSPECTIVE

Would people go to school for many years to become physicians if they could make as much money and gain as much respect working as street cleaners? Functionalists say no, which is partly why they believe that a stratified society is universal.

In the view of Kingsley Davis and Wilbert Moore (1945), society must distribute its members among a variety of social positions. It must not only make sure that these positions are filled but also see that they are filled by people with the appropriate talents and abilities. Rewards, including money and prestige, are based on the importance of a position and the relative scarcity of qualified personnel. Yet this assessment often devalues work

As the reality television series *Ice Road Truckers,* now in its seventh season, suggests, long-haul truck drivers take pride in their low-prestige job. According to the conflict perspective, the cultural beliefs that form a society's dominant ideology, such as the popular image of the truck driver as hero, help the wealthy to maintain their power and control at the expense of the lower classes.

performed by certain segments of society, such as women's work in the home or in occupations traditionally filled by women, or low-status work in fast-food outlets.

Davis and Moore argue that stratification is universal and that social inequality is necessary so that people will be motivated to fill functionally important positions. But critics say that unequal rewards are not the only means of encouraging people to fill critical positions and occupations. Personal pleasure, intrinsic satisfaction, and value orientations also motivate people to enter particular careers. Functionalists agree, but they note that society must use some type of reward to motivate people to enter unpleasant or dangerous jobs and professions that require a long training period. This response does not address stratification systems in which status is largely inherited, such as slave or caste societies. Moreover, even if stratification is inevitable, the functionalist explanation for differential rewards does not explain the wide disparity between the rich and the poor (R. Collins 1975; Kerbo 2012).

CONFLICT PERSPECTIVE

The writings of Karl Marx lie at the heart of conflict theory. Marx viewed history as a continuous struggle between the oppressors and the oppressed, which ultimately would culminate in an egalitarian, classless society. In terms of stratification, he argued that under capitalism, the dominant class—the bourgeoisie—manipulates the economic and political systems in order to maintain control over the exploited proletariat. Marx did not believe that stratification was inevitable, but he did see inequality and oppression as inherent in capitalism (E. O. Wright et al. 1982; E. O. Wright 2011).

Like Marx, contemporary conflict theorists believe that human beings are prone to conflict over scarce resources such as wealth, status, and power. However, Marx focused primarily on class conflict; more recent theorists have extended the analysis to include conflicts based on gender, race, age, and other dimensions. British sociologist Ralf Dahrendorf (1929–2009) is one of the most influential contributors to the conflict approach.

Dahrendorf (1959) has modified Marx's analysis of capitalist society to apply to modern capitalist societies. For Dahrendorf, social classes are groups of people who share common interests resulting from their authority relationships. In identifying the most powerful groups in society, he includes not only the bourgeoisie—the owners of the means of production—but also the managers of industry, legislators, the judiciary, heads of the government bureaucracy, and others. In that respect, Dahrendorf has merged Marx's emphasis on class conflict with Weber's recognition that power is an important element of stratification (Cuff et al. 1990).

Conflict theorists, including Dahrendorf, contend that the powerful of today, like the bourgeoisie of Marx's time, want society to run smoothly so that they can enjoy their privileged positions. Because the status quo suits those with wealth, status, and power, they have a clear interest in preventing, minimizing, or controlling societal conflict.

One way for the powerful to maintain the status quo is to define and disseminate the society's dominant ideology. The term **dominant ideology** describes a set of cultural beliefs and practices that helps to maintain powerful social, economic, and political interests. For Marx, the dominant ideology in a capitalist society served the interests of the ruling class. From a conflict perspective, the social significance of the dominant ideology is that not only do a society's most powerful groups and institutions control

TABLE 8-2 SOCIOLOGICAL PERSPECTIVES ON SOCIAL STRATIFICATION

Tracking Sociological Perspectives

	Functionalist	Conflict	Interactionist
Purpose of social stratification	Facilitates filling of social positions	Facilitates exploitation	Influences people's lifestyles
Attitude toward social inequality	Necessary to some extent	Excessive and growing	Influences intergroup relations
Analysis of the wealthy	Talented and skilled, creating opportunities for others	Use the dominant ideology to further their own interests	Exhibit conspicuous consumption and conspicuous leisure

wealth and property; even more important, they control the means of producing beliefs about reality through religion, education, and the media (Abercrombie et al. 1980, 1990; Robertson 1988).

The powerful, such as leaders of government, also use limited social reforms to buy off the oppressed and reduce the danger of challenges to their dominance. For example, minimum-wage laws and unemployment compensation unquestionably give some valuable assistance to needy men and women. Yet these reforms also serve to pacify those who might otherwise rebel. Of course, in the view of conflict theorists, such maneuvers can never entirely eliminate conflict, since workers will continue to demand equality, and the powerful will not give up their control of society.

Conflict theorists see stratification as a major source of societal tension and conflict. They do not agree with Davis and Moore that stratification is functional for a society or that it serves as a source of stability. Rather, conflict sociologists argue that stratification will inevitably lead to instability and social change (R. Collins 1975; L. Coser 1977).

Table 8-2 summarizes and compares the three major perspectives on social stratification.

LENSKI'S VIEWPOINT

Let's return to the question posed earlier—Is stratification universal?—and consider the sociological response. Some form of differentiation is found in every culture, from the most primitive to the most advanced industrial societies of our time. Sociologist Gerhard Lenski, in his sociocultural evolution approach, described how economic systems change as their level of technology becomes more complex, beginning with hunting and gathering and culminating eventually with industrial society.

In subsistence-based hunting-and-gathering societies, people focus on survival. While some inequality and differentiation are evident, a stratification system based on social class does not emerge because there is no real wealth to be claimed. As a society advances technologically, it becomes capable of producing a considerable surplus of goods. The emergence of surplus resources greatly expands the possibilities for inequality in status, influence, and power, allowing a well-defined, rigid social class system to develop. To minimize strikes, slowdowns, and industrial sabotage, the elites may share a portion of the economic surplus with the lower classes, but not enough to reduce their own power and privilege.

As Lenski argued, the allocation of surplus goods and services controlled by those with wealth, status, and power reinforces the social inequality that accompanies stratification systems. While this reward system may once have served the overall purposes of society, as functionalists contend, the same cannot be said for the large disparities separating the haves from the have-nots in current societies. In contemporary industrial society, the degree of social and economic inequality far exceeds what is needed to provide for goods and services (Lenski 1966; Nolan 2004; Nolan and Lenski 2009).

Read each question carefully and then select or provide the best answer.

1. In Karl Marx's view, the destruction of the capitalist system will occur only if the working class first develops
   a. bourgeois consciousness.
   b. false consciousness.
   c. class consciousness.
   d. caste consciousness.

2. Which of the following were viewed by Max Weber as analytically distinct components of stratification?
   a. conformity, deviance, and social control
   b. class, status, and power
   c. class, caste, and age
   d. class, prestige, and esteem

3. Which sociological perspective argues that stratification is universal and that social inequality is necessary so that people will be motivated to fill socially important positions?
   a. the functionalist perspective
   b. the conflict perspective
   c. the interactionist perspective
   d. the labeling perspective

4. In the _____ system of stratification, or feudalism, peasants were required to work land leased to them by nobles in exchange for military protection and other services.

5. Karl Marx viewed _____ differentiation as the crucial determinant of social, economic, and political inequality.

Answers

1 (c); 2 (b); 3 (a); 4 estate; 5 class

Consider these questions to get a deeper understanding of the material.

1. In your view, does the extent of social inequality in the United States serve a useful function, or is it mostly harmful? Explain.

2. Give some examples of conspicuous consumption that you have observed in your own personal experience (i.e., not from movies or TV). Are they obvious or subtle?

RECAP

LO 25-1 Define stratification and describe the four general systems of stratification.

- Stratification—the structured ranking of groups of people that perpetuates unequal economic rewards and power in a society—exists to some degree in all cultures.
- Systems of social stratification include slavery, castes, the estate system, and social classes.

- Slavery is based on the idea that persons can be used as property. Castes are rigid, immobile hereditary ranks from which there is virtually no chance of escape. The estate system is based on strict division between land owners and servants, as typified by the feudalism of the Middle Ages.
- A class system is a system of social ranking based largely on economic status and permitting some degree of movement between classes.

LO 25-2 Describe Rossides's five-class model as applied to the United States.

- Sociologist Daniel Rossides describes the class system of the United States as consisting of five classes: upper, upper-middle, lower-middle, working, and lower. In addition to income level, the classes tend to share other characteristics.
- Although seemingly based on achieved status, the class system is influenced to an ever-increasing degree by ascribed statuses such as race, gender, and disability.
- The middle class in the United States is under economic pressure, with about half its members rising to a higher class and half to a lower class. The U.S. working class is declining in size as service and technical jobs replace the trades and manual labor.
- The increasing inequality between the wealthiest class and the rest of the citizenry is causing class conflict.

LO 25-3 Analyze stratification using the views of Marx and Weber and the major sociological perspectives.

- Karl Marx saw that differences in access to the means of production created social, economic, and political inequality, as well as two distinct classes, owners and laborers.
- Max Weber identified three analytically distinct components of stratification: class, status group, and power.
- Functionalists argue that stratification is necessary to motivate people to fill society's important positions. Conflict theorists see stratification as a major source of societal tension and conflict. Interactionists stress the importance of social class in determining a person's lifestyle.

KEY TERMS

Achieved status A social position that a person attains largely through his or her own efforts.

Ascribed status A social position assigned to a person by society without regard for the person's unique talents or characteristics.

Bourgeoisie Karl Marx's term for the capitalist class, comprising the owners of the means of production.

Capitalism An economic system in which the means of production are held largely in private hands and the main incentive for economic activity is the accumulation of profits.

Caste A hereditary rank, usually religiously dictated, that tends to be fixed and immobile.

Class A group of people who have a similar level of wealth and income.

Class consciousness In Karl Marx's view, a subjective awareness held by members of a class regarding their common vested interests and the need for collective political action to bring about social change.

Class system A social ranking based primarily on economic position in which achieved characteristics can influence social mobility.

Conspicuous consumption Purchasing goods not to survive but to flaunt one's superior wealth and social standing.

Dominant ideology A set of cultural beliefs and practices that helps to maintain powerful social, economic, and political interests.

Estate system A system of stratification under which peasants were required to work land leased to them by nobles in exchange for military protection and other services. Also known as *feudalism*.

False consciousness A term used by Karl Marx to describe an attitude held by members of a class that does not accurately reflect their objective position.

Income Salaries and wages.

Power The ability to exercise one's will over others.

Proletariat Karl Marx's term for the working class in a capitalist society.

Slavery A system of enforced servitude in which some people are owned by other people.

Social inequality A condition in which members of society have differing amounts of wealth, prestige, or power.

Status group People who have the same prestige or lifestyle, independent of their class positions.

Stratification A structured ranking of entire groups of people that perpetuates unequal economic rewards and power in a society.

Wealth An inclusive term encompassing all a person's material assets, including land, stocks, and other types of property.

MODULE 26 Stratification by Social Class

P Prepare Learning Objectives

LO 26-1 Summarize the methods used by sociologists to measure stratification.

LO 26-2 Describe the distribution of income and wealth in the United States.

O Organize Module Outline

Measuring Social Class
    The Objective Method
    Gender and Occupational Prestige
    Multiple Measures
Income and Wealth

We continually assess how wealthy people are by looking at the cars they drive, the houses they live in, the clothes they wear, and so on. Yet it is not so easy to locate an individual within our social hierarchies as it would be in slavery or caste systems of stratification. To determine someone's class position, sociologists use several measures.

Study Alert

Remember that *prestige*, the respect and admiration that an occupation elicits in society, is independent of the particular individual who holds the job, whereas *esteem* refers to the reputation that a specific individual has earned within an occupation.

LO 26-1 Measuring Social Class

Sociologists tend to favor statistical methods of measuring social class because these are based on quantifiable categories independent of subjective assessments by either researchers or the people under consideration. These measures generally rely on what is called the objective method.

THE OBJECTIVE METHOD

In the **objective method** of measuring social class, class is viewed largely as a statistical category. Researchers assign individuals to social classes on the basis of criteria such as occupation, education, income, and place of residence. The key to the objective method is that the *researcher,* rather than the person being classified, identifies an individual's class position.

The first step in using this method is to decide what indicators or causal factors will be measured objectively, whether wealth, income, education, or occupation. The prestige ranking of occupations has proved to be a useful indicator of a person's class position. For one thing, it is much easier to determine accurately than income or wealth. The term **prestige** refers to the respect and admiration that an occupation holds in a society. "My daughter, the physicist" connotes something very different from "my daughter, the waitress." Prestige is independent of the particular individual who occupies a job, a characteristic that distinguishes it from esteem. **Esteem** refers to the reputation that a specific person has earned within an occupation. Therefore, one can say that the position of president of the United States has high prestige, even though it has been occupied by people with varying degrees of esteem. A hairdresser may have the esteem of his clients, but he lacks the prestige of a corporate executive.

From the perspective of . . .

A Female Bank Manager How comfortable would you be introducing your partner or husband to your professional friends if that person was an auto mechanic? Discuss your feelings.

Table 8-3 ranks the prestige of a number of well-known occupations. In a series of national surveys, sociologists assigned prestige rankings to about 500 occupations, ranging from surgeon to panhandler. The highest possible prestige score was 100; the lowest was 0. Surgeon, physician, lawyer, dentist, and college professor were the most highly regarded occupations. Sociologists have used such data to assign prestige rankings to virtually all jobs and have found a stability in rankings from 1925 to the present. Similar studies in other countries have also developed useful prestige rankings of occupations (Nakao and Treas 1994).

GENDER AND OCCUPATIONAL PRESTIGE

For many years, studies of social class tended to neglect the occupations and incomes of *women* as determinants of social rank. With more than half of all married women now working outside the home, this approach seems outmoded. How should we judge class or status in dual-career families—by the occupation regarded as having greater prestige, the average, or some other combination of the two? Sociologists—in particular, feminist sociologists in Great Britain—are drawing on new approaches to assess women's social class standing. One approach is to focus on the individual (rather than the family

TABLE 8-3 PRESTIGE RANKINGS OF OCCUPATIONS

Occupation	Score	Occupation	Score
Physician	86	Bank teller	50
College professor	78	Electrician	49
Lawyer	76	Farm manager	48
Dentist	74	Insurance agent	47
Banker	72	Secretary	46
Architect	71	Mail carrier	42
Airline pilot	70	Farmer	41
Clergy	69	Correctional officer	40
Registered nurse	66	Carpenter	40
High school teacher	63	Barber	38
Legislator	61	Child care worker	36
Pharmacist	61	Hotel clerk	32
Elementary school teacher	60	Bus driver	32
Veterinarian	60	Truck driver	30
Police officer or detective	60	Salesworker (shoes)	28
Prekindergarten teacher	60	Waiter and waitress	28
Accountant	57	Cook (short-order)	28
Librarian	55	Bartender	25
Firefighter	53	Garbage collector	17
Funeral director	52	Janitor	16
Social worker	52	Newspaper vendor	15

Note: 100 is the highest and 0 the lowest possible prestige score.
Source: General Social Survey 2012.

or household) as the basis for categorizing a woman's class position. Thus, a woman would be classified according to her own occupational status rather than that of her spouse (O'Donnell 1992).

Another feminist effort to measure the contribution of women to the economy reflects a more clearly political agenda. International Women Count Network, a global grassroots feminist organization, has sought to give a monetary value to women's unpaid work. Besides providing symbolic recognition of women's role in labor, this value would also be used to calculate pension and other benefits, which are usually based on wages received. The United Nations has placed an $11 trillion price tag on unpaid labor by women, largely in child care, housework, and agriculture. Whatever the figure, the continued undercounting of many workers' contributions to a family and to an entire economy means that virtually all measures of stratification are in need of reform (United Nations Development Programme 1995; United Nations Economic and Social Council 2010; Wages for Housework Campaign 1999).

MULTIPLE MEASURES

Another complication in measuring social class is that advances in statistical methods and computer technology have multiplied the factors used to define class under the objective method. No longer are sociologists limited to annual income and education in evaluating a person's class position. Today, studies use as criteria the value of homes, sources of income, assets, years in present occupations, neighborhoods, and considerations regarding dual careers. Adding these variables will not necessarily paint a different picture of class differentiation in the United States, but it does allow sociologists to measure class in a more complex and multidimensional way. When researchers use multiple measures, they typically speak of **socioeconomic status (SES)**, a measure of social class that is based on income, education, and occupation. To determine the socioeconomic status of a young person, such as a college student under age 25, they use *parental* income, education, and occupation.

Whatever the technique used to measure class, the sociologist is interested in real and often dramatic differences in power, privilege, and opportunity in a society. The study of stratification is a study of inequality. Nowhere is the truth of that statement more evident than in the distribution of income and wealth.

FIGURE 8-2 MEAN HOUSEHOLD INCOME BY QUINTILE

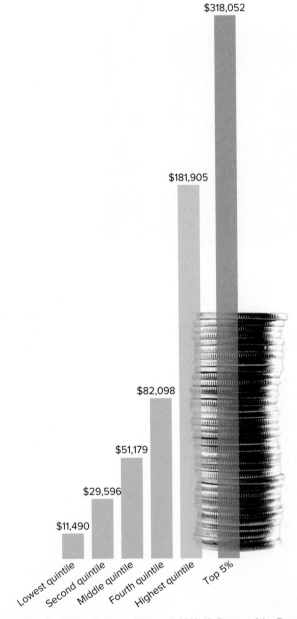

$318,052
$181,905
$82,098
$51,179
$29,596
$11,490

Lowest quintile Second quintile Middle quintile Fourth quintile Highest quintile Top 5%

Source: Data for 2012 in DeNavas-Walt et al. 2013:40; Bureau of the Census 2011d: Table H-3.

LO 26-2 Income and Wealth

By all measures, income in the United States is distributed unevenly. Nobel Prize–winning economist Paul Samuelson has described the situation in the following words: "If we made an income pyramid out of building blocks, with each layer portraying $500 of income, the peak would be far higher than Mount Everest, but most people would be within a few feet of the ground" (Samuelson and Nordhaus 2010:324).

Recent data support Samuelson's analogy. In 2012, the median household income in the United States was $51,017. In other words, half of all households had higher incomes that year and half had lower incomes. However, this fact does not fully convey the income disparities in our society. We can get some sense of income inequality by contrasting this median (middle) income with the mean arithmetic average, which in 2012 was $71,274. The mean is so much higher than the median because some people make a lot more money than others, which draws the mean up. Thus, the mean is a less useful statistic than the median for describing the average, or typical, income (DeNavas-Walt et al. 2013:33).

We can gain additional insight into income inequality in the United States by looking at the relative placement of households within the income distribution. One of the most common ways of doing so is to line up all income-earning households from low to high and then break them into quintiles, or fifths. Because there are approximately 122 million households in the United States, each quintile includes an equal number of about 24 million households. This method gives us a sense of the average income within each quintile, along with the percentage of the nation's total income earned in each quintile.

As Figure 8-2 shows, looking at the population in this way reveals a significant degree of income inequality. The mean income for households in the lowest quintile is $11,490; in the top quintile, it is $181,905. If we were to move up to the highest end of the income distribution, we would find that the top 0.01 percent of taxpayers—about 15,000 households—make incomes of at least $11.5 million a year. Collectively, they control 6 percent of the nation's total income (DeNavas-Walt et al. 2013:41; Sloan 2009:27).

There has been a modest redistribution of income in the United States over the past 80 years, but not always to the benefit of the poor or even the middle class. From 1929 through 1970, the government's economic and tax policies shifted some income to the poor. However, in the past four decades—especially in the 1980s and in the decade from 2001 through 2010—federal tax policies favored the affluent. Moreover, while the salaries of highly skilled workers and professionals have continued to rise, the wages of less skilled workers have *decreased* when controlled for inflation.

Careful economic analysis has shown that over the past 30 years, federal and state tax policies have tended to accentuate this trend toward income inequality. During one 25-year period, the top 1 percent of income earners *after taxes* saw their incomes rise 228 percent, compared to only 21 percent for households in the middle quintile. Little wonder that the middle class is shrinking (Billitteri 2009; A. Sherman 2007).

Globalization is often blamed for this growing inequality, because it has forced less skilled workers to compete with lower-paid foreign-born workers. While that is true, research suggests that the number of displaced workers who are reemployed at similarly paid or even higher-paid jobs roughly equals the number of workers whose earnings drop (S. Zimmerman 2008a). The growing inequality in income is mirrored in increasing inequality in wealth. Consider the years between 1980 and 2010. During this period of less than a generation, the real net worth of middle-income earners rose only 2 percent, while that of low-income families dropped 7 percent. Yet for upper-income families, net worth climbed 87 percent. The pattern is clear: the biggest winners have been the affluent (Pew Research Center 2012b:92).

Indeed, wealth is distributed much more unevenly than income in the United States. A 2009 Federal Reserve Bank study showed that half the population controls 2.5 percent of the nation's wealth; the other half controls over 97 percent (Figure 8-3). Put another way, the wealth of the top 1 percent exceeds the collective wealth of the bottom 90 percent.

Researchers have also found a dramatic disparity in the wealth of African Americans and Hispanics compared to that of Whites. The median wealth of White households is now 18 times the median wealth of Latino households and 20 times that of Blacks. Furthermore, evidence suggests that the gap is widening (Pew Social and Demographic Trends 2011; T. Shapiro et al. 2010).

FIGURE 8-3 DISTRIBUTION OF WEALTH IN THE UNITED STATES

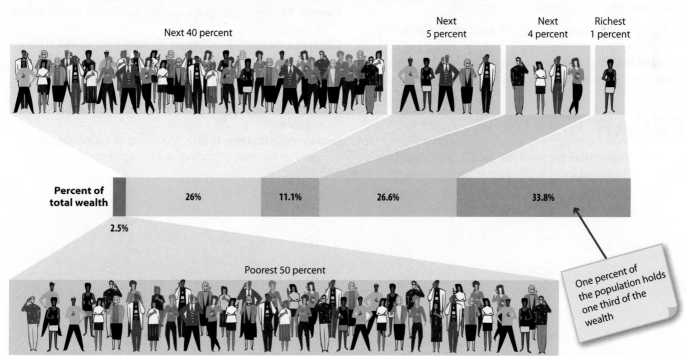

Source: Data for 2007, as reported in a 2009 Federal Reserve Bank study. See Kennickell 2009:35.

Read each question carefully and then select or provide the best answer.

1. The key advantage of the objective method of measuring social class is that an individual's class standing is identified by:
   a. researchers using statistics.
   b. government officials using electoral data.
   c. sociologists using professional judgment.
   d. the individuals being classified.

2. The respect or admiration that an occupation holds in a society is referred to as
   a. status.
   b. esteem.
   c. prestige.
   d. ranking.

3. The measure of social class most commonly used by sociologists that is based on income, education, and occupation is called _____ _____.

Answers

1 (a); 2 (c); 3 socioeconomic status

R Rethink

Consider these questions to get a deeper understanding of the material.

1. To what degree do you believe that students are motivated by the prestige of their intended occupations?

2. Within the occupational category "teachers," what do you think are the primary reasons the prestige ranking of high school teachers is higher than the ranking of prekindergarten teachers? Do you think gender is a factor? Why or why not?

RECAP

LO 26-1 Summarize the methods used by sociologists to measure stratification.

- In the objective method of measuring, class is viewed essentially as a statistical category, depending on such factors as occupation, education, income, and place of residence.
- The relationship of occupation to social class is related to the prestige of the position in society, as well as the salary that it commands and the education that it requires.
- Categorizing a woman's social class by occupation has been complicated by a reluctance to consider her own occupation rather than her spouse's in the calculation, and by the comparatively low prestige associated with many occupations traditionally held by women.
- The use of computers has led to the consideration of multiple measures in determining social class, especially income, education, and occupation. Researchers typically refer to such factors as measures of socioeconomic status (SES).

LO 26-2 Describe the distribution of income and wealth in the United States.

- One consequence of social class in the United States is that both income and wealth are distributed unevenly.
- Analysis of income trends since 1980 reveals that federal and state tax policies have increased income inequality in favor of the wealthy—a fact *not* substantially due to increased globalization and competition.
- The divide between rich and poor is matched by the divide between White and non-White households, which shows signs of increasing in the next decade.

KEY TERMS

Esteem The reputation that a specific person has earned within an occupation.

Objective method A technique for measuring social class that assigns individuals to classes on the basis of criteria such as occupation, education, income, and place of residence.

Prestige The respect and admiration that an occupation holds in a society.

Socioeconomic status (SES) A measure of social class that is based on income, education, and occupation.

MODULE 27 Poverty

W Work

About 15 percent of the people in the United States live below the poverty line established by the federal government. In 2012, no fewer than 46.5 million people were living in poverty. The economic boom of the 1990s passed these people by. A Bureau of the Census report shows that one in five households has trouble meeting basic needs, from paying the utility bills to buying dinner (Bauman 1999; DeNavas-Walt et al. 2013).

One contributor to the United States' high poverty rate has been the large number of workers employed at minimum wage. At current minimum wage rates, which are quite low, most workers cannot make ends meet. The Social Policy section at the end of this module will examine minimum wage laws and their effect on people who are living in poverty. However, the minimum wage is only one aspect of a much larger problem in the United States, which includes a shortage both of well-paid jobs and skilled workers who can do those jobs. Typically, workers earn the minimum wage for unskilled work.

Sociologists have long had an interest in the impact of substandard work on society, beginning with the writings of Karl Marx, Émile Durkheim, and Max Weber. Their interest increased with the global economic decline that began in 2008, which trapped many people in jobs they did not want or left them unemployed. Box 8-1 considers recent sociological work on *precarious work*.

In this module, we'll consider just how social scientists define *poverty*. We'll also take a closer look at the people who fall into that category—including the working poor.

8-1 PRECARIOUS WORK

In 2008 Jim Marshall, age 39, lost his job in Detroit's faltering auto industry. Figuring that job prospects had to be better elsewhere, he moved to Florida. But by May 2009 Jim was homeless, living in a tent city just north of St. Petersburg. "My parents always taught me to work hard in school, graduate high school, go to college, get a degree and you'll do fine. You'll do better than your parents' generation," Marshall says. "I did all those things. . . . For a while, I did have that good life, but nowadays that's not the reality" (Bazar 2009:A2).

Jim's story is all too common. He is one of the millions of Americans who have been reduced to doing **precarious work**—employment that is poorly paid, and from the worker's perspective, insecure and unprotected. People who engage in precarious work often cannot support a household, and they are vulnerable to falling into poverty.

Even before economists recognized the economic downturn in 2009, there was ample statistical evidence that precarious work was increasing, despite the fact that the unemployment rate remained steady. In his presidential address to the ASA, Arne L. Kalleberg offered the following five social indicators:

1. *A decline in the average length of time workers remain with an employer.* This trend has been especially noticeable among older White men, who in the past were protected by employers.
2. *An increase in long-term unemployment.* The proportion of workers who remained unemployed after six months rose in the 2000s, when the number of manufacturing jobs shrank and fewer new jobs were created.
3. *A decrease in job security.* Given the increase in long-term unemployment and the decrease in average time spent with an employer, workers became increasingly insecure about their ability to replace a lost job.
4. *An increase in outsourcing and temporary work.* To meet cyclical fluctuations in supply and demand, employers have turned more and more to nontraditional labor sources. Today, virtually any job can be outsourced, including accounting, legal, and military services.

To meet cyclical fluctuations in supply and demand, employers have turned more and more to nontraditional labor sources. Today, virtually any job can be outsourced, including accounting, legal, and military services.

5. *A shift in risk from employers to employees.* Few companies offer traditional pensions anymore. Employees are being asked to shoulder at least part of the cost and risk not only of their retirement investments, but of their health insurance plans as well.

Precarious workers are seeking political recognition by using social media, as well as other forms of communication, to draw attention to their plight. The Occupy Wall Street movement, which included some precarious workers, relied on social media. In Italy, clothing workers mounted a satirical runway show to underscore the precariousness of work in their industry. Their stunt created a flash of coverage, bringing attention to precarious work across all media and outlets, from the printed press to web applications and from mainstream to alternative media.

What can be done to revitalize labor markets so that fewer workers end up doing substandard work—or at least, so that those who do will suffer less from it? Denmark is one country that has tried to deal with the problem. Although the government there cannot make jobs more secure, it does provide significant assistance to the unemployed. Help finding a job, significant income compensation (90 percent of a worker's previous wage for one year, without conditions), and subsidized education and training are all available to Danish workers who have lost their jobs.

Let's Discuss

1. Has the trend toward increasing reliance on precarious work touched your family or friends? Has anyone you know been unemployed longer than six months?
2. Looking forward to your own career, can you think of a strategy for avoiding precarious work, frequent job loss, and long-term unemployment?

Sources: European Metalworkers' Federation 2010; Fudge and Owens 2006; Kalleberg 2009, 2012; Mattoni 2012; Purser 2013; Somavia 2008; Westergaard-Nielsen 2008.

LO **27-1** Studying Poverty

The efforts of sociologists and other social scientists to better understand poverty are complicated by the difficulty of defining it. This problem is evident even in government programs that conceive of poverty in either absolute or relative terms. **Absolute poverty** refers to a minimum level of subsistence that no family should be expected to live below.

One commonly used measure of absolute poverty is the federal government's *poverty line,* a money income figure that is adjusted annually to reflect the consumption requirements of families based on their size and composition. The poverty line serves as an official definition of which people are poor. In 2012, for example, any family of four (two adults and two children) with a combined income of $23,283 or less fell below the poverty line. This definition determines which individuals and families will be eligible for certain government benefits (DeNavas-Walt et al. 2013:59).

Although by absolute standards, poverty has declined in the United States, it remains higher than in many other industrial nations. As Figure 8-4 shows, a comparatively high proportion of U.S. households is poor, meaning that they are unable to purchase basic consumer goods. If anything, this cross-national comparison understates the extent of poverty in the United States, since U.S. residents are likely to pay more for housing, health care, child care, and education than residents of other countries, where such expenses are often subsidized.

In contrast, **relative poverty** is a floating standard of deprivation by which people at the bottom of a society, whatever their lifestyles, are judged to be disadvantaged *in comparison with the nation as a whole.* Therefore, even if the poor of 2014 are better off in absolute terms than the poor of the 1930s or 1960s, they are still seen as deserving of special assistance.

Debate has been growing over the accuracy of the federal government's measure of poverty, which has remained largely unchanged since 1963. If noncash benefits such as Medicare, Medicaid, tax credits, food stamps (the Supplemental Nutrition Assistance Program, or SNAP), public housing, and health care and other employer-provided fringe benefits were included, the reported poverty rate would be lower. On the other hand, if out-of-pocket medical expenses and mandatory work expenses for transportation and child care were included, the poverty rate would be higher. Furthermore, although the current poverty measure does consider family size, it does not consider a household's location, whether in a relatively expensive city like New York or in a less expensive rural area. Nor does it consider whether a householder pays rent or a mortgage installment, lives at home or with someone else.

To address some of these shortcomings, in 2010 the federal government launched a second statistic called the Supplemental Poverty Measure (SPM), which will be used to estimate economic hardship. The SPM is a relative poverty measure that is based on a broad range of changing household resources and expenses. It was calculated beginning in late 2011, but will not replace the poverty line in determining a household's eligibility for benefits (Blank 2011; Short 2012).

> # Study Alert
>
> Remember that *absolute poverty* refers to the minimum level of subsistence that no family should be expected to live below, whereas *relative poverty* describes a floating standard of deprivation where people at the lower end of society are judged to be disadvantaged in comparison to the society as a whole.

FIGURE 8-4 POVERTY IN SELECTED COUNTRIES

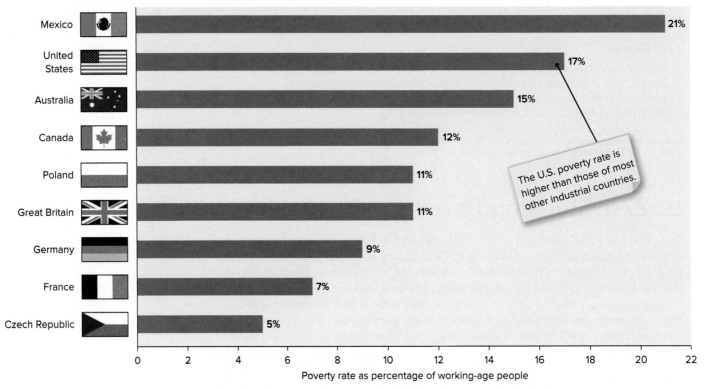

Note: Data are averages for late 2000s, as reported in 2013. Poverty threshold is 50 percent of a nation's median household income.
Source: Organisation for Economic Co-Operation and Development 2013a.

WHO ARE THE POOR?

Not only does the category of the poor defy any simple definition; it counters the common stereotypes about "poor people." For example, many people in the United States believe that the poor are able to work but will not. Yet 40 percent of poor adults *do* work outside the home—27 percent of them full time—compared to 65 percent of all adults. Such stereotypes lead to the criminalization of the poor.

Though many of the poor live in urban slums, a majority live outside those poverty-stricken areas. Poverty is no stranger in rural areas, from Appalachia to hard-hit farming regions to Native American reservations. Table 8-4 provides additional statistical information regarding low-income people in the United States.

FEMINIZATION OF POVERTY

Since World War II, an increasing proportion of the poor people of the United States have been women, many of whom are divorced or never-married mothers. In 1959, female householders accounted for 26 percent of the nation's poor; by 2012, that figure had risen to 50 percent (see Table 8-4). This alarming trend, known as the **feminization of poverty**, is evident not just in the United States but around the world.

About half of all women living in poverty in the United States are in transition, coping with an economic crisis caused by the departure, disability, or death of a husband. The other half tend to be economically dependent either on the welfare system or on friends and relatives living nearby. A major factor in the feminization of poverty has been the increase in families with women as single heads of the household. Conflict theorists and other observers trace the higher rates of poverty among women to three distinct factors: the difficulty in finding affordable child care, sexual harassment, and sex discrimination in the labor market (Burns 2010).

THE UNDERCLASS

In 2012, 43 percent of poor people in the United States were living in central cities. These highly visible urban residents are the focus of most government efforts to alleviate poverty. Yet according to many observers, the plight of the urban poor is growing worse, owing to the devastating interplay of inadequate education and limited employment prospects. Traditional employment opportunities in the industrial sector are largely closed to the unskilled poor. Past and present discrimination heightens these problems for those low-income urban residents who are Black or Hispanic.

Along with other social scientists, sociologist William Julius Wilson (1996, 2012a, 2012b) and his colleagues (2004) have used the term **underclass** to describe the long-term poor who lack training and skills. According to an analysis of census data, 10.3 million people live in extremely impoverished areas. Although not all of them are poor, living in such disadvantaged neighborhoods means limited educational opportunities, greater exposure to crime and health risks, reduced access to private investment, and higher prices for goods and services. About 38 percent of the population in these neighborhoods is Black, 30 percent Hispanic, and 26 percent White non-Hispanic (Bishaw 2011).

Those statistics may sound high, but they could climb higher. Some scholars are predicting that the recent economic downturn may swell the ranks of the underclass, increasing the proportion of the U.S. population that they represent. Indeed, the recession seems to have accelerated the demise of less efficient, less profitable firms. When the downturn is over, jobs will not return to declining industries.

Analyses of the poor in general reveal that they are not a static social class. The overall composition of the poor changes continually, because some individuals and families near the top edge of poverty move above the poverty level after a year or two, while others slip below it. Still, hundreds of thousands of people remain in poverty for many years at a time. Blacks and Latinos are more likely than Whites to be persistently poor. Both Latinos and Blacks are less likely than Whites to leave the welfare rolls as a result of welfare reform (Jäntti 2009; Sampson 2011).

LO 27-2 EXPLAINING POVERTY

Why is it that poverty pervades a nation of such vast wealth? In 2013, poverty levels matched those of 50 years earlier. Sociologist Herbert Gans (1995), who has applied functionalist analysis to the existence of poverty, argues that various segments of society actually *benefit* from the existence of the poor. Gans has identified a number of social, economic, and political functions that the poor perform for society (Porter 2013):

- The presence of poor people means that society's dirty work—physically dirty or dangerous, dead-end and underpaid, undignified and menial jobs—will be performed at low cost.
- Poverty creates jobs for occupations and professions that serve the poor. It creates both legal employment (public health experts, welfare caseworkers) and illegal jobs (drug dealers, numbers runners).

TABLE 8-4 WHO ARE THE POOR IN THE UNITED STATES?

Group	Percentage of the Population of the United States	Percentage of the Poor of the United States
Age		
Under 18 years old	24%	35%
18 to 64 years old	63	57
65 years and older	13	8
Race-Ethnicity		
Whites (non-Hispanic)	63	41
Blacks	13	23
Hispanics	17	29
Asians and Pacific Islanders	5	4
Family Composition		
Couples with male householders	73	39
Female householders	19	50
People with Disabilities	8	16

Note: People with disabilities includes ages 18–64.
Source: Data for 2012 in DeNavas-Walt et al. 2013:14, 17.

Even if this single parent works her way up the ladder, supporting her family will still be difficult.

- The identification and punishment of the poor as deviants upholds the legitimacy of conventional social norms and mainstream values regarding hard work, thrift, and honesty.

- Within a relatively hierarchical society, the existence of poor people guarantees the higher status of the rich. As psychologist William Ryan (1976) noted, affluent people may justify inequality (and gain a measure of satisfaction) by *blaming the victims* of poverty for their disadvantaged condition.

- Because of their lack of political power, the poor often absorb the costs of social change. Under the policy of deinstitutionalization, mental patients released from long-term hospitals have been transferred primarily to low-income communities and neighborhoods. Similarly, halfway houses for rehabilitated drug abusers, rejected by more affluent communities, often end up in poorer neighborhoods.

In Gans's view, then, poverty and the poor actually satisfy positive functions for many nonpoor groups in the United States.

LO **27-3** Life Chances

Max Weber saw class as being closely related to people's **life chances**—that is, their opportunities to provide themselves with material goods, positive living conditions, and favorable life experiences (Gerth and Mills 1958). Life chances are reflected in measures such as housing, education, and health. Occupying a higher social class in a society improves your life chances and brings greater access to social rewards. In contrast, people in the lower social classes are forced to devote a larger proportion of their limited resources to the necessities of life. In some cases, life chances are a matter of life and death. According to a medical study published in 2011, in the United States, approximately 133,000 deaths a year can be attributed to individual poverty, and another 119,000 to income inequality. That is over a quarter million deaths per year caused by severely limited resources (Galea et al. 2011).

In times of danger, the affluent and powerful have a better chance of surviving than people of ordinary means. When the supposedly unsinkable British ocean liner *Titanic* hit an iceberg in 1912, it was not carrying enough lifeboats to accommodate all passengers. Plans had been made to evacuate only first- and second-class passengers. About 62 percent of the first-class passengers survived the disaster. Despite a rule that women and children would go first, about a third of those passengers were male. In contrast, only 25 percent of the third-class passengers survived. The first attempt to alert them to the need to abandon ship came well after other passengers had been notified. In an ironic demonstration of continuing social inequality, a luxury travel organization called Bluefish recently charged passengers $60,000 each to view the underwater remains of the *Titanic* from a deep-sea submersible (Butler 1998; Crouse 1999; Dickler 2011; Riding 1998).

Class position also affects people's vulnerability to natural disasters. When Hurricane Katrina hit the Gulf Coast of the United States in 2005, affluent and poor people alike became its victims. However, poor people who did not own automobiles (100,000 of them in New Orleans

Class position affects people's vulnerability to disasters. When the ill-fated *Titanic* sank in 1912, many more first-class passengers than third-class passengers survived. This photograph, taken recently on the ocean floor, shows the remains of a first-class cabin on the luxury liner.

alone) were less able than others to evacuate in advance of the storm. The poor who survived its fury had no nest egg to draw on, and thus were more likely than others to accept relocation wherever social service agencies could place them—sometimes hundreds or thousands of miles from home. Those who were able to return are still dealing with the toxic debris left behind (Bullard and Wright 2009).

Wealth, status, and power may not ensure happiness, but they certainly provide additional ways of coping with problems and disappointments. For this reason, the opportunity for advancement—for social mobility—is of special significance to those on the bottom of society. Most people want the rewards and privileges that are granted to high-ranking members of a culture. What can society do to increase their social mobility? One strategy is to offer financial aid to college students from low-income families, on the theory that education lifts people out of poverty. Yet such programs are not having as great an effect as their authors once hoped.

LO 27-3 Social Mobility

In the movie *Maid in Manhattan,* Jennifer Lopez plays the lead in a modern-day Cinderella story, rising from the lowly status of chambermaid in a big-city hotel to a company supervisor and the girlfriend of a well-to-do politician. The ascent of a person from a poor background to a position of prestige, power, or financial reward is an example of social mobility. Formally defined, the term **social mobility** refers to the movement of individuals or groups from one position in a society's stratification system to another. But how significant—how frequent, how dramatic—is mobility in a class society such as the United States?

OPEN VERSUS CLOSED STRATIFICATION SYSTEMS

Sociologists use the terms *open stratification system* and *closed stratification system* to indicate the degree of social mobility in a society. An **open system** implies that the position of each individual is influenced by his or her *achieved* status. Such a system encourages competition among members of society. The United States is moving toward this ideal type as the government attempts to reduce the barriers faced by women, racial and ethnic minorities, and people born in lower social classes. Even in the midst of the economic downturn of 2008–2009, nearly 80 percent of people in the United States felt they could get ahead (Economic Mobility Project 2009).

At the other extreme of social mobility is the **closed system**, which allows little or no possibility of individual social mobility. The slavery and caste systems of stratification are examples of closed systems. In such societies, social placement is based on *ascribed* statuses, such as race or family background, which cannot be changed.

TYPES OF SOCIAL MOBILITY

An elementary school teacher who becomes a police officer moves from one social position to another of the same rank. Each occupation has the same prestige ranking: 60 on a scale ranging from a low of 0 to a high of 100 (see Table 8-3). Sociologists call this kind of movement **horizontal mobility**. However, if the teacher were to become a lawyer (prestige ranking of 76), he or she would experience **vertical mobility**, the movement of an individual from one social position to another of a different rank. Vertical mobility can also involve moving *downward* in a society's stratification system, as would be the case if the teacher became a bank teller (ranking of 50). Pitirim Sorokin ([1927] 1959) was the first sociologist to distinguish between horizontal and vertical mobility. Most sociological analysis, however, focuses on vertical rather than horizontal mobility.

One way of examining vertical social mobility is to contrast its two types, intergenerational and intragenerational mobility. **Intergenerational mobility** involves changes in

FIGURE 8-5 INTERGENERATIONAL INCOME MOBILITY

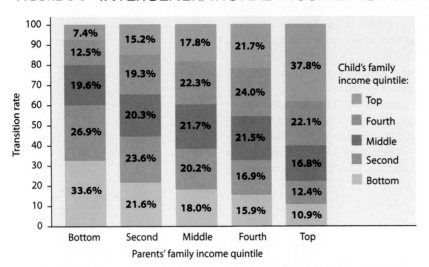

Over a 25-year period, adult children often end up in the same income bracket as their parents. For example, as the first column shows, only 7 percent of those who begin in the bottom quintile reach the top quintile as adults; their story is one of rags to riches. By comparison, a third of the people in their quintile (33 percent) stay at the bottom, where they began.

Source: Mazumder 2008:11.

the social position of children relative to their parents. Thus, a trash collector whose father was a physician provides an example of downward intergenerational mobility. The celebrated movie star Leonardo DiCaprio, who was raised by a single mother in a neighborhood frequented by drug dealers and prostitutes, illustrates upward intergenerational mobility. Because education contributes significantly to upward mobility, any barrier to the pursuit of advanced degrees can definitely limit intergenerational mobility.

Figure 8-5 shows intergenerational mobility based on income. In 1978–1980, a national survey looked at the family income of 6,000 young people. Two decades later, in 1997–2003, researchers followed up on those young adults and their income. The results showed a strong stickiness in both the bottom and top quintiles, or fifths, of the income distribution. Just over 33 percent of those whose parents were in the bottom quintile and 37 percent of those who were in the top quintile remained in the same quintile as adults. Yet the study also showed mobility: almost 66 percent of those in the bottom quintile moved up, and over 60 percent of those at the top experienced downward mobility.

Among men born in the 1960s, this consistent intergenerational mobility resulted largely from economic growth. On average, these men earned more than their fathers did at the same age; their family incomes improved as well. However, the trend has not continued into the next generation. Currently, young men are earning less than their fathers did at the same age—about 12 percent less. Family incomes are slightly higher than in the last generation, but only because women have moved into the paid labor force to supplement their husbands' earnings. With so few women left to join the labor force, most families will need to increase their wages to raise their incomes further (Sawhill and Haskins 2009).

Intragenerational mobility involves changes in social position within a person's adult life. A woman who begins work as a teacher's aide and eventually becomes superintendent of the school district experiences upward intragenerational mobility. A man who becomes a taxicab driver after his accounting firm goes bankrupt undergoes downward intragenerational mobility.

SOCIAL MOBILITY IN THE UNITED STATES

The belief in upward mobility is an important value in our society. Does that mean that the United States is indeed the land of opportunity? Not unless such ascriptive characteristics as race, gender, and family background have ceased to be significant in determining one's future prospects. We can see the impact of these factors in the occupational structure.

[**Study Alert**

Be able to differentiate different types of social mobility, including intergenerational and occupational mobility.]

Occupational Mobility Two sociological studies conducted a decade apart offer insight into the degree of mobility in the nation's occupational structure (Blau and Duncan 1967; Featherman and Hauser 1978). Taken together, these investigations lead to several noteworthy conclusions. First, occupational mobility (both intergenerational and intragenerational) has been common among males. Approximately 60 to 70 percent of sons are employed in higher-ranked occupations than their fathers.

Second, although there is a great deal of mobility in the United States, much of it is minor. That is, people who reach an occupational level above or below that of their parents usually advance or fall back only one or two out of a possible eight occupational levels. Thus, the child of a laborer may become an artisan or a technician, but he or she is less likely to become a manager or professional. The odds against reaching the top are extremely high unless one begins from a relatively privileged position.

From the perspective of . . .

A High School Guidance Counselor Would you advise a high school student to pursue a college degree if you knew the high cost would be a serious stretch for the family and result in substantial debt for the student? What factors would influence your decision?

The Impact of Education Another conclusion of both studies is that education plays a critical role in social mobility. The impact of formal schooling on adult status is even greater than that of family background (although as we have seen, family background influences the likelihood that one will receive higher education). Furthermore, education represents an important means of intergenerational mobility. A person who was born into a poor family but who graduates from college has a one in five chance of entering the top fifth of all income earners as an adult (Isaacs et al. 2008).

The impact of education on mobility has diminished somewhat in the past decade, however. An undergraduate degree—a BA or a BS— serves less as a guarantee of upward mobility now than it did in the past, simply because more and more entrants into the job market hold such a degree. Moreover, intergenerational mobility is declining, since there is no longer such a stark difference between generations. In earlier decades, many high school–educated parents successfully sent their children to college, but today's college students are increasingly likely to have college-educated parents (Sawhill and Morton 2007).

The Impact of Race and Ethnicity Sociologists have long documented the fact that the class system is more rigid for African Americans than it is for members of other racial groups. African American men who have good jobs, for example, are less likely than White men to see their adult children attain the same status. The cumulative disadvantage of discrimination plays a significant role in the disparity between the two groups' experiences. Compared to White households, the relatively modest wealth of African American households means that adult African American children are less likely than adult White children to receive financial support from their parents. Indeed, young African American couples are much more likely than young White couples to be assisting their parents—a sacrifice that hampers their social mobility.

If this lawyer were the daughter of a car mechanic, her rise to the upper-middle class would illustrate intergenerational mobility. If she had begun as a paralegal and worked her way up the occupational ladder, her career would illustrate intragenerational mobility.

Mary Barra, CEO of General Motors, began her career in 1980 as a plant engineer. In 2014 she reached the top of the corporate ladder. Despite equal opportunity laws, occupational barriers still limit women's climb to the top. As of January 2014, women ran just 25 of the Fortune 500 companies; men ran the other 475.

Not surprisingly, African Americans are more likely than Whites to experience downward intergenerational mobility, and less likely to move up the social ladder. A study of people born in the 1980s and 1990s found that based on their projected adult incomes, 68 percent of Whites should reach the middle class or better by age 40, compared to 34 percent of African Americans. If we focus on the ability of Blacks to climb out of poverty compared to Whites, the differences become even more marked.

The African American middle class has grown over the past few decades, due to economic expansion and the benefits of the civil rights movement of the 1960s. Yet many of these middle-class households have little savings, a fact that puts them in danger during times of crisis. We noted earlier that recession hits Black and Latino households harder than White households. Studies have consistently shown that downward mobility is significantly higher for Blacks than it is for Whites (Conley 2010; Oliver and Shapiro 2006; Sawhill et al. 2012; Sernau 2001; Wessel 2012; W. Wilson 1996).

The Latino population is not doing much better. According to one analysis, the median wealth of White non-Hispanic households is 18 times that of Hispanic households. This lopsided wealth ratio is the largest since the government first published the data in the 1980s. Continuing immigration accounts for part of the disparity: most of the new arrivals are destitute. But even the wealthiest 10 percent of Latino households have only a third as much net worth as the top 5 percent of White households (Kochhar et al. 2011).

The Impact of Gender Studies of mobility, even more than those of class, have traditionally ignored the significance of gender, but some research findings are now available that explore the relationship between gender and mobility.

Women's employment opportunities are much more limited than men's. Moreover, according to recent research, women whose skills far exceed the jobs offered them are more likely than men to withdraw entirely from the paid labor force. Their withdrawal violates an assumption common to traditional mobility studies: that most people will aspire to upward mobility and seek to make the most of their opportunities.

In contrast to men, women have a rather large range of clerical occupations open to them. But the modest salary ranges and few prospects for advancement in many of these positions limit the possibility of upward mobility. Self-employment as shopkeepers, entrepreneurs, independent professionals, and the like—an important road to upward mobility for men—is more difficult for women, who find it harder to secure the necessary financing. Although sons commonly follow in the footsteps of their fathers, women are unlikely to move into their fathers' positions. Consequently, gender remains an important factor in shaping social mobility. Women in the United States (and in other parts of the world) are especially likely to be trapped in poverty, unable to rise out of their low-income status (Beller 2009; Heilman 2001).

On the positive side, though today's women lag behind men in employment, their earnings have increased faster than their mothers' did at a comparable age, so that their incomes are substantially higher. The one glaring exception to this trend is the daughters of low-income parents. Because these women typically care for children—many as single parents—and sometimes for other relatives as well, their mobility is severely restricted (Isaacs 2007b).

LO 27-4 SOCIAL POLICY and Stratification

We have seen that researchers rely on a number of tools, from time-tested observational research and use of existing sources to the latest in computer technologies. Because in the real world, sociological research can have far-reaching consequences for public policy and public welfare, we will evaluate its impact on minimum wage laws.

MINIMUM WAGE LAWS

Who works for the minimum wage? A generation ago, many of those who earned the minimum wage were teens who worked after school and on weekends. Today, only 12 percent of minimum wage workers are under age 20. A third of them are over 40.

Morris Cornley, 57, works as a delivery driver at Jimmy John's in Kansas City, Missouri. Cornley, who makes $7.35 an hour, takes home about $370 after taxes every two weeks. His wages are supplemented by $1,000 a month in military disability pay plus $46 a month in food stamps. Cornley's rent is $475 a month. "I struggle to pay all the bills at one time," he says. "I'm not really living—I'm surviving" (P. Davidson 2013:7; Dube 2013a).

Cornley's case is typical: by itself, the minimum wage simply is not high enough to support workers. This shortfall in income has severe consequences. In the United States, the large number of workers who are employed at minimum wage contributes to our high poverty rate and to the presence of an underclass.

Not only is the minimum wage too low; it also tends to shrink in value. Although the federal government has repeatedly raised the minimum—from 75 cents an hour in 1950 to $7.25 in 2009—in terms of its real value after inflation, the minimum wage often has not kept pace with the cost of living. Since the current minimum wage was enacted, it has lost 6 percent of its spending power; in real terms, it is now below its level in 1968 (*The Economist* 2013d).

The federal minimum wage does not apply to certain jobs, such as those for which employees receive tips. Wait persons, nail salon workers, and parking attendants receive a minimum wage of $2.13. It also does not apply in states and cities that require employers to pay a higher minimum wage. Table 8-5 summarizes the current minimum wage rates in those states.

Applying Sociology to the Minimum Wage Conflict theorists argue that low-wage workers are vulnerable in other ways beyond the struggle to pay their bills. Although the minimum wage is the law, it is not always enforced. Many low-wage earners may fear that they could lose their jobs if they complain to authorities that they are receiving less than the minimum wage.

Low-wage workers are also vulnerable to *wage theft*—the deliberate withholding of wages they have earned. Employers may shortchange workers of their rightful income by asking them to work "off the clock" (without

TABLE 8-5 MINIMUM WAGE RATES BY STATE

Hourly	Minimum Wage
$7.25	*Federal minimum wage*
7.40	Michigan
7.50	Maine, Missouri, New Mexico
7.75	Alaska
7.79	Florida
7.90	Arizona, Montana
7.95	Ohio
8.00	California, Colorado, Massachusetts, New York, Rhode Island
8.25	District of Columbia, Illinois, Nevada, New Jersey
8.70	Connecticut
8.73	Vermont
9.10	Oregon
9.32	Washington

Note: Minimum wage rates as of July 1, 2014. In states with rates that are lower than the federal minimum (Arkansas, Georgia, Minnesota, and Wyoming), employers must pay the federal minimum wage.
Sources: Bureau of the Census 2011a: Table 653; Department of Labor 2013a; Loecke 2014.

pay), by failing to pay them time and half for overtime, by stealing their tips, by misclassifying them as independent contractors, or by taking illegal deductions from their paychecks. Employers may also limit workers' wages by pressuring them not to file for workers' compensation after on-the-job injuries. According to a survey of people in various low-wage occupations, workers lose about 15 percent of their pay through such wage violations (Bernhardt et al. 2009).

Interactionists note that wages are only one kind of reward for work; the social contact that workers have on the job can also be beneficial. Depending on the workplace, the impact of the minimum wage on employees' lives can vary. Studies have shown that some low-wage workplaces offer a positive environment. Especially for younger workers, who see their wages as "spending money," work is a place to socialize with friends, away from their parents' watchful eyes. However, other studies have found high levels of alienation among minimum wage workers. Although well-paid workers can also feel alienated, at least they have the comfort of earning a livable wage (Bessen-Cassino 2013).

Initiating Minimum Wage Policy Few people would argue that low-wage workers should not be paid more. Instead, they disagree about the implications of such pay raises. Will a higher minimum wage result in higher prices for consumers? Will the extra pay that workers have to spend stimulate the economy? Will employers hire fewer workers or cut back on the number of hours they offer to minimum wage workers? Would other measures, such as the earned-income tax credit, better address the needs of the working poor? These concerns arise every time an increase in the minimum wage is debated, whether the increase is $3 an hour, $6 an hour, or $10 an hour (Neumark 2007).

Research shows that the effects of a change in the minimum wage are exceedingly complex. To predict the effects of a new increase in the minimum wage, economists have studied the impact of past increases. They have also examined the impact of changes in state minimum wage rates, both within the state and in neighboring states. The results of these studies have been far from conclusive, however.

Even if the minimum wage does have an economic impact, many other economic and social variables must be taken into account, including economic conditions in general. Moreover, economists do not necessarily agree on the effects of these other variables. For example, some studies note that certain wage hikes coincided with an economic slowdown; others note that the slowdowns affected primarily manufacturing—a sector that employs few minimum wage workers. No such slowdown has been observed in retail services or accommodation and food services, which together hire nearly two-thirds of all minimum wage workers. According to a recent Federal Reserve study, increasing the minimum wage to $9.25 would both increase spending by low-wage workers and decrease spending by consumers facing higher prices. Overall, it would increase consumer spending by $48 billion a year (Aaronson and French 2013; Dube 2013b).

In his 2013 State of the Union message, President Obama proposed raising the minimum wage to $9 an hour by 2015—a change that would affect an estimated 15 million workers. Critics of the proposal argue that it would raise labor costs for businesses, which would then hire fewer workers. Public opinion seems to support the president's proposal, however. A recent national survey found that although 25 percent of respondents oppose raising the federal minimum wage, 33 percent favor raising it to $9, and 36 percent favor raising it to $10.10. Women, people with lower incomes, and those under age 30 are more likely than others to favor these changes (S. Greenhouse 2013:34; Peterson 2013; White House 2013).

In the United States, changes in the minimum wage require legislative action, which often lags the need for a wage hike by years. Some labor specialists suggest that the United States should adopt a different model, like those used in Great Britain and some other nations. Such a model would either tie the minimum wage to an economic indicator like inflation or create an independent board of economists to set its level (*The Economist* 2013d).

Many people argue that raising the minimum wage is not all that should be done for low-wage workers. These people advocate for a **living wage**, or a wage that meets workers' basic needs, allowing them to maintain a safe, decent standard of living within their community. Because community needs differ significantly from place to place, a living wage must vary in response to regional differences. For a single adult in Lincoln, Nebraska, a living wage might be $8.08; in Gainesville, Florida, it might be $9.27; in Los Angeles, it might be $11.37; and in New York City, $12.75. If the single adult is supporting a child, the living wage would more than double (National Employment Law Project 2013).

Workers and supporters of a living wage have mounted a public campaign on behalf of the idea. In 2013, from August through the holiday shopping season, they protested outside fast-food restaurants and big-box stores, calling for a minimum wage of $15 an hour. Industry spokespersons claimed that such a steep jump in the wage would increase the cost of a $3 hamburger by 60 cents; others countered with an estimate closer to 30 cents (Dewan 2013; Dube 2013a).

While politicians debated the policy, critics expressed concern over the potential loss of jobs, and employers cut back their hiring just as the economy was beginning to improve. Meanwhile, McDonald's advised workers to take a second job to make ends meet, but failed to consider workers' child care expenses and the cost of their health insurance. About the same time, managers of a Walmart store in Ohio launched a food drive to ensure that employees would have enough food to eat (P. Davidson 2013).

E Evaluate

Read each question carefully and then select or provide the best answer.

1. Approximately how many people in the United States live below the poverty line established by the federal government?
   a. 5 percent
   b. 10 percent
   c. 15 percent
   d. 25 percent

2. Which sociologist has applied functionalist analysis to the existence of poverty and argues that various segments of society actually benefit from the existence of the poor?
   a. Émile Durkheim
   b. Max Weber
   c. Karl Marx
   d. Herbert Gans

3. A trash collector whose father was a physician is an example of
   a. downward intergenerational mobility.
   b. upward intergenerational mobility.
   c. downward intragenerational mobility.
   d. upward intragenerational mobility.

4. _____ poverty is the minimum level of subsistence that no family should be expected to live below, whereas _____ poverty is a floating standard of deprivation by which people at the bottom of a society, whatever their lifestyles, are judged to be disadvantaged in comparison with the nation as a whole.

5. Max Weber used the term _____ _____ to refer to people's opportunities to provide themselves with material goods, positive living conditions, and favorable life experiences.

Answers

1 (c); 2 (d); 3 (a); 4 Absolute, relative; 5 life chances

R Rethink

Consider these questions to get a deeper understanding of the material.

1. In what ways do people's life chances affect society as a whole?

2. Which factor—education, occupation, race and ethnicity, or gender—do you expect will have the greatest impact on your own social mobility? Explain.

RECAP

LO 27-1 Explain how poverty is determined and describe the people living in poverty.

- The usual measure of poverty in the United States is the poverty line, intended to reflect the minimum requirements of families. Despite annual adjustments, the poverty line has fallen out of step with reality, since the method of calculating it has remained unchanged since 1963.
- Many who live in poverty are full-time workers struggling to support their families at minimum-wage jobs with no long-term security.
- Since World War II, the number of women who are in poverty has risen significantly—a trend referred to as the feminization of poverty.

LO 27-2 Analyze the social implications of poverty.

- The long-term poor—those who lack the training and skills to lift themselves out of poverty—form an underclass.
- The underclass lacks the training and skills to improve their condition, and their prospects are limited because they live in disadvantaged neighborhoods, lack educational opportunities, are exposed to crime and health risks, have low access to private investment, and pay higher prices for goods and services.
- Poverty is generally considered to be harmful to society. However, according to a controversial functionalist analysis, poverty actually serves a beneficial social, economic, and political function for those who are not poor.

LO 27-3 Demonstrate how life chances and social mobility are linked to stratification.

- Life chances are related to social class. Occupying a high social position improves a person's life chances.
- Social mobility is more likely to be found in an open system that emphasizes achieved status than in a closed system that emphasizes ascribed status. Race, gender, and family background are important factors in social mobility—even in open systems.
- Social mobility may be horizontal (e.g., change to a job of equal prestige) or vertical (e.g., change to a higher-prestige job). Vertical mobility may be intergenerational (i.e., children's status differs from their parents' status) or intragenerational (i.e., a change in status within one lifetime).
- Although upward mobility is a key American value, actual mobility is limited by ascriptive factors such as race,

gender, and family background. Education has historically played a key role in enabling social mobility.

LO 27-4 Discuss the minimum wage issue in relation to social stratification, poverty, and mobility.

- The large number of workers who are employed at minimum wage contributes to the high poverty rate in the United States, and to the presence of an underclass.
- Because the minimum wage does not keep pace with the cost of living, some people have begun to advocate instead for a *living wage* that will meet workers' basic needs, allowing them to maintain a safe, decent standard of living and fostering social mobility.

KEY TERMS

Absolute poverty A minimum level of subsistence that no family should be expected to live below.

Closed system A social system in which there is little or no possibility of individual social mobility.

Feminization of poverty A trend in which women constitute an increasing proportion of the poor people of both the United States and the world.

Horizontal mobility The movement of an individual from one social position to another of the same rank.

Intergenerational mobility Changes in the social position of children relative to their parents.

Intragenerational mobility Changes in social position within a person's adult life.

Life chances The opportunities people have to provide themselves with material goods, positive living conditions, and favorable life experiences.

Living wage A wage that meets workers' basic needs, allowing them to maintain a safe, decent standard of living within their community.

Open system A social system in which the position of each individual is influenced by his or her achieved status.

Precarious work Employment that is poorly paid, and from the worker's perspective, insecure and unprotected.

Relative poverty A floating standard of deprivation by which people at the bottom of a society, whatever their lifestyles, are judged to be disadvantaged *in comparison with the nation as a whole.*

Social mobility Movement of individuals or groups from one position in a society's stratification system to another.

Underclass The long-term poor who lack training and skills.

Vertical mobility The movement of an individual from one social position to another of a different rank.

The Case of . . . Treading Water

Fiona Murray works as a receptionist in an upscale dental practice. "Most of our clients are budding millionaires," she reports, "but I make $16 an hour and San Francisco is a pricey city to live in." Murray and her 10-year-old son live in a one-bedroom apartment in a lower-class neighborhood. "It's a real melting pot, which I like," Murray says, "but our apartment is cramped, I sleep on the sofa, and stuff is constantly breaking down."

Murray studied communications in college but never finished her degree. "I couldn't afford it," she says. "My parents had a little money to help me. I worked and took out loans, but after a while, I thought 'What's the point?' I was already $10,000 in debt, and very few grads in my department were getting jobs." Murray admits she sometimes daydreams about going back to school, studying something that might improve her situation. "But then I think 'I've got a son,' and college tuition keeps skyrocketing. I can barely manage now."

Murray says the worst part of her situation is the pressure to act like she's got it all together, like she's got money. "For example, because the dental practice serves an upscale crowd, I'm expected to dress well, which means expensive," she says. "I try to find cheap stuff that *looks* nice, but I resent spending money my son and I need so that some rich people never have to see my truth."

1. How is Murray's story an example of the feminization of poverty?

2. Considering the factors that contribute to a shrinking middle class, do you think Murray is treading water as the title of the case study implies, or is she actually sliding downhill? Explain your thinking.

3. Describe Murray's job in terms of both prestige and esteem.

4. Do you think Murray is an example of someone living in relative poverty? Why or why not?

5. If San Francisco were to suffer a major earthquake, how might Murray's socioeconomic status affect her life chances?

Managing Your Time Wisely

The life of a modern college student is busy, with constant juggling of classes, homework, one or more jobs, and family life. If you "take things as they come," you may get swamped by a confusing array of tasks, obligations, promises, and worry. Effective time management becomes, in this scenario, not a luxury but a life-saver. Here are some tips.

 **Prepare**

- Use a calendar religiously—the one on your phone or computer or a paper calendar.
- Keep a daily time log to record how you actually spend your time.
- List and rank your priorities for the semester.

 **Organize**

- Use AT MOST two calendars: one that is with you at all times and an "official" calendar onto which you transfer everything you have to do.
- Use the official calendar to create a daily To-Do list.

 **Work**

- Enter on your calendar *everything* you have to do, including sleep time, appointments, and obligations.
- Practice long-range forward planning. If you have a major assignment due on May 3, work backwards and enter on your calendar dates for planning, research, writing, and review.
- Leave room for unexpected events (e.g., a car repair, an illness).
- Schedule regular rest and exercise time. This is essential: Your calendar may run from 7 to midnight, but you can't.
- Schedule in "reward time." If you can, end Friday's schedule at 3 p.m. If this is impossible, schedule reward time to follow big events, such as a final exam.
- Keep to your schedule. Don't waste time and don't procrastinate (literally, putting off till tomorrow what you need to do today).
- Learn how to say "No, thanks!" to things that will interfere with your schedule, no matter how appealing they may be.

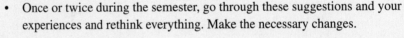 **Evaluate**

- Each week, evaluate what is and isn't working.
- If you need a different calendar, get one. If your calendar is confusing, color-code it.
- If you are overextended, adjust your work hours or class load.
- Are you wasting time? Identify invisible time drains and take action. You may have to check your Facebook page or Twitter feed less often or turn your phone off during study hours.

 **Rethink**

- Once or twice during the semester, go through these suggestions and your experiences and rethink everything. Make the necessary changes.

em POWER me

Are You An Effective Time Manager?

There's no denying that modern life is busy. You have many things on your plate: school, work, exercise, friends, and hopefully, sleep. Getting a handle on your time—the hours you have available and how you use them—is the key to managing your life successfully. Place a check in the appropriate column to rate how true each of the following items is for you, then use the scale here to score your answers:

Always: 2

Sometimes: 1

Never: 0

	Always	Sometimes	Never
1. Some interruption or crisis always seems to stop me from accomplishing my goals.			
2. I check my Facebook page and Twitter feed frequently throughout the day.			
3. I jot down test dates and other important stuff I have to do in the margins of my notebook or on scrap paper.			
4. My work hours and class load don't really leave time for anything else.			
5. I start writing papers or studying for exams the night before they're due.			
6. I'm often too tired to get my work done.			
7. I don't keep a To-Do list. I just tackle whatever suits my mood.			
8. I put off tasks that I must do but just can't find the motivation to do.			
9. I usually study wherever I happen to be until someone I know shows up.			
10. I have no idea where my time goes.			

SCORE: Add up your total points.

0-5: You make the most of your time and organize your priorities.

6-10: You have some good time-management habits, but you could improve.

11 or more: You are prone to procrastination, disorganization, and easily distracted. Consider the tips in the P.O.W.E.R. Study Strategies: Managing Your Time Wisely to help you better control your use of time.

9 Racial and Ethnic Inequality

Sociology at **WORK** COMMUNITY COLLEGE RECRUITER

PAUL CHEN visits more than a dozen high schools each year to talk to students about their future plans and encourage them to consider enrolling in a course of study at the local college where he works. "I like to feel that our college reflects the real world, so I'm always on the lookout for what might be called non-traditional students," he says. "Grades and test scores have their place, but talent comes in many packages." As an example, Chen points to a young man he recently recruited from an urban school. "The resources of the school are nil and there aren't high expectations for the kids," Chen says. "This student's grades weren't brilliant, but he had organized a battle of the bands for disaster relief in Haiti. He hopes to work in public health in Africa. I look at this student and I don't see an 'average' boy. I see a young man who can take an idea and make it happen. I see a person who hasn't had the breaks himself, but hopes to improve the lives of others. I see exactly the kind of student I want to have here on our campus." ■

Looking Ahead

WHAT IS PREJUDICE, AND HOW IS IT INSTITUTIONALIZED IN THE FORM of discrimination? In what ways have race and ethnicity affected the experience of immigrants from other countries? What are the fastest-growing minority groups in the United States today? In this chapter we will focus on the meaning of race and ethnicity. We will begin by identifying the basic characteristics of a minority group and distinguishing between racial and ethnic groups. Then we will examine the dynamics of prejudice and discrimination. After considering four sociological perspectives on race and ethnicity, we'll take a look at common patterns of intergroup relations. The following module will describe the major racial and ethnic groups in the United States. Finally, in the Social Policy section we will explore the issue of global immigration.

MODULE 28 Minority, Racial, and Ethnic Groups

 **Prepare** Learning Objectives

LO 28-1 Define and differentiate minority groups, racial groups, and ethnic groups.
LO 28-2 Distinguish between prejudice and discrimination and explain why "race neutrality" amounts to covert racism.

 **Organize** Module Outline

Minority Groups
Race
　　Social Construction of Race
　　Recognition of Multiple Identities

Ethnicity
Prejudice and Discrimination
    Prejudice
    Color-Blind Racism
    Discriminatory Behavior
    The Privileges of the Dominant
    Institutional Discrimination

Sociologists frequently distinguish between racial and ethnic groups. The term **racial group** describes a group that is set apart from others because of physical differences that have taken on social significance. Whites, African Americans, and Asian Americans are all considered racial groups in the United States. While race does turn on physical differences, it is the culture of a particular society that constructs and attaches social significance to those differences, as we will see later. Unlike racial groups, an **ethnic group** is set apart from others primarily because of its national origin or distinctive cultural patterns. In the United States, Puerto Ricans, Jews, and Polish Americans are all categorized as ethnic groups (Table 9-1).

LO 28-1 Minority Groups

A numerical minority is any group that makes up less than half of some larger population. The population of the United States includes thousands of numerical minorities, including television actors, green-eyed people, tax lawyers, and descendants of the Pilgrims who arrived on the *Mayflower.* However, these numerical minorities are not considered to be minorities in the sociological sense; in fact, the number of people in a group does not necessarily determine its status as a social minority (or a dominant group). When sociologists define a minority group, they are concerned primarily with the economic and political power, or powerlessness, of that group. A **minority group** is a subordinate group whose members have significantly less control or power over their own lives than the members of a dominant or majority group have over theirs.

Sociologists have identified five basic properties of a minority group: unequal treatment, physical or cultural traits, ascribed status, solidarity, and in-group marriage (Wagley and Harris 1958):

1. Members of a minority group experience unequal treatment compared to members of a dominant group. For example, the management of an apartment complex may refuse to rent to African Americans, Hispanics, or Jews. Social inequality may be created or maintained by prejudice, discrimination, segregation, or even extermination.

2. Members of a minority group share physical or cultural characteristics that distinguish them from the dominant group. Each society arbitrarily decides which characteristics are most important in defining groups.

3. Membership in a minority (or dominant) group is not voluntary; people are born into the group. Thus, race and ethnicity are considered *ascribed* statuses.

4. Minority group members have a strong sense of group solidarity. William Graham Sumner, writing in 1906, noted that people make distinctions between members of their own group (the *in-group*) and everyone else (the *out-group*). When a group is the object of long-term prejudice and discrimination, the feeling of "us versus them" can and often does become extremely intense.

5. Members of a minority group generally marry others from the same group. A member of a dominant group is often unwilling to marry into a supposedly inferior minority group. In addition, the minority group's sense of solidarity encourages marriage within the group and discourages marriage to outsiders.

Study Alert

Be sure you can distinguish among a *racial group* (set apart due to physical differences that have assumed social significance), an *ethnic group* (set apart because of national origin or distinct cultural patterns), and a *minority group* (a group whose members are subordinate to a dominant group in the power and control they have over their own lives).

TABLE 9-1 RACIAL AND ETHNIC GROUPS IN THE UNITED STATES, 2010

Classification	Number in Thousands	Percentage of Total Population
Racial Groups		
Whites (non-Hispanic)	195,371	60.3
Blacks/African Americans	37,686	12.2
Native Americans, Alaskan Natives	2,247	0.7
Asian Americans	15,553	5.0
Chinese	3,347	1.1
Asian Indians	2,843	0.9
Filipinos	2,556	0.8
Vietnamese	1,548	0.5
Koreans	1,424	0.5
Japanese	763	0.2
Pacific Islanders, Native Hawaiians	1,847	0.6
Other Asian Americans	1,225	0.5
Arab Americans	1,517	0.5
Two or more races	9,009	2.9
Ethnic Groups		
White ancestry		
Germans	49,341	16.0
Irish	35,664	11.6
English	26,873	8.7
Italians	17,486	5.7
Poles	9,757	3.2
French	9,159	3.0
Scottish and Scots-Irish	9,122	3.0
Jews	6,452	2.1
Hispanics (or Latinos)	50,478	16.4
Mexican Americans	31,798	10.3
Puerto Ricans	4,624	1.5
Cubans	1,785	0.6
Salvadorans	1,648	0.5
Dominicans	1,415	0.5
Guatemalans	1,044	0.3
Other Hispanics	8,164	2.7
TOTAL (all groups)	**308,746**	

Note: Arab American population excluded from White total. All data are for 2010. Percentages do not total 100 percent, and when subcategories are added they do not match totals in major categories because of overlap between groups (e.g., Polish American Jews or people of mixed ancestry such as Irish and Italian).
Sources: American Community Survey 2011:Table C04006; Asi and Beaulieu 2013; DellaPergola 2012; Ennis et al. 2011; Hixson et al. 2012; Hoeffel et al. 2012; Humes et al. 2011; T. Norris et al. 2012.

LO **28-1** Race

Many people think of race as a series of biological classifications. However, research shows that is not a meaningful way of differentiating people. Genetically, there are no systematic differences between the races that affect people's social behavior and abilities. Instead, sociologists use the term *racial group* to refer to those minorities (and the corresponding dominant groups) who are set apart from others by obvious physical differences. But what is an "obvious" physical difference? Each society labels those differences that people consider important, while ignoring other characteristics that could serve as a basis for social differentiation.

SOCIAL CONSTRUCTION OF RACE

Because race is a social construction, the process of defining races typically benefits those who have more power and privilege than others. In the United States, we see differences in both skin color and hair color. Yet people learn informally that differences in skin color have a dramatic social and political meaning, whereas differences in hair color do not.

When observing skin color, many people in the United States tend to lump others rather casually into the traditional categories of "Black," "White," and "Asian." Subtle differences in skin color often go unnoticed. In many nations of Central America and South America, in contrast, people recognize color gradients on a continuum from light to dark skin color. Brazil has approximately 40 color groupings, while in other countries people may be described as "Mestizo Hondurans," "Mulatto Colombians," or "African Panamanians." What we see as "obvious" differences, then, are subject to each society's social definitions.

The largest racial minorities in the United States are African Americans (or Blacks), Native Americans (or American Indians), and Asian Americans (Japanese Americans, Chinese Americans, and other Asian peoples). Figure 9-1 provides information about the population of racial and ethnic groups in the United States over the past five centuries, projected through 2060.

Given current population patterns, it is clear that the nation's diversity will continue to increase. In 2011, for the first time ever, census data revealed that the majority of all children ages three and under are now either Hispanic or non-White. This turning point marks the beginning of a pattern in which the nation's minority population will slowly become the majority. By 2050, if not sooner, the majority of all school-age children in the United States will belong to racial or ethnic minority groups (Frey 2011).

Racial definitions are crystallized through what Michael Omi and Howard Winant (1994) have called **racial formation**, a sociohistorical process in which racial categories are created, inhabited, transformed, and destroyed. In this process, those who have power define groups of people according to a racist social structure. The creation of a reservation system for Native Americans in the late 1800s, which later influenced Charles Trimble's life and work, is one example of racial formation. Federal officials combined what were distinctive tribes into a single racial group, which we refer to today as Native Americans. The extent and frequency with which peoples are subject to racial formation is such that no one escapes it.

Another example of racial formation from the 1800s was known as the "one-drop rule." If a person had even a single drop of "Black blood," that person was defined and

From the perspective of . . .

A Police Officer As the number of multiracial children born in the United States continues to increase, would you expect the number of hate crimes committed to decrease? Why or why not?

viewed as Black, even if he or she *appeared* to be White. Clearly, race had social significance, enough so that White legislators established official standards about who was "Black" and who was "White."

The one-drop rule was a vivid example of the *social construction of race*—the process by which people come to define a group as a race based in part on physical characteristics, but also on historical, cultural, and economic factors. For example, in the 1800s, immigrant groups such as Italian and Irish Americans were not at first seen as being "White," but as foreigners who were not necessarily trustworthy. The social construction of race is an ongoing process that is subject to debate, especially in a diverse society such as the United States, where each year increasing numbers of children are born to parents of different racial backgrounds.

RECOGNITION OF MULTIPLE IDENTITIES

In 1900, in an address to the Anti-Slavery Union in London, scholar W. E. B. DuBois predicted that "the color line" would become the foremost problem of the 20th century. DuBois, born a free Black man in 1868, had witnessed prejudice and discrimination throughout the United States. His comment was prophetic. Today, over a century later, race and ethnicity still carry enormous weight in the United States (DuBois [1900] 1969).

The color line has blurred significantly since 1900, however. Interracial marriage is no longer forbidden by law and custom. Thus, Geetha Lakshmi-narayanan, a native of Ann Arbor, Michigan, is both White and Asian Indian. Often mistaken for a Filipina or Latina, she has grown accustomed to the blunt question "What are you?" (Navarro 2005).

In the late 20th century, with immigration from Latin America rising, the fluid nature of racial formation became evident. Suddenly, people were speaking about the "Latin Americanization" of the United States, or about a biracial, Black/White society being replaced by a triracial one. In the 2010 Census, over 9 million people in the United States (or about 2.9 percent of the population) reported that they were of two or more races. Half the people classified as multiracial were under age 18, suggesting that this segment of the population will grow in the years to come. People who claimed both White and American Indian ancestry were the largest group of multiracial residents (Bonilla-Silva 2004; Humes et al. 2011).

This statistical finding of millions of multiracial people obscures how individuals are often

FIGURE 9-1

RACIAL AND ETHNIC GROUPS IN THE UNITED STATES, 1500–2060 (PROJECTED)

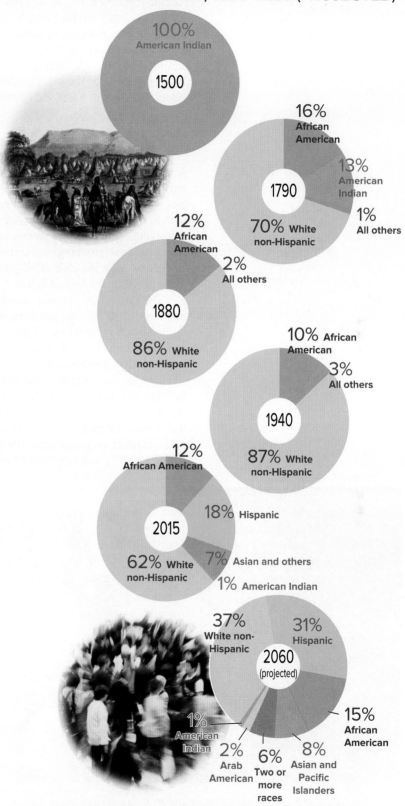

The racial and ethnic composition of what is today the United States has been undergoing change not just for the past 50 years, but for the past 500. Five centuries ago the land was populated only by indigenous Native Americans.

Note: Data for 2010 and 2060, African American and others, are for non-Hispanics.
Sources: Author's estimate; Bureau of the Census 2004a, 2012e:Table 4, 2013b; Humes et al. 2011.

asked to handle their identity. For example, the enrollment forms for government programs typically include only a few broad racial-ethnic categories. This approach to racial categorization is part of a long history that dictates single-race identities. Still, many individuals, especially young adults, struggle against social pressure to choose a single identity, and instead openly embrace multiple heritages. Public figures, rather than hide their mixed ancestry, now flaunt it. Singer Mariah Carey celebrates her Irish American background, and President Barack Obama speaks of being born in Hawaii to a Kenyan father and a White mother from Kansas. Tiger Woods, the world's best-known professional golfer, considers himself both Asian and African American.

LO 28-1 Ethnicity

An ethnic group, unlike a racial group, is set apart from others because of its national origin or distinctive cultural patterns. Among the ethnic groups in the United States are peoples with a Spanish-speaking background, referred to collectively as *Latinos* or *Hispanics,* such as Puerto Ricans, Mexican Americans, Cuban Americans, and other Latin Americans. Other ethnic groups in this country include Jewish, Irish, Italian, and Norwegian Americans. Although these groupings are convenient, they serve to obscure differences *within* ethnic categories (as in the case of Hispanics), as well as to overlook the mixed ancestry of so many people in the United States.

The distinction between racial and ethnic minorities is not always clear-cut. Some members of racial minorities, such as Asian Americans, may have significant cultural differences from other racial groups. At the same time, certain ethnic minorities, such as Latinos, may have obvious physical differences that set them apart from other ethnic groups in the United States.

Despite categorization problems, sociologists continue to feel that the distinction between racial groups and ethnic groups is socially significant. In most societies, including the United States, socially constructed physical differences tend to be more visible than ethnic differences. Partly as a result of this fact, stratification along racial lines is more resistant to change than stratification along ethnic lines. Over time, members of an ethnic minority can sometimes become indistinguishable from the majority—although the process may take generations and may never include all members of the group. In contrast, members of a racial minority find it much more difficult to blend in with the larger society and gain acceptance from the majority.

LO 28-2 Prejudice and Discrimination

Looking at the United States in the 21st century, some people wonder aloud if race and ethnicity are still relevant to social stratification. After all, African Americans have served as secretary of state, secretary of defense, and chairman of the Joint Chiefs of Staff; the office of attorney general has been held by both an African American and a Hispanic. Most notably, an African American now serves as president. As historic as these leaders' achievements have been, however, in every case their elevation meant that they left behind a virtually all-White government department or assembly.

At the same time, college campuses across the United States have been the scene of bias-related

The inauguration of President Barack Obama in 2009 was clearly historic. To put its significance in perspective, however, Obama's Senate seat was the only one held by a Black man when he left it to become president. Four years later, more than half of White voters in the 2012 presidential election—59 percent—cast their ballots for candidates other than Obama.

incidents. Student-run newspapers and radio stations have ridiculed racial and ethnic minorities; threatening literature has been stuffed under the doors of minority students; graffiti endorsing the views of White supremacist organizations such as the Ku Klux Klan have been scrawled on university walls. In some cases, there have even been violent clashes between groups of White and Black students (Southern Poverty Law Center 2010). What causes such ugly incidents?

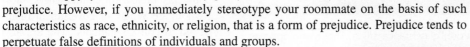

Today, some children of mixed-race families identify themselves as biracial or multiracial, rejecting efforts to place them in a single racial category.

PREJUDICE

Prejudice is a negative attitude toward an entire category of people, often an ethnic or racial minority. If you resent your roommate because he or she is sloppy, you are not necessarily guilty of prejudice. However, if you immediately stereotype your roommate on the basis of such characteristics as race, ethnicity, or religion, that is a form of prejudice. Prejudice tends to perpetuate false definitions of individuals and groups.

Sometimes prejudice results from **ethnocentrism**—the tendency to assume that one's own culture and way of life represent the norm or are superior to all others. Ethnocentric people judge other cultures by the standards of their group, which leads quite easily to prejudice against cultures they view as inferior.

One important and widespread ideology that reinforces prejudice is **racism**, the belief that one race is supreme and all others are innately inferior. When racism prevails in a society, members of subordinate groups generally experience prejudice, discrimination, and exploitation. In 1990, as concern mounted about racist attacks in the United States, Congress passed the Hate Crimes Statistics Act. As a result, hate crimes are now beginning to be reported and investigated in much the same way as conventional crimes against property and people.

Prejudice is also rooted in racial and ethnic **stereotypes**— unreliable generalizations about all members of a group that do not recognize individual differences within the group. The dominant or majority group creates these stereotypes through the process of racial formation. As the interactionist William I. Thomas (1923) noted, the dominant group's "definition of the situation" is often so powerful, it can mold the individual personality. That is, people respond not only to the objective features of a situation or person, but to the *social meaning* that situation or person carries. Thus, the false images or stereotypes created by the dominant group can become real in their consequences.

COLOR-BLIND RACISM

Over the past three generations, nationwide surveys have consistently shown growing support among Whites for integration, interracial dating, and the election of minority group members to public office—including the presidency of the United States. How can this trend be explained, given the persistence of residential segregation and the commission of thousands of hate crimes every year? The answer, to some extent, is that prejudice and discriminatory

Even successful members of minority groups, like Jeremy Lin, point guard for the Houston Rockets, are subjected to ethnic slurs. "Chink in the Armor" proclaimed a headline on ESPN's website in 2012 after Lin, who had spearheaded a multigame winning streak, had a bad night. The network later apologized for the remark.

People in need of help crowd a government public assistance office. Those who oppose government welfare programs but support other forms of government assistance, such as financial aid to college students, may be exhibiting color-blind racism.

attitudes are no longer expressed as freely as they once were. Often, they are couched in terms of equal opportunity.

Color-blind racism is the use of the principle of race neutrality to defend a racially unequal status quo. Proponents of race neutrality claim they believe that everyone should be treated equally. However, the way they apply the principle to government policy is anything but neutral. Proponents of this approach oppose affirmative action, public welfare assistance, and to a large extent, government-funded health insurance, all of which they see largely as favors to minority groups. Yet they do not object to practices that privilege Whites, such as college admissions criteria that give preference to the relatives of alumni. Nor do they oppose tax breaks for homeowners, most of whom are White, or government financial aid to college students, who are also disproportionately White. Though race neutrality is not based on theories of racial superiority or inferiority, then, the idea that society should be color-blind only perpetuates racial inequality.

Color-blind racism has also been referred to as "covert racism." Although its proponents rarely speak of racism, other indicators of social status, such as social class or citizenship, tend to become proxies for race. Thus, many White people can convince themselves that they are not racist—nor do they know anyone who is—and yet remain prejudiced against "welfare mothers" and "immigrants." They can conclude, mistakenly, that racial tolerance, or even racial and ethnic equality, has been achieved.

Researchers who have surveyed White attitudes toward African Americans over the past several decades have reached two inescapable conclusions. First, people's attitudes do change. In periods of social upheaval, dramatic attitudinal shifts can occur within a single generation. Second, less racial progress was made in the late 20th and early 21st centuries than in the relatively brief period of the 1950s and 1960s. Today, economically disadvantaged groups such as African Americans and Latinos have become so closely associated with urban decay, homelessness, welfare, and crime that those problems are now viewed as racial issues, even if they are not labeled as such. The tendency to *blame the victims* of these social ills complicates their resolution, especially at a time when government's ability to address social problems is limited by recession, antitax initiatives, and concern over terrorism. In short, the color line is still in place, even if more and more people refuse to acknowledge its existence (Ansell 2008; Bonilla-Silva 2006; Coates 2008; M. King 2007; Quillian 2006; Winant 1994).

DISCRIMINATORY BEHAVIOR

Prejudice often leads to **discrimination**, the denial of opportunities and equal rights to individuals and groups because of prejudice or other arbitrary reasons. Say that a White corporate president with a prejudice against Asian Americans has to fill an executive position. The most qualified candidate for the job is a Vietnamese American. If the president refuses to hire this candidate and instead selects an inferior White candidate, he or she is engaging in an act of racial discrimination.

Prejudiced *attitudes* should not be equated with discriminatory *behavior*. Although the two are generally related, they are not identical; either condition can be present without the other. A prejudiced person does not always act on his or her biases. The White corporate president, for example, might choose—despite his or her stereotypes—to hire the Vietnamese American. That would be prejudice without discrimination. On the other hand, a White

Study Alert

Remember that *color-blind racism*, which argues that some people who see themselves as race-neutral and are proponents of everyone being treated the same, may actually mask covert racism, because it perpetuates racial inequality.

corporate president with a completely respectful view of Vietnamese Americans might refuse to hire them for executive posts out of fear that biased clients would take their business elsewhere. In that case, the president's action would constitute discrimination without prejudice.

A field experiment by sociologist Devah Pager, then a doctoral candidate at the University of Wisconsin–Madison, documented racial discrimination in hiring. Pager sent four polite, well-dressed young men out to look for an entry-level job in Milwaukee, Wisconsin. All were 23-year-old college students, but they presented themselves as high school graduates with similar job histories. Two of the men were Black and two were White. One Black applicant and one White applicant claimed to have served 18 months in jail for a felony conviction—possession of cocaine with intent to distribute.

As one might expect, the four men's experiences with 350 potential employers were vastly different. Predictably, the White applicant with a purported prison record received only half as many callbacks as the other White applicant—17 percent compared to 34 percent. But as dramatic as the effect of his criminal record was, the effect of his race was more significant. Despite his prison record, he received slightly more callbacks than the Black applicant *with no criminal record* (17 percent compared to 14 percent). Race, it seems, was more of a concern to potential employers than a criminal background.

The implications of this research are not limited to any one city, such as Milwaukee. Similar studies have confirmed discriminatory handling of job applications in Chicago; New York City; Long Island, New York; San Diego; and Washington, D.C. Over time, the cumulative effect of such differential behavior by employers contributes to significant differences in income. Figure 9-2 vividly illustrates the income inequality between White men and almost everyone else (Pager 2007; Pager et al. 2009).

FIGURE 9-2 U.S. MEDIAN INCOME BY RACE, ETHNICITY, AND GENDER

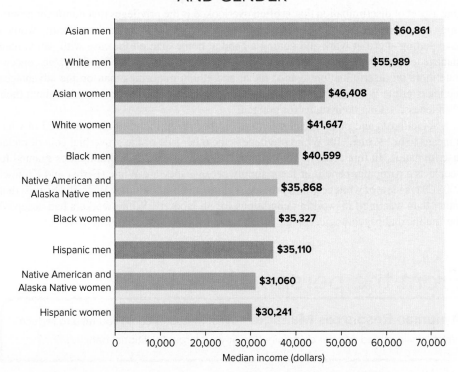

Even at the highest levels of schooling, the income gap remains between Whites and Blacks. Education also has little apparent effect on the income gap between male and female workers. Even a brief analysis reveals striking differences in earning power between White men and women, especially African American, Native American, and Hispanic women.

Note: Data released in 2013 for income earned in 2012. Median income is from all sources and is limited to year-round, full-time workers at least 25 years old (American Indian data for 16 years or older). Data for White men and women are for non-Hispanics.
Sources: American Community Survey 2013a:Table B20017C; DeNavas-Walt et al. 2013:PINC-03.

If race serves as a barrier, why do Asian American men earn slightly more income than White men (see Figure 9-2)? Not all Asian American men earn high incomes; indeed, some Asian American groups, such as Laotians and Vietnamese, have high levels of poverty. Nevertheless, a significant number of Asian Americans have advanced degrees that qualify them for highly paid jobs, and which raise the median income for the group as a whole. Although these highly educated Asian Americans earn a lot of money, they do not earn quite as much as their White counterparts, however. With a doctorate holder in the family, the typical Asian American family earns an estimated $124,000, compared to $140,000 for a White family (DeNavas-Walt et al. 2013:FINC-01).

Sometimes racial and ethnic discrimination is overt. Internet forums like Craigslist .org or Roommate.com feature classified ads that state "African Americans and Arabians tend to clash with me" or "Clean, Godly Christian men only." While anti-discrimination laws prevent such notices from being published in the newspapers, existing law has not caught up with online bigotry in hiring and renting (Liptak 2006).

Discrimination persists even for the most educated and qualified minority group members from the best family backgrounds. Despite their talents and experiences, they sometimes encounter attitudinal or organizational bias that prevents them from reaching their full potential. The term **glass ceiling** refers to an invisible barrier that blocks the promotion of a qualified individual in a work environment because of the individual's gender, race, or ethnicity (R. Schaefer 2014).

In early 1995, the federal Glass Ceiling Commission issued the first comprehensive study of barriers to promotion in the United States. The commission found that glass ceilings continue to block women and minority group men from top management positions in the nation's industries.

THE PRIVILEGES OF THE DOMINANT

One aspect of discrimination that is often overlooked is the privileges that dominant groups enjoy at the expense of others. For instance, we tend to focus more on the difficulty women have getting ahead at work and getting a hand at home than on the ease with which men manage to make their way in the world and avoid household chores. Similarly, we concentrate more on discrimination against racial and ethnic minorities than on the advantages members of the White majority enjoy. Indeed, most White people rarely think about their "Whiteness," taking their status for granted.

Sociologists and other social scientists are becoming increasingly interested in what it means to be "White," for White privilege is the other side of the proverbial coin of racial discrimination. In this context, **White privilege** refers to rights or immunities granted to people as a particular benefit or favor simply because they are White (Ferber and Kimmel 2008). This view of whiteness as a privilege echoes an observation by W. E. B. DuBois, that rather than wanting fair working conditions for all laborers, White workers had accepted the "public and psychological wage" of whiteness ([1935] 1962:700).

From the perspective of . . .

A Human Resources Manager What measures could you take to reduce White privilege and gender discrimination at your large, traditional banking firm?

The feminist scholar Peggy McIntosh (1988) became interested in White privilege after noticing that most men would not acknowledge that there were privileges attached to being male—even if they would agree that being female had its disadvantages. Did White people suffer from a similar blind spot regarding their racial privilege? she wondered. Intrigued, McIntosh began to list all the ways in which she benefited from her Whiteness. She soon realized that the list of unspoken advantages was long and significant.

White people are accustomed to seeing other White people in professional positions and jobs with authority and prestige. Whiteness *does* have its privileges.

McIntosh found that as a White person, she rarely needed to step out of her comfort zone, no matter where she went. If she wished to, she could spend most of her time with people of her race. She could find a good place to live in a pleasant neighborhood, buy the foods she liked to eat from almost any grocery store, and get her hair styled in almost any salon. She could attend a public meeting without feeling that she did not belong, that she was different from everyone else.

McIntosh discovered, too, that her skin color opened doors for her. She could cash checks and use credit cards without suspicion, browse through stores without being shadowed by security guards. She could be seated without difficulty in a restaurant. If she asked to see the manager, she could assume he or she would be of her race. If she needed help from a doctor or a lawyer, she could get it.

McIntosh also realized that her Whiteness made the job of parenting easier. She did not need to worry about protecting her children from people who didn't like them. She could be sure that their schoolbooks would show pictures of people who looked like them, and that their history texts would describe White people's achievements. She knew that the television programs they watched would include White characters.

Finally, McIntosh had to admit that others did not constantly evaluate her in racial terms. When she appeared in public, she didn't need to worry that her clothing or behavior might reflect poorly on White people. If she was recognized for an achievement, it was seen as her achievement, not that of an entire race. And no one ever assumed that the personal opinions she voiced should be those of all White people. Because McIntosh blended in with the people around her, she wasn't always onstage.

These are not all the privileges White people take for granted as a result of their membership in the dominant racial group in the United States. As Devah Pager's study showed, White job seekers enjoy a tremendous advantage over equally well-qualified—even better-qualified—Blacks. Whiteness *does* carry privileges—to a much greater extent than most White people realize (Fitzgerald 2008; Picca and Feagin 2007).

INSTITUTIONAL DISCRIMINATION

Discrimination is practiced not only by individuals in one-to-one encounters but also by institutions in their daily operations. Social scientists are particularly concerned with the ways in which structural factors such as employment, housing, health care, and government operations maintain the social significance of race and ethnicity. **Institutional discrimination** refers to the denial of opportunities and equal rights to individuals and groups that results from the normal operations of a society. This kind of discrimination consistently affects certain racial and ethnic groups more than others.

The Commission on Civil Rights (1981:9–10) has identified various forms of institutional discrimination:

- Rules requiring that only English be spoken at a place of work, even when it is not a business necessity to restrict the use of other languages.

- Preferences shown by law and medical schools in the admission of children of wealthy and influential alumni, nearly all of whom are White.

- Restrictive employment-leave policies, coupled with prohibitions on part-time work, that make it difficult for the heads of single-parent families (most of whom are women) to obtain and keep jobs.

In some cases, even seemingly neutral institutional standards can have discriminatory effects. African American students at a midwestern state university protested a policy under which fraternities and sororities that wished to use campus facilities for a dance were required to pay a $150 security deposit to cover possible damages. They complained that the policy had a discriminatory impact on minority student organizations. Campus police countered that the university's policy applied to all student groups interested in using the facilities. However, since the overwhelmingly White fraternities and sororities at the school had their own houses, which they used for dances, the policy indeed affected only the African American and other minority organizations.

Attempts have been made to eradicate or compensate for institutional discrimination. The 1960s saw the passage of many pioneering civil rights laws, including the landmark 1964 Civil Rights Act (which prohibits discrimination in public accommodations and publicly owned facilities on the basis of race, color, creed, national origin, and gender). Yet today, voting rights are still an issue in some states (Box 9-1).

For more than 40 years, affirmative action programs have been instituted to overcome past discrimination. **Affirmative action** refers to positive efforts to recruit minority group

Before passage of the Civil Rights Act (1964), segregation of public accommodations was the norm throughout the South. Whites used the most up-to-date bathrooms, waiting rooms, and even drinking fountains, while Blacks ("Colored") were directed to older facilities in inferior condition. Such separate but unequal arrangements are a blatant example of institutional discrimination.

Research Today

9-1 INSTITUTIONAL DISCRIMINATION IN THE VOTING BOOTH

Eddie Lee Holloway Jr. has been voting since he was 18. Now, decades later, he is having trouble not only casting his ballot but receiving disability benefits. Because of a clerical error that was made when he was born—Eddie's birth certificate names him Eddie Junior Holloway—the state of Wisconsin will not allow him to vote. Eddie's social security card shows his correct name, as does an expired Illinois photo ID. His father's name, Eddie Lee Holloway, appears on his birth certificate. Still, the state government will not recognize him as a U.S. citizen. Like a lot of non-White Americans, Eddie has lost his birthright to institutional discrimination.

How should government establish the authenticity of a person's right to vote? Today, many states have begun to require a government-issued ID bearing a photograph, presumably to prevent voter fraud. Other states will accept any photo ID (see the figure). In the past, voters usually did not need to show any kind of identification at the polls; their identity was established at the time they registered to vote.

Courts have been reluctant to uphold the new voter ID laws, for not all eligible voters can easily obtain these credentials. Such laws disproportionately disenfranchise the elderly and members of minority groups, simply because they do not have a driver's license. According to national surveys, 25 percent of African American citizens and 16 percent of Latino citizens do not have a valid government-issued photo ID, compared to 8 percent of White citizens. These findings fit the definition of institutional discrimination, in that *through the normal operations of society*—in this case, the holding of elections—people of color are more likely than others to be denied their rights. Indeed, research into who can and cannot vote suggests the

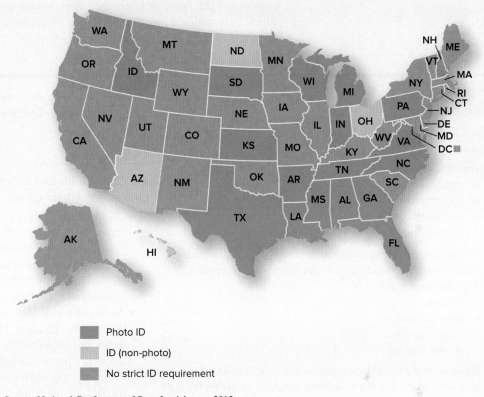

MAPPING LIFE NATIONWIDE

VOTER ID REQUIREMENTS

- Photo ID
- ID (non-photo)
- No strict ID requirement

Source: National Conference of State Legislatures 2013.

existence of institutional discrimination in our national elections.

Why the sudden emphasis on establishing voters' identity? There is little evidence to suggest that people have been impersonating eligible voters at the polls.

> *Such laws disproportionately disenfranchise the elderly and members of minority groups, simply because they do not have a driver's license.*

Yet surveys show that most Americans prefer strict voter ID enforcement, whether or not such tactics constitute institutional discrimination. In 2013 a national telephone survey found that 70 percent of likely U.S. voters believe that all voters should be required to prove their identity before

being allowed to vote. Only 25 percent opposed such a requirement.

These findings are one more example of the painful underlying context of American intergroup relations. Institutional discrimination consistently imposes more hindrances on, and awards fewer benefits to, certain racial and ethnic groups compared to others.

Let's Discuss

1. Are you a registered voter? If so, how does your local polling place verify voters' identity? Have you ever had difficulty establishing your identity on election day?
2. Why are citizens and state legislators suddenly so concerned about requiring voters to establish their identity?

Sources: ACLU 2013; Brennan Center 2006, 2013; Dade 2012; Rasmussen Reports 2013.

members or women for jobs, promotions, and educational opportunities. Many people resent these programs, arguing that advancing one group's cause merely shifts the discrimination to another group. By giving priority to African Americans in admissions, for example, schools may overlook more qualified White candidates. In many parts of the country and many sectors of the economy, affirmative action is being rolled back, even though it was never fully implemented.

Discriminatory practices continue to pervade nearly all areas of life in the United States today. In part, that is because various individuals and groups actually *benefit* from racial and ethnic discrimination in terms of money, status, and influence. Discrimination permits members of the majority to enhance their wealth, power, and prestige at the expense of others. Less qualified people get jobs and promotions simply because they are members of the dominant group. Such individuals and groups will not surrender these advantages easily.

E Evaluate

Read each question carefully and then select or provide the best answer.

1. Racism is a form of which of the following?
   a. ethnocentrism
   b. discrimination
   c. prejudice
   d. stereotyping

2. Suppose that a White employer refuses to hire a qualified Vietnamese American but hires an inferior White applicant. This decision is an act of
   a. prejudice.
   b. ethnocentrism.
   c. discrimination.
   d. stigmatization.

3. Suppose that a workplace requires that only English be spoken, even when it is not a business necessity to restrict the use of other languages. This requirement would be an example of
   a. prejudice.
   b. scapegoating.
   c. a self-fulfilling prophecy.
   d. institutional discrimination.

4. _____ are unreliable generalizations about all members of a group that do not recognize individual differences within the group.

5. Sociologists use the term _____ to refer to a negative attitude toward an entire category of people, often an ethnic or racial minority.

Answers
1 (c); 2 (c); 3 (d); 4 Stereotypes; 5 prejudice

R Rethink

Consider these questions to get a deeper understanding of the material.

1. Why does the social construction of race defy the traditional notion of race as a biological category?

2. Which would be more socially significant, the elimination of prejudice or the elimination of discrimination?

RECAP

LO 28-1 Define and differentiate minority groups, racial groups, and ethnic groups.

- According to sociologists, the five basic properties of minority groups are unequal treatment, physical or cultural traits, ascribed status, solidarity, and in-group marriage. When sociologists define a minority group, they are concerned primarily with the economic and political power (or powerlessness) of the group.
- Race is a social construction rather than a genetic or biological classification. The attachment of meaning by powerful, privileged people to physical differences between races is a process called "racial formation."
- Ethnicity is based on national origin and distinctive cultural traits, but ethnicity is routinely blurred in countries like the United States, with the result that few clear ethnic markers remain after a comparatively short time.

LO 28-2 Distinguish between prejudice and discrimination and explain why "race neutrality" amounts to covert racism.

- Prejudice is a negative attitude (literally a "pre-judgment") toward a category of people, typically a racial or ethnic minority. Ethnocentrism, racism, and racial and ethnic stereotypes are usually at the root of prejudice.
- Discrimination is unfair behavior toward individuals and groups because of prejudice or other arbitrary reasons. Prejudice often but not always leads to discrimination.
- In what is called "color-blind racism," prejudiced people use the principle of racial neutrality to mask underlying racial prejudice. Proponents of "racial neutrality" criticize and resent benefits accorded to minority groups while silently enjoying the benefits routinely accorded to majority group members.
- Another form of discrimination is institutional discrimination, which is the denial of opportunities and equal treatment to individuals and groups that results from the normal operations of a society.

KEY TERMS

Affirmative action Positive efforts to recruit minority group members or women for jobs, promotions, and educational opportunities.

Color-blind racism The use of the principle of race neutrality to defend a racially unequal status quo.

Discrimination The denial of opportunities and equal rights to individuals and groups because of prejudice or other arbitrary reasons.

Ethnic group A group that is set apart from others primarily because of its national origin or distinctive cultural patterns.

Ethnocentrism The tendency to assume that one's own culture and way of life represent the norm or are superior to all others.

Glass ceiling An invisible barrier that blocks the promotion of a qualified individual in a work environment because of the individual's gender, race, or ethnicity.

Institutional discrimination The denial of opportunities and equal rights to individuals and groups that results from the normal operations of a society.

Minority group A subordinate group whose members have significantly less control or power over their own lives than the members of a dominant or majority group have over theirs.

Prejudice A negative attitude toward an entire category of people, often an ethnic or racial minority.

Racial formation A sociohistorical process in which racial categories are created, inhabited, transformed, and destroyed.

Racial group A group that is set apart from others because of physical differences that have taken on social significance.

Racism The belief that one race is supreme and all others are innately inferior.

Stereotype An unreliable generalization about all members of a group that does not recognize individual differences within the group.

White privilege Rights or immunities granted to people as a particular benefit or favor simply because they are White.

MODULE 29 Sociological Perspectives on Race and Ethnicity

P Prepare | Learning Objectives

LO 29-1 Analyze racial and ethnic inequality using the functionalist, conflict, labeling, and interactionist perspectives.

LO 29-2 Describe the patterns of intergroup relations, as defined by sociologists.

O Organize | Module Outline

Functionalist Perspective
Conflict Perspective
Labeling Perspective
Interactionist Perspective
Spectrum of Intergroup Relations
    Segregation
    Amalgamation
    Assimilation
    Pluralism

Relations among racial and ethnic groups lend themselves to analysis from four major sociological perspectives. Viewing race from the macro level, functionalists observe that racial prejudice and discrimination serve positive functions for dominant groups. Conflict theorists see the economic structure as a central factor in the exploitation of minorities. Labeling theorists note the way in which minorities are singled out for differential treatment by law enforcement officers. On the micro level, interactionist researchers stress the manner in which everyday contact between people from different racial and ethnic backgrounds contributes to tolerance or hostility.

LO **29-1** Functionalist Perspective

What possible use could racial bigotry have? Functionalist theorists, while agreeing that racial hostility is hardly to be admired, point out that it serves positive functions for those who practice discrimination.

Anthropologist Manning Nash (1962) has identified three functions of racially prejudiced beliefs for the dominant group:

1. Racist views provide a moral justification for maintaining an unequal society that routinely deprives a minority group of its rights and privileges. Southern Whites justified slavery by believing that Africans were physically and spiritually subhuman and devoid of souls.

2. Racist beliefs discourage the subordinate minority from attempting to question its lowly status, which would be to question the very foundations of society.

3. Racial myths suggest that any major societal change (such as an end to discrimination) would only bring greater poverty to the minority and lower the majority's standard of living. As a result, racial prejudice grows when a society's value system (one underlying a colonial empire or slavery, for example) is threatened.

Although racial prejudice and discrimination may serve the powerful, such unequal treatment can also be dysfunctional for a society, and even for the dominant group. Sociologist Arnold Rose (1951) has outlined four dysfunctions that are associated with racism:

1. A society that practices discrimination fails to use the resources of all individuals. Discrimination limits the search for talent and leadership to the dominant group.

2. Discrimination aggravates social problems such as poverty, delinquency, and crime, and places the financial burden of alleviating those problems on the dominant group.

3. Society must invest a good deal of time and money to defend its barriers to the full participation of all members.

4. Racial prejudice and discrimination often undercut goodwill and friendly diplomatic relations between nations.

LO **29-1** Conflict Perspective

Conflict theorists would certainly agree with Arnold Rose that racial prejudice and discrimination have many harmful consequences for society. Sociologists such as Oliver Cox (1948), Robert Blauner (1972), and Herbert M. Hunter (2000) have used the **exploitation theory** (or *Marxist class theory*) to explain the basis of racial subordination in the United States. Karl Marx viewed the exploitation of the lower class as a basic part of the capitalist economic system. From a Marxist point of view, racism keeps minorities in low-paying jobs, thereby supplying the capitalist ruling class with a pool of cheap labor. Moreover, by forcing racial minorities to accept low wages, capitalists can restrict the wages of *all* members of the proletariat. Workers from the dominant group who demand higher wages can always be replaced by minorities who have no choice but to accept low-paying jobs.

The conflict view of race relations seems persuasive in a number of instances. Japanese Americans were the object of little prejudice until they began to enter jobs that brought them into competition with Whites. The movement to keep Chinese immigrants out of the United States became most fervent during the latter half of the 19th century, when Chinese and Whites fought over dwindling work opportunities. Both the enslavement of Blacks and the extermination and removal westward of Native Americans were economically motivated.

However, the exploitation theory is too limited to explain prejudice in its many forms. Not all minority groups have been exploited to the same extent. In addition, many groups (such as the Quakers and the Mormons) have been victimized by prejudice for other than economic reasons. Still, as Gordon Allport (1979:210) concludes, the exploitation theory correctly "points a sure finger at one of the factors involved in prejudice, . . . rationalized self-interest of the upper classes."

LO 29-1 Labeling Perspective

One practice that fits both the conflict perspective and labeling theory is racial profiling. **Racial profiling** is any arbitrary action initiated by an authority based on race, ethnicity, or national origin rather than on a person's behavior. Generally, racial profiling occurs when law enforcement officers, including customs officials, airport security, and police, assume that people who fit a certain description are likely to be engaged in illegal activities. Beginning in the 1980s with the emergence of the crack cocaine market, skin color became a key characteristic in racial profiling. This practice is often based on very explicit stereotypes. For example, one federal antidrug initiative encouraged officers to look specifically for people with dreadlocks and for Latino men traveling together.

Today, authorities continue to rely on racial profiling, despite overwhelming evidence that it is misleading. A recent study showed that Blacks are still more likely than Whites to be frisked and handled with force when they are stopped. Yet Whites are more likely than Blacks to possess weapons, illegal drugs, or stolen property (Farrell and McDevitt 2010).

In U.S. retail stores, Black customers have different experiences from White customers. They are more likely than Whites to have their checks or credit cards refused and more likely to be profiled by security personnel.

Research on the ineffectiveness of racial profiling, coupled with calls by minority communities to end the stigmatization, has led to growing demands to end the practice. But these efforts came to an abrupt halt after the September 11, 2001, terrorist attacks on the United States, when suspicions arose about Muslim and Arab immigrants. Foreign students from Arab countries were summoned for special questioning by authorities. Legal immigrants who were identified as Arab or Muslim were scrutinized for possible illegal activity and prosecuted for violations that authorities routinely ignored among immigrants of other ethnicities and faiths. National surveys have found little change since 2001 in public support for profiling of Arab Americans at airports. In 2010, 53 percent of Americans favored "ethnic and religious profiling" of air travelers—even those who are U.S. citizens—together with more intensive security checks of passengers who fit certain profiles (Zogby 2010).

LO 29-1 Interactionist Perspective

A Hispanic woman is transferred from a job on an assembly line to a similar position working next to a White man. At first, the White man is patronizing, assuming that she must be incompetent. She is cold and resentful; even when she needs assistance, she refuses to admit it. After a week, the growing tension between the two leads to a bitter quarrel. Yet over time, each slowly comes to appreciate the other's strengths and talents. A year after they begin working together, these two workers become respectful friends. This story is an example of what interactionists call the *contact hypothesis* in action.

The **contact hypothesis** states that in cooperative circumstances, interracial contact between people of equal status will cause them to become less prejudiced and to abandon old stereotypes. People begin to see one another as individuals and discard the broad generalizations characteristic of stereotyping. Note the phrases *equal status* and *cooperative circumstances*. In the story just told, if the two workers had been competing for one vacancy as a supervisor, the racial hostility between them might have worsened (Allport 1979; Fine 2008).

As Latinos and other minorities slowly gain access to better-paying and more responsible jobs, the contact hypothesis may take on even greater significance. The trend in our society is toward increasing contact between individuals from dominant and subordinate groups. That may be one way of eliminating—or at least reducing—racial and ethnic stereotyping and prejudice. Another may be the establishment of interracial coalitions, an idea suggested by sociologist William Julius Wilson (1999). To work, such coalitions would obviously need to be built on an equal role for all members.

Table 9-2 summarizes the four major sociological perspectives on race. No matter what the explanation for racial and ethnic distinctions—functionalist, conflict, labeling, or interactionist—these socially constructed inequalities can have powerful consequences in the form of prejudice and discrimination. In the next section, we will see how inequality based on the ascribed characteristics of race and ethnicity can poison people's interpersonal relations, depriving whole groups of opportunities others take for granted.

Study Alert

Remember that the *contact hypothesis* depends on equal status and cooperative circumstances for people of different races to set aside their prejudices and recognize each other as individuals.

Tracking Sociological Perspectives

TABLE 9-2 **SOCIOLOGICAL PERSPECTIVES ON RACE AND ETHNICITY**

Perspective	Emphasis
Functionalist	The dominant majority benefits from the subordination of racial minorities.
Conflict	Vested interests perpetuate racial inequality through economic exploitation.
Labeling	People are profiled and stereotyped based on their racial and ethnic identity.
Interactionist	Cooperative interracial contacts can reduce hostility.

LO 29-2 Spectrum of Intergroup Relations

Racial and ethnic groups can relate to one another in a wide variety of ways, ranging from friendships and intermarriages to hostility, from behaviors that require mutual approval to behaviors imposed by the dominant group.

One devastating pattern of intergroup relations is **genocide**—the deliberate, systematic killing of an entire people or nation. This term describes the killing of 1 million Armenians by Turkey beginning in 1915. It is most commonly applied to Nazi Germany's extermination of 6 million European Jews, as well as gays, lesbians, and the Roma ("Gypsies"), during World War II. The term *genocide* is also appropriate in describing the United States' policies toward Native Americans in the 19th century. In 1800, the Native American (or American Indian) population of the United States was about 600,000; by 1850, it had been reduced to 250,000 through warfare with the U.S. cavalry, disease, and forced relocation to inhospitable environments.

The *expulsion* of a people is another extreme means of acting out racial or ethnic prejudice. In 1979, for example, the government of Vietnam expelled nearly 1 million ethnic Chinese from the country. The action resulted partly from centuries of hostility between Vietnam and neighboring China.

More recently (beginning in 2009), France expelled over 10,000 ethnic Roma (or Gypsies) who had immigrated from their home countries of Bulgaria and Romania. The action appeared to violate the European Union's ban against targeting ethnic groups, as well as its policy of "freedom of movement" throughout the EU. In 2011, the EU withdrew the threat of legal action when the French government modified its policy to apply only to those Roma who lived in "illegal camps." However, many observers saw the concession as a thinly veiled attempt to circumvent the EU's long-standing human rights policies.

In a variation of expulsion, called *secession,* failure to resolve an ethnic or racial conflict results in the drawing of formal boundaries between the groups. In 1947, India was partitioned into two separate countries in an attempt to end violent conflict between Hindus and Muslims. The predominantly Muslim areas in the north became the new country of Pakistan; the rest of India became predominantly Hindu.

Secession, expulsion, and genocide are extreme behaviors, clustered on the negative end of what is called the Spectrum of Intergroup Relations (Figure 9-3). More typical intergroup relations follow four identifiable patterns: (1) segregation, (2) amalgamation, (3) assimilation, and (4) pluralism. Each pattern defines the dominant group's actions and the minority group's responses. Intergroup relations are rarely restricted to only one of the four patterns, although invariably one does tend to dominate. Think of these patterns primarily as ideal types.

French police remove a member of the Roma minority who is resisting deportation to his home country. The expulsion of certain racial or ethnic groups is an extreme result of prejudice.

Study Alert

Be able to differentiate between genocide, expulsion, and secession, all of which perpetuate racial and ethnic prejudice.

SEGREGATION

Separate schools, separate seating on buses and in restaurants, separate washrooms, even separate drinking fountains—these were all part of the lives of African Americans in the South when segregation ruled early in the 20th century. **Segregation** refers to the physical separation of two groups of people in terms of residence, workplace, and social events. Generally, a dominant group imposes this pattern on a minority group. Segregation is rarely complete, however. Intergroup contact inevitably occurs, even in the most segregated societies.

From 1948 (when it received its independence) to 1990, the Republic of South Africa severely restricted the movement of Blacks and other non-Whites by means of a wide-ranging system of segregation known as **apartheid**. Apartheid even included the creation of separate homelands where Blacks were expected to live. However, decades of local resistance to apartheid, combined with international pressure, led to marked political changes in the 1990s. In 1994, a prominent Black activist, Nelson Mandela, was elected South Africa's president in the first election in which Blacks (the majority of the nation's population) were allowed to vote. Mandela had spent almost 28 years in South African prisons for his anti-apartheid activities. His election was widely viewed as the final blow to South Africa's oppressive policy of segregation.

FIGURE 9-3 SPECTRUM OF INTERGROUP RELATIONS

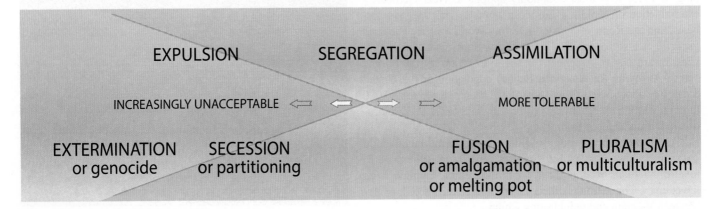

EXPULSION · SEGREGATION · ASSIMILATION

INCREASINGLY UNACCEPTABLE ⟸ ⟸ ⟹ ⟹ MORE TOLERABLE

EXTERMINATION
or genocide · SECESSION
or partitioning · FUSION
or amalgamation
or melting pot · PLURALISM
or multiculturalism

Source: Prepared by author, Richard T. Schaefer.

In contrast to the enforced segregation in South Africa, the United States exemplifies an unmandated but nevertheless persistent separation of the races. In their book *American Apartheid,* sociologists Douglas Massey and Nancy Denton (1993) described segregation in U.S. cities using 1990 census data. As the book's title suggests, the racial makeup of U.S. neighborhoods resembles the rigid government-imposed segregation that prevailed for so long in South Africa.

Analysis of recent census data shows continuing segregation despite the nation's racial and ethnic diversity. To measure the degree of separation between groups, scholars use a segregation index that ranges from 0 (complete integration) to 100 (complete segregation). The index value indicates the percentage of the minority group that needs to move for the minority group to be distributed exactly as Whites. For example, a segregation index of 60 for Blacks–Whites would mean that 60 percent of all African Americans need to move to achieve the same racial distribution as Whites.

Table 9-3 shows the eight most segregated metropolitan areas in the United States; all have large African American, Latino, and Asian American populations. Blacks and Whites are most separated from each other in Detroit; Whites and Latinos, in the Los Angeles/Long Beach metropolitan area. Asians and Whites are most segregated in the New Brunswick, New Jersey area. Roughly half to three quarters of the population in these areas would need to move in order to even the distribution of racial/ethnic groups throughout the city and surrounding suburbs.

Over the last 40 years, Black–White segregation has declined only modestly. Hispanic–White and Asian–White segregation, although they are lower, have not changed significantly in the last 30 years. Even when we consider social class, the pattern of minority group segregation persists, despite the occasional multiracial neighborhood (Bureau of the Census 2010b; Frey 2011; Krysan et al. 2008; Wilkes and Iceland 2004).

AMALGAMATION

Amalgamation happens when a majority group and a minority group combine to form a new group. Through intermarriage over several generations, various groups in society combine to form a new group. This pattern can be expressed as A + B + C → D, where A, B, and C represent different groups in a society, and D signifies the end result, a unique cultural-racial group unlike any of the initial groups (W. Newman 1973).

The belief in the United States as a "melting pot" became compelling in the first part of the 20th century, particularly since that image suggested that the nation had an almost divine mission to amalgamate various groups into one people. However, in actuality, many residents were not willing to include Native Americans, Jews, African Americans, Asian Americans, and Irish Roman Catholics in the melting pot. Therefore, this pattern does not adequately describe dominant–subordinate relations in the United States. There *has* been a significant increase in interracial marriage among Whites, Blacks, Asians, and Hispanics in recent years.

TABLE 9-3 SEGREGATED METROPOLITAN AMERICA

Black–White	Hispanic–White	Asian–White
1. Detroit 79.6	1. Los Angeles/Long Beach 63.4	1. Edison/New Brunswick, NJ 53.7
2. Milwaukee 79.6	2. New York/White Plains 63.1	2. New York/White Plains 49.5
3. New York/White Plains 79.1	3. Newark 62.6	3. Houston 48.7
4. Newark 78.0	4. Boston 62.0	4. Los Angeles/Long Beach 47.6
5. Chicago/Naperville 75.9	5. Salinas, CA 60.0	5. Boston 47.4
6. Philadelphia 73.7	6. Philadelphia 58.8	6. Sacramento, CA 46.8
7. Miami/Miami Beach 73.0	7. Chicago/Naperville 57.0	7. San Francisco 46.7
8. Cleveland 72.6	8. Oxford/Ventura, CA 54.5	8. Warren/Farmington Hills, MI 46.3

Note: The higher the value, the more segregated the metropolitan area.
Source: Logan and Stults 2011.

ASSIMILATION

In India, many Hindus complain about Indian citizens who copy the traditions and customs of the British. In France, people of Arab and African origin, many of them Muslim, complain they are treated as second-class citizens—a charge that provoked riots in 2005 and again in 2012. And in the United States, some Italian Americans, Polish Americans, Hispanics, and Jews have changed their ethnic-sounding family names to names that are typically found among White Protestant families.

Assimilation is the process through which a person forsakes his or her cultural tradition to become part of a different culture. Generally, it is practiced by a minority group member who wants to conform to the standards of the dominant group. Assimilation can be described as a pattern in which A + B + C → A. The majority, A, dominates in such a way that members of minorities B and C imitate it and attempt to become indistinguishable from it (W. Newman 1973).

Today, members of racial and ethnic minorities still struggle with the question of whether to assimilate. Too often, those who do assimilate face continued prejudice and discrimination. Race and ethnicity, as much as class, affect people's place and status in a stratification system, not only in this country, but throughout the world. High incomes, a good command of English, and hard-earned professional credentials do not always override racial and ethnic stereotypes or protect those who fit them from the sting of racism.

A recent comparison study of immigrant groups in the United States, Canada, and Europe found that for the most part, assimilation has progressed further in the United States than in Europe, although more slowly than in Canada. In the United States, the rate of assimilation has generally been constant across groups. However, the recent recession has hampered new groups' ability to move into a broad range of jobs (Myers and Pitkin 2011; Vigdor 2011).

PLURALISM

In a pluralistic society, a subordinate group does not have to forsake its lifestyle and traditions to avoid prejudice or discrimination. **Pluralism** is based on mutual respect for one another's cultures among the various groups in a society. This pattern allows a minority group to express its own culture and still participate without prejudice in the larger society. Earlier, we described amalgamation as A + B + C → D, and assimilation as A + B + C → A. Using this same approach, we can conceive of pluralism as A + B + C → A + B + C. All the groups coexist in the same society (W. Newman 1973).

In the United States, pluralism is more of an ideal than a reality. There are distinct instances of pluralism—the ethnic neighborhoods in major cities, such as Koreatown, Little Tokyo, Andersonville (Swedish Americans), and Spanish Harlem—yet there are also limits to cultural freedom. To survive, a society must promote a certain consensus among its members regarding

> **Study Alert**
>
> Know the characteristics of each of the four typical patterns of intergroup relationships: *segregation, amalgamation, assimilation,* and *pluralism.*

basic ideals, values, and beliefs. Thus, if a Hungarian immigrant to the United States wants to move up the occupational ladder, he or she cannot avoid learning the English language.

Switzerland exemplifies the modern pluralistic state. There, the absence of both a national language and a dominant religious faith leads to a tolerance for cultural diversity. In addition, various political devices safeguard the interests of ethnic groups in a way that has no parallel in the United States. In contrast, Great Britain has had difficulty achieving cultural pluralism in a multiracial society. East Indians, Pakistanis, and Blacks from the Caribbean and Africa experience prejudice and discrimination within the dominant White society there. Some British advocate cutting off all Asian and Black immigration, and a few even call for expulsion of those non-Whites currently living in Britain.

E Evaluate

Read each question carefully and then select or provide the best answer.

1. Working together as computer programmers for an electronics firm, a Hispanic woman and a Jewish man overcome their initial prejudices and come to appreciate each other's strengths and talents. This scenario is an example of
   a. the contact hypothesis.
   b. a self-fulfilling prophecy.
   c. amalgamation.
   d. reverse discrimination.

2. Intermarriage over several generations, resulting in various groups combining to form a new group, would be an example of
   a. amalgamation.
   b. assimilation.
   c. segregation.
   d. pluralism.

3. Alphonso D'Abruzzo changed his name to Alan Alda. His action is an example of
   a. amalgamation.
   b. assimilation.
   c. segregation.
   d. pluralism.

4. The legalized segregation of Whites from others in South Africa, known as _____, remained in force until decades of resistance led by Nelson Mandela ended the practice.

5. _____ is the pattern of intergroup relations that is based on mutual respect for one another's different cultures. It is more a dream than a reality in the United States.

Answers
1 (a); 2 (a); 3 (b); 4 apartheid; 5 Pluralism (or Multiculturalism)

R Rethink

Consider these questions to get a deeper understanding of the material.

1. Describe an example of labeling with which you are personally familiar.

2. Give examples of amalgamation, assimilation, segregation, and pluralism that you have seen on your campus or in your workplace.

RECAP

LO 29-1 Analyze racial and ethnic inequality using the functionalist, conflict, labeling, and interactionist perspectives.

- Functionalists point out that discrimination is both functional and dysfunctional for a society. Conflict theorists explain racial subordination through exploitation theory. Labeling theorists focus on the ways that minorities are treated differently by government security officials. Interactionists pose the contact hypothesis as a means of reducing prejudice and discrimination.
- Racial profiling is any arbitrary action initiated by an authority based on race, ethnicity, or national origin rather than on a person's behavior. Based on false stereotypes of certain racial and ethnic groups, the practice is not an effective way to fight crime.

LO 29-2 Describe the patterns of intergroup relations, as defined by sociologists.

- Four patterns describe typical intergroup relations in North America and elsewhere: segregation, amalgamation, assimilation, and pluralism. Pluralism remains more of an ideal than a reality.
- Segregation refers to the physical separation of groups of people. In amalgamation, groups of people combine through intermarriage to become a new group.
- Assimilation is the process by which people in a minority group give up their cultural traditions to become part of the dominant culture. Under pluralism, or multiculturalism, different groups, including the dominant group, show mutual respect for one another's cultures while participating in the larger society.

KEY TERMS

Amalgamation The process through which a majority group and a minority group combine to form a new group.

Apartheid A former policy of the South African government, designed to maintain the separation of Blacks and other non-Whites from the dominant Whites.

Assimilation The process through which a person forsakes his or her cultural tradition to become part of a different culture.

Contact hypothesis An interactionist perspective which states that in cooperative circumstances, interracial contact between people of equal status will reduce prejudice.

Exploitation theory A Marxist theory that views racial subordination in the United States as a manifestation of the class system inherent in capitalism.

Genocide The deliberate, systematic killing of an entire people or nation.

Pluralism Mutual respect for one another's cultures among the various groups in a society, which allows minorities to express their cultures without experiencing prejudice.

Racial profiling Any arbitrary action initiated by an authority based on race, ethnicity, or national origin rather than on a person's behavior.

Segregation The physical separation of two groups of people in terms of residence, workplace, and social events; often imposed on a minority group by a dominant group.

MODULE 30 Race and Ethnicity in the United States

P Prepare | Learning Objectives

LO 30-1 Describe major racial and ethnic populations in the United States.

LO 30-2 Analyze the immigration issue in the United States and other countries from the functionalist, conflict, and feminist perspectives.

O Organize | Module Outline

African Americans
Native Americans
Asian Americans
    Chinese Americans
    Asian Indians
    Filipino Americans
    Vietnamese Americans
    Korean Americans
    Japanese Americans
Arab Americans
Latinos
    Mexican Americans
    Puerto Ricans
    Cuban Americans
    Central and South Americans
Jewish Americans
White Ethnics
Social Policy and Racial and Ethnic Inequality
    Global Immigration

Few societies have a more diverse population than the United States; the nation is truly a multiracial, multiethnic society. Of course, that has not always been the case. The population of what is now the United States has changed dramatically since the arrival of European settlers in the 1600s, as Figure 9-1 shows. Immigration, colonialism, and in the case of Blacks, slavery determined the racial and ethnic makeup of our present-day society.

Today, the largest racial minorities in the United States are African Americans, Native Americans, and Asian Americans. The largest ethnic groups are Latinos, Jews, and the various White ethnic groups. Figure 9-4 shows where the major racial and ethnic minorities are concentrated.

LO **30-1** African Americans

"I am an invisible man," wrote Black author Ralph Ellison in his novel *Invisible Man* (1952:3). "I am a man of substance, of flesh and bone, fiber and liquids—and I might even be said to possess a mind. I am invisible, understand, simply because people refuse to see me."

Over five decades later, many African Americans still feel invisible. Despite their large numbers, they have long been treated as second-class citizens. Currently, by the standards of the federal government, more than 1 out of every 4 African Americans—as opposed to 1 out of every 11 White non-Hispanics—is poor (DeNavas-Walt et al. 2011:15).

MAPPING LIFE NATIONWIDE

FIGURE 9-4 MINORITY POPULATION BY COUNTY

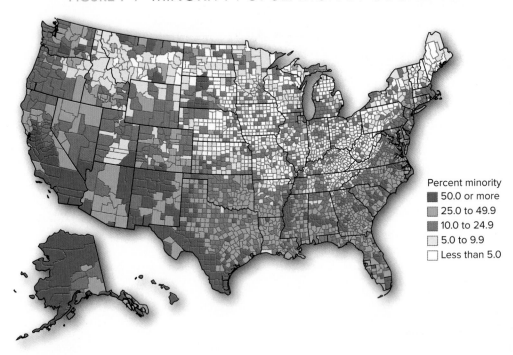

Percent minority
- 50.0 or more
- 25.0 to 49.9
- 10.0 to 24.9
- 5.0 to 9.9
- Less than 5.0

In four states (California, Hawaii, New Mexico, and Texas) and the District of Columbia, as well as in about one out of every nine counties, minorities constitute the numerical majority.

Source: Jones-Puthoff 2013:slide 5.

Contemporary institutional discrimination and individual prejudice against African Americans are rooted in the history of slavery in the United States. Many other subordinate groups had little wealth and income, but as sociologist W. E. B. DuBois ([1909] 1970) and others have noted, enslaved African Americans were in an even more oppressive situation, because by law they could not own property and could not pass on the benefits of their labor to their children. Today, increasing numbers of African Americans and sympathetic Whites are calling for *slave reparations* to compensate for the injustices of forced servitude. Reparations could include official expressions of apology from governments such as the United States, ambitious programs to improve African Americans' economic status, or even direct payments to descendants of slaves (D. Williams and Collins 2004).

The end of the Civil War did not bring genuine freedom and equality for Blacks. The Southern states passed Jim Crow laws to enforce official segregation, and the Supreme Court upheld them as constitutional in 1896. In addition, Blacks faced the danger of lynching campaigns, often led by the Ku Klux Klan, during the late 1800s and early 1900s. From a conflict perspective, Whites maintained their dominance formally through legalized segregation and informally by means of vigilante terror and violence (Franklin and Higginbotham 2011).

During the 1960s, a vast civil rights movement emerged, with many competing factions and strategies for change. The Southern Christian Leadership Conference (SCLC), founded by Dr. Martin Luther King Jr., used nonviolent civil disobedience to oppose segregation. The National Association for the Advancement of Colored People (NAACP) favored use of the courts to press for equality for African Americans. But many younger Black leaders, most notably Malcolm X, turned toward an ideology of Black power. Proponents of **Black power** rejected the goal of assimilation into White middle-class society. They defended the beauty and dignity of Black and African cultures and supported the creation of Black-controlled political and economic institutions (Ture and Hamilton 1992).

Despite numerous courageous actions to achieve Black civil rights, Black and White citizens are still separate, still unequal. From birth to death, Blacks suffer in terms of their life chances. Life remains difficult for millions of poor Blacks, who must attempt to survive in ghetto areas shattered by high unemployment and abandoned housing. Today the median household income of Blacks is still 60 percent that of Whites, and the unemployment rate among Blacks is more than twice that of Whites.

Some African Americans—especially middle-class men and women—have made economic gains over the past 50 years. For example, data show that the number of African Americans in management increased nationally from 2.4 percent of the total in 1958 to 6.4 percent in 2010. Yet Blacks still represent only 7 percent or less of all physicians, engineers, scientists, lawyers, judges, and marketing managers (Bureau of Labor Statistics 2013b:Table 11).

From the perspective of . . .

A Real Estate Agent How would you handle sellers who, though they say nothing openly, discourage non-White families from taking an interest in buying their house?

LO 30-1 Native Americans

Today, about 2.2 million Native Americans represent a diverse array of cultures distinguishable by language, family organization, religion, and livelihood. The outsiders who came to the United States—European settlers—and their descendants came to know these

Native American artists often break new ground to represent their life experiences. Dunne-Za member Brian Jungen used Nike shoes to make this three-dimensional piece, which suggests both his Pacific Northwest culture and his family's practice of stretching their modest means by reusing everything.

native peoples' forefathers as "American Indians." By the time the Bureau of Indian Affairs (BIA) was organized as part of the War Department in 1824, Indian–White relations had already included more than two centuries of hostile actions that had led to the virtual elimination of native peoples (see Figure 9-1). During the 19th century, many bloody wars wiped out a significant part of the Indian population. By the end of the century, schools for Indians—operated by the BIA or by church missions—prohibited the practice of Native American cultures. Yet at the same time, such schools did little to make the children effective members of White society.

Today, life remains difficult for members of the 554 tribal groups in the United States, whether they live in cities or on reservations. For example, one Native American teenager in six has attempted suicide—a rate four times higher than the rate for other teenagers. Traditionally, some Native Americans have chosen to assimilate and abandon all vestiges of their tribal cultures to escape certain forms of prejudice. However, by the 1990s, an increasing number of people in the United States were openly claiming a Native American identity. Since 1960, the federal government's count of Native Americans has tripled.

Native Americans have made some progress in redressing their past mistreatment. In 2009, the federal government settled a 13-year-old lawsuit for the recovery of lease payments due on tribal lands used by the government for oil and gas exploration and grazing. Although the $3.4 billion settlement was large, it was long overdue—some of the government's debts dated back to 1887—and from the perspective of tribal leaders, it was too little, too late. The United States is not the only country that has tried to redress the government's past actions toward indigenous peoples. For example, in 1967, the government of Australia extended citizenship and voting rights to the Aboriginal people, along with access to welfare and unemployment benefits.

The introduction of gambling on Indian reservations has transformed the lives of some Native Americans. Native Americans got into the gaming industry in 1988, when Congress passed the Indian Gambling Regulatory Act. The law stipulates that states must negotiate agreements with tribes interested in commercial gaming; they cannot prevent tribes from engaging in gambling operations, even if state law prohibits such ventures. The income from these lucrative operations is not evenly distributed, however. About two-thirds of recognized Indian tribes are not involved in gambling ventures. Those tribes that earn substantial revenues from gambling constitute a small fraction of Native Americans (Conner and Taggart 2009).

Like Native Americans, many native peoples living in the United States have successfully established their autonomy, gaining control over their resources and business enterprises.

LO 30-1 Asian Americans

Asian Americans are a diverse group, one of the fastest-growing segments of the U.S. population (up 43 percent between 2000 and 2010). Among the many groups of Americans of Asian descent are Vietnamese Americans, Chinese Americans, Japanese Americans, and Korean Americans (Figure 9-5).

Asian Americans are also economically diverse. There are rich and poor Japanese Americans, rich and poor Filipino Americans, and so forth. In fact, Southeast Asians living in the United States have the highest rate of welfare dependency of any racial or ethnic group. According to a study published in 2011, poverty rates are particularly high among the adult children of Cambodian, Hmong, and Thai immigrants to the United States. Though Asian Americans have substantially more schooling than other ethnic groups, their median income is only slightly higher than Whites' income, and their poverty rate is higher. In 2012, for every Asian American household with an annual income of $150,000 or more, there was another earning less than $20,000 a year (DeNavas-Walt et al. 2013; Takei and Sakamoto 2011).

The fact that as a group, Asian Americans work in the same occupations as Whites suggests that they have been successful—and many have. However, there are some differences between the two groups. Asian immigrants, like other minorities and immigrants before them, are found disproportionately in low-paying service occupations. At the same time, better-educated Asian Americans are concentrated near the top in professional and managerial positions, although they rarely reach the pinnacle. Instead, they hit the glass ceiling, or try to "climb a broken ladder," as some put it.

Ironically, Asian Americans are often held up as an unqualified success story. According to popular belief, they have succeeded in adapting to mainstream U.S. culture despite past prejudice and discrimination, and without resorting to confrontations with Whites. This portrayal of Asian Americans as a **model** or **ideal minority** ignores their economic diversity. It also carries an implicit critique of Blacks, Hispanics, and other groups who have not fared as well as the model minority.

CHINESE AMERICANS

Unlike African slaves and Native Americans, the Chinese were initially encouraged to immigrate to the United States. From 1850 to 1880, thousands of Chinese immigrated to this country, lured by job opportunities created by the discovery of gold. However, as employment possibilities decreased and competition for mining jobs grew, the Chinese became the target of a bitter campaign to limit their numbers and restrict their rights. Chinese laborers were exploited, then discarded.

In 1882, Congress enacted the Chinese Exclusion Act, which prevented Chinese immigration and even forbade Chinese in the United States to send for their families. As a result, the Chinese population declined steadily until after World War II. More recently, the descendants of the 19th-century immigrants have been joined by a new influx from Hong Kong and Taiwan. These groups may contrast sharply in their degree of assimilation, desire to live in Chinatowns, and feelings about this country's relations with the People's Republic of China.

Currently, over 3 million Chinese Americans live in the United States. Some Chinese Americans have entered lucrative occupations, yet many immigrants struggle to survive under living and working conditions that belie the model-minority stereotype. New York City's Chinatown district is filled with illegal sweatshops in which recent immigrants—many of them Chinese women—work for minimal wages. Outside of Chinatown, 23 percent of Asian Americans fall into the low-income category. At the other end of the income distribution, barely 5 percent of Chinatown's residents earn more than $100,000 a year, compared to 25 percent of Asian Americans who live elsewhere in New York City (Logan et al. 2002; Wong 2006).

ASIAN INDIANS

After Chinese Americans, the second-largest Asian American group, immigrants from India and their descendants, numbers over 2.8 million. It is difficult to generalize about Asian Indian Americans because Asian Indians are such a diverse population. India, a country of more than 1.2 billion people that is fast becoming the most populous nation in the world, is multiethnic. Perhaps because Asian Indian immigrants feel threatened by mainstream U.S. culture, religious orthodoxy is often stronger among first-generation immigrants to the United States than it is in India. New immigrants try to practice their religion just as they did in India rather than join congregations already established by other immigrant groups.

Maintaining family traditions is a major challenge for Asian Indian immigrants to the United States. Family ties remain strong despite their immigration—so much so that many Asian Indians feel more connected to their relatives in India than Americans do to relatives nearby. These *Desi* (pronounced day-see, colloquial for people who trace their ancestry to South Asia, especially India) are particularly concerned about the erosion of

FIGURE 9-5 **ASIAN AMERICAN AND PACIFIC ISLANDER POPULATION BY ORIGIN**

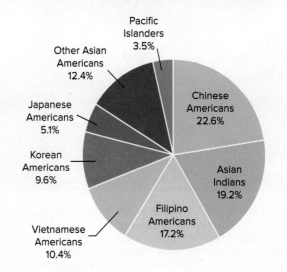

Pacific Islanders 3.5%
Other Asian Americans 12.4%
Japanese Americans 5.1%
Korean Americans 9.6%
Vietnamese Americans 10.4%
Filipino Americans 17.2%
Asian Indians 19.2%
Chinese Americans 22.6%

Sources: Census 2010 data in Hixson et al. 2012:Table 2.5; Hoeffel et al. 2012:Tables 2, 3.

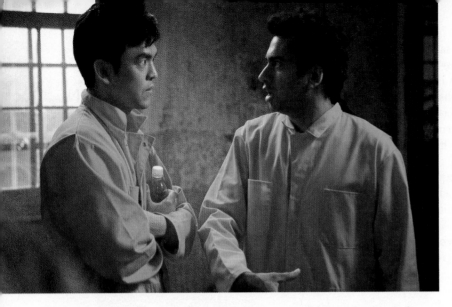

Asian Americans rarely head the casts of motion pictures, unless those films feature the martial arts. Two exceptions to the rule are John Cho and Kal Penn, who co-star in the successful Harold & Kumar movies. Penn is the stage name used by Kalpen Modi, the son of Asian Indian immigrants to the United States. In 2009, President Obama appointed Modi associate director of the Office of Public Engagement, where he served as a liaison to the Asian American and Pacific Islander communities.

traditional family authority. Indian American children dress like their peers, go to fast-food restaurants, and even eat hamburgers, rejecting the vegetarian diet typical of both Hindus and many Asian Indian Muslims. Sons do not feel the extent of responsibility to the family that tradition dictates. Daughters, whose occupations and marriage partners the family could control in India, assert their right to choose their careers, and even their husbands (Rangaswamy 2005).

FILIPINO AMERICANS

Filipinos are the third-largest Asian American group in the United States, with nearly 2.6 million people. For geographic reasons, social scientists consider them to be of Asian extraction, but physically and culturally this group also reflects centuries of Spanish and U.S. colonial rule, as well as the more recent U.S. military occupation.

Filipinos began immigrating to the United States as American nationals when the U.S. government gained possession of the Philippine Islands at the end of the Spanish–American War (1899). When the Philippines gained their independence in 1948, Filipinos lost their unrestricted immigration rights, although farmworkers were welcome to work in Hawai'i's pineapple groves. Aside from this exception, immigration was restricted to 50 to 100 Filipinos a year until 1965, when the Immigration Act lifted the strict quotas.

Today, a significant percentage of Filipino immigrants are well-educated professionals who work in the field of health care. Although they are a valuable human resource in the United States, their immigration has long drained the medical establishment in the Philippines. When the U.S. Immigration and Naturalization Service stopped giving preference to physicians, Filipino doctors began entering the country as nurses—a dramatic illustration of the incredible income differences between the two countries. Like other immigrant groups, Filipino Americans save much of their income and send a significant amount of money, called **remittances,** back to their extended families.

For several reasons, Filipino Americans have not coalesced in a single formal social organization, despite their numbers. Their strong loyalty to the family (*sa pamilya*) and to the church—particularly Roman Catholicism—reduces their need for a separate organization. Moreover, their diversity complicates the task of uniting the Filipino American community, which reflects the same regional, religious, and linguistic distinctions that divide their homeland. Thus, the many groups that Filipino Americans have organized tend to be club-like or fraternal in nature. Because those groups do not represent the general population of Filipino Americans, they remain largely invisible to Anglos. Although Filipinos remain interested in events in their homeland, they also seek to become involved in broader, non-Filipino organizations and to avoid exclusive activities (Bonus 2000; Kang 1996; Lau 2006; Padilla 2008).

VIETNAMESE AMERICANS

Vietnamese Americans came to the United States primarily during and after the Vietnam War—especially after U.S. withdrawal from the conflict in 1975. Refugees from the communist government in Vietnam, assisted by local agencies, settled throughout the United States, tens of thousands of them in small towns. Over time, however, Vietnamese Americans have gravitated toward the larger urban areas, establishing Vietnamese restaurants and grocery stores in their ethnic enclaves there.

In 1995, the United States resumed normal diplomatic relations with Vietnam. Gradually, the *Viet Kieu,* or Vietnamese living abroad, began to return to their old country to visit, but usually not to take up permanent residence. Today, more than 35 years after the end of the Vietnam War, sharp differences of opinion remain among Vietnamese Americans, especially the older ones, concerning the war and the present government of Vietnam (Pfeifer 2008).

KOREAN AMERICANS

At over 1.4 million, the population of Korean Americans now exceeds that of Japanese Americans. Yet Korean Americans are often overshadowed by other groups from Asia.

Today's Korean American community is the result of three waves of immigration. The initial wave arrived between 1903 and 1910, when Korean laborers migrated to Hawai'i. The second wave followed the end of the Korean War in 1953; most of those immigrants were wives of U.S. servicemen and war orphans. The third wave, continuing to the present, has reflected the admissions priorities set up in the 1965 Immigration Act. These well-educated immigrants arrive in the United States with professional skills. Yet because of language difficulties and discrimination, many must settle at least initially for positions of lower responsibility than those they held in Korea and must suffer through a period of disenchantment. Stress, loneliness, and family strife may accompany the pain of adjustment.

In the early 1990s, the apparent friction between Korean Americans and another subordinate racial group, African Americans, attracted nationwide attention. Conflict between the two groups was dramatized in Spike Lee's 1989 movie *Do the Right Thing.* The situation stemmed from Korean Americans' position as the latest immigrant group to cater to the needs of inner-city populations abandoned by those who have moved up the economic ladder. This type of friction is not new; generations of Jewish, Italian, and Arab merchants have encountered similar hostility from what to outsiders seems an unlikely source— another oppressed minority (K. Kim 1999).

JAPANESE AMERICANS

Approximately 763,000 Japanese Americans live in the United States. As a people, they are relatively recent arrivals. In 1880, only 148 Japanese lived in the United States, but by 1920 there were more than 110,000. Japanese immigrants—called the *Issei* (pronounced ee-say), or first generation—were usually males seeking employment opportunities. Many Whites saw them (along with Chinese immigrants) as a "yellow peril" and subjected them to prejudice and discrimination.

In 1941, the attack on Hawai'i's Pearl Harbor by Japan had severe repercussions for Japanese Americans. The federal government decreed that all Japanese Americans on the West Coast must leave their homes and report to "evacuation camps." In effect, Japanese Americans became scapegoats for the anger that other people in the United States felt concerning Japan's role in World War II. By August 1943, in an unprecedented application of guilt by virtue of ancestry, 113,000 Japanese Americans had been forced into hastily built camps. In striking contrast, only a few German Americans and Italian Americans were sent to evacuation camps (Hosokawa 1969).

In 1983, a federal commission recommended government payments to all surviving Japanese Americans who had been held in detention camps. The commission reported that the detention was motivated by "race prejudice, war hysteria, and a failure of political leadership." It added that "no documented acts of espionage, sabotage, or fifth-column activity were shown to have been committed" by Japanese Americans. In 1988, President Ronald Reagan signed the Civil Liberties Act, which required the federal government to issue individual apologies for all violations of Japanese Americans' constitutional rights, and established a $1.25 billion trust fund to pay reparations to the approximately 77,500 surviving Japanese Americans who had been interned (Department of Justice 2000).

LO **30-1** Arab Americans

Arab Americans are immigrants, and their descendants, from the 22 nations of the Arab world. As defined by the League of Arab States, these are the nations of North Africa and what is popularly known as the Middle East, including Lebanon, Syria, Palestine, Morocco, Iraq, Saudi Arabia, and Somalia. Not all residents of those countries are Arab; for example, the Kurds, who live in northern Iraq, are not Arab. And some Arab Americans may have immigrated to the United States from non-Arab countries such as Great Britain or France, where their families have lived for generations.

The Arabic language is the single most unifying force among Arabs, although not all Arabs, and certainly not all Arab Americans, can read and speak Arabic. Moreover, the language has evolved over the centuries so that people in different parts of the Arab world speak different dialects. Still, the fact that the Koran (or Qur'an) was originally written in Arabic gives the language special importance to Muslims, just as the Torah's compilation in Hebrew gives that language special significance to Jews.

Estimates of the size of the Arab American community differ widely. Nearly 4 million people of Arab ancestry reside in the United States. Among those who identify themselves as Arab Americans, the most common country of origin is Lebanon, followed by Syria, Egypt, and Palestine. In 2000, these four countries of origin accounted for two-thirds of all Arab Americans. Their rising numbers have led to the development of Arab retail centers in several cities, including Dearborn and Detroit, Michigan; Los Angeles; Chicago; New York City; and Washington, D.C.

In Chicago, a young Muslim woman sports an "I Love New York" T-shirt. Across the United States, racial and ethnic diversity has increased dramatically.

As a group, Arab Americans are extremely diverse. Many families have lived in the United States for several generations; others are foreign born. Their points of origin range from the metropolis of Cairo, Egypt, to the rural villages of Morocco. Despite the stereotype, most Arab Americans are *not* Muslim (Figure 9-6). Nor can Arab Americans be characterized as having a specific family type, gender role, or occupational pattern (David 2004, 2008).

In spite of this great diversity, profiling of potential terrorists at airports has put Arab and Muslim Americans under special surveillance. For years, a number of airlines and law enforcement authorities have used appearance and ethnic-sounding names to identify and take aside Arab Americans and search their belongings. After the terrorist attacks of September 2001, criticism of this practice declined as concern for the public's safety mounted.

LO **30-1** Latinos

Together, the various groups included under the general category *Latinos* represent the largest minority in the United States. There are more than 50 million Hispanics in this country, including 32 million Mexican Americans, more than 4 million Puerto Ricans, and smaller numbers of Cuban Americans and people of Central and South American origin (Figure 9-7). The latter group represents the fastest-growing and most diverse segment of the Hispanic community.

According to Census Bureau data, the Latino population now outnumbers the African American population in 6 of the 10 largest metropolitan areas of the United States: New York City, Los Angeles, Chicago, Dallas–Fort Worth, Houston, and Miami–Fort Lauderdale. The rise of the Hispanic population of the United States—fueled by comparatively high birthrates and immigration levels—has Latinos beginning to flex their muscles as voters. In the 2012 presidential election, Latinos accounted for more than 10 percent of eligible voters. As Hispanics age and immigrants become citizens, their presence in the voting booth will be felt even more strongly (Bureau of the Census 2011a:Table 23 on page 31; Lopez 2011).

The various Latino groups share a heritage of Spanish language and culture, which can cause serious problems in their assimilation. An intelligent student whose first language is Spanish may be presumed slow or even unruly by English-speaking schoolchildren, and frequently by English-speaking teachers as well. The labeling of Latino children as underachievers, as learning disabled, or as emotionally disturbed can act as a self-fulfilling prophecy for some children. Bilingual education aims at easing the educational difficulties experienced by Hispanic children and others whose first language is not English.

The educational difficulties of Latino students certainly contribute to Hispanics' generally low economic status. In 2012, about 17 percent of all Hispanic households earned less than $15,000, compared to 11 percent of White non-Hispanic households; the poverty rate was 25.6 percent for Hispanics, compared to 9.7 percent for White non-Hispanics. Although Latinos are not as affluent as White non-Hispanics, a middle class is beginning to emerge (DeNavas-Walt et al. 2013:14, 34, 38).

MEXICAN AMERICANS

The largest Latino population is Mexican Americans, who can be further subdivided into those descended from residents of the territories annexed after the Mexican American War of 1848 and those who have immigrated from Mexico to the United States. The opportunity for a Mexican to earn in one hour what it would take an entire day to earn in Mexico has pushed millions of legal and illegal immigrants north.

Many people view Mexican Americans as primarily an immigrant group. Since at least 2000, however, the number of Mexican Americans who were born in the United States has far exceeded those who immigrated here. Overall, Mexican Americans accounted for 42 percent of the nation's population growth in the decade 2000–2010. Two-thirds of them were born here; the other third were new arrivals (Bureau of the Census 2011a:8; Pew Hispanic Center 2011).

PUERTO RICANS

The second-largest segment of Latinos in the United States is Puerto Ricans. Since 1917, residents of Puerto Rico have held the status of American citizens; many have migrated to New York and other eastern cities. Unfortunately, Puerto Ricans have experienced serious poverty both in the United States and on the island. Those who live in the continental United States earn barely half the family income of Whites. As a result, a reverse migration began in the 1970s, when more Puerto Ricans were leaving for the island than were coming to the mainland (Torres 2008).

Politically, Puerto Ricans in the United States have not been as successful as Mexican Americans in organizing for their rights. For many mainland Puerto Ricans—as for many residents of the island—the paramount political issue is the destiny of Puerto Rico itself: should it continue in its present commonwealth status, petition for admission to the United States as the 51st state, or attempt to become an independent nation? This question has divided Puerto Rico for decades and remains a central issue in Puerto Rican elections. In a 1998 referendum, voters supported a "none of the above" option, effectively favoring continuation of the commonwealth status over statehood or independence.

FIGURE 9-6 ARAB AMERICAN RELIGIOUS AFFILIATIONS

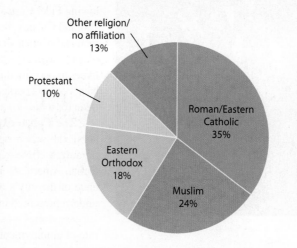

Unlike Arabs in other parts of the world, most Arab Americans are Christian.

Notes: Roman/Eastern Catholic includes Roman Catholic, Maronite, and Melkite (Greek Catholic); Eastern Orthodox includes Antiochian, Syrian, Greek, and Coptic; Muslim includes Sunni, Shi'a, and Druze.
Source: Arab American Institute 2010, based on 2002 Zogby International Survey.

FIGURE 9-7 HISPANIC POPULATION BY ORIGIN

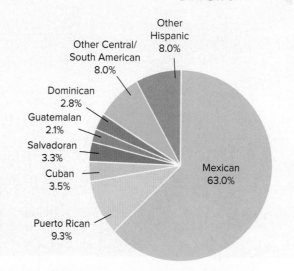

Note: "Other Hispanic" includes Spanish Americans and Latinos identified as mixed ancestry as well as other Central and South Americans not otherwise indicated by specific country.
Source: 2010 census data in Ennis et al. 2011:33. All nationalities with more than 1 million are represented.

CUBAN AMERICANS

Cuban immigration to the United States dates back as far as 1831, but it began in earnest following Fidel Castro's assumption of power in the Cuban revolution (1959). The first wave of 200,000 Cubans included many professionals with relatively high levels of schooling; these men and women were largely welcomed as refugees from communist tyranny. However, more recent waves of immigrants have aroused growing concern, partly because they were less likely to be skilled professionals. Throughout these waves of immigration, Cuban Americans have been encouraged to locate around the United States. Nevertheless, many continue to settle in (or return to) metropolitan Miami, Florida, with its warm climate and proximity to Cuba.

The Cuban experience in the United States has been mixed. Some detractors worry about the vehement anticommunism of Cuban Americans and the apparent growth of an organized crime syndicate that engages in the drug trade and ganglike violence. Recently, Cuban Americans in Miami have expressed concern over what they view as the indifference of the city's Roman Catholic hierarchy. Like other Hispanics, Cuban Americans are underrepresented in leadership positions within the church. Also—despite many individual success stories—as a group, Cuban Americans in Miami remain behind Whites in income, rate of employment, and proportion of professionals (Masud-Piloto 2008).

CENTRAL AND SOUTH AMERICANS

Immigrants from Central and South America are a diverse population that has not been closely studied. Indeed, most government statistics treat members of this group collectively as "other," rarely differentiating among them by nationality. Yet people from Chile and Costa Rica have little in common other than their hemisphere of origin and the Spanish language—if that. The fact is, not all Central and South Americans speak Spanish. Immigrants from Brazil, for example, speak Portuguese; immigrants from French Guyana speak French; and immigrants from Suriname speak Dutch.

Racially, many of the nations of Central and South America follow a complex classification system that recognizes a multitude of color gradients. Experience with this multiracial system does not prepare immigrants to the United States for the stark Black–White racial divide that characterizes U.S. society. Beyond their diversity in color and language, immigrants from Central and South America are differentiated by social class distinctions, religious differences, urban or rural upbringings, and dialects. Some of them may come from indigenous populations, especially in Guatemala and Belize. If so, their social identity would be separate from any national allegiance.

In short, social relations among Central and South Americans, who collectively number nearly 7 million people, defy generalization. The same can be said about their relations with other Latinos and with non-Latinos. Central and South Americans do not form, nor should they be expected to form, a cohesive group. Nor do they easily form coalitions with Cuban Americans, Mexican Americans, or Puerto Ricans.

Sonia Sotomayor was born in the Bronx, New York, of Puerto Rican parents. In 2009 she became the first Hispanic, and one of only 4 women, ever to be appointed to the U.S. Supreme Court. Of the other 108 justices, 2 have been African American men and 106 have been White men.

LO 30-1 Jewish Americans

Jews constitute about 2 percent of the population of the United States. They play a prominent role in the worldwide Jewish community, because the United States has the world's largest concentration of Jews. Like the Japanese, many Jewish immigrants came to this country and became white-collar professionals in spite of prejudice and discrimination.

Anti-Semitism—anti-Jewish prejudice—has often been vicious in the United States, although rarely so widespread and never so formalized as in Europe. In many cases, Jews have been used as scapegoats for other people's failures. Not surprisingly, Jews have not achieved equality in the United States. Despite high levels of education and professional training, they are still conspicuously absent from the top management of large corporations (except for the few firms founded by Jews). Nonetheless, a national survey in 2009 showed that one out of four people in the United States blames "the Jews" for the financial crisis. In addition, private social clubs and fraternal groups frequently continue to limit membership to Gentiles (non-Jews), a practice upheld by the Supreme Court in the 1964 case *Bell v. Maryland* (Malhotra and Margalit 2009).

The Anti-Defamation League (ADL) of B'nai B'rith coordinates an annual tally of reported anti-Semitic incidents. Although the number has fluctuated, in 2012 the tabulation of

For practicing Jews, the Hebrew language is an important part of religious instruction. This young pupil learns the Hebrew alphabet with a Jewish teacher.

the total reported incidents of harassment, threats, vandalism, and assaults came to 927. Some incidents were inspired and carried out by neo-Nazi skinheads—groups of young people who champion racist and anti-Semitic ideologies. Such threatening behavior only intensifies the fears of many Jewish Americans, who remember the Holocaust—the extermination of 6 million Jews by the Nazi Third Reich during World War II (Anti-Defamation League 2013).

As is true for other minorities discussed in this chapter, Jewish Americans face the choice of maintaining ties to their long religious and cultural heritage or becoming as indistinguishable as possible from Gentiles. Many Jews have tended to assimilate, as is evident from the rise in marriages between Jews and Christians. In marriages that occurred in the 1970s, more than 70 percent of Jews married Jews or people who converted to Judaism. In marriages since 1996, that proportion has dropped to 53 percent. This trend means that today, American Jews are almost as likely to marry a Gentile as a Jew. For many, religion is a nonissue—neither parent practices religious rituals. Two-thirds of the children of these Jewish–Gentile marriages are not raised as Jews. Finally, in 2005, two-thirds of Jews felt that the biggest threat to Jewish life was anti-Semitism; only one-third named intermarriage as the biggest threat (American Jewish Committee 2005; Sanua 2007).

LO 30-1 White Ethnics

A significant segment of the population of the United States is made up of White ethnics whose ancestors arrived from Europe within the last century and a half. The nation's White ethnic population includes about 49 million people who claim at least partial German ancestry, 36 million Irish Americans, 17 million Italian Americans, and 10 million Polish Americans, as well as immigrants from other European nations. Some of these people continue to live in close-knit ethnic neighborhoods, whereas others have largely assimilated and left the "old ways" behind.

Many White ethnics today identify only sporadically with their heritage. **Symbolic ethnicity** refers to an emphasis on concerns such as ethnic food or political issues rather than on deeper ties to one's ethnic heritage. It is reflected in the occasional family trip to an ethnic bakery, the celebration of a ceremonial event such as St. Joseph's Day among Italian Americans, or concern about the future of Northern Ireland among Irish Americans. Such practices are another example of the social construction of race and ethnicity. Except in cases in which new immigration reinforces old traditions, symbolic ethnicity tends to decline with each passing generation (Alba 1990; Winter 2008).

White Americans often express their ethnicity with special celebrations, such as this Scandinavian Festival parade in Junction City, Oregon. Participants proudly display the flag of Denmark.

Although the White ethnic identity may be a point of pride to those who share it, they do not necessarily celebrate it at the expense of disadvantaged minorities. It is all too easy to assume that race relations are a zero-sum game in which one group gains at the expense of the other. Rather, the histories of several White ethnic groups, such as the Irish and the Italians, show that once marginalized people can rise to positions of prestige and influence (Alba 2009).

That is not to say that White ethnics and racial minorities have not been antagonistic toward one another because of economic competition—an interpretation that agrees with the conflict approach to sociology. As Blacks, Latinos, and Native Americans emerge from the lower class, they must compete with working-class Whites for jobs, housing, and educational opportunities. In times of high unemployment or inflation, any such competition can easily generate intense intergroup conflict.

In many respects, the plight of White ethnics raises the same basic issues as that of other subordinate people in the United States. How ethnic can people be—how much can they deviate from an essentially White, Anglo-Saxon, Protestant norm—before society punishes them for their willingness to be different? Our society does seem to reward people for assimilating, yet as we have seen, assimilation is no easy process. In the years to come, more and more people will face the challenge of fitting in, not only in the United States but around the world, as the flow of immigrants from one country to another continues to increase. In the Social Policy section that follows, we focus on global immigration and its implications for the future.

LO 30-2 SOCIAL POLICY and Racial and Ethnic Inequality

We have seen that researchers rely on a number of tools, from time-tested observational research and use of existing sources to the latest in computer technologies. Because in the real world, sociological research can have far-reaching consequences for public policy and public welfare, we'll evaluate its impact on global immigration.

GLOBAL IMMIGRATION

Worldwide, immigration is at an all-time high. Each year, about 191 million people move from one country to another—a number that is roughly the equivalent of the total populations of Russia and Italy. A million of these immigrants enter the United States legally, to join the 13 percent of the U.S. population who are foreign born. Perhaps more significantly, one-fourth of the U.S. labor force is foreign born—the largest proportion in at least 120 years (Motel and Patten 2012).

Globally, these mass migrations have had a tremendous social impact. The constantly increasing numbers of immigrants and the pressure they put on job opportunities and welfare capabilities in the countries they enter raise troubling questions for many of the world's economic powers. Who should be allowed in? At what point should immigration be curtailed (United Nations 2009)?

The migration of people is not uniform across time or space. At certain times, war or famine may precipitate large movements of people, either temporarily or permanently. Temporary dislocations occur when people wait until it is safe to return to their home areas. However, more and more migrants who cannot make an adequate living in their home nations are making permanent moves to developed nations. The major migration streams flow into North America, the oil-rich areas of the Middle East, and the industrial economies of western Europe and Asia. Currently, seven of the world's wealthiest nations (including Germany, France, the United Kingdom, and the United States) shelter about one-third of the world's migrant population, but less than one-fifth of the world's total population. As long as disparities in job opportunities exist among countries, there is little reason to expect this international trend to reverse.

One consequence of global immigration is the emergence of **transnationals**—immigrants who sustain multiple social relationships that link their societies of origin with the society of settlement. The industrial tycoons of the early 20th century, whose power outmatched that of many nation-states, were among the world's first transnationals. Today, millions of people, many of very modest means, move back and forth between countries much as commuters do between city and suburbs. More and more of these people have dual citizenship. Rather than being shaped by allegiance to one country, their identity is rooted in their struggle to survive—and in some instances prosper—by transcending international borders (Croucher 2004; Sassen 2005).

Countries that have long been a destination for immigrants, such as the United States, usually have policies regarding who has preference to enter. Often, clear racial and ethnic biases are built into these policies. In the 1920s, U.S. policy gave preference to people from western Europe, while making it difficult for residents of southern and eastern Europe, Asia, and Africa to enter the country. During the late 1930s and early 1940s, the federal government refused to lift or loosen restrictive immigration quotas in order to allow Jewish refugees to escape the terror of the Nazi regime. In line with this policy, the SS *St. Louis,* with more than 900 Jewish refugees on board, was denied permission to land in the United States in 1939. The ship was forced to sail back to Europe, where it is estimated that at least a few hundred of its passengers later died at the hands of the Nazis (Morse 1967; G. Thomas and Witts 1974).

Since the 1960s, U.S. policy has encouraged the immigration of relatives of U.S. residents as well as of people who have desirable skills. This change has significantly altered the pattern of sending nations. Previously, Europeans dominated, but for the past 50 years, immigrants have come primarily from Latin America and Asia. Thus, an ever-growing proportion of the U.S. population will be Asian or Hispanic (Figure 9-8). To a large degree, fear and resentment of growing racial and ethnic diversity is a key factor in opposition to immigration. In many nations, people are concerned that the new arrivals do not reflect their own cultural and racial heritage.

Applying Sociology to Immigration Research suggests that immigrants adapt well to life in the United States, becoming an asset to the nation's economy. In some areas, heavy immigration may drain a local community's resources, but in other areas it revitalizes the local economy.

Despite people's fears, immigration performs many valuable functions. For the receiving society, it alleviates labor shortages, as it does in health care and technology in the United States. For the sending nation, migration can relieve an economy unable to support large numbers of people. Often overlooked is the large amount of money (*remittances*) that immigrants send *back* to their home nations.

Immigration can be dysfunctional as well. Although studies generally show that it has a positive impact on the receiving nation's economy, areas that accept high concentrations of immigrants may find it difficult to meet short-term social service needs. And when migrants with skills or educational potential leave developing countries, their departure can be dysfunctional for those nations. No amount of payments sent back home can make up for the loss of valuable human resources from poor nations (Borjas et al. 2006; Kochhar 2006; Sum et al. 2006).

FIGURE 9-8 ## LEGAL MIGRATION TO THE UNITED STATES, 1820–2010

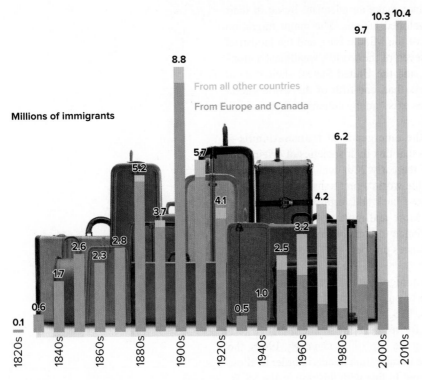

Millions of immigrants

From all other countries

From Europe and Canada

For the past four decades, the majority of immigrants to the United States have come from outside Europe and Canada.

Source: Office of Immigration Statistics 2013 and author's estimates for projection to 2020.

Conflict theorists note how much of the debate over immigration is phrased in economic terms. The debate intensifies when the arrivals are of a different racial or ethnic background from the host population. For example, Europeans often refer to "foreigners," but the term does not necessarily mean one of foreign birth. In Germany, "foreigners" refers to people of non-German ancestry, even if they were *born* in Germany; it does not refer to people of German ancestry born in another country, who may choose to return to their mother country. Fear and dislike of "new" ethnic groups divides countries throughout the world.

The feminist perspective pays special attention to the role that women play in global immigration. Immigrant women face all the challenges that immigrant men do, and some additional ones. Typically, they bear the responsibility for obtaining services for their families, particularly their children. Because the men are likely to be consumed with work, the women are left to navigate through the bureaucratic tangle of schools, city services, and medical facilities, as well as the unfamiliar stores and markets they must visit to feed their families. Women who need special medical services or are victims of domestic violence are often reluctant to seek outside help. Yet they are more likely than the men to serve as the liaison between their households and community and religious associations. Also, because many new immigrants view the United States as a dangerous place to raise a family, women must be especially watchful over their children's lives (Hondagneu-Sotelo 2003).

Initiating Immigration Policy The long border with Mexico provides ample opportunity for illegal immigration into the United States. Throughout the 1980s, the public perception that the United States had lost control of its borders grew. Feeling pressure for immigration control, Congress ended a decade of debate by approving the Immigration Reform and Control Act of 1986. The act marked a historic change in the nation's immigration policy. For the first time, the hiring of illegal aliens was outlawed, and employers caught violating the law became subject to fines and even prison sentences. Just as significant a change was the extension of amnesty and legal status to many illegal immigrants already living in the United States. More than 20 years later, however, the act appears to have had mixed results. Substantial numbers of illegal immigrants continue to enter the country each year, with an estimated 11 million or more present at any given time—a marked increase since 2000, when their number was estimated at close to 8 million (Passel et al. 2013).

In 2010, frustrated by the continuing flow of illegal immigrants across the Mexican border, Arizona enacted a law empowering police to detain without authorization people whom they reasonably suspect of being illegal immigrants and to verify their immigration status. Immediately, opponents charged that the new law would lead to racial profiling. In 2012 the Supreme Court upheld the right of police to check the immigration status of anyone they stop or detain if they have a "reasonable suspicion" that the person has entered the country illegally. The debate continues between those seeking to tighten border controls and those advocating reform of the nation's immigration laws. Legal experts question whether state enforcement of immigration law is constitutional. Although implementation of the law has been problematic, it has highlighted the resolve of those seeking to tighten control of the nation's borders. It has also galvanized those seeking to reform the nation's immigration law.

In recent years Latinos have staged massive marches to pressure Congress to speed up the naturalization process and allow illegal immigrants to gain legal residency. Despite this political pressure, little action has been taken or even debated. The presidential election of 2012 saw the Democrats' strength among Hispanic voters grow at Republicans' expense, further encouraging the two parties to agree on immigration reform. Any new policy is likely to be linked to additional steps to strengthen the U.S.–Mexican border, while still facilitating the entry of workers needed in U.S. industries.

The entire world feels the overwhelming impact of globalization on immigration patterns. The European Union agreement of 1997 gave the governing commission authority to propose a Europe-wide policy on immigration. An EU policy that allows residents of one EU country to live and work in another EU country is expected to complicate efforts by sending nations, such as Turkey, to become members of the EU. Immigrants from Turkey's predominantly Muslim population are not welcome in many EU countries (Denny 2004).

In the wake of the attacks of September 11, 2001, on the World Trade Center and the Pentagon, immigration procedures were complicated by the need to detect potential terrorists. Illegal immigrants especially, but even legal immigrants, have felt increased scrutiny by government officials around the world. For would-be immigrants to many nations, the wait to receive the right to enter a country—even to join relatives—has increased substantially, as immigration officials scrutinize more closely what were once routine applications.

The intense debate over immigration reflects deep value conflicts in the cultures of many nations. One strand of our culture, for example, has traditionally emphasized egalitarian principles and a desire to help people in time of need. At the same time, hostility to potential immigrants and refugees—whether the Chinese in the 1880s, European Jews in the 1930s and 1940s, or Mexicans, Haitians, and Arabs today—reflects not only racial, ethnic, and religious prejudice, but a desire to maintain the dominant culture of the in-group by keeping out those viewed as outsiders.

Despite a decline in illegal immigration to the United States since the economic downturn that began in 2007, the number of people deported has increased due to greater pressure to identify illegal immigrants. These suspected illegal immigrants are being detained in California.

E Evaluate

Read each question carefully and then select or provide the best answer.

1. In which of the following racial or ethnic groups has one teenager in every six attempted suicide?
   a. African Americans
   b. Asian Americans
   c. Native Americans
   d. Latinos

2. Advocates of *Marxist class theory* argue that the basis for racial subordination in the United States lies within the capitalist economic system. Another representation of this point of view is reflected in which of the following theories?
   a. exploitation
   b. functionalist
   c. interactionist
   d. contact

3. After the Civil War, the Southern states passed "_____ _____," laws to enforce official segregation, and the Supreme Court upheld them as constitutional in 1896.

4. In the 1960s, proponents of _____ _____ rejected the goal of assimilation into White, middle-class society. They defended the beauty and dignity of Black and African cultures and supported the creation of Black-controlled political and economic institutions.

5. Asian Americans are held up as a(n) _____ or _____ minority group, supposedly because despite past suffering from prejudice and discrimination, they have succeeded economically, socially, and educationally without resorting to political and violent confrontations with Whites.

6. Together, the various groups included under the general category _____ represent the largest minority group in the United States.

Answers
1 (c); 2 (a); 3 Jim Crow; 4 Black power; 5 model, ideal; 6 Latinos (or Hispanics)

Consider these questions to get a deeper understanding of the material.

1. Many ethnic cultures routinely display and celebrate their cultural identities. Why do White ethnic identities seem more elusive?

2. To what extent has U.S. society achieved pluralism? Give examples from your own experience to support your opinion.

RECAP

LO 30-1 Describe major racial and ethnic populations in the United States.

- Contemporary prejudice and discrimination against African Americans are rooted in the history of slavery in the United States.
- Asian Americans are commonly viewed as a model or ideal minority, a false stereotype that is not necessarily beneficial to members of that group.
- Arab Americans experience suspicion and have been subject to racial profiling, especially since the attacks on the World Trade Center and the Pentagon in 2001.
- The various groups included under the general term *Latinos* represent the largest ethnic minority in the United States.
- Jewish Americans have long been a vital part of U.S. culture, but they continue to experience anti-Semitism in this country.

LO 30-2 Analyze the immigration issue in the United States and other countries from the functionalist, conflict, and feminist perspectives.

- Immigration can be both functional and dysfunctional for the sending and receiving nation. For the receiving society, immigration can alleviate labor shortages in key areas but put pressure on social services. For the sending nation, it can relieve pressure on economies experiencing high general unemployment but deprive those economies of individuals with education and skills.
- Conflict theorists note that opposition to immigration, always couched in economic terms, intensifies when the immigrants are of a different racial or ethnic background from the receiving population. The feminist perspective focuses on the role that women play in global immigration.
- Worldwide, immigration is at an all-time high, fueling controversy not only in the United States but in the European Union as well. A new kind of immigrant, the transnational, moves back and forth across international borders in search of a better job or an education.

KEY TERMS

Anti-Semitism Anti-Jewish prejudice.

Black power A political philosophy, promoted by many younger Blacks in the 1960s, that supported the creation of Black-controlled political and economic institutions.

Model, or **ideal minority** A subordinate group whose members supposedly have succeeded economically, socially, and educationally despite past prejudice and discrimination, and without resorting to political and violent confrontations with Whites.

Remittances The monies that immigrants return to their families of origin. Also called *migradollars*.

Symbolic ethnicity An ethnic identity that emphasizes concerns such as ethnic food or political issues rather than deeper ties to one's ethnic heritage.

Transnational An immigrant who sustains multiple social relationships that link his or her society of origin with the society of settlement.

The Case of . . . Different Strokes

Rosa and Elena Martinez are sisters, born two years apart, who grew up in Arizona. "As little kids, we were real close," Elena says, "but in our teens, we began going our own ways." Rosa, who now calls herself "Rose Martin," agrees. "I have lots of ambition," Rose says. "But I could see I would never get anywhere if I refused to adopt American ways. I'm not in Mexico. I'm here. If I want to make it big, I need to accept the values of the mainstream culture."

Elena says her sister's attitude bothers her. "Okay, she wants to be a hotshot financial advisor," Elena says. "But you don't change your name to achieve things. You take pride in who you are. You honor your roots. You respect others and you insist on respect for yourself." Elena knows the United States is far from realizing this ideal, but she insists that for every person who adopts it, there is one less roadblock to a pluralistic society. "I work as an assistant to an architect. My dream is to be an architect who designs cityscapes that encourage cultural exchange. Have I ever had to deal with prejudice? Sure. Have I ever faced sexism? Absolutely. My Irish boss was the worst. At first. But when he gave me attitude, I said, "Hey, America once had trouble accepting the Irish. Times change. People change. Together, you and I can make this company great."

1. What pattern of intergroup relations has each of the Martinez sisters adopted?

2. Do you feel Rose is justified in saying she needs to adopt the values of the mainstream culture to succeed? Why or why not?

3. Why does Elena remind her boss that Americans once discriminated against the Irish?

4. Do you agree with Elena that mutual respect between cultures is achievable in the United States? Why or why not?

5. Do you think Rose, in her attempt to blend in with the dominant culture, will be granted White privilege, or will she still be vulnerable to discrimination? Explain your thinking.

Catch the Critical Thinking Habit

Sociology demands critical thinking. You will often have to react to unexpected, controversial ideas orally or in writing. Ideas may come from your reading, your instructor, or your classmates, and you may agree or disagree with them. The habit of thinking critically consists of considering new ideas intelligently and responding reasonably—and once you develop the habit, it will serve you not only in sociology, but in other classes and in life. Here are some tips for developing the critical thinking habit.

 **Prepare**

- When faced with a new idea, opinion, or argument, take a few minutes to gather whatever facts you know about the topic.

 **Organize**

- Based on what you know, make a preliminary decision on whether you agree or disagree with the idea. Be prepared to alter your initial opinion in the face of good arguments and evidence.

 **Work**

- Learn to distinguish facts from opinions. Facts are verifiable, whereas opinions are subject to argument and counter-opinions.
- Question every statement. The main question to ask is not *Is this true?* but *How can I know if this is true?* This is a matter of looking for logical arguments and supporting evidence.
- Determine if an argument proceeds logically or if steps are missing. Be sure the argument proceeds from A to B to C to D, and not from A to D.
- Determine if the evidence is trustworthy. Look at any numbers or statistics that are offered. Do they make sense? Were there enough subjects in the study? Are the numbers convincing? *Are* there any numbers?
- Remember the difference between cause and correlation. If necessary, reread the opening chapter of this book.
- Consider the source. Is the evidence from a trusted source (such as a scientific journal) or from unnamed sources? Are the persons stating the evidence trustworthy? Are they experts in the field? Do they seem generally impartial, or do they seem predisposed toward one point of view?
- Beware of biases—even your own. Look for personal, deeply held opinions in others and in yourself. Keep an open mind and be ready to learn something.
- If you have an emotional reaction to what someone says, such as anger or offense, don't deny it. Manage it: stay rational and respectful, but speak up.
- Don't be afraid of seeming unintelligent. Fear shouldn't stifle your opinions. Take intellectual risks!

Evaluate

- Look at your own argument and try to refute it. Seek out holes and gaps and do your best to plug them.

Rethink

- If your argument is evaluated, hear or read the instructor's or your classmates' remarks clearly. Learn to profit from criticism.

Are You a Critical Thinker?

Developing critical thinking skills—the ability to interpret, analyze, make inferences, evaluate, explain, and sift for bias—is crucial to making sense, and use, of what you read, hear, and see. To assess your own skills in this area, consider the following statements, then check "That's Me" or "Not Me" after each. To find your score, use this scale:

That's Me = 0
Not Me = 1

	That's Me	Not Me
1. I think all "facts" are just someone's opinion.		
2. Statistics are the one thing you can rely on.		
3. When I read two conflicting reports, I go with the one that seems more convincing.		
4. Unlike people, I think most books and newspapers are free from bias.		
5. I usually draw conclusions about an issue based on my own experience and feelings.		
6. I find it difficult to explain my ideas to others.		
7. I get my facts from my favorite TV news program or news website.		
8. I never watch or listen to the news. It's just a bunch of random events.		
9. I'm not a fan of mystery shows. I can never follow the clues.		
10. Predictions are a waste of time. One never knows what will happen.		

SCORE:

9-10: You use critical thinking skills to sift and evaluate what you read, see, and hear. You're also careful not to let your own biases influence your overall judgment.

6-8: You have developed some good critical thinking skills, but filling in your "gaps" will benefit your studies and your life.

5 or less: Making sense of what you read and hear is challenging, but as you learn to practice the critical thinking skills listed in the P.O.W.E.R. Study Strategies: Catch the Critical Thinking Habit, you will start to develop the mental habits you need to succeed.

10 Stratification by Gender

MODULE 31 The Social Construction of Gender

MODULE 32 Women: The Oppressed Majority

Sociology at WORK   HUMAN RESOURCES MANAGER

KARA NOONAN is the human resources manager at a technology research and development company. It's her job to supervise payroll, evaluate and promote employees, and make salary decisions. But the most exciting aspect of the job, Noonan says, is the company's new talent management program, which she helped develop and oversees. Noonan's talent management program is designed to hire a more diverse staff—more diverse in gender, race, and ethnicity. "What I'm really seeking is a diversity of *ideas*," she says. "People from different backgrounds bring different perspectives, and we need that to keep us fresh." Noonan wants to build what she calls "talent teams" to address the strategic needs of the business. "I'm not looking for people who fit the company's culture but people who *create* that culture," she explains. "In our line of work, if you stop innovating, you're dead."■

Looking Ahead

IN THIS CHAPTER WE WILL STUDY HOW VARIOUS CULTURES, INCLUDING our own, assign women and men to particular social roles. Then we will consider sociological explanations for gender stratification. We will see that around the world, women constitute an oppressed majority of the population. We'll learn that women have developed a collective consciousness of their oppression and the way in which their gender combines with other factors to create social inequality. Finally, we will close the chapter with a Social Policy section on the controversy over a woman's right to abortion.

MODULE 31 The Social Construction of Gender

P Prepare **Learning Objectives**

LO 31-1 Explain the meaning of the phrase "the social construction of gender."

LO 31-2 Describe women's and men's gender roles and the process of gender-role socialization in the United States.

LO 31-3 Analyze the functionalist, conflict, feminist, and interactionist explanations of gender stratification.

O Organize **Module Outline**

Are Gender Roles Socially Constructed?
   Gender Roles in the United States
   Cross-Cultural Perspective

Sociological Perspectives on Gender
   Functionalist Perspective
   Conflict Perspective
   Feminist Perspective
   Intersections with Race, Class, and Other Social Factors
   Interactionist Perspective

W Work

LO 31-1 Are Gender Roles Socially Constructed?

How many airline passengers do you think are startled on hearing a female captain's voice from the cockpit? What do we make of a father who announces that he will be late for work because his son has a routine medical checkup? Consciously or unconsciously, we are likely to assume that flying a commercial plane is a *man's* job and that most parental duties are, in fact, a *woman's*. Gender is such a routine part of our everyday activities that we typically take notice only when someone deviates from conventional behavior and expectations.

Although a few people begin life with an unclear sexual identity, the overwhelming majority begin with a definite sex and quickly receive societal messages about how to behave. In fact, virtually all societies have established social distinctions between females and males that do not inevitably result from biological differences between the sexes (such as women's reproductive capabilities).

In studying gender, sociologists are interested in the gender-role socialization that leads females and males to behave differently. In Chapter 4, **gender roles** were defined as expectations regarding the proper behavior, attitudes, and activities of males and females. The application of dominant gender roles leads to many forms of differentiation between women and men. Both sexes are capable of learning to cook and sew, yet most Western societies determine that women should perform those tasks. Both men and women are capable of learning to weld and to fly airplanes, but those functions are generally assigned to men.

As we will see throughout this chapter, however, social behavior does not mirror the mutual exclusivity suggested by these gender roles. Nor are gender roles independent: in real life, the way men behave influences women's behavior, and the way women behave affects men's behavior. Thus, most people do not display strictly "masculine" or "feminine" qualities all the time. Indeed, such standards can be ambiguous. For instance, though men are supposed to be unemotional, they are allowed to become emotional when their favorite athletic team wins or loses a critical game. Yet our society still focuses on "masculine" and "feminine" qualities as if men and women must be evaluated in those terms. Despite recent inroads by women into male-dominated occupations, our construction of gender continues to define significantly different expectations for females and males.

Gender roles are evident not only in our work and behavior but also in how we react to others. We are constantly "doing gender" without realizing it. If the father mentioned earlier sits in the doctor's office with his son in the middle of a workday, he will probably receive approving glances from the receptionist and from other patients. "Isn't he a wonderful father?" runs through their minds. But if the boy's mother leaves *her* job and sits with the son in the doctor's office, she will not receive such silent applause.

We socially construct our behavior so as to create or exaggerate male/female differences. For example, men and women come in a variety of heights, sizes, and ages. Yet traditional norms regarding marriage and even casual dating tell us that in heterosexual couples,

the man should be older, taller, and wiser than the woman. As we will see throughout this chapter, such social norms help to reinforce and legitimize patterns of male dominance.

LO 31-2 GENDER ROLES IN THE UNITED STATES

Gender-Role Socialization Male babies get blue blankets; females get pink ones. Boys are expected to play with trucks, blocks, and toy soldiers; girls receive dolls and kitchen goods. Boys must be masculine—active, aggressive, tough, daring, and dominant—but girls must be feminine—soft, emotional, sweet, and submissive. These traditional gender-role patterns have been influential in the socialization of children in the United States.

From the perspective of . . .

An Elementary School Teacher   How would you handle the group of boys who tend to dominate everything, from choosing teams for a soccer game (girls last, always) to bullying the smaller, quieter boys?

An important element in traditional views of proper "masculine" and "feminine" behavior is **homophobia**, fear of and prejudice against homosexuality. Homophobia contributes significantly to rigid gender-role socialization, since many people stereotypically associate male homosexuality with femininity and lesbianism with masculinity. Consequently, men and women who deviate from traditional expectations about gender roles are often presumed to be gay. Despite the advances made by the gay liberation movement, the continuing stigma attached to homosexuality in our culture places pressure on all males (whether gay or not) to exhibit only narrow masculine behavior and on all females (whether lesbian or not) to exhibit only narrow feminine behavior (Seidman 1994).

It is *adults,* of course, who play a critical role in guiding children into those gender roles deemed appropriate in a society. Parents are normally the first and most crucial agents of socialization. But other adults, older siblings, the mass media, and religious and educational institutions also exert an important influence on gender-role socialization, in the United States and elsewhere.

It is not hard to test how rigid gender-role socialization can be. Just try transgressing some gender norm—say, by smoking a cigar in public if you are female, or by carrying a purse if you are male. That was exactly the assignment given to sociology students at the University of Colorado and Luther College in Iowa. Professors asked students to behave in ways that they thought violated the norms of how a man or woman should act. The students had no trouble coming up with gender-norm transgressions (Table 10-1), and they kept careful notes on others' reactions to their behavior, ranging from amusement to disgust (Nielsen et al. 2000).

Women's Gender Roles How does a girl come to develop a feminine self-image, while a boy develops one that is masculine? In part, they do so by identifying with females and males in their families and neighborhoods and in the media. If a young girl regularly sees female television characters of all ages and body types, she is likely to grow up with a normal body image. And it will not hurt if the women she knows—her mother, sister, parents' friends, and neighbors—are comfortable with their body types, rather than constantly obsessed with their weight. In contrast, if this young girl sees only wafer-thin actresses and models on television, her self-image will be quite different. Even if she grows up to become a well-educated professional, she may secretly regret falling short of the media stereotype—a thin, sexy young woman in a bathing suit.

In our society, men and women receive different messages about the ideal body image. For women, the Miss America pageant promotes a very slim, statuesque physique. For men, "action figures" like the G.I. Joe doll promote an exaggerated muscularity typical of professional wrestlers (Angier 1998; Byrd-Bredbenner and Murray 2003).

TABLE 10-1 AN EXPERIMENT IN GENDER NORM VIOLATION BY COLLEGE STUDENTS

Norm If by Women	Norm If by Men
Send men flowers	Wear fingernail polish
Spit in public	Do needlepoint in public
Use men's bathroom	Throw Tupperware party
Buy jock strap	Cry in public
Buy/chew tobacco	Have pedicure
Talk knowledgeably about cars	Apply to babysit
Open doors for men	Shave body hair

In an experiment testing gender-role stereotypes, sociology students were asked to behave in ways that might be regarded as violations of gender norms, and to keep notes on how others reacted. This is a sample of their choices of behavior over a seven-year period. Do you agree that these actions test the boundaries of conventional gender behavior?

Source: Nielsen et al. 2000:287.

Television is far from alone in stereotyping women. Studies of children's books published in the United States in the 1940s, 1950s, and 1960s found that females were significantly underrepresented in central roles and illustrations. Virtually all female characters were portrayed as helpless, passive, incompetent, and in need of a strong male caretaker. Studies of picture books published from the 1970s through the present have found some improvement, but males still dominate the central roles. While males are portrayed as a variety of characters, females tend to be shown mostly in traditional roles, such as mother, grandmother, or volunteer, even if they also hold nontraditional roles, such as working professional (Etaugh 2003).

Traditional gender roles have restricted females more severely than males. This chapter shows how women have been confined to subordinate roles in the political and economic institutions of the United States. Yet it is also true that gender roles have restricted males.

Men's Gender Roles Stay-at-home fathers? Until recent decades such an idea was unthinkable. Yet in a 2012 nationwide survey, 22 percent of men said they preferred to stay at home and take care of the house and family. That lifestyle preference is much more common among women, however; 44 percent of women said they preferred to stay at home. But while people's conceptions of gender roles are obviously changing, the fact is that men who stay home to care for their children are still an unusual phenomenon. For every stay-at-home dad there are 38 stay-at-home moms (Fields 2004:11–12; Saad 2012).

While attitudes toward parenting may be changing, studies show little change in the traditional male gender role. Men's roles are socially constructed in much the same way as women's are. Family, peers, and the media all influence how a boy or man comes to view his appropriate role in society. The male gender role, besides being antifeminine (no "sissy stuff"), includes proving one's masculinity at work and sports—often by using force in dealing with others—as well as initiating and controlling all sexual relations (Coontz 2012).

Males who do not conform to the socially constructed gender role face constant criticism and even humiliation, both from children when they are boys and from adults as men. It can be agonizing to be treated as a "chicken" or a "sissy" as a youth—particularly if such remarks come from one's father or brothers. And grown men who pursue nontraditional occupations, such as preschool teaching or nursing, must constantly deal with others' misgivings and strange looks. In one study, interviewers found that such men frequently had to alter their behavior in order to minimize others' negative reactions. One 35-year-old nurse reported that he had to claim he was "a carpenter or something like that" when he "went clubbing," because women weren't interested in getting to know a male nurse. The subjects made similar accommodations in casual exchanges with other men (Cross and Bagilhole 2002:215).

At the same time, boys who successfully adapt to cultural standards of masculinity may grow up to be inexpressive men who cannot share their feelings with others. They remain forceful and tough, but as a result they are also closed and isolated. In fact, a small but growing body of scholarship suggests that for men as well as women, traditional gender roles may be disadvantageous. In many communities across the nation, girls seem to outdo boys in high school, grabbing a disproportionate share of the leadership positions, from valedictorian to class president to yearbook editor—everything, in short, except captain of the boys' athletic teams. Their advantage continues after high school. In the 1980s, girls in the United States became more likely than boys to go to college. Since then, women have consistently accounted for 54 to 55 percent of first-year students at community colleges and four-year colleges. This trend is projected to continue through at least 2021 (Hussar and Bailey 2013:Table 30).

Aside from these disadvantages, many men find that traditional masculinity does not serve them well in the job market. The growth of a service economy over the past two generations has created a demand for skills, attitudes, and behaviors that are the antithesis of traditional masculinity. Increasingly, this sector is the place where low-skilled men must look for jobs. As a British study showed, many out-of-work men are reluctant to engage in the kind of sensitive, deferential behavior required by service sector jobs (Nixon 2009).

In the past 40 years, inspired in good part by the contemporary feminist movement (examined later in the chapter), increasing numbers of men in the United States have criticized the restrictive aspects of the traditional male gender role. Some men have taken strong public positions in support of women's struggle for full equality and have even organized voluntary associations for the purpose. However, their actions have been countered by other men who feel they are unfairly penalized by laws related to alimony, child support and custody, family violence, and affirmative action (Kimmel 2008; National Organization for Men Against Sexism 2012).

Research on gender roles has shown that in fact there is no single, simple characterization of the male gender role. Australian sociologist R. W. Connell (1987, 2002, 2005) has spoken of **multiple masculinities**,

Gender roles serve to discourage men from entering certain low-paying female-dominated occupations, such as child care. Only 5 percent of day care workers are male.

10-1 WOMEN IN COMBAT WORLDWIDE

In 2012 an estimated 250,000 women, or about 16 percent of the nation's armed forces, served in the U.S. military. Yet these women had never been allowed to fight alongside men—at least, not officially.

For some time now, women in uniform have been serving—and dying—in supportive roles on the warfront. In 2004 Tammy Duckworth, an Army reservist, was serving as a co-pilot in Iraq when a rocket-propelled grenade took down her Black Hawk helicopter. Duckworth, who was severely injured in the attack, received the Purple Heart. She now serves as a U.S. congresswoman from Illinois.

Although the Army does recognize women for their distinguished service— Duckworth was promoted to major soon after the attack—historically, the official prohibition against women serving in combat has prevented them from receiving full credit for their service. In the U.S. Army, the most desirable jobs and career paths require combat experience. Because women officially could not serve in combat positions until 2013, they have been shut out of many types of duty that might interest them. Little wonder that today, the top brass at the Pentagon is almost exclusively male.

Conflict theorists call this obstacle to women's advancement in the Army (their official exclusion from combat) the **brass ceiling**. They note that for women, second-class service in dangerous jobs is nothing new. Historically, both women and racial minorities have often served under hazardous conditions without full recognition.

In 2013, recognizing the injustice of the situation, the Army finally lifted the ban on women serving directly in ground combat. From a sociological point of view, the decision can be related to past directives regarding other minority groups. Functionalists would note that historically, African Americans, Asian Americans, and gays and lesbians were excluded from combat based in part on the fear that their presence would prove dysfunctional. That is, prejudice against those groups would cause conflict in military units, which would undermine their effectiveness on the battlefield. When experience with those minority groups proved that such fears were unfounded, the Army dropped its exclusionary policies.

Among women, opposition to full service can also be related to the fixed gender roles women and men have traditionally played, which reflect stereotypical images of masculinity and femininity.

Interactionists find that women feel empowered by the experience of combat. Despite their full-fledged service, however, these women are often pushed into roles based on traditional gender expectations. In Israel, sociologist Orlee Hauser (2011) interviewed female soldiers aged 18 to 31. She found that like women in the civilian workforce, many female soldiers became the targets of sexual harassment. In active war zones, these women were more likely than men to be assigned educational or training duties, or to perform what was essentially social work. Off the battlefield, women reported being asked to choose a new carpet or bake a cake.

In a national opinion poll taken immediately after the Army's announcement that women would be allowed in combat, an overwhelming 75 percent of U.S. voters supported the decision. There was little difference between men and women on the subject. On the question of whether the change would increase the military's effectiveness, however, the poll showed a sizable gender difference. Among women, 46 percent thought that it would enhance the military's effectiveness; only 36 percent of men held that opinion. All in all, women were less likely than men to see

In 2004 Army reservist Tammy Duckworth, now a member of Congress, was co-piloting a Black Hawk helicopter in Iraq when a rocket-propelled grenade hit the aircraft and severely wounded her; she lost both legs. At the time, although women in uniform often served in dangerous roles, they were officially banned from combat operations.

the decision as a concern for the armed forces.

Historically, both women and racial minorities have often served under hazardous conditions without full recognition.

Nevertheless, the argument over who gets to participate in the military, or indeed any organization, is directly related to its effectiveness. In response to such concerns, the Army is expected to review the training requirements for all recruits, male and female. Some physical standards may be rethought, and lowered if they are found to be unnecessarily high. Psychological and intellectual standards may be strengthened.

The United States is hardly a trailblazer in deciding to allow women in combat. Women have served in combat positions not just in Israel, but in many other countries. Soviet women did so in World War II, although they are not allowed in combat today in Russia. Israel has assigned women to combat regularly since the late 1990s. Australia, Canada, China, Denmark, France, Germany, the Netherlands, and North Korea have also opened up combat to women. Although it would be incorrect to assume that the transition has been smooth—indeed, in Canada and Israel, it happened under court order—the new gender-integrated combat units are proving to be capable and effective on the battlefield.

As in other countries that have opened up combat to women, the new policy in the United States will go through a long period of implementation. At the time of the announcement, Pentagon officials stressed that the standards for combat positions would be "gender-neutral." Strength tests, such as the ability to repeatedly load 55-pound tank shells, might limit women's access to certain positions. Similarly, women would face the same qualifications as men for admission to elite units like the Navy SEALs or the Army Rangers and Green Berets.

Let's Discuss

1. Have you or a woman you know experienced combat? If so, describe the challenges and opportunities women faced on or near the battlefield. Do you agree that women should be allowed to serve in combat without restrictions? Explain your reasoning.
2. What do you think will be the military effect of women's presence in combat roles? Will the Army be stronger or weaker as a result of the new policy? Justify your position.

Sources: Bowman 2013; Domi 2013; Hauser 2011; Llana and Eulich 2013; Mulrine 2012; Myre 2013; Quinnipiac University 2013.

---

meaning that men play a variety of gender roles, including a nurturing-caring role and an effeminate-gay role, in addition to their traditional gender role of dominating women. Nevertheless, society reinforces their traditional, dominating role more than any other role (McCormack 2010).

Few aspects of contemporary life dramatize contemporary gender roles more than modern warfare. Box 10-1 looks at women's roles in today's military.

Gender and Human Sexuality How do gender roles affect a person's sexuality? Separating sex from gender is of course impossible. Yet it would be incorrect simply to equate males with stereotypically masculine expressions of sexuality, or females with stereotypically feminine expressions of sexuality.

Over time, social norms regarding sexual behavior have changed as gender roles have changed, becoming more ambiguous. Today, popularly coined words like *metrosexual* and *bromance* suggest that men should feel comfortable embracing traditionally feminine tastes or developing deep friendships with other men. Similarly, society is beginning to accept not only same-sex couples, but individuals whose gender and identity do not fit a simple either/or pattern, such as bisexuals and transgendered people.

As we saw in Chapter 7, society uses labels such as "good kids" and "delinquents" to condone or sanction certain behaviors by certain groups of people. The same is true of sexual behaviors. In Chapter 11, on the family, we will see how society uses labels to brand specific sexual behaviors as deviant. Traditionally, those labels have derived from gender-role distinctions.

Study Alert

Keep in mind that multiple masculinities characterize the wide range of gender roles men engage in, including a nurturing-caring role and an effeminate-gay role, as well as the socially reinforced, traditional role of dominating women.

CROSS-CULTURAL PERSPECTIVE

To what extent do actual biological differences between the sexes contribute to the cultural differences associated with gender? This question brings us back to the debate over "nature versus nurture." In assessing the alleged and real differences between men and women, it is useful to examine cross-cultural data.

Around the world, anthropologists have documented highly diverse constructions of gender that do not always conform to our ideals of masculinity and femininity. Beginning with the path-breaking work of Margaret Mead ([1935] 2001) and continuing through contemporary fieldwork, these scholars have shown that gender roles can vary greatly from one physical environment, economy, and political system to the next.

Being harassed or groped on public transit is a problem for women all over the world. In Tokyo, separate subway cars are reserved for women to protect them from sex offenses.

In any society, gender stratification requires not only individual socialization into traditional gender roles within the family, but also the promotion and support of those traditional roles by other social institutions, such as religion and education. Moreover, even with all major institutions socializing the young into conventional gender roles, every society has women and men who resist and successfully oppose the stereotypes: strong women who become leaders or professionals, gentle men who care for children, and so forth. It seems clear that differences between the sexes are not dictated by biology. Indeed, the maintenance of traditional gender roles requires constant social controls—and those controls are not always effective.

We can see the social construction of gender roles in process in societies strained by war and social upheaval. U.S. troops were sent to Afghanistan primarily to quell terrorist operations, but also to improve women's rights in a country where social protections and the rule of law have broken down. In this patriarchal society wracked by poverty and war, Afghani women have never been secure; their appearance in public is especially dangerous. Not only is violence against women common in Afghanistan; it is seldom investigated or prosecuted, even in the most severe cases. Victims of violence risk being charged with adultery if they report the crime to authorities. Thanks to UN intervention on women's behalf, however, Afghanis are beginning to recognize that violence against women is a social problem (Organisation for Economic Co-Operation and Development 2012b).

LO 31-3 Sociological Perspectives on Gender

Cross-cultural studies indicate that societies dominated by men are much more common than those in which women play the decisive role. Sociologists have turned to all the major theoretical perspectives to understand how and why these social distinctions are established. Each approach focuses on culture rather than biology as the primary determinant of gender differences. Yet in other respects, advocates of these sociological perspectives disagree widely.

FUNCTIONALIST PERSPECTIVE

Functionalists maintain that gender differentiation has contributed to overall social stability. Sociologists Talcott Parsons and Robert Bales (1955) argued that to function most effectively, the family requires adults who specialize in particular roles. They viewed the traditional gender roles as arising out of the need to establish a division of labor between marital partners.

Parsons and Bales contended that women take the expressive, emotionally supportive role and men the instrumental, practical role, with the two complementing each other. **Expressiveness** denotes concern for the maintenance of harmony and the internal emotional affairs of the family. **Instrumentality** refers to an emphasis on tasks, a focus on more distant goals, and a concern for the external relationship between one's family and other social institutions. According to this theory, women's interest in expressive goals frees men for instrumental tasks, and vice versa. Women become anchored in the family as wives, mothers, and household managers; men become anchored in the occupational world outside the home. Of course, Parsons and Bales offered this framework in the 1950s, when many more women were full-time homemakers than is true today. These theorists did not explicitly endorse traditional gender roles, but they implied that dividing tasks between spouses was functional for the family as a unit.

Given the typical socialization of women and men in the United States, the functionalist view is initially persuasive. However, it would lead us to expect girls and women who have no interest in children to become babysitters and mothers. Similarly, males who love spending time with children might be programmed into careers in the business world. Such differentiation might harm the individual who does not fit into prescribed roles, as well as deprive society of the contributions of many talented people who feel confined by gender stereotyping. Moreover, the functionalist approach does not convincingly explain why men should be assigned categorically to the instrumental role and women to the expressive role.

CONFLICT PERSPECTIVE

Viewed from a conflict perspective, the functionalist approach masks the underlying power relations between men and women. Parsons and Bales never explicitly presented the expressive and instrumental roles as being of unequal value to society, yet their inequality is quite evident. Although social institutions may pay lip service to women's expressive skills, men's instrumental skills are more highly rewarded, whether in terms of money or prestige. Consequently, according to feminists and conflict theorists, any division of labor by gender into instrumental and expressive tasks is far from neutral in its impact on women.

Conflict theorists contend that the relationship between females and males has traditionally been one of unequal power, with men in a dominant position over women. Men may originally have become powerful in preindustrial times because their size, physical strength, and freedom from childbearing duties allowed them to dominate women physically. In contemporary societies, such considerations are not so important, yet cultural beliefs about the sexes are long established, as anthropologist Margaret Mead and feminist sociologist Helen Mayer Hacker (1951, 1974) both stressed. Such beliefs support a social structure that places males in controlling positions.

Conflict theorists, then, see gender differences as a reflection of the subjugation of one group (women) by another group (men). If we use an analogy to Marx's analysis of class conflict, we can say that males are like the bourgeoisie, or capitalists; they control most of the society's wealth, prestige, and power. Females are like the proletariat, or workers; they can acquire valuable resources only by following the dictates of their bosses. Men's work is uniformly valued; women's work (whether unpaid labor in the home or wage labor) is devalued.

Conflict theorists emphasize that men's work is uniformly valued, whereas women's work (whether unpaid labor in the home or wage labor) is devalued. This woman is removing pencils from a conveyor belt at General Pencil Co.'s factory in Jersey City, New Jersey.

FEMINIST PERSPECTIVE

A significant component of the conflict approach to gender stratification draws on feminist theory. Although use of the term *feminist theory* is comparatively recent, the critique of women's position in society and culture goes back to some of the earliest works that have influenced sociology. Among the most important are Mary Wollstonecraft's *A*

Vindication of the Rights of Women (originally published in 1792), John Stuart Mill's *The Subjection of Women* (originally published in 1869), and Friedrich Engels's *The Origin of the Family, Private Property, and the State* (originally published in 1884).

Engels, a close associate of Karl Marx, argued that women's subjugation coincided with the rise of private property during industrialization. Only when people moved beyond an agrarian economy could males enjoy the luxury of leisure and withhold rewards and privileges from women. Drawing on the work of Marx and Engels, many contemporary feminist theorists view women's subordination as part of the overall exploitation and injustice that they see as inherent in capitalist societies. Some radical feminist theorists, however, view the oppression of women as inevitable in *all* male-dominated societies, whether they are labeled capitalist, socialist, or communist (Feuer 1989; Tuchman 1992; Tucker 1978:734–759).

Feminist sociologists would find little to disagree with in the conflict theorists' perspective, but are more likely to embrace a political agenda. Rather than be caught up in discussing progress toward gender equality over the last generation, they would draw attention to the need for greater progress. Feminists would also argue that until the 1970s, the very discussion of women and society, however well meant, was distorted by the exclusion of women from academic thought, including sociology. We have noted the many accomplishments of Jane Addams and Ida Wells-Barnett, but they generally worked outside the discipline, focusing on what we would now call applied sociology and social work. At the time, their efforts, while valued as humanitarian, were seen as unrelated to the research and conclusions being reached in academic circles, which of course were male academic circles (Andersen 2007; J. Howard 1999; Ridgeway 2011).

INTERSECTIONS WITH RACE, CLASS, AND OTHER SOCIAL FACTORS

Contemporary feminists recognize the differential treatment of some women not only because of their gender, but also because of the intersection of their race, ethnicity, and socioeconomic status. Simply put, Whites dominate these poor, non-White women because they are non-White; men dominate them because they are women; and the affluent dominate them because they are poor. The African American feminist theorist Patricia Hill Collins (2000) has termed the convergence of social forces that contributes to the subordinate status of these low-status women the **matrix of domination** (Figure 10-1).

Gender, race, and social class are not the only sources of oppression in the United States, though they profoundly affect women and people of color. Other forms of categorization and stigmatization that might be included in the matrix are sexual orientation, religion, disability, and age. If we apply the matrix to the world as a whole, we might add citizenship status or perceived colonial or neocolonial status to the list (Winant 2006).

Though feminists have addressed themselves to the needs of minority women, these women are oppressed much more by their race and ethnicity than by their gender. The question for Latinas (Hispanic women), African American women, Asian American women, and Native American women appears to be whether they should unite with their brothers against racism or challenge them for their sexism. The answer is that our society must eradicate both sexism and racism (Beisel and Kay 2004; Breines 2007; C. Epstein 1999).

The discussion of gender roles among African Americans has always provoked controversy. Advocates of Black nationalism contend that feminism only distracts women from participating fully in the African American struggle. The existence of feminist groups among Blacks, in their view, simply divides the Black community, thereby serving the dominant White majority. In contrast, Black feminists such as bell hooks (1994) argue that little is to be gained by accepting the gender-role divisions of the dominant society, which place women in a separate, subservient position. Though the media commonly portray Black women in a negative light—as illiterates, welfare queens, or prostitutes—Black feminists emphasize that it is not solely Whites and the White-dominated media who focus

FIGURE 10-1 **MATRIX OF DOMINATION**

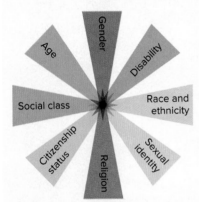

The matrix of domination illustrates how several social factors, including gender, social class, and race and ethnicity, can converge to create a cumulative impact on a person's social standing.

Source: Developed by author.

on such negative images. Black men (most recently, Black male rap artists) have also portrayed Black women in a negative way (Threadcraft 2008; Wilkins 2012).

Historically, Native Americans stand out as an exception to the patriarchal tradition in North America. At the time of the European settlers' arrival, Native American gender roles varied greatly from tribe to tribe. Southern tribes, for reasons unclear to today's scholars, were usually matriarchal and traced their descent through the mother. European missionaries, who sought to make the native peoples more like Europeans, set out to transform this arrangement, which was not entirely universal. Like members of other groups, some Native American women have resisted gender stereotypes (Marubbio 2006).

Latinas are usually considered as part of either the Hispanic or feminist movements, and their distinctive experience ignored. In the past, they have been excluded from decision making in the two social institutions that most affect their daily lives: the family and the church. Particularly in the lower class, the Hispanic family suffers from the pervasive tradition of male domination. And the Catholic Church relegates women to supportive roles, while reserving the leadership positions for men (Browne 2001; De Anda 2004).

Prior to this chapter, much of our discussion has focused on the social effects of race and ethnicity, coupled with poverty, low incomes, and meager wealth. The matrix of domination highlights the confluence of these factors with gender discrimination, which we must include to fully understand the plight of women of color.

INTERACTIONIST PERSPECTIVE

While functionalists and conflict theorists who study gender stratification typically focus on macro-level social forces and institutions, interactionist researchers tend to examine gender stratification on the micro level of everyday behavior. The key to this approach is the way gender is socially constructed in everyday interactions. We "do gender" by reinforcing traditionally masculine and feminine actions. For example, a man "does masculinity" by opening a door for his girlfriend; she "does femininity" by consenting to his assistance. Obviously, the social construction of gender goes beyond these relatively trivial rituals. Interactionists recognize, too, that people can challenge traditional gender roles. A female golfer who uses the men's tees and a man who actively arranges a birthday luncheon at work are redoing gender (Deutsch 2007; West and Zimmerman 1987).

One continuing subject of investigation is the role of gender in cross-sex conversations (sometimes referred to as "crosstalk"), specifically the idea that men interrupt women more than women interrupt men. Interestingly, empirical research does not clearly support this assertion. True, people in positions of authority or status—who are much more likely to be male than female—dominate interpersonal conversations. That does not necessarily mean that women per se cannot be heard, however. Future research results may deemphasize the clichéd advice that women must speak up and focus instead on the situational structures that cast men in dominant positions (Cameron 2007; Hyde 2005; Tannen 1990).

Table 10-2 summarizes the major sociological perspectives on gender.

Study Alert

The matrix of domination describes the convergence of social forces—gender, race/ethnicity, and socioeconomic status—that contributes to the subordinate status of low-status women.

TABLE 10-2 SOCIOLOGICAL PERSPECTIVES ON GENDER

Tracking Sociological Perspectives

Theoretical Perspective	Emphasis
Functionalist	Gender differentiation contributes to social stability
Conflict	Gender inequality is rooted in the female–male power relationship
Feminist	Women's subjugation is integral to society and social structure
Interactionist	Gender distinctions and "doing gender" are reflected in people's everyday behavior

Read each question carefully and then select or provide the best answer.

1. Both males and females are physically capable of learning to cook and sew, yet most Western societies determine that women should perform these tasks. This illustrates the operation of
   a. gender roles.
   b. sociobiology.
   c. homophobia.
   d. comparable worth.

2. An important element in traditional views of proper "masculine" and "feminine" behavior is fear of homosexuality. This fear, along with accompanying prejudice, is referred to as
   a. lesbianism.
   b. femme fatalism.
   c. homophobia.
   d. claustrophobia.

3. The most crucial agents of socialization in teaching gender roles in the United States are
   a. peers.
   b. teachers.
   c. media personalities.
   d. parents.

4. Talcott Parsons and Robert Bales contend that women take the _____, emotionally supportive role in the family and that men take the _____, practical role, with the two complementing each other.

5. A significant component of the _____ approach to gender stratification draws on feminist theory.

Answers

1 (a); 2 (c); 3 (d); 4 expressive, instrumental; 5 conflict

Consider these questions to get a deeper understanding of the material.

1. Compare the social construction of gender with the social construction of race.

2. Which aspects of the functionalist and conflict perspectives on gender make the most sense to you? Explain.

RECAP

LO 31-1 Explain the meaning of the phrase "the social construction of gender."

- In the United States, the social construction of gender continues to define significantly different expectations for females and males.
- Gender roles show up in our work and behavior and in how we react to others. Throughout history, these roles have restricted women much more than they have men.

- Though men may exhibit a variety of different gender roles, called multiple masculinities, society reinforces their traditional role of dominating women.

LO 31-2 Describe women's and men's gender roles and the process of gender-role socialization in the United States.

- Anthropologists have found highly diverse constructions of gender from one culture to another. However, in any society, gender stratification entails that males and females are socialized into traditional roles within the family, which are reinforced by social institutions such as religion and education.
- Anthropological research points to the importance of cultural conditioning rather than biology in defining the social roles of males and females.
- In the United States, girls are socialized to be soft, weak, and emotional, while boys are socialized to be tough, strong, and unemotional. Both sexes suffer from the boxes into which gender roles confine them.

LO 31-3 Analyze the functionalist, conflict, feminist, and interactionist explanations of gender stratification.

- Functionalists maintain that sex differentiation contributes to overall social stability, but conflict theorists, often drawing on the insights of feminist theory, charge that the relationship between females and males is one of unequal power, with men dominating women. This dominance shows up in people's everyday interactions.
- Many women experience differential treatment, not only because of their gender but because of their race, ethnicity, and social class as well. Patricia Hill Collins has termed this convergence of social forces the matrix of domination.
- As one example of their micro-level approach to the study of gender stratification, interactionists have analyzed men's verbal dominance over women through conversational interruptions.

KEY TERMS

Brass ceiling An invisible barrier that blocks the promotion of a woman in the military because of her official (not necessarily actual) exclusion from combat.

Expressiveness Concern for the maintenance of harmony and the internal emotional affairs of the family.

Gender role Expectations regarding the proper behavior, attitudes, and activities of males and females.

Homophobia Fear of and prejudice against homosexuality.

Instrumentality An emphasis on tasks, a focus on more distant goals, and a concern for the external relationship between one's family and other social institutions.

Matrix of domination The cumulative impact of oppression because of race and ethnicity, gender, and social class, as well as religion, sexual orientation, disability, age, and citizenship status.

Multiple masculinities A variety of male gender roles, including nurturing-caring and effeminate-gay roles, that men may play along with their more pervasive traditional role of dominating women.

Women: The Oppressed Majority

LO 32-1 Summarize the status of women today and the effects of sex discrimination worldwide.

LO 32-2 Compare and contrast the labor force participation and compensation of U.S. men and women in various occupations.

LO 32-3 Describe major developments in the rise of feminism in the United States, including the effects of the abortion debate.

Sexism and Sex Discrimination
The Status of Women Worldwide
Women in the Workforce of the United States
    Labor Force Participation
    Compensation
    Social Consequences of Women's Employment
Emergence of a Collective Consciousness
Social Policy and Gender Stratification
    The Battle over Abortion from a Global Perspective

Many people, both male and female, find it difficult to conceive of women as a subordinate and oppressed group. Yet take a look at the political structure of the United States: women remain noticeably underrepresented. Following the 2012 elections, for example, only 5 of the nation's 50 states had a female governor (Arizona, New Hampshire, New Mexico, Oklahoma, and South Carolina).

Women have made slow but steady progress in certain political arenas. In 1981, out of 535 members of Congress, there were only 21 women: 19 in the House of Representatives and 2 in the Senate. In contrast, the Congress that held office following the 2012 elections had 98 women: 78 in the House and 20 in the Senate. Yet the membership and leadership of Congress remain overwhelmingly male.

In October 1981, Sandra Day O'Connor was sworn in as the nation's first female Supreme Court justice. Still, no woman has ever served as president of the United States, vice president, or chief justice of the Supreme Court.

LO 32-1 Sexism and Sex Discrimination

Just as African Americans are victimized by racism, women in our society are victimized by sexism. **Sexism** is the ideology that one sex is superior to the other. The term is generally used to refer to male prejudice and discrimination against women. In Chapter 9, we noted that Blacks can suffer from both individual acts of racism and institutional discrimination.

Institutional discrimination was defined as the denial of opportunities and equal rights to individuals and groups that results from the normal operations of a society. In the same sense, women suffer from both individual acts of sexism (such as sexist remarks and acts of violence) and institutional sexism.

It is not simply that particular men in the United States are biased in their treatment of women. All the major institutions of our society—including the government, armed forces, large corporations, the media, universities, and the medical establishment—are controlled by men. These institutions, in their normal, day-to-day operations, often discriminate against women and perpetuate sexism. For example, if the central office of a nationwide bank sets a policy that single women are a bad risk for loans—regardless of their incomes and investments—that bank will discriminate against women in state after state. It will do so even at branches where loan officers hold no personal biases toward women, but are merely "following orders."

From the perspective of . . .

A U.S. Army Officer What measures could you take to foster respect for your female troops, and to make it clear that harassment and rape will not be tolerated?

Our society is run by male-dominated institutions, yet with the power that flows to men come responsibility and stress. Men have higher reported rates of certain types of mental illness than women, and a greater likelihood of death due to heart attack or stroke. The pressure on men to succeed, and then to remain on top in the competitive world of work, can be especially intense. That is not to suggest that gender stratification is as damaging to men as it is to women. But it is clear that the power and privilege men enjoy are no guarantee of personal well-being.

LO 32-1 The Status of Women Worldwide

According to a detailed overview of the status of the world's women, issued by the World Bank in 2012, the lives of girls and women have changed dramatically over the past quarter century. Progress has been limited in some respects, however. In many parts of the world, women still lag far behind men in their earnings and in their ability to speak out politically (World Bank 2012b).

This critique applies to Western as well as non-Western countries. Although Westerners tend to view some societies—for example, Muslim countries—as being particularly harsh toward women, that perception is actually an overgeneralization. Muslim countries are exceedingly varied and complex and do not often fit the stereotypes created by the Western media.

Regardless of culture, however, women everywhere suffer from second-class status. It is estimated that women grow half the world's food, but they rarely own land. They constitute one-third of the world's paid labor force, but are generally found in the lowest-paying jobs. Single-parent households headed by women, which appear to be on the rise in many nations, are typically found in the poorest sections of the population. The feminization of poverty has become a global phenomenon. As in the United States, women around the world are underrepresented politically.

Despite these challenges, women are not responding passively. They are mobilizing, individually and collectively. Given the significant underrepresentation of women in government offices and national legislatures, however, the task is difficult.

Not surprisingly, there is a link between the wealth of industrialized nations and the poverty of women in developing countries. Viewed from a conflict perspective or through the lens of Immanuel Wallerstein's world systems analysis, the economies of developing nations are controlled and exploited by industrialized countries and multinational corporations

FIGURE 10-2 GENDER INEQUALITY IN HOUSEWORK

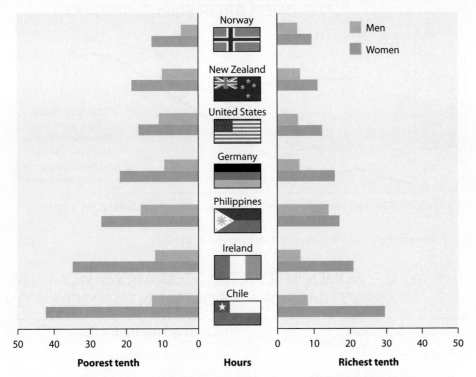

Around the world, rich or poor, women do much more housework than men.

Note: Housework includes laundry, grocery shopping, dinner preparation, and care for sick family members.
Source: Adapted from Heisig 2011:84.

based in those countries. Much of the exploited labor in developing nations, especially in the nonindustrial sector, is performed by women. Women workers typically toil long hours for low pay, but contribute significantly to their families' incomes (Chubb et al. 2008).

In industrialized countries, women's unequal status can be seen in the division of housework, as well as in the jobs they hold and the pay they earn. Sociologist Jan Paul Heisig analyzed gender inequality among the rich (the top decile in income) and the poor (the bottom decile) in 33 industrialized countries. Typically, poor men did more housework than rich men, but as Figure 10-2 shows, rich or poor, men did much less housework than women. The recent economic recession accentuated this unequal division of housework. Obviously, being unemployed leaves both men and women with more time for household chores. However, unemployed women do double the amount of extra housework as unemployed men (Gough and Killewald 2011).

LO 32-2 Women in the Workforce of the United States

Nearly 40 years ago, the U.S. Commission on Civil Rights (1976:1) concluded that the passage in the Declaration of Independence proclaiming that "all men are created equal" has been taken too literally for too long—especially with respect to women's opportunities for employment. In this section we will see how gender bias has limited women's opportunities for employment outside the home, at the same time that it forces them to carry a disproportionate burden inside the home.

LABOR FORCE PARTICIPATION

Women's participation in the paid labor force of the United States increased steadily throughout the 20th century and into the 21st century (Figure 10-3). Today, millions of

FIGURE 10-3 TRENDS IN U.S. WOMEN'S PARTICIPATION IN THE PAID LABOR FORCE, 1890–2011

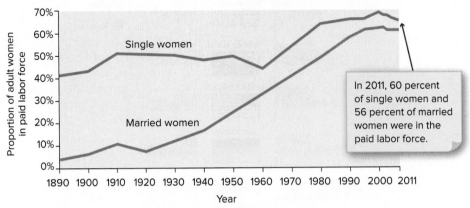

In 2011, 60 percent of single women and 56 percent of married women were in the paid labor force.

Source: Bureau of the Census 1975; Bureau of Labor Statistics 2013a:Table 4.

TABLE 10-3 U.S. WOMEN IN SELECTED OCCUPATIONS: WOMEN AS A PERCENTAGE OF ALL WORKERS IN THE OCCUPATION

Underrepresented		Overrepresented	
Firefighters	3%	High school teachers	57%
Aircraft pilots and engineers	4	Cashiers	72
Police officers	13	Social workers	81
Civil engineers	14	Elementary teachers	81
Clergy	21	File clerks	81
Chefs and head cooks	22	Librarians	87
Dentists	24	Tellers	87
Computer systems analysts	31	Word processors and typists	89
Lawyers	31	Registered nurses	91
Physicians	34	Receptionists	92
Athletes, coaches, and umpires	37	Child care workers	95
Postal mail carriers	38	Dental hygienists	99

Note: Women constitute 47 percent of the entire labor force.
Source: Data for 2012 reported in Bureau of Labor Statistics 2013b: Table 11.

women—married or single, with or without children, pregnant or recently having given birth—are in the labor force.

Overall, 58 percent of adult women in the United States were in the labor force in 2011, compared to 41 percent in 1970. For men, the data were 71 percent in 2011, compared to 76 percent in 1970 (Bureau of Labor Statistics 2013a:Table 4).

Still, women entering the job market find their options restricted in important ways. Women are *underrepresented* in occupations historically defined as "men's jobs," which often carry much greater financial rewards and prestige than women's jobs. For example, in 2011, women accounted for approximately 47 percent of the paid labor force of the United States, yet they constituted only 14 percent of civil engineers, 31 percent of computer systems analysts, and 34 percent of physicians (Table 10-3).

Such occupational segregation is not unique to the United States but typical of industrial countries. In Great Britain, for example, only 6 percent of engineers are women, while 71 percent of cashiers and 88 percent of nurses are women (Office for National Statistics 2013).

Women from all groups and men from minority groups sometimes encounter attitudinal or organizational bias that prevents them from reaching their full potential. As we saw in Chapter 9, the term **glass ceiling** refers to an invisible barrier that blocks the promotion of a qualified individual in a work environment because of the individual's gender, race, or ethnicity. Furthermore, women and minority men confront not only a glass ceiling that limits their upward mobility, but glass walls that reduce their ability to move horizontally into fast-track jobs that lead directly up to the highest rungs on the corporate ladder. A study of the *Fortune* 500 largest corporations in the United States showed that in 2013, barely 16 percent of the seats on their boards of directors were held by women (Alliance for Board Diversity 2013).

When women do gain entry to corporate boards of directors, the response in the financial world is not entirely positive. Despite objective tests that show strong financial performance under gender-diverse leadership, some investors tend to balk. Research by Frank Dobbin and Jiwook Jung (2010) shows that small investors often sell their shares when women become corporate leaders, apparently falling for the stereotype that associates males with success. This sell pattern is not characteristic of larger investors, who have long argued that gender-diverse leadership is good for business.

This type of inequality is not unique to the United States. Worldwide, women hold less than 1 percent of corporate managerial positions. In recognition of the underrepresentation of women on boards of directors, the Norwegian legislature established minimum quotas for the number of female board members. As the architects of the plan put it, "instead of assuming what people *can't* do at work, provide opportunities for employees to prove what they can do." The goal was not complete equity for women, but 40 percent representation by 2008. By 2012 the percentage stood at 18 percent (European PWN 2012).

COMPENSATION

He works. She works. Both are physicians—a high-status occupation with considerable financial rewards. He makes $140,000. She makes $88,000.

These median annual earnings for physicians in the United States were released by the Census Bureau. They are typical of the results of the bureau's detailed study of occupations and income. Take air traffic controllers. He makes $67,000; she makes $56,000. Or housekeepers: he makes $19,000; she makes $15,000. What about teachers' assistants? He makes $20,000; she makes $15,000. Statisticians at the bureau looked at the median annual earnings for no fewer than 821 occupations ranging from dishwasher to chief executive. After adjusting for workers' ages, education, and work experience, they came to an unmistakable conclusion: across the board, there is a substantial gender gap in the median earnings of full-time workers.

From the perspective of . . .

A Policy Analyst What arguments, besides the basic one of fairness, could you make in support of equal pay for women?

Men do not always earn more than women for doing the same work. Researchers at the Census Bureau found 2 occupations out of 821 in which women typically earn about 1 percent more income than men: hazardous materials recovery and telecommunications line installation. These two occupations employed less than 1 out of every 1,000 workers the bureau studied. Forecasting analyses show no convincing evidence that the wage gap is narrowing.

What accounts for these yawning wage gaps between men and women in the same occupation? Scholars at the Census Bureau studied the following characteristics of men and women in the same occupation:

- Age and degree of formal education
- Marital status and the presence of children at home

- Specialization within the occupation (for example, family practice versus surgical practice)
- Years of work experience
- Hours worked per year

Taking all these factors into consideration reduced the pay gap between men and women by only 3 cents. Women still earned 80 cents for every dollar earned by men. In sum, the disparity in pay between men and women cannot be explained by pointing to women's career choices (Government Accountability Office 2003; Weinberg 2004, 2007).

Legally, sex discrimination in wage payments is difficult to prove. Witness the case of former Goodyear worker Lilly Ledbetter, who learned 19 years after she was hired that she was being paid less than men doing the same job. Ledbetter sued and was awarded damages, only to have the Supreme Court overturn the decision on the grounds that she made her claim more than six months after the first discriminatory paycheck was issued. Congress relaxed this restriction in 2009 (Pear 2009).

Not all the obstacles women face in the workplace originate with management. Unfortunately, many workers, both male and female, would prefer not to work for a woman.

What happens to men who enter traditionally women's occupations? Research shows that the glass ceiling that women face does not appear to hamper them. Instead, men who enter traditionally female occupations are more likely than women to rise to the top. Male elementary teachers become principals; male nurses become supervisors. The term **glass escalator** refers to this advantage men experience in occupations dominated by women. Whereas women who enter traditionally male occupations may be seen as tokens, men who move out of sex-typical jobs are likely to be advantaged.

This difference between the sexes is associated with a pay differential. A national study released in 2013 found that among full-time, year-round registered nurses, females earn 7 percent less on average than their male counterparts. Even when specializations are considered, pay differences remain; they are even greater among the highest paid nurses, such as nurse anaesthetists (Budig 2002; Bureau of the Census 2013c).

SOCIAL CONSEQUENCES OF WOMEN'S EMPLOYMENT

Today, many women face the challenge of trying to juggle work and family. Their situation has many social consequences. For one thing, it puts pressure on child care facilities, public financing of day care, and even the fast-food industry, which provides many of the meals women used to prepare themselves. For another, it raises questions about what responsibility male wage earners have in the household.

Who does the housework when women become productive wage earners? Studies indicate that there is a clear gender gap in the performance of housework, although it has been narrowing (see Figure 10-2). Women do more housework and spend more time on child care than men do, whether on a workday or a nonworkday. Taken together, then, a woman's workday on and off the job is much longer than a man's (Sayer et al. 2004).

Sociologist Arlie Hochschild (1990, 2005, 2012) has used the phrase **second shift** to describe the double burden—work outside the home followed by child care and housework—that many women face and few men share equitably. Unfortunately, today's workplace is becoming a 24/7 virtual office thanks to the advent of mobile information technologies. As these devices take over what little personal time employees have left, the physical toll on women becomes even more burdensome.

What is life like for these women? On the basis of interviews with and observations of 52 couples over an eight-year period, Hochschild reports that the wives (and not their husbands) drive home from the office while planning domestic schedules and play dates for children—and then begin their second shift. Drawing on national studies, she concludes that women spend 15 fewer hours each week in leisure activities than their husbands. In a year, these women work an extra month of 24-hour days because of the second shift; over a dozen years, they work an extra year of 24-hour days. Hochschild found that the married couples she studied were fraying at the edges, and so were their careers and their

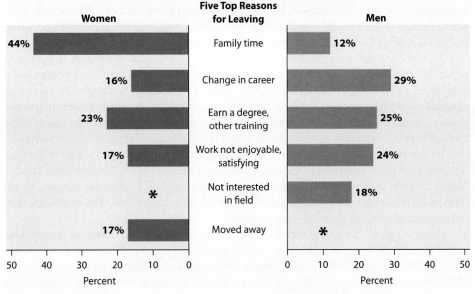

FIGURE 10-4 WHY LEAVE WORK?

Five Top Reasons for Leaving

Women		Men
44%	Family time	12%
16%	Change in career	29%
23%	Earn a degree, other training	25%
17%	Work not enjoyable, satisfying	24%
*	Not interested in field	18%
17%	Moved away	*

* Not one of top 5 reasons

Note: Based on a representative Harris Interactive survey of "highly qualified" workers, defined as those with a graduate degree, a professional degree, or a high honors undergraduate degree.
Source: Adapted by author, Richard Schaefer, based on data in Hewlett and Luce 2005.

marriages. With such reports in mind, many feminists have advocated greater governmental and corporate support for child care, more flexible family leave policies, and other reforms designed to ease the burden on the nation's families (Eby et al. 2010).

The greater amounts of time women put into caring for their children, and to a lesser degree into housework, take a special toll on women who are pursuing careers. In a survey published in the *Harvard Business Review,* about 40 percent of women indicated that they had voluntarily left work for months or years, compared to only 24 percent of men. As Figure 10-4 shows, women were much more likely than men to take time off for family reasons. Even women in the most prestigious professions have difficulty balancing home and work responsibilities.

LO 32-3 Emergence of a Collective Consciousness

Feminism is an ideology that favors equal rights for women. The feminist movement of the United States was born in upstate New York, in a town called Seneca Falls, in the summer of 1848. On July 19, the first women's rights convention began, attended by Elizabeth Cady Stanton, Lucretia Mott, and other pioneers in the struggle for women's rights. This first wave of *feminists,* as they are currently known, battled ridicule and scorn as they fought for legal and political equality for women. They were not afraid to risk controversy on behalf of their cause; in 1872, Susan B. Anthony was arrested for attempting to vote in that year's presidential election.

Ultimately, the early feminists won many victories, among them the passage and ratification of the Nineteenth Amendment to the Constitution, which granted women the right to vote in national elections beginning in 1920. But suffrage did not lead to other reforms in women's social and economic position, and in the early and middle 20th century the women's movement became a much less powerful force for social change.

The second wave of feminism in the United States emerged in the 1960s and came into full force in the 1970s. In part, the movement was inspired by three pioneering books arguing for women's rights: Simone de Beauvoir's *The Second Sex,* Betty Friedan's *The*

Feminine Mystique, and Kate Millett's *Sexual Politics.* In addition, the general political activism of the 1960s led women—many of whom were working for Black civil rights or against the war in Vietnam—to reexamine their own powerlessness. The sexism often found within even allegedly progressive and radical political circles convinced many women that they needed to establish a movement for women's liberation (Stansell 2011).

As more and more women became aware of sexist attitudes and practices, including attitudes they themselves had accepted through socialization into traditional gender roles, they began to challenge male dominance. A sense of sisterhood, much like the class consciousness that Marx hoped would emerge in the proletariat, became evident. Individual women identified their interests with those of the collectivity *women.* No longer were women happy in submissive, subordinate roles ("false consciousness" in Marxist terms).

By the 1980s, however, the movement's influence was beginning to wane. In 1998, in a provocative cover illustration, the editors of *Time* magazine asked "Is Feminism Dead?" Young women, they wrote, seemed to take women's improved status for granted, to see their mothers' struggles for equal rights as irrelevant to their own lives. Fewer women, they noted, were identifying themselves as feminists.

How do today's women perceive the movement? According to a national survey done in 2013, about 23 percent of women (and 12 percent of men) call themselves feminists. There is little reason to believe that younger women are less willing to accept the label than older women. Perhaps more telling is the fact that 32 percent of women and 42 percent of men think the term *feminist* has negative connotations.

Is feminism dead? Many feminists resent that question, because it seems to imply that all their concerns have been resolved. Today's feminists argue that they have moved beyond early criticism that the movement was too obsessed with the concerns of White middle-class women, that it marginalized African American feminists and others. Indeed, current polling shows that African American and Latino women are more likely than others to call themselves feminists. Recognizing the legal and economic victories they have made over the last 40 years, feminists are now working to improve women's lives in nonindustrial countries, where they focus on eliminating malnutrition, starvation, extreme poverty, and violence (Breines 2007; Schnittker et al. 2003; Swanson 2013).

LO 32-3 **SOCIAL POLICY** and Gender Stratification

We have seen that researchers rely on a number of tools, from simple observational research to the latest in computer technologies. Because in the real world sociological research can have far-reaching consequences for public policy and public welfare, we'll consider its impact on the battle over abortion.

THE BATTLE OVER ABORTION FROM A GLOBAL PERSPECTIVE

Few issues seem to stir as much intense conflict as abortion. A critical victory in the struggle for legalized abortion in the United States came in 1973, when the Supreme Court granted women the right to terminate pregnancies. This ruling, known as *Roe v. Wade,* was based on a woman's right to privacy. The Court's decision was generally applauded by pro-choice groups, which believe women should have the right to make their own decisions about their bodies and should have access to safe and legal abortions. It was bitterly condemned by those opposed to abortion. For these pro-life groups, abortion is a moral and often a religious issue. In their view, human life begins at the moment of conception, so that its termination through abortion is essentially an act of murder.

The debate that has followed *Roe v. Wade* revolves around prohibiting abortion altogether, or at the very least, limiting it. In 1979, for example, Missouri required parental consent for minors wishing to obtain an abortion, and the Supreme Court upheld the law.

Parental notification and consent have become especially sensitive issues in the debate. Pro-life activists argue that the parents of teenagers should have the right to be notified about—and to permit or prohibit—abortions. In their view, parental authority deserves full support at a time when the traditional nuclear family is embattled. However, pro-choice activists counter that many pregnant teenagers come from troubled families where they have been abused. These young women may have good reason to avoid discussing such explosive issues with their parents.

In the United States, people support a woman's right to a legal abortion, but with reservations. According to a 2012 national survey, 52 percent say that abortion should be legal in any case; 28 percent, legal only under certain circumstances; and 18 percent, illegal in all cases. There is no gender difference in opinion on this issue: women and men hold similar views on the legality of abortion (Saad 2013).

The United States is not alone in debating abortion. Latin American countries typically have the strictest measures against the practice, but occasionally changes occur. In 2007, Mexico loosened decade-old restrictions to permit legal abortions during the first three months of a pregnancy, for any reason (M. Davis 2010).

Applying Sociology to the Abortion Issue Sociologists see gender and social class as the defining issues surrounding abortion. That is, the intense conflict over abortion reflects broader differences over women's position in society. Feminists involved in defending abortion rights typically believe that men and women are essentially similar. They support women's full participation in work outside the home and oppose all forms of sex discrimination. Feminists also claim that pregnancy and childbirth have been socially constructed by male-centered health care systems and patriarchal religious traditions. In contrast, most antiabortion activists believe that men and women are fundamentally different. In their view, men are best suited to the public world of work, while women are best suited to the demanding and crucial task of rearing children. These activists are troubled by women's growing participation in work outside the home, which they view as destructive to the family, and ultimately to society (Lorber 2005).

Another obstacle facing the poor is access to abortion providers. In the face of vocal pro-life sentiment, fewer and fewer hospitals throughout the world are allowing physicians to perform abortions, except in extreme cases. Moreover, some doctors who work in clinics, intimidated by death threats and murders, have stopped performing abortions. For poor people in rural areas, this reduction in service makes it more difficult to locate and travel to a facility that will accommodate their wishes. Viewed from a conflict perspective, this is one more financial burden that falls especially heavily on low-income women.

These obstacles are compounded by state and local policies that further hamper the doctors and clinics that provide abortions: building requirements and bans on public funding; restrictions or outright bans on public health insurance, such as Medicaid and Obamacare. Other policies, such as long waiting periods and required ultrasound tests, are meant to discourage women from seeking abortions. These requirements have become more onerous since 2000. By 2014, the 15 states labeled "supportive" in Figure 10-5 had no more than one such requirement on the books; the 27 states labeled "opposed" had adopted most if not all of them. About 56 percent of the country's population lives in those 27 states. People who take a right-to-life position see these states' restrictions as part of an effort "to create and sustain a culture of life" (Guttmacher Institute 2014; Paulson 2013).

Initiating the Abortion Policy In 1973 the Supreme Court supported the general right to terminate a pregnancy by a narrow 5–4 majority. Although pro-life activists continue to hope for an overruling of *Roe v. Wade,* they have focused in the interim on weakening the decision through tactics such as limiting the use of fetal tissue in medical experiments and prohibiting certain late-term abortions, which they term "partial-birth" abortions. The Supreme Court continues to hear cases involving such restrictions.

What is the policy in other countries? As in the United States, many European nations responded to public opinion and liberalized abortion laws beginning in the 1970s. However, many of those nations limit the procedure to the first 12 weeks of a pregnancy. (The United

FIGURE 10-5 STATE ABORTION-RELATED POLICIES, 2000–2014

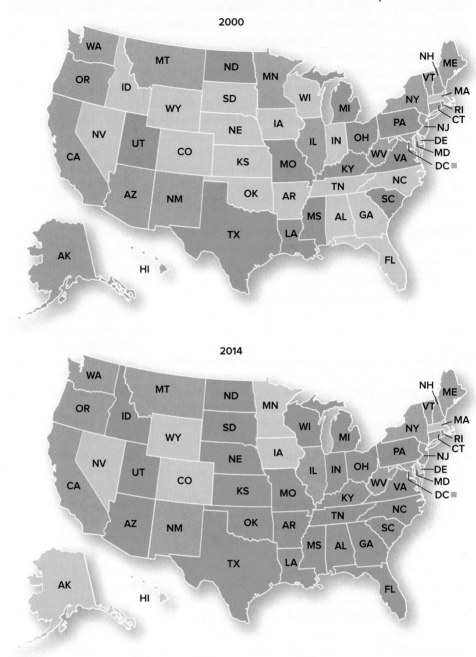

Note: Policies in place as of January 2014.
Source: Gold and Nash 2012; Guttmacher Institute 2014.

States, in contrast, allows abortions up to about the 24th week and beyond.) Inspired by the strong antiabortion movement in the United States, antiabortion activists in Europe have become more outspoken, especially in Great Britain, France, Portugal, Spain, Italy, and Germany.

The policies of the United States are intertwined with those of developing nations. From the 1980s through January 2009, members of Congress who opposed abortion successfully blocked foreign aid to countries that might use the funds to encourage abortion. Yet developing nations generally have the most restrictive abortion laws. As Figure 10-6

FIGURE 10-6   THE GLOBAL DIVIDE ON ABORTION

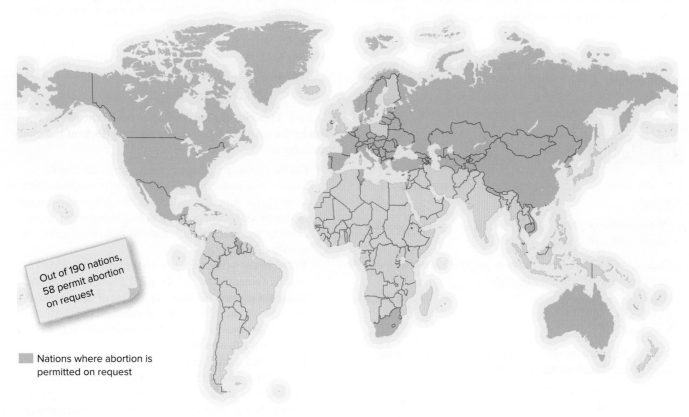

Out of 190 nations, 58 permit abortion on request

Nations where abortion is permitted on request

Note: Data current as of March 2013.
Source: Developed by the author, Richard Schaefer, based on United Nations Population Division 2013.

shows, it is primarily in Africa, Latin America, and parts of Asia that women are not allowed to terminate a pregnancy on request. As might be expected, illegal abortions are most common in those nations. An estimated quarter of the world's women live in countries where abortion is illegal or is permitted only if a woman's life is in jeopardy. Indeed, the rate of abortions in countries with legal restrictions on the procedure matches the rate in countries that permit it. Hence, 40 percent of abortions worldwide—about 16 million procedures each year—are performed illegally (P. Baker 2009; Guttmacher Institute 2008).

E Evaluate

Read each question carefully and then select or provide the best answer.

1. Which sociological perspective distinguishes between instrumental and expressive roles?
   a. functionalist perspective
   b. conflict perspective
   c. interactionist perspective
   d. labeling theory

2. Contemporary feminists recognize the differential treatment of some women not only because of their gender, but also because of their

   a. race.
   b. ethnicity.
   c. socioeconomic status.
   d. all of the above

3. The sense of sisterhood that became evident during the rise of the contemporary feminist movement resembled the Marxist concept of
   a. alienation.
   b. dialectics.
   c. class consciousness.
   d. false consciousness.

4. Women from all groups and men from minority groups sometimes encounter attitudinal or organizational bias that prevents them from reaching their full potential. This is known as the _____ _____.

5. Sociologist Arlie Hochschild has used the phrase _____ _____ to describe the double burden that many women face and few men share equitably: work outside the home followed by child care and housework.

Answers

1 (a); 2 (d); 3 (c); 4 glass ceiling; 5 second shift

R Rethink

Consider these questions to get a deeper understanding of the material.

1. What are the challenges to comparing the status of women across different nations?

2. Today, is feminism more likely to produce social change or respond to social change? Explain.

RECAP

LO 32-1 Summarize the status of women today and the effects of sex discrimination worldwide.

- Women around the world live and work with pervasive sexism and institutional discrimination, stuck in the lowest-paying jobs and rarely owning land in spite of growing half the world's food.
- The number of single-parent families appears to be on the rise globally, and most are headed by poor women. This phenomenon has been called "the feminization of poverty."
- Despite some progress, women in many parts of the world still lag behind men in earnings and in the ability to speak out politically.

LO 32-2 Compare and contrast the labor force participation and compensation of U.S. men and women in various occupations.

- In the United States today, almost as many women as men participate in the paid labor force, but women are underrepresented in managerial positions and underpaid compared to men in the same jobs.
- Women sometimes encounter organizational bias that hinders their advancement in the corporate world. This has

been called the *glass ceiling,* an invisible barrier to upward movement.

- As women have taken on more and more hours of paid employment outside the home, they have been only partially successful in getting their husbands to take on more homemaking duties, including child care. The result is that most working women work what sociologist Arlie Hochschild has called the *second shift:* an evening of child care and housework following a full day of paid work.

LO 32-3 Describe major developments in the rise of feminism in the United States, including the effects of the abortion debate.

- During two major waves of feminism in the United States—one in the mid-1800s and one in the mid-1900s—women experienced a collective consciousness—a sense of sisterhood—in opposition to long-entrenched sexist attitudes and practices that support male dominance and female subservience.
- Today, many women agree with the positions of the feminist movement but reject the label *feminist,* apparently taking for granted the improved status of women.
- The issue of abortion has bitterly divided the United States (as well as other nations), pitting pro-choice activists against pro-life activists.
- The abortion issue has mobilized many women in a new spirit of feminism directed against paternalistic attitudes and practices enforced by predominantly male legislators and jurists that limit women's control over their own health decisions.

KEY TERMS

Feminism An ideology that favors equal rights for women.

Glass ceiling An invisible barrier that blocks the promotion of a qualified individual in a work environment because of the individual's gender, race, or ethnicity.

Glass escalator The advantage men experience in occupations dominated by women.

Institutional discrimination The denial of opportunities and equal rights to individuals and groups that results from the normal operations of a society.

Second shift The double burden—work outside the home followed by child care and housework—that many women face and few men share equitably.

Sexism The ideology that one sex is superior to the other.

The Case of . . . Switching It Up

When Steve Jacobs was downsized out of his job as a claims adjuster for an insurance company, his wife, Mia, jumped at the chance to turn her "hobby" into a full-time career. "Staying home with our three kids, I had become involved in all the usual school projects and extracurriculars. That meant I was always baking for one fundraiser or another," Mia says. "Over the years, I realized two things: I was good at it, and I enjoyed it."

At first, Steve was weary of his wife's plan for "Mia's Cakes." But she showed him her business plan. She would rent commercial oven space. Hire an assistant only during the wedding season. Make her own deliveries. "She really had the thing thought out," Steve says. "And she'd made projections based on the real numbers of similar businesses. I was surprised, and impressed."

As Mia began making cakes—and money—Steve took over most of the household chores and ferried the kids to their afterschool activities. "It sounds simple," he says, "but housework is never-ending and kids need a *lot*, not just your time, but *you*." Still, Steve found himself enjoying the new bond with his kids. "I even enjoy finding ways to streamline the work that needs to be done around here," he says. "To tell you the truth, I always hated insurance, and I hated going to the office every day. But, if you're a guy, that's what you're supposed to do."

1. If Mia had wanted to resume a career she'd had before the kids rather than start a new business, what challenges might she have encountered?

2. Why do you think Steve was surprised that Mia had developed a smart, detailed business plan?

3. How does Steve exemplify the theory of multiple masculinities?

4. When meeting Steve for the first time, how do you think men will react to his announcement that he's a stay-at-home dad? What about women?

Writing Essays and Papers

As a sociology student, you will have to write essays and papers in which you discuss an important issue; state an opinion; argue your opinion, citing evidence and using logical reasoning to support it; and draw a conclusion. To do this, you will use the critical thinking skills that we discussed in the previous P.O.W.E.R. Study Strategy—but this time, in writing. Here's how to do it.

- Before you write a word, read your assignment. Carefully. Several times. Think about the topic, recalling what you already know.

- Brainstorm ideas about the topic *without filtering them.* For about 15 minutes, write down anything and everything that comes to mind.
- Use a visual concept map, which graphically shows how concepts are related to one another, to organize your notes into categories: facts, opinions, major ideas, supporting ideas, evidence, counterarguments, and conclusions.

W Work

- Write down a simple statement of your main idea—for example: *This paper will discuss income inequality in the United States.*
- Write down a *thesis statement,* in which you state the opinion that you will argue in the rest of the paper—for example: *The growing income and wealth gap between the rich and everyone else is a ticking bomb that is due to explode.* Your job in the paper is to turn your opinion into fact through the use of evidence and logic.
- Write down ideas on how you plan to support your thesis. Write down at least three sources of evidence (e.g., books, articles, online editorials). These should come from trustworthy sources. You don't have to have quotations yet—just where you intend to find them.
- Write a conclusion that you plan to reach in the end. (*Unless we do X, the result will be Y.*) This may change as you do your research, but it is good to have a point to aim for.
- Outline your argument. Be sure it follows a clear and logical path—for example: (1) evidence of an income gap; (2) evidence that the gap is growing; (3) evidence that the gap is doing harm; (4) evidence of increasing public reaction against the gap; and (5) your conclusion.
- Flesh it out: Do your research, gather your facts and evidence, and add substance to each paragraph. You should have an introductory paragraph, three to five support and discussion paragraphs, and a concluding paragraph.
- As you make statements, remember to ask, *How do I know this is true?*

- Read your draft paper. Check it for sense, typos, spelling, word choice, and grammar. Ask someone else to read it, too. Then revise.
- Is your logic clear? Have you left any steps out? Did you convince yourself?

R Rethink

- When your instructor returns your paper, read the comments carefully. If you don't understand something, ask about it.
- Don't be discouraged. Learn something from every paper.

Are You a Strategic Writer?

Writing top-grade essays and papers requires thought and organization. Hint: Starting a paper three hours before it's due may get the job done, but probably not *well* done. To rate your skills in this area, check the appropriate box after each item, then add up your score using this scale:

Always = 2
Sometimes = 1
Rarely = 0

	Always	Sometimes	Rarely
1. I give myself time to brainstorm ideas for my paper so that I can choose the best ones.			
2. My thesis statement is a clearly expressed opinion that I will argue in my paper.			
3. I make a list of the sources I will use before I start writing.			
4. The first thing I do is to read through the assignment several times to make sure I understand what is expected.			
5. Part of my prep is to make a concept map of my main ideas. Then, I add evidence, opinions, and counterarguments.			
6. I give myself time to revise my paper.			
7. I outline the argument I will use in my paper to check that it makes sense.			
8. I use at least three reliable sources. My papers are not rehashes of material on the web.			
9. I write a conclusion before I start my paper, so I will have a sense of where I'm going, even if my conclusion gets revised as I work.			
10. I check my paper over for any gaps in evidence or logic.			

SCORE:

17–20: You understand how important the upfront thought and organization work is to writing a great paper. You also know that review and revision strengthen and streamline your argument.

13–16: You may be strong in planning but slapdash in execution. Or, you may jump in without preparation but have good writing skills, which more planning would polish. Either way, use the items here to fill in your weak spots.

12 or below: Writing good papers will become a lot easier if you follow the ideas in this chapter's P.O.W.E.R. Study Strategies: Writing Essays and Papers.

11 The Family and Human Sexuality

MODULE 33 Global View of the Family

MODULE 34 Marriage and Family

MODULE 35 Trends in Family Life and Sexuality

Sociology at WORK COUPLES THERAPIST

ROBIN HAMADA is part of a family therapy practice in Seattle. "I do what used to be known as marriage counseling, but now is often called couples counseling," she says. Hamada has a lengthy waiting list. "I try to refer people to other therapists because a relationship in trouble can't wait two or three years, but everyone I know is full up," Hamada says. "Intimate relationships are under a lot of strain today. Two parents working or the flipside, losing their jobs. Mortgage foreclosures. Stolen pensions. Boomerang kids invading the empty nest. Step-kids. Adopted kids. Love can take a real beating out there."

Another sign of the times is the number of lesbian and gay couples Hamada counsels. "It's been fascinating," she says. "All this ruckus about gay marriage. Well, from where I sit, all couples, whatever their orientation, experience the same conflicts. There's always the question of how power will be shared. Then there are the specific issues of money, sex, and how to raise the kids. As painful as these situations are, I find a kind of beauty in our universal human need to try to build a life with another person." ■

Looking Ahead

THIS CHAPTER ADDRESSES FAMILY AND HUMAN SEXUALITY IN THE United States and other parts of the world. We will begin by looking at the family as an institution and considering it from the functionalist, conflict, interactionist, and feminist points of view. We'll examine variations in marital patterns and family life, including child rearing, paying particular attention to the increasing numbers of people in dual-income and single-parent families. Next, we'll examine divorce in the United States and consider diverse lifestyles such as cohabitation and marriage without children. We'll conclude by discussing the complexity of human sexual behavior, and the growing acceptance of lesbian and gay relationships. Finally, in the Social Policy section we'll confront the controversial issue of gay marriage.

MODULE 33 Global View of the Family

P Prepare <u>Learning Objectives</u>

LO 33-1 Describe the types of family arrangements that exist in different cultures.

LO 33-2 Explain different kinship and authority patterns prevalent in families around the world.

LO 33-3 Analyze the family using the functionalist, conflict, interactionist, and feminist perspectives.

Among Tibetans, a woman may be married simultaneously to more than one man, usually brothers. This system allows sons to share the limited amount of good land. Among the Betsileo of Madagascar, a man has multiple wives, each one living in a different village where he cultivates rice. Wherever he has the best rice field, that wife is considered his first or senior wife. Among the Yanomami of Brazil and Venezuela, it is considered proper to have sexual relations with your opposite-sex cousins if they are the children of your mother's brother or your father's sister. But if your opposite-sex cousins are the children of your mother's sister or your father's brother, the same practice is considered to be incest (Haviland et al. 2008; Kottak 2011).

LO **33-1** Universal Principles

As these examples illustrate, there are many variations in the family from culture to culture. Despite the differences, however, the family is a universal social institution, found in every culture. A **family** can be defined as a set of people related by blood, marriage or some other agreed-on relationship, or adoption, who share the primary responsibility for reproduction and caring for members of society. Certain general principles concerning its composition, kinship patterns, and authority patterns are universal.

COMPOSITION: WHAT IS THE FAMILY?

The family of today is not what it was a century ago, or even a generation ago. New roles, new gender distinctions, and new child-rearing patterns have all combined to create new forms of family life. Today, for example, more and more women are taking the breadwinner's role, whether married or as a single parent. Blended families—the result of divorce and remarriage—are almost the norm. And many people are seeking intimate relationships without being married, whether in gay partnerships or in cohabiting arrangements (Cherlin 2009, 2011). The word *family* is inadequate to describe some of these arrangements, including cohabiting partners, same-sex marriages, and single-parent households. In 2011, the nation crossed a major threshold: the majority of births to women under age 30 occurred outside of marriage (Cherlin 2011; Wildsmith et al. 2011).

Many people still think of the family in very narrow terms—as a married couple and their unmarried children living together. However, this is but one type of family, what sociologists refer to as a **nuclear family**. The term *nuclear family* is well chosen, since this type of family serves as the nucleus, or core, on which larger family groups are built.

Most people in the United States see the nuclear family as the preferred family arrangement. Yet by 2000, only about a third of the nation's family households fit this model. The proportion of households in the United States that is composed of married couples with children at home has decreased steadily over the past 40 years and is expected to continue shrinking. At the same time, the number of single-parent households has increased (Figure 11-1).

From the perspective of . . .

A Preschool Teacher What are some ways you can demonstrate and foster respect for the variety of family patterns (extended families, single parents, gay/lesbian parents, stepparents) represented by your students?

A family in which relatives—such as grandparents, aunts, or uncles—live in the same home as parents and their children is known as an **extended family**. Although not common, such living arrangements do exist in the United States. The structure of the extended family offers certain advantages over that of the nuclear family. Crises such as death, divorce, and illness put less strain on family members, since more people can provide assistance and emotional support. In addition, the extended family constitutes a larger economic unit than the nuclear family. If the family is engaged in a common enterprise—a farm or a small business—the additional family members may represent the difference between prosperity and failure.

In considering these different family types, we have limited ourselves to the form of marriage that is characteristic of the United States—monogamy. The term **monogamy** describes a form of marriage in which an individual has only one partner. Until recently, the societal expectation was that the couple would be a man and a woman. Increasingly, however, same-sex couples are entering legal marriages. Regardless, observers, noting the high rate of divorce in the United States, have suggested that "serial monogamy" is a more accurate description of the form marriage takes in this country. In **serial monogamy**, a person may have several spouses in a lifetime, but only one spouse at a time.

Some cultures allow an individual to have several husbands or wives simultaneously. This form of marriage is known as **polygamy**. In fact, most societies throughout the world, past and present, have preferred polygamy to monogamy. According to a mid-20th century analysis of 565 societies, polygamy was preferred in more than 80 percent. While polygamy declined steadily through most of the 20th century, in at least five countries in Africa 20 percent of men still have polygamous marriages (Murdock 1949, 1957; Population Reference Bureau 1996).

There are two basic types of polygamy. According to Murdock, the most common—endorsed by the majority of cultures he sampled—is *polygyny*. **Polygyny** refers to the marriage of a man to more than one woman at the same time. The wives are often sisters, who are expected to hold similar values and have already had experience sharing a household. In polygynous

FIGURE 11-1 **U.S. HOUSEHOLDS BY FAMILY TYPE, 1970–2012**

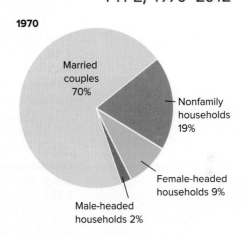

1970

Married couples 70%

Nonfamily households 19%

Female-headed households 9%

Male-headed households 2%

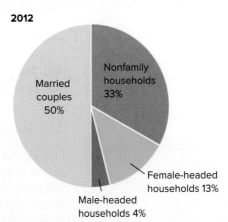

2012

Married couples 50%

Nonfamily households 33%

Female-headed households 13%

Male-headed households 4%

Note: Nonfamily households include women and men living alone or exclusively with people to whom they are not related, as in a college dormitory, homeless shelter, or military base.
Source: Bureau of the Census 1981:2; Vespa et al. 2013:5, also Table HH1.

societies, relatively few men actually have multiple spouses. Most individuals live in monogamous families; having multiple wives is viewed as a mark of status.

The other principal variation of polygamy is **polyandry**, in which a woman may have more than one husband at the same time. Such is the case in the culture of the Nyinba. Polyandry, however, is exceedingly rare today, though it is accepted in some extremely poor societies. Like many other societies, polyandrous cultures devalue the social worth of women (Zeitzen 2008).

By the end of the 20th century, polygamy had been relegated to the margins of U.S. society, and to discussion of other cultures. Recently, however, it has resurfaced. As the concept of marriage is redefined to include same-sex marriage, Mormon fundamentalists and Muslims who practice polygamy have asked why it should not also embrace polygamy. Some support this perspective; others suspect that the issue is being raised by those who oppose same-sex marriage. This is certainly not the first time that family cultural practices have collided with social norms (Keenan 2013).

LO 33-2 KINSHIP PATTERNS: TO WHOM ARE WE RELATED?

Many of us can trace our roots by looking at a family tree or by listening to elderly family members talk about their lives—and about the lives of ancestors who died long before we were born. Yet a person's lineage is more than simply a personal history; it also reflects societal patterns that govern descent. In every culture, children encounter relatives to whom they are expected to show an emotional attachment. The state of being related to others is called **kinship**. Kinship is culturally learned, however, and is not totally determined by biological or marital ties. For example, adoption creates a kinship tie that is legally acknowledged and socially accepted.

The family and the kin group are not necessarily one and the same. Whereas the family is a household unit, kin do not always live together or function as a collective body on a daily basis. Kin groups include aunts, uncles, cousins, in-laws, and so forth. In a society such as the United States, the kinship group may come together only rarely, for a wedding or funeral. However, kinship ties frequently create obligations and responsibilities. We may feel compelled to assist our kin, and we may feel free to call on them for many types of aid, including loans and babysitting.

How do we identify kinship groups? The principle of descent assigns people to kinship groups according to their relationship to a mother or father. There are three primary ways of determining descent. The United States follows the system of **bilateral descent**, which means that both sides of a person's family are regarded as equally important. For example, no higher value is given to the brothers of one's father than to the brothers of one's mother.

Most societies—according to George Murdock, 64 percent—give preference to one side of the family or the other in tracing descent. In **patrilineal** (from the Latin *pater,* "father") **descent**, only the father's relatives are significant in terms of property, inheritance, and emotional ties. Conversely, in societies that favor **matrilineal** (from the Latin *mater,* "mother") **descent**, only the mother's relatives are significant.

New forms of reproductive technology will necessitate a new way of looking at kinship. Today, a combination of biological and social processes can "create" a family member, requiring that more distinctions be made about who is related to whom.

AUTHORITY PATTERNS: WHO RULES?

Imagine that you have recently married and must begin to make decisions about the future of your new family. You and your spouse face many questions. Where will you live? How will you furnish your home? Who will do the cooking, the shopping, the cleaning? Whose friends will be invited to dinner? Each time a decision must be made, an issue is raised: Who has the power to make the decision? In simple terms, who rules the family? Conflict theorists examine these questions in the context of traditional gender stratification, under which men have held a dominant position over women.

Societies vary in the way power is distributed within the family. A society that expects males to dominate in all family decision making is termed a **patriarchy**. In patriarchal societies, such as Iran, the eldest male often wields the greatest power, although wives are expected to be treated with respect and kindness. An Iranian woman's status is typically defined by her relationship to a male relative, usually as a wife or daughter. In many patriarchal societies, women find it more difficult to obtain a divorce than a man does. In contrast, in a **matriarchy**, women have greater authority than men. Matriarchies, which are very uncommon, emerged among Native American tribal societies and in nations in which men were absent for long periods because of warfare or food-gathering expeditions (Farr 1999).

Although spouses in an egalitarian family may not share all their decisions, they regard themselves as equals. This pattern of authority is becoming more common in the United States.

In a third type of authority pattern, the **egalitarian family**, spouses are regarded as equals. That does not mean, however, that all decisions are shared in such families. Wives may hold authority in some spheres, husbands in others. Many sociologists believe the egalitarian family has begun to replace the patriarchal family as the social norm in the United States.

LO 33-3 Sociological Perspectives on the Family

Do we really need the family? Over a century ago, Friedrich Engels ([1884] 1959), a colleague of Karl Marx, described the family as the ultimate source of social inequality because of its role in the transfer of power, property, and privilege. More recently, conflict theorists have argued that the family contributes to societal injustice, denies women opportunities that are extended to men, and limits freedom in sexual expression and mate selection. In contrast, the functionalist view focuses on the ways in which the family gratifies the needs of its members and contributes to social stability. The interactionist view considers the intimate, face-to-face relationships that occur in the family. And the feminist approach examines the role of the wife and mother, especially in the absence of an adult male.

FUNCTIONALIST PERSPECTIVE

The family performs six paramount functions, first outlined nearly 80 years ago by sociologist William F. Ogburn (Ogburn and Tibbits 1934):

1. **Reproduction.** For a society to maintain itself, it must replace dying members. In this sense, the family contributes to human survival through its function of reproduction.

2. **Protection.** In all cultures, the family assumes the ultimate responsibility for the protection and upbringing of children.

3. **Socialization.** Parents and other kin monitor a child's behavior and transmit the norms, values, and language of their culture to the child.

4. **Regulation of sexual behavior.** Sexual norms are subject to change both over time (for instance, in the customs for dating) and across cultures (compare strict Saudi Arabia to

the more permissive Denmark). However, whatever the time period or cultural values of a society, standards of sexual behavior are most clearly defined within the family circle.

5. **Affection and companionship.** Ideally, the family provides members with warm and intimate relationships, helping them to feel satisfied and secure. Of course, a family member may find such rewards outside the family—from peers, in school, at work— and may even perceive the home as an unpleasant or abusive setting. Nevertheless, we expect our relatives to understand us, to care for us, and to be there for us when we need them.

6. **Provision of social status.** We inherit a social position because of the family background and reputation of our parents and siblings. The family presents the newborn child with an ascribed status based on race and ethnicity that helps to determine his or her place within society's stratification system. Moreover, family resources affect children's ability to pursue certain opportunities, such as higher education.

Traditionally, the family has fulfilled a number of other functions, such as providing religious training, education, and recreational outlets. But Ogburn argued that other social institutions have gradually assumed many of those functions. Education once took place at the family fireside; now it is the responsibility of professionals working in schools and colleges. Even the family's traditional recreational function has often been transferred to outside groups such as soccer leagues, athletic clubs, and Twitter.

CONFLICT PERSPECTIVE

Conflict theorists view the family not as a contributor to social stability, but as a reflection of the inequality in wealth and power that is found within the larger society. Feminist and conflict theorists note that the family has traditionally legitimized and perpetuated male dominance. Throughout most of human history—and in a wide range of societies— husbands have exercised overwhelming power and authority within the family. Not until the first wave of contemporary feminism in the United States, in the mid-1800s, was there a substantial challenge to the historic status of wives and children as the legal property of husbands.

While the egalitarian family has become a more common pattern in the United States in recent decades—owing in good part to the activism of feminists beginning in the late 1960s and early 1970s—male dominance over the family has hardly disappeared. Sociologists have found that while married men are increasing their involvement in child care, their wives still perform a disproportionate amount of it. Furthermore, for every stay-at-home dad there are 38 stay-at-home moms. And unfortunately, many husbands reinforce their power and control over wives and children through acts of domestic violence (Fields 2004:11–12; Garcia-Moreno et al. 2005; Sayer et al. 2004).

Conflict theorists also view the family as an economic unit that contributes to societal injustice. The family is the basis for transferring power, property, and privilege from one generation to the next. Although the United States is widely viewed as a land of opportunity, social mobility is restricted in important ways. Children inherit the privileged or less-than-privileged social and economic status of their parents (and in some cases, of earlier generations). The social class of parents significantly influences children's socialization experiences and the degree of protection they receive. Thus, the socioeconomic status of a child's family will have a marked influence on his or her nutrition, health care, housing, educational opportunities, and in many respects, life chances as an adult. For this reason, conflict theorists argue that the family helps to maintain inequality.

INTERACTIONIST PERSPECTIVE

Interactionists focus on the micro level of family and other intimate relationships. They are interested in how individuals interact with one another, whether they are cohabiting partners or longtime married couples. For example, in a study of both Black and White two-parent households, researchers found that when fathers are more involved with their children (reading to them, helping them with homework, or restricting their television viewing), the children have fewer behavior problems, get along better with others, and are more responsible (Mosley and Thomson 1995).

Another interactionist study might examine the role of the stepparent. The increased number of single parents who remarry has sparked an interest in those who are helping to raise other people's children. Studies have found that stepmothers are more likely than stepfathers to accept the blame for bad relations with their stepchildren. Interactionists theorize that stepfathers (like most fathers) may simply be unaccustomed to interacting directly with children when the mother isn't there (Bray and Kelly 1999; F. Furstenberg and Cherlin 1991).

FEMINIST PERSPECTIVE

Because "women's work" has traditionally focused on family life, feminist sociologists have taken a strong interest in the family as a social institution. Research on gender roles in child care and household chores has been extensive. Sociologists have looked particularly closely at how women's work outside the home impacts their child care and housework— duties Arlie Hochschild (1990, 2005, 2012) has referred to as the "second shift." Today, researchers recognize that for many women, the second shift includes the care of aging parents as well.

Feminist theorists have urged social scientists and social agencies to rethink the notion that families in which no adult male is present are automatically a cause for concern, or even dysfunctional. They have also contributed to research on single women, single-parent households, and lesbian couples. In the case of single mothers, researchers have focused on the resiliency of many such households, despite economic stress. According to Velma McBride Murray and her colleagues (2001) at the University of Georgia, such studies show that among African Americans, single mothers draw heavily on kinfolk for material resources, parenting advice, and social support. Considering feminist research on the family as a whole, one researcher concluded that the family is the "source of women's strength" (V. Taylor et al. 2009).

Finally, feminists who take the interactionist perspective stress the need to investigate neglected topics in family studies. For instance, in a growing number of dual-income households, the wife earns a higher income than the husband. In 2005, a study of 58 married couples revealed that 26 percent of the wives earned more than their husbands. In 1981, the proportion was just 16 percent. Yet beyond individual case studies, little research has been done on how these families may differ from those in which the husband is the major breadwinner (Wills and Risman 2006).

Table 11-1 summarizes the four major theoretical perspectives on the family.

[Study Alert]

Use Table 11-1 to help you to understand the different sociological perspectives on the family.

Interactionists are particularly interested in the ways in which parents relate to each other and to their children. The close and loving relationship illustrated here is one of the foundations of a strong family.

Tracking Sociological Perspectives

TABLE 11-1 SOCIOLOGICAL PERSPECTIVES ON THE FAMILY

Theoretical Perspective	Emphasis
Functionalist	The family as a contributor to social stability Roles of family members
Conflict	The family as a perpetuator of inequality Transmission of poverty or wealth across generations
Interactionist	Relationships among family members
Feminist	The family as a perpetuator of gender roles Female-headed households

E Evaluate

Read each question carefully and then select or provide the best answer.

1. Alice, age seven, lives in a private home with her parents, her grandmother, and her aunt. Alice's family is an example of a(n)
   a. nuclear family.
   b. dysfunctional family.
   c. extended family.
   d. polygynous family.

2. In which form of marriage may a person have several spouses in his or her lifetime, but only one spouse at a time?
   a. serial monogamy
   b. monogamy
   c. polygamy
   d. polyandry

3. According to the functionalist perspective, which of the following is *not* one of the paramount functions performed by the family?
   a. mediation
   b. reproduction
   c. regulation of sexual behavior
   d. affection and companionship

4. As _____ theorists point out, the social class of couples and their children significantly influences the socialization experiences to which the children are exposed and the protection they receive.

5. _____ focus on the micro level of family and other intimate relationships; for example, they are interested in whether people are cohabiting partners or are longtime married couples.

Answers

1 (c); 2 (a); 3 (a); 4 conflict; 5 Interactionists

R Rethink

Consider these questions to get a deeper understanding of the material.

1. From a woman's point of view, what are the economic advantages and disadvantages of monogamous, polygamous, and polyandrous families? What are the advantages and disadvantages of each of these family situations for men?

2. How would functionalist, conflict, interactionist, and feminist theorists explain a polygamous family structure?

RECAP

LO 33-1 Describe the types of family arrangements that exist in different cultures.

- Although the family is a universal institution, types of families vary from culture to culture and even within the same culture.
- The multigenerational structure of the extended family can offer certain advantages over that of the nuclear family.
- Both monogamy (one partner) and polygamy (more than one partner) are forms of marriage practiced widely. Polygyny (multiple wives) is much more common than polyandry (multiple husbands). In the United States, polygamy is very rare, but serial monogamy is more prevalent than lifelong monogamy.

LO 33-2 Explain different kinship and authority patterns prevalent in families around the world.

- Societies determine kinship by descent from both parents (bilateral descent), from the father only (patrilineal descent), or from the mother only (matrilineal descent).
- The bilateral descent model of the United States is in the minority. Most modern societies are either patrilineal or matrilineal.

- Societies in which males dominate family decision making are called patriarchies, while women-led families are called matriarchies.
- In the United States, a third model, the egalitarian family in which authority is shared, appears to be gaining ground on the patriarchal pattern of domination as the social norm.

LO 33-3 Analyze the family using the functionalist, conflict, interactionist, and feminist perspectives.

- William F. Ogburn, writing from the functionalist perspective, outlined six basic functions of the family: reproduction, protection, socialization, regulation of sexual behavior, affection and companionship, and the provision of social status.
- Conflict theorists argue that male dominance of the family contributes to societal injustice and denies women opportunities that are extended to men.
- Interactionists focus on how individuals interact in the family and in other intimate relationships.
- Feminists stress the need to broaden research on the family. Like conflict theorists, they see the family's role in socializing children as the primary source of sexism.

KEY TERMS

Bilateral descent A kinship system in which both sides of a person's family are regarded as equally important.

Egalitarian family An authority pattern in which spouses are regarded as equals.

Extended family A family in which relatives—such as grandparents, aunts, or uncles—live in the same home as parents and their children.

Family A set of people related by blood, marriage, or some other agreed-on relationship, or adoption, who share the primary responsibility for reproduction and caring for members of society.

Kinship The state of being related to others.

Matriarchy A society in which women dominate in family decision making.

Matrilineal descent A kinship system in which only the mother's relatives are significant.

Monogamy A form of marriage in which an individual has only one partner.

Nuclear family A married couple and their unmarried children living together.

Patriarchy A society in which men dominate in family decision making.

Patrilineal descent A kinship system in which only the father's relatives are significant.

Polyandry A form of polygamy in which a woman may have more than one husband at the same time.

Polygamy A form of marriage in which an individual may have several husbands or wives simultaneously.

Polygyny A form of polygamy in which a man may have more than one wife at the same time.

Serial monogamy A form of marriage in which a person may have several spouses in his or her lifetime, but only one spouse at a time.

MODULE 34 Marriage and Family

P Prepare Learning Objectives

LO 34-1 Describe variations in marital patterns and family life in the United States and other cultures.

LO 34-2 Discuss the various child-rearing patterns prevalent in U.S. family life today.

O Organize Module Outline

Courtship and Mate Selection
    Aspects of Mate Selection
    The Love Relationship
Variations in Family Life and Intimate Relationships
    Social Class Differences
    Racial and Ethnic Differences

W Work

Currently, over 95 percent of all men and women in the United States marry at least once during their lifetimes. Historically, the most consistent aspect of family life in this country has been the high rate of marriage. In fact, despite the high rate of divorce, there are some indications of a miniboom in marriages of late.

In this module, we will examine various aspects of love, marriage, and parenthood in the United States and contrast them with cross-cultural examples. Though we're used to thinking of romance and mate selection as strictly a matter of individual preference, sociological analysis tells us that social institutions and distinctive cultural norms and values also play an important role.

LO 34-1 Courtship and Mate Selection

In the past, most couples met their partners through family or friends in their neighborhood or workplace. Today, however, many couples meet on the Internet, through online dating services.

Internet romance is only the latest courtship practice. In the central Asian nation of Uzbekistan and many other traditional cultures, courtship is defined largely through the interaction of two sets of parents, who arrange marriages for their children. Typically, a young Uzbekistani woman will be socialized to eagerly anticipate her marriage to a man whom she has met only once, when he is presented to her family at the time of the final inspection of her dowry. In the United States, in contrast, courtship is conducted primarily by individuals who have a romantic interest in each other. In our culture, courtship often requires these individuals to rely heavily on intricate games, gestures, and signals. Despite such differences, courtship—whether in the United States, Uzbekistan, or elsewhere—is influenced by the norms and values of the larger society (C. Williams 1995).

One unmistakable trend in mate selection is that the process appears to be taking longer today than in the past. A variety of factors, including concerns about financial security and personal independence, has contributed to this delay in marriage. Back in 1966, men were typically under age 23 and women under 21 when they were first married. In 2013, the average age was 29 for men and close to 27 years for women (Bureau of the Census 2013b). Most people are now well into their 20s before they marry, both in the United States and in most other countries (Figure 11-2).

Although most interracial couples are not as visible as Robert De Niro and Grace Hightower, such unions are becoming increasingly common and accepted. They are also blurring the definitions of race. Will the children of these couples be considered Black or White? Why do you think so?

ASPECTS OF MATE SELECTION

Many societies have explicit or unstated rules that define potential mates as acceptable or unacceptable. These norms can be distinguished in terms of endogamy and exogamy. **Endogamy** (from the Greek *endon,* "within") specifies the groups within which a spouse must be found and prohibits marriage with others. For example, in the United States, many people are expected to marry within their racial, ethnic, or religious group, and are strongly discouraged or even prohibited from marrying outside the group. Endogamy is intended to reinforce the cohesiveness of the group by suggesting to the young that they should marry someone "of their own kind."

Even in the United States, interracial and interethnic marriages are still the exception. According to a report released in 2012, among newly married White couples, about 9 percent marry someone of a different race or ethnicity. Among African American couples the proportion is 17 percent; among Latinos, 26 percent; and among Asian Americans, 28 percent (W. Wang 2012).

In contrast, **exogamy** (from the Greek *exo,* "outside") requires mate selection outside certain groups, usually one's family or certain kinfolk. The **incest taboo**, a social norm common to virtually all societies, prohibits sexual relationships between certain culturally specified relatives. For those of us in the United States, this taboo means that we must marry outside the nuclear family. We cannot marry our siblings, and in most states we cannot marry our first cousins.

Another factor that influences the selection of a marriage partner is **homogamy**, the conscious or unconscious tendency to select a mate with personal characteristics similar to one's own. The "like marries like" rule can be seen in couples with similar personalities and cultural interests. However, mate selection is unpredictable. Though some people may follow the homogamous pattern, others observe the "opposites attract" rule: one person is dependent and submissive—almost childishly so—while the other is dominant and controlling.

THE LOVE RELATIONSHIP

Today's generation of college students seems more likely to hook up or cruise in large packs than to engage in the romantic dating relationships of their parents' and grandparents' generations. Still, at some point in their adult lives, the great majority of today's students will meet someone they love and enter into a long-term relationship that focuses on creating a family.

Parents in the United States tend to value love highly as a rationale for marriage, so they encourage their children to develop intimate relationships based on love and affection. Songs, films, books, magazines, television shows, and even cartoons and comic books reinforce the theme of love. At the same time, our society expects parents and peers to help a person confine his or her search for a mate to "socially acceptable" members of the opposite sex.

Though most people in the United States take the importance of falling in love for granted, the coupling of love and marriage is by no means a cultural universal. Many of the world's cultures give priority in mate selection to factors other than romantic feelings. In societies with *arranged marriages* engineered by parents or religious authorities, economic considerations play a significant role. The newly married couple is expected to develop a feeling of love *after* the legal union is formalized, if at all (J. Lee 2013).

FIGURE 11-2

MEDIAN AGE AT FIRST MARRIAGE IN EIGHT COUNTRIES

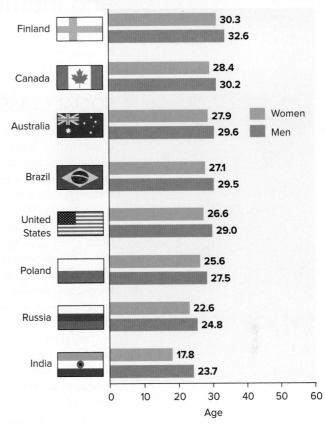

Sources: Bureau of the Census 2013b; United Nations Statistics Division (2013). *Demographic Yearbook 2013.* New York: United Nations.

Study Alert

Be able to distinguish among *endogamy* (specifies the groups within which a spouse may be chosen and prohibits marriage outside these groups), *exogamy* (requires marriage outside certain groups, usually family members), and *homogamy* (the tendency to marry someone with similar personal characteristics).

LO 34-1 Variations in Family Life and Intimate Relationships

Within the United States, social class, race, and ethnicity create variations in family life. Studying these variations will give us a more sophisticated understanding of contemporary family styles in our country.

SOCIAL CLASS DIFFERENCES

Various studies have documented the differences in family organization among social classes in the United States. In the upper class, the emphasis is on lineage and maintenance of family position. If you are in the upper class, you are not simply a member of a nuclear family, but rather a member of a larger family tradition (think of the Rockefellers or the Kennedys). As a result, upper-class families are quite concerned about what they see as proper training for children.

Lower-class families do not often have the luxury of worrying about the "family name"; they must first struggle to pay their bills and survive the crises often associated with a life of poverty. Such families are more likely to have only one parent at home, which creates special challenges in child care and financial management. Children from lower-class families typically assume adult responsibilities—including marriage and parenthood—at an earlier age than children from affluent homes. In part, that is because they may lack the money needed to remain in school.

Social class differences in family life are less striking today than they once were. In the past, family specialists agreed that the contrasts in child-rearing practices were pronounced. Lower-class families were found to be more authoritarian in rearing children and more inclined to use physical punishment. Middle-class families were more permissive and more restrained in punishing their children. And compared to lower-class families, middle-class families tended to schedule more of their children's time, or even to overstructure it. However, these differences may have narrowed as more and more families from all social classes turned to the same books, magazines, and even television talk shows for advice on rearing children (Kronstadt and Favreault 2008; Luster et al. 1989; J. Sherman and Harris 2012).

Among the poor, women often play a significant role in the economic support of the family. Men may earn low wages, may be unemployed, or may be entirely absent from the family. In 2012, 31 percent of all families headed by women with no husband present fell below the federal government's poverty line. In comparison, the poverty rate for married couples was only 6.2 percent. The disproportionate representation of female-headed households among the poor is a persistent and growing trend, referred to by sociologists as the *feminization of poverty* (DeNavas-Walt et al. 2013:17).

Finally, in her book *The Accordion Family*, Katherine S. Newman (2012) noted that the accordion or boomerang family differs by social class. An upper-middle-class family can afford to provide space to an adult child who is working toward an advanced degree. Less privileged families tend to hang on to their adult children for the labor or income they can contribute to the family's welfare.

Many racial and ethnic groups appear to have distinctive family characteristics. However, racial and class factors are often closely related. In examining family life among racial and ethnic minorities, keep in mind that certain patterns may result from class as well as cultural factors.

RACIAL AND ETHNIC DIFFERENCES

The subordinate status of racial and ethnic minorities in the United States profoundly affects their family lives. For example, the lower incomes of African Americans, Native Americans, most Hispanic groups, and selected Asian American groups make creating and maintaining successful marital unions a difficult task. The economic restructuring of the past 60 years, described by sociologist William Julius Wilson (1996, 2009) and others, has especially affected people living in inner cities and desolate rural areas, such as reservations. Furthermore, the immigration policy of the United States has complicated the successful relocation of intact families from Asia and Latin America.

The African American family suffers from many negative and inaccurate stereotypes. It is true that in a significantly higher proportion of Black than White families, no husband is present in the home (Figure 11-3). Yet Black single mothers often belong to stable, functioning kin networks, which mitigate the pressures of sexism and racism. Members of these networks—predominantly female kin such as mothers, grandmothers, and aunts—ease financial strains by sharing goods and services. In addition to these strong kinship bonds, Black family life has emphasized deep religious commitment and high aspirations for achievement (DuBois [1909] 1970; F. Furstenberg 2007).

Like African Americans, Native Americans draw on family ties to cushion many of the hardships they face. On the Navajo reservation, for example, teenage parenthood is not regarded as the crisis that it is elsewhere in the United States. The Navajo trace their descent matrilineally. Traditionally, couples reside with the wife's family after marriage, allowing the grandparents to help with the child rearing. While the Navajo do not approve of teenage parenthood, the deep emotional commitment of their extended families provides a warm home environment for children, even when no father is present or involved (Dalla and Gamble 2001; John 2012).

Sociologists also have taken note of differences in family patterns among other racial and ethnic groups. For example, Mexican American men have been described as exhibiting a sense of virility, personal worth, and pride in their maleness that is called **machismo**. Mexican Americans are also described as being more familistic than many other subcultures. **Familism** (or *familismo*) refers to pride in the extended family, expressed through the maintenance of close ties and strong obligations to kinfolk outside the immediate family. Traditionally, Mexican Americans have placed proximity to their extended families above other needs and desires.

Although familism is often seen as a positive cultural attribute, it may also have negative consequences. Sociologists who have studied the relatively low college application rates of Hispanic students have found they have a strong desire to stay at home. Even the children of college-educated parents express this preference, which diminishes the likelihood of their getting a four-year degree and dramatically reduces the possibility that they will apply to a selective college.

These family patterns are changing, however, in response to changes in Latinos' social class standing, educational achievements, and occupations. Like other Americans, career-oriented Latinos in search of a mate but short on spare time are turning to Internet sites. As Latinos and other groups assimilate into the dominant culture of the United States, their family lives take on both the positive and negative characteristics associated with White households (Negroni 2012; Suárez and Perez 2012).

FIGURE 11-3 RISE OF SINGLE-PARENT FAMILIES IN THE UNITED STATES, 1970–2010

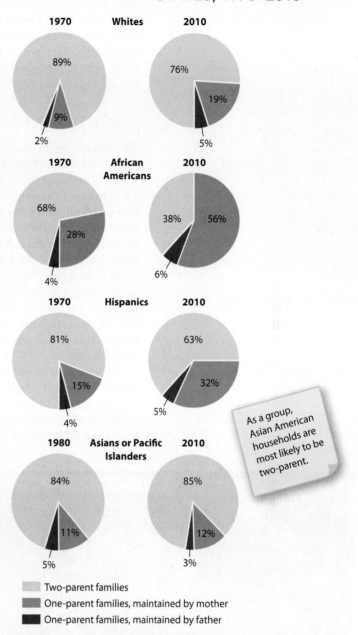

Two-parent families

One-parent families, maintained by mother

One-parent families, maintained by father

As a group, Asian American households are most likely to be two-parent.

Note: Families are groups with children under 18. Early data for Asian Americans are for 1980. Hispanics can be of any race. Not included are unrelated people living together with no children present. All data exclude the 11 percent of children in nonparental households.
Sources: Bureau of the Census 2008a:56, 2010c: Table FG10.

LO 34-2 Child-Rearing Patterns

The Nayars of southern India acknowledge the biological role of fathers, but the mother's eldest brother is responsible for her children. In contrast, uncles play only a peripheral role in child care in the United States. Caring for children is a universal function of the family, yet the ways in which different societies assign this function to family members can vary significantly. Even within the United States, child-rearing patterns are varied. We'll take a look here at parenthood and grandparenthood, adoption, dual-income families, single-parent families, and stepfamilies.

PARENTHOOD AND GRANDPARENTHOOD

The socialization of children is essential to the maintenance of any culture. Consequently, parenthood is one of the most important (and most demanding) social roles in the United States. Sociologist Alice Rossi (1968, 1984) has identified four factors that complicate the transition to parenthood and the role of socialization. First, there is little anticipatory socialization for the social role of caregiver. The normal school curriculum gives scant attention to the subjects most relevant to successful family life, such as child care and home maintenance. Second, only limited learning occurs during the period of pregnancy itself. Third, the transition to parenthood is quite abrupt. Unlike adolescence, it is not prolonged; unlike the transition to work, the duties of caregiving cannot be taken on gradually. Finally, in Rossi's view, our society lacks clear and helpful guidelines for successful parenthood. There is little consensus on how parents can produce happy and well-adjusted offspring—or even on what it means to be well adjusted. For these reasons, socialization for parenthood involves difficult challenges for most men and women in the United States.

In some homes, the full nest holds grandchildren. By 2009, 9 percent of White children, 17 percent of Black children, and 14 percent of Hispanic children lived with at least one grandparent. In about a third of these homes, no parent was present to assume responsibility for the youngsters. Special difficulties are inherent in such relationships, including legal custodial concerns, financial issues, and emotional problems for adults and youths alike. It is not surprising that support groups such as Grandparents as Parents have emerged to provide assistance (Kreider and Ellis 2011).

ADOPTION

In a legal sense, **adoption** is the transfer of the legal rights, responsibilities, and privileges of parenthood to a new legal parent or parents. In many cases, these rights are transferred from a biological parent or parents (often called birth parents) to an adoptive parent or parents. Every year, about 135,000 children are adopted (Child Welfare Information 2011).

Viewed from a functionalist perspective, government has a strong interest in encouraging adoption. Policymakers, in fact, have both a humanitarian and a financial stake in the process. In theory, adoption offers a stable family environment for children who otherwise might not receive

When nine-year-old Blake Brunson shows up for a basketball game, so do his *eight* grandparents—the result of his parents' remarriages. Blended families can be very supportive to children, but what message do they send to them on the permanency of marriage?

satisfactory care. Moreover, government data show that unwed mothers who keep their babies tend to be of lower socioeconomic status and often require public assistance to support their children. The government can lower its social welfare expenses, then, if children are transferred to economically self-sufficient families. From an interactionist perspective, however, adoption may require a child to adjust to a very different family environment and parental approach to child rearing.

There are two legal methods of adopting an unrelated person: the adoption may be arranged through a licensed agency, or in some states it may be arranged through a private agreement sanctioned by the courts. Adopted children may come from the United States or from abroad. In 2012, over 8,600 children entered the United States as the adopted children of U.S. citizens (Bureau of Consular Affairs 2013).

Having a new child is a major adjustment for everyone in the family; adopting a child is an even bigger adjustment. If the adopted child comes from another culture and is racially or ethnically different from the adopting family, the challenge is that much greater. Box 11-1 describes research on the adjustment that occurs when a U.S. family adopts a child from South Korea.

The 2010 earthquake in Haiti drew attention to the foreign perspective on international adoptions, which is not always positive. When well-meaning people from the United States arrived in Haiti to rescue alleged orphans and arrange for their adoption in other countries, government officials objected. Some of the children, it turned out, were not orphans; their parents were simply too poor to care for them. For the governments of overstressed developing nations, adoption can be both a solution and a problem.

Adoption is controversial not only abroad but at home as well. In some cases, those who adopt children are not married. In 1995, an important court decision in New York held that a couple does not need to be married to adopt a child. Under this ruling, unmarried heterosexual couples, lesbian couples, and gay couples can all adopt children in New York. Today, most states permit gay and lesbian couples to adopt. Significant restrictions or outright prohibitions exist in Mississippi, Nebraska, and Utah (ACLU 2014).

For every child who is adopted, many more remain the wards of state-sponsored child protective services. At any given time, around half a million children in the United States are living in foster care. Every year, about 52,000 of them are adopted; another 101,000 are eligible and waiting to be adopted (Department of Health and Human Services 2013).

DUAL-INCOME FAMILIES

The idea of a family consisting of a wage-earning husband and a wife who stays at home has largely given way to the dual-income household. Among married people between ages 25 and 64, 96 percent of the men and 69 percent of the women were in the labor force in 2010 (Bureau of the Census 2011a: Table 597).

Why has there been such a rise in the number of dual-income couples? A major factor is economic need, coupled with a desire by both men *and* women to pursue their careers. Evidence of this trend can be found in the rise in the number of married couples living apart for reasons other than marital discord. The 3.6 million couples who now live apart represent 1 out of every 33 marriages. More than half of them live farther than 100 miles apart, and half

Miles Harvey reads to his children via Skype. Harvey, who is happily married, lives 900 miles from his family in Chicago. He accepted a job in New Orleans for economic reasons.

11-1 TRANSRACIAL ADOPTION: THE EXPERIENCE OF CHILDREN FROM KOREA

Caleb Littell was born in South Korea and adopted by a White couple in the United States as an infant. He joined a loving family in the predominantly White suburb of Renton, Washington, just outside Seattle. Now in his 30s, Caleb always knew that he was loved and fiercely wanted by his parents. Still, he struggled with his identity. Why did he look different from his parents? Why was he adopted? What did it mean to be Korean? These questions didn't trouble him at home, but at school and in the wider community, where he was often teased for being "Oriental" or "Asian."

Transracial adoption raises special challenges.

His White parents, whom he identified with, didn't see him as different from themselves, he reasoned, yet people outside the family did—why? Caleb wasn't just hurt; he was confused.

This story, recounted by educator Mia Tuan and sociologist Jiannbin Lee Shiao, is all too familiar to children who have experienced **transracial adoption**, the adoption of a non-White child by White parents or a Hispanic child by non-Hispanics. According to a 2011 estimate, there are about 300,000 such children under age 16 in the United States today. Although this type of adoption has occurred for generations, it became more common in the 1990s with the increase in international adoptions. About 85 percent of international adoptions are transracial.

Although no single case is typical, the lifelong socialization of the transracially adopted child does present some special challenges. A child's relationship to his or her parents is an ascribed status, as is ethnicity or race. Korean children who were adopted by White families find that when they move outside their protective nuclear families, their ascribed identities are immediately questioned. Sociologists and other researchers point out that their experience reflects contemporary racial and ethnic relations in the United States. That is to say, these children find acceptance and opportunity as well as intolerance and conflict in their new home country.

Now in his 30s, Caleb always knew that he was loved and fiercely wanted by his parents. Still, he struggled with his identity.

Assessing the long-term success of transracial adoption is difficult, since the outcomes of raising children in general are complex. The researcher must separate normal parenting problems from transracial parenting problems. One common transracial parenting problem is that White parents may lack the individual experiences, and at first the resources, to transmit positive identity messages to their adopted children. For advice, parents often turn to support groups and online chat rooms. Some send their children to *heritage camps*, which have emerged over the last 30 years to immerse children in cultural experiences reflective of their cultural background, be it African, Asian, or Hispanic. Besides offering language instruction, such camps allow children to socialize with others who were transracially adopted. The degree and quality of support from other relatives and from the surrounding community is also important to the children's adjustment.

In terms of the children's adult identity, there is no single outcome. Adult Korean American adoptees may describe themselves as "Korean American," "Caucasian, except when looking in the mirror, " or "Amerasian trying to be White." Research indicates that their identification with Korea is weak, although it has strengthened a bit among more recent adoptees, as support structures have improved. Few of them really learn to speak the Korean language or to truly enjoy Korean food.

Let's Discuss

1. As a child, did you know anyone who may have been transracially adopted? If so, did the child fit in well with his or her peers? Relate your answer to the community you grew up in.
2. Compare the experience of transracial adoption to the experience of entering a blended family. From the child's point of view, what might be the advantages and disadvantages of each? From the parents' point of view, what might be the challenges of each?

Sources: Freundlich and Lieberthal 2000; Kreider 2011; Randolph and Holtzman 2010; Tuan and Shiao 2011; Woon 2005.

of those live 1,000 or more miles apart. Of course, couples living apart are nothing new; men have worked at transient jobs for generations as soldiers, truck drivers, or traveling salesmen. Now, however, the woman's job is often the one that creates the separation. The existence of such household arrangements reflects an acceptance of the egalitarian family type (Higgins et al. 2010; Holmes 2009; Silverman 2009).

SINGLE-PARENT FAMILIES

The 2004 *American Idol* winner Fantasia Barrino's song "Baby Mama" offers a tribute to young single mothers—a subject she knows about. Barrino was 17 when she became pregnant with her daughter. Though critics charged that the song sends the wrong message to teenage girls, Barrino says it is not about encouraging teens to have sex. Rather, she sees the song as an anthem for young mothers courageously trying to raise their children alone (Cherlin 2006).

Most households in the United States do not consist of two parents living with their unmarried children.

In recent decades, the stigma attached to unwed mothers and other single parents has significantly diminished. **Single-parent families**, in which only one parent is present to care for the children, can hardly be viewed as a rarity in the United States. In 2010, a single parent headed about 24 percent of White families with children under 18, 37 percent of Hispanic families with children, and 62 percent of African American families with children (see Figure 11-3).

The lives of single parents and their children are not inevitably more difficult than life in a traditional nuclear family. It is as inaccurate to assume that a single-parent family is necessarily deprived as it is to assume that a two-parent family is always secure and happy. Nevertheless, life in a single-parent family can be extremely stressful, in both economic and emotional terms. A family headed by a single mother faces especially difficult problems when the mother is a teenager.

Why might low-income teenage women wish to have children and face the obvious financial difficulties of motherhood? Viewed from an interactionist perspective, these women tend to have low self-esteem and limited options; a child may provide a sense of motivation and purpose for a teenager whose economic worth in our society is limited at best. Given the barriers that many young women face because of their gender, race, ethnicity, and class, many teenagers may believe they have little to lose and much to gain by having a child.

According to a widely held stereotype, "unwed mothers" and "babies having babies" in the United States are predominantly African American. However, this view is not entirely accurate. African Americans account for a disproportionate share of births to unmarried women and teenagers, but the majority of all babies born to unmarried teenage mothers are born to White adolescents. Moreover, since 1980, birthrates among Black teenagers have generally declined (J. Martin et al. 2009).

Although 84 percent of single parents in the United States are mothers, the number of households headed by single fathers more than quadrupled from 1980 to 2013. Though single mothers often develop social networks, single fathers are typically more isolated. In addition, they must deal with schools and social service agencies that are more accustomed to women as custodial parents (Bureau of the Census 1981, 2013d).

STEPFAMILIES

Approximately 45 percent of all people in the United States will marry, divorce, and then remarry. The rising rates of divorce and remarriage have led to a noticeable increase in stepfamily relationships.

The exact nature of blended families has social significance for adults and children alike. Certainly resocialization is required when an adult becomes a stepparent or a child becomes a stepchild and stepsibling. Moreover, an important distinction must be made between first-time stepfamilies and households where there have been repeated divorces, breakups, or changes in custodial arrangements.

From the perspective of . . .

A Wedding Planner How would you manage the seating for a sit-down dinner at the wedding reception of a couple where the bride is the daughter of a single mother who has recently married a man with three children and two stepchildren, and the groom has a mother, a father, and two stepfathers, plus a brother and three stepsisters?

In evaluating the rise of stepfamilies, some observers have assumed that children would benefit from remarriage because they would be gaining a second custodial parent, and would potentially enjoy greater economic security. However, after reviewing many studies of stepfamilies, sociologist Andrew J. Cherlin (2010) concluded that children whose parents have remarried do not have higher levels of well-being than children in divorced single-parent families.

Stepparents can play valuable and unique roles in their stepchildren's lives, but their involvement does not guarantee an improvement in family life. In fact, standards may decline. Studies suggest that children raised in families with stepmothers are likely to have less health care, education, and money spent on their food than children raised by biological mothers. The measures are also negative for children raised by stepfathers, but only half as negative as in the case of stepmothers. These results don't mean that stepmothers are "evil"—it may be that the stepmother holds back out of concern for seeming too intrusive, or relies mistakenly on the biological father to carry out parental duties (Schmeeckle 2007; Schmeeckle et al. 2006).

E Evaluate

Read each question carefully and then select or provide the best answer.

1. Which norm requires mate selection outside certain groups, usually one's own family or certain kinfolk?
   a. exogamy
   b. endogamy
   c. matriarchy
   d. patriarchy

2. According to the discussion of social class differences in family life and intimate relationships, which of the following statements is true?
   a. Social class differences in family life are more striking than they once were.
   b. The upper class emphasizes lineage and maintenance of family position.

   c. Among the poor, women usually play an insignificant role in the economic support of the family.
   d. In examining family life among racial and ethnic minorities, most patterns result from cultural, but *not* class, factors.

3. In the United States, the *majority* of all babies born to unmarried teenage mothers are born to whom?
   a. African American adolescents
   b. White adolescents
   c. Latina adolescents
   d. Asian American adolescents

4. The rule of _____ specifies the groups within which a spouse must be found and prohibits marriage with others.

5. Viewed from the _____ perspective, the government has a strong interest in encouraging adoption.

Answers

1 (a); 2 (b); 3 (b); 4 endogamy; 5 functionalist

Consider these questions to get a deeper understanding of the material.

1. How do both cultural and socioeconomic factors contribute to the following trends: later age of first marriage, the increasing number of extended-family households, and the boomerang generation?

2. Explain mate selection from the functionalist and interactionist perspectives.

RECAP

LO 34-1 Describe variations in marital patterns and family life in the United States and other cultures.

- People select mates in a variety of ways. In some societies, marriages are arranged; in others, people choose their own mates. Some societies require mates to be chosen within a certain group (endogamy) or outside certain groups (exogamy). And consciously or unconsciously, many people look for a mate with similar personal characteristics (homogamy).

- In the United States, premarital relationships may be casual, but the love relationship remains the primary rationale for marriage.

- Despite societal changes, upper-class families in the United States still place emphasis on lineage and the preservation of family position.

- The frequent absence of Black fathers in the United States has caused Black single mothers to develop stable, functioning kin networks that help to ease financial burdens and the pressures of child rearing.

- The culture of *familismo*, or pride in the extended family, has led many Mexican American men to maintain close ties and obligations to kinfolk outside the immediate family and to place proximity to the extended family above other needs and desires.

LO 34-2 Discuss the various child-rearing patterns prevalent in U.S. family life today.

- Because most new parents have little formal preparation for parenthood and the transition to parenthood is abrupt, their new social role confronts them with challenges that must be met through improvisation rather than anticipatory socialization.

- Functionalists assert that the government has a strong interest in encouraging and supporting adoptions instead of either single parenthood or institutional care.

- Currently, in the majority of all married couples in the United States, both husband and wife work outside the home. This leads to challenges for their children and for the parent with primary care responsibilities.

- Single-parent families account for an increasing proportion of U.S. families. Children in single-parent households are not necessarily deprived, but their parent often experiences high levels of economic and emotional stress.

- The rising rates of divorce and remarriage have led to a corresponding increase in stepfamily relationships, with all their challenges.

KEY TERMS

Adoption In a legal sense, the transfer of the legal rights, responsibilities, and privileges of parenthood to a new legal parent or parents.

Endogamy The restriction of mate selection to people within the same group.

Exogamy The requirement that people select a mate outside certain groups.

Familism (*Familismo*) Pride in the extended family, expressed through the maintenance of close ties and strong obligations to kinfolk outside the immediate family.

Homogamy The conscious or unconscious tendency to select a mate with personal characteristics similar to one's own.

Incest taboo The prohibition of sexual relationships between certain culturally specified relatives.

Machismo A sense of virility, personal worth, and pride in one's maleness.

Single-parent family A family in which only one parent is present to care for the children.

Transracial adoption The adoption of a non-White child by White parents or a Hispanic child by non-Hispanics.

MODULE 35 Trends in Family Life and Sexuality

🅆 Work

Recent developments in U.S. society have led to significant changes in customary attitudes and practices relating to marriage and sexuality. Since the 1950s, such changes have been explosive as wave after wave of social revolution rippled through U.S. culture. We will discuss two categories of change in this module: the increase in divorce rates and the evolving definition of the nature and limits of permissible human sexuality.

LO 35-1 Divorce

In the United States, the pattern of family life includes commitments both to marriage and to self-expression and personal growth. Needless to say, the tension between those competing commitments can undermine a marriage, working against the establishment of a lasting relationship. This approach to family life is distinctive to the United States. In some nations, such as Italy, the culture strongly supports marriage and discourages divorce. In others, such as Sweden, people treat marriage the same way as cohabitation, and both arrangements are just as lasting (Cherlin 2009).

STATISTICAL TRENDS IN DIVORCE

Just how common is divorce? Surprisingly, this is not a simple question; divorce statistics are difficult to interpret. The media frequently report that one out of every two marriages ends in divorce, but that figure is misleading. It is based on a comparison of all divorces that occur in a single year (regardless of when the couples were married) with the number of new marriages in the same year.

Sources: Bureau of the Census 1975:64; Centers for Disease Control and Prevention 2012b.

In many countries, divorce began to increase in the late 1960s but then leveled off; since the late 1980s, it has declined by 30 percent. (Figure 11-4 shows the pattern in the United States.) This trend is due partly to the aging of the baby boomer population and the corresponding decline in the proportion of people of marriageable age. But it also indicates an increase in marital stability in recent years (Coontz 2006).

Getting divorced obviously does not sour people on marriage. About 63 percent of all divorced people in the United States have remarried. Women are less likely than men to remarry because many retain custody of their children after a divorce, which complicates a new adult relationship (Bianchi and Spain 1996; Saad 2004).

Some people regard the nation's high rate of remarriage as an endorsement of the institution of marriage, but it does lead to the new challenges of a kin network composed of both current and prior marital relationships. Such networks can be particularly complex if children are involved or if an ex-spouse remarries.

FACTORS ASSOCIATED WITH DIVORCE

Perhaps the most important factor in the increase in divorce over the past hundred years has been the greater social *acceptance* of divorce. It is no longer considered necessary to endure an unhappy marriage. More important, various religious denominations have relaxed their negative attitudes toward divorce, so that most religious leaders no longer treat it as a sin.

The growing acceptance of divorce is a worldwide phenomenon. A decade ago, Sunoo, South Korea's foremost matchmaking service, had no divorced clients. Few Koreans divorced; those who did felt social pressure to resign themselves to the single life. But in one recent seven-year period, South Korea's divorce rate doubled. Today, 15 percent of Sunoo's membership are divorced (Onishi 2003; United Nations Statistics Division 2009: Table 23).

In the United States, several factors have contributed to the growing social acceptance of divorce:

- Most states have adopted more liberal divorce laws in the past three decades. No-fault divorce laws, which allow a couple to end their marriage without fault on either side (by specifying adultery, for instance), accounted for an initial surge in the divorce rate after they were introduced in the 1970s, but appear to have had little effect beyond that.

- Divorce has become a more practical option in newly formed families, since families tend to have fewer children now than in the past.

- A general increase in family incomes, coupled with the availability of free legal aid to some poor people, has meant that more couples can afford costly divorce proceedings.

- As society provides greater opportunities for women, more and more wives are becoming less dependent on their husbands, both economically and emotionally. They may feel more able to leave a marriage if it seems hopeless.

IMPACT OF DIVORCE ON CHILDREN

Divorce is traumatic for all involved, but it has special meaning for the more than 1 million children whose parents divorce each year. Of course, for some of these children, divorce signals the welcome end to a very dysfunctional relationship. Perhaps that is why a national study that tracked 6,332 children both before and after their parents' divorce found that their behavior did not suffer from the marital breakups. Other studies have shown greater unhappiness among children who live amid parental conflict than among children whose parents are divorced. Still, it would be simplistic to assume that children are automatically better off following the breakup of their parents' marriage. The interests of the parents do not necessarily serve children well (H. Kim 2011; Zi 2007).

LO 35-2 Diverse Lifestyles

Marriage is no longer the presumed route from adolescence to adulthood. Instead, it is treated as just one of several paths to maturity. As a result, the marriage ceremony has lost much of its social significance as a rite of passage. The nation's marriage rate has declined since 1960 because people are postponing marriage until later in life, and because more couples, including same-sex couples, are deciding to form partnerships without marriage (Haq 2011).

COHABITATION

In the United States, testing the marital waters by living together before making a commitment is a common practice among marriage-wary 20- and 30-somethings. The tremendous increase in the number of male–female couples who choose to live together without marrying, a practice called **cohabitation**, is one of the most dramatic trends of recent years.

About half of all *currently* married couples in the United States say that they lived together before marriage. This percentage is likely to increase. The number of households in the United States that are headed by unmarried opposite-sex couples has been rising steadily; in 2012 it was 7.8 million. About 40 percent of cohabiting couples' households included children under age 18—nearly the same proportion as married couples' households (Jacobsen et al. 2012; Kreider 2010; Vespa et al. 2013:22).

From the perspective of . . .

A Bank Loan Officer Would you consider a cohabiting couple to be a greater risk for a mortgage loan than a married couple? Why or why not?

In much of Europe, cohabitation is so common that the general sentiment seems to be "Love, yes; marriage, maybe." In Iceland, 62 percent of all children are born to single mothers; in France, Great Britain, and Norway, about 40 percent. Government policies in these countries make few legal distinctions between married and unmarried couples or households. Perhaps as a result, partnerships between cohabiting adults are not necessarily brief or lacking in commitment. Children born to a cohabiting couple in Sweden, for example, are less likely than children born to a cohabiting couple in the United States to see their parents break up (Cherlin 2009; Lyall 2002; M. Moore 2006).

People tend to associate cohabitation with younger, childless couples. Although that stereotype may have been accurate a generation or more ago, it is not now. Since 1970, the number of unmarried couples with children has increased 12-fold.

Periodically, legislators attempt to bolster the desirability of a lifelong commitment to marriage. In 2002, President George W. Bush backed funding for an initiative to promote marriage among those who receive public assistance. Under the Healthy Marriage Initiative, the federal government created a resource center that promoted marriage-related programs. Critics charged that the effort was underfunded or an inappropriate mission for the federal government. The Obama administration has indicated a desire to continue the initiative, renaming it the Healthy Marriage and Responsible Fatherhood Initiative. As the name implies, the initiative extends grants to programs that strengthen fathers' ties with their children and partners. It has also established pilot projects to serve formerly incarcerated parents and their families, designed to provide activities that strengthen their marriages and encourage responsible parenting and economic stability (Jayson 2009; Office of Family Assistance 2014).

REMAINING SINGLE

Looking at TV programs today, you would be justified in thinking that most households are composed of singles. Although that is not the case, it is true that more and more people in the United States are postponing entry into a first marriage. Over one out of three households with children in the United States is a single-parent household. Even so, less than 4 percent of women and men in the United States are likely to remain single throughout their lives (Bureau of the Census 2011c).

The trend toward maintaining a single lifestyle for a longer period is related to the growing economic independence of young people. This trend is especially significant for women. Freed from financial needs, women don't necessarily have to marry to enjoy a satisfying life. Divorce, late marriage, and longevity also figure into this trend.

There are many reasons why a person may choose not to marry. Some singles do not want to limit their sexual intimacy to one lifetime partner. Some men and women do not want to become highly dependent on any one person—and do not want anyone depending heavily on them. In a society that values individuality and self-fulfillment, the single lifestyle can offer certain freedoms that married couples may not enjoy. Even divorced parents may not feel the need to remarry. Andrew J. Cherlin (2009) contends that a single parent who connects with other adults, such as grandparents, to form a solid, supportive relationship for child rearing should not feel compelled to re-partner.

Nevertheless, remaining single represents a clear departure from societal expectations; indeed, it has been likened to "being single on Noah's Ark." A single adult must confront the inaccurate view that he or she is always lonely, is a workaholic, or is immature. These stereotypes help to support the traditional assumption in the United States and most other societies that to be truly happy and fulfilled, a person must get married and raise a family. To counter these societal expectations, singles have formed numerous support groups (Hertz 2006; Klinenberg 2012; Lundquist 2006).

MARRIAGE WITHOUT CHILDREN

There has been a modest increase in childlessness in the United States. According to census data, about 16 to 17 percent of women will now complete their childbearing years without having borne any children, compared to 10 percent in 1980. As many as 20 percent of women in their 30s expect to remain childless (Biddlecom and Martin 2006).

Childlessness within marriage has generally been viewed as a problem that can be solved through such means as adoption and artificial insemination. More and more couples today, however, choose not to have children and regard themselves as child-free rather than childless. They do not believe that having children automatically follows from marriage, nor do they feel that reproduction is the duty of all married couples. Childless couples have formed support groups (with names like No Kidding) and set up websites.

Economic considerations have contributed to this shift in attitudes; having children has become quite expensive. According to a government estimate made for 2012, the average middle-class family will spend $241,080 to feed, clothe, and shelter a child from birth to age 18. If the child attends college, that amount could double, depending on the college chosen. In 1960, parents spent only 2 percent of their income on child care and education; now they spend 16 percent, reflecting the rising dependence on nonfamily child care. Aware of the financial pressures, some couples are weighing the advantages of a child-free marriage (Lino 2013).

Childless couples are beginning to question current practices in the workplace. While applauding employers' efforts to provide child care and flexible work schedules, some nevertheless express concern about tolerance of employees who leave early to take children to doctors, ball games, or after-school classes. As more dual-career couples enter the paid labor force and struggle to balance career and familial responsibilities, conflicts with employees who have no children may increase (Biddlecom and Martin 2006).

LO 35-3 Human Sexuality

Human sexuality spans a broad range of behaviors, including some that are not condoned by particular societies. From the sociologist's perspective, however, sexuality is not limited to physical behaviors, but includes the beliefs, values, and social norms that collectively govern its expression. For example, most societies seek to restrict sexual expression to marriage because of its effect on the family, particularly the welfare of women and children (C. Schneider 2008).

Although human sexuality is expressed in all societies, the way it is sanctioned differs widely, both geographically and historically. In South Africa, following the end of apartheid in 1990, legislators removed barriers to interracial cohabitation and marriage. Then in 1998 they passed the Recognition of Customary Marriages Act, which legalized polygamy among some African tribal groups, but not among Muslims and other religious groups. Finally, under the Civil Union Act of 2006, they granted gay and lesbian couples the same rights and responsibilities as opposite-sex couples (Stacey 2011).

Clearly, sexual attitudes and practices change over time. The publication of Alfred Kinsey's first study of human sexuality in 1948 profoundly shocked Americans. Today, online sites routinely solicit descriptions of almost any kind of human sexuality. Besides the new cultural openness about sex, medical advances have encouraged what many refer to as a sexual revolution. For example, the development of oral contraceptives ("the pill") in 1965 and of remedies for erectile dysfunction (Viagra and other such drugs) in 1998 reduced the risk and increased the likelihood of frequent sexual activity. Today, the sexual practices of young people are in many ways more daring than those of earlier generations.

LABELING AND HUMAN SEXUALITY

We have seen how society singles out certain groups of people by labeling them in positive or negative ways—as "good kids" or "delinquents," for example. Labeling theorists have also studied how labels are used to sanction certain sexual behaviors as "deviant."

The definition of deviant sexual behavior has varied significantly over time and from one culture to another. Until 1973, the

Lady Gaga's 2011 hit single "Born This Way" was written as an anthem to diversity and acceptance of all people, including gays and lesbians.

American Psychiatric Association considered homosexuality a "sociopathic personality disorder," which in effect meant that homosexuals should seek therapy. Two years later, however, the association removed homosexuality from its list of mental illnesses. Today, the organization publicly proclaims that "being gay is just as healthy as being straight." To use Goffman's term, mental health professionals have removed the *stigma* from this form of sexual expression. As a result, in the United States and many other countries, consensual sex between same-sex adults is no longer a crime (American Psychological Association 2008; International Gay and Lesbian Human Rights Commission 2010).

Despite the change in health professionals' attitudes, however, the social stigma of homosexuality lingers. As a result, many people prefer the more positive terms *gay* and *lesbian*. Others, in defiance of the stigma, have proudly adopted the pejorative term *queer* in a deliberate reaction to the ridicule they have borne because of their sexual identity. Still others maintain that constructing one's sexual identity as either homosexual or heterosexual is too limiting. Indeed, such labels ignore those who are *bisexual,* or sexually attracted to both sexes.

Another group whose sexual identity does not fit into the usual categories is *transgendered persons,* or those people whose current gender identity does not match their physical identity at birth. Some transgendered persons see themselves as both male and female. Others, called *transsexuals,* may take hormones or undergo surgery in an effort to draw physically closer to their chosen gender identity. Transgendered persons are sometimes confused with *transvestites,* or cross-dressers who wear the clothing of the opposite sex. Transvestites are typically men, either gay or heterosexual, who choose to wear women's clothing.

The use of these terms even in a positive or nonjudgmental way is problematic, since they imply that human sexuality can be confined in neat, mutually exclusive categories. Moreover, the destigmatization of these labels tends to reflect the influence of the socially privileged—that is, the affluent—who have the resources to overcome the stigma. In contrast, the traditional Native American concept of the *two spirit,* a personality that blends the masculine and the feminine, has been largely ridiculed or ignored (Gilley 2006; Wentling et al. 2008).

What does constitute sexual deviance, then? The answer to this question seems to change with each generation. Today, U.S. laws allow married women to accuse their husbands of rape, when a generation ago such an offense was not recognized. Similarly, *pedophilia*—an adult having sex with a minor—is generally regarded with disgust today, even when it is consensual. Yet in many countries, fringe groups now speak positively of "intergenerational sex," arguing that "childhood" is not a biological given (Hendershott 2002).

Though pedophilia and some other aspects of sexual expression are still against the law, the meaning of the labels is beginning to blur. Although child pornography is both illegal and abhorrent to most people, many fashion advertisements in mainstream magazines seem to verge on it. And while sex work and sex trafficking seem wrong to most of us, society tolerates and even regulates many aspects of those activities (Barton 2006).

Study Alert

Know the differences among transgendered persons (people whose current gender identity differs from their physical identity at birth), transsexuals (who may take hormones or have surgery to become physically more like their chosen gender), and transvestites (people who wear clothing traditionally worn by the opposite sex, typically men who may be gay or heterosexual).

LESBIAN AND GAY RELATIONSHIPS

Twenty-one-year-old Parke, a junior in college, grew up in a stable, loving family. A self-described fiscal conservative, he credits his parents with instilling in him a strong work ethic. Sound like an average child of an average family? The only break with traditional expectations in this case is that Parke is the son of a lesbian couple (P. Brown 2004).

The lifestyles of lesbians and gay men are varied. Some live in long-term, monogamous relationships; others live alone or with roommates. Some remain in "empty-shell" heterosexual marriages and do not publicly acknowledge their homosexuality. Others live with children from a former marriage or with adopted children. Based on election exit polls, researchers for the National Health and Social Life Survey and the Voter News Service estimate that 2 to 5 percent of the adult population identify themselves as either

FIGURE 11-5 SAME-SEX COUPLE HOUSEHOLDS
AS PERCENT OF ALL HOUSEHOLDS

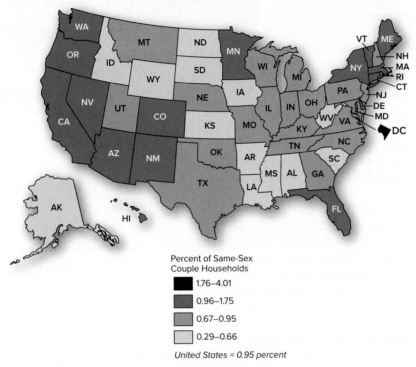

Percent of Same-Sex
Couple Households

■ 1.76–4.01
■ 0.96–1.75
■ 0.67–0.95
□ 0.29–0.66

United States = 0.95 percent

About 600,000 same-sex couples lived in the United States in 2010.

Source: 2010 American Community Survey data in Lofquist 2011:4.

gay or lesbian. An analysis of the 2010 Census shows about 600,000 gay households, and a gay and lesbian adult population approaching 10 million (Figure 11-5) (Laumann et al. 1994b:293; Lofquist 2011).

The last few years have seen dramatic changes in legal discrimination against lesbian, gay, bisexual, and transgender (LGBT) people. Although significant barriers remain, especially in family law and in publicly expressed prejudicial attitudes, progress has been made in other areas. Increasingly, businesses are seeing the benefit of hiring LGBT people. In 2012 the CIA began active recruitment in the LGBT community—a sharp departure from the past, when the CIA and other federal agencies routinely denied security clearances to gay men and women. As a result, a 2012 survey showed that 91 percent of gay men and lesbians in the United States are experiencing greater acceptance of their lifestyle (G. Allen 2012; S. Page 2012).

One remaining and highly publicized issue is prohibitions against gay marriage. The inability to marry denies gay people many rights that married couples take for granted, from the ability to make decisions for an incapacitated partner to the right to receive government benefits to dependents, such as Social Security payments. Though gay couples consider themselves families just like the straight couples who live down the street, they are often treated as if they are not.

Precisely because of such inequities, many gay and lesbian couples are now demanding the right to marry with increasing success. In the Social Policy section that follows, we will examine the highly controversial issue of gay marriage.

LO 35-3 SOCIAL POLICY and the Family

We have seen that researchers rely on a number of tools, from simple observational research to the latest in computer technologies. Because in the real world sociological research can have far-reaching consequences for public policy and public welfare, we'll consider its impact on gay marriage.

GAY MARRIAGE

In the United States, attitudes toward marriage are complex. As always, society and popular culture suggest that a young man or woman should find the perfect mate, settle down and marry, have children, and live happily ever after. But young people are also bombarded by messages implying the frequency of adultery and the acceptability of divorce. In this atmosphere, the idea of same-sex marriage strikes some people as only the latest of many attacks on traditional marriage. To others, it seems an overdue acknowledgment of the formal relationships that faithful, monogamous gay couples have long maintained.

What has made gay marriage the focus of national attention? Events in two states brought the issue to the forefront. In 1999, Vermont gave gay couples the legal benefits of marriage through civil union, but stopped short of calling the arrangement a marriage. Then, in 2003, the Massachusetts Supreme Court ruled 4–3 that under the state's constitution, gay couples have the right to marry—a ruling the U.S. Supreme Court has refused to review. Almost immediately, gay couples began crossing state lines to get married in Massachusetts.

As of 2013, an estimated 124,000 gay and lesbian couples in the United States are married and raising more than 30,000 children. Now that some of them have been legally married 10 years or more, scholars are beginning to study their family experiences compared to those of opposite-sex couples (Rodriquez and Gatlin 2014).

In a 2014 national survey, 55 percent of respondents said marriage between same-sex couples should be recognized by law. Another 42 percent said such arrangements should not be recognized (McCarthy 2014).

Applying Sociology to Gay Marriage Functionalists have traditionally seen marriage as a social institution that is closely tied to human reproduction. Same-sex marriage would at first appear not to fit that arrangement. However, many same-sex couples are entrusted with the socialization of young children, whether or not their relationship is recognized by the state. Functionalists also wonder whether religious views toward marriage can be ignored. The courts have focused on civil marriage, but religious views are hardly irrelevant, even in a country like the United States, which observes a separation between religion and the state. Indeed, religious teachings have led even some staunch supporters of gay rights to oppose same-sex marriage on spiritual grounds.

Conflict theorists have charged that denial of the right to marry reinforces the second-class status of gays and lesbians. Some have compared the ban on gay marriage to past policies that until 1967 banned interracial marriage in 32 states.

Interactionists generally avoid the policy question and focus instead on the nature of same-sex households. They ask many of the same questions about gay partner relations and child rearing that they ask about conventional couples. Of course, much less research has been done on same-sex households than on other families, but the studies published to date raise the same issues as those that apply to conventional married couples, plus a few more. For gay couples, the support or opposition of family, co-workers, and friends looms large (Dundas and Kaufman 2000; Dunne 2000; B. Powell et al. 2010).

Queer theorists see these issues as significant, arguing that they are often understudied by researchers (although that is beginning to change). In particular, queer theorists point to the relative lack of high-quality research on LGBT households and their relationship to the larger society, not to mention non-LGBT relatives. As the campaign for same-sex marriage gains momentum, some scholars see a need to focus on gay men and lesbians who do not fit the new "gay norm," who reject the desire to create a nuclear family household. Continuing to focus on the margins of society, queer theorists argue for more attention to people of color, the working class, the poor, and immigrants in the LGBT community (Mignon Moore and Stambolis-Ruhstorfer 2013).

Initiating Gay Marriage Policy The United States is not the first nation to consider this issue. In 2001, the Netherlands became the first nation to legalize same-sex marriage. In less than 14 years, 15 other nations followed: Argentina, Belgium, Brazil, Canada, Denmark, France, Great Britain, Iceland, New Zealand, Norway, Portugal, South Africa, Spain, Sweden, and Uruguay. Typically, same-sex couples account for 2 to 3 percent of all marriages in these nations (R. Taylor 2013).

FIGURE 11-6 GAY MARRIAGE RECOGNITION BY STATE

Authorizes same-sex marriage

Prohibits same-sex marriage

* Legal challenges underway and gay marriage likely to be recognized.

Note: Recognition has been instituted state-by-state by state legislative action, statewide referendum, state supreme courts, or federal appeals court. Also recognized by 10 American Indian tribes.
Sources: As of October 12, 2014; Human Rights Campaign 2014 and various news reports during October 2014.

In the United States, marriage has traditionally been under the jurisdiction of state lawmakers. However, in 1996, responding to conservatives, Congress enacted the Defense of Marriage Act (DOMA). The act defined marriage as a union between one man and one woman and allowed states and the federal government to deny legal recognition of same-sex marriages. Despite criticism from the gay community and those who support the recognition of same-sex marriage, the measure proved popular with the public.

Then in 2013, by a 5–4 vote in *United States v. Windsor,* the Supreme Court struck down a key section of DOMA, in effect declaring that the federal government must recognize gay marriage in the 12 states where it was legal at the time. As of October 2014, 31 states and the District of Columbia were issuing marriage licenses to same-sex couples (Figure 11-6). In states that have yet to recognize gay marriage, the ruling in *United States v. Windsor* has kept the movement toward legalization going.

At the local level, opponents to gay marriage are finding new ways to declare their views. There is growing evidence that some photographers, wedding cake bakers, and florists are refusing to provide their services at same-sex wedding and civil union ceremonies. Their discriminatory rejection of customers based on sexual identification raises complex legal questions that must await future court decisions (Dimrock et al. 2013; Koppel and Jones 2013).

Not everyone in the LGBT community sees the legalization of same-sex marriage as necessarily the central issue. Assimilation—the process through which individuals forsake their own heritage to become a part of a different culture—has emerged as a hot issue in the gay community. Some argue that in promoting marriage equality, LGBT people are merely trying to assimilate, to become like the oppressor and adopt the oppressor's social conventions. Many fear that such efforts will detract from efforts to help more marginalized gays and lesbians, such as people of color, transgender people, and those who prefer forms of intimacy other than marriage (Bernstein and Taylor 2013).

Read each question carefully and then select or provide the best answer.

1. The trend of persons choosing to remain single for a long period is connected to which of the following social developments?
   a. the rising divorce rate among young married people
   b. high mortgage rates for new home buyers
   c. increasing financial independence among young people
   d. financial penalties in the tax code associated with marrying

2. Which of the following statements about cohabitation is true?
   a. Cohabitation is more common in the United States than in Europe.
   b. About half of all currently married U.S. couples cohabited before they married.
   c. The U.S. cohabitation rate rose in the late 1960s but has been dropping steadily.
   d. The majority of cohabiting couples' households include children under age 18.

3. Which of the following factors is associated with the high divorce rate in the United States?
   a. the liberalization of divorce laws
   b. the fact that contemporary families have fewer children than earlier families did
   c. the general increase in family incomes
   d. all of the above

4. The state of _____ became the first state to recognize gay couples' right to marry because of a court ruling in 2003.

5. People whose gender identity does not match their physical identity at birth are called _____ persons.

Answers
1 (c); 2 (b); 3 (d); 4 Massachusetts; 5 transgendered

Consider these questions to get a deeper understanding of the material.

1. In a society that maximizes the welfare of all family members, how easy should it be for couples to divorce? How easy should it be to get married?

2. How is cohabitation similar to marriage? How is it different? Could gay and lesbian couples achieve all the benefits of marriage without actually marrying? Why or why not?

RECAP

LO 35-1 Explain the causes and effects of the increased divorce rate in the United States.

- The U.S. divorce rate began to rise in the late 1960s and has since leveled off slightly. Divorce remains common, as does remarriage.
- Among the factors that contribute to the rising divorce rate in the United States are greater social acceptance of divorce and the liberalization of divorce laws in many states.
- Sociological studies have found that the behavior and happiness of children of divorced parents are similar to those of children who live amid parental conflict.

LO 35-2 Discuss the impact of diverse lifestyles on the family as a social institution.

- Marriage is no longer assumed to be the only way that two people begin a shared life. More and more people in the United States and Europe are living together without marrying, a practice known as cohabitation.
- People are staying single longer, largely because independent young people can afford to do so. Still, the vast majority of people marry at some point during their lives.
- Some married couples are deciding not to have children because they value their independence and feel no need to reproduce. Such couples constantly confront the common societal view that childless couples must be unable—rather than merely unwilling—to have children.

LO 35-3 Analyze policy concerning sexual behavior using a sociological lens.

- Gradually, much sexual behavior that was once labeled deviant is gaining social acceptance in the United States and elsewhere. Homosexuals, bisexuals, transgendered persons, transsexuals, and transvestites have all ventured slowly into the daylight, although all of these statuses still carry a social stigma.
- Because homosexuality has traditionally been labeled a deviant behavior, gay and lesbian couples face significant discrimination, including the denial of their right to marry, although this is beginning to change in the United States.
- The gay marriage movement, which would confer equal rights on gay and lesbian couples and their dependents, is strongly opposed by conservative religious and political groups, but is gaining acceptance within the United States.

KEY TERMS

Cohabitation The practice of living together as a male–female couple without marrying.

The Case of . . . All in the Family

It's a full house at the home of Tori Reese and her husband Moses Allard. Tori has two daughters from a previous marriage, the younger one just out of college. Moses has three children by his first wife. "When we met, our youngest children were juniors in high school," Tori says. "We thought the years of heavy-duty parenting were behind us. We thought, 'Okay, maybe now it's about us.'" But eighteen months later, Tori's mother suffered a stroke that left her partially paralyzed. "There was no money to put her in a good care facility," Tori says, "so I brought her home. Moses built a lovely little porch off her room, and she enjoys sitting out there."

Tori and Moses had just settled in with her mother, when Moses's eldest son showed up on their doorstep, laid off from his job and broke. They gave him the room next to Tori's mom, and Moses put him to work. "I run a construction crew, build houses," Moses says. "Luckily, he showed up when I had some hours to give."

"We thought, 'Okay, Moses's son will get on his feet in a year or so,'" Tori says, "but then my daughter called. Her boyfriend ran off and she was pregnant. I just said, 'You can't be clear across the country, no family out there. Come on home.'" Now, Tori's daughter and new grandson are watching Moses's son build a two-story "guesthouse" in the backyard. When it's finished, the daughter and her new baby will have the top floor. Moses's son and his new wife will occupy the lower apartment. Tori smiles. "I'm just waiting to see who shows up next."

1. What positive outcomes does their extended family offer to each member of the Tori-Moses household?

2. Do you think parents should make room for adult children who return home? Why or why not?

3. Do you think Tori's pregnant daughter made a wise choice in returning home? What might her life have been like as a single parent far from her family?

4. If Tori and Moses had been wealthy, what other options might they have had for handling each of their family "crises"?

Taking Sociology Tests

Test-taking is a source of anxiety for many students. If you've been doing your home-work, you should have nothing to worry about but the unknown. These strategies should help you minimize the unknowns about the content and about the testing situation.

- The best way to prepare is to study. Read notes, handouts, previous tests and assignments, and the textbook.
- Ask your instructor how long the test will be, what it will cover, and how many of each kind of test question it will contain.
- Practice answering questions. Have your study group divide up the content that will be covered and prepare questions to ask one another.
- Get a good night's sleep before the test and plan to arrive early.

- The best way to study is with a study group. Form or join one now.
- Gather the supplies you'll need for the test: pencils, scratch paper, a watch (you may not be allowed to keep your phone), etc.

- Look over the test. How many questions are there, and how many of each type? Knowing this will enable you to pace yourself.
- Read the directions closely and completely before you work on answering questions.
- Answer the easiest questions first. Mark any questions you skip so you can find them later. Move on.
- For multiple-choice questions, read the question part carefully. Look for tricky words like *not* and *except*.
- If you see a choice that you know is right, first check if "all of the above" is one of the other choices. If it is, check the other answers before making your final choice.
- Cross out answers that you can immediately eliminate. You're trying to narrow your odds to 50–50 at the worst.
- For short-answer questions, if you can't immediately come up with the answer, mark the question as skipped and continue. Keep moving.
- For essay questions, recall what you've learned about constructing essays: topic, opinion, support (evidence and logic), conclusion. Use your time well, but always take a couple of minutes upfront for brainstorming.
- In your essay, write down as much as you can. You may get partial credit.
- Be sure to return to the questions you skipped the first time through.
- Manage anxiety. No one is completely calm about tests. Keep it under control and you'll do fine.

- Save time at the end of the test to check your work. Really.

- When you get your grade, rethink what went right and what went wrong with your test preparation and your test-taking. Consider what you did well and what you could have done better.

Test Your Test-Taking Skills

Have you ever received an average or poor grade on a test and felt like you knew as much about the subject as the students who aced it? Test-taking is a skill, like writing a great paper, that you can learn. To see where you need to brush up, rate each of the following items "That's Me" or "Not Me," then use this scale to find your score:

That's Me = 1

Not Me = 0

	That's Me	Not Me
1. I study all night before a test, then load up on caffeine and head off to the exam.		
2. I sort of look over everything before a test because you never know what the instructor will ask.		
3. I often spend so much time on a difficult question that I don't get to the last section of the test.		
4. Multiple-choice questions are so confusing because it seems like most of the answers could be right.		
5. When I finish the last question, I just turn in the exam and leave, happy to get out of there.		
6. I hate essay questions. I end up trying to write about everything the book covered.		
7. Tests make me so nervous that everything just sort of goes out of my head.		
8. I try to answer the hardest questions first so I can get them out of the way.		
9. When reading the passages on a multiple-choice test, I get lost in all the words and can't figure out what's important.		
10. I never participate in study groups because it takes too much preparation.		

SCORE:

0–1   Taking tests poses no problems for you. You prepare, get a good night's sleep, and use your time wisely in the exam room.

2–4   You have the basics of test-taking, but you could pick up a few more tips to help you show what you know.

5–10 Find out what the best test takers know by reviewing the tips in this chapter's P.O.W.E.R. Study Strategies: Taking Sociology Tests.

Health and the Environment

12

Sociology at WORK ENVIRONMENTAL ANALYST

JAKE BARBER works for an environmental nonprofit agency in Oregon. "Our focus is sustainability practices," Barber says. "We gather info to create a big picture of what's sustainable for the earth and what's sustainable for human, animal, and beneficial insect life." Over the past two years, Barber has spent his working hours reading up on genetically modified crops and foods (GMOs).

"GMO plants were developed to engineer crops that are resistant to pests and drought," Barber says. "They were supposed to raise crop yields and save the developing world from starvation. That's not an inconsiderable promise, but it's also not the whole story." Barber's concerns, having analyzed hundreds of studies, are that GMOs threaten variety in plant life and encourage the development of chemical-resistant weeds and pests. "There's also evidence for human health concerns, such as GMOs' contribution to obesity and possible harm to vital organs," Barber says. "My job is to weigh all the evidence in light of what's necessary for the sustainability of life on our planet, and to get the word out so that individuals, organizations, and policymakers can make informed decisions." ■

Looking Ahead

WHAT DEFINES A HEALTHY ENVIRONMENT? HOW IS THE ENVIRONMENT connected to our health as a society? How do health and health care vary from one social class to another and from one nation to another? In this chapter, we present a sociological overview of health, illness, health care, and medicine as a social institution. We begin by examining how functionalists, conflict theorists, interactionists, and labeling theorists look at health-related issues. Then we study the distribution of diseases in a society by social class, race and ethnicity, gender, and age.

We'll look too at the evolution of the U.S. health care system. We will analyze the interactions among physicians, nurses, and patients; alternatives to traditional health care; the role of government in providing health care services to the needy; and the issues people with mental illness face.

Later in the chapter, we will examine the environmental problems facing the world in the 21st century, and we will draw on the functionalist and conflict perspectives to better understand environmental issues. We'll see that it is important not to oversimplify the relationship between health and the environment. Finally, in the Social Policy section we explore the recently renewed interest in environmentalism.

MODULE 36 Sociological Perspectives on Health and Illness

 **Prepare** Learning Objective

LO 36-1 Analyze health and illness using the functionalist, conflict, interactionist, and labeling approaches.

 **Organize** Module Outline

Definitions of Health and Wellness
    Functionalist Perspective
    Conflict Perspective
    Interactionist Perspective
    Labeling Perspective

 **Work**

LO 36-1 Definitions of Health and Wellness

How can we define health? Imagine a continuum with health on one end and death on the other. In the preamble to its 1946 constitution, the World Health Organization defined **health** as a "state of complete physical, mental, and social well-being, and not merely the absence of disease and infirmity" (Leavell and Clark 1965:14). In this definition, the "healthy" end of the continuum represents an ideal rather than a precise condition.

Along the continuum, individuals define themselves as healthy or sick on the basis of criteria established by themselves and relatives, friends, co-workers, and medical practitioners. Health and illness, in other words, are socially constructed. They are rooted in culture and are defined by claims makers—people who describe themselves as healthy or ill—as well as by a broad range of interested parties, including health care providers, pharmaceutical firms, and even food providers (Conrad and Barker 2010).

Because health is socially constructed, we can consider how it varies in different situations or cultures. Why is it that you may consider yourself sick or well when others do not agree? Who controls definitions of health and illness in our society, and for what ends? What are the consequences of viewing yourself (or of being viewed) as ill or disabled? By drawing on four sociological perspectives—functionalism, conflict theory, interactionism, and labeling theory—we can gain greater insight into the social context that shapes definitions of health and the treatment of illness.

FUNCTIONALIST PERSPECTIVE

Illness entails breaks in our social interactions, both at work and at home. From a functionalist perspective, being sick must therefore be controlled, so that not too many people are released from their societal responsibilities at any one time. Functionalists contend that an overly broad definition of illness would disrupt the workings of a society.

Sickness requires that one take on a social role, if only temporarily. The **sick role** refers to societal expectations about the attitudes and behavior of a person viewed as being ill. Sociologist Talcott Parsons (1951, 1975), well known for his contributions to functionalist theory, outlined the behavior required of people who are considered sick. They are exempted from their normal, day-to-day responsibilities and generally do not suffer blame for their condition. Yet they are obligated to try to get well, which includes seeking competent professional care. This obligation arises from the common view that illness is dysfunctional, because it can undermine social stability. Attempting to get well is particularly

Health practices vary from one country to another. Unlike people in most other societies, the Japanese often wear surgical masks in public, to protect themselves from disease or pollution. The practice began in 1919, when the worldwide Spanish flu epidemic became a public health menace. Today mask-wearing persists even when there is no public health threat.

important in the world's developing countries. Modern automated industrial societies can absorb a greater degree of illness or disability than horticultural or agrarian societies, in which the availability of workers is far more critical (Conrad and Leiter 2013).

According to Parsons's theory, physicians function as *gatekeepers* for the sick role. They verify a patient's condition either as "illness" or as "recovered." The ill person becomes dependent on the physician, because the latter can control valued rewards (not only treatment of illness, but also excused absences from work and school). Parsons suggests that the physician–patient relationship is somewhat like that between parent and child. Like a parent, the physician helps the patient to enter society as a full and functioning adult (Weitz 2009).

The concept of the sick role is not without criticism. First, patients' judgments regarding their own state of health may be related to their gender, age, social class, and ethnic group. For example, younger people may fail to detect warning signs of a dangerous illness, while elderly people may focus too much on the slightest physical malady. Second, the sick role may be more applicable to people who are experiencing short-term illnesses than to those with recurring, long-term illnesses. Finally, even simple factors, such as whether a person is employed, seem to affect one's willingness to assume the sick role—as does the impact of socialization into a particular occupation or activity. For example, beginning in childhood, athletes learn to define certain ailments as "sports injuries" and therefore do not regard themselves as "sick." Nonetheless, sociologists continue to rely on Parsons's model for functionalist analysis of the relationship between illness and societal expectations of the sick (Curry 1993).

CONFLICT PERSPECTIVE

Conflict theorists observe that the medical profession has assumed a preeminence that extends well beyond whether to excuse a student from school or an employee from work. Sociologist Eliot Freidson (1970:5) has likened the position of medicine today to that of state religions yesterday—it has an officially approved monopoly of the right to define health and illness and to treat illness. Conflict theorists use the term *medicalization of society* to refer to the growing role of medicine as a major institution of social control (Conrad 2009; McKinlay and McKinlay 1977; Zola 1972, 1983).

The Medicalization of Society Social control involves techniques and strategies for regulating behavior in order to enforce the distinctive norms and values of a culture. Typically, we think of informal social control as occurring within families and peer groups, and formal social control as being carried out by authorized agents such as police officers, judges, school administrators, and employers. Viewed from a conflict perspective, however, medicine is not simply a "healing profession"; it is a regulating mechanism.

How does medicine manifest its social control? First, medicine has greatly expanded its domain of expertise in recent decades. Physicians now examine a wide range of issues, among them sexuality, old age, anxiety, obesity, child development, alcoholism, and drug addiction. We tolerate this expansion of the boundaries of medicine because we hope that these experts can bring new "miracle cures" to complex human problems, as they have to the control of certain infectious diseases.

From the perspective of . . .

A Health Insurance Agent How might the medicalization of society affect the services your company is expected to cover and the overall cost of insurance premiums?

In defining these new conditions, physicians determine and control the course of treatment, and even affect patients' views of themselves. Once a problem is viewed using this **medical model**, it becomes more difficult for common people to join the discussion and exert influence on decision making. It also becomes more difficult to view these issues as being shaped by social, cultural, or psychological factors, rather than simply by physical or medical factors (Caplan 1989; Conrad 2009).

Second, medicine serves as an agent of social control by retaining absolute jurisdiction over many health care procedures. It has even attempted to guard its jurisdiction by placing health care professionals such as chiropractors and nurse-midwives outside the realm of acceptable medicine. Despite the fact that midwives first brought professionalism to child delivery, they have been portrayed as having invaded the "legitimate" field of obstetrics, in both the United States and Mexico. Nurse-midwives have sought licensing as a way to achieve professional respectability, but physicians continue to exert power to ensure that midwifery remains a subordinate occupation (Scharnberg 2007).

Inequities in Health Care The medicalization of society is but one concern of conflict theorists as they assess the workings of health care institutions. As we have seen throughout our introduction to sociology, in analyzing any issue, conflict theorists seek to determine who benefits, who suffers, and who dominates at the expense of others. Viewed from a conflict perspective, glaring inequities exist in health care delivery in the United States. For example, poor areas tend to be underserved because medical services concentrate where people are wealthy.

Similarly, from a global perspective, obvious inequities exist in health care delivery. Today, the United States has about 24 physicians per 10,000 people, while African nations have fewer than 1 per 10,000. This situation is only worsened by the **brain drain**—the immigration to the United States and other industrialized nations of skilled workers, professionals, and technicians who are desperately needed in their home countries. As part of this brain drain, physicians, nurses, and other health care professionals have come to the United States from developing countries such as India, Pakistan, and various African states. Conflict theorists view their emigration out of the Third World as yet another way in which the world's core industrialized nations enhance their quality of life at the expense of developing countries. One way the developing countries suffer is in lower life expectancy. In Africa and much of Latin America and Asia, life expectancy is far lower than in industrialized nations (World Bank 2013).

Conflict theorists emphasize that inequities in health care have clear life-and-death consequences. From a conflict perspective, the dramatic differences in *infant mortality rates* around the world (Figure 12-1) reflect, at least in part, unequal distribution of health care resources based on the wealth or poverty of various nations. The **infant mortality rate** is the number of deaths of infants under 1 year old per 1,000 live births in a given year. This measure is an important indicator of a society's level of health care; it reflects prenatal nutrition, delivery procedures, and infant screening measures. Still, despite the wealth of the United States, at least 48 nations have *lower* infant mortality rates. Conflict theorists point out that unlike the United States, these countries offer some form of government-supported health care for all citizens, which typically leads to greater availability and use of prenatal care.

The growing concern about obesity among the young has focused attention on their eating habits and their need for exercise. Concern about obesity is a sign of the medicalization of society.

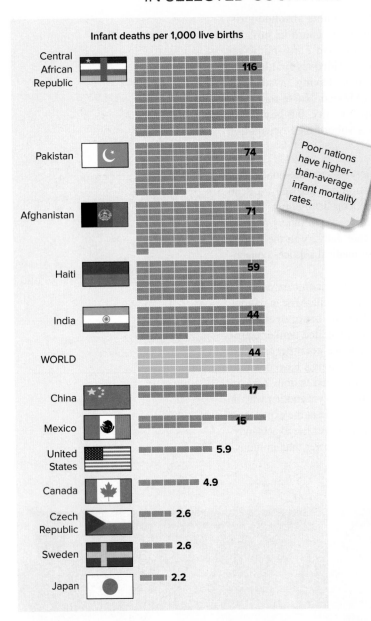

FIGURE 12-1 INFANT MORTALITY RATES IN SELECTED COUNTRIES

Infant deaths per 1,000 live births

Central African Republic	116
Pakistan	74
Afghanistan	71
Haiti	59
India	44
WORLD	44
China	17
Mexico	15
United States	5.9
Canada	4.9
Czech Republic	2.6
Sweden	2.6
Japan	2.2

Poor nations have higher-than-average infant mortality rates.

Source: Haub and Kaneda 2013.

INTERACTIONIST PERSPECTIVE

From an interactionist point of view, patients are not passive; often, they actively seek the services of a health care practitioner. In examining health, illness, and medicine as a social institution, then, interactionists engage in micro-level study of the roles played by health care professionals and patients. Interactionists are particularly interested in how physicians learn to play their occupational role. For example, in one of his earliest works, sociologist Howard Becker took the perspective that medical education socialized students into the role of doctor as much as it transferred medical knowledge to them (H. Becker et al. 1961).

Following this approach, Brenda Beagan (2001) found that the technical language students learn in medical school becomes the basis for the script they follow as novice physicians. The familiar white coat is their costume—one that helps them to appear confident and professional at the same time that it identifies them as doctors to patients and other staff members. Beagan found that many medical students struggle to project the appearance of competence that they think their role demands. More recently, she has considered how medical personnel interact with patients undergoing sex-change procedures and hormonal therapy to conform their bodies to their deeply held sexual identities. Because most health care providers receive little or no prior formal education in this complex undertaking, they learn from experienced colleagues. More than in most clinical situations, they may also be "educated" by the patients themselves (Beagan et al. 2013).

Sometimes patients play an active role in health care by *failing* to follow a physician's advice. For example, some patients stop taking medications long before they should. Some take an incorrect dosage on purpose, and others never even fill their prescriptions. Such noncompliance results in part from the prevalence of self-medication in our society; many people are accustomed to self-diagnosis and self-treatment. On the other hand, patients' active involvement in their health care can sometimes have very *positive* consequences. Some patients read books about preventive health care techniques, attempt to maintain a healthful and nutritious diet, carefully monitor any side effects of medication, and adjust the dosage based on perceived side effects.

LABELING PERSPECTIVE

Labeling theory helps us to understand why certain people are *viewed* as deviants, "bad kids," or criminals, whereas others whose behavior is similar are not. Labeling theorists also suggest that the designation "healthy" or "ill" generally involves social definition by others. Just as police officers, judges, and other regulators of social control have the power to define certain people as criminals, health care professionals (especially physicians) have the power to define certain people as sick. Moreover, like labels that suggest nonconformity or criminality, labels that are associated with illness commonly reshape how others treat us and how we see ourselves. Our society attaches serious consequences to labels that suggest less-than-perfect physical or mental health (H. Becker 1963; C. Clark 1983; H. Schwartz 1994).

A historical example illustrates perhaps the ultimate extreme in labeling social behavior as a sickness. As enslavement of Africans in the United States came under increasing attack in the 19th century, medical authorities provided new rationalizations for the oppressive practice. Noted physicians published articles stating that the skin color of Africans deviated from "healthy" white skin coloring because Africans suffered from congenital leprosy. Moreover, the continuing efforts of enslaved Africans to escape from their White masters were classified as an example of the "disease" of drapetomania (or "crazy run-aways"). The prestigious *New Orleans Medical and Surgical Journal* suggested that the remedy for this "disease" was to treat slaves kindly, as one might treat children. Apparently, these medical authorities would not entertain the view that it was healthy and sane to flee slavery or join in a slave revolt (T. Szasz 2010).

Similarly, labeling theorists suggest that other behaviors viewed today as mental illnesses may not really be illnesses. Instead, the individual's problems arise from living in society, not from physical maladies. From this perspective, a variety of life experiences treated as illnesses today may not be illnesses at all. Premenstrual syndrome, post-traumatic stress disorders, and hyperactivity are examples of medically recognized disorders that labeling theorists would consider questionable.

Probably the most noteworthy medical example of labeling is the case of homosexuality. For years, psychiatrists classified being gay or lesbian not as a lifestyle but as a mental disorder subject to treatment. This official sanction became an early target of the growing gay and lesbian rights movement in the United States. In 1974, members of the American Psychiatric Association voted to drop homosexuality from the standard manual on mental disorders (Conrad 2009).

Table 12-1 summarizes four major sociological perspectives on health and illness. Although they may seem quite different, two common themes unite them. First, any person's health or illness is more than an organic condition, since it is subject to the interpretation of others. The impact of culture, family and friends, and the medical profession means that health and illness are not purely biological occurrences, but sociological occurrences as well. Second, since members of a society (especially industrial societies) share the same health care delivery system, health is a group and societal concern. Although health may be defined as the complete well-being of an individual, it is also the result of one's social environment, as the next section will show (Cockerham 2012).

Study Alert

Use Table 12-1 to help you distinguish the differences among the functionalist, conflict, interactionist, and labeling perspectives on health and illness.

TABLE 12-1 SOCIOLOGICAL PERSPECTIVES ON HEALTH AND ILLNESS

Tracking Sociological Perspectives

	Functionalist	Conflict	Interactionist	Labeling
Major emphasis	Control of the number of people who are considered sick	Overmedicalization Gross inequities in health care	Doctor–patient relationship Interaction of medical staff	Definition of illness and health
Controlling factors	Physician as gatekeeper	Medical profession Social inequities	Medical profession	Medical profession
Proponents	Talcott Parsons	Thomas Szasz Irving Zola	Howard Becker	Thomas Szasz

Read each question carefully and then select or provide the best answer.

1. Which sociologist developed the concept of the sick role?
   a. Émile Durkheim
   b. Talcott Parsons
   c. C. Wright Mills
   d. Erving Goffman

2. Regarding health care inequities, the conflict perspective would note that
   a. physicians serve as gatekeepers for the sick role, either verifying a patient's condition as "illness" or designating the patient as "recovered."
   b. patients play an active role in health care by failing to follow a physician's advice.
   c. emigration out of the Third World by physicians is yet another way that the world's core industrialized nations enhance their quality of life at the expense of developing countries.
   d. the designation "healthy" or "ill" generally involves social definition by others.

3. Which of the following terms do conflict theorists use in referring to the growing role of medicine as a major institution of social control?
   a. the sick role
   b. the medicalization of society
   c. medical labeling
   d. epidemiology

4. From a(n) _____ perspective, "being sick" must be controlled so as to ensure that not too many people are released from their societal responsibilities at any one time.

5. The immigration to the United States and other industrialized nations of skilled workers, professionals, and technicians who are desperately needed by their home countries is known as the _____ _____.

Answers

1 (b); 2 (c); 3 (b); 4 functionalist; 5 brain drain

Consider these questions to get a deeper understanding of the material.

1. Define the term "health" from the functionalist, conflict, and interactionist perspectives.

2. Describe an occasion on which people you know disagreed about a socially applied medical label. What was the label, and why did people disagree?

RECAP

LO 36-1 Analyze health and illness using the functionalist, conflict, interactionist, and labeling approaches.

- Health and illness are social constructions that are rooted in culture and based on criteria established by professionals and nonprofessionals alike.
- According to Talcott Parsons's functionalist perspective, physicians function as gatekeepers for the sick role, either verifying a person's condition as "illness" or designating the person as "recovered."
- Conflict theorists use the term *medicalization of society* to refer to medicine's growing role as a major institution of social control.
- Labeling theorists suggest that the designation of a person as "healthy" or "ill" generally involves social definition by others. These definitions affect how others see us and how we view ourselves.

KEY TERMS

Brain drain The immigration to the United States and other industrialized nations of skilled workers, professionals, and technicians who are desperately needed in their home countries.

Health As defined by the World Health Organization, a state of complete physical, mental, and social well-being, and not merely the absence of disease and infirmity.

Infant mortality rate The number of deaths of infants under 1 year old per 1,000 live births in a given year.

Labeling theory An approach to deviance that attempts to explain why certain people are viewed as deviants while others engaged in the same behavior are not.

Medical model An approach in which medical experts define illness or disease, determine and control the course of treatment, and even affect patients' view of themselves.

Sick role Societal expectations about the attitudes and behavior of a person viewed as being ill.

MODULE 37 Social Epidemiology and Health

LO **37-1** Studying Health and Disease

Social epidemiology is the study of the distribution of disease, impairment, and general health status across a population. Initially, epidemiologists concentrated on the scientific study of epidemics, focusing on how they started and spread. Contemporary social epidemiology is much broader in scope, concerned not only with epidemics but also with nonepidemic diseases, injuries, drug addiction and alcoholism, suicide, and mental illness. Epidemiologists have taken on the new role of tracking bioterrorism. In 2001, they mobilized to trace the anthrax outbreak and prepare for any terrorist use of smallpox or other lethal microbes. Epidemiologists draw on the work of a wide variety of scientists and researchers, among them physicians, sociologists, public health officials, biologists, veterinarians, demographers, anthropologists, psychologists, and meteorologists.

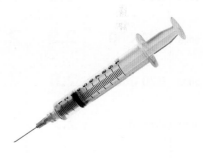

Epidemiologists have found that worldwide, an estimated 35 million people were infected with HIV at the end of 2013. Women account for a growing proportion of new cases of HIV/AIDS, especially among racial and ethnic minorities. Although the spread of AIDS is stabilizing, with fewer new cases reported, the disease is not evenly distributed. Those areas that are least equipped to deal with it—the developing nations of sub-Saharan Africa—face the greatest challenge (Figure 12-2).

When disease data are presented as rates, or as the number of reports per 100,000 people, they are called **morbidity rates**. (The term **mortality rate** refers to the rate of *death* in a given population.) Sociologists find morbidity rates useful because they reveal that a specific disease occurs more frequently in one segment of a population than another. As we shall see, social class, race, ethnicity, gender, and age can all affect a population's morbidity rates.

LO 37-2 SOCIAL CLASS

Social class is clearly associated with differences in morbidity and mortality rates. Studies in the United States and other countries have consistently shown that people in the lower classes have higher rates of mortality and disability than others.

Why is class linked to health? Crowded living conditions, substandard housing, poor diet, and stress all contribute to the ill health of many low-income people in the United States. In certain instances, poor education may lead to a lack of awareness of measures necessary to maintain good health. Financial strains are certainly a major factor in the health problems of less affluent people.

From the perspective of . . .

A Health Care Provider How would you explain the importance of preventative care to a 25-year-old who feels great?

What is particularly troubling about social class differences is that they appear to be cumulative. Little or no health care in childhood or young adulthood is likely to mean more illness later in life. The longer that low income presents a barrier to adequate health care, the more chronic and difficult to treat illness becomes (Pampel et al. 2010; Phelan et al. 2010).

Another reason for the link between social class and health is that the poor—many of whom belong to racial and ethnic minorities—are less able than others to afford quality medical care. The affluent are more likely than others to have health insurance, either because they can afford it or because they have jobs that provide it. Pharmacists report that people purchase only those medications they "need the most," or buy in small quantities, such as four pills at a time. Even for children, many of whom are eligible for government-subsidized health insurance, coverage varies widely, ranging from 96.2 percent in Massachusetts and Maine to 83.5 percent in Alaska (Figure 12-3).

Finally, in the view of Karl Marx and contemporary conflict theorists, capitalist societies such as the United States care more about maximizing profits than they do about the health and safety of industrial workers. As a result, government agencies do not take forceful action to regulate conditions in the workplace, and workers suffer many preventable job-related injuries and illnesses. As we will see later in this module, research also shows that the lower classes are more vulnerable to environmental pollution than are the affluent, not only where they work but where they live.

LO 37-2 RACE AND ETHNICITY

The health profiles of many racial and ethnic minorities reflect the social inequality evident in the United States. The poor economic and environmental conditions of groups such as African Americans, Hispanics, and Native Americans are manifested in high morbidity and mortality rates for those groups. It is true that some diseases, such as sickle-cell anemia among Blacks, have a clear genetic basis. But in most instances, environmental factors contribute to the differential rates of disease and death.

As noted earlier, infant mortality is regarded as a primary indicator of health care. There is a significant gap in the United States between the infant mortality rates of African Americans and Whites. Generally, the rate of infant death is more than twice as high among Blacks (MacDorman and Mathews 2009).

The medical establishment is not exempt from racism. Unfortunately, the media often focus on obvious forms of racism, such as hate crimes, while overlooking more insidious forms in social institutions like the medical establishment. Minorities

FIGURE 12-2 **AIDS BY THE NUMBERS WORLDWIDE**

	New infections (children)	New HIV infections (millions)	AIDS related deaths (millions)	People accessing treatment (millions)
2001	550 000	3.4		
2002	560 000	3.3		
2003	560 000	3.1		
2004	550 000	3.0	2.3	
2005	540 000	2.9	2.3	1.3
2006	520 000	2.8	2.3	2.0
2007	480 000	2.7	2.2	2.9
2008	450 000	2.6	2.1	4.1
2009	400 000	2.6	2.0	5.3
2010	360 000	2.5	1.9	6.6
2011	310 000	2.5	1.8	8.1
2012	260 000	2.3	1.6	9.7

Source: UNAIDS 2013.

FIGURE 12-3 PERCENTAGE OF CHILDREN WITHOUT HEALTH INSURANCE

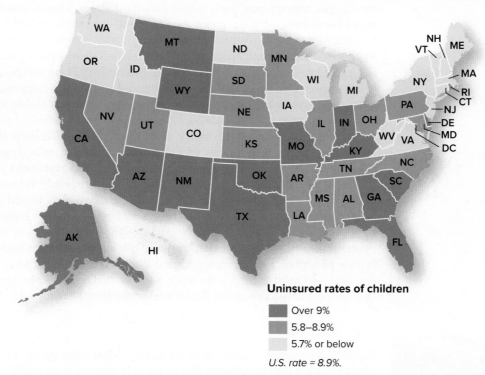

Uninsured rates of children

- ■ Over 9%
- ■ 5.8–8.9%
- ☐ 5.7% or below

U.S. rate = 8.9%.

Note: In 2012, children under 18 years without private or government health insurance, not covered by Medicaid, Medicare, or military health care.
Source: DeNavas-Walt et al. 2013: Table HI05.

receive inferior medical care even when they are insured. Despite having access to care, Blacks, Latinos, and Native Americans are treated unequally as a result of racial prejudice and differences in the quality of various health care plans. Furthermore, national clinical studies have shown that even allowing for differences in income and insurance coverage, racial and ethnic minorities are less likely than other groups to receive both standard health care and life-saving treatment for conditions such as HIV infection (Centers for Disease Control and Prevention 2011b; Long and Masi 2009).

Drawing on the conflict perspective, sociologist Howard Waitzkin (1986) suggests that racial tensions also contribute to the medical problems of Blacks. In his view, the stress that results from racial prejudice and discrimination helps to explain the higher rates of hypertension found among African Americans (and Hispanics) compared to Whites. Hypertension—twice as common in Blacks as in Whites—is believed to be a critical factor in Blacks' high mortality rates from heart disease, kidney disease, and stroke (Centers for Disease Control and Prevention 2011b).

Some Mexican Americans and many other Latinos adhere to cultural beliefs that make them less likely than others to use the established medical system. They may interpret their illnesses according to ***curanderismo,*** or traditional Latino folk medicine—a form of holistic health care and healing. *Curanderismo* influences how one approaches health care and even how one defines illness. Most Hispanics probably use *curanderos,* or folk healers, infrequently, but perhaps 20 percent rely on home remedies. Some define such illnesses as *susto* (fright sickness) and *atague* (fighting attack) according to folk beliefs. Because these complaints often have biological bases, sensitive medical practitioners need to deal with them carefully in order to diagnose and treat illnesses accurately. Moreover, it would be a mistake to blame the poor health care that Latinos receive on cultural differences. Latinos are much more likely to seek treatment for pressing medical problems at clinics and emergency rooms than they are to receive regular preventive care through a family physician (Centers for Disease Control and Prevention 2011b; Durden and Hummer 2006; Trotter and Chavira 1997).

> **Study Alert**
>
> Be able to identify how poor economic and environmental conditions play a role in the high morbidity and mortality rates of racial and ethnic minorities in the United States.

LO 37-2 GENDER

A large body of research indicates that compared with men, women experience a higher occurrence of many illnesses, although they tend to live longer. There are some variations—for example, men are more likely to have parasitic diseases, whereas women are more likely to become diabetic—but as a group, women appear to be in poorer health than men.

The apparent inconsistency between the ill health of women and their greater longevity deserves an explanation, and researchers have advanced a theory. Women's lower rate of cigarette smoking (reducing their risk of heart disease, lung cancer, and emphysema), lower consumption of alcohol (reducing the risk of auto accidents and cirrhosis of the liver), and lower rate of employment in dangerous occupations explain about one-third of their greater longevity than men. Moreover, some clinical studies suggest that the differences in morbidity may actually be less pronounced than the data show. Researchers argue that women are much more likely than men to seek treatment, to be diagnosed as having a disease, and thus to have their illnesses reflected in the data examined by epidemiologists.

From a conflict perspective, women have been particularly vulnerable to the medicalization of society, with everything from birth to beauty being treated in an increasingly medical context. Such medicalization may contribute to women's higher morbidity rates compared to those of men. Ironically, even though women have been especially affected by medicalization, medical researchers have often excluded them from clinical studies. Female physicians and researchers charge that sexism lies at the heart of such research practices, and insist there is a desperate need for studies of female subjects (Centers for Disease Control and Prevention 2011b; Rieker and Bird 2000).

LO 37-2 AGE

Health is the overriding concern of the elderly. Most older people in the United States report having at least one chronic illness, but only some of those conditions are potentially life threatening or require medical care. At the same time, health problems can affect the quality of life of older people in important ways. Almost half of older people in the United States are troubled by arthritis, and many have visual or hearing impairments that can interfere with the performance of everyday tasks.

Older people are also especially vulnerable to certain mental health problems. Alzheimer's disease, the leading cause of dementia in the United States, afflicts an estimated 5.4 million people age 65 or over—that is, 13 percent of that segment of the population. While some individuals with Alzheimer's exhibit only mild symptoms, the risk of severe problems resulting from the disease rises substantially with age (Alzheimer's Association 2012).

Not surprisingly, older people in the United States (age 75 and older) are five times more likely to use health services than younger people (ages 15–24). The disproportionate use of the U.S. health care system by older people is a critical factor in all discussions about the cost of health care and possible reforms of the health care system (Bureau of the Census 2011a).

In sum, to achieve greater access and reduce health disparities, federal health officials must overcome inequities that are rooted not just in age, but in social class, race and ethnicity, and gender. If that were not enough, they must also deal with a geographical disparity in health care resources.

E Evaluate

Read each question carefully and then select or provide the best answer.

1. Which one of the following nations has the lowest infant mortality rate?
   a. the United States
   b. Mozambique
   c. Canada
   d. Japan

2. Compared with Whites, Blacks have higher death rates from
   a. heart disease.
   b. diabetes.
   c. cancer.
   d. all of the above.

3. Which theorist notes that capitalist societies, such as the United States, care more about maximizing profits

than they do about the health and safety of industrial workers?

a. Thomas Szasz
b. Karl Marx
c. Erving Goffman
d. Talcott Parsons

4. A _____ _____ studies the effects of social class, race and ethnicity, gender, and age on the distribution of disease, impairment, and general health across a population.

5. Sociologists find it useful to consider _____ rates because they reveal that a specific disease occurs more frequently among one segment of a population compared with another.

Answers

1 (d); 2 (d); 3 (b); 4 social epidemiologist; 5 morbidity

R Rethink

Consider these questions to get a deeper understanding of the material.

1. Which is a more important factor in the adequate delivery of health care, race or gender? Explain.

2. What are some likely social consequences of passage of the Patient Protection and Affordable Care Act of 2010 (also called Obamacare)?

RECAP

LO 37-1 Explain what is meant by social epidemiology.

- Historically, epidemiologists focused on the scientific study of the origins and spread of epidemics.
- Contemporary social epidemiology is concerned not only with epidemics but also with nonepidemic diseases, injuries, drug addiction and alcoholism, suicide, and mental illness.

LO 37-2 Describe how social class, race, ethnicity, gender, and age can affect the overall health of populations.

- Studies have consistently shown that people in the lower social classes have higher rates of mortality and disability than others.
- Racial and ethnic minorities have higher rates of morbidity and mortality than Whites. Women tend to be in poorer health than men but to live longer. Older people are especially vulnerable to mental health problems, such as Alzheimer's disease.

KEY TERMS

Curanderismo Latino folk medicine, a form of holistic health care and healing.
Morbidity rate The rate of disease in a given population.
Mortality rate The rate of death in a given population.
Social epidemiology The study of the distribution of disease, impairment, and general health status across a population.

MODULE 38 Physical and Mental Health Care in the United States

P Prepare Learning Objectives

LO 38-1 Describe the history and practices of the health care system in the United States.

LO 38-2 Summarize alternatives to traditional health care and explain the role of government in U.S. health care.

LO 38-3 Discuss the foundation and development of mental health treatment in the United States.

As the entire nation is well aware, the costs of health care have skyrocketed. In 1997, total expenditures for health care in the United States crossed the trillion-dollar threshold—more than four times the 1980 total (Figure 12-4). In 2000, the amount spent on health care equaled that spent on education, defense, prisons, farm subsidies, food stamps, and foreign aid combined. By the year 2020, total expenditures for health care in the United States are expected to exceed $4.6 trillion. The rising costs of medical care are especially burdensome in the event of catastrophic illnesses or confinement to a nursing home. Bills of tens of thousands of dollars are not unusual in the treatment of cancer, Alzheimer's disease, and other chronic illnesses requiring custodial care.

The health care system of the United States has moved far beyond the days when general practitioners living in a neighborhood or community made house calls and charged modest fees for their services. How did health care become a big business involving nationwide hospital chains and marketing campaigns? How have these changes reshaped the interactions between doctors, nurses, and patients? We will address these questions in this module.

LO **38-1** A Historical View

Today, state licensing and medical degrees confer an authority on medical professionals that is maintained from one generation to the next. However, health care in the United States has not always followed this model. The "popular health movement" of the 1830s and 1840s emphasized preventive care and what is termed "self-help." Strong criticism was voiced of "doctoring" as a paid occupation. New medical philosophies or sects established their own medical schools and challenged the authority and methods of more traditional doctors. By the 1840s, most states had repealed medical licensing laws.

In response, through the leadership of the American Medical Association (AMA), founded in 1848, "regular" doctors attacked lay practitioners, sectarian doctors, and female physicians in general. Once they had institutionalized their authority through standardized programs of education and licensing, they conferred it on all who successfully completed their programs. The authority of the physician no longer depended on lay attitudes or on the person occupying the sick role; increasingly, it was built into the structure of the medical profession and the health care system. As the institutionalization of health care proceeded, the medical profession gained

FIGURE 12-4 **TOTAL HEALTH CARE EXPENDITURES IN THE UNITED STATES, 1970–2020 (PROJECTED)**

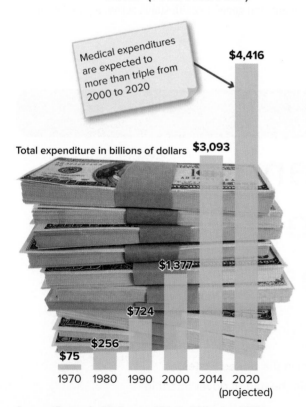

Medical expenditures are expected to more than triple from 2000 to 2020

$4,416

Total expenditure in billions of dollars $3,093

$1,377

$724

$256

$75

1970 1980 1990 2000 2014 2020 (projected)

Sources: Centers for Medicare and Medicaid Services 2013a, 2013b: Table 1.

control over both the market for its services and the various organizational hierarchies that govern medical practice, financing, and policymaking. By the 1920s, physicians controlled hospital technology, the division of labor of health personnel, and indirectly, other professional practices such as nursing and pharmacy (R. Coser 1984).

Patients have traditionally relied on medical personnel to inform them of health care issues, but increasingly they are turning to the media for health care information. Recognizing this change, pharmaceutical firms are advertising their prescription drugs directly to potential customers through television and magazines. The Internet is another growing source for patient information. Medical professionals are understandably suspicious of these new sources of information.

Today, consumers get more than their health care information in new ways. Over the past decade, they have discovered a new way to access traditional medicine: going to the store (Box 12-1).

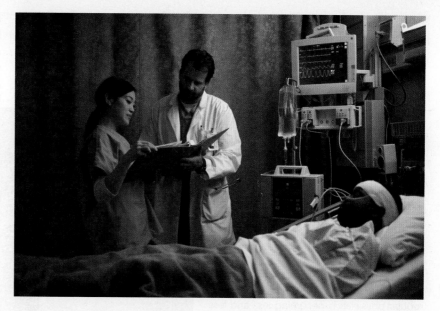

As if the status differences between nurses and physicians were not clear to all, the more colorful uniform of nurses and the formal white doctor's coat reinforce the distinction.

LO 38-1 Physicians, Nurses, and Patients

Traditionally, physicians have held a position of dominance in their dealings with both patients and nurses. The functionalist and interactionist perspectives offer a framework for understanding the professional socialization of physicians as it relates to patient care. Functionalists suggest that established physicians and medical school professors serve as mentors or role models who transmit knowledge, skills, and values to the passive learner—the medical student. Interactionists emphasize that students are molded by the medical school environment as they interact with their classmates.

Both approaches argue that the typical training of physicians in the United States leads to rather dehumanizing physician–patient encounters. As Dr. Lori Arviso Alvord, a Navajo physician, writes in *The Scalpel and the Silver Bear,* "I had been trained by a group of physicians who placed much more emphasis on their technical abilities and clinical skills than on their abilities to be caring and sensitive" (Alvord and Van Pelt 1999:13). Despite many efforts to formally introduce a humanistic approach to patient care into the medical school curriculum, patient overload and cost-cutting by hospitals have tended to undercut positive relations. Moreover, widespread publicity about malpractice suits and high medical costs has further strained the physician–patient relationship. Interactionists have closely examined compliance and negotiation between physician and patient. They concur with Talcott Parsons's view that the relationship is generally asymmetrical, with doctors holding a position of dominance and controlling rewards.

Just as physicians have maintained dominance in their interactions with patients, they have controlled interactions with nurses. Despite their training and professional status, nurses commonly take orders from physicians. Traditionally, the relationship between doctors and nurses has paralleled the male dominance of the United States: most physicians have been male, while virtually all nurses have been female.

Like other women in subordinate roles, nurses have been expected to perform their duties without challenging the authority of men. Psychiatrist Leonard Stein (1967) refers to this process as the *doctor–nurse game.* According to the rules of this "game," the nurse must never openly disagree with the physician. When she has recommendations concerning a patient's care, she must communicate them indirectly, in a deferential tone. For example, if asked by a hospital's medical resident, "What sleeping medication has been helpful to Mrs. Brown in the past?" (an indirect request for a recommendation), the nurse will respond with a disguised recommendation, such as "Pentobarbital 100 mg was quite

Greeting cards are in aisle 7; vaccinations, in aisle 4. Today, over 1,200 health clinics are located in retail stores throughout the United States, including Walgreens, CVS, and Walmart. Staffed by nurse-practitioners and nurses with advanced degrees, these in-store clinics treat a limited menu of complaints, including sore throats, ear infections, pinkeye, and non-complicated respiratory conditions. And the nurses do write prescriptions.

What are the implications of these new clinics for traditional health care? Having a regular physician is becoming less and less common in the United States, given the many people who lack health insurance, as well as the frequent changes in corporate health plans. Like it or not, the physician you see this year simply may not be available to you next year. Under these circumstances, retail medical care may not pose much of a challenge to traditional medical practices.

For three acute conditions—sore throat, middle ear infection, and urinary tract infection—retail clinics delivered the same or better-quality care than traditional medical settings.

What about the quality of care offered at in-store clinics? Recently, researchers compared the care delivered in retail clinics to the care available in doctors' offices, urgent care departments, and emergency rooms. For three acute conditions—sore throat, middle ear infection, and urinary tract infection—they found that retail clinics delivered the same or better-quality care than traditional medical settings, including preventive care during or after the first visit. Costs were much lower, especially compared to those in emergency rooms.

In-store clinics are another example of **McDonaldization**, the process by which the principles of bureaucratization have increasingly shaped organizations worldwide. McDonaldization offers the benefit of clearly stated services and prices, but the drawback of impersonality. Family doctors note that 40 percent of clinic patients have a family physician. Yet given the shortcomings of health care delivery in the United States, it is difficult to argue against an innovative new method of providing health care.

Let's Discuss

1. Have you ever been treated at an in-store clinic? If so, were you satisfied with the care you received? What about the price you paid—was it reasonable?
2. Evaluate the emergence of clinics from a functionalist and then a conflict perspective. On balance, do you think these clinics are a benefit to society?

Sources: Pickert 2009; RAND 2010; Ritzer 2013:63–64.

---

effective night before last." Her careful response allows the physician to authoritatively restate the same prescription as if it were *his* idea.

Like nurses, female physicians have traditionally found themselves in a subordinate position because of their gender, but that is slowly changing as their numbers increase.

LO 38-2 Alternatives to Traditional Health Care

In traditional forms of health care, people rely on physicians and hospitals for the treatment of illness. Yet at least one out of every three adults in the United States attempts to maintain good health or respond to illness through the use of alternative health care techniques.

For example, in recent decades interest has been growing in *holistic* (also spelled *wholistic*) medical principles, first developed in China. **Holistic medicine** refers to therapies in which the health care practitioner considers the person's physical, mental, emotional, and spiritual characteristics. The individual is regarded as a totality rather than a collection of interrelated organ systems. Treatment methods include massage, chiropractic medicine, acupuncture (which involves the insertion of fine needles into surface points), respiratory exercises, and the use of herbs as remedies. Nutrition, exercise, and visualization may also be used to treat ailments that are generally treated through medication or hospitalization (Sharma and Bodeker 1998).

Practitioners of holistic medicine do not necessarily function totally outside the traditional health care system. Some have medical degrees and rely on X-rays and EKG machines for diagnostic assistance. Others who staff holistic clinics, often referred to as *wellness clinics,* reject the use of medical technology. The recent resurgence of holistic medicine comes amid widespread recognition of the value of nutrition and the dangers of overreliance on prescription drugs (especially those used to reduce stress, such as Valium).

The medical establishment—professional organizations, research hospitals, and medical schools—has generally served as a stern protector of traditionally accepted health care techniques. However, a major breakthrough occurred in 1992 when the federal government's National Institutes of Health—the nation's major funding source for biomedical research—opened the National Center for Complementary and Alternative Medicine, empowered to accept grant requests. NIH-sponsored national surveys found that one in four adults in the United States had used some form of "complementary and alternative medicine" during the previous month or year. Examples included acupuncture, folk medicine, meditation, yoga, homeopathic treatments, megavitamin therapy, and chiropractic treatment. When prayer was included as an alternative or complementary form of medicine, the proportion of adults who used alternative medicine rose to over 62 percent (Figure 12-5).

On the international level, the World Health Organization (WHO) has begun to monitor the use of alternative medicine around the world. According to WHO, 80 percent of people who live in the poorest countries in the world use some form of alternative medicine, from herbal treatments to the services of a faith healer. In most countries, these treatments are largely unregulated, even though some of them can be fatal. For example, kava kava, an herbal tea used in the Pacific Islands to relieve anxiety, can be toxic to the liver in concentrated form. However, other alternative treatments have been found to be effective in the treatment of serious diseases, such as malaria and sickle-cell anemia. WHO's goal is to compile a list of such practices, as well as to encourage the development of universal training programs and ethical standards for practitioners of alternative medicine. To date, the organization has published findings on about 100 of the 5,000 plants believed to be used as herbal remedies (McNeil 2002).

LO 38-2 The Role of Government

Not until the 20th century did health care receive federal aid. The first significant involvement was the 1946 Hill-Burton Act, which provided subsidies for building and improving hospitals, especially in rural areas. A far more important change came with the enactment in 1965 of two wide-ranging government assistance programs: Medicare, which is essentially a compulsory health insurance plan for the elderly, and Medicaid, which is a noncontributory federal and state insurance plan for the poor. These programs greatly expanded federal involvement in health care financing for needy men, women, and children.

> **Study Alert**
>
> Remember that *holistic medicine* often uses alternative medical approaches when treating a person's physical, mental, emotional, and spiritual health.

FIGURE 12-5 **USE OF COMPLEMENTARY AND ALTERNATIVE MEDICINE**

Diets	3.6 %
Yoga	6.1 %
Massage	8.3%
Chiropractic	8.6%
Meditation	9.4%
Prayer group	9.6%
Deep breathing	12.7%
Natural products	17.1%
Prayer/others	24.4%
Prayer/self	43.0%

Note: Data from 2007 survey, except for prayer data from 2002 survey.
Source: P. Barnes et al. 2004, 2008.

Tensions ran high as the Supreme Court heard arguments on the constitutionality of controversial new federal health care legislation. These citizens are indicating their opposition to the 2010 Affordable Care Act.

Given the high rates of illness and disability among elderly people, Medicare has had a huge impact on the health care system. Initially, Medicare simply reimbursed health care providers such as physicians and hospitals for the billed costs of their services. However, in 1983, as the overall costs of Medicare increased dramatically, the federal government introduced a price-control system. Under this system, private hospitals often transfer patients whose treatment may be unprofitable to public facilities. In fact, many private hospitals have begun to conduct "wallet biopsies"— that is, to investigate the financial status of potential patients. Those judged undesirable are then refused admission or dumped. Although a federal law passed in 1987 made it illegal for any hospital receiving Medicare funds to dump patients, the practice continues (E. Gould 2007; Light 2004).

The 2010 Affordable Care Act improved health insurance coverage for people of all ages, especially young adults, who were allowed to remain longer on their parents' policies. President Obama's administration had pushed for the act in response to several problems, including high out-of-pocket costs for the uninsured and the inability of people with preexisting conditions to get insurance. In 2012 the Supreme Court upheld the federal government's authority to implement the law's provisions. Opponents of the legislation, which they dubbed "Obamacare," have vowed to seek legislative changes to the law and to make further legal challenges in 2014. Critics complain that the act is too expensive for taxpayers, and unnecessarily—perhaps even unconstitutionally—dictates citizens' health care decisions.

LO 38-3 What Is Mental Illness?

Like other illnesses, mental disorders affect not just individuals and their families, but society as a whole. In industrial economies, mental disorders are a significant cause of disability. Thus, as a British medical journal declared in connection with the Global Mental Health Summit, there can be "no health without mental health" (Prince et al. 2007).

Sadly, the words *mental illness* and *insanity* evoke dramatic and often inaccurate images of emotional problems. Though the media routinely emphasize the most violent behavior of those with emotional disturbances, mental health and mental illness can more appropriately be viewed as a continuum of behavior that we ourselves move along. Using this definition, we can consider a person to have a mental disorder "if he or she is so disturbed that coping with routine, everyday life is difficult or impossible." The term **mental illness** should be reserved for a disorder of the brain that disrupts a person's thinking, feeling, and ability to interact with others (J. Coleman and Cressey 1980:315; National Alliance on Mental Illness 2008).

Traditionally, people in the United States have maintained a negative and suspicious view of those with mental disorders. Holding the status of "mental patient" or even "former mental patient" can have unfortunate and undeserved consequences. Voting rights are denied in some instances, acceptance for jury duty is problematic, and past emotional problems are an issue in divorce and custody cases. Moreover, content analysis of network television programs and films shows that mentally ill characters are uniformly portrayed in a demeaning and derogatory fashion; many are labeled as "criminally insane," "wackos," or "psychos." From an interactionist perspective, a key social institution is shaping social behavior by manipulating symbols and intensifying people's fears about the mentally ill (Diefenbach and West 2007).

In 2012, a tragic mass shooting at an elementary school in Newtown, Connecticut, led to renewed scrutiny of the role of mental illness in incidents of gun violence. The shooter was said to have had a mental illness, for which he apparently went untreated. As a result, some people argued that to curb gun violence, legislators should focus on mental health rather than on gun control. Unfortunately, such public debates tend to perpetuate the false assumption that people with mental illness are dangerous, furthering the *stigma* associated with their illness. The term **stigma**, coined by the interactionist Erving Goffman (1963), describes the labels society uses to devalue members of certain social groups.

A review of the available survey data shows that over time, the general public has become more sophisticated about mental illness, and perhaps a bit more open to disclosure, recognition, and response to mental health problems. Yet since 1950, people have become much more likely to associate "violence" with "mental illness," despite overwhelming evidence to the contrary. In fact, the vast majority of people with psychiatric disorders *do not* commit violent acts. Only 4 percent of violent crimes in the United States can be attributed to people with mental illness (R. Friedman 2012; Nocera 2012; Pescosolido 2013).

Certainly many in the mental health community would welcome expanded services for those with mental illness, especially given the billions of dollars that were cut from mental health programs during the recession. However, members of this community have questioned hastily drawn-up proposals that would lower the threshold for involuntary commitment or broaden the requirements for reporting potentially dangerous patients to the authorities. Their concerns may not receive a fair hearing, though, because the mental health community is far less powerful politically than the advocacy groups representing gun owners and sellers (E. Goode and Healy 2013).

Despite the stigmatization of mental illness, more people are seeking care and professional assistance than in the past. In the military services, the depression and post-traumatic stress that many veterans experience is receiving growing attention. And increasingly, legislators are recognizing the need to provide services for all who suffer from mental illness (Kessler et al. 2006; Tanielian 2009).

LO 38-3 THEORETICAL MODELS OF MENTAL DISORDERS

In studying mental illness, we can draw on both the medical model and a more sociological approach derived from labeling theory. Each model rests on distinctive assumptions regarding treatment of people with mental disorders.

According to the medical model, mental illness is rooted in biological causes that can be treated through medical intervention. Problems in brain structure or in the biochemical balance in the brain, sometimes due to injury and sometimes due to genetic inheritance, are thought to be at the bottom of these disorders. The U.S. Surgeon General (1999) released an exhaustive report on mental health in which he declared that the accumulated weight of scientific evidence leaves no doubt about the physical origins of mental illness.

That is not to say that social factors do not contribute to mental illness. Just as culture affects the occurrence of illness and its treatment, so too it can affect mental illness. In fact, the very definition of mental illness differs from one culture to the next. Mainstream U.S. culture, for instance, considers hallucinations highly abnormal. However, many traditional cultures view them as evidence of divine favor and confer a special status on those who experience them. As we have noted throughout this textbook,

In 2011, actress Catherine Zeta-Jones announced that she was being treated for bipolar disorder, a condition she shares with an estimated 2 percent of the U.S. population. The stigma of mental illness is slowly diminishing as celebrities come forward to reveal they are being treated for various mental disorders.

For generations, many thousands of people with mental illness were effectively removed from society and placed in residential facilities. The now abandoned Harlem Valley Psychiatric Center in Dover, New York, which operated from 1924 to 1993, included 80 buildings; at its peak it housed 5,000 patients.

a given behavior may be viewed as normal in one society, disapproved of but tolerated in a second, and labeled as sick and heavily sanctioned in a third.

A major focus of the controversy over the medical model is the *Diagnostic and Statistical Manual of Mental Disorders (DSM),* which came out in its fifth edition in 2013 (*DSM-5*). The *DSM,* which was introduced in 1952 by the American Psychiatric Association (APA), is intended to establish standard criteria for diagnosing mental disorders. Over time, however, the classification of various conditions has changed, seeming to undercut the notion that mental disorders are fixed medical conditions. A 1987 revision, for example, dropped the diagnosis "sexual orientation disturbance," ending the treatment of homosexuality as a curable disorder. In *DSM-5,* binge eating and some forms of hoarding have been added to the list of disorders, and bereavement has been removed as a symptom of depression.

Importantly, the *DSM* is more than an academic volume. The categories it sets forth become the basis for insurance coverage, special educational and behavioral services, and medical prescriptions, and may qualify those with a diagnosis for disability benefits. Although supporters of the *DSM* acknowledge its limitations, they stress the need for practitioners to reach a consensus on the definition and treatment of mental disorders (American Psychiatric Association 2013; Satel 2013; Scheid 2013).

In contrast to the medical model, labeling theory suggests that some behaviors that are viewed as mental illnesses may not really be illnesses. For example, the U.S. Surgeon General's report (1999:5) notes that "bereavement symptoms" of less than two months' duration do not qualify as a mental disorder, but beyond that they may be redefined. Sociologists would see this approach to bereavement as labeling by those with the power to affix labels rather than as an acknowledgment of a biological condition.

Psychiatrist Thomas Szasz ("Sahz"), in his book *The Myth of Mental Illness* (2010), advanced the view that numerous personality disorders are not diseases, but simply patterns of conduct labeled as disorders by significant others. The response to Szasz's challenging thesis was sharp: the commissioner of the New York State Department of Hygiene demanded his dismissal from his university position because Szasz did not "believe" in mental illness. But many sociologists embraced his model as a logical extension of examining individual behavior in a social context.

In sum, the medical model is persuasive because it pinpoints the causes of mental illness and offers treatment for disorders. Yet proponents of the labeling perspective maintain that mental illness is a distinctively social process, whatever other processes are involved. From a sociological perspective, the ideal approach to mental illness integrates the insights of labeling theory with those of the medical approach (Horwitz 2002; Scheid 2013).

LO 38-3 Patterns of Care

For most of human history, those who suffered from mental disorders were deemed the responsibility of their families. Yet mental illness has been a matter of governmental concern much longer than physical illness has. That is because severe emotional disorders threaten stable social relationships and entail prolonged incapacitation. As early as the 1600s, European cities began to confine the insane in public facilities along with the poor and criminals. Prisoners, indignant at being forced to live with "lunatics," resisted this approach. The isolation of people with mental illness from others in the same facility and from the larger society soon made physicians the central and ultimate authority over their welfare.

A major policy development in caring for those with mental disorders came with the passage of the Community Mental Health Centers Act (1963). The CMHC program, as it is known, not only increased the federal government's involvement in the treatment of people with mental illness. It also established community-based mental health centers to treat clients on an *outpatient* basis, thereby allowing them to continue working and living at home. The program showed that outpatient treatment could be more effective than the institutionalized programs of state and county mental hospitals.

Expansion of the federally funded CMHC program decreased inpatient care. By the 1980s, community-based mental health care had replaced hospitalization as the typical form of treatment. Across the United States, deinstitutionalization of the mentally ill reached dramatic proportions. Deinstitutionalization had been conceived as a social reform that would effectively reintegrate the mentally ill into the outside world. However, the authentic humanitarian concern behind the approach proved to be a convenient front for politicians whose goal was simply to cut costs. In 1950, 339 people per 100,000 population resided in state psychiatric hospitals. By 2010 the number had declined to 14 per 100,000 (Kelly 2009; Szabo 2013; Torrey 2013).

In a marked shift from public policy over the past three decades, several states have recently made it easier to commit mental patients to hospitals involuntarily. These changes have come in part because community groups and individual residents have voiced increasing fear and anger about the growing number of people with mental illness who are homeless and living in their midst, many of them on the streets. All too often, the severely mentally ill end up in jail or prison after committing crimes that lead to their prosecution. Ironically, family members of these men and women with mental illness complain that they cannot get adequate treatment for their loved ones *until* they have committed violent acts. Nevertheless, civil liberties advocates and voluntary associations of people with mental illness worry about the risks of denying people their constitutional rights, and cite horror stories about the abuses people have experienced during institutionalization (Marquis and Morain 1999; Shogren 1994).

The Mental Health Parity and Addiction Equity Act of 2008, which took effect in 2010, requires insurers to extend comparable benefits for mental and physical health care. This congressional effort to ensure equal treatment for mental health patients is not the first or only such effort. Although the act has helped to dispel the stigma associated with mental illness, most mental health providers agree that true parity in financial benefits for those with mental disorders has not been achieved. For example, the act exempts group health insurance plans if providing comparable mental health benefits would increase premiums by 1 percent or more. Higher co-pays, deductibles, and out-of-pocket maximums also have undercut the legislation's effectiveness (Health Cost Institute 2013; Hernandez and Uggen 2012).

Finally, although mental health care is often considered to be qualitatively different from other types of health care, many of the observations that apply to traditional medicine also apply to mental health care. For example, African Americans, Latinos, and American Indians have higher rates for several mental disorders, but are much less likely than Whites to receive treatment. Documented prejudice by practitioners contributes to the disparity, along with inadequate insurance and geographic isolation. In both rural and inner-city areas, mental health care is difficult to access and often poor in quality, especially for members of minority groups (McGuire and Miranda 2008).

E Evaluate

Read each question carefully and then select or provide the best answer.

1. Placing sole power to educate and award medical licenses in the hands of the American Medical Association is an example of the
   a. socialization of health care.
   b. stigmatization of health care.
   c. institutionalization of health care.
   d. democratization of health care.

2. Which program is essentially a compulsory health insurance plan for the elderly?
   a. Medicare
   b. Medicaid
   c. Blue Cross
   d. Healthpac

3. _____ medicine refers to therapies in which the health care practitioner considers the patient's physical, mental, emotional, and spiritual state.

4. Traditionally, the relationship between doctors and nurses has paralleled the pattern of _____ dominance in the larger society.

5. The system of reimbursement used by Medicare has contributed to the controversial practice of "_____," under which patients whose treatment may be unprofitable are transferred by private hospitals to public facilities.

Answers

R Rethink

Consider these questions to get a deeper understanding of the material.

1. Explain the dominance of physicians in the health care system from a conflict perspective.

2. In the United States, a nation with a world-renowned medical system, why do so many people seek alternative forms of health care?

RECAP

LO 38-1 Describe the history and practices of the health care system in the United States.

- The American Medical Association, through its monopoly of physician education and licensing, has institutionalized health care and gained control over the profession.
- The preeminent role of physicians in the U.S. health care system has given them a position of dominance in their dealings with nurses and patients, who are socialized not to contradict or question their pronouncements.
- The institutionalized approach to medicine has been criticized for dehumanizing the physician–patient relationship and turning the physician–nurse relationship into a power game.

LO 38-2 Summarize alternatives to traditional health care and explain the role of government in U.S. health care.

- Largely because of the high cost and impersonality of institutionalized medicine, many people have turned to alternative health care techniques, such as holistic medicine, acupuncture, homeopathic treatments, and self-help groups.

- The World Health Organization (WHO) has begun to compile a list of alternative medical practices and to encourage the development of training programs and ethical standards for practitioners.
- The federal government only recently entered the health care arena, instituting Medicare and Medicaid in 1965 and the Affordable Care Act ("Obamacare") in 2010.

LO 38-3 Discuss the foundation and development of mental health treatment in the United States.

- Mental disorders may be viewed from two different perspectives, the medical model and the sociological model, which is based on labeling theory. The medical model holds that mental illness is biologically caused, while the sociological model suggests that societal labels are attached to some behaviors that may not be illnesses.
- In the United States, society has traditionally taken a negative, suspicious attitude toward people with mental disorders, attaching a stigma to them even after they have been treated and cured.
- As mental health treatment shifted from hospitalization to deinstitutionalization with care from community mental health centers, funding dropped noticeably. Deinstitutionalization became a way to cut costs without treating patients. Unfortunately, this has led to an unfounded fear of mental patients living without restraint in the larger society.
- Mental health care shares with physical health care the discriminatory treatment of African American, Latino, and American Indian patients, as compared with White patients.

KEY TERMS

Holistic medicine Therapies in which the health care practitioner considers the person's physical, mental, emotional, and spiritual characteristics.

McDonaldization The process by which the principles of bureaucratization have increasingly shaped organizations worldwide.

Mental illness A disorder of the brain that disrupts a person's thinking, feeling, and ability to interact with others.

Stigma A label used to devalue members of certain social groups.

MODULE 39 Sociological Perspectives on the Environment

W Work

We have seen that the environment people live in has a noticeable effect on their health. Those who live in stressful, overcrowded places suffer more from disease than those who do not. Likewise, people have a noticeable effect on their environment. Around the world, increases in population, together with the economic development that accompanies them, have had serious environmental consequences. We can see signs of despoliation almost everywhere: our air, our water, and our land are being polluted, whether we live in St. Louis, Mexico City, or Lagos, Nigeria.

Though environmental problems may be easy to identify, devising socially and politically acceptable solutions to them is much more difficult. In this module we will see what sociologists have to say about the trade-off between economic growth and development and its effects on the environment. In the Social Policy section we will look more closely at specific environmental issues.

TABLE 12-2 WORLD POPULATION GROWTH

Population Level	Time Taken to Reach New Population Level	Year of Attainment
First billion	Human history before 1800	1800
Second billion	130 years	1930
Third billion	30 years	1960
Fourth billion	14 years	1974
Fifth billion	13 years	1987
Sixth billion	12 years	1999
Seventh billion	12 years	2011
Eighth billion	13 years	2024
Ninth billion	21 years	2045

Two centuries of rapid population growth have placed enormous pressure on the environment. Even more significant, however, has been the growth of human consumption and waste, both natural and manufactured.

Sources: Population Reference Bureau and United Nations in Kunzig 2011.

LO 39-1 Human Ecology

Human ecology is an area of study that is concerned with the interrelationships between people and their environment. As the environmentalist Barry Commoner (1971:39) put it, "Everything is connected to everything else." Human ecologists focus on how the physical environment shapes people's lives and on how people influence the surrounding environment.

There is no shortage of illustrations of the interconnectedness of people and their environment. For example, scientific research has linked pollutants in the physical environment to people's health and behavior. The increasing occurrence of asthma, lead poisoning, and cancer have all been tied to human alterations to the environment. Similarly, the rise in melanoma (skin cancer) diagnoses has been linked to global warming. Ecological changes in our food and diet have been related to early obesity and diabetes. And finally, global population growth has had a huge impact on the environment (Table 12-2).

With its view that "everything is connected to everything else," human ecology stresses the trade-offs inherent in every decision that alters the environment. In facing the environmental challenges of the 21st century, government policymakers and environmentalists must determine how they can fulfill humans' pressing needs for food, clothing, and shelter while preserving the environment.

LO 39-1 Conflict Perspective on the Environment

Can you identify these slowly sinking replicas of world-famous landmarks? Greenpeace staged the publicity stunt to draw attention to global warming during climate talks in Cancún, Mexico, in 2010.

World systems analysis shows how a growing share of the human and natural resources of developing countries is being redistributed to the core industrialized nations. This process only intensifies the destruction of natural resources in poorer regions of the world. From a conflict perspective, less affluent nations are being forced to exploit their mineral deposits, forests, and fisheries in order to meet their debt obligations. The poor turn to the only means of survival available to them: they plow mountain slopes, burn plots in tropical forests, and overgraze grasslands (Pellow and Brehm 2013).

Brazil exemplifies this interplay between economic troubles and environmental destruction. Each year more than 5.7 million acres of forest are cleared for crops and livestock. The elimination of the rain forest affects worldwide weather patterns, heightening the gradual warming of the earth. These socioeconomic patterns, with their harmful environmental consequences, are evident not only in Latin America but in many regions of Africa and Asia.

Conflict theorists are well aware of the environmental implications of land use policies in the Third World, but they contend that focusing on the developing countries is ethnocentric. First, throughout most of history, developed countries have been the major source of greenhouse gas emissions. As Figure 12-6 shows, only recently have developing nations begun to emit greenhouse gases in the same quantities as developed nations. (Greenhouse gas emissions will be discussed in more detail later.)

Second, the industrialized nations of North America and Europe account for only 12 percent of the world's population but are responsible for 60 percent of worldwide consumption. Who, these theorists ask, is more to blame for environmental deterioration: the poverty-stricken and "food-hungry" populations of the world or the "energy-hungry" industrialized nations? The money that residents of developed countries spend on ocean cruises each year could provide clean drinking water for everyone on the planet. Ice cream expenditures in Europe alone could be used to immunize every child in the world. Thus, conflict theorists charge, the most serious threat to the environment comes from the global consumer class (Pellow and Brehm 2013).

Allan Schnaiberg (1994) further refined this analysis by shifting the focus from affluent consumers to the capitalist system as the cause of environmental troubles. In his view, a capitalist system creates a "treadmill of production" because of its inherent

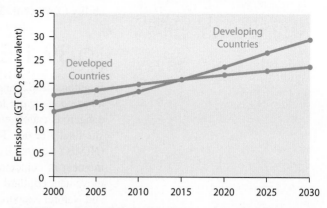

FIGURE 12-6   PROJECTED GREENHOUSE GAS EMISSIONS

By 2015, total greenhouse gas emissions from developing countries are expected to exceed those from developed countries.

Source: Environmental Protection Agency 2012.

From the perspective of . . .

A Landfill Operator   What relationship do you see between the promotion of endless consumption and the current state of the environment?

need to build ever-expanding profits. This treadmill necessitates the creation of increasing demand for products, the purchase of natural resources at minimal cost, and the manufacturing of products as quickly and cheaply as possible—no matter what the long-term environmental consequences. Indeed, over a century ago, Max Weber predicted that rampant industrialism would continue until "the last ton of fossil fuel has burnt to ashes" ([1904] 2011:157).

LO 39-1 Ecological Modernization

Critics of the human ecological and conflict models argue that they are too rooted in the past. People who take these approaches, they charge, have become bogged down in addressing existing practices. Instead, proponents of **ecological modernization**, an approach that emerged in the 1980s, focus on the alignment of environmentally favorable practices with economic self-interest through constant adaptation and restructuring (Mol 2010; Mol and Sonnenfeld 2000; Mol et al. 2009).

Ecological modernization can occur on both the macro and micro levels. On a macro level, adaptation and restructuring can mean reintegrating industrial waste back into the production process. On a micro level, it can mean reshaping individual lifestyles, including human consumption patterns. In a sense, those who practice ecological modernization seek to refute the oft-expressed notion that being environmentally conscious means "going back to nature" or "living off the grid." Even modest changes in production and consumption patterns, they believe, can increase environmental sustainability (York et al. 2010).

LO 39-1 Environmental Justice

In autumn 1982, nearly 500 African Americans participated in a six-week protest against a hazardous waste landfill in North Carolina. Their protests and legal actions against the dangerous cancer-causing chemicals continued until 2002, when decontamination of the site finally began. This 20-year battle could be seen as yet another "not in my backyard" (NIMBY) event. But today, the Warren County struggle is viewed as a transformative moment in contemporary environmentalism: the beginning of the *environmental justice* movement (Bullard 1993; McGurty 2000; North Carolina Department of Environmental and Natural Resources 2008).

Environmental justice is a legal strategy based on claims that racial minorities are subjected disproportionately to environmental hazards. Some observers have heralded environmental justice as the "new civil rights of the 21st century" (Kokmen 2008:42). Since the start of the environmental justice movement, activists and scholars have discovered other environmental disparities that break along racial and social class lines. In general, poor people and people of color are much more likely than others to be victimized by the everyday consequences of our built environment, including the air pollution from expressways and incinerators.

Sociologists Paul Mohai and Robin Saha (2007) examined over 600 identified hazardous waste treatment, storage, and disposal facilities in the United States. They found that non-Whites and Latinos make up 43 percent of the people who live within one mile of these dangerous sites. Skeptics often argue that minorities move near such sites because of low housing prices. However, two recent longitudinal (long-term) research studies, done over 30- and 50-year periods, found that toxic facilities tend to be located in minority communities (Mohai et al. 2009:413).

The environmental justice movement has become globalized, for several reasons. In many nations, activists have noticed similar patterns in the location of hazardous waste sites. These groups have begun to network across international borders, to share their tactics and remedies. Their unified approach is wise, because the offending corporations are often multinational entities; influencing their actions, much less prosecuting them, is difficult. As we have noted before, the global warming debate often focuses criticism on developing nations like China and India, rather than on established industrial giants with a long history of greenhouse gas emissions (Pellow and Brehm 2013).

Sociologists, then, have emphasized both the interconnectedness of humans and the environment and the divisiveness of race and social class in their work on humans and their alteration of the environment. Scientists, too, have taken different approaches, disagreeing sharply on the likely outcomes of environmental change. When these disagreements threaten to affect government policy and economic regulations, they become highly politicized.

Environmental justice draws attention to the fact that the poor, along with racial and ethnic minorities, are more likely than the rich to live near refineries, waste dumps, and other environmental hazards.

LO 39-2 Environmental Issues

Around the world, people are recognizing the need to address challenges to the environment. Yet in the United States, survey respondents do not see environmental issues as the most pressing of concerns, and they often balk at proposed solutions. Unfortunately, framing environmental issues as "problems" may prevent people from seeing environmental deterioration as the by-product of both institutional practices and their own behavior. Thus, in a 2013 national survey, 41 percent of respondents thought the seriousness of global warming was generally exaggerated (Saad 2013b).

We will discuss the enormous challenge of global warming next, along with three broad areas of environmental concern. Two of them, air and water pollution, are thought to be contributors to global warming.

AIR POLLUTION

Worldwide, more than 1 billion people are exposed to potentially health-damaging levels of air pollution. Unfortunately, in cities around the world, residents have come to accept smog and polluted air as normal. Urban air pollution is caused primarily by emissions from automobiles and secondarily by emissions from electric power plants and heavy industries. Smog not only limits visibility; it also can lead to health problems as uncomfortable as eye irritation and as deadly as lung cancer. Such problems are especially severe in developing countries.

Although people are capable of changing their behavior, they are unwilling to make such changes permanent. During the 1984 Olympics in Los Angeles, residents were asked to carpool and stagger their work hours to relieve traffic congestion and improve the quality of the air athletes would breathe. These changes resulted in a remarkable 12 percent drop in ozone levels. But when the Olympians left, people reverted to their normal behavior and the ozone levels climbed back up. Similarly, in the 2008 Olympics, China took drastic action to ensure that Beijing's high levels of air pollution did not mar the games. Construction work in the city ceased, polluting factories and power plants closed down, and roads were swept and sprayed with water several times a day. This temporary solution hardly solved China's ongoing problem, however (A. Jacobs 2010).

On an everyday basis—that is, when cities are not holding down their emissions because of global sports events—air pollution remains a serious issue. Today, half of all people live in countries where they are exposed to dangerously high levels of air pollution, either short-term or year-round. Solutions range from community efforts to clean up power plants and enforce or strengthen air quality standards to individual actions, like driving less often or using less electricity (American Lung Association 2011).

WATER POLLUTION

Throughout the United States, dumping of waste materials by industries and local governments has polluted streams, rivers, and lakes. Consequently, many bodies of water have become unsafe for drinking, fishing, and swimming. Around the world, pollution of the oceans is an issue of growing concern. Such pollution results regularly from waste dumping and is made worse by fuel leaks from shipping and occasional oil spills. When the oil tanker Exxon *Valdez* ran aground in Prince William Sound, Alaska, in 1989, its cargo of more than 11 million gallons of crude oil spilled into the sound and washed onto the shore, contaminating 1,285 miles of shoreline. All together, about 11,000 people joined in a massive cleanup effort that cost over $2 billion. Globally, oil

Images like this one have been combined with scientific data to draw attention to global warming.

Vacation in an unspoiled paradise! Increasingly, people from developed countries are turning to ecotourism as an environmentally friendly way to see the world. The new trend bridges the interests of environmentalists and businesspeople, especially in developing countries. These birdwatchers, accompanied by a local guide, are vacationing in Uganda.

tanker spills occur regularly. The oil spilled from BP's Deepwater Horizon oil platform in 2010 is estimated at *sixteen times* or more that of the Exxon *Valdez* (ITOPF 2006; Shapley 2010).

Less dramatic than large-scale accidents or disasters, but more common in many parts of the world, are problems with the basic water supply. The situation is worsened by heavy, widespread pollution of surface and groundwater by towns, industries, agriculture, and mining operations. In Egypt, a typical example, agricultural and industrial waste pours into the Nile. Every year about 17,000 Egyptian children die from diarrhea and dehydration after contact with the river's polluted water. Although water conditions in North America are not as deadly, from 2000 through 2014 the western United States and Canada experienced moderate to exceptional drought and an escalating demand for water (Hengeveld 2012; National Oceanic and Atmospheric Administration 2014).

CLIMATE CHANGE

Climate change is an observable alteration of the global atmosphere that affects natural weather patterns over several decades or longer. Periods of climate change occurred well before humans walked the earth. Recently, climate change has included rapid *global warming.*

The term **global warming** refers to the significant rise in the earth's surface temperatures that occurs when industrial gases like carbon dioxide turn the planet's atmosphere into a virtual greenhouse. These *greenhouse gas emissions,* which also include methane, nitrous oxide, and ozone, trap heat in the lower atmosphere. Even one additional degree of warmth in the globe's average surface temperature can increase the likelihood of wildfires, shrinkage of rivers and lakes, expansion of deserts, and torrential downpours, including typhoons and hurricanes. Greenhouse gas emissions are highest per capita in industrialized nations like the United States, Russia, and Japan, where energy consumption in the form of coal and oil is high. Because of their large populations and their reliance on these fossil fuels, just three nations—China, the United States, and India—account for half of all greenhouse gas emissions (Myers and Kulish 2013).

"The End of Snow?" asked a newspaper headline during the 2014 Winter Olympics. Although snow will not disappear from the earth, climatologists predict that finding suitable sites for the snow-dependent international competition will become increasingly difficult. Of the 19 cities that have hosted the Winter Olympics in the past, as few as 10 might be cold enough to do so in 2050, and just 6 in 2100. For people digging out from the record snowfalls of 2013–2014, that prediction might have seemed laughable, but the global trend is toward reduced snowfall. Decline in the snowpack is now jeopardizing half of all ski resorts in the northeastern United States; if it continues, they may not be viable 30 years from now. Similar trends are threatening ski resorts in the western United States. More important, snowpack is not just for skiers; the spring runoff from melting snow is critical to maintaining water supplies (Fox 2014).

Although scientific concern over global warming has heated up, climate change remains low on policymakers' list of concerns. The problem seems abstract, and in many countries, officials think that the real impact of any action they may take depends on decisive action by other nations. The Kyoto Protocol (1997) was intended to reduce global emissions of heat-trapped gases, which can contribute to global warming and climate change. To date, 191 countries are party to the accord; the United States and

Canada are the only major nations that have failed to ratify it. Opponents of the protocol argue that doing so would place the nation at a disadvantage in the global marketplace. The United States has attempted to address global warming and climate change in other ways, including bilateral agreements with China to reduce the two nations' emissions. However, these efforts regularly bog down amidst conflict over other political and economic issues.

In writing about the global environment, activists often assert, "We're all in this together." Though we are all in this together, the reality is that globally, the most vulnerable countries tend to be the poorest. Developing nations are more likely than others to have economies that are built on limited resources or on a small number of crops that are vulnerable to drought, flood, and fluctuations in worldwide demand (Nordhaus and Shellenberger 2007; Revkin 2007).

We can view global warming from the point of view of world systems analysis. Historically, core nations have been the major emitters of greenhouse gases. Today, however, manufacturing has moved to semi-periphery and periphery nations, where greenhouse gas emissions are escalating. Ironically, many of the forces that are now calling for a reduction in the human activity that contributes to global warming are located in core nations, which have contributed disproportionately to the problem. We want our hamburgers, but we decry the destruction of the rain forests to create grazing land for cattle. We want inexpensive clothes and toys, but we condemn developing countries for depending on coal-fired power plants. Coal-fired power generation is expected to increase from 2 to 4 percent a year for decades to come, tripling between 2010 and 2050 and surpassing oil as the world's primary energy source (L. Smith 2011).

What are the causes of this global environmental crisis? Some observers, such as Paul Ehrlich and Anne Ehrlich, see the pressure of world population growth as the central factor in environmental deterioration. They argue that population control is essential in preventing widespread starvation and environmental decay.

Barry Commoner, a biologist, counters that the primary cause of environmental ills is the increasing use of technological innovations that are destructive to the environment—among them plastics, detergents, synthetic fibers, pesticides, herbicides, and chemical fertilizers. Conflict theorists see the despoliation of the environment through the lens of world systems analysis. And interactionists stress efforts by informed individuals and groups to reduce their carbon footprint—that is, their daily or even lifetime production of greenhouse gases—through careful selection of the goods they consume (Carbon Trust 2012; Commoner 1990, 2007; Ehrlich and Ellison 2002).

THE IMPACT OF GLOBALIZATION

Globalization can be both good and bad for the environment. On the negative side, it can create a race to the bottom, as polluting companies relocate to countries with less stringent environmental standards. Similarly, globalization allows multinationals to reap the resources of developing countries for short-term profit. From Mexico to China, the industrialization that often accompanies globalization has increased pollution of all types.

Yet globalization can have a positive impact, as well. As barriers to the international movement of goods, services, and people fall, multinational corporations have an incentive to carefully consider the cost of natural resources. Overusing or wasting resources makes little sense, especially when they are in danger of depletion (Gallagher 2009; Kwong 2005).

One reflection of the interplay between globalization and the environment is the emergence of **environmental refugees**, people who have been displaced by rising seas, destructive storms, expanding deserts, water shortages, and high levels of toxic pollutants. Europe in particular is beginning to see an influx of such immigrants from developing nations. Viewed through the lens of world systems analysis, periphery countries may become overburdened by environmental problems, precipitating either migrations to industrial nations or conflicts that cause mass displacements of their populations. Even within the United States, environmental change prompts migrations. In the western United States, drought has displaced people whose livelihood once centered on freshwater fishing and irrigated crops. And in Alaska, rising waters caused by ice melt are displacing many of the Native peoples who live in coastal regions and along waterways (Susan F. Martin 2013; National Public Radio 2013).

Against these potentially negative effects of globalization we must note the potential for new jobs in what are called green industries. Installing solar panels, weatherizing homes, brewing biofuels, building hybrid cars, growing organic foods, manufacturing organic garments, and erecting giant wind turbines are all classified as *green-collar jobs.* However, skeptics question how many such jobs will be created, and to what degree they will offset job losses in pollution-prone industries like oil, gas, and coal mining (S. Greenhouse 2008b; R. Pinderhughes 2008).

LO 39-3 SOCIAL POLICY and the Environment

We have seen that researchers rely on a number of tools, from simple observational research to the latest in computer technologies. Because in the real world sociological research can have far-reaching consequences for public policy and public welfare, we'll consider its impact on the battle over the environment.

ENVIRONMENTALISM

On April 22, 1970, in a dramatic manifestation of growing grassroots concern over preservation of the environment, an estimated 25 million people turned out to observe the nation's first Earth Day. Two thousand communities held planned celebrations, and more than 2,000 colleges and 10,000 schools hosted environmental teach-ins. In many parts of the United States, citizens marched on behalf of specific environmental causes. That same year, the activism of these early environmentalists convinced Congress to establish the Environmental Protection Agency. The Clean Air, Clean Water, and Endangered Species acts soon followed (Brulle and Jenkins 2008).

Sociologist Manuel Castells (2010a:72) has declared environmentalism "the most comprehensive, influential movement of our time." Several social trends helped to mobilize the environmental movement. First, the activist subculture of the 1960s and early 1970s encouraged people, especially young people, to engage in direct action regarding social issues. Second, the dissemination of scientific knowledge about serious environmental problems like oil spills and air pollution alarmed many Americans. And third, the growing popularity of outdoor recreation increased the number of people who were concerned about the environment. In this climate of broad-based interest in environmental issues, many organizations that had once focused narrowly on the conservation of natural resources evolved into full-fledged environmental groups (Dunlap and Mertig 1991).

Today, Earth Day has been enshrined on the calendars of city councils, zoos, and museums worldwide. Environmental issues have also moved up the agenda of mainstream political parties. Increasingly, efforts to publicize environmental concerns and create support for action have moved to the Internet. Although times have changed, two beliefs continue to galvanize environmentalists: the environment is in dire need of protection, and the government must take strong action in response. Although environmentalists recognize that they must "think locally" and monitor their own carbon footprints, they also see preservation of the environment as a global challenge. They note that while significant progress has been made toward environmental protection, government regulation of the environment has been curtailed in some ways (Brulle and Jenkins 2008; Rootes 2007; Sieber et al. 2006).

The general public has a mixed reaction to environmental issues. On the one hand, many people question the scientific arguments behind the theory of climate change. On the other, many recognize that there is a trade-off between cheap energy and preserving the environment (Figure 12-7). The public seems evenly divided on the issue.

FIGURE 12-7 **THE ENVIRONMENT VERSUS ENERGY PRODUCTION**

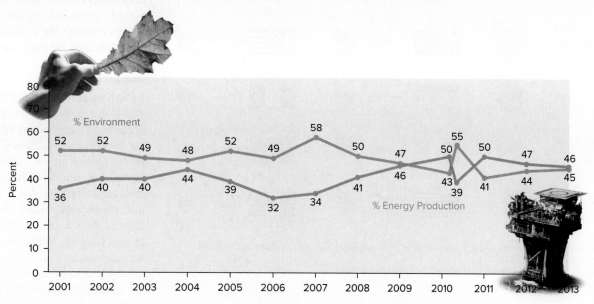

Source: Saad, 2013; J. Jones 2013.

In times of economic stress, people tend to put off or ignore environmental concerns. Thus, there seems to be little public enthusiasm for the positive, forward-looking approach of ecological modernization. Not surprisingly, the political debate over the environmental movement grew more partisan between 2000 and 2012: Democrats became more sympathetic and Republicans more antagonistic (Dunlap 2010).

Today's college students show less interest in the environment than students of past decades. In 2012, 26.5 percent of first-year college students in the United States wanted to clean up the environment—down from 45.9 percent in 1972. And as Figure 12-8 shows, U.S. high school students' interest in the issue does not compare favorably with that of teens in other major countries. In a 30-nation comparative study, 15-year-olds in the United States tied those in another country for 22nd place in their knowledge of environmental issues (Pryor et al. 2007, 2013).

Applying Sociology to Environmentalism Even those who support environmentalists' goals are troubled by the fact that nationwide, the most powerful environmental organizations are predominantly White, male-dominated, and affluent. One study notes that while women are overrepresented in the environmental movement (particularly in grassroots environmental groups), men continue to hold most of the high-profile upper-management positions in mainstream national organizations. The perceived middle-class orientation of the movement is especially relevant given the class, racial, and ethnic factors associated with environmental hazards. As we saw earlier in the context of environmental justice, low-income communities and areas with significant minority populations are more likely than affluent White communities to be located near waste sites. Sociologists Liam Downey and Brian Hawkins (2008) found that an average Black household with an income of $50,000 to $60,000 a year coped with higher levels of pollution than an average White household with an income of less than $10,000 a year.

Viewed from a conflict perspective, this disproportionate exposure of the poor and minorities to environmental pollutants can act as a disincentive for others to take action. As Andrew Szasz (2007) noted in his book *Shopping Our Way to Safety,* more affluent households can try to avoid exposing themselves and their children to health hazards by drinking bottled spring water, installing water and air filters in their homes, and buying organic food. Unfortunately, these individual actions have the unintended consequence of weakening collective environmental efforts.

Another concern, from the conflict perspective, is the fact that many environmental movements either do not include the poor and minorities or do not address their

FIGURE 12-8 ARE U.S. TEENS GREEN ENOUGH?

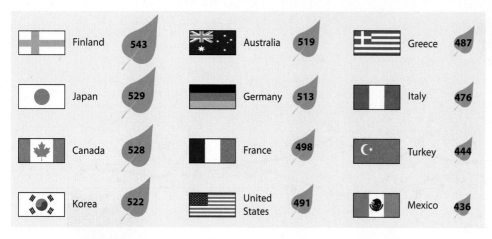

Finland	543	Australia	519	Greece	487
Japan	529	Germany	513	Italy	476
Canada	528	France	498	Turkey	444
Korea	522	United States	491	Mexico	436

Note: Mean score for 15-year-old students' knowledge of environmental issues such as climate change and biodiversity. Mean score was 543.
Source: Organisation for Economic Co-operation and Development 2009b.

concerns. Although environmental justice issues have been well publicized, environmentalists do not always consider the implications of their demands for excluded groups (Rudel et al. 2011).

Initiating Environmental Policy

The global economic downturn that began in 2008 has been a mixed blessing for environmentalists. Currently, public opinion in the United States favors economic growth over environmental protection. Yet at the same time, the recent recession has sharply reduced the use of fossil fuels such as coal and oil. Moreover, the federal government's efforts to stimulate economic activity have emphasized the creation of green-collar jobs. By one estimate, every $1 billion invested in well-conceived green programs generates over 30,000 jobs and $450 million in cost savings per year. More specific environmental measures, such as raising federal gas mileage standards for automobiles, face a tough battle in Congress (Houser et al. 2009).

Environmentalism has moved onto a much bigger stage than the one it occupied on the first Earth Day. In 2008, for the first time, the leaders of the G8 economic powers (the United States, Japan, Germany, Great Britain, France, Italy, Canada, and Russia) set an explicit long-term target for eliminating greenhouse gases, which scientists have long warned were warming the planet. "Long-term" may be an understatement: their target date for cutting greenhouse gases in half is 2050. Environmentalists sharply criticized the G8's failure to set specific goals for the nearer term. The challenge is significant, given the fact that G8 emissions *increased* 35 percent over the preceding 15 years (Longhofer and Schofer 2010; Stolberg 2008).

Conventional wisdom holds that concern for environmental quality is limited to wealthy industrialized nations. However, the results of a 47-nation survey show that around the world, people are increasingly reluctant to ignore environmental issues. Concern has risen sharply in Latin America and Europe, as well as in Japan and India. The survey also noted a general increase in the percentage of people who cite pollution and environmental problems as a top global threat. Many people in other countries blame the United States, and to a lesser extent China, for environmental problems, and look to Washington, D.C., for a solution. Time will tell whether policymakers in the United States or elsewhere will address their concern for the environment (Pew Global Attitudes Project 2007).

 **Evaluate**

Read each question carefully and then select or provide the best answer.

1. Which of the following approaches stresses the alignment of environmentally favorable practices with economic self-interest?
   a. conflict theory
   b. human ecology
   c. ecological modernization
   d. environmental justice

2. Conflict theorists would contend that blaming developing countries for the world's environmental deterioration contains an element of
   a. ethnocentrism.
   b. xenocentrism.
   c. separatism.
   d. goal displacement.

3. The biologist _____ _____ blames environmental degradation primarily on technological innovations such as plastics and pesticides.

4. Regarding environmental problems, four broad areas of concern stand out: _____ pollution, _____ pollution, _____ _____, and _____.

5. _____ _____ is a legal strategy based on claims that racial minorities are subjected disproportionately to environmental hazards.

Answers

1 (c); 2 (a); 3 Barry Commoner; 4 air, water, global warming (or climate change), globalization; 5 Environmental justice

R Rethink

Consider these questions to get a deeper understanding of the material.

1. How are the physical and human environments connected in your neighborhood or community?

2. Which issue is more significant in your local community, air or water pollution? Why?

RECAP

LO 39-1 Explain environmental issues using the human ecology, conflict, and environmental justice perspectives.

- Today's environmental issues stem from trade-offs between economic development and the effects of that development on the environment.
- Human ecology is an area of study that focuses on how the physical environment shapes people's lives and how people simultaneously shape the environment.
- Conflict theorists charge that the most serious threat to the environment comes from exploitive demands that Western industrialized nations impose on less affluent nations.
- Environmental justice is a legal strategy that attempts to address the disproportionate subjection of minorities to environmental hazards.

LO 39-2 Describe the nature and extent of environmental problems, including how globalization and technology affect the environment.

- Four broad areas of environmental concern are air pollution, water pollution, climate change (global warming), and globalization. Though globalization can contribute to environmental woes, it can also have beneficial effects.

- The most promising solutions to these problems depend on a large-scale change of behavior by a substantial portion of the world's population. Unfortunately, a sustainable change of large magnitude has so far proven impossible to accomplish.

LO 39-3 Analyze the impact of environmentalism on social policy.

- Since the first Earth Day in 1970, a grassroots environmental movement has energized people to make local efforts and initiate public policies to improve environmental conditions.
- Many environmental arguments have been met with denial of the science that underlies them and a conservative rejection of the use of taxes to fund environmental projects.
- Environmentalism has been criticized as an elite social movement dominated by affluent White people from industrialized countries. Increasingly, however, people of all races, ethnicities, social classes, and nationalities have become concerned about global warming and the threat it poses to our planet's health.

KEY TERMS

Climate change An observable alteration of the global atmosphere that affects natural weather patterns over several decades or longer.

Ecological modernization The alignment of environmentally favorable practices with economic self-interest through constant adaptation and restructuring.

Environmental justice A legal strategy based on claims that racial minorities are subjected disproportionately to environmental hazards.

Environmental refugee A person who has been displaced by rising seas, destructive storms, expanding deserts, water shortages, or high levels of toxic pollutants.

Global warming A significant rise in the earth's surface temperatures that occurs when industrial gases like carbon dioxide turn the planet's atmosphere into a virtual greenhouse.

Human ecology An area of study that is concerned with the interrelationships between people and their environment.

The Case of . . . A Cure for the Blues

Eva Duval suffered from depression into her mid-20s. "I was always feeling sort of 'gray,'" she says. At 16, her parents sent her to a therapist. "It was nice to have someone to talk to," she says, "but it didn't change things. I couldn't say exactly what was wrong. My family was fine, I had a few friends, but . . ." In college, her doctor suggested looking into antidepressants. "I did some online research and what I found really scared me," Duval says. "Some of those drugs actually *killed* people. I told my doctor I was feeling better and he never brought it up again."

After college, Duval worked in a bookstore. "I didn't have the energy to look for work so I just took the first job I applied for," she says. Six months later, her boss took her out for coffee. "She said, 'You're my best employee but you always seem sad.'" Duval's boss suggested a book about holistic medicine. "That book changed my life," Duval says. "It made me see that all of me—mind, body, emotions—functioned *together*. What I ate affected how I thought. How I felt influenced my immune system. It made perfect sense but no one had ever suggested it before."

On the basis of what she read, Duval had a thyroid function panel done, which showed she was borderline hypothyroid, a condition that might have accounted for her depression. "The doctor suggested a synthetic hormone, but it had potential side effects and I hated the idea of being on a drug for life," Duval says, "so I made some basic changes to my life. Daily exercise, no processed foods, no sugar, no gluten. I researched basic vitamin needs, and made sure I got them." A year later, Duval says she feels great. "For the first time, I have energy. I wake up happy."

1. Why do you think no doctor had ever mentioned the mind–body connection to Duval?

2. Duval's doctors had suggested antidepressants and synthetic hormone drugs. Do you think the United States is a drug-dependent culture? Why or why not?

3. More people are relying on the Internet to diagnose their symptoms and evaluate harmful side effects of drugs. What do you feel are the pros and cons of this approach?

4. How did traditional Western medicine assist Duval in finding her "cure"?

Managing Stress

Stress is unavoidable, especially for busy college students. In the POWER Study Strategies in Chapter 8, we discussed one essential skill for de-stressing the student life-style: time management. Here we address the stress issue more generally.

- Keep your body in good shape, and your mind will follow. Exercise regularly, even for only 15 minutes a day.
- Eat smart. Try to eat fresh food, not fast food, and vegetables and fruit in abundance.
- Cut down on sugary soft drinks and coffee. Caffeine increases stress.

- List everything in your life that is causing stress. Then organize the list in order of stress, from most to least, and work on your major stressors first.

- Take control. Stress arises when we feel out of control, so take charge of the situation. For instance, if two big assignments are due on the same day, talk to one of your instructors, make your case, and ask for a later due date. If that doesn't work, talk to the other one.

- Don't break your commitments, renegotiate them. If you have too much on your plate, adjust schedules, divide the work into parts, lessen the scope of the work, or make other changes. If you simply break your commitments, your guilt may add to your stress.
- Redefine the stressor as an opportunity. For example, if you have to learn a new computer program or routine very quickly, redefine the situation as a learning opportunity. Chances are your new skill will come in handy in another course or another setting sooner than you think.
- Don't dwell on the past. If you got a bad grade on a test last week, let it go and resolve to do better the next time. *Don't relive what you can't revise.*
- Get support. Talk to family, friends, classmates, or counselors and vent your stress. Even if they do no more than listen and nod, this can help. And who knows? They may even have some good ideas to de-stress the situation.
- Relax. Use relaxation techniques, such as meditation or yoga. Find a good self-help relaxation routine on the web and try it out. Relaxation is a proven way to break the stranglehold of stress.

- Monitor your mood and your stress level every morning. If you need to do more to reduce stress, return to these suggestions and try something new.

- Rethink stress itself—and make peace with it. What would life be without it? Challenges bring stress, and a life without challenges would be dull.
- Don't sweat the small stuff—and you may be surprised at how much of your stress is small stuff. Keep it in perspective.

Do You Manage Stress or Does It Manage You?

None of us is able to arrange life exactly the way we would like. Demands crop up. The unexpected happens. Even good opportunities can feel like a burden if they come at a difficult time. No one has total control of events, but everyone can control how they handle the resulting stress. To evaluate your stress management skills, check the appropriate response after each of the following items, then use this scale to find your score:

Rarely = 0

Sometimes = 1

Frequently = 2

	Rarely	Sometimes	Frequently
1. My typical dinner is takeout fajitas, a 32-ounce soft drink, and a quart of Ben & Jerry's.			
2. I run and run all the time, but I always seem to fall further behind.			
3. I feel like there's no point to trying when I get a bad grade.			
4. I get distressed because it seems like there's always something on my to-do list.			
5. I can't talk about my stress. Everyone I know has it all together and I don't want to look like a loser.			
6. I drink a lot of coffee to get me through my busy days.			
7. I get very anxious before starting something new—a class, a job, a major change in routine.			
8. I can't remember the last time I took a day off or had a real night's sleep.			
9. I have no idea what's stressing me out. I just feel overwhelmed.			
10. I would love to get outside but I have to stay glued to my desk until all my work is done.			

SCORE:

0–5 You manage your stress effectively. You understand what causes it and how to minimize it.

6–10 You have some stress management skills, but your inconsistent approach to coping with life's demands means you suffer more than is necessary.

11 or more You need to take stress management seriously. Not only for your class performance, but for your health. Check the tips in this chapter's P.O.W.E.R. Study Strategies: Managing Stress and start breathing easier.

Education

13

Sociology at **WORK** ESL TEACHER

EMILIA JUAREZ is an elementary school ESL (English as a second language) teacher in California. Her students are native Spanish, Japanese, and Mandarin speakers. "My job is to teach these children how to speak, read, write, and understand English, so they can comprehend the lessons in their regular classroom," she says. Juarez speaks fluent Spanish and has studied the varied cultures of all her students. "It's like they said in the '60s, you need to know where your students are coming from if you want to understand and help them."

Juarez uses a curriculum that takes a big-picture approach to English study. "I teach basic skills through the usual channels: textbooks, videos, quizzes," she says. "I also use a computer game designed to teach grammar. It's a 'painless' way to learn something dry." Juarez enjoys taking her students on field trips where they practice their speaking and listening skills in real-life situations. "I see my role as helping these kids to show what they know," she says. "It's a huge challenge for a child, trying to take instruction and perform in a second language. Most of my kids are really bright and capable. My job is to make them competent in English so that their natural gifts shine through." ■

Looking Ahead

IN THIS CHAPTER, WE WILL LOOK AT THE SOCIAL FUNCTIONS OF education. We'll begin with a discussion of the four sociological perspectives on education: functionalist, conflict, feminist, and interactionist. We'll look at schools as formal organizations—as bureaucracies and subcultures of teachers and students. We'll also examine homeschooling, a movement away from institutionalized education and its much-publicized failures. Finally, in the Social Policy section we'll discuss Title IX, one of the most effective—and controversial—federal laws designed to increase gender equity in education.

MODULE 40 Sociological Perspectives on Education

 **Prepare** Learning Objectives

LO 40-1 Describe the manifest and latent functions of schools, according to the functionalist view.

LO 40-2 Analyze education using the conflict, feminist, and interactionist perspectives.

W Work

When learning is explicit and formalized—when some people consciously teach, while others adopt the role of learner—the process of socialization is called **education**. Education, like religion and the family, is a cultural universal.

Besides being a major industry in the United States, education is the social institution that formally socializes members of our society. In the past few decades, increasing proportions of people have obtained high school diplomas, college degrees, and advanced professional degrees. Figure 13-1 shows the proportion of the college-educated population in selected countries.

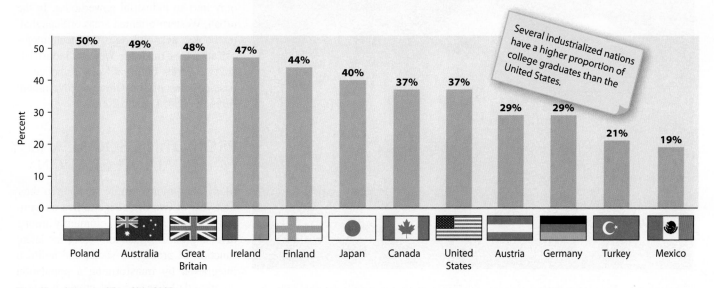

FIGURE 13-1 **CURRENT HIGHER EDUCATION GRADUATION RATES (BA/BS), SELECTED COUNTRIES**

Several industrialized nations have a higher proportion of college graduates than the United States.

Note: For adults ages 25 to 64 in 2009.
Source: Organisation for Economic Co-Operation and Development 2012c:Table A3.

Throughout the world, education has become a vast and complex social institution that prepares citizens for the roles demanded by other social institutions, such as the family, government, and the economy. The functionalist, conflict, feminist, and interactionist perspectives offer distinctive views of education as a social institution.

LO 40-1 Functionalist Perspective

Like other social institutions, education has both manifest (open, stated) and latent (hidden) functions. The most basic *manifest* function of education is the transmission of knowledge. Schools teach students how to read, speak foreign languages, and repair automobiles. Another important manifest function is the bestowal of status. Because many believe this function is performed inequitably, we will consider it later, in the section on the conflict view of education.

In addition to these manifest functions, schools perform a number of *latent* functions: transmitting culture, promoting social and political integration, maintaining social control, and serving as an agent of change.

TRANSMITTING CULTURE

As a social institution, education performs a rather conservative function—transmitting the dominant culture. Schooling exposes each generation of young people to the existing beliefs, norms, and values of their culture. In our society, we learn respect for social control and reverence for established institutions, such as religion, the family, and the presidency. Of course, this statement is true of many other cultures as well. While schoolchildren in the United States are hearing about the accomplishments of George Washington and Abraham Lincoln, British children are hearing about the distinctive contributions of Queen Elizabeth I and Winston Churchill.

Sometimes nations reassess the ways in which they transmit culture to students. In the last decade, the Chinese government revised the nation's history curriculum. Students are now taught that the Chinese Communist Party, not the United States, played a central role in defeating Japan in World War II. No mention is made of the estimated 30 million Chinese who died from famine because of party founder Mao Zedong's disastrous Great Leap Forward (1958–1962), a failed effort to transform China's agrarian economy into an industrial powerhouse. In the urban, Western-oriented areas of Shanghai, textbooks acknowledge the technological advances made in Western industrialized countries but avoid any criticism of past policies of the Chinese government (French 2004; J. Kahn 2006).

Although the school Harry Potter attends in the film *Harry Potter and the Deathly Hallows: Part 2* is fictitious, like real schools, it transmits a socially sanctioned culture to students.

PROMOTING SOCIAL AND POLITICAL INTEGRATION

Many institutions require students in their first year or two of college to live on campus, to foster a sense of community among diverse groups. Education serves the latent function of promoting social and political integration by transforming a population composed of diverse racial, ethnic, and religious groups into a society whose members share—to some extent—a common identity. Historically, schools in the United States have played an important role in socializing the children of immigrants into the norms, values, and beliefs of the dominant culture. From a functionalist perspective, the common identity and social integration fostered by education contribute to societal stability and consensus (Touraine 1974).

In the past, the integrative function of education was most obvious in its emphasis on promoting a common language. Immigrant children were expected to learn English. In some instances, they were even forbidden to speak their native language on school grounds. More recently, bilingualism has been defended both for its educational value and as a means of encouraging cultural diversity. However, critics argue that bilingualism undermines the social and political integration that education has traditionally promoted.

In response to a high pregnancy rate among adolescent girls, many schools now offer sex education courses that promote abstinence as well as safe sex. When schools attempt to remedy negative social trends, they are serving as an agent of social change.

MAINTAINING SOCIAL CONTROL

In performing the manifest function of transmitting knowledge, schools go far beyond teaching skills like reading, writing, and mathematics. Like other social institutions, such as the family and religion, education prepares young people to lead productive and orderly lives as adults by introducing them to the norms, values, and sanctions of the larger society.

Through the exercise of social control, schools teach students various skills and values essential to their future positions in the labor force. They learn punctuality, discipline, scheduling, and responsible work habits, as well as how to negotiate the complexities of a bureaucratic organization. As a social institution, education reflects the interests of both the family and another social institution, the economy. Students are trained for what is ahead, whether it be the assembly line or a physician's office. In effect, then, schools serve as a transitional agent of social control, bridging the gap between parents and employers in the life cycle of most individuals (Bowles and Gintis 1976; Cole 1988).

Schools direct and even restrict students' aspirations in a manner that reflects societal values and prejudices. School administrators may allocate ample funds for athletic programs but give much less support to music, art, and dance. Teachers and guidance counselors may encourage male students to pursue careers in the sciences but steer female students into careers as early childhood teachers. Such socialization into traditional gender roles can be viewed as a form of social control.

SERVING AS AN AGENT OF CHANGE

So far, we have focused on the conservative functions of education—on its role in transmitting the existing culture, promoting social and political integration, and maintaining social control. Yet education can also stimulate or bring about desired social change. Sex education classes were introduced to public schools in response to the soaring pregnancy rate among teenagers. Affirmative action in admissions—giving priority to females or minorities—has been endorsed as a means of countering racial and sexual discrimination. And Project Head Start, an early childhood program that serves

> **Study Alert**
>
> It is important to understand the ways in which schools act as agents of social control.

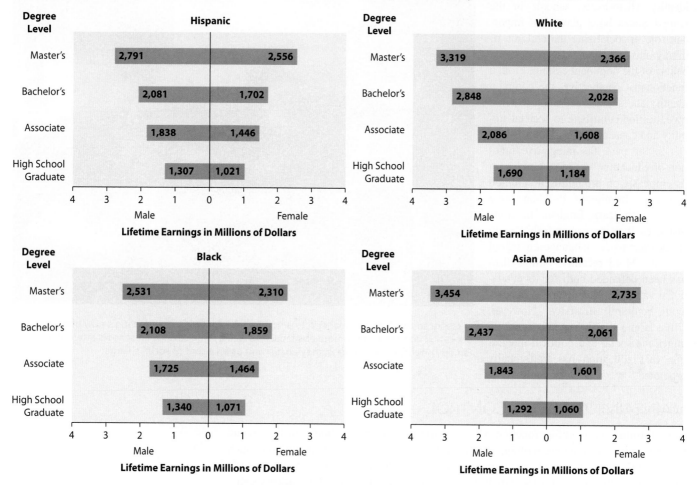

FIGURE 13-2 LIFETIME EARNINGS BY RACE, GENDER, AND DEGREE LEVEL

Note: Estimates for lifetime earnings for full-time, year-round workers ages 25 to 64 based on the American Community Survey for 2006–2008. Data are for Hispanics, non-Hispanic Whites, Blacks, and Asian Americans. Data points shown in thousands of dollars.
Source: Julian and Kominski 2011:6.

more than 904,000 children annually, has sought to compensate for the disadvantages in school readiness experienced by children from low-income families (Bureau of the Census 2011a:Table 574).

These educational programs can and have transformed people's lives. For example, continued formal education has had a positive effect on the income people earn; median earnings rise significantly with each step up the educational ladder. Consider the significance of those increased earnings when they stretch over an entire lifetime. Obviously, racial, ethnic, and gender differences in income are also significant. Yet as significant as those inequalities are, the best indicator of a person's lifetime earnings is still the number of years of formal schooling that person has received (Figure 13-2) (Julian and Kominski 2011; Wessel and Banchero 2012).

Numerous sociological studies have revealed that additional years of formal schooling are also associated with openness to new ideas and liberal social and political viewpoints. Sociologist Robin Williams points out that better-educated people tend to have greater access to factual information, to hold more diverse opinions, and to possess the ability to make subtle distinctions in analysis. Formal education stresses both the importance of qualifying statements (in place of broad generalizations) and the need at least to question (rather than simply accept) established truths and practices. The scientific method, which relies on *testing* hypotheses, reflects the questioning spirit that characterizes modern education (R. Williams et al. 1964).

LO **40-2** Conflict Perspective

The functionalist perspective portrays contemporary education as a basically benign institution. For example, it argues that schools rationally sort and select students for future high-status positions, thereby meeting society's need for talented and expert personnel. In contrast, the conflict perspective views education as an instrument of elite domination. Conflict theorists point out the sharp inequalities that exist in the educational opportunities available to different racial and ethnic groups. In 2014, the nation marked the 60th anniversary of the Supreme Court's landmark decision *Brown v. Board of Education,* which declared unconstitutional the segregation of public schools. Yet today, our schools are still characterized by racial isolation. For example, although White students account for just over half the nation's school enrollment, the typical White student attends a school where three-quarters of his or her peers are White. Fully 15 percent of Black students and 14 percent of Latino students attend what have been termed "apartheid schools," where Whites make up less than 1 percent of the enrollment. And despite the dramatic suburbanization of African American and Hispanic families in recent decades, across the nation, 80 percent of Latino students and 74 percent of Black students still attend majority non-White schools—that is, schools that are 50 to 100 percent minority (Orfield et al. 2012).

Conflict theorists also argue that the educational system socializes students into values dictated by the powerful, that schools stifle individualism and creativity in the name of maintaining order, and that the level of change they promote is relatively insignificant. From a conflict perspective, the inhibiting effects of education are particularly apparent in the "hidden curriculum" and the differential way in which status is bestowed.

THE HIDDEN CURRICULUM

Schools are highly bureaucratic organizations, as we will see later. To maintain order, many teachers rely on rules and regulations. Unfortunately, the need for control and discipline can take precedence over the learning process. Teachers may focus on obedience to the rules as an end in itself, in which case students and teachers alike become victims of what Philip Jackson (1968) has called the *hidden curriculum.*

The term **hidden curriculum** refers to standards of behavior that are deemed proper by society and are taught subtly in schools. According to this curriculum, children must not speak until the teacher calls on them and must regulate their activities according to the clock or bells. In addition, they are expected to concentrate on their own work rather than to assist other students who learn more slowly. A hidden curriculum is evident in schools around the world. For example, Japanese schools offer guidance sessions that seek to improve the classroom experience and develop healthy living skills. In effect, these sessions instill values and encourage behavior that is useful in the Japanese business world, such as self-discipline and openness to group problem solving and decision making (Okano and Tsuchiya 1999).

In a classroom that is overly focused on obedience, value is placed on pleasing the teacher and remaining quiet rather than on creative thought and academic learning. Habitual obedience to authority may result in the type of distressing behavior documented by Stanley Milgram in his classic obedience studies.

CREDENTIALISM

Sixty years ago, a high school diploma was the minimum requirement for entry into the paid labor force of the United States. Today, a college diploma is virtually the bare minimum. This change reflects the process of **credentialism**—a term used to describe an increase in the lowest level of education needed to enter a field.

In recent decades, the number of occupations that are viewed as professions has risen. Credentialism is one symptom of this trend. Employers and occupational associations typically contend that such changes are a logical response to the increasing complexity of many jobs. However, in many cases, employers raise the degree requirements for a position simply because all applicants have achieved the existing minimum credential (David K. Brown 2001; Hurn 1985).

Conflict theorists observe that credentialism may reinforce social inequality. Applicants from poor and minority backgrounds are especially likely to suffer from the escalation of qualifications, since they lack the financial resources needed to obtain degree after degree. In addition, upgrading of credentials serves the self-interest of the two groups most responsible for this trend. Educational institutions profit from prolonging the investment of time and money that people make by staying in school. Moreover, as C. J. Hurn (1985) has suggested, current jobholders have a stake in raising occupational requirements, since credentialism can increase the status of an occupation and lead to demands for higher pay. Max Weber anticipated this possibility as early as 1916, concluding that the "universal clamor for the creation of educational certificates in all fields makes for the formation of a privileged stratum in businesses and in offices" (Gerth and Mills 1958:240–241).

BESTOWAL OF STATUS

Sociologists have long recognized that schooling is central to social stratification. Both functionalist and conflict theorists agree that education performs the important function of bestowing status. According to Kingsley Davis and Wilbert E. Moore (1945), society must distribute its members among a variety of social positions. Education can contribute to this process by sorting people into appropriate levels and courses of study that will prepare them for positions in the labor force.

As noted earlier, an increasing proportion of people in the United States are obtaining high school diplomas, college degrees, and advanced professional degrees. From a functionalist perspective, this widening bestowal of status is beneficial not only to particular recipients but to society as a whole.

Conflict theorists are far more critical of the *differential* way in which education bestows status. They stress that schools sort pupils according to their social class backgrounds. Although the educational system helps certain poor children to move into middle-class professional positions, it denies most disadvantaged children the same educational opportunities afforded to children of the affluent. In this way, schools tend to preserve social class inequalities in each new generation. Higher education in particular acts more like a sieve that sorts people out of the educated classes than a social ladder that helps all with ambition to rise (Alon 2009; Giroux 1988; Sacks 2007).

The status that comes with advanced training is not cheap and has been getting progressively more expensive for several decades. Over the past 30 years, average tuition and fees at community colleges have risen at a relatively modest pace that matches the inflation rate (Figure 13-3). The increases have been greater at four-year institutions. At the same time as tuition has been increasing, financial aid has become more difficult to obtain.

Even a single school can reinforce class differences by putting students in tracks. The term **tracking** refers to the practice of placing students in specific curriculum groups on the basis of their test scores and other criteria. Tracking begins very early, often in reading groups during first grade. The practice can reinforce the disadvantages that children from less affluent families may face if they haven't been exposed to reading materials, computers, and other forms of educational stimulation during their early childhood years. To ignore this connection between tracking and students' race and social class is to fundamentally misunderstand how schools perpetuate the existing social structure.

Not surprisingly, most recent research on tracking raises questions about its effectiveness, especially for low-ability students. In one study of low-income schools in California, researchers discovered a staggering difference between students who were tracked and those who were not. At one school, all interested students were allowed to enroll in advanced placement (AP) courses, not just those who were selected by the administration. Half the open enrollment students scored high enough to qualify for college credit—a much higher proportion than in selective programs, in which only 17 percent of students qualified for college credit. Tracking programs do not necessarily identify those students with the potential to succeed (B. Ellison 2008; Sacks 2007).

> ## Study Alert
>
> Remember a downside of tracking: it potentially reinforces the disadvantages faced by children from less affluent families.

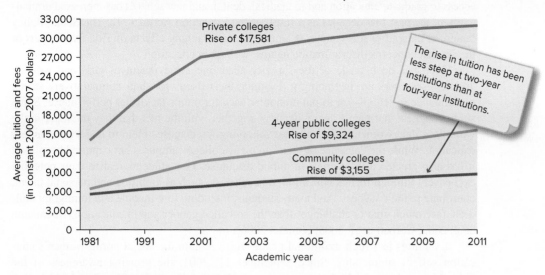

FIGURE 13-3 TUITION COSTS, 1981–2011

Private colleges
Rise of $17,581

The rise in tuition has been less steep at two-year institutions than at four-year institutions.

4-year public colleges
Rise of $9,324

Community colleges
Rise of $3,155

Sources: National Center for Education Statistics 2013.

Conflict theorists hold that the educational inequalities produced by tracking are designed to meet the needs of modern capitalist societies. Samuel Bowles and Herbert Gintis (1976) have argued that capitalism requires a skilled, disciplined labor force, and that the educational system of the United States is structured with that objective in mind. Citing numerous studies, they offer support for what they call the **correspondence principle**. According to this approach, schools promote the values expected of individuals in each social class and perpetuate social class divisions from one generation to the next. Thus, working-class children, assumed to be destined for subordinate positions, are likely to be placed in high school vocational and general tracks, which emphasize close supervision and compliance with authority. In contrast, young people from more affluent families are likely to be directed to college preparatory tracks, which stress leadership and decision making—the skills they are expected to need as adults (McLanahan and Percheski 2008).

LO **40-2** Feminist Perspective

The educational system of the United States, like many other social institutions, has long been characterized by discriminatory treatment of women. In 1833, Oberlin College became the first institution of higher learning to admit female students—some 200 years after the first men's college was established. But Oberlin believed that women should aspire to become wives and mothers, not lawyers and intellectuals. In addition to attending classes, female students washed men's clothing, cared for their rooms, and served them at meals. In the 1840s, Lucy Stone, then an Oberlin undergraduate and later one of the nation's most outspoken feminist leaders, refused to write a commencement address because it would have been read to the audience by a male student.

In the 20th century, sexism in education showed up in many ways—in textbooks with negative stereotypes of women, counselors' pressure on female students to prepare for "women's work," and unequal funding for women's and men's athletic programs. But perhaps nowhere was educational discrimination more evident than in the employment of teachers. The positions of university professor and college administrator, which hold relatively high status in the United States, were generally filled by men. Public school teachers, who earn much lower salaries, were largely female.

Women have made great strides in one area: the proportion of women who continue their schooling. As recently as 1969, twice as many men as women received college

degrees; today, women outnumber men at college commencements. Moreover, women's access to graduate education and to medical, dental, and law schools has increased dramatically in the past few decades as a result of the Education Act of 1972. The Social Policy feature at the end of this chapter examines the far-reaching effects of Title IX, the part of the act that concerns discrimination against women in education.

Much has been made of the superior academic achievement of girls and women. Today, researchers are beginning to examine the reasons for their comparatively strong performance in school—or to put it another way, for men's lackluster performance. Some studies suggest that men's aggressiveness, together with the fact that they do better in the workplace than women, even with less schooling, predisposes them to undervalue higher education. While the "absence of men" on many college campuses has captured headlines, it has also created a false crisis in public discourse. Few students realize their potential exclusively through formal education; other factors, such as ambition and personal talent, contribute to their success. And many students, including low-income and immigrant children, face much greater challenges than the so-called gender gap in education (Buchmann et al. 2008; Corbett et al. 2008; Kimmel 2006).

In cultures in which traditional gender roles remain the social norm, women's education suffers appreciably. Since September 11, 2001, the growing awareness of the Taliban's repression of Afghan women has dramatized the gender disparities in education in developing nations. Research has demonstrated that women are critical to economic development and good governance, and that education is instrumental in preparing them for those roles. Educating women, especially young girls, yields high social returns by lowering birthrates and improving agricultural productivity through better management (I. Coleman 2004).

LO 40-2 Interactionist Perspective

High school students know who they are—the kids who qualify for a free lunch. So stigmatized are they that in some schools, these students will buy a bit of food in the cash line or simply go without eating to avoid being labeled a "poor kid." School officials in San Francisco are so concerned about their plight that they are moving to cashless cafeterias, in which everyone, rich or poor, uses a debit card (Pogash 2008).

The labeling approach suggests that if we treat people in particular ways, they may fulfill our expectations. Children who are labeled as "troublemakers" may come to view themselves as delinquents. Similarly, a dominant group's stereotyping of racial minorities may limit their opportunities to break away from expected roles.

In Tokyo, parents escort their daughter to an admissions interview at a highly competitive private school. Some Japanese families enroll children as young as 2 years of age in cram schools. Like parents in the United States, Japanese parents know that higher education bestows status.

Can the labeling process operate in the classroom? Because interactionist researchers focus on micro-level classroom dynamics, they have been particularly interested in this question. Sociologist Howard S. Becker (1952) studied public schools in low-income and affluent areas of Chicago. He noticed that administrators expected less of students from poor neighborhoods, and wondered if teachers accepted their view. A decade later, in *Pygmalion in the Classroom,* psychologist Robert Rosenthal and school principal Lenore Jacobson (1968, 1992) documented what they referred to as a **teacher-expectancy effect**—the impact that a teacher's expectations about a student's performance may have on the student's actual achievements. This effect is especially evident in the lower grades (through Grade 3).

Studies in the United States have revealed that teachers wait longer for an answer from a student they believe to be a high achiever and are more likely to give such children a second chance. In one experiment, teachers' expectations were even shown to have an impact on students' athletic achievements. Teachers obtained better athletic performance—as measured in

TABLE 13-1 SOCIOLOGICAL PERSPECTIVES ON EDUCATION

Theoretical Perspective	Emphasis
Functionalist	Transmission of the dominant culture
	Integration of society
	Promotion of social norms, values, and sanctions
	Promotion of desirable social change
Conflict	Domination by the elite through unequal access to schooling
	Hidden curriculum
	Credentialism
	Bestowal of status
Interactionist	Teacher-expectancy effect
Feminist	Treatment of female students
	Role of women's education in economic development

the number of sit-ups or push-ups performed—from those students of whom they *expected* higher numbers. Despite the controversial nature of these findings, researchers continue to document the existence of the teacher-expectancy effect. Interactionists emphasize that ability alone may be less predictive of academic success than one might think (Babad and Taylor 1992; Brint 1998; Rosenthal and Jacobson 1992:247–262).

Table 13-1 summarizes the four major theoretical perspectives on education.

From the perspective of . . .

An Elementary Teacher In what ways could the teacher-expectancy effect, regarding gender roles, play out in the classroom?

E Evaluate

Read each question carefully and then select or provide the best answer.

1. Most recent research on ability grouping raises questions about its
   a. effectiveness, especially for lower-achieving students.
   b. failure to improve the prospects of higher-achieving students.
   c. tendency to mix lower- and higher-achieving students in similar classes.
   d. lack of correspondence with teacher expectancies.

2. Fifty years ago, a high school diploma was the minimum requirement for entry into the paid labor force of the United States. Today, a college diploma is virtually the bare minimum. This change reflects the process of
   a. tracking.
   b. credentialism.
   c. the hidden curriculum.
   d. the correspondence principle.

3. Samuel Bowles and Herbert Gintis have argued that capitalism requires a skilled, disciplined labor force and that the educational system of the United States is structured with

that objective in mind. Citing numerous studies, they offer support for what they call
a. tracking.
b. credentialism.
c. the correspondence principle.
d. the teacher-expectancy effect.

4. The teacher-expectancy effect is most closely associated with
a. the functionalist perspective.
b. the conflict perspective.
c. the interactionist perspective.
d. the feminist perspective.

5. Schools perform a variety of _____ functions, such as transmitting culture, promoting social and political integration, and maintaining social control.

Answers

1 (a); 2 (b); 3 (c); 4 (c); 5 latent

R Rethink

Consider these questions to get a deeper understanding of the material.

1. How do the functions of integration and social control reinforce each other? How do they work against each other?

2. What are the functions and dysfunctions of tracking in schools? In what ways might tracking have a positive impact on the self-concepts of various students? In what ways might it have a negative impact?

RECAP

LO 40-1 Describe the manifest and latent functions of schools, according to the functionalist view.

- The transmission of knowledge and bestowal of status are manifest functions of education.
- Among the latent functions of education are the conservative functions of transmitting culture, promoting social and political integration, and maintaining social control.
- Another latent function—serving as an agent of social change—is less conservative in nature. In performing this function, schools foster creativity and even subversive thinking.

LO 40-2 Analyze education using the conflict, feminist, and interactionist perspectives.

- In the view of conflict theorists, education serves as an instrument of elite domination by creating standards for entry into occupations, bestowing status unequally, and tracking students into class-influenced career paths. The means through which schools perform this function has been termed "the hidden curriculum."
- Feminist theorists point to the historical discrimination against women practiced in school curricula and employment practices, contrasting this with the increase in the number of women who continue their schooling in college and the higher academic achievement of girls and women compared to their male counterparts.
- Interactionists note that labeling of students perpetuates social stigmatization, which can be adopted by teachers who openly expect more from affluent students than from poorer ones.
- Teacher expectations about a student's performance can sometimes have an impact on the student's actual achievements, becoming a self-fulfilling prophecy. This has been called the teacher-expectancy effect.

KEY TERMS

Correspondence principle The tendency of schools to promote the values expected of individuals in each social class and to perpetuate social class divisions from one generation to the next.

Credentialism An increase in the lowest level of education needed to enter a field.

Education A formal process of learning in which some people consciously teach, while others adopt the social role of learner.

Hidden curriculum Standards of behavior that are deemed proper by society and are taught subtly in schools.

Teacher-expectancy effect The impact that a teacher's expectations about a student's performance may have on the student's actual achievements.

Tracking The practice of placing students in specific curriculum groups on the basis of their test scores and other criteria.

MODULE 41 Schools as Formal Organizations

P Prepare | Learning Objectives

LO 41-1 Explain the bureaucratization of schools and its impact on teaching and learning.

LO 41-2 Analyze the roles that teachers and students play in formal schooling.

O Organize | Module Outline

Bureaucratization of Schools
Teachers: Employees and Instructors
Student Subcultures
Homeschooling
Social Policy and Education
    The Debate over Title IX

W Work

Nineteenth-century educators would be amazed at the scale of schools in the United States in the 21st century. The nation has about 15 million high school students today, compared to 10 million in 1961 and 5 million in 1931 (Bureau of the Census 2011a:Table 246; 2012c: Table H S-20).

In many respects, today's schools, when viewed as an example of a formal organization, are similar to factories, hospitals, and business firms. Like those organizations, schools do not operate autonomously; they are influenced by the market of potential students. This statement is especially true of private schools, but could have broader impact if acceptance of voucher plans and other school choice programs increases. The parallels between schools and other types of formal organizations will become more apparent as we examine the bureaucratic nature of schools, teaching as an occupation, and the student subculture (Dougherty and Hammack 1992).

LO 41-1 Bureaucratization of Schools

It simply is not possible for a single teacher to transmit culture and skills to children of varying ages who will enter many diverse occupations. The growing number of students being served by school systems and the greater degree of specialization required within a technologically complex society have combined to bureaucratize schools.

Max Weber noted five basic characteristics of bureaucracy, all of which are evident in the vast majority of schools, whether at the elementary, secondary, or even college level:

1. **Division of labor.** Specialized experts teach particular age levels and specific subjects. Public elementary and secondary schools now employ instructors whose sole responsibility is to work with children with learning disabilities or physical impairments.

2. **Hierarchy of authority.** Each employee of a school system is responsible to a higher authority. Teachers must report to principals and assistant principals and may also be supervised by department heads. Principals are answerable to a superintendent of schools, and the superintendent is hired and fired by a board of education.

3. **Written rules and regulations.** Teachers and administrators must conform to numerous rules and regulations in the performance of their duties. This bureaucratic trait can become dysfunctional; the time invested in completing required forms could instead be spent in preparing lessons or conferring with students.

4. **Impersonality.** As class sizes have swelled at schools and universities, it has become more difficult for teachers to give personal attention to each student. In fact, bureaucratic norms may actually encourage teachers to treat all students in the same way, despite the fact that students have distinctive personalities and learning needs.

5. **Employment based on technical qualifications.** At least in theory, the hiring of instructors is based on professional competence and expertise. Promotions are normally dictated by written personnel policies; people who excel may be granted lifelong job security through tenure.

Functionalists take a generally positive view of the bureaucratization of education. Teachers can master the skills needed to work with a specialized clientele, since they no longer are expected to cover a broad range of instruction. The chain of command within schools is clear. Students are presumably treated in an unbiased fashion because of uniformly applied rules. Finally, security of position protects teachers from unjustified dismissal. In general, then, functionalists stress that the bureaucratization of education increases the likelihood that students, teachers, and administrators will be dealt with fairly—that is, on the basis of rational and equitable criteria.

In contrast, conflict theorists argue that the trend toward more centralized education has harmful consequences for disadvantaged people. The standardization of educational curricula, including textbooks, will generally reflect the values, interests, and lifestyles of the most powerful groups in our society, and may ignore those of racial and ethnic minorities. In addition, the disadvantaged, more so than the affluent, will find it difficult to sort through complex educational bureaucracies and to organize effective lobbying groups. Therefore, in the view of conflict theorists, low-income and minority parents will have even less influence over citywide and statewide educational administrators than they have over local school officials (Bowles and Gintis 1976; Katz 1971).

Sometimes schools can seem overwhelmingly bureaucratic, with the effect of stifling rather than nourishing intellectual curiosity in students. This concern has led many parents and policymakers to push for school choice programs—allowing parents to choose the school that suits their children's needs, and forcing schools to compete for their "customers."

In the United States, another significant countertrend to the bureaucratization of schools is the availability of education over the Internet. Increasingly, colleges and universities are reaching out via the web, offering entire courses and even majors to students in the comfort of their homes. Online curricula provide flexibility for working students and others who may have difficulty attending conventional classes because of distance or disability. Research on this type of learning is just beginning, so the question of whether teacher–student contact can thrive online remains to be settled. Computer-mediated instruction may also have an impact on instructors' status as employees, which we will discuss next, as well as on alternative forms of education like homeschooling.

Despite efforts to establish positive relationships among students and between teachers and students, many young people view their schools as impersonal institutions.

LO **41-2** Teachers: Employees and Instructors

Whether they serve as instructors of preschoolers or of graduate students, teachers are employees of formal organizations with bureaucratic structures. There is an inherent conflict in serving as a professional in a bureaucracy. The organization follows the principles of hierarchy and expects adherence to its rules, but professionalism demands the individual responsibility of the practitioner. This conflict is very real for teachers, who experience all the positive and negative consequences of working in bureaucracies.

A teacher undergoes many perplexing stresses every day. While teachers' academic assignments have become more specialized, the demands on their time remain diverse and contradictory. Conflicts arise from serving as an instructor, a disciplinarian, and an employee of a school district at the same time. In too many schools, discipline means dealing with violence. (See Box 13-1.) Burnout is one result of these stresses: between a quarter and a third of new teachers quit within their first three years, and as many as half leave poor urban schools in their first five years (Wallis 2008).

Given these difficulties, does teaching remain an attractive profession in the United States? In 2012, 3.2 percent of male first-year college students and 8.2 percent of women indicated that they were interested in becoming either elementary or high school teachers. These figures are dramatically lower than the 11 percent of first-year male students and 37 percent of first-year female students who held those occupational aspirations in 1966 (Pryor et al. 2007:76, 122; 2013).

Undoubtedly, economic considerations enter into students' feelings about the attractiveness of teaching. In 2012, the average salary for all public elementary and secondary school teachers in the United States was reported at $55,418, placing teachers somewhere near the average of all the nation's wage earners. In most other industrialized countries, teachers' salaries are higher in relation to the general standard of living. Of course, teachers' salaries vary considerably from state to state (Figure 13-4), and even more from one school district to another. Nevertheless, the economic reward for teaching is miniscule compared to some career options: the CEO of a major corporation makes more money in a day than the average teacher makes in a year.

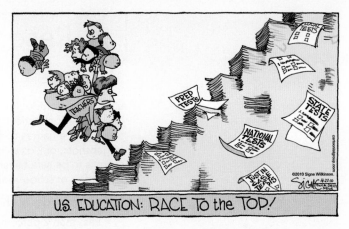

From preschool through high school, teachers face a variety of challenges, including preparing students for standardized tests.

MAPPING LIFE NATIONWIDE

FIGURE 13-4 **AVERAGE SALARY FOR TEACHERS**

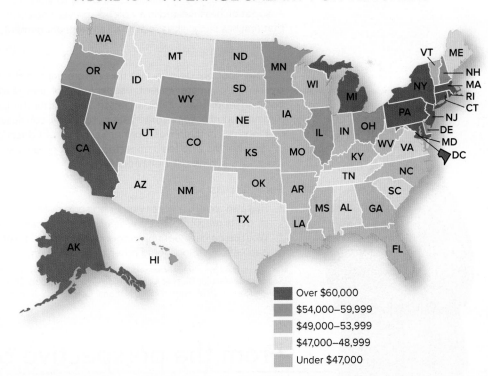

Legend:
- Over $60,000
- $54,000–59,999
- $49,000–53,999
- $47,000–48,999
- Under $47,000

State averages for teacher salaries range from a low of $38,804 in South Dakota to a high of $73,998 in New York.

Note: Data released in 2012 for 2011–2012.
Source: National Education Association 2012.

13-1 VIOLENCE IN THE SCHOOLS

Littleton, Colorado; Red Lake, Minnesota; Jonesboro, Arkansas; West Paducah, Kentucky; Newtown, Connecticut; Edinboro, Pennsylvania; Springfield, Oregon—these are now more than just the names of small towns and medium-size cities. They resonate with the sound of gunshots, or kids killing kids on school grounds. As a result, people no longer perceive schools to be safe havens. But how accurate is that impression?

Studies of school violence put the recent spate of school killings in perspective:

- 17 homicides of children ages 5 to 18 occurred at school during the 2009–2010 year.

- Less than 2 percent of youth homicides occur at school.

- About 7 percent of teachers report being threatened with injury or physically attacked by a student from their school.

Schools, then, are safer than neighborhoods, but people are still unnerved by the perception of an alarming rise in school violence generated by heavy media coverage of recent incidents. Some conflict theorists object to the huge outcry about recent violence in schools. After all, they note, violence in and around inner-city schools has a long history. It seems that only when middle-class White children are the victims does school violence become a plank on the national policy agenda. When violence hits the middle class, the problem is viewed not as an extension of delinquency but a structural issue in need of legislative remedies such as gun control (see the Social Policy section in Chapter 7).

Feminists observe that virtually all the offenders in these incidents are male, and in some instances, such as the case in Jonesboro, the victims are disproportionately female. The precipitating factor in the violence is often a broken-off dating relationship—yet another example of the violence of men against women (or in this case, boys against girls).

Increasingly, efforts to prevent school violence are focusing on the ways in which the socialization of young people contributes to violence. For example, the American Medical Association has invested in a violence-prevention curriculum for elementary school students that teaches social skills related to anger management, impulse control, and empathy.

A child has a less than one in a million chance of being killed at school.

Some people believe that a key ingredient in the prevention of violence, in and out of school, is greater parental supervision of and responsibility for their children. In her book *A Tribe Apart*, Patricia Hersch documents the lives of eight teens growing up in a Virginia suburb over a three-year period. Her conclusion: children need meaningful adult relationships in their lives. Former Secretary of Education Richard Riley cites studies showing that youths who feel connected to their parents and schools are less likely than others to engage in high-risk behaviors.

Let's Discuss

1. Has a shooting or other violent episode ever occurred at your school? If so, how did students react? Do you feel safer at school than at home, as experts say you are?
2. What steps have administrators at your school taken to prevent violence? Have they been effective, or should other steps be taken?

Sources: Centers for Disease Control and Prevention 2008b, 2013; Department of Education 1999, 2004; Donohue et al. 1998; Hersch 1998; National Center for Education Statistics 2002.

From the perspective of . . .

A School Administrator What measures, besides salary increases, could be taken to make teaching a more attractive profession?

The status of any job reflects several factors, including the level of education required, financial compensation, and the respect given the occupation by society. The teaching profession is feeling pressure in all three of these areas. First, the level of formal schooling required for teaching remains high, and the public has begun to call for new competency examinations. Second, the statistics just cited demonstrate that teachers' salaries are significantly lower than those of many professionals and skilled workers. Third, the overall prestige of the teaching profession has declined in the past decade. Many teachers have become disappointed and frustrated and have left the educational world for careers in other professions.

Student subcultures are more diverse today than in the past. Many adults are returning to college to obtain further education, advance their careers, or change their line of work.

LO 41-2 Student Subcultures

An important latent function of education relates directly to student life: schools provide for students' social and recreational needs. Education helps toddlers and young children to develop interpersonal skills that are essential during adolescence and adulthood. In their high school and college years, students may meet future husbands and wives and establish lifelong friendships. It is important to remember that these informal aspects of schools, community colleges, and universities do not exist independently of schools' explicit educational functions. Furthermore, informal social systems can be as important as the academic system in determining students' positive and negative outcomes (Crosnoe 2011).

When people observe high schools, community colleges, or universities from the outside, students appear to constitute a cohesive, uniform group. However, the student subculture is actually quite complex and diverse. High school cliques and social groups may crop up according to race, social class, physical attractiveness, placement in courses, athletic ability, and leadership roles in the school and community. In his classic community study of "Elmtown," August B. Hollingshead (1975) found some 259 distinct cliques in a single high school. The cliques, whose average size was five, were centered on the school itself, on recreational activities, and on religious and community groups.

Amid these close-knit and often rigidly segregated cliques, gay and lesbian students are particularly vulnerable. Peer group pressure to conform is intense at this age. Although coming to terms with one's sexuality is difficult for all adolescents, it can be downright dangerous for those whose sexual orientation does not conform to societal expectations.

Teachers and administrators are becoming more sensitized to these issues. Perhaps more important, some schools are creating gay–straight alliances (GSAs), school-sponsored support groups that bring gay teens together with sympathetic straight peers. Begun in Los Angeles in 1984, these programs numbered nearly 3,000 nationwide in 2005; most were founded after the murder of Matthew Shepard, a gay college student, in 1998. In some districts parents have objected to these organizations, but the same court rulings that protect the right of conservative Bible groups to meet on school grounds also protect GSAs. In 2003, the gay–straight movement reached a milestone when the New York City public schools moved an in-school program for gays, bisexuals, and transgendered students to a separate school. The Harvey Milk High School was named in memory of San Francisco's first openly gay city supervisor, who was assassinated in 1978 (Gay, Lesbian and Straight Education Network 2012).

We can find a similar diversity of student groups at the college level. Burton Clark and Martin Trow (1966) and more recently, Helen Lefkowitz Horowitz (1987) have identified four distinctive subcultures among college students:

1. The *collegiate* subculture focuses on having fun and socializing. These students define what constitutes a "reasonable" amount of academic work (and what amount of work is "excessive" and leads to being labeled a "grind"). Members of the collegiate subculture have little commitment to academic pursuits. Athletes often fit into this subculture.

FIGURE 13-5 COLLEGE CAMPUSES BY RACE AND ETHNICITY: THEN, NOW, AND IN THE FUTURE

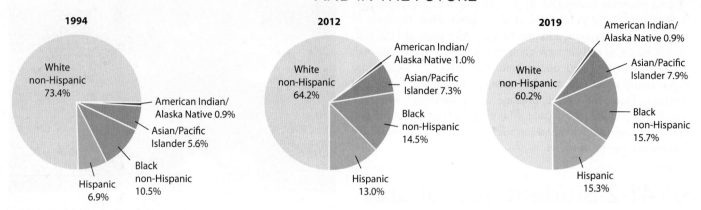

Note: Percentages do not add to 100 due to rounding error. Nonresident aliens whose race/ethnicity is unknown excluded.
Source: Hussar and Bailey 2011:Table 29.

2. The *academic* subculture identifies with the intellectual concerns of the faculty and values knowledge for its own sake.

3. The *vocational* subculture is interested primarily in career prospects and views college as a means of obtaining degrees that are essential for advancement.

4. Finally, the *nonconformist* subculture is hostile to the college environment and seeks ideas that may or may not relate to academic studies. This group may find outlets through campus publications or issue-oriented groups.

Each college student is eventually exposed to these competing subcultures and must determine which (if any) seems most in line with his or her feelings and interests.

The typology used by the researchers reminds us that school is a complex social organization—almost like a community with different neighborhoods. Of course, these four subcultures are not the only ones evident on college campuses in the United States. For example, one might find subcultures of Vietnam veterans or former full-time homemakers at community colleges and four-year commuter institutions. And as more and more students from minority groups decide to continue their formal education beyond high school, subcultures based on race and ethnicity will become more evident. As Figure 13-5 shows, college campuses are becoming increasingly diverse.

Sociologist Joe R. Feagin has studied a distinctive collegiate subculture: Black students at predominantly White universities. These students must function academically and socially within universities where there are few Black faculty members or administrators, where harassment of Blacks by campus police is common, and where curricula place little emphasis on Black contributions. Feagin (1989:11) suggests that "for minority students life at a predominantly White college or university means long-term encounters with pervasive whiteness." In Feagin's view, Black students at such institutions experience both blatant and subtle racial discrimination, which has a cumulative impact that can seriously damage the students' confidence (see also Feagin et al. 1996).

LO **41-2** Homeschooling

When most people think of school, they think of bricks and mortar and the teachers, administrators, and other employees who staff school buildings. But for an increasing number of students in the United States, home is the classroom and the teacher is a parent. About 1.5 million students are now being educated at home. That is about 3 percent of the K–12 school population. For these students, the issues of bureaucratization and social structure are less significant than they are for public school students (Grady et al. 2010).

In the 1800s, after the establishment of public schools, families that taught their children at home lived in isolated environments or held strict religious views that were at odds with the secular environment of public schools. But today, homeschooling is attracting a broader range of families not necessarily tied to organized religion. Poor academic quality, peer pressure, and school violence are motivating many parents to teach their children at home. In addition, some immigrants choose homeschooling as a way to ease their children's transition to a new society. For example, the growing Arab American population recently joined the movement toward homeschooling (MacFarquhar 2008; National Center for Education Statistics 2009).

While supporters of homeschooling believe children can do just as well or better in homeschools as in public schools, critics counter that because homeschooled children are isolated from the larger community, they lose an important chance to improve their social-ization skills. But proponents of homeschooling claim their children benefit from contact with others besides their own age group. They also see homeschools as a good alternative for children who suffer from attention-deficit/hyperactivity disorder (ADHD) and learning disorders (LDs). Such children often do better in smaller classes, which present fewer dis-tractions to disturb their concentration.

Quality control is an issue in homeschooling. While homeschooling is legal in all 50 states, 10 states require no notification that a child will be homeschooled, and another 14 require notification only. Other states may require parents to submit their children's curricula or test scores for professional evaluation. Despite the lack of uniform standards, a research review by the Home School Legal Defense Association (2005) reports that homeschooled students score higher than others on standardized tests, in every subject and every grade.

Who are the people who are running homeschools? In general, they tend to have higher-than-average incomes and educational levels. Most are two-parent families, and their children watch less television than average—both factors that are likely to support superior educational performance. The same students, with the same support from their parents, would probably do just as well in the public schools. As research has repeat-edly shown, small classes are better than big classes, and strong parental and community involvement is key (R. Cox 2003:28).

Whatever the controversy over homeschooling in the United States, it is much less serious than in some other nations. In 2010, the U.S. Immigration and Naturalization Service began granting political asylum to German families who homeschool their chil-dren, in violation of their country's constitution. German parents can be fined and impris-oned for homeschooling their children (Francis 2010).

LO 41-2 SOCIAL POLICY and Education

We have seen that researchers rely on a number of tools, from time-tested observational research and use of existing sources to the latest in computer technologies. Because in the real world, sociological research can have far-reaching consequences for public policy and public welfare, we will evaluate its impact on gender equality in education.

THE DEBATE OVER TITLE IX

Few federal policies have had such a visible effect on education as Title IX, which man-dates gender equity in education in federally funded schools. Congressional amendments to the Education Act of 1972 have brought significant changes for both men and women at all levels of schooling. Title IX eliminated sex-segregated classes, prohibited sex discrimi-nation in admissions and financial aid, and mandated that girls receive more opportunities to play sports, in proportion to their enrollment and interest.

Today, Title IX is still one of the more controversial attempts ever made by the fed-eral government to promote equality for all citizens. Its consequences for the funding of college athletics programs are hotly debated, while its real and lasting effects on college admissions and employment are often forgotten.

The issues addressed by Title IX pertain to the principle of fair treatment of males and females under the law. The government decided in 1972, and in reconsiderations of the law subsequently, to support gender equity by imposing stringent standards of conformance on schools receiving federal aid. Since most public institutions fall into this category, institutions have had to devise strategies to make male-dominated sports and other educational programs fall into compliance with the law.

Under this landmark legislation, to receive federal funds, a school or college must pass one of three tests. First, the numbers of male and female athletes must be proportional to the numbers of men and women enrolled at the school. Second, lacking that, the school must show a continuing history of expanding opportunities for female athletes. Or third, the school must demonstrate that the level of female participation in sports meets female students' level of interest or ability.

Schools with major collegiate sports teams, especially football teams, have had to scramble to balance those teams' large squads of male athletes with increased numbers of female sports participants. Some institutions have tried with mixed success to meet one of the second two equity tests under the law: demonstrating a continuing history of expanding opportunities or assessing the level of female students' interest or ability. Others have opted to increase the number of sports available to women or to both sexes on their campuses. And some have had to take the poisonous step—supremely unpopular with alumni groups that provide substantial support to institutions with strong male sports teams—of cutting some male sports (e.g., wrestling) or opening participation in those sports to women (e.g., fencing).

The law has produced notable results. Participation by women in university academic areas formerly considered the preserve of men, such as law and the sciences, has increased dramatically. Furthermore, women's enrollment in sports such as basketball, soccer, swimming, track, and lacrosse has skyrocketed at many institutions. Still, the law remains controversial, mostly because of its effects on male athletes—and the alumni support that is jeopardized if a school chooses to cut or diminish an athletic program that has traditionally been dominated by men.

Applying Sociology to Title IX Supporters of Title IX believe that the law has opened up academic areas and athletic opportunities to a previously underserved body of students. They see the main argument in favor of the law as the prevention of discrimination against a group of students based on their ascribed status as women rather than on any achieved status or merit. Quite simply, supporters argue that the law addresses a fundamental inequity and combats both bias and discrimination in education. The facts support the argument that women have benefited from the law: for example, between 1972, when Title IX was passed, and 2013, the number of girls participating in high school athletics jumped from 300,000 to over 3.2 million.

Critics, focusing mainly on the effect of the law on organized collegiate sports, charge that men's teams have suffered from proportional funding of women's teams and athletic scholarships, since schools with tight athletic budgets can expand women's sports only at the expense of men's sports. They argue that enforcing equity on behalf of one group—women—has resulted in "reverse discrimination" against another group—men. Supporters of the law reply that "equity" means just that and that redressing an existing imbalance is not discrimination, but fairness.

Furthermore, supporters argue that the increased funding for women's sports has benefited men in some ways, too. In terms of coaching and administration, men have increasingly replaced women as directors of women's sports since Title IX was passed. Today only 19 percent of collegiate women's athletic administrators are women, compared to over 90 percent in the early 1970s. No national data exists for high school sports leadership, but an analysis of Minnesota youth soccer found that only 15 percent of head coaches were women.

Looking at the issue from another angle, some sociologists caution that the social effects of sports on college campuses are not all positive for women athletes. Michael A. Messner, professor of sociology at the University of Southern California, points to some troubling results of a survey by the Women's Sports Foundation. The study shows that teenage girls who play sports simply for fun have more positive body images than girls who don't play sports. But those who are "highly involved" in sports are more likely than other girls to take steroids and to become risk-takers. "Everyone has tacitly agreed, it seems, to view men's sports as the standard to which women should strive to have equal access," Messner writes. He is skeptical of a system that propels a lucky few college athletes to stardom each year while leaving the majority, many of them African American, without a career or an education. Certainly that was not the kind of equal opportunity legislators envisioned when they wrote Title IX.

Initiating Gender Equity Policy in Education Title IX remains the law of the land, despite continued efforts to water it down or downright repeal it. The most recent attempt to revise the law occurred under President George W. Bush, who formed a panel in 2002, named "the Commission on Opportunity in Athletics," to review the law and propose changes.

When draft versions of portions of the commission's report were released to reporters, two members of the commission—both women—issued a minority report condemning some of the proposed changes to the law for using deceptive counting schemes to help colleges appear to be in compliance with the law while in fact flouting it. Supported by a number of women's groups and prominent individual women, a "Save Title IX" campaign was launched which eventually succeeded—for now—in derailing all attempts to weaken the law.

The lesson is clear. Title IX remains controversial and resides perpetually in the gun sights of opponents. Proponents of the law must be as determined as opponents are persistent if Title IX, which has benefited so many young women, is to remain in effect.

E Evaluate

Read each question carefully and then select or provide the best answer.

1. Which of the following is NOT one of the basic characteristics of bureaucracy, as enumerated by Max Weber?
   a. written rules and regulations
   b. hierarchy of authority
   c. focus on credentialism
   d. impersonality

2. Which of the following desirable characteristics of teachers conflicts with the increasing bureaucratization of teaching?
   a. individual responsibility and independence
   b. strong subject-matter knowledge
   c. central role as social control agents
   d. clear expectation of high standards

3. Compared with traditional school-based learning, what advantage does Internet-based education provide?
   a. higher level of academic quality and accountability
   b. increased one-on-one interaction with instructors
   c. higher level of informal contact with fellow students
   d. increased flexibility for working students

4. Parents who homeschool their children most often
   a. have above-average income levels and better educations.
   b. have lower-than-average income levels.
   c. have fewer ties to the community than parents who send their children to public schools.
   d. face the most opposition in the United States as opposed to other countries, where homeschooling is more typical.

5. The four distinctive subcultures that have been identified in U.S. colleges are _____, _____, _____, and _____.

Answers

1 (c); 2 (a); 3 (d); 4 (a); 5 collegiate, academic, vocational, nonconformist

R Rethink

Consider these questions to get a deeper understanding of the material.

1. Select two functions of education and suggest how they could be fulfilled through homeschooling.

2. How would functionalists, conflict theorists, and interactionists view the existence of student subcultures on college campuses?

RECAP

LO 41-1 Explain the bureaucratization of schools and its impact on teaching and learning.

- Schools exhibit the five basic characteristics of bureaucracy: division of labor, hierarchy of authority, written rules and regulations, impersonality, and employment based on technical qualifications. This arrangement meets with the approval of functionalists.

- In contrast, conflict theorists argue that standardized curricula and educational bureaucracies have harmful consequences for disadvantaged people.
- School choice programs and Internet-based education are suggested by some as positive countertrends to the bureaucratization of schools, but these have disadvantages as well.

LO 41-2 Analyze the roles that teachers and students play in formal schooling.

- Teachers serve simultaneously as employees of formal bureaucracies and instructors of students. These roles are somewhat contradictory, since bureaucratic organization is meant to foster compliance to rules and hierarchy, while the teaching profession is supposed to be based on independent, professional thinking and decision making.

- Sociologists have identified four distinctive subcultures among college students: collegiate, academic, vocational, and nonconformist. While student subcultures are more diverse today than previously, Black students at predominantly White colleges experience overt and subtle racial discrimination that can jeopardize their college careers.
- Problems in the public school system, including poor academic quality, peer pressure, and violence, have led some parents to homeschool their children.

The Case of . . . The Wrong Side of the Tracks

Before Shakur Taylor's family moved out of Baltimore, he went to an inner-city school that was 95 percent Black. Now, he attends high school in a Maryland suburb that is 85 percent White. "My Baltimore school was in a dumpy building where the water pipes kept breaking," Taylor recalls. "We had lots of kids in each class and never enough books to go around. My new school is this modern steel and glass palace with a fine arts wing and plenty of everything." Taylor admits he likes the space and having a locker that isn't broken. "But it's not like the old school was all bad and this one is all good," he says. "In my old school, we were all Black kids, so we all got taught the same things. Maybe nobody on the outside expected much from us, but we had some teachers who expected a lot. Here, I'm definitely a minority. They track kids here and they put me in what they call the 'business track.' It's supposed to be a nice way of saying 'not college material.' I guess I should be glad they didn't dump me in 'vocational.' Everyone knows that's the bottom rung." Taylor says he gets the watered-down version of the college-track courses plus practical math and data entry. "The business track doesn't have some of the courses I would need to get to college, so my decision's been made for me," he says. "I didn't even get to take a test when I came here. They just took one look at my skin and the fact that I qualify for free lunch, and they figured, 'With a little work, this boy could maybe run a Kwik-E-Mart.'"

1. Does the tracking system in Taylor's new school perpetuate social-class divisions? Explain your thinking.

2. How might the teacher-expectancy effect play out in each of the school's three tracks: college, business, and vocational?

3. If Taylor's school used testing to place students in the various tracks, would that validate their placements? Why or why not?

4. Do you think there are actions Taylor can take to "rise above" the track he was placed in and attend college if he chooses? What would you recommend?

Speaking in Public

You may never have to deliver a major public address, but in class you'll be expected to summarize opinions and argue positions in front of the class. If this terrifies you, console yourself with the knowledge that you're not alone. In fact, there are few things that people fear more than public speaking—including death! The fact that *glossophobia*—to give it its scientific name—is so universal can actually help you get over it.

- Remember that everyone in your audience—including your instructor—hates public speaking. This means that they will absolutely be on your side.
- Before you speak, define your main point. What do you want your audience to take away from your presentation?

- If you have time to prepare, create an outline or note cards. Use key words, not sentences and paragraphs. Then practice using them while speaking.
- If possible, create charts, graphs, or slides to help convey your thoughts.
- If you have to speak without preparation, STALL. Gather your papers, look at your notebook, clear your throat, walk slowly to the front of the room—whatever it takes to gain a few seconds. Use this time to define your message and prepare a few talking points.

- Remember that your audience is on your side. They want you to succeed.
- Breathe normally—don't take short, nervous breaths. If you hyperventilate, you will lose physical control and start to shake.
- Control your voice. One common technique is to speak in a "radio voice"—a voice pitched a tiny bit lower and stronger than your usual voice.
- Stand tall. If you slouch, your breathing will be shortened and you'll find yourself gasping for air.
- Leave room between sentences. Try to slow yourself down, avoiding the natural desire to get through your presentation as quickly as possible.
- Make "false eye contact" with your audience. Focus on a point in their foreheads or hairlines. They'll think you're looking right at them.
- Alternatively, find a few friends in the audience and play directly to them.
- Some "glossophobes" imagine that they're playing a part—like an actor delivering lines. In this way, they make the audience seem to vanish.
- Glance at your notes occasionally, but don't bury yourself in them.
- Practice avoiding "um," "er," "like," "you know," and similar fillers. If you *absolutely* need fillers, make them silent: Try just swallowing.

- Ask people who heard you to evaluate your presentation. Act on their feedback the next time you have to speak in public.

- Now that it's over, ask yourself, *Did I communicate my main message?* If not, work on doing better the next time.

em POWER me

Are You Ready to Speak Up?

Do your instructors routinely downgrade you for not participating in class discussions? Would you rather have your fingernails pulled out one by one than make an oral presentation to the class? While public speaking may never be completely jitter-free, there are techniques and strategies that will calm your nerves and improve your delivery. Rank each of the following items according to how often it's true for you; then use this scale to find your score:

Frequently = 2

Sometimes = 1

Rarely = 0

	Frequently	Sometimes	Rarely
1. I use an outline or note cards with key words when making an oral presentation.			
2. I focus on an object at the back of the room or a friend's face when speaking in front of the class.			
3. I use a tape recorder to practice oral presentations, and listen for any weak spots I can improve in my speech.			
4. I prepare a chart or graph to use as a visual aid so that I don't have to keep a lot of figures in my head.			
5. I speak slowly and remember to take breaths so that my thoughts don't get tangled.			
6. I role-play with a study partner, taking turns explaining a concept or defending a point of view.			
7. I glance at my notes during a presentation, but don't read directly from them.			
8. During a class discussion, I jot down a few key points I wish to make before speaking.			
9. In preparing an oral presentation, I begin by deciding what my main message to my audience will be.			

SCORE:

15–18 Regardless of how you feel beforehand, you are prepared to speak when the situation calls for it. You know the points you wish to make and you present them clearly to your audience.

11–14 You do some preparation before speaking and make use of one or two effective speaking techniques, but you can improve your delivery.

10 or less Resist the impulse to run and hide. Study the tips and techniques in the items above; then turn to this chapter's P.O.W.E.R. Study Strategies: Speaking in Public for more ideas.

14 Social Change in the Global Community

MODULE 42 Social Movements
MODULE 43 Social Change
MODULE 44 Global Social Change

Sociology at WORK COMMUNITY ORGANIZER

LIAM BYRNES is a community organizer in Brooklyn. He spends his days on the streets, talking to community members about the conditions of their local schools. "This isn't the affluent part of the borough," Byrnes says. "These people can't afford to send their kids to private schools, and the public schools they have are in a sorry state. Crumbling buildings. Crowded classrooms. Outdated textbooks." Byrnes has collected data on each of the local schools, including rankings on standardized tests and dropout rates. "I share what I know with the people in the community and encourage them to tell me their stories," he says. "Then we discuss what needs to be done and ways we might make that happen."

Byrnes sees his primary role as being that of a mover and shaker. "I'm there to put the issue on the table," he explains. "I get people thinking and talking, then I take the role of facilitator, arranging meetings, putting the community in touch with the appropriate government agencies." Byrnes believes that real change always starts at the local level. "Government is an abstract thing to most people," he says. "I help them to discover that regular people *do* have power when they act together."

Looking Ahead

SOCIAL CHANGE HAS BEEN DEFINED AS SIGNIFICANT ALTERATION OVER time in behavior patterns and culture (W. Moore 1967). How does social change happen? Is the process unpredictable, or can we make certain generalizations about it? Has globalization contributed to social change? In this chapter we examine the process of social change, with special emphasis on the impact of globalization. We begin with *social movements*—collective efforts to bring about deliberate social change. We will see that recent advances in communications technology have allowed some social movements to circle the world. Next, we examine three theories of social change: the evolutionary, functionalist, and conflict perspectives. Then we discuss vested interests, which often attempt to block changes they see as threatening. And we recognize the influence of globalization in spreading social change around the world, noting the rapid social change that has occurred over a matter of decades in the Middle Eastern city-state of Dubai. Finally, we turn to the unanticipated social change that occurs when innovations such as new technologies sweep through society. The chapter closes with a Social Policy section on a controversial aspect of global social change, the creation of *transnationals*—immigrants with an allegiance to more than one nation.

MODULE 42 Social Movements

P Prepare Learning Objectives

LO 42-1 Describe social movements in terms of relative deprivation theory, resource mobilization theory, and gender.

LO 42-2 Explain what is meant by *new social movements*.

LO 42-3 Analyze the impact of new communications technology on social movements.

W Work

LO 42-1 The Emergence of Social Movements

In 2010, protesters in London disguised themselves as characters in the movie *Avatar* to draw attention to the plight of an indigenous tribe in India. The Dongria Kondh people's way of life, the protesters charged, was threatened by a multinational corporation's plan to construct a mine on their land. The Indian government blocked the project, agreeing with protesters that it would have violated the tribe's rights.

Although such factors as the physical environment, population, technology, and social inequality serve as sources of change, it is the *collective* effort of individuals organized into social movements that ultimately leads to change. Sociologists use the term **social movement** to refer to an organized collective activity to bring about or resist fundamental change in an existing group or society (Benford 1992). Herbert Blumer (1955:19) recognized the special importance of social movements when he defined them as "collective enterprises to establish a new order of life."

In many nations, including the United States, social movements have had a dramatic impact on the course of history and the evolution of the social structure. Consider the actions of abolitionists, suffragists, civil rights workers, activists opposed to the war in Vietnam, and Occupy Wall Street protesters. Members of each social movement stepped outside traditional channels for bringing about social change, yet each had a noticeable influence on public policy. In Eastern Europe, equally dramatic collective efforts helped to topple communist regimes in a largely peaceful manner, in nations that many observers had thought were "immune" to such social change (Ramet 1991).

Though social movements imply the existence of conflict, we can also analyze their activities from a functionalist perspective. Even when they are unsuccessful, social movements contribute to the formation of public opinion. Initially, people thought the ideas of Margaret Sanger and other early advocates of birth control were radical, yet contraceptives are now widely available in the United States.

Because social movements know no borders, even nationalistic movements are deeply influenced by global events. Increasingly, social movements are taking on an international dimension from the start. Global enterprises, in particular, lend themselves to targeting through international mobilization, whether they are corporations like McDonald's or governmental bodies like the World Trade Organization. Global activism is not new, however; it began with the writing of Karl Marx, who sought to mobilize oppressed peoples in other industrialized countries. Today, activist networking is facilitated by the Internet. Participation in transnational activism is much more widespread now than in the past, and passions are quicker to ignite.

How and why do social movements emerge? Obviously, people are often discontented with the way things are. What causes them to organize at a particular moment in a collective effort to effect change? Sociologists rely on two explanations for why people mobilize: the relative deprivation and resource mobilization approaches.

RELATIVE DEPRIVATION APPROACH

Those members of a society who feel most frustrated and disgruntled by social and economic conditions are not necessarily the worst off in an objective sense. Social scientists have long recognized that what is more significant is the way in which people *perceive* their situation. As Karl Marx pointed out, although the misery of the workers was important to their perception of their oppressed state, so was their position *in relation to* the capitalist ruling class (Marx and Engels [1847] 1955).

The term **relative deprivation** is defined as the conscious feeling of a negative discrepancy between legitimate expectations and present actualities (J. Wilson 1973). In other words, things aren't as good as you hoped they would be. Such a state may be characterized by scarcity rather than a complete lack of necessities (as we saw in the distinction between absolute and relative poverty in Chapter 8). A relatively deprived person is dissatisfied because he or she feels downtrodden relative to some appropriate reference group. Thus, blue-collar workers who live in two-family houses on small plots of land—though hardly at the bottom of the economic ladder—may nevertheless feel deprived in comparison to corporate managers and professionals who live in lavish homes in exclusive suburbs.

In addition to the feeling of relative deprivation, two other elements must be present before discontent will be channeled into a social movement. People must feel that they have a *right* to their goals, that they deserve better than what they have. At the same time, the disadvantaged group must perceive that its goals cannot be attained through conventional means. This belief may or may not be correct. Whichever is the case, the group will not mobilize into a social movement unless there is a shared perception that members can end their relative deprivation only through collective action (D. Morrison 1971).

From the perspective of . . .

A Classroom Teacher   What does the concept of relative deprivation suggest your students who qualify for free lunch vouchers may be feeling?

Critics of this approach have noted that people don't need to feel deprived to be moved to act. In addition, this approach fails to explain why certain feelings of deprivation are transformed into social movements, whereas in similar situations, no collective effort is

made to reshape society. Consequently, in recent years, sociologists have paid increasing attention to the forces needed to bring about the emergence of social movements (Alain 1985; Finkel and Rule 1987; Orum and Dale 2009).

RESOURCE MOBILIZATION APPROACH

It takes more than desire to start a social movement. It helps to have money, political influence, access to the media, and personnel. The term **resource mobilization** refers to the ways in which a social movement utilizes such resources. Indeed, the success of a movement for change will depend in good part on what resources it has and how effectively it mobilizes them. In other words, recruiting adherents and marshalling resources is critical to the growth and success of social movements (D. Miller 2014; Tilly 1964, 2003; Walder 2009).

Leadership is a central factor in the mobilization of the discontented into social movements. Often, a movement will be led by a charismatic figure, such as Dr. Martin Luther King Jr. As Max Weber described it in 1904, *charisma* is that quality of an individual that sets him or her apart from ordinary people. Of course, charisma can fade abruptly, which helps to account for the fragility of certain social movements (Morris 2000).

Many social movements are mobilized by institutional insiders. During the nationwide debate of the Obama administration's plan for health care reform in 2009, for example, health insurance companies encouraged their employees to attend the forums arranged by the White House. Managers distributed "Town Hall Tips" that included a list of concerns employees could raise and suggestions on how to make their comments as personal as possible, by talking about their own health issues (E. Walker 2010).

Why do certain individuals join a social movement while others who are in similar situations do not? Some of them are recruited to join. Karl Marx recognized the importance of recruitment when he called on workers to become *aware* of their oppressed status and to develop a class consciousness. Like theorists of the resource mobilization approach, Marx held that a social movement (specifically, the revolt of the proletariat) would require leaders to sharpen the awareness of the oppressed. They would need to help workers to overcome feelings of **false consciousness**, or attitudes that did not reflect workers' objective position, in order to organize a revolutionary movement. Similarly, one of the challenges faced by women's liberation activists of the late 1960s and early 1970s was to convince women that they were being deprived of their rights and of socially valued resources.

GENDER AND SOCIAL MOVEMENTS

Sociologists point out that gender is an important element in understanding social movements. In our male-dominated society, women find it more difficult than men to assume leadership positions in social movement organizations. Though women often serve disproportionately as volunteers in these movements, their work is not always recognized, nor are their voices as easily heard as men's. Gender bias causes the real extent of their influence to be overlooked. Indeed, traditional examination of the sociopolitical system tends to focus on such male-dominated corridors of power as legislatures and corporate boardrooms, to the neglect of more female-dominated domains such as households, community-based groups, and faith-based networks. However, efforts to influence family values, child rearing, relationships between parents and schools, and spiritual values are clearly significant to a culture and society (Ferree and Merrill 2000; Noonan 1995).

Scholars of social movements now realize that gender can affect even the way we view organized efforts to bring about or resist change. For example, an emphasis on using rationality and cold logic to achieve goals helps to obscure the importance of passion and emotion in successful social movements. It would be difficult to find any movement—from labor battles to voting rights to animal rights—in which passion was not part of the consensus-building force. Yet calls for a more serious study of the role of emotion are frequently seen as applying only to the women's movement, because emotion is traditionally thought of as being feminine (Ferree and Merrill 2000; V. Taylor 1999, 2004).

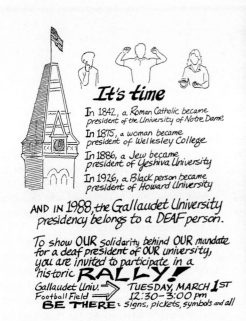

Gallaudet University in Washington, D.C., is the only four-year liberal arts college for deaf students in the United States. A leaflet (left) was distributed in 1988 as part of a successful effort by students, faculty, and alumni to force the appointment of the university's first deaf president. In 2007, after that president's retirement, students protested once again over the election process (right). The mobilization of resources, including leaflets, is one key to the success of a social movement.

LO 42-2 NEW SOCIAL MOVEMENTS

Beginning in the late 1960s, European social scientists observed a change in both the composition and the targets of emerging social movements. Previously, traditional social movements had focused on economic issues, often led by labor unions or by people who shared the same occupation. However, many social movements that have become active in recent decades—including the contemporary women's movement, the peace movement, and the environmental movement—do not have the social class roots typical of the labor protests in the United States and Europe over the past century (Tilly 1993, 2004).

The term **new social movement** refers to an organized collective activity that addresses values and social identities, as well as improvements in the quality of life. These movements may be involved in developing collective identities. Many have complex agendas that go beyond a single issue, and even cross national boundaries. Educated, middle-class people are significantly represented in some of these new social movements, such as the women's movement and the movement for lesbian and gay rights. Box 14-1 describes the women's movements in South Korea and India.

New social movements generally do not view government as their ally in the struggle for a better society. While they typically do not seek to overthrow the government, they may criticize, protest, or harass public officials. Researchers have found that members of new social movements show little inclination to accept established authority, even scientific or technical authority. This characteristic is especially evident in the environmental and anti–nuclear power movements, whose activists present their own experts to counter those of government or big business (Garner 1996; Polletta and Jasper 2001; A. Scott 1990).

The environmental movement is one of many new movements with a worldwide focus (see the Social Policy section in Chapter 12). In their efforts to reduce air and water pollution, curtail global warming, and protect endangered animal species, environmental activists have realized that strong regulatory measures within a single country are not sufficient. Similarly, labor union leaders and human rights advocates cannot adequately address exploitative sweatshop conditions in a developing country if multinational corporations can simply move their factories to another country, where workers earn even less. Whereas traditional views of social movements tended to emphasize resource mobilization on a local level, new social movement theory offers a broader, global perspective on social and political activism.

14-1 WOMEN'S SOCIAL MOVEMENTS IN SOUTH KOREA AND INDIA

Women have long played a significant role in social movements. Scholars have taken two different approaches to studying these movements: a macro-level, national approach and a more local approach to new social movements.

The macro-level approach has proved useful in studying the women's movement in South Korea. In 1987, a nationwide movement that included a variety of women's organizations toppled the country's longtime authoritarian ruler. In the democratic environment that followed his overthrow, women joined together in Korean Women's Association United (KWAU) to seek a voice on issues involving families, the environment, education, and sexuality, including sexual harassment and assault. The KWAU staged public demonstrations, held hearings, and presented petitions. Recognizing the women's right to be heard, the national government created special commissions to focus specifically on women's issues.

Eventually, the women's movement in South Korea became an institutionalized collaborator with the central government, even receiving government grants. Progress on women's issues has not been steady, however, as some administrations have been less friendly than others to the KWAU. To gain traction, the KWAU reached out to the United Nations in its efforts to further women's social equality, and to other international bodies, such as those seeking to curb human trafficking.

In the last 10 years, groups of younger women, often based on college campuses,

have questioned the KWAU's ability to speak for them. These women charge that the KWAU has in effect become part of the state, and by extension, "part of the problem." Disabled women and lesbians, for example, feel unrepresented by the KWAU. And an organization of prostitutes has argued for the decriminalization of sex work—a position clearly at odds with the KWAU's stance against human trafficking.

From workers' rights to the voting booth, from education to freedom from sexual violence, women's issues are an increasingly common feature of politics in both India and South Korea.

In India, the women's social movement tends to be locally based, often in farming communities, where about 71 percent of the nation's 1.2 billion people live. As in other parts of the developing world, rural families in India are quite poor. For decades, villagers have been moving to the cities in hopes of earning a better income, only to be exploited in sweatshops and multinational factories. In the mid-1980s, 5,000 striking textile workers returned to their rural villages to mobilize support for their movement. As the strike wore on, some of those women remained in the villages and sought work on government drought-relief projects. However, there weren't enough jobs for the villagers, much less for the striking textile workers.

This experience inspired a new social movement in rural India. With unemployment

threatening an expanded population in rural villages, activists formed what came to be called the *Shoshit, Shetkari, Kashtakari, Kamgar, Mukti Sangharsh* (SSKKMS), which means "exploited peasants, toilers, workers liberation struggle." The movement's initial goal was to provide drought relief for farmers, but the deeper goal was to empower rural residents.

Indian women have also worked to improve their families' lot through microfinance programs. They have marched on government offices to demand that at least a third of the seats in Parliament and the state assemblies be reserved for them. Clearly, Indian women's traditional role of maintaining their households' health and nutrition is critical to their families' survival. Thus, their leadership in seeking improved living conditions is winning them new respect in India's patriarchal society.

From workers' rights to the voting booth, from education to freedom from sexual violence, women's issues are an increasingly common feature of politics in both India and South Korea.

Let's Discuss

1. What do you think might explain the differences between women's social movements and issues in South Korea and in India?
2. What would happen if "powerless" people in the United States formed a social movement of their own? Would it succeed? Why or why not?

Sources: Hur 2011; Korean Women's Association United 2010; Sengupta 2009; Subramaniam 2006; Suh 2011; Working Women's Forum 2012.

Table 14-1 summarizes the sociological approaches that have contributed to social movement theory. Each has added to our understanding of the development of social movements.

LO 42-3 Communications and the Globalization of Social Movements

Today, through global text-messaging and the Internet, social activists can reach a large number of people around the world almost instantaneously, with relatively little effort and expense. The Internet's listservs and chat rooms—a form of social networking—allow organizers of social movements to enlist like-minded people without face-to-face contact, or even simultaneous interaction (Calhoun 1998; Kavada 2005).

Moreover, television and the Internet, as contrasted with books and newspapers, often convey a false sense of intimacy reinforced by immediacy, as we can see when people seem to be personally affected by the latest celebrity news. The latest technology brings us together to act and react in an electronic global village (Della Porta and Tarrow 2005; Garner 1999).

This sense of online togetherness extends to social movements, which more and more are being mounted on the web. Through the instantaneous communication that is possible over the Internet, Mexican Zapatistas and other groups of indigenous peoples can transform their cause into an international lobbying effort, and Greenpeace organizers can link environmental activists throughout the world via video recorded on members' cell phones.

Sociologists have begun to refer to such electronic enhancement of established social movements as **computer-mediated communication (CMC)**. Computer-mediated communication may be defined as communicative interaction through two or more networked devices, such as a computer or cell phone. The term applies to a variety of text-based or video interactions, including e-mails, chat rooms, and text messages, some of which may be supported by social media. This kind of electronic communication strengthens a group's solidarity, allowing fledgling social movements to grow and develop faster than they might otherwise. Thus the face-to-face contact that once was critical to a social movement is no longer necessary. However, the legitimacy of such online movements is a matter of opinion (Castells 2010b; Niezen 2005).

The new global communications technology also helps to create enclaves of similarly minded people. Alex Steffen (2008), editor of the book *World Changing,* notes that

TABLE 14-1

CONTRIBUTIONS TO SOCIAL MOVEMENT THEORY

Approach	Emphasis
Relative deprivation	Social movements are especially likely to arise when expectations are frustrated.
Resource mobilization	The success of social movements depends on which resources are available and how effectively they are used.
New social movement	Social movements arise when people are motivated by value issues and social identity questions.

Summing Up

Rural residents of Mongolia pose outside their home with their satellite dish. In the 21st century, technology links people in even the remotest areas. In 2008 protesters rocked Mongolia's capital in anger over election fraud. Two years later, they gathered to demand more equitable distribution of the nation's mining wealth. In both cases, people from rural areas organized for action on the Internet.

the Internet is changing the way people relate to one another across vast distances, allowing small, focused audiences to become part of a global conversation. In doing so, they may find a common purpose. These social connections happen because of the Internet's technological structure. Websites are not autonomous and independent; they are connected by a global electronic network. One website generally lists a variety of other sites that serve as links. For example, seeking information on domestic partnerships may lead you to an electronic enclave that is supportive of cohabitation between men and women or to an enclave that is supportive of gay and lesbian couples. New developments in communications technology have clearly broadened the way we interact with one another (Calhoun 1998).

E Evaluate

Read each question carefully and then select or provide the best answer.

1. You are a student and do not own a car. All your close friends who are attending your college or university have vehicles of their own. You feel downtrodden and dissatisfied. You are experiencing
   a. relative deprivation.
   b. resource mobilization.
   c. false consciousness.
   d. depression.

2. It takes more than desire to start a social movement; it helps to have money, political influence, access to the media, and workers. The ways in which a social movement uses such things are referred to collectively as
   a. relative deprivation.
   b. false consciousness.
   c. resource mobilization.
   d. economic independence.

3. Karl Marx held that leaders of social movements must help workers overcome feelings of
   a. class consciousness.
   b. false consciousness.
   c. socialist consciousness.
   d. surplus value.

4. Organized collective activities that promote autonomy and self-determination, as well as improvements in the quality of life, are referred to as
   a. new social movements.
   b. social revolutions.
   c. resource mobilizations.
   d. crazes.

5. A person suffering from relative deprivation is dissatisfied because he or she feels downtrodden relative to some appropriate _____ group.

Answers

1 (a); 2 (c); 3 (b); 4 (a); 5 reference

R Rethink

Consider these questions to get a deeper understanding of the material.

1. What aspects of traditional gender roles explain the roles that women and men typically play in social movements?

2. What might be some drawbacks of global communications technology?

RECAP

LO 42-1 Describe social movements in terms of relative deprivation theory, resource mobilization theory, and gender.

- Social movements—organized activity to bring change—are more structured than other forms of collective behavior and persist over longer periods.
- A group will not mobilize into a social movement without a shared perception that its relative deprivation can be ended only through collective action.
- The success of a social movement depends in good part on effective resource mobilization. A key mobilization factor is leadership.
- Gender plays a role in the operation of social movements. Bias has caused the contributions of women, who serve disproportionately as volunteers in social movements, to be undervalued compared to the more noticeable leadership roles typically occupied by men.

LO 42-2 Explain what is meant by *new social movements*.

- New social movements are organized activities addressing values rather than improvements in the quality of life, which had been the traditional focus of labor-led, national social movements before the 1960s.
- New social movements tend to focus on more than just economic issues, and often cross national boundaries.

LO 42-3 Analyze the impact of new communications technology on social movements.

- Advances in communications technology—especially the Internet—have had a major impact on social movements.

- The immediacy of online communication has brought a sense of togetherness to social movements whose participants are geographically distant.
- Computer-mediated communication strengthens solidarity, enables rapid growth and spread, facilitates recruitment and membership, and leads to the sharing of ideas and strategies among members of social movements.

KEY TERMS

Computer-mediated communication (CMC) Communicative interaction through two or more networked devices, such as a computer or cell phone. The term applies to a variety of text-based or video interactions, including e-mails, chat rooms, and text messages, some of which may be supported by social media.

False consciousness A term used by Karl Marx to describe an attitude held by members of a class that does not accurately reflect their objective position.

New social movement An organized collective activity that addresses values and social identities, as well as improvements in the quality of life.

Relative deprivation The conscious feeling of a negative discrepancy between legitimate expectations and present actualities.

Resource mobilization The ways in which a social movement utilizes such resources as money, political influence, access to the media, and personnel.

Social change Significant alteration over time in behavior patterns and culture, including norms and values.

Social movement An organized collective activity to bring about or resist fundamental change in an existing group or society.

MODULE 43 Social Change

P Prepare Learning Objectives

LO 43-1 Analyze social change according to the evolutionary, functionalist, and conflict theories.

LO 43-2 Describe the factors that create resistance to social change.

O Organize Module Outline

Theories of Social Change
    Evolutionary Theory
    Functionalist Perspective
    Conflict Perspective
Resistance to Social Change
    Economic and Cultural Factors
    Resistance to Technology

W Work

A new millennium provides the occasion to offer explanations of social change. But what constitutes a "significant" alteration? Certainly the dramatic rise in formal education in the last century represents a change that has had profound social consequences. Other social changes that have had long-term and important consequences include the emergence of slavery as a system of stratification, the Industrial Revolution, and the increased

TABLE 14-2 THE UNITED STATES: A CHANGING NATION

Population	1850	1940	1960	2012
Total in millions	23.2	132.1	180.7	308.8
Percentage under age 15	41%	25%	31%	20%
Education	**1850**	**1940**	**1960**	**2012**
Percentage not completing high school or equivalent	88%	18%	13%	7%
Percentage ages 19–24 enrolled in higher education	Under 1%	8%	40%	41%
Labor Force Participation	**1850**	**1940**	**1960**	**2011**
Men in their 20s	94%	88%	86%	81%
Women in their 20s	22%	39%	74%	76%
Health	**1850**	**1940**	**1960**	**2010**
Physicians per 100,000 population	176	133	150	272
Life expectancy at birth, in years	38	63	70	78.7
Technology	**1870**	**1940**	**1960**	**2011**
Copyrights issued	5,600	176,997	243,926	670,000
Patents issued	12,127	42,238	47,170	253,155
Family	**1890**	**1940**	**1960**	**2013**
Median age at first marriage				
Men	26	24	23	29
Women	22	22	20	28.6
Number of children born per family	3.25	2.7	3.65	1.9

Note: Data are comparable, although definitions vary. Definition of the United States changes between 1850 and 1940 and between 1940 and 1960. Earliest date for children born per family is 1905.
Sources: Author, based on federal data collected in Bureau of the Census 2011a, 2012f, 2013b; Bureau of Labor Statistics 2013a; National Center for Education Statistics 2013; National Center for Health Statistics 2013: Tables 10, 18; Sutch and Carter 2006; United States Copyright Office 2012; United States Patent and Trademark Office 2012; World Bank 2013.

participation of women in the paid labor forces of the United States and Europe. Social change often follows the introduction of a new technology. Social change can occur so slowly as to be almost undetectable to those it affects, but it can also happen with breathtaking rapidity. As Table 14-2 shows, some changes that have occurred in U.S. society over the past century and a half have been relatively slow or slight; others have been rapid or striking in magnitude.

LO **43-1** Theories of Social Change

Explanations of social change are clearly a challenge in the diverse and complex world we inhabit today. Nevertheless, theorists from several disciplines have sought to analyze social change. In some instances, they have examined historical events to arrive at a better understanding of contemporary changes. We will review three theoretical approaches to change—evolutionary, functionalist, and conflict—and then take a look at resistance to social change.

EVOLUTIONARY THEORY

The pioneering work of Charles Darwin (1809–1882) in biological evolution contributed to 19th-century theories of social change. Darwin's approach stresses a continuing progression of successive life-forms. For example, human beings came at a later stage of evolution than reptiles and represent a more complex form of life. Social theorists seeking an analogy to this biological model originated **evolutionary theory**, in which society is viewed as moving in a definite direction. Early evolutionary theorists generally agreed that society was progressing inevitably toward a higher state. As might be expected, they concluded in ethnocentric fashion that their behavior and culture were more advanced than those of earlier civilizations.

Auguste Comte (1798–1857), a founder of sociology, was an evolutionary theorist of change. He saw human societies as moving forward in their thinking, from mythology to the scientific method. Similarly, Émile Durkheim ([1893] 1933) maintained that society progressed from simple to more complex forms of social organization.

Today, evolutionary theory influences sociologists in a variety of ways. For example, it has encouraged sociobiologists to investigate the behavioral links between humans and other animals. It has also influenced human ecology, the study of the interaction between communities and their environment (Maryanski 2004).

FUNCTIONALIST PERSPECTIVE

Because functionalist sociologists focus on what *maintains* a system, not on what changes it, they might seem to offer little to the study of social change. Yet as the work of sociologist Talcott Parsons demonstrates, functionalists have made a distinctive contribution to this area of sociological investigation.

Parsons (1902–1979), a leading proponent of the functionalist perspective, viewed society as being in a natural state of equilibrium. By "equilibrium," he meant that society tends toward a state of stability or balance. Parsons would view even prolonged labor strikes or civilian riots as temporary disruptions in the status quo rather than as significant alterations in social structure. Therefore, according to his **equilibrium model**, as changes occur in one part of society, adjustments must be made in other parts. If not, society's equilibrium will be threatened and strains will occur.

Reflecting the evolutionary approach, Parsons (1966) maintained that four processes of social change are inevitable. *Differentiation* refers to the increasing complexity of social organization. The transition from medicine man to physician, nurse, and pharmacist is an illustration of differentiation in the field of health. This process is accompanied by *adaptive upgrading*, in which social institutions become more specialized in their purposes. The division of physicians into obstetricians, internists, surgeons, and so forth is an example of adaptive upgrading.

The next process Parsons identified is the *inclusion* of groups that were previously excluded because of their gender, race, ethnicity, or social class. Medical schools have practiced inclusion by admitting increasing numbers of women and African Americans. Finally, Parsons contends that societies experience *value generalization,* the development of new values that tolerate and legitimate a greater range of activities. The acceptance of preventive and alternative medicine is an example of value generalization: society has broadened its view of health care. All four processes identified by Parsons stress consensus—societal agreement on the nature of social organization and values (B. Johnson 1975; Wallace and Wolf 1980).

Although Parsons's approach explicitly incorporates the evolutionary notion of continuing progress, the dominant theme in his model is stability. Society may change, but it remains stable through new forms of integration. For example, in place of the kinship ties that provided social cohesion in the past, people develop laws, judicial processes, and new values and belief systems.

CONFLICT PERSPECTIVE

The functionalist perspective minimizes the importance of change. It emphasizes the persistence of social life and sees change as a means of maintaining society's equilibrium (or balance). In contrast, conflict theorists contend that social institutions and practices persist

On the outskirts of Buenos Aires, Argentina, a squatter settlement forms a stark contrast to the gleaming skyscrapers in the wealthy downtown area. Marxists and conflict theorists see social change as a way of overcoming the kind of social inequality evident in this photograph.

because powerful groups have the ability to maintain the status quo. Change has crucial significance, since it is needed to correct social injustices and inequalities.

Karl Marx accepted the evolutionary argument that societies develop along a particular path. However, unlike Comte and Spencer, he did not view each successive stage as an inevitable improvement over the previous one. History, according to Marx, proceeds through a series of stages, each of which exploits a class of people. Ancient society exploited slaves; the estate system of feudalism exploited serfs; modern capitalist society exploits the working class. Ultimately, through a socialist revolution led by the proletariat, human society will move toward the final stage of development: a classless communist society, or "community of free individuals," as Marx described it in 1867 in *Das Kapital* (see Bottomore and Rubel 1956:250).

As we have seen, Marx had an important influence on the development of sociology. His thinking offered insights into such institutions as the economy, the family, religion, and government. The Marxist view of social change is appealing because it does not restrict people to a passive role in responding to inevitable cycles or changes in material culture. Rather, Marxist theory offers a tool for those who wish to seize control of the historical process and gain their freedom from injustice. In contrast to functionalists' emphasis on stability, Marx argues that conflict is a normal and desirable aspect of social change. In fact, change must be encouraged as a means of eliminating social inequality (Lauer 1982).

One conflict theorist, Ralf Dahrendorf (1958), has noted that the contrast between the functionalist perspective's emphasis on stability and the conflict perspective's focus on change reflects the contradictory nature of society. Human societies are stable and long-lasting, yet they also experience serious conflict. Dahrendorf found that the functionalist and conflict perspectives were ultimately compatible, despite their many points of disagreement. Indeed, Parsons spoke of new functions that result from social change, and Marx recognized the need for change so that societies could function more equitably.

Table 14-3 summarizes the differences between the three major perspectives on social change.

TABLE 14-3 SOCIOLOGICAL PERSPECTIVES ON SOCIAL CHANGE

Evolutionary	Social change moves society in a definite direction, frequently from simple to more complex.
Functionalist	Social change must contribute to society's stability.
	Modest adjustments must be made to accommodate social change.
Conflict	Social change can correct social injustices and inequalities.

LO **43-2** Resistance to Social Change

Efforts to promote social change are likely to meet with resistance. In the midst of rapid scientific and technological innovations, many people are frightened by the demands of an ever-changing society. Moreover, certain individuals and groups have a stake in maintaining the existing state of affairs.

Social economist Thorstein Veblen (1857–1929) coined the term **vested interests** to refer to those people or groups who will suffer in the event of social change. For example, in 2010 President Obama proposed scuttling NASA's Constellation project, whose primary goal was to return humans to the moon. Although many people expressed disappointment with the decision to abandon manned space flights, key opposition came from just 27 members of Congress. All represented districts in Alabama and Texas that were home to large suppliers to the project. Ironically, many of those representatives had gone on record as opponents of large federal spending projects. In general, those with a disproportionate share of society's wealth, status, and power, such as members of Congress and representatives of big business, have a vested interest in preserving the status quo (Friedman 2010; Veblen 1919).

From the perspective of . . .

An Environmental Activist What are some examples of vested interests who oppose measures to clean up the environment and reverse climate change?

ECONOMIC AND CULTURAL FACTORS

Economic factors play an important role in resistance to social change. For example, it can be expensive for manufacturers to meet high standards for the safety of products and workers, and for the protection of the environment. Conflict theorists argue that in a capitalist economic system, many firms are not willing to pay the price of meeting strict safety and environmental standards. They may resist social change by cutting corners or by pressuring the government to ease regulations.

Communities, too, protect their vested interests, often in the name of "protecting property values." The abbreviation *NIMBY* stands for "not in my backyard," a cry often heard when people protest landfills, prisons, nuclear power facilities, and even bike trails and group homes for people with developmental disabilities. The targeted community may not challenge the need for the facility, but may simply insist that it be located elsewhere. The "not in my backyard" attitude has become so common that it is almost impossible for policymakers to find acceptable locations for facilities such as hazardous-waste dumps (Jasper 1997).

On the world stage, what amounts to a "not on planet Earth" campaign has emerged. Members of this movement stress many issues, from profiteering to nuclear proliferation, from labor rights to the eradication of poverty and disease. Essentially an antiglobalization movement, it manifests itself at international meetings of trade ministers and heads of state.

Like economic factors, cultural factors frequently shape resistance to change. William F. Ogburn (1922) distinguished between material and nonmaterial aspects of culture. *Material culture* includes inventions, artifacts, and technology; *nonmaterial culture* encompasses ideas, norms, communications, and social organization. Ogburn pointed out that one cannot devise methods for controlling and using new technology before the introduction of a technique. Thus, nonmaterial culture typically must respond to changes in material culture. Ogburn introduced the term **culture lag** to refer to the period of maladjustment when the nonmaterial culture is still struggling to adapt to new material conditions. One example is the Internet. Its rapid, uncontrolled growth raises questions about whether to regulate it, and if so, how much.

3D printers are now widely available, although still expensive, and are used increasingly to transmit both designs and objects. This bust of a *Star Wars* film character was constructed by a 3D printer in Bangalore, India, in 2014.

In certain cases, changes in material culture can strain the relationships between social institutions. For example, new means of birth control have been developed in recent decades. Large families are no longer economically necessary, nor are they commonly endorsed by social norms. However, certain religious faiths, among them Roman Catholicism, continue to extol large families and to disapprove methods of limiting family size, such as contraception and abortion. This issue represents a lag between aspects of material culture (technology) and nonmaterial culture (religious beliefs). Conflicts may also emerge between religion and other social institutions, such as government and the educational system, over the dissemination of birth control and family-planning information (Riley et al. 1994a, 1994b).

RESISTANCE TO TECHNOLOGY

Technology is cultural information about the ways in which the material resources of the environment may be used to satisfy human needs and desires. Technological innovations are examples of changes in material culture that often provoke resistance. The *Industrial Revolution*, which took place largely in England during the period 1760 to 1830, was a scientific revolution focused on the application of nonanimal sources of power to labor tasks. As this revolution proceeded, societies came to rely on new inventions that facilitated agricultural and industrial production and on new sources of energy, such as steam. In some industries, the introduction of power-driven machinery reduced the need for factory workers and made it easier for factory owners to cut wages.

Strong resistance to the Industrial Revolution emerged in some countries. In England, beginning in 1811, masked craft workers took extreme measures: they mounted nighttime raids on factories and destroyed some of the new machinery. The government hunted these rebels, known as **Luddites**, and ultimately banished or hung them. In a similar effort in France, angry workers threw their *sabots* (wooden shoes) into factory machinery to destroy it, giving rise to the term *sabotage*. While the resistance of the Luddites and the French workers was short-lived and unsuccessful, they have come to symbolize resistance to technology.

Are we now in the midst of a second industrial revolution, with a contemporary group of Luddites engaged in resisting? Many sociologists believe that we are living in a *postindustrial society*. It is difficult to pinpoint exactly when this era began. Generally, it is viewed as having begun in the 1950s, when for the first time the majority of workers in industrial societies became involved in services rather than in the actual manufacture of goods.

Just as the Luddites resisted the Industrial Revolution, people in many countries have resisted postindustrial technological changes. The term *neo-Luddites* refers to those who are wary of technological innovations and who question the incessant expansion of industrialization, the increasing destruction of the natural and agrarian world, and the "throw-it-away" mentality of contemporary capitalism, with its resulting pollution of the environment (Volti 2010).

A new slang term, *urban amish,* refers specifically to those who resist technological devices that have become part of our daily lives, such as cell phones. Such people insist that whatever the presumed benefits of industrial and postindustrial technology, such technology has distinctive social costs and may represent a danger to both the future of the human species and our planet (Bauerlein 1996; Rifkin 1995; Sale 1996; Slack and Wise 2007; Snyder 1996; Urban Dictionary 2012).

Other people will resist a new technology simply because they find it difficult to use or because they suspect that it will complicate their lives. Both these objections are especially true of new information and media technologies. Whether it is TiVo, the iPhone, or even the latest digital camera, many consumers are leery of these so-called must-have items.

Read each question carefully and then select or provide the best answer.

1. Nineteenth-century theories of social change reflect the pioneering work in biological evolution done by
   a. Albert Einstein.
   b. Harriet Martineau.
   c. James Audubon.
   d. Charles Darwin.

2. According to Talcott Parsons's equilibrium model, during which process do social institutions become more specialized in their purposes?
   a. differentiation
   b. adaptive upgrading
   c. inclusion
   d. value generalization

3. Which of the following terms did William F. Ogburn use to refer to the period of maladjustment during which the nonmaterial culture is still struggling to adapt to new material conditions?
   a. economic shift
   b. political turmoil
   c. social change
   d. culture lag

4. Talcott Parsons used the term _____ to refer to the increasing complexity of social organization.

5. Social economist Thorstein Veblen coined the term _____ _____ to refer to those people or groups who will suffer in the event of social change.

Answers

1 (d); 2 (b); 3 (d); 4 differentiation; 5 vested interests

Consider these questions to get a deeper understanding of the material.

1. Which perspective on social change—evolutionary, functionalist, or conflict—do you find most convincing? Why?

2. Which do you think play more of a role in resistance to social change, economic or cultural factors? Why?

RECAP

LO 43-1 Analyze social change according to the evolutionary, functionalist, and conflict theories.

- Early advocates of the evolutionary theory of social change believed that society was progressing inevitably toward a higher state.

- Talcott Parsons, a leading advocate of the functionalist perspective, viewed society as being in a natural state of equilibrium or balance. In his equilibrium model, he identified four processes by which societies accommodate change while maintaining balance: differentiation, adaptive upgrading, inclusion, and value generalization.

- Conflict theorists see change as having crucial significance, since it is needed to break up the status quo and correct social injustices and inequalities.

LO 43-2 Describe the factors that create resistance to social change.

- Because people with a disproportionate share of society's wealth, status, and power are likely to suffer from social change, they have a stake in maintaining the status quo. Such people, whom Veblen called vested interests, will resist change.

- Economic factors also cause resistance to social change—factors such as expense, community values, and the protectionism of the "not-in-my-backyard" reaction to proposed changes.

- Cultural factors such as fear of the new can cause a temporary period during which resistance to change is typical. The period of maladjustment when nonmaterial culture is still struggling to adapt to new material conditions is known as culture lag.

- Technology itself can cause resistance due to an ingrained suspicion of mechanized tools and gadgets. People who resist technology just because it is technology are called Luddites.

KEY TERMS

Culture lag A period of maladjustment when the nonmaterial culture is still struggling to adapt to new material conditions.

Equilibrium model The functionalist view that society tends toward a state of stability or balance.

Evolutionary theory A theory of social change that holds that society is moving in a definite direction.

Luddites Rebellious craft workers in 19th-century England who destroyed new factory machinery as part of their resistance to the Industrial Revolution.

Technology Cultural information about the ways in which the material resources of the environment may be used to satisfy human needs and desires.

Vested interests Those people or groups who will suffer in the event of social change, and who have a stake in maintaining the status quo.

MODULE 44 Global Social Change

W Work

The recent past has been a truly dramatic time in history to consider global social change. Maureen Hallinan (1997), in her presidential address to the American Sociological Association, asked those present to consider just a few of the recent events: the collapse of communism; terrorism in various parts of the world, including the United States; major regime changes and severe economic disruptions in Africa, the Middle East, and Eastern Europe; the spread of AIDS; and the computer revolution. Just a few months after her remarks came the first verification of the cloning of a complex animal, Dolly the sheep.

LO 44-1 Anticipating Change

In this era of massive social, political, and economic change, global in scale, is it possible to predict change? Some technological changes seem obvious, but the collapse of communist governments in the former Soviet Union and Eastern Europe in the early 1990s took people by surprise. Yet prior to the Soviet collapse, sociologist Randall Collins (1986, 1995), a conflict theorist, had observed a crucial sequence of events that most observers had missed.

In seminars as far back as 1980, and in a book published in 1986, Collins had argued that Soviet expansionism had resulted in an overextension of resources, including disproportionate spending on military forces. Such an overextension will strain a regime's stability. Moreover, geopolitical theory suggests that nations in the middle of a geographic region, such as the Soviet Union, tend to fragment into smaller units over time. Collins predicted that the coincidence of social crises on several frontiers would precipitate the collapse of the Soviet Union.

And that is just what happened. In 1979, the success of the Iranian revolution had led to an upsurge of Islamic fundamentalism in nearby Afghanistan, as well as in Soviet republics with substantial Muslim populations. At the same time, resistance to communist rule was growing both throughout Eastern Europe and within the Soviet Union itself. Collins had predicted that the rise of a dissident form of communism within the Soviet Union might facilitate the breakdown of the regime. Beginning in the late 1980s, Soviet leader Mikhail Gorbachev chose not to use military power and other types of repression to crush dissidents in Eastern Europe. Instead, he offered plans for democratization and social reform of Soviet society, and seemed willing to reshape the Soviet Union into a loose federation of somewhat autonomous states. But in 1991, six republics on the western periphery declared their independence, and within months the entire Soviet Union had formally disintegrated into Russia and a number of other independent nations.

In her presidential address, Maureen Hallinan (1997) cautioned that we need to move beyond the restrictive models of social change—the linear view of evolutionary theory and the assumptions about equilibrium in the functionalist perspective. Hallinan noted that upheavals and major shifts do occur, and that sociologists must learn to predict their occurrence, as Collins did with the Soviet Union. Imagine, for example, the dramatic nonlinear social change that accompanies the transformation of a small, undeveloped principality into a major financial and communications hub called Dubai.

SOCIAL CHANGE IN DUBAI

The story of Dubai, a Middle Eastern principality the size of Rhode Island, is a tale of two cities. When the Maktoum family took control of Dubai (pronounced Doo-Bye) in 1883, it was a pearl-fishing village on the Persian Gulf. But in 1966, the discovery of oil changed everything. When the state's oil reserves proved too limited to fund significant economic and social change, Dubai reinvented itself as a free-trade oasis. By 2000 it had become a tax-free information-technology hub. In less than a single generation—barely a decade—Dubai had transformed itself into what *Forbes* magazine calls the richest city in the world. This is a place that in the late 1950s had no electricity and no paved roads.

Wide-eyed journalists have described Dubai's air-conditioned indoor ski run, open year-round in a country where the daytime temperature averages 92 degrees. Then there is the 160-story Burj Khalifa, which opened in 2010; at a half-mile high, it is by far the world's tallest building. At one point, so much of the city was under construction that 10 percent of the world's construction cranes were located there.

A constitutional monarchy, Dubai is no democratic utopia—there are no contested elections, and there is little public opposition to the government. Socially, however, Dubai is relatively progressive for an Arab state. Women are encouraged to work, and there is little separation of the sexes, as is common in neighboring states. Alcohol is freely available, speech is relatively free, and the media are largely uncensored.

The citizens of Dubai share its affluence: they receive cheap electricity, free land and water, free health care and education (including graduate study abroad), as well

From 1990 to 2008, the area surrounding the Emirates Golf Club in Dubai changed dramatically.

as an average subsidy of $55,000 per year. They pay no income or property taxes. Ironically, the government handouts that citizens enjoy mean that most have little interest in competitive work, so high-skilled positions tend to go to foreigners. The social consequences of Dubai's wealth have been less than benign, however. Environmentally, the cost of its lavish lifestyle is exorbitant. Dubai ranks at the top of the list in terms of its greenhouse gas emissions, at twice the level of the United States and triple the global average.

Another significant social problem, hidden from the investment bankers and tourists who visit Dubai, is the treatment of immigrant laborers. About 95 percent of Dubaians are foreigners from India, Pakistan, the Philippines, Sri Lanka, North Korea, Bangladesh, China, and Yemen. A million of them—seven times the number of Dubai nationals—come from India alone. These migrant laborers sold everything they owned to come to Dubai and take jobs stacking bricks, watering lawns, and cleaning floors. The pay is good relative to their home countries—$275 a month for a skilled electrician—but very poor compared to what the lowest-paid citizen of Dubai earns. At best, an immigrant must work two years just to break even.

There is little government oversight of working or living conditions in Dubai, both of which are poor. For foreign workers seeking to escape the slums in distant deserts, one-bedroom apartments rent for $1,400 per month. In 2008, fire investigators found 500 laborers living in a house built for a single family. Little wonder that late in 2009, when Dubai's economic expansion ground to a halt, foreign workers were heading home at an estimated rate of 5,000 a day.

The global economic downturn that began in 2008 has been particularly savage to Dubai. Having borrowed heavily and invested not always wisely, both the government and major companies are groaning under a debt load that is heavier than even the United States' or Europe's. By 2010, however, Dubai's economy was back on the move, although a bit moderated. The state's story is hardly finished. At the beginning of the second decade of the 21st century, the well-to-do are still flying lobster in for extravagant parties. Overworked foreign laborers, although many fewer of them remain, are still earning wages well above those available in their home countries. Political analysts note that Dubai is the most stable country in the Arab world, with a measured tolerance for outside cultural influences and an intolerance for corruption (Alderman 2010; Ali 2010; Gill 2011; Gorney 2014; Harman 2009; Krane 2009, 2010; McGirk 2009; Rogan 2009; Tatchell 2009).

LO 44-2 Technology and the Future

Technological advances—the airplane, the automobile, the television, the atomic bomb, and more recently, the computer, digital media, and the cell phone—have brought striking changes to our cultures, our patterns of socialization, our social institutions, and our day-to-day social interactions. Technological innovations are, in fact, emerging and being accepted with remarkable speed.

In the past generation alone, industrial countries have seen a major shift in consumer technologies. No longer do we buy electronic devices to last for even 10 years. Increasingly, we buy them with the expectation that within as little as 3 years, we will need to upgrade to an entirely new technology, whether it be a handheld device or a home computer. Of course, there are those

Meet your new teacher! A humanoid robot interacts with school pupils. "Saya" can call the rolls, display six basic expressions—surprise, fear, disgust, anger, happiness, and sadness—and speak basic phrases. Some people think robots provide a solution to the shortage of skilled laborers, but others question their ability to care for people.

people who either reject the latest gadgets or become frustrated trying to adapt to them. And then there are the **"tech-no's"**—people who resist the worldwide movement toward electronic networking. Those who become tech-no's are finding that it is a life choice that sets them apart from their peers, much like deciding to be "child free" (Darlin 2006; Kornblum 2007).

In the following sections, we examine various aspects of our technological future and consider their impact on social change, including the social strain they will cause. We focus in particular on recent developments in computer technology, electronic censorship, and biotechnology.

COMPUTER TECHNOLOGY

The past decade witnessed an explosion of computer technology in the United States and around the world. Its effects were particularly noteworthy with regard to the Internet, the world's largest computer network. In 2012 the Internet reached 2.3 billion users, compared to just 50 million in 1996.

The Internet evolved from a computer system built in 1962 by the U.S. Defense Department to enable scholars and military researchers to continue their government work even if part of the nation's communications system were destroyed by a nuclear attack. Until a generation ago, it was difficult to gain access to the Internet without holding a position at a university or a government research laboratory. Today, however, virtually anyone can reach the Internet with a phone line, a computer, and a modem. People buy and sell cars, trade stocks, auction off items, research new medical remedies, vote, and track down long-lost friends online—to mention just a few of the thousands of possibilities.

"We have to move - they're putting in a cell phone tower here."

Finding a place where you can't receive a text message is getting harder and harder.

Unfortunately, not everyone can get onto the information highway, especially not the less affluent. Moreover, this pattern of inequality is global. The core nations that Immanuel Wallerstein described in his world systems analysis have a virtual monopoly on information technology; the peripheral nations of Asia, Africa, and Latin America depend on the core nations both for technology and for the information it provides. For example, North America, Europe, and a few industrialized nations in other regions possess almost all the world's *Internet hosts*—computers that are connected directly to the worldwide network.

What is the solution to this global disconnect between the haves and the have-nots? Some people have suggested giving everyone a computer—or at least, everyone who can't afford one.

Another unsettling aspect of technological innovation is the possibility that such advances could eliminate people's jobs. This concern is not new; throughout the 20th century, first machines and then sophisticated robots took the place of human workers. Today, with software becoming steadily more sophisticated and affordable, the pace of technological innovation is increasing. Researchers at Oxford University looked at 702 occupations in the United States in terms of the worker's role in manipulating objects, thinking with originality, negotiating with or persuading others, and gauging others' emotions and reactions. They then used their findings to predict the likelihood that existing or foreseeable technologies could automate those 702 jobs within the next decade or two. Table 14-4 summarizes a portion of their research.

These predictions are by no means airtight; changes in many variables could affect the researchers' probability estimates. For example, even if a technology can be developed to perform a specific skill, access to cheap labor or relatively high technological costs could prevent automation of that skill. Labor organizing could also defer such an outcome. Nevertheless, around 47 percent of total U.S. employment falls into the high-risk category, in danger of being automated within the next decade or two.

TABLE 14-4 JOBS PROJECTED TO BE ELIMINATED BY COMPUTERIZATION

Unlikely to Be Eliminated by Technology (probability under 0.5 percent)

Emergency management directors
Mental health and substance abuse social workers
Audiologists
First-line supervisors of firefighters
Dietitians and nutritionists
Choreographers
Physicians and surgeons
Elementary school teachers

Likely to Be Eliminated by Technology (probability over 98 percent)

Models
Bookkeepers, accountants, and auditing clerks
Credit analysts
Umpires, referees, and other sports officials
Photographic process workers
Tax preparers
Cargo and freight agents
Watch repairers
Hand embroiderers and sewers

Note: Probability that an occupation could be computerized in the next decade or two. Occupations selected from those extremely likely or unlikely to be computerized on a list of 702 U.S. occupations.
Source: Data from Appendix in Frey and Osborne 2013.

PRIVACY AND CENSORSHIP IN A GLOBAL VILLAGE

Today, new technologies like robots, cars that can park themselves, and smartphones with map applications are bringing about sweeping social change. While much of that change is beneficial, there are some negative effects. Recent advances in computer technology have made it increasingly easy for business firms, government agencies, and even criminals to retrieve and store information about everything from our buying habits to our web-surfing patterns. In public places, at work, and on the Internet, surveillance devices now track our every move, be it a keystroke or an ATM withdrawal. At the same time that these innovations have increased others' power to monitor our behavior, they have raised fears that they might be misused for criminal or undemocratic purposes. In short, new technologies threaten

not just our privacy, but our freedom from crime and censorship (O'Harrow Jr. 2005).

In recent years, concern about the criminal misuse of personal information has been underscored by the loss of some huge databases. In the midst of the 2013 holiday shopping season, for example, the credit card records of an estimated 40 million shoppers at Target and other major retailers were compromised.

From a sociological point of view, the complex issues of privacy and censorship can be considered illustrations of culture lag. As usual, the material culture (technology) is changing faster than the nonmaterial culture (norms for controlling the use of technology). Too often, the result is an anything-goes approach to the use of new technologies.

Legislation regarding the surveillance of electronic communications has not always upheld citizens' right to privacy. In 1986, the federal government passed the Electronic Communications Privacy Act, which outlawed the surveillance of telephone calls except with the permission of both the U.S. attorney general and a federal judge. Telegrams, faxes, and e-mail did not receive the same degree of protection, however. Then in 2001, one month after the terrorist attacks of September 11, Congress passed the Patriot Act, which relaxed existing legal checks on surveillance by law enforcement officers. As a result, federal agencies are now freer to gather electronic data, including credit-card receipts and banking records. In 2005, Americans learned that the National Security Agency was covertly monitoring phone calls with the cooperation of major U.S. telecommunications companies. Four years later, a federal court ruled that wiretapping without warrants is legal (Eckenwiler 1995; Lichtblau 2009; Vaidhyanathan 2008).

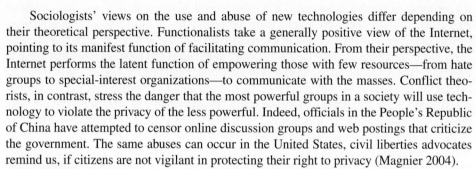

From the perspective of . . .

A Bank Manager   What benefits does online banking offer your customers? What risks?

Sociologists' views on the use and abuse of new technologies differ depending on their theoretical perspective. Functionalists take a generally positive view of the Internet, pointing to its manifest function of facilitating communication. From their perspective, the Internet performs the latent function of empowering those with few resources—from hate groups to special-interest organizations—to communicate with the masses. Conflict theorists, in contrast, stress the danger that the most powerful groups in a society will use technology to violate the privacy of the less powerful. Indeed, officials in the People's Republic of China have attempted to censor online discussion groups and web postings that criticize the government. The same abuses can occur in the United States, civil liberties advocates remind us, if citizens are not vigilant in protecting their right to privacy (Magnier 2004).

Another source of controversy is the widespread use of GPS devices to track the location of cars or even people, not to mention the electronic tracking of handheld communications devices. Technology allows you to tweet your whereabouts to your friends, but should others, including the government, be able to home in on you? Put another way, is your location at any given moment covered by the Fourth Amendment to the U.S. Constitution, which protects your right to privacy? Both public opinion and court rulings on this question remain divided. The issue is yet another example of culture lag, or the time it takes for society to reconcile a new technology with traditional cultural values and behavior (Zipp 2009).

If anything, people seem to be less vigilant today about maintaining their privacy than they were before the information age. Young people who have grown up browsing the Internet seem to accept the existence of the cookies and spyware they may pick up while surfing. They have become accustomed to adult surveillance of their conversation in electronic chat rooms. Many see no risk in providing personal information about themselves to the strangers they meet online. Little wonder that college professors find their students do not appreciate the political significance of their right to privacy (Turkle 2004).

Study Alert

Understand the ways in which sociologists' views on the use and abuse of new technologies differ depending on their theoretical perspective.

BIOTECHNOLOGY AND THE GENE POOL

Another field in which technological advances have spurred global social change is biotechnology. Sex selection of fetuses, genetically engineered organisms, cloning of sheep, cows, and some small animals—these have been among the significant yet controversial scientific advances in the field of biotechnology. George Ritzer's (2013) concept of McDonaldization applies to the entire area of biotechnology. Just as the fast-food concept has permeated society, no phase of life now seems exempt from therapeutic or medical intervention. In fact, sociologists view many aspects of biotechnology as an extension of the recent trend toward the medicalization of society. Through genetic manipulation, the medical profession is expanding its turf still further (Clarke et al. 2003; Human Genome Project 2012).

One notable success of biotechnology—an unintended consequence of modern warfare—has been progress in the treatment of traumatic injuries. In response to the massive numbers of soldiers who survived serious injury in Iraq and Afghanistan, military doctors and therapists have come up with electronically controlled prosthetic devices. Their innovations include artificial limbs that respond to thought-generated nerve impulses, allowing amputees to move legs, arms, and even individual fingers. These applications of computer science to the rehabilitation of the injured will no doubt be extended to civilians (J. Ellison 2008; Gailey 2007).

One startling biotechnological advance is the possibility of altering human behavior or physical traits through genetic engineering. Fish and plant genes have already been mixed to create frost-resistant potato and tomato crops. More recently, human genes have been implanted in pigs to provide humanlike kidneys for organ transplant. William F. Ogburn probably could not have anticipated such scientific developments when he wrote of culture lag over 80 years earlier. However, advances like these or even the successful cloning of sheep illustrate again how quickly material culture can change, and how nonmaterial culture moves more slowly in absorbing such changes.

Although today's biotechnology holds itself out as totally beneficial to human beings, it is in constant need of monitoring. Biotechnological advances have raised many difficult ethical and political questions, among them the desirability of tinkering with the gene pool, which could alter our environment in unexpected and unwanted ways. In particular, controversy has been growing concerning genetically modified (GM) food, an issue that arose in Europe but has since spread to other parts of the world, including the United States. The idea behind the technology is to increase food production and make agriculture more economical. But critics use the term *Frankenfood* (as in "Frankenstein") to refer to everything from breakfast cereals made from genetically engineered grains to fresh GM tomatoes. Members of the antibiotech movement object to tampering with nature, and are concerned about the possible health effects of GM food. Supporters of genetically modified food include not just biotech companies, but those who see the technology as a way to help feed the burgeoning populations of Africa and Asia (Petersen 2009; World Health Organization 2009).

In contrast, less expensive and controversial technologies can further agriculture where it is needed more, in the developing world. Consider cell phones. Unlike most new technologies, the majority of the world's cell phones are used in *less* developed countries. Relatively cheap and not as dependent as computers on expensive communications infrastructure, cell phones are common in the world's poorest areas. In Uganda, farmers use them to check weather forecasts and commodity prices. In South Africa, laborers use them to look for work. Researchers at the London Business School have found that in developing countries, a 10 percent increase in cell phone use is correlated with a 0.6 percent rise in GDP (Bures 2011).

While farmers in the developing world use cell phones to improve their incomes, others set out for foreign countries. The Social Policy section that follows considers *transnationals,* immigrants who travel back and forth between the developing and developed worlds, forging human rather than technological links.

LO 44-3 SOCIAL POLICY and Globalization

We have seen that researchers rely on a number of tools, from simple observational research to the latest in computer technologies. Because in the real world sociological research can have far-reaching consequences for public policy and public welfare, we'll consider its impact on transnationals.

TRANSNATIONALS

Around the world, new communications technologies—cell phones, the World Wide Web—have definitely hastened the process of globalization. Yet without human capital, these innovations would not have spurred the huge increase in global trade and development that occurred over the last several decades. Who are the people behind the trend toward globalization? Often, they are people who see a business opportunity abroad and strike out on their own to take advantage of it. In the process, many of them become migrants.

To facilitate trade and investment with other countries, migrants often exploit their social connections and their familiarity with their home language and culture. In Southeast Asia, for example, Chinese migrants dominate the trade with China; in Africa, Indian migrants dominate. Some migrants invest directly in their home countries to get the manufactured goods they sell abroad. Opportunities abound, and those with capital and good business skills can become quite wealthy (Guest 2011).

The millions of migrant laborers who leave home in search of a better life also play a role in the global economy, filling jobs where there are shortages in the labor market. Although they do not become wealthy working as landscapers or short-order cooks, they consider themselves better off than they were in the old country. Unfortunately, citizens of the host countries often react negatively to the migrants' arrival, worrying that they will take jobs away from the native-born.

As of 2013, 232 million people, or about 3 percent of the world's population, were international migrants. That is more than double the number in 1970. The rest of the world's population were "stayers"—that is, people who continued to live in the countries where they were born (United Nations 2013).

Figure 14-1 shows the worldwide movement of workers with and without the legal right to immigrate. Several areas, such as the European Union, have instituted international agreements that provide for the free movement of laborers. But in most other parts of the world, immigration restrictions give foreign workers only temporary status. Despite such legal restrictions, the labor market has become an increasingly global one. Just as globalization has integrated government policies, cultures, social movements, and financial markets, it has unified what were once discrete national labor markets. So today, for example, immigrants from at least eight different countries work in one small Middle Eastern state, Dubai.

Globalization has changed the immigrant experience as well as the labor market. In generations past, immigrants read foreign language newspapers to keep in touch with events in their home countries. Today, the Internet gives them immediate access to their countries and kinfolk. In this global framework, immigrants are less likely than they were

FIGURE 14-1 LABOR MIGRATION

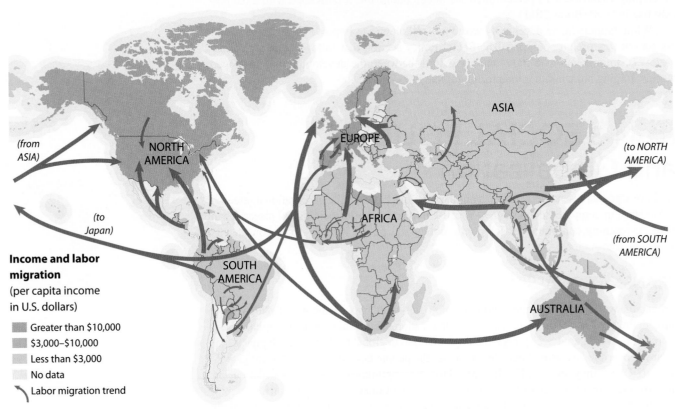

Income and labor migration

(per capita income in U.S. dollars)

- Greater than $10,000
- $3,000–$10,000
- Less than $3,000
- No data
- Labor migration trend

Source: National Geographic 2005:16.

in the past to think of themselves as residents of just one country. **Transnationals** are immigrants who sustain multiple social relationships that link their societies of origin with their societies of settlement (P. Levitt and Jaworsky 2007).

Applying Sociology to the Transnational Issue As with other issues, sociologists differ in their opinion of transnationals, depending on their theoretical perspective. Functionalists see the free flow of immigrants, even when it is legally restricted, as one way for economies to maximize their use of human labor. Given the law of supply and demand, they note, countries with too few workers will inevitably attract laborers, while those with too many will become unattractive to residents.

Conflict theorists charge that globalization and international migration have increased the economic gulf between developed and developing nations. Today, residents of North America, western Europe, Australia, and Japan consume 32 times more resources than the billions of people who live in developing countries. Through tourism and the global reach of the mass media, people in the poorer countries have become aware of the affluent lifestyle common in developed nations—and of course, many of them now aspire to it (L. Smith 2011).

Interactionists are interested in the day-to-day relationships transnationals have with the people around them, from those of their country of origin to those of the host country and fellow workers from other countries. These scholars are studying transnationals' involvement in local ethnic organizations, to see whether their membership facilitates or retards their integration into the host society. They have discovered that members of global social networks provide one another with mutual support and trust.

Transnationals also participate in social movements. Many transnationals immigrate either to a country with greater political freedom (for example, an Iranian immigrant to

Great Britain) or from a more tolerant society (for example, a Filipino worker in Dubai). In these situations, transnational migrants often monitor social movements that interest them via computer. They may also facilitate the growth of a social movement from a distance, by providing information, money, or both (Aunio and Staggenborg 2011).

Another question of interest to interactionists is how transnationals see themselves—how they see their own identities as well as those of their children. In effect, transnationals negotiate their identities, depending on which social network they belong to at the moment. Some sociologists note that while being a transnational can be exhilarating, it can also isolate a person, even in a city of millions. Others worry that transnationals may become so cosmopolitan that they will lose touch with their national identities (Calhoun 2003; Evergeti and Zontini 2006; Plüss 2005; Portes et al. 2008; Rajan and Sharma 2006; Tilly 2007).

Initiating Policy Affecting Transnationals Although connecting to two societies can be an enriching experience, transnationals face continuing adjustment problems in their new home countries. As we saw with Dubai, immigrant laborers often face difficult living and working conditions. Some sending countries, such as Indonesia and the Philippines, have created national agencies to ensure the protection of their workers abroad. Their objective is ambitious, given that funding for the agencies is limited, and diplomatic and legal challenges complicate their task (United Nations Development Programme 2009:102–104).

Another unresolved transnational issue is voter eligibility. Not all nations allow dual citizenship; even those countries that do may not allow absent nationals to vote. The United States and Great Britain are rather liberal in this regard, permitting dual citizenship and allowing émigrés to continue to vote. Mexico, in contrast, has been reluctant to allow citizens who have emigrated to vote. Mexican politicians worry that the large number of Mexicans who live abroad (especially those in the United States) might vote differently from local voters, causing different outcomes (P. Levitt and Jaworsky 2007; Sellers 2004).

Finally, the controversial issue of illegal immigration has yet to be settled, perhaps because of culture lag. That is, both public attitudes and government policies (nonmaterial culture) have not kept pace with, much less adjusted to, the increasing ease of migration around the globe (material culture). Though globalization has created a global labor market—one that many countries depend on, legal or illegal—the general public's attitude toward illegal immigrants remains hostile, especially in the United States.

E Evaluate

Read each question carefully and then select or provide the best answer.

1. In developing countries, which of the following new technological tools has been the most widely adopted and influential?
   a. robotic workers
   b. laptop computers
   c. cell phones
   d. teleconferencing

2. People who resist the global movement toward involvement in electronic networking are known by which nickname?
   a. Luddites
   b. tech-no's
   c. nimbys
   d. NOPEs

3. Which sociological perspective sees transnationals as a way for economies to maximize their use of human labor?
   a. functionalist
   b. conflict
   c. interactionist
   d. feminist

4. In 2011, the U.S. Congress passed the _____ Act, which relaxed existing legal checks on surveillance by law enforcement officers. Federal agencies are now free to gather data electronically, including credit card receipts and banking records.

5. The _____ perspective would stress the danger that the most powerful groups in a society will use technology to violate the privacy of the less powerful.

Answers
1 (c); 2 (b); 3 (a); 4 Patriot; 5 conflict

Consider these questions to get a deeper understanding of the material.

1. Which aspect of biotechnology do you find most promising? Most unsettling? Explain.

2. Do you think that people should be more or less free to cross international borders to find better working and living conditions? Why?

RECAP

LO 44-1 Discuss the nature and extent of global social change.

- We are living in a time of sweeping social, political, and economic change—change that occurs not just on a local or national basis, but on a global scale.
- Old models of evolutionary social change and equilibrium must be abandoned in the face of dramatic social change that is following a nonlinear developmental pattern.
- Rapid social change in Dubai, for example, has brought unusual levels of domestic prosperity and many technological advances, but at the price of extravagant greenhouse gas emissions and inequitable social conditions for non-native workers.

LO 44-2 Summarize advances and concerns stemming from the global spread of technology.

- Technological changes have brought significant advances to society, especially to societies in developed countries. However, with every advance come new concerns and issues.

- Computer technology threatens to transfer a significant portion of the business economy from human hands and minds to computers, worsening the employment picture for those who have been displaced.
- Technology has made it increasingly easy for individuals, companies, and government agencies to retrieve our personal information, greatly reducing our privacy while endangering our security.
- Recent advances in biotechnology have raised difficult ethical questions about genetic engineering of food and humans.

LO 44-3 Analyze issues associated with the emergence of the transnational as a new type of immigrant.

- Globalization has increased the international migration of laborers, producing a new kind of immigrant, called the transnational.
- Transnationals sustain multiple social relationships that link their societies of origin with their societies of settlement.

KEY TERMS

Tech-no's People who resist the worldwide movement toward electronic networking.

Transnational An immigrant who sustains multiple social relationships that link his or her society of origin with the society of settlement.

The Case of . . . The Good Fight

Caitlin Abbott proudly displays her "I am one of the 99 Percent" button. "I got it in New York at an Occupy Wall Street rally," Abbott says. "I just happened to be passing by, but I liked the idea of it immediately. To me, it says, 'Hey, don't forget all the regular people. We *are* the majority.'"

Abbott donated five dollars to Occupy but her real passion is directed at early childhood education. "I volunteer in a first-grade classroom two mornings a week," Abbott says. "It's made me realize what a big advantage some kids have over others right from the start. Not every kid has a comfy home or books, or a parent who has time to read to them." Abbott talked to the classroom teacher about her observations. "She told me that for 10 years the school district had a terrific early education program, but then it got cut. No money," Abbott says. "I kept thinking about that. Why cut something so important to so many kids?" Abbott started digging around and learned that funding for early education programs was being cut in many districts across the nation. "I got most of my information online," she says. "That's also where I started connecting with other people who share my concerns." Abbott began going to rallies to protest the cuts. "Now, I help write leaflets to explain our position, and I go door-to-door to collect money and tell people what I saw in the classroom," she says. "You shouldn't have to fight for something good for little kids, but you do, so I will."

1. How is the movement to increase spending for early education typical of a new social movement?

2. What role did technology play in forging Abbott's commitment to fight for early education?

3. In terms of resource mobilization, who would you expect to provide leadership for early education spending and how might this group use the media effectively?

4. How might cutting spending for early education create feelings of relative deprivation?

Study Strategies

Powering Up Your Life

By using the P.O.W.E.R. Study Strategies at the end of each chapter of this book, you have seen the benefits of the P.O.W.E.R. system as applied to your major tasks as a sociology student. The P.O.W.E.R. system can also be used throughout your life to help you deal effectively with major life tasks: getting a job, finding a place to live, doing well at work, participating in family life, and serving your community. Here is a compilation of the general principles that you have been exposed to in the Study Strategies of this book.

 **Prepare**

- Take the time to define your objectives before you begin working on a task. For any complex task, this will *gain* you time, not *cost* you time.

 **Organize**

- Gather the tools you'll need to meet your goals, including physical and mental tools. Think of the steps you will have to go through to complete the task.
- Consider whether it will be best to work alone or as part of a group.

 **Work**

- When reading, think first about what you know already. Then read carefully, taking time to absorb important points and make useful notes.
- Improve your memory by using memory tricks (mnemonics)—the sillier and more striking the better. Check out lists on the Internet to get you started. Make mnemonics a routine part of your life.
- Use what you know about your learning style and personality type to work more effectively. If you're an *introverted reader,* don't try to be an *outgoing toucher.*
- When taking notes, remember that less is more. Stick to the essentials. Always ask: *Why is this important?* and *How does this relate to me and my life?* This will help you to retain important concepts.
- Manage your time wisely. Use a calendar and plan thoroughly—but allow flexibility in your plan and leave time for rest and relaxation.
- Think critically. When you hear or read a claim, always ask: *How can I know if this is true?*
- When writing, remember the basic outline: topic, thesis, opinion, support (evidence and logic), and conclusion.
- Find out as much as you can about a test before you take it. When you receive the test, look it over, plan your use of time, and answer questions strategically.
- Take control of your stress level. Practice relaxation techniques, don't live in the past, and get support when you need it. You are not alone.
- When speaking publicly, control your voice and breathing. Stand tall and relax. Remember that your audience is on your side. Begin by stating your topic and/or thesis clearly.

Evaluate

- As you work on any big task, pause from time to time and evaluate how the work is going. Are you on target to accomplish both your short- and long-term goals?

Rethink

- After you have completed your task and implemented your plan, take the time to look back and rethink what worked and what didn't as you worked on it, and what is going well and what isn't now that you are living with what you did. Then change—slightly or completely—what isn't working.

Have You Mastered the Study Skills?

Your success as a student depends on integrating the wide variety of skills we have looked at in the P.O.W.E.R. Study Strategies. To evaluate your skills overall, and identify any remaining areas that need improvement, answer the following items, then use this scale to find your score:

That's Me = 1

Not Me = 0

	That's Me	Not Me
1. I read through my class notes and review the textbook in preparation to complete a homework assignment.		
2. When reading or listening, I often pause to consider whether an author's or speaker's statements are fact or opinion.		
3. When I have too many commitments, I renegotiate what I can and make realistic adjustments to my schedule.		
4. I jot down key concepts in class and draw diagrams to show how the important ideas are related.		
5. I break big projects into smaller steps and use a calendar to record when each step must be accomplished to meet my deadline.		
6. I use flash cards, acronyms, and other memory tricks to help me recall key ideas, facts, and lists.		
7. When faced with a decision, I list all my alternatives and write down the pros and cons of each.		
8. I outline my argument and gather the relevant facts and evidence before writing a paper.		
9. I brainstorm to gather as many possible solutions as I can when faced with a problem to solve.		
10. I prepare an outline on note cards when I have to make an oral presentation.		

SCORE:

8 to 10 Congratulations! You have developed an array of critical thinking, planning, and problem-solving skills that will help you succeed in life as well as in the classroom.

6–7 You have a core of skills to help you achieve your goals. Take note of any areas that need improvement and get going.

5 or less Review the P.O.W.E.R. Study Strategies at the end of each chapter in this book to find the tools that will help you achieve your goals.

GLOSSARY

Numbers following the definitions indicate modules where the terms were defined. Consult the index for further page references.

A

Absolute poverty A minimum level of subsistence that no family should be expected to live below. (Module 27)

Achieved status A social position that a person attains largely through his or her own efforts. (Modules 15, 25)

Adoption In a legal sense, the transfer of the legal rights, responsibilities, and privileges of parenthood to a new legal parent or parents. (Module 34)

Affirmative action Positive efforts to recruit minority group members or women for jobs, promotions, and educational opportunities. (Module 28)

Agrarian society The most technologically advanced form of preindustrial society. Members engage primarily in the production of food, but increase their crop yields through technological innovations such as the plow. (Module 18)

Alienation A condition of estrangement or dissociation from the surrounding society. (Module 17)

Amalgamation The process through which a majority group and a minority group combine to form a new group. (Module 29)

Anomie Durkheim's term for the loss of direction felt in a society when social control of individual behavior has become ineffective. (Modules 1, 22)

Anomie theory of deviance Robert Merton's theory of deviance as an adaptation of socially prescribed goals or of the means governing their attainment, or both. (Module 22)

Anticipatory socialization Processes of socialization in which a person rehearses for future positions, occupations, and social relationships. (Module 14)

Anti-Semitism Anti-Jewish prejudice. (Module 30)

Apartheid A former policy of the South African government, designed to maintain the separation of Blacks and other non-Whites from the dominant Whites. (Module 29)

Applied sociology The use of the discipline of sociology with the specific intent of yielding practical applications for human behavior and organizations. (Module 3)

Argot Specialized language used by members of a group or subculture. (Module 10)

Ascribed status A social position assigned to a person by society without regard for the person's unique talents or characteristics. (Modules 15, 25)

Assimilation The process through which a person forsakes his or her cultural tradition to become part of a different culture. (Module 29)

Authority Institutionalized power that is recognized by the people over whom it is exercised. (Module 50)

B

Basic sociology Sociological inquiry conducted with the objective of gaining a more profound knowledge of the fundamental aspects of social phenomena. Also known as *pure sociology*. (Module 3)

Big data The rapid collection and analysis of enormous amounts of information by supercomputers. (Module 21)

Bilateral descent A kinship system in which both sides of a person's family are regarded as equally important. (Module 33)

Bilingualism The use of two languages in a particular setting, such as the workplace or schoolroom, treating each language as equally legitimate. (Module 10)

Black power A political philosophy, promoted by many younger Blacks in the 1960s, that supported the creation of Black-controlled political and economic institutions. (Module 30)

Bourgeoisie Karl Marx's term for the capitalist class, comprising the owners of the means of production. (Module 25)

Brain drain The immigration to the United States and other industrialized nations of skilled workers, professionals, and technicians who are desperately needed in their home countries. (Module 36)

Brass ceiling An invisible barrier that blocks the promotion of a woman in the military because of her official (not necessarily actual) exclusion from combat. (Module 31)

Bureaucracy A component of formal organization that uses rules and hierarchical ranking to achieve efficiency. (Module 17)

Bureaucratization The process by which a group, organization, or social movement becomes increasingly bureaucratic. (Module 17)

C

Capitalism An economic system in which the means of production are held largely in private hands and the main incentive for economic activity is the accumulation of profits. (Modules 25, 49)

Caste A hereditary rank, usually religiously dictated, that tends to be fixed and immobile. (Module 25)

Causal logic The relationship between a condition or variable and a particular consequence, with one leading to the other. (Module 4)

Charismatic authority Max Weber's term for power made legitimate by a leader's exceptional personal or emotional appeal to his or her followers. (Module 50)

Class A group of people who have a similar level of wealth and income. (Module 25)

Class consciousness In Karl Marx's view, a subjective awareness held by members of a class regarding their common vested interests and the need for collective political action to bring about social change. (Module 25)

Class system A social ranking based primarily on economic position in which achieved characteristics can influence social mobility. (Module 25)

Classical theory An approach to the study of formal organizations that views workers as being motivated almost entirely by economic rewards. (Module 17)

Climate change An observable alteration of the global atmosphere that affects natural weather patterns over several decades or longer. (Module 39)

Clinical sociology The use of the discipline of sociology with the specific intent of altering social relationships or restructuring social institutions. (Module 3)

Closed system A social system in which there is little or no possibility of individual social mobility. (Module 27)

Coalition A temporary or permanent alliance geared toward a common goal. (Module 16)

Code of ethics The standards of acceptable behavior developed by and for members of a profession. (Module 6)

Cognitive theory of development Jean Piaget's theory that children's thought progresses through four stages of development. (Module 12)

Cohabitation The practice of living together as a male–female couple without marrying. (Module 35)

Colonialism The maintenance of political, social, economic, and cultural domination over a people by a foreign power for an extended period. (Module 45)

Color-blind racism The use of the principle of race neutrality to defend a racially unequal status quo. (Module 28)

Communism As an ideal type, an economic system under which all property is communally owned and no social distinctions are made on the basis of people's ability to produce. (Module 49)

Computer-mediated communication (CMC) Communicative inter-action through two or more networked devices, such as a computer or cell phone. The term applies to a variety of text-based or video inter-actions, including e-mails, chat rooms, and text messages, some of which may be supported by social media. (Module 42)

Conflict perspective A sociological approach that assumes that social behavior is best understood in terms of tension between groups over power or the allocation of resources, including housing, money, access to services, and political representation. (Module 2)

Conformity Going along with peers—individuals of our own status who have no special right to direct our behavior. (Module 22)

Conspicuous consumption Purchasing goods not to survive but to flaunt one's superior wealth and social standing. (Module 25)

Contact hypothesis An interactionist perspective which states that in cooperative circumstances, interracial contact between people of equal status will reduce prejudice. (Module 29)

Content analysis The systematic coding and objective recording of data, guided by some rationale. (Module 5)

Control group The subjects in an experiment who are not introduced to the independent variable by the researcher. (Module 5)

Control theory A view of conformity and deviance that suggests that our connection to members of society leads us to systematically con-form to society's norms. (Module 23)

Control variable A factor that is held constant to test the relative impact of an independent variable. (Module 4)

Corporate welfare Tax breaks, bailouts, direct payments, and grants that the government gives to corporations. (Module 46)

Correlation A relationship between two variables in which a change in one coincides with a change in the other. (Module 4)

Correspondence principle A term used by Bowles and Gintis to refer to the tendency of schools to promote the values expected of individuals in each social class and to perpetuate social class divisions from one generation to the next. (Module 40)

Counterculture A subculture that deliberately opposes certain aspects of the larger culture. (Module 10)

Creationism A literal interpretation of the Bible regarding the cre-ation of humanity and the universe, used to argue that evolution should not be presented as established scientific fact. (Module 48)

Credentialism An increase in the lowest level of education needed to enter a field. (Module 40)

Crime A violation of criminal law for which some governmental authority applies formal penalties. (Module 24)

Cultural capital Noneconomic goods, such as family background and education, which are reflected in a knowledge of language and the arts. (Module 1)

Cultural convergence The flow of content across multiple media, and the accompanying migration of media audiences. (Module 19)

Cultural relativism The viewing of people's behavior from the per-spective of their own culture. (Module 7)

Cultural transmission A school of criminology that argues that criminal behavior is learned through social interactions. (Module 22)

Cultural universal A common practice or belief found in every culture. (Module 7)

Culture The totality of learned, socially transmitted customs, knowledge, material objects, and behavior. (Module 7)

Culture industry The worldwide media industry that standardizes the goods and services demanded by consumers. (Module 7)

Culture lag A period of maladjustment when the nonmaterial culture is still struggling to adapt to new material conditions. (Modules 9, 21, 43)

Culture shock The feeling of surprise and disorientation that people experience when they encounter cultural practices that are different from their own. (Module 10)

Culture war The polarization of society over controversial cultural elements. (Module 8)

Curanderismo Latino folk medicine, a form of holistic health care and healing. (Module 37)

D

Degradation ceremony An aspect of the socialization process within some total institutions, in which people are subjected to humiliating rituals. (Module 14)

Deindustrialization The systematic, widespread withdrawal of investment in basic aspects of productivity, such as factories and plants. (Module 52)

Democracy In a literal sense, government by the people. (Module 50)

Denomination A large, organized religion that is not officially linked to the state or government. (Module 48)

Dependency theory An approach that contends that industrialized nations continue to exploit developing countries for their own gain. (Module 45)

Dependent variable The variable in a causal relationship that is sub-ject to the influence of another variable. (Module 4)

Deviance Behavior that violates the standards of conduct or expecta-tions of a group or society. (Module 22)

Dictatorship A government in which one person has nearly total power to make and enforce laws. (Module 50)

Differential association A theory of deviance proposed by Edwin Sutherland that holds that violation of rules results from exposure to attitudes favorable to criminal acts. (Module 22)

Differential justice Differences in the way social control is exercised over different groups. (Module 22)

Diffusion The process by which a cultural item spreads from group to group or society to society. (Module 9)

Digital divide The relative lack of access to the latest technologies among low-income groups, racial and ethnic minorities, rural resi-dents, and the citizens of developing countries. (Module 19)

Discovery The process of making known or sharing the existence of an aspect of reality. (Module 9)

Discrimination The denial of opportunities and equal rights to individuals and groups because of prejudice or other arbitrary reasons. (Module 28)

Dominant ideology A set of cultural beliefs and practices that helps to maintain powerful social, economic, and political interests. (Modules 8, 19, 25)

Double consciousness The division of an individual's identity into two or more social realities. (Module 1)

Downsizing Reductions taken in a company's workforce as part of deindustrialization. (Module 52)

Dramaturgical approach A view of social interaction, popularized by Erving Goffman, in which people are seen as theatrical performers. (Modules 2, 12)

Dysfunction An element or process of a society that may disrupt the social system or reduce its stability. (Module 2)

E

Ecclesia A religious organization that claims to include most or all members of a society and is recognized as the national or official religion. (Module 48)

Ecological modernization The alignment of environmentally favorable practices with economic self-interest through constant adaptation and restructuring. (Module 39)

Economic system The social institution through which goods and services are produced, distributed, and consumed. (Module 49)

Education A formal process of learning in which some people consciously teach, while others adopt the social role of learner. (Module 40)

Egalitarian family An authority pattern in which spouses are regarded as equals. (Module 33)

Elite model A view of society as being ruled by a small group of individuals who share a common set of political and economic interests. (Module 51)

Endogamy The restriction of mate selection to people within the same group. (Module 34)

Environmental justice A legal strategy based on claims that racial minorities are subjected disproportionately to environmental hazards. (Module 39)

Environmental refugee A person who has been displaced by rising seas, destructive storms, expanding deserts, water shortages, or high levels of toxic pollutants. (Module 39)

Equilibrium model Talcott Parsons's functionalist view that society tends toward a state of stability or balance. (Module 43)

Established sect J. Milton Yinger's term for a religious group that is the outgrowth of a sect, yet remains isolated from society. (Module 48)

Estate system A system of stratification under which peasants were required to work land leased to them by nobles in exchange for military protection and other services. Also known as *feudalism*. (Module 25)

Esteem The reputation that a specific person has earned within an occupation. (Module 26)

Ethnic group A group that is set apart from others primarily because of its national origin or distinctive cultural patterns. (Module 28)

Ethnocentrism The tendency to assume that one's own culture and way of life represent the norm or are superior to all others. (Modules 7, 28)

Ethnography The study of an entire social setting through extended systematic fieldwork. (Module 5)

Evolutionary theory A theory of social change that holds that society is moving in a definite direction. (Module 43)

Exogamy The requirement that people select a mate outside certain groups. (Module 34)

Experiment An artificially created situation that allows a researcher to manipulate variables. (Module 5)

Experimental group The subjects in an experiment who are exposed to an independent variable introduced by a researcher. (Module 5)

Exploitation theory A Marxist theory that views racial subordination in the United States as a manifestation of the class system inherent in capitalism. (Module 29)

Expressiveness Concern for the maintenance of harmony and the internal emotional affairs of the family. (Module 31)

Extended family A family in which relatives—such as grandparents, aunts, or uncles—live in the same home as parents and their children. (Module 33)

F

Face-work A term used by Erving Goffman to refer to the efforts people make to maintain the proper image and avoid public embarrassment. (Module 12)

False consciousness A term used by Karl Marx to describe an attitude held by members of a class that does not accurately reflect their objective position. (Modules 25, 42)

Familism (*Familismo*) Pride in the extended family, expressed through the maintenance of close ties and strong obligations to kinfolk outside the immediate family. (Module 34)

Family A set of people related by blood, marriage or some other agreed-on relationship, or adoption, who share the primary responsibility for reproduction and caring for members of society. (Module 33)

Feminism An ideology that favors equal rights for women. (Module 32)

Feminist perspective A sociological approach that views inequity in gender as central to all behavior and organization. (Module 2)

Feminization of poverty A trend in which women constitute an increasing proportion of the poor people of both the United States and the world. (Module 27)

Folkway A norm governing everyday behavior whose violation raises comparatively little concern. (Module 8)

Force The actual or threatened use of coercion to impose one's will on others. (Module 50)

Formal norm A norm that has been written down and that specifies strict punishments for violators. (Module 8)

Formal organization A group designed for a special purpose and structured for maximum efficiency. (Module 17)

Formal social control Social control that is carried out by authorized agents, such as police officers, judges, school administrators, and employers. (Module 22)

Functionalist perspective A sociological approach that emphasizes the way in which the parts of a society are structured to maintain its stability. (Module 2)

Fundamentalism An emphasis on doctrinal conformity and the literal interpretation of sacred texts. (Module 48)

G

Gatekeeping The process by which a relatively small number of people in the media industry control what material eventually reaches the audience. (Module 19)

Gemeinschaft A term used by Ferdinand Tönnies to describe a close-knit community, often found in rural areas, in which strong personal bonds unite members. (Module 18)

Gender role Expectations regarding the proper behavior, attitudes, and activities of males and females. (Modules 13, 31)

Generalized other A term used by George Herbert Mead to refer to the attitudes, viewpoints, and expectations of society as a whole that a child takes into account in his or her behavior. (Module 12)

Genocide The deliberate, systematic killing of an entire people or nation. (Module 29)

Gesellschaft A term used by Ferdinand Tönnies to describe a community, often urban, that is large and impersonal, with little commitment to the group or consensus on values. (Module 18)

Glass ceiling An invisible barrier that blocks the promotion of a qualified individual in a work environment because of the individual's gender, race, or ethnicity. (Modules 28, 32)

Glass escalator The advantage men experience in occupations dominated by women. (Module 32)

Global warming A significant rise in the earth's surface temperatures that occurs when industrial gases like carbon dioxide turn the planet's atmosphere into a virtual greenhouse. (Module 39)

Globalization The worldwide integration of government policies, cultures, social movements, and financial markets through trade and the exchange of ideas. (Modules 3, 45)

Goal displacement Overzealous conformity to official regulations of a bureaucracy. (Module 17)

Group Any number of people with similar norms, values, and expectations who interact with one another on a regular basis. (Module 16)

H

Hate crime A criminal offense committed because of the offender's bias against a race, religion, ethnic group, national origin, or sexual orientation. Also referred to as *bias crime*. (Module 24)

Hawthorne effect The unintended influence that observers of experiments can have on their subjects. (Module 5)

Health As defined by the World Health Organization, a state of complete physical, mental, and social well-being, and not merely the absence of disease and infirmity. (Module 36)

Hidden curriculum Standards of behavior that are deemed proper by society and are taught subtly in schools. (Module 40)

Holistic medicine Therapies in which the health care practitioner considers the person's physical, mental, emotional, and spiritual characteristics. (Module 38)

Homogamy The conscious or unconscious tendency to select a mate with personal characteristics similar to one's own. (Module 34)

Homophobia Fear of and prejudice against homosexuality. (Module 31)

Horizontal mobility The movement of an individual from one social position to another of the same rank. (Module 27)

Horticultural society A preindustrial society in which people plant seeds and crops rather than merely subsist on available foods. (Module 18)

Human ecology An area of study that is concerned with the interrelationships between people and their environment. (Module 39)

Human relations approach An approach to the study of formal organizations that emphasizes the role of people, communication, and participation in a bureaucracy and tends to focus on the informal structure of the organization. (Module 17)

Hunting-and-gathering society A preindustrial society in which people rely on whatever foods and fibers are readily available in order to survive. (Module 18)

Hyperconsumerism The practice of buying more than we need or want, and often more than we can afford; a preoccupation of postmodern consumers. (Modules 18, 19)

Hyper-local media Reporting that is highly local and typically Internet-based. (Module 19)

Hypothesis A speculative statement about the relationship between two or more variables. (Module 4)

I

Ideal type A construct or model for evaluating specific cases. (Modules 1, 17)

Impression management A term used by Erving Goffman to refer to the altering of the presentation of the self in order to create distinctive appearances and satisfy particular audiences. (Module 12)

Incest taboo The prohibition of sexual relationships between certain culturally specified relatives. (Module 34)

Income Salaries and wages. (Module 25)

Independent variable The variable in a causal relationship that causes or influences a change in another variable. (Module 4)

Index crimes The eight types of crime tabulated each year by the FBI in the *Uniform Crime Reports:* murder, rape, robbery, assault, burglary, theft, motor vehicle theft, and arson. (Module 24)

Industrial society A society that depends on mechanization to produce its goods and services. (Modules 18, 49)

Infant mortality rate The number of deaths of infants under 1 year old per 1,000 live births in a given year. (Module 36)

Influence The exercise of power through a process of persuasion. (Module 50)

Informal economy Transfers of money, goods, or services that are not reported to the government. (Module 49)

Informal norm A norm that is generally understood but not precisely recorded. (Module 8)

Informal social control Social control that is carried out casually by ordinary people through such means as laughter, smiles, and ridicule. (Module 22)

In-group Any group or category to which people feel they belong. (Module 16)

Innovation The process of introducing a new idea or object to a culture through discovery or invention. (Module 9)

Institutional discrimination The denial of opportunities and equal rights to individuals and groups that results from the normal operations of a society. (Modules 28, 32)

Instrumentality An emphasis on tasks, a focus on more distant goals, and a concern for the external relationship between one's family and other social institutions. (Module 31)

Intelligent design (ID) The idea that life is so complex that it could only have been created by intelligent design. (Module 48)

Interactionist perspective A sociological approach that generalizes about everyday forms of social interaction in order to explain society as a whole. (Module 2)

Intergenerational mobility Changes in the social position of children relative to their parents. (Module 27)

Interview A face-to-face, phone, or online questioning of a respondent to obtain desired information. (Module 5)

Intragenerational mobility Changes in social position within a person's adult life. (Module 27)

Invention The combination of existing cultural items into a form that did not exist before. (Module 9)

Iron law of oligarchy A principle of organizational life developed by Robert Michels, under which even a democratic organization will eventually develop into a bureaucracy ruled by a few individuals. (Module 17)

K

Kinship The state of being related to others. (Module 33)

L

Labeling theory An approach to deviance that attempts to explain why certain people are viewed as deviants while others engaged in the same behavior are not. (Modules 22, 36)

Labor union Organized workers who share either the same skill or the same employer. (Module 18)

Laissez-faire A form of capitalism under which people compete freely, with minimal government intervention in the economy. (Module 49)

Language An abstract system of word meanings and symbols for all aspects of culture; includes gestures and other nonverbal communication. (Module 8)

Latent function An unconscious or unintended function that may reflect hidden purposes. (Module 2)

Law Governmental social control. (Modules 8, 22)

Liberation theology Use of a church, primarily Roman Catholic, in a political effort to eliminate poverty, discrimination, and other forms of injustice from a secular society. (Module 47)

Life chances Max Weber's term for the opportunities people have to provide themselves with material goods, positive living conditions, and favorable life experiences. (Module 27)

Life course approach A research orientation in which sociologists and other social scientists look closely at the social factors that influence people throughout their lives, from birth to death. (Module 14)

Living wage A wage that meets workers' basic needs, allowing them to maintain a safe, decent standard of living within their community. (Module 27)

Looking-glass self A concept used by Charles Horton Cooley that emphasizes the self as the product of our social interactions. (Module 12)

Luddites Rebellious craft workers in 19th-century England who destroyed new factory machinery as part of their resistance to the Industrial Revolution. (Module 43)

M

Machismo A sense of virility, personal worth, and pride in one's maleness. (Module 34)

Macrosociology Sociological investigation that concentrates on large-scale phenomena or entire civilizations. (Module 1)

Manifest function An open, stated, and conscious function. (Module 2)

Mass media Print and electronic means of communication that carry messages to widespread audiences. (Module 19)

Master status A status that dominates others and thereby determines a person's general position in society. (Module 15)

Material culture The physical or technological aspects of our daily lives. (Module 9)

Matriarchy A society in which women dominate in family decision making. (Module 33)

Matrilineal descent A kinship system in which only the mother's relatives are significant. (Module 33)

Matrix of domination The cumulative impact of oppression because of race and ethnicity, gender, and social class, as well as religion, sexual orientation, disability, age, and citizenship status. (Module 31)

McDonaldization The process by which the principles of bureaucratization have increasingly shaped organizations worldwide. (Module 38)

Mechanical solidarity A collective consciousness that emphasizes group solidarity, characteristic of societies with minimal division of labor. (Module 18)

Medical model An approach in which medical experts define illness or disease, determine and control the course of treatment, and even affect patients' views of themselves. (Module 36)

Mental illness A disorder of the brain that disrupts a person's thinking, feeling, and ability to interact with others. (Module 38)

Microfinancing Lending small sums of money to the poor so they can work their way out of poverty. (Module 52)

Microsociology Sociological investigation that stresses the study of small groups, often through experimental means. (Module 1)

Midlife crisis A stressful period of self-evaluation that begins at about age 40. (Module 14)

Minority group A subordinate group whose members have significantly less control or power over their own lives than the members of a dominant or majority group have over theirs. (Module 28)

Model, or ideal, minority A subordinate group whose members supposedly have succeeded economically, socially, and educationally despite past prejudice and discrimination, and without resorting to political and violent confrontations with Whites. (Module 30)

Modernization The far-reaching process through which periphery nations move from traditional or less developed institutions to those characteristic of more developed societies. (Module 45)

Modernization theory A functionalist approach that proposes that modernization and development will gradually improve the lives of people in developing nations. (Module 45)

Monarchy A form of government headed by a single member of a royal family, usually a king, queen, or some other hereditary ruler. (Module 50)

Monogamy A form of marriage in which an individual has only one partner. (Module 33)

Monopoly Control of a market by a single business firm. (Module 49)

Morbidity rate The rate of disease in a given population. (Module 37)

Mores Norms deemed highly necessary to the welfare of a society. (Module 8)

Mortality rate The rate of death in a given population. (Module 37)

Multinational corporation A commercial organization that is headquartered in one country but does business throughout the world. (Module 45)

Multiple masculinities A variety of male gender roles, including nurturing-caring and effeminate-gay roles, that men may play along with their more pervasive traditional role of dominating women. (Module 31)

N

Narcotizing dysfunction The phenomenon in which the media provide such massive amounts of coverage that the audience becomes numb and fails to act on the information, regardless of how compelling the issue. (Module 19)

Natural science The study of the physical features of nature and the ways in which they interact and change. (Module 1)

Naturally occurring retirement community (NORC) An area that has gradually become an informal center for senior citizens. (Module 14)

Neocolonialism Continuing dependence of former colonies on foreign countries. (Module 45)

New religious movement (NRM) or cult A small, secretive religious group that represents either a new religion or a major innovation of an existing faith. (Module 48)

New social movement An organized collective activity that addresses values and social identities, as well as improvements in the quality of life. (Module 42)

Nonmaterial culture Ways of using material objects, as well as customs, beliefs, philosophies, governments, and patterns of communication. (Module 9)

Nonverbal communication The sending of messages through the use of gestures, facial expressions, and postures. (Module 2)

Norm An established standard of behavior maintained by a society. (Module 8)

Nuclear family A married couple and their unmarried children living together. (Module 33)

O

Obedience Compliance with higher authorities in a hierarchical structure. (Module 22)

Objective method A technique for measuring social class that assigns individuals to classes on the basis of criteria such as occupation, education, income, and place of residence. (Module 26)

Observation A research technique in which an investigator collects information through direct participation, by closely watching a group or community. (Module 5)

Offshoring The transfer of work to foreign contractors. (Module 52)

Oligarchy A form of government in which a few individuals rule. (Module 50)

Open system A social system in which the position of each individual is influenced by his or her achieved status. (Module 27)

Operational definition An explanation of an abstract concept that is specific enough to allow a researcher to assess the concept. (Module 4)

Opinion leader Someone who influences the opinions and decisions of others through day-to-day personal contact and communication. (Module 20)

Organic solidarity A collective consciousness that rests on mutual interdependence, characteristic of societies with a complex division of labor. (Module 18)

Organized crime The work of a group that regulates relations between criminal enterprises involved in illegal activities, including prostitution, gambling, and the smuggling and sale of illegal drugs. (Module 24)

Out-group A group or category to which people feel they do not belong. (Module 16)

P

Patriarchy A society in which men dominate in family decision making. (Module 33)

Patrilineal descent A kinship system in which only the father's relatives are significant. (Module 33)

Peace The absence of war, or more broadly, a proactive effort to develop cooperative relations among nations. (Module 50)

Personality A person's typical patterns of attitudes, needs, characteristics, and behavior. (Module 11)

Peter principle A principle of organizational life, originated by Laurence J. Peter, according to which every employee within a hierarchy tends to rise to his or her level of incompetence. (Module 17)

Pluralism Mutual respect for one another's cultures among the various groups in a society, which allows minorities to express their cultures without experiencing prejudice. (Module 29)

Pluralist model A view of society in which many competing groups within the community have access to government, so that no single group is dominant. (Module 51)

Political system The social institution that is founded on a recognized set of procedures for implementing and achieving society's goals. (Module 49)

Politics In Harold Lasswell's words, "who gets what, when, and how." (Module 50)

Polyandry A form of polygamy in which a woman may have more than one husband at the same time. (Module 33)

Polygamy A form of marriage in which an individual may have several husbands or wives simultaneously. (Module 33)

Polygyny A form of polygamy in which a man may have more than one wife at the same time. (Module 33)

Postindustrial society A society whose economic system is engaged primarily in the processing and control of information. (Module 18)

Postmodern society A technologically sophisticated society that is preoccupied with consumer goods and media images. (Module 18)

Power The ability to exercise one's will over others. (Modules 25, 50)

Power elite A term used by C. Wright Mills to refer to a small group of military, industrial, and government leaders who control the fate of the United States. (Module 51)

Precarious work Employment that is poorly paid, and from the worker's perspective, insecure and unprotected. (Modules 27, 52)

Prejudice A negative attitude toward an entire category of people, often an ethnic or racial minority. (Module 28)

Prestige The respect and admiration that an occupation holds in a society. (Module 26)

Primary group A small group characterized by intimate, face-to-face association and cooperation. (Module 16)

Profane The ordinary and commonplace elements of life, as distinguished from the sacred. (Module 47)

Professional criminal A person who pursues crime as a day-to-day occupation, developing skilled techniques and enjoying a certain degree of status among other criminals. (Module 24)

Proletariat Karl Marx's term for the working class in a capitalist society. (Module 25)

Protestant ethic Max Weber's term for the disciplined work ethic, this-worldly concerns, and rational orientation to life emphasized by John Calvin and his followers. (Module 47)

Q

Qualitative research Research that relies on what is seen in field or naturalistic settings more than on statistical data. (Module 5)

Quantitative research Research that collects and reports data primarily in numerical form. (Module 5)

Queer theory The study of society from the perspective of a broad spectrum of sexual identities, including heterosexuality, homosexuality, and bisexuality. (Module 2)

Questionnaire A printed or written form used to obtain information from a respondent. (Module 5)

R

Racial formation A sociohistorical process in which racial categories are created, inhabited, transformed, and destroyed. (Module 28)

Racial group A group that is set apart from others because of physical differences that have taken on social significance. (Module 28)

Racial profiling Any arbitrary action initiated by an authority based on race, ethnicity, or national origin rather than on a person's behavior. (Module 29)

Racism The belief that one race is supreme and all others are innately inferior. (Module 28)

Random sample A sample for which every member of an entire population has the same chance of being selected. (Module 4)

Rational-legal authority Power made legitimate by law. (Module 50)

Reference group Any group that individuals use as a standard for evaluating themselves and their own behavior. (Module 16)

Relative deprivation The conscious feeling of a negative discrepancy between legitimate expectations and present actualities. (Module 42)

Relative poverty A floating standard of deprivation by which people at the bottom of a society, whatever their lifestyles, are judged to be disadvantaged *in comparison with the nation as a whole*. (Module 27)

Reliability The extent to which a measure produces consistent results. (Module 4)

Religion According to Émile Durkheim, a unified system of beliefs and practices relative to sacred things. (Module 47)

Religious belief A statement to which members of a particular religion adhere. (Module 48)

Religious experience The feeling or perception of being in direct contact with the ultimate reality, such as a divine being, or of being overcome with religious emotion. (Module 48)

Religious ritual A practice required or expected of members of a faith. (Module 48)

Remittances The monies that immigrants return to their families of origin. Also called *migradollars*. (Module 30)

Representative democracy A form of government in which certain individuals are selected to speak for the people. (Module 50)

Research design A detailed plan or method for obtaining data scientifically. (Module 5)

Resocialization The process of discarding former behavior patterns and accepting new ones as part of a transition in one's life. (Module 14)

Resource mobilization The ways in which a social movement utilizes such resources as money, political influence, access to the media, and personnel. (Module 42)

Rite of passage A ritual marking the symbolic transition from one social position to another. (Module 14)

Role conflict The situation that occurs when incompatible expectations arise from two or more social positions held by the same person. (Module 15)

Role exit The process of disengagement from a role that is central to one's self-identity in order to establish a new role and identity. (Module 15)

Role strain The difficulty that arises when the same social position imposes conflicting demands and expectations. (Module 15)

Role taking The process of mentally assuming the perspective of another and responding from that imagined viewpoint. (Module 12)

S

Sacred Elements beyond everyday life that inspire awe, respect, and even fear. (Module 47)

Sample A selection from a larger population that is statistically representative of that population. (Module 4)

Sanction A penalty or reward for conduct concerning a social norm. (Modules 8, 23)

Sandwich generation The generation of adults who simultaneously try to meet the competing needs of their parents and their children. (Module 14)

Sapir-Whorf hypothesis A hypothesis concerning the role of language in shaping our interpretation of reality. It holds that language is culturally determined. (Module 8)

Science The body of knowledge obtained by methods based on systematic observation. (Module 1)

Scientific management approach Another name for the classical theory of formal organizations. (Module 17)

Scientific method A systematic, organized series of steps that ensures maximum objectivity and consistency in researching a problem. (Module 4)

Second shift The double burden—work outside the home followed by child care and housework—that many women face and few men share equitably. (Module 32)

Secondary analysis A variety of research techniques that make use of previously collected and publicly accessible information and data. (Module 5)

Secondary group A formal, impersonal group in which there is little social intimacy or mutual understanding. (Module 16)

Sect A relatively small religious group that has broken away from some other religious organization to renew what it considers the original vision of the faith. (Module 48)

Secularization The process through which religion's influence on other social institutions diminishes. (Module 47)

Segregation The physical separation of two groups of people in terms of residence, workplace, and social events; often imposed on a minority group by a dominant group. (Module 29)

Self According to George Herbert Mead, a distinct identity that sets us apart from others. (Module 12)

Serial monogamy A form of marriage in which a person may have several spouses in his or her lifetime, but only one spouse at a time. (Module 33)

Sexism The ideology that one sex is superior to the other. (Module 32)

Sick role Societal expectations about the attitudes and behavior of a person viewed as being ill. (Module 36)

Significant other A term used by George Herbert Mead to refer to an individual who is most important in the development of the self, such as a parent, friend, or teacher. (Module 12)

Single-parent family A family in which only one parent is present to care for the children. (Module 34)

Slavery A system of enforced servitude in which some people are owned by other people. (Module 25)

Social capital The collective benefit of social networks, which are built on reciprocal trust. (Modules 1, 19)

Social change Significant alteration over time in behavior patterns and culture, including norms and values. (Module 42)

Social constructionist perspective An approach to deviance that emphasizes the role of culture in the creation of the deviant identity. (Module 22)

Social control The techniques and strategies for preventing deviant human behavior in any society. (Module 22)

Social disorganization theory The theory that crime and deviance are caused by the absence or breakdown of communal relationships and social institutions. (Module 22)

Social epidemiology The study of the distribution of disease, impairment, and general health status across a population. (Module 37)

Social inequality A condition in which members of society have differing amounts of wealth, prestige, or power. (Modules 3, 25)

Social institution An organized pattern of beliefs and behavior centered on basic social needs. (Module 16)

Social interaction The ways in which people respond to one another. (Module 15)

Social mobility Movement of individuals or groups from one position in a society's stratification system to another. (Module 27)

Social movement An organized collective activity to bring about or resist fundamental change in an existing group or society. (Module 42)

Social network A series of social relationships that links a person directly to others, and through them indirectly to still more people. (Module 16)

Social role A set of expectations for people who occupy a given social position or status. (Module 15)

Social science The study of the social features of humans and the ways in which they interact and change. (Module 1)

Social structure The way in which a society is organized into predictable relationships. (Module 15)

Socialism An economic system under which the means of production and distribution are collectively owned. (Module 49)

Socialization The lifelong process in which people learn the attitudes, values, and behaviors appropriate for members of a particular culture. (Module 11)

Societal-reaction approach Another name for *labeling theory*. (Module 22)

Society A fairly large number of people who live in the same territory, are relatively independent of people outside their area, and participate in a common culture. (Module 7)

Sociobiology The systematic study of how biology affects human social behavior. (Module 7)

Sociocultural evolution Long-term social trends resulting from the interplay of continuity, innovation, and selection. (Module 18)

Socioeconomic status (SES) A measure of social class that is based on income, education, and occupation. (Module 26)

Sociological imagination An awareness of the relationship between an individual and the wider society, both today and in the past. (Module 1)

Sociology The scientific study of social behavior and human groups. (Module 1)

Status A term used by sociologists to refer to any of the full range of socially defined positions within a large group or society. (Module 15)

Status group A term used by Max Weber to refer to people who have the same prestige or lifestyle, independent of their class positions. (Module 25)

Stereotype An unreliable generalization about all members of a group that does not recognize individual differences within the group. (Modules 19, 28)

Stigma A label used to devalue members of certain social groups. (Module 22, 38)

Stratification A structured ranking of entire groups of people that perpetuates unequal economic rewards and power in a society. (Module 25)

Subculture A segment of society that shares a distinctive pattern of customs, rules, and traditions that differs from the pattern of the larger society. (Module 10)

Survey A study, generally in the form of an interview or questionnaire, that provides researchers with information about how people think and act. (Module 5)

Symbol A gesture, object, or word that forms the basis of human communication. (Module 8)

Symbolic ethnicity An ethnic identity that emphasizes concerns such as ethnic food or political issues rather than deeper ties to one's ethnic heritage. (Module 30)

T

Teacher-expectancy effect The impact that a teacher's expectations about a student's performance may have on the student's actual achievements. (Module 40)

Technology Cultural information about the ways in which the material resources of the environment may be used to satisfy human needs and desires. (Modules 9, 18, 43)

Tech-no's People who resist the worldwide movement toward electronic networking. (Module 44)

Terrorism The use or threat of violence against random or symbolic targets in pursuit of political aims. (Module 50)

Theory In sociology, a set of statements that seeks to explain problems, actions, or behavior. (Module 1)

Total institution A term coined by Erving Goffman to refer to an institution that regulates all aspects of a person's life under a single authority, such as a prison, the military, a mental hospital, or a convent. (Module 14)

Totalitarianism Virtually complete government control and surveillance over all aspects of a society's social and political life. (Module 50)

Tracking The practice of placing students in specific curriculum groups on the basis of their test scores and other criteria. (Module 40)

Traditional authority Legitimate power conferred by custom and accepted practice. (Module 50)

Trained incapacity The tendency of workers in a bureaucracy to become so specialized that they develop blind spots and fail to notice obvious problems. (Module 17)

Transnational An immigrant who sustains multiple social relationships that link his or her society of origin with the society of settlement. (Modules 30, 44)

Transnational crime Crime that occurs across multiple national borders. (Module 24)

Transracial adoption The adoption of a non-White child by White parents or a Hispanic child by non-Hispanics. (Module 34)

U

Underclass The long-term poor who lack training and skills. (Module 27)

V

Validity The degree to which a measure or scale truly reflects the phenomenon under study. (Module 4)

Value A collective conception of what is considered good, desirable, and proper—or bad, undesirable, and improper—in a culture. (Module 8)

Value neutrality Max Weber's term for objectivity of sociologists in the interpretation of data. (Module 6)

Variable A measurable trait or characteristic that is subject to change under different conditions. (Module 4)

Verstehen The German word for "understanding" or "insight"; used by Max Weber to stress the need for sociologists to take into account the subjective meanings people attach to their actions. (Module 1)

Vertical mobility The movement of an individual from one social position to another of a different rank. (Module 27)

Vested interests Veblen's term for those people or groups who will suffer in the event of social change, and who have a stake in maintaining the status quo. (Module 43)

Victimization survey A questionnaire or interview given to a sample of the population to determine whether people have been victims of crime. (Module 24)

Victimless crime A term used by sociologists to describe the willing exchange among adults of widely desired but illegal goods and services. (Module 24)

W

War Conflict between organizations that possess trained combat forces equipped with deadly weapons. (Module 50)

Wealth An inclusive term encompassing all a person's material assets, including land, stocks, and other types of property. (Module 25)

White-collar crime Illegal acts committed by affluent, "respectable" individuals in the course of business activities. (Module 24)

White privilege Rights or immunities granted to people as a particular benefit or favor simply because they are White. (Module 28)

World systems analysis The global economy as an interdependent system of economically and politically unequal nations. (Module 45)

REFERENCES

A

Aaronson, Daniel, and Eric French. 2013. "How Does a Federal Minimum Wage Hike Affect Aggregate Household Spending?" Chicago Fed Letter (August). Accessed December 20 at http://www.chicagofed.org/digital_assets/publications/chicago_fed_letter/2013/cflaugust2013_313.pdf.

ABC Television. 2013. "Arkansas Schools to Start Moment of Silence when Classes Begin." August 2. Accessed September 8, 2013 at http://www.4029tv.com.

Abercrombie, Nicholas, Bryan S. Turner, and Stephen Hill, eds. 1990. Dominant Ideologies. Cambridge, MA: Unwin Hyman.

———, Stephen Hill, and Bryan S. Turner. 1980. The Dominant Ideology Thesis. London: Allen and Unwin.

Aberle, David F., A. K. Cohen, A. K. Davis, M. J. Leng, Jr., and F. N. Sutton. 1950. "The Functional Prerequisites of a Society." Ethics 60 (January):100–111.

ACLU. 2013. "Frank v. Walker: Fighting Voter Suppression in Wisconsin." November 4. Accessed December 30 at https://www.aclu.org/voting-rights/frank-v-walker-fighting-voter-suppression-wisconsin.

———. 2014. "Map of States with Restrictions on Adoption or Fostering by LGB People." Accessed January 18 at https://www.aclu.org/lgbt-rights/map-states-restrictions-adoption-or-fostering-lgb-people.

Acosta, R. Vivian, and Linda Jean Carpenter. 2001. "Women in Intercollegiate Sport: A Longitudinal Study: 1977–1998." Pp. 302–308 in Sport in Contemporary Society: An Anthology, 6th ed., edited by D. Stanley Eitzen. New York: Worth.

Adams, Tracey L. 2010. "Gender and Feminization in Health Care Professions." Sociology Compass 4 (July):454–465.

Adams, Tyrene L., and Stephen A. Smith. 2008. Electronic Tribes: The Virtual Worlds of Geeks, Gamas, Shamans, and Scammers. Austin: University of Texas Press.

Addams, Jane. 1910. Twenty Years at Hull-House. New York: Macmillan.

———. 1930. The Second Twenty Years at Hull-House. New York: Macmillan.

Adler, Patricia A., and Peter Adler. 2007. "The Demedicalization of Self-Injury: From Psychopathology to Sociological Deviance." Journal of Contemporary Ethnography 36 (October):537–570.

———, and ———. 2011. The Tender Cut: Inside the Hidden World of Self-Injury. New York: New York University Press.

———, ———, and John M. Johnson. 1992. "Street Corner Society Revisited." Journal of Contemporary Ethnography 21 (April):3–10.

Adorno, Theodor. [1971] 1991. The Culture Industry. London: Routledge.

Agence France-Presse. 2013. "World Watches American TV, Not Always Legally." September 21. Accessed November 23, 2013 at http://www.rawstory.com/rs/2013/09/21/world-watches-american-tv-not-always-legally/.

Alain, Michel. 1985. "An Empirical Validation of Relative Deprivation." Human Relations 38 (8):739–749.

Alba, Richard D. 1990. Ethnic Identity: The Transformation of White America. New Haven, CT: Yale University Press.

———. 2009. Blurring the Color Line: The New Chance for a More Integrated America. Cambridge, MA: Harvard University Press.

Albas, Cheryl, and Daniel Albas. 1996. "An Invitation to the Ethnographic Study of University Examination Behavior: Concepts, Methodology and Implications." Canadian Journal of Higher Education 26 (3):1–26.

Albas, Daniel, and Cheryl Albas. 1988. "Aces and Bombers: The Post-Exam Impression Management Strategies of Students." Symbolic Interaction 11 (Fall):289–302.

Albrecht, Gary L. 2004. "Disability: Sociological Perspectives." Pp. 3710–3713 in International Encyclopedia of the Social and Behavioral Sciences, edited by Neil J. Smelser and Paul B. Baltes. New York: Elsevier.

Albrecht, Karl. 2014. "The Information Revolution's Broken Promises." Futurist (March–April):22–28.

Alderman, Liz. 2010. "Rapid Growth in Dubai Outstrips Its Resources." New York Times, October 28, pp. D1, D5.

———. 2012. "Starbucks on the Seine." New York Times, March 30, pp. B1, B8.

Ali, Syed. 2010. "Permanent Impermanence." Contexts (Spring):26–31.

Allen, Bem P. 1978. Social Behavior: Fact and Falsehood. Chicago: Nelson-Hall.

Allen, Greg. 2012. "Mission Diversify: CIA Begins LGBT Recruiting." December 2. Accessible at www.wbur.org.

Alliance for Board Diversity. 2013. Missing Pieces: Women and Minorities on Fortune 500 Boards. 2012 Alliance for Board Diversity Census. Accessible at http://theabd.org/2012_ABD%20Missing_Pieces_Final_8_15_13.pdf.

Allport, Gordon W. 1979. The Nature of Prejudice. 25th anniversary ed. Reading, MA: Addison-Wesley.

Alon, Sigal. 2009. "The Evolution of Class Inequality in Higher Education: Competition, Exclusion, and Adaptation." American Sociological Review 74 (October):731–755.

Alvord, Lori Arviso, and Elizabeth Cohen Van Pelt. 1999. The Scalpel and the Silver Bear. New York: Bantam Books.

Alwin, Duane F. 2002. "Generations X, Y, and Z: Are They Changing America?" Contexts (Fall–Winter):42–51.

Alzheimer's Association. 2012. 2012 Alzheimer's Disease Facts and Figures. Accessed March 25 at http://www.alzheimers_disease_facts_and_figures.asp.

American Academy of Cosmetic Surgery. 2010. "New Survey Indicates More than 17 Million Cosmetic Procedures Performed Last Year in U.S." Chicago: AACS.

American Academy of Pediatrics. 2011. "Media Use by Children Younger Than 2 Years." Pediatrics 128 (November):1040–1045.

———. 2013. "Children, Adolescents, and the Media." Pediatrics 132 (November):958–959.

American Community Survey. 2011. "American Community Survey 2010." Accessible at www.census.gov/acs/www/.

———. 2013a. "American Community Survey 2012." Data released August 2013 and accessible at www.census.gov.

———. 2013b. "Survey Methodology Main." Accessible at www.census.gov/acs/www/methodology/methodology_main/.

American Jewish Committee. 2005. 2005 Annual Survey of American Jewish Opinion. New York: AJC.

American Lung Association. 2011. "State of the Air 2011." Accessed March 26, 2012 (www.stateoftheair.org).

American Psychiatric Association. 2013. Diagnostic and Statistical Manual of Mental Disorders, Fifth Edition (DSM-5(TM)). Arlington VA: American Psychiatric Publishing.

American Psychological Association. 2008. "Being Gay Is Just as Healthy as Being Straight." Accessed February 25 (www.apa.org).

American Sociological Association. 1999. Code of Ethics. Reprinted 2008. Washington DC: ASA.

———. 2005. "Need Today's Data Yesterday." Accessed December 17 (www.asanet.org).

———. 2009. 21st Century Careers with an Undergraduate Degree in Sociology. Washington, DC: ASA.

———. 2014. Current Sections. Accessed January 2 (www.asanet.org/sections/list.cfm).

Anatale, Alex, Atsushi Yamanaka, and Didier Nkurikiyimfura. 2013. "The Metamorphosis to a Knowledge-Based Society: Rwanda." Chapter 2.2 in *The Global Information Technology Report 2013: Growth and Jobs in a Hyperconnected World*, edited by Beñat Bilbao-Osorio, Soumitra Dutta, and Bruno Lanvin. April 10. Geneva: World Economic Forum. Accessible at http://www.weforum.org/reports/global-information-technology-report-2013.

Andersen, Margaret. 2007. *Thinking about Women: Sociological Perspectives on Sex and Gender.* 7th ed. New York: Allyn and Bacon.

Anderson, Elijah. 1990. *Streetwise: Race, Class, and Change in an Urban Community.* Chicago: University of Chicago Press.

Anderson, Gretchen. 2009. *Love, Actually: A National Survey of Adults 18+ on Love, Relationships, and Romance.* Washington, DC: AARP.

Anderson, John Ward, and Molly Moore. 1993. "The Burden of Womanhood." *Washington Post National Weekly Edition* 10 (March 22–28):6–7.

Anderson, Warwick. 2003. *The Cultivation of Whiteness: Science, Health and Racial Destiny in Australia.* New York: Perseus.

Andrews, Lori. 2012. "Facebook Is Using You." *New York Times,* February 5, Sunday Review, p. 7.

Angier, Natalie. 1998. "Drugs, Sports, Body Image and G.I. Joe." *New York Times,* December 22, pp. D1, D3.

Angwin, Julia. 2010. "The Web's New Gold Mine: Your Secrets." *Wall Street Journal,* July 31, pp. W1, W2.

———. 2012. "Digital-Privacy Rules Taking Shape." *Wall Street Journal,* March 26. Accessible at http://online.wsj.com/news/articles/SB10001424052702303404704577305473061190762.

———, and Jennifer Valentino-DeVries. 2010a. "Race Is On to 'Fingerprint' Phones, PCs." *Wall Street Journal,* December 1, pp. A1, A15.

Ansell, Amy E. 2008. "Color Blindness." Pp. 320–321, vol. 1, in *Encyclopedia of Race, Ethnicity, and Society,* edited by Richard T. Schaefer. Thousand Oaks, CA: Sage.

Anti-Defamation League. 2013. *2012 Audit of Anti-Semitic Incidents.* Accessible at http://www.adl.org.

Arab American Institute. 2010. "Demographics." Accessed March 7 (www.aaiusa.org/arab-americans/22/demographics).

Archer, Patrick, and Bryan Orr. 2011. "Class Identification in Review: Past Perspectives and Future Directions." *Sociology Compass* 5 (January):104–115.

Argetsinger, Amy, and Jonathan Krim. 2002. "Stopping the Music." *Washington Post National Weekly Edition* 20 (December 2):20.

Armer, J. Michael, and John Katsillis. 1992. "Modernization Theory." Pp. 1299–1304, vol. 4, in *Encyclopedia of Sociology,* edited by Edgar F. Borgatta and Marie L. Borgatta. New York: Macmillan.

Ash, Timothy Garton. 2007. "Welcome to a Mixed-Up World." *Globe and Mail* (Toronto), July 14, p. A19.

Asi, Maryam, and Daniel Beaulieu. 2013. *Arab Households in the United States 2006–2010.* ACSBR/10-20. Accessible at http://www.census.gov.

Aslanian, Sasha. 2006. "Researchers Still Learning from Romania's Orphans." NPR, September 16. Accessed September 25, 2013 at http://www.npr.org/templates/story/story.php?storyi=6089477.

Association of Theological Schools. 2013. "Annual Data Tables 2012–2013." Table 2-12A. Accessed January 25, 2014 at http://docs.ats.edu/uploads/resources/insitutional-data/annual-data-tables/2012-2013-annual-data-tables.pdf.

Atchley, Robert C. 1976. *The Sociology of Retirement.* New York: Wiley.

Attwood, Bain. 2003. *Rights for Aborigines.* Crows Nest, Australia: Allen and Unwin.

Aunio, Anna-Lisa, and Suzanne Staggenborg. 2011. "Transnational Linkages and Movement Communities." *Sociology Compass* 5 (5):364–375.

Austin, Chammie. 2009. *Impression Management.* Accessed January 11, 2012 (www.education.com/reference/article/impression-management).

Australia. 1997. "Bringing Them Home: Report of the National Inquiry into the Separation of Aboriginal and Torres Strait Islander Children from Their Families." Accessible at www.humanrights.gov.au.

———. 2008. "Apology to Australia's Indigenous Peoples, House of Representatives, Parliament House, Canberra." Accessed February 13 (www.pm.gov.au/media/speech/2008/speech_0073.cfm).

Avon. 2013. "Experience Avon's History." Accessed February 26 at http://www.avoncompany.com/aboutavon/history/index.html.

Azumi, Koya, and Jerald Hage. 1972. *Organizational Systems.* Lexington, MA: Heath.

B

Babad, Elisha Y., and P. J. Taylor. 1992. "Transparency of Teacher Expectancies across Language, Cultural Boundaries." *Journal of Educational Research* 86:120–125.

Bacon Lovers' Talk. 2009. "Bacon Lovers' Talk." Accessed February 4 (www.bacontalk.com/).

Bado-Fralick, Nikki and Rebecca Sachs Norris. 2010. *Toying with God: The World of Religious Games and Dolls.* Waco, TX: Baylor University Press.

Bagby, Ihsam. 2012. *The American Mosque 2011.* Washington, DC: Council on American-Islamic Relations.

Bajaj, Vikas. 2011a. "15 Years in Microcredit Has Suffered a Black Eye." *New York Times,* January 6, p. B3.

———. 2011b. "Luster Dims for a Public Microlender." *New York Times,* May 11, pp. 1, 4.

Baker, Peter. 2009. "Obama Reverses Rules on U.S. Abortion Aid." *New York Times,* January 24.

Baker, Therese L. 1999. *Doing Social Research.* 3rd ed. New York: McGraw-Hill.

Baran, Stanley. 2014. *Introduction to Mass Communication: Media Literacy and Culture.* 8th ed. New York: McGraw-Hill.

Barnes, Patricia, Barbara Bloom, and Richard Nahin. 2008. "Complementary and Alternative Medicine Use among Adults and Children: United States, 2007." *National Health Statistics Reports,* December 10.

———, Eve Powell-Griner, Ken McFann, and Richard L. Nation. 2004. "Complementary and Alternative Medicine Use among Adults: United States, 2002." *Advance Data from Vital and Health Statistics,* No. 343. Hyattsville, MD: National Center for Health Statistics.

Barnes, Taylor. 2009. "Rise of the Shadow Economy." *Christian Science Monitor,* November 8, pp. 30–31.

Barnett, W. Steven, Megan E. Carolan, Jen Fitzgerald, and James H. Squires. 2013. *The State of Preschool 2012: State Preschool Yearbook.* New Brunswick, NJ: National Institute for Early Education Research.

Barrett, David B., Todd M. Johnson, and Peter F. Crossing. 2008. "The 2007 Annual Megacensus of Religions." Chicago: Encyclopaedia Britannica.

Bartlett, Thomas. 2009. "How the International Essay Mill Has Changed Cheating." *Chronicle of Higher Education,* March 20, pp. A1, A22–A25.

———. 2011. "A Database Named Desire: 2 Scientists Examine Online Searches for Sex." *Chronicle of Higher Education* 57 (August 12):A12.

Barton, Bernadette. 2006. *Stripped: Inside the Lives of Exotic Dancers.* New York: New York University Press.

Basulto, Dominic. 2011. "Popping the 'Supercommittee' 'Filter Bubble.'" *Washington Post* (November 3). Accessed November 11 (www.washingtonpost.com/blogs/innovations/post/popping-the-supercommittee-filter-bubble/2010/12/20glQAMfcviM_blog.html).

Baudrillard, Jean. [1970] 1998. *The Consumer Society.* London: Sage.

Bauerlein, Monika. 1996. "The Luddites Are Back." *Utne Reader* (March–April):24, 26.

Bauman, Kurt J. 1999. "Extended Measures of Well-Being: Meeting Basic Needs." *Current Population Reports,* ser. P-70, no. 67. Washington, DC: U.S. Government Printing Office.

Bazar, Emily. 2009. "Tent Cities Filling up with Casualties of the Economy." *USA Today,* May 5, pp. 1A–2A.

BBC News. 2005. "Indonesian Village Report: January 12, 2005." Accessed January 19 (www.theworld.org).

Beagan, Brenda L. 2001. " 'Even If I Don't Know What I'm Doing I Can Make It Look Like I Know What I'm Doing': Becoming a Doctor in the 1990s." *Canadian Review of Sociology and Anthropology* 38:275–292.

———, Alana Chiasson, Cheryl Fiske, Stephanie Forseth, Alisha Hosein, Marianne Myers, and Janine Stang. 2013. "Working with Transgender Clients: Learning from Others to Improve Occupational Therapy Practice." *Canadian Journal of Occupational Therapy* 80(2):82–91.

Bearman, Peter S., James Moody, and Katherine Stovel. 2004. "Chains of Affection: The Structure of Adolescent Romantic and Sexual Networks." *American Journal of Sociology* 110 (July):44–91.

Becker, Anne E. 2007. "Facets of Acculturation and Their Diverse Relations to Body Shape Concerns in Fiji." *International Journal of Eating Disorders* 40 (1):42–50.

Becker, Howard S. 1952. "Social Class Variations in the Teacher-Pupil Relationship." *Journal of Educational Sociology* 25 (April):451–465.

———. 1963. *The Outsiders: Studies in the Sociology of Deviance.* New York: Free Press.

——— (ed.). 1964. *The Other Side: Perspectives on Deviance.* New York: Free Press.

———, Blanche Geer, Everett C Hughes, and Anselm Strauss. 1961. *Boys in White: Student Culture in Medical School.* Chicago: University of Chicago Press.

Beddoes, Zanny Milton. 2012. "For Richer, for Poorer." *The Economist* (October 13): Special Report.

Beisel, Nicola, and Tamara Kay. 2004. "Abortion, Race, and Gender in Nineteenth-Century America." *American Sociological Review* 69 (4):498–518.

Belkin, Douglas, and Caroline Porter. 2012. "Web Profiles Haunt Students." *Wall Street Journal,* October 4, p. A3.

Bell, Daniel. 1953. "Crime as an American Way of Life." *Antioch Review* 13 (Summer):131–154.

———. [1973] 1999. *The Coming of Post-Industrial Society: A Venture in Social Forecasting.* With new foreword. New York: Basic Books.

Bell, Wendell. 1981. "Modernization." Pp. 186–187 in *Encyclopedia of Sociology.* Guilford, CT: DPG Publishing.

Beller, Emily. 2009. "Bringing Intergenerational Social Mobility Research into the Twenty-first Century: Why Mothers Matter." *America Sociological Review* 74 (August):507–528.

Benford, Robert D. 1992. "Social Movements." Pp. 1880–1887, vol. 4, in *Encyclopedia of Sociology,* edited by Edgar F. Borgatta and Marie Borgatta. New York: Macmillan.

Bergen, Raquel Kennedy. 2006. *Marital Rape: New Research and Directions.* Harrisburg, PA: VAW Net.

Berger, Peter, and Thomas Luckmann. 1966. *The Social Construction of Reality.* New York: Doubleday.

Berman, Paul. 2003. *Terror and Liberalism.* New York: Norton.

Bernhardt, Annette, et al. (10 additional co-authors). 2009. *Broken Laws, Unprotected Workers.* New York: Ford, Joyce, Haynes, and Russell Sage Foundations.

Bernstein, Elizabeth. 2007. "Colleges Move Boldly on Student Drinking." *Wall Street Journal,* December 6, pp. D1, D2.

Bernstein, Mary, and Verta Taylor, eds. 2013. *The Marrying Kind?* Minneapolis: University of Minnesota Press.

Bessen-Cassino, Yasemin. 2013. "Cool Store Bad Jobs." *Contexts* (Fall):42–47.

Best, Joel. 2004. *Deviance: Career of a Concept.* Belmont, CA: Wadsworth Thomson.

Bhagat, Chetan. 2007. *One Night at the Call Centre.* London: Black Swan.

Bialik, Carol. 2010. "Seven Careers in a Lifetime? Think Twice, Researchers Say." *Wall Street Journal,* September 4, p. A6.

Bianchi, Suzanne M., and Daphne Spain. 1996. "Women, Work, and Family in America." *Population Bulletin* 51 (December).

Biddlecom, Ann, and Steven Martin. 2006. "Childless in America." *Contexts* 5 (Fall):54.

Bielby, Denise D., and C. Lee Harrington. 2008. *Global TV: Exporting Television and Culture in the World Market.* New York: New York University Press.

Bilbao-Osorio, Benñat, Soumitra Dutta, and Bruno Lanvin, eds. 2013. *The Global Information Technology Report 2013: Growth and Jobs in a Hyperconnected World.* April 10. Geneva: World Economic Forum. Accessible at http://www.weforum.org/reports/global-information-technology-report-2013.

Billboard. 2012. "The Year in Music 2012—Charts, Ringtones." Accessed February 11 at www.billboard.com.

Billitteri, Thomas, J. 2009. "Middle-Class Squeeze." *CQ Researcher* 19 (March 6):201–224.

Bishaw, Aleyayehu. 2011. "Areas with Concentrated Poverty: 2006–2010." *American Community Survey Briefs.* Issued December 2011 ACSBR/10-17. Accessible at http://www.census.gov/prod/2011pubs/acsbr10-17.pdf.

Bitler, Marianne, and Hilary W. Hoynes. 2010. "The State of the Safety Net in the Post-Welfare Reform Era." Paper prepared for Brooking Papers on Economic Activity, Washington, DC, September 16–20.

Black, Donald. 1995. "The Epistemology of Pure Sociology." *Law and Social Inquiry* 20 (Summer): 829–870.

Blais, Allison, and Lynn Rasic. 2011. *A Place of Remembrance: Official Book of the National September 11 Memorial.* Washington, DC: National Geographic.

Blank, Rebecca M. 2010. "Middle Class in America." *Focus* 27 (Summer):1–8.

———. 2011. *Changing Inequality.* Berkeley: University of California Press.

Blau, Peter M., and Otis Dudley Duncan. 1967. *The American Occupational Structure.* New York: Wiley.

Blauner, Robert. 1972. *Racial Oppression in America.* New York: Harper and Row.

Blumberg, Stephen J., and Julian V. Luke. 2007. "Coverage Bias in Traditional Telephone Surveys of Low-Income and Young Adults." *Public Opinion Quarterly* 71 (5):734–749.

Blumer, Herbert. 1955. "Collective Behavior." Pp. 165–198 in *Principles of Sociology,* 2nd ed., edited by Alfred McClung Lee. New York: Barnes and Noble.

———. 1969. *Symbolic Interactionism: Perspective and Method.* Englewood Cliffs, NJ: Prentice Hall.

Boase, Jeffery, John B. Horrigan, Barry Wellman, and Lee Rainie. 2006. *The Strength of Internet Ties.* Washington, DC: Pew Internet and American Life Project.

Boje, David M. 1995. "Stories of Storytelling Organization: A Postmodern Analysis of Disney as 'Tamara-Land.'" *Academy of Management Journal* 38:997–1035.

Bonilla-Silva, Eduardo. 2004. "From Bi-Racial to Tri-Racial: Towards a New System of Racial Stratification in the USA." *Ethics and Racial Studies* 27 (November):931–950.

———. 2006. *Racism without Racists.* Lanham, MD: Rowman and Littlefield.

Bonus, Rick. 2000. *Locating Filipino Americans: Ethnicity and the Cultural Politics of Space.* Philadelphia: Temple University Press.

Borjas, George S., Jeffrey Grogger, and Gordon H. Hanson. 2006. "Immigration and African-American Employment Opportunities: The Response of Wages, Employment, and Incarceration to Labor Supply Shocks." Working Paper 12518. Cambridge, MA: National Bureau of Economic Research.

Boston Area Research Initiative. 2013. "Housing Issues." Accessible at http://www.bostonarearesearchinitiative.net.

Bottomore, Tom, and Maximilien Rubel, eds. 1956. *Karl Marx: Selected Writings in Sociology and Social Philosophy.* New York: McGraw-Hill.

Bourdieu, Pierre, and Jean-Claude Passerson. 1990. *Reproduction in Education, Society and Culture.* 2nd ed. London. Sage. Originally published as *La reproduction.*

Boushey, Heather. 2005. *Student Debt: Bigger and Bigger.* Washington, DC: Center for Economic and Policy Research.

Bowles, Samuel, and Herbert Gintis. 1976. *Schooling in Capitalistic America: Educational Reforms and the Contradictions of Economic Life.* New York: Basic Books.

Bowman, Thomas. 2013. "As Qualified Men Dwindle, Military Looks for a Few Good Women." March 23. Accessible at http://www.npr.org/2013/03/25/174966070/

as-qualified-men-dwindle-military-looks-for-a-few-good-women.

Boy Scouts of America. 2010. "2009 Annual Report." Accessed November 10, 2011 (www.scouting.org).

Brady Campaign. 2013. "2013 State Rankings." Accessed February 16 at www.bradycampaign.org/xshare/stateleg/scorecard/2011/2011_brady_campaign_state_scorecard_rankings.pdf.

Brady, Erik. 2010. "Title IX Model Survey Policy to Be Rescinded." *USA Today,* April 20, p. C1.

Brandchannel.com. 2013. "Browse by Brand or Film." Accessed February 11 at http://www.branchannel.com/brandcameo_films.asp?movie_year=2-12.

Brannigan, Augustine. 1992. "Postmodernism." Pp. 1522–1525 in *Encyclopedia of Sociology,* vol. 3, edited by Edgar F. Borgatta and Marie L. Borgatta. New York: Macmillan.

Bray, James H., and John Kelly. 1999. *Stepfamilies: Love, Marriage, and Parenting in the First Decade.* New York: Broadway Books.

Brazier, Chris, and Amir Hamed, eds. 2007. *The World Guide.* 11th ed. Oxford, UK: New Internationalist.

Breines, Winifred. 2007. "Struggling to Connect: White and Black Feminism in the Movement Years." *Contexts* 6 (Winter):18–24.

Brennan Center. 2006. *Citizens Without Proof.* New York: Brennan Center for Justice at NYU School of Law.

———. 2013. *Election 2012 Laws Roundup.* Accessed January 13 at http://www.brennancenter.org.

Brewer, Rose M., and Nancy A. Heitzeg. 2008. "The Racialization of Criminal Punishment." *American Behavioral Scientist* 51 (January):625–644.

Brewis, Alexandra, Amber Wutich, Ashlan Falletta-Cowden, and Isa Rodriguez-Soto. 2011. "Body Norms and Fat Stigma in Global Perspective." *Current Anthropology* 52 (April):269–276.

Brint, Steven. 1998. *Schools and Societies.* Thousand Oaks, CA: Pine Forge Press.

Britannica Online. 2011. "Worldwide Adherents of All Religions by Six Continental Areas. Mid-2010." Accessed March 28.

Brown, David. 2009. "Doing a Number on Surveys." *Washington Post National Weekly Edition* 26 (January 19):37.

Brown, David K. 2001. "The Social Sources of Educational Credentialism: Status Cultures, Labor Markets, and Organizations." *Sociology of Education* 74 (Extra issue):19–34.

Brown, Geoff. 2008a. "Cities under Fire." *Johns Hopkins Public Health* (Fall).

———. 2008b. "Building a Safer Gun." *John Hopkins Public Health* (Fall).

Brown, Patricia Leigh. 2004. "For Children of Gays, Marriage Brings Joy." *New York Times,* March 19, p. A13.

Brown, Robert McAfee. 1980. *Gustavo Gutierrez.* Atlanta: John Knox.

Browne, Irene, ed. 2001. *Latinas and African American Women at Work: Race, Gender, and Economic Inequality.* New York: Russell Sage Foundation.

Brubaker, Bill. 2008. "Social Insecurity: Many People's Numbers Are Readily Available Online to Identity Thieves." *Washington Post National Weekly Edition,* January 14, p. 34.

Brulle, Robert, and J. Craig Jenkins. 2008. "Fixing the Bungled U.S. Environmental Movement." *Contexts* 7 (Spring):14–18.

Bryman, Alan. 1995. *Disney and His Worlds.* London: Routledge.

Buchmann, Claudia, Thomas A. DiPrete, and Anne McDaniel. 2008. "Gender Inequalities in Education." *Annual Review of Sociology* 34:319–337.

Buckingham, David. 2007. "Selling Childhood? Children and Consumer Culture." *Journal of Children and Media* 1 (1):15–24.

Buddeberg-Fischer, Barbara, Marina Stamm, Claus Buddeberg, Georg Bauer, Oliver Hämmig, Michaela Knecht, and Richard Klafhofer. 2012. "The Impact of Gender and Parenthood on Physicians' Careers—Professional and Personal Situation Seven Years After Graduation." *BMC Health Services Research* 10:40.

Budig, Michelle J. 2002. "Male Advantage and the Gender Composition of Jobs: Who Rides the Glass Escalator?" *Social Problems* 49 (2):258–277.

Bullard, Robert D. 1993. *Dumping in Dixie: Race, Class, and Environmental Quality.* 2nd ed. Boulder, CO: Westview Press.

———, and Beverly Wright. 2009. *Race, Place, and Environmental Justice after Hurricane Katrina.* Boulder, CO: Westview Press.

Burawoy, Michael. 2005. "For Public Sociology." *American Sociological Review* 70 (February): 4–28.

Bureau of the Census. 1975. *Historical Statistics of the United States, Colonial Times to 1970.* Washington, DC: U.S. Government Printing Office.

———. 1981. "Statistical Abstract of the United States, 1980." Accessible at www.census.gov/compendia/statlab/.

———. 2004a. *Statistical Abstract of the United States, 2004–2005.* Washington, DC: U.S. Government Printing Office.

———. 2005b. "American Fact Finder: Places with United States." Accessed December 12 (http://factfinder.census.gov).

———. 2008a. *Statistical Abstract of the United States, 2008.* Washington, DC: U.S. Government Printing Office.

———. 2008c. "America's Families and Living Arrangements 2008." Accessed at www.census.gov/population/www/socdemo/hh-fam/cps2008.html.

———. 2010b. "America's Families and Living Arrangements: 2010." Released January. Accessible at www.census.gov/population/www/socdemo/hh-fam/cps2010.html.

———. 2010c. "America's Families and Living Arrangements, 2010." Accessible at http://www.census.gov/population/www/socdemo/hh-fam/cps2010.html.

———. 2011a. *Statistical Abstract of the United States, 2012.* Washington, DC: U.S. Government Printing Office.

———. 2011c. "Census Bureau Releases Estimate of Same-Sex Married Couples." Accessible at www.census.gov/newsroom/releases/archives/2010_census/cb11-cn181.html.

———. 2011d. "Current Population Survey, Annual Social and Economic Supplements." Washington, DC: U.S. Government Printing Office.

———. 2011e. "America's Families and Living Arrangements: 2011" November 3. Accessible at www.census.gov/newsroom/releases/archives/families_households/cb11-183.html.

———. 2011f. "Voting and Registration in the Elections of November 2012—Detailed Tables." Accessible at http://www.census.gov/hhes/www/socdemo/voting/publications/p20/2012/tables.html.

———. 2012c. "Graphs on Historical Voting Trends." February 15. Accessible at www.census.gov/newsroom/releases/archives/voting/cb12-tps08.html.

———. 2012e. "Annual Estimates of the Resident Population." Accessible at http://www.census.gov/popest/data/national/asrh/2011/index.html.

———. 2012f. "Age and Sex Composition in the United States: 2012." Accessible at http://www.census.gov/population/age/data/2012comp.html.

———. 2013a. "2012 American Community Survey." Accessible at www.census.gov.

———. 2013b. "Estimated Median Age at First Marriage, by Sex: 1890 to the Present." Accessible at http://www.census.gov/hhes/families/data/marital.html.

———. 2013c. "Men in Nursing Occupations." American Community Survey Highlight Report. February 2012. Accessible at www.census.gov.

———. 2013d. "America's Families and Living Arrangements: 2013: Children (C table series): tabC3-all." Accessible at www.census.gov.

Bureau of Consular Affairs. 2013. FY 2012 Annual Report on Intercountry Adoption, January 2013. Washington, DC: Bureau of Consular Affairs, U.S. Department of State.

Bureau of Labor Statistics. 2003. "Women at Work: A Visual Essay." *Monthly Labor Review* (October):45.

———. 2010. "Economic News Release: Number of Jobs Held." Accessible at www.bls.gov/news.release/nlsoy.nr0.htm.

———. 2012. "Part-Time Employment Rates by Sex, Selected Countries, 2010." Chart 2.7 in *Charting International Labor Comparisons.* September 2012. Accessible at http://www.bls.gov/fls/chartbook/2012/chartbook2012.pdf.

———. 2012c. "Employment Characteristics and Families Summary." April 26. Accessible at www.bls.gov/news.release/famee.nr0.htm.

———. 2013a. *Women in the Labor Force: A Databook*. February 2013. Accessible at http://www.bls.gov/cps/wlf-databook-2012.pdf.

———. 2013b. "Labor Force Statistics from the Current Population Survey. Table 11. Employed Persons by Detailed Occupation, Sex, Race, and Hispanic or Latino Ethnicity." February 6. Accessible at http://www.bls.gov/cps/tables.htm.

———. 2014. *Employment Situation—January 2014*. Washington, DC: U.S. Government Printing Office.

Bures, Frank. 2011. "Can You Hear Us Now?" *Utne Reader* (March–April):8–9, 11.

Burger, Jerry M. 2009. "Replicating Milgram: Would People Still Obey Today?" *American Psychologist* 64 (January):1–11.

Burger King. 2009. "Whopper Sacrifice." Accessed February 4 (www.whoppersacrifice.com/).

Burns, Melinda. 2010. "Workfare and the Low-Wage Woman." *Miller-McClune* (November–December):76–81.

Butler, Daniel Allen. 1998. *"Unsinkable": The Full Story*. Mechanicsburg, PA: Stackpole Books.

Byrd-Bredbenner, Carol, and Jessica Murray. 2003. "Comparison of the Anthropometric Measurements of Idealized Female Body Images in Media Directed to Men, Women, and Mixed Gender Audiences." *Topics in Clinical Nutrition* 18 (2):117–129.

C

Calhoun, Craig. 1998. "Community without Propinquity Revisited." *Sociological Inquiry* 68 (Summer):373–397.

———. 2003. "Belonging in the Cosmopolitan Imaginary." *Ethnicities* 3 (December):531–553.

Cali, Billie E., Jill M. Coleman, and Catherine Campbell. 2013. "Stranger Danger? Women's Self-Protection Intent and the Continuing Stigma of Online Dating." *Cyberpsychology, Behavior, and Social Networking* 16 (December):853–857.

Cameron, Deborah. 2007. *The Myth of Mars and Venus*. Oxford: Oxford University Press.

Campbell, Mary, Robert Haveman, Gary Sandefur, and Barbara Wolte. 2005. "Economic Inequality and Educational Attainment across a Generation." *Focus* 23 (Spring):11–15.

Campo-Flores, Arian. 2013. "Street Vendors Battle Limits." *Wall Street Journal*, January 22, p. A3.

Caplan, Ronald L. 1989. "The Commodification of American Health Care." *Social Science and Medicine* 28 (11):1139–1148.

Caplow, Theodore, and Louis Hicks. 2002. *Systems of War and Peace*. 2nd ed. Lanham, MD: University Press of America.

Carbon Trust. 2012. "About the Carbon Trust." Accessed March 27 (www.carbontrust.co.uk/about-carbon-trust/pages/default.aspx).

Carey, Anne R., and Karl Gelles. 2010. "What Viewers Enjoy Most about Watching the Super Bowl on TV." *USA Today*, February 5, p. A1; *Gallup Poll* (May):3.

Carlton-Ford, Steve. 2010. "Major Armed Conflicts, Militarization, and Life Chances." *Armed Forces and Society* 36 (October):864–899.

Carr, Nicholas. 2010. "Tracking Is an Assault on Liberty, with Real Dangers." *Wall Street Journal*, August 7, pp. W1, W2.

Carroll, Joseph. 2006. "Public National Anthem Should Be Sung in English." *Gallup Poll* (May):3.

Caruso, Eugene M., Dobromir A. Rahnev, and Mahzarin R. Banaji. 2009. "Using Conjoint Analysis to Detect Discrimination: Revealing Covert Preferences from Overt Choices." *Social Cognition* 27 (1):128–137.

Castells, Manuel. 2001. *The Internet Galaxy: Reflections on the Internet, Business, and Society*. New York: Oxford University Press.

———. 2010a. *The Rise of the Network Society*. 2nd ed. With a new preface. Malden, MA: Wiley-Blackwell.

———. 2010b. *The Power of Identity*. 2nd ed. With a new preface. Malden, MA: Wiley-Blackwell.

———. 2012. *Networks of Outrage and Hope: Social Movements in the Internet Age*. Cambridge, UK: Polity.

Cauchon, Dennis. 2009. "Women Gain in Historic Job Shift." *USA Today*, September 3, p. A1.

CBS News. 1979. Transcript of *Sixty Minutes* segment, "I Was Only Following Orders." March 31, pp. 2–8.

Center for Academic Integrity. 2006. *CAI Research*. Accessed January 10 (www.academicintegrity.org).

Center for Community Initiatives. 2012a. "Northeast Florida Center for Community Initiatives (CCI)." Accessed January 3 (www.unf.edu/coas/cci/).

———. 2012b. "Magnolia Grant Objectives 2012." Accessed April 11 (htpp://aries.unfcsd.unf.edu/Magnolia/2012/objectives2012.php).

Centers for Disease Control and Prevention. 2010. "Binge Drinking among High School Students and Adults—United States, 2009." Washington, DC: CDC. Accessible at http://www.cdc.gov/mmwr/preview/mmwrhtml/mm5939a4.htm?s_cid=mm5939a4_w.

———. 2011b. *Health Disparities and Inequalities Report—United States, 2011*.

———. 2012a. *Vital Signs:* Binge Drinking. January 2012. Accessible at www.cdc.gov/vitalsigns/BingeDrinking.

———. 2012b. "National Marriage and Divorce Rate Trends." Accessed February 24 (www.cdc.gov/nchs/nvss/marriage_divorce_tables.htm).

Centers for Medicare and Medicaid Services. 2013a. "NHE Historical and Projections 1965–2022." Accessible at http://www.cms.gov/Research-Statistics-Data-and-Systems/Statistics-Trends-and-Reports/NationalHealthExpendData/index.html.

———. 2013b. "NHE Projections 2012-2022." Accessible at http://www.cms.gov/Research-Statistics-Data-and-Systems/Statistics-Trends-and-Reports/NationalHealthExpendData/index.html.

Chalfant, H. Paul, Robert E. Beckley, and C. Eddie Palmer. 1994. *Religion in Contemporary Society*. 3rd ed. Itasca, IL: F. E. Peacock.

Chambliss, William. 1973. "The Saints and the Roughnecks." *Society* 11 (November–December): 24–31.

Chan, Sewell. 2009. "City Unveils Facebook Page to Encourage Condom Use." *New York Times*, February 12, p. A32.

Charrad, Mounira M. 2011. "Gender in the Middle East: Islam, State, Agency." *Annual Review of Sociology* 37:417–437

Chase-Dunn, Christopher, and Peter Grimes. 1995. "World-Systems Analysis." Pp. 387–417 in *Annual Review of Sociology*, 1995, edited by John Hagan. Palo Alto, CA: Annual Reviews.

———, Yukio Kawano, and Benjamin D. Brewer. 2000. "Trade Globalization Since 1795: Waves of Integration in the World System." *American Sociological Review* 65 (February):77–95.

Cheng, Shu-Ju Ada. 2003. "Rethinking the Globalization of Domestic Service." *Gender and Society* 17 (2):166–186.

Cherlin, Andrew J. 2003. "Should the Government Promote Marriage?" *Contexts* 2 (Fall):22–29.

———. 2006. On Single Mothers "Doing" Family. *Journal of Marriage and Family* 68 (November):800–803.

———. 2009. *The Marriage-Go-Round: The State of Marriage and the Family in America Today*. New York: Knopf.

———. 2010. *Public and Private Families: An Introduction*. 6th ed. New York: McGraw-Hill.

———. 2011. "The Increasing Complexity of Family Life in the United States." September 8. Accessible at www.prb.org/Articles/2011/us-complex-family-life.aspx?p=1.

Child Welfare Information. 2011. *How Many Children Were Adopted in 2007 and 2008?* Washington, DC: U.S. Government Printing Office.

Chin, Kolin. 1996. *Chinatown Gangs: Extortion, Enterprise, and Ethnicity*. New York: Oxford University Press.

Choney, Suzanne. 2010. "Mobile Giving for Chile Pales Compared to Haiti." MSNBC. March 12, 2010. Accessible at www.msnmb.msn.com/ed/35822836/ns/technology_and_science-wireless/t/mobile-giving-chile-pales-compared-haiti.

Chrisafis, Angelique. 2013. "Faith War Enters Private Spheres." *The Guardian Weekly* (September 8):30–31.

Christakis, Nicholas A., and James H. Fowler. 2007. "The Spread of Obesity in a Large Social Network over 32 Years." *New England Journal of Medicine* 357 (July 26):370–379.

———, and ———. 2009. *Connected: The Amazing Power of Social Networks and How They Shape Our Lives*. New York: Harper.

Chronic Poverty Research Centre. 2009. *The Chronic Poverty Report 2008–09: Escaping Poverty Traps.* Geneva: Chronic Poverty Research Centre.

Chu, Henry. 2005. "Tractors Crush Heart of a Nation." *Los Angeles Times,* July 10, p. A9.

Chu, Kathy. 2010. "Vietnam's Market Grows Up." *USA Today,* August 23, p. B3.

Chubb, Catherine, Simone Melis, Louisa Potter, and Raymond Storry. 2008. *The Global Gender Pay Gap.* London: Incomes Data Services.

Chung, Esther K., Leny Mathew, Amy C. Rothkopf, Irma T. Elo, James C. Cayne, and Jennifer F. Culhane. 2009. "Parenting Attitudes and Infant Spanking: The Influence of Childhood Experiences." *Pediatrics* 124 (August):278–286.

Clark, Burton, and Martin Trow. 1966. "The Organizational Context." Pp. 17–70 in *The Study of College Peer Groups,* edited by Theodore M. Newcomb and Everett K. Wilson. Chicago: Aldine.

Clark, Candace. 1983. "Sickness and Social Control." Pp. 346–365 in *Social Interaction: Readings in Sociology,* 2nd ed., edited by Howard Robboy and Candace Clark. New York: St. Martin's Press.

Clarke, Adele E., Janet K. Shim, Laura Maro, Jennifer Ruth Fusket, and Jennifer R. Fishman. 2003. "Bio Medicalization: Technoscientific Transformations of Health, Illness, and U.S. Biomedicine." *American Sociological Review* 68 (April):161–194.

Clayton, Mark. 2011. "The New Cyber Arms Race." *Christian Science Monitor,* March 7, pp. 26–71.

Clemmitt, Marcia. 2005. "Intelligent Design." *CQ Researcher* 15 (July 29): 637–660.

Clifford, Stephanie. 2009a. "Teaching Teenagers about Harassment." *New York Times,* January 27, p. B1.

Clinard, Marshall B., and Robert F. Miller. 1998. *Sociology of Deviant Behavior.* 10th ed. Fort Worth, TX: Harcourt Brace.

Clymer, Adam. 2000. "College Students Not Drawn to Voting or Politics, Poll Shows." *New York Times,* January 2, p. A14.

Coates, Rodney. 2008. "Covert Racism in the USA and Globally." *Sociology Compass* 2:208–231.

Cockerham, William C. 2012. *Medical Sociology.* 12th ed. Upper Saddle River, NJ: Prentice Hall.

Coffman, Katherine B., Lucas C. Coffman, Keith M. Marzilli Ericson. 2013. "The Size of the LGBT Population and the Magnitude of Anti-Gay Sentiment Are Substantially Underestimated." NBER Working Paper No. 19508. Accessible at http://www.nber.org/papers/w19508.

Cole, Mike. 1988. *Bowles and Gintis Revisited: Correspondence and Contradiction in Educational Theory.* Philadelphia: Falmer.

Coleman, Isobel. 2004. "The Payoff from Women's Rights." *Foreign Affairs* 83 (May–June):80–95.

Coleman, James William. 2006. *The Criminal Elite: Understanding White-Collar Crime.* 6th ed. New York: Worth.

———, and Donald R. Cressey. 1980. *Social Problems.* New York: Harper and Row.

College Board Advocacy and Policy Center. 2012. *Trends in College Pricing.* New York: CBAPC.

Collins, Daryl, Jonathan Morduch, Stuart Rutherford, and Orlanda Ruthven. 2009. *Portfolios of the Poor: How the World's Poor Live on $2 a Day.* Princeton, NJ: Princeton University Press.

Collins, Patricia Hill. 2000. *Black Feminist Thought: Knowledge, Consciousness, and the Politics of Empowerment.* Revised 10th anniv. 2nd ed. New York: Routledge.

Collins, Randall. 1975. *Conflict Sociology: Toward an Explanatory Sociology.* New York: Academic Press.

———. 1980. "Weber's Last Theory of Capitalism: A Systematization." *American Sociological Review* 45 (December):925–942.

———. 1986. *Weberian Sociological Theory.* New York: Cambridge University Press.

———. 1995. "Prediction in Macrosociology: The Case of the Soviet Collapse." *American Journal of Sociology* 100 (May):1552–1593.

Colucci, Jim. 2008. "All the World's a Screen." *Watch!* (June):50–53.

Commission on Civil Rights. 1976. *Fulfilling the Letter and Spirit of the Law: Desegregation of the Nation's Public Schools.* Washington, DC: U.S. Government Printing Office.

———. 1976. *A Guide to Federal Laws and Regulations Prohibiting Sex Discrimination.* Washington, DC: U.S. Government Printing Office.

———. 1981. *Affirmative Action in the 1980s: Dismantling the Process of Discrimination.* Washington, DC: U.S. Government Printing Office.

Commoner, Barry. 1971. *The Closing Circle.* New York: Knopf.

———. 1990. *Making Peace with the Planet.* New York: Pantheon.

———. 2007. "At 90, an Environmentalist from the 70's Still Has Hope." *New York Times,* June 19, p. D2.

Conley, Dalton. 2010. *Being Black, Living in the Red.* 10th anniversary edition. Berkeley: University of California Press.

Connell, R. W. 1987. *Gendered Power: Society, the Person, and Sexual Politics.* Stanford, CA: Stanford University Press.

———. 2002. *Gender.* Cambridge, UK: Polity Press.

———. 2005. *Masculinities.* 2nd ed. Berkeley: University of California Press.

Conner, Thaddieus, and William A. Taggart. 2009. "The Impact of Gaming on the Indian Nations in New Mexico." *Social Science Quarterly* 90 (March):52–70.

Conrad, Peter, ed. 2009. *The Medicalization of Society: On the Transformation of Human Conditions into Treatable Disorders.* 11th ed. Baltimore, MD: Johns Hopkins University.

———, and Kristin K. Barker. 2010. "The Social Construction of Illness: Key Insights and Policy Implications." *Journal of Health and Social Behavior* 51 (5):567–579.

———, and Valerie Leiter. 2013. *The Sociology of Health and Illness: Critical Perspectives.* 9th ed. New York: Worth.

Cooky, Cheryl, and Nicole M. LaVoi. 2012. "Playing but Losing." *Contexts* (Winter):42–46.

Cooley, Charles. H. 1902. *Human Nature and the Social Order.* New York: Scribner.

Coontz, Stephanie. 2006. "A Pop Quiz on Marriage." *New York Times,* February 19, p. 12.

———. 2012. "The Myth of Male Decline." *New York Times,* September 30 (Section SR), pp. 1, 8.

Cooper, K., S. Day, A. Green, and H. Ward. 2007. "Maids, Migrants and Occupational Health in the London Sex Industry." *Anthropology and Medicine* 14 (April):41–53.

Corbett, Christianne, Catherine Hill, and Andresse St. Rose. 2008. *Where the Girls Are: The Facts about Gender Equity in Education.* Washington, DC: American Association of University Women.

Coser, Lewis A. 1977. *Masters of Sociological Thought: Ideas in Historical and Social Context.* 2nd ed. New York: Harcourt, Brace and Jovanovich.

Coser, Rose Laub. 1984. "American Medicine's Ambiguous Progress." *Contemporary Sociology* 13 (January):9–13.

Côté, James E. 2000. *Arrested Adulthood: The Changing Nature of Identity and Maturity in the Late World.* New York: New York University.

Couch, Carl J. 1996. *Information Technologies and Social Orders.* Edited with an introduction by David R. Maines and Shing-Ling Chien. New York: Aldine de Gruyter.

Council on Foreign Relations. 2009. "Public Opinion on Global Issues." Accessible at www.cfr.org/public-opinion.

Cox, Oliver C. 1948. *Caste, Class, and Race: A Study in Social Dynamics.* Detroit: Wayne State University Press.

Cox, Rachel S. 2003. "Home Schooling Debate." *CQ Researcher* 13 (January 17):25–48.

Crabtree, Steve. 2010. *Religiosity Highest in World's Poorest Nations.* August 31. Accessible at www.gallup.com.

Crosnoe, Robert. 2011. *Fitting in, Standing out: Navigating the Social Challenges of High School to Get an Education.* New York: Cambridge University Press.

Cross, Simon, and Barbara Bagilhole. 2002. "Girls' Jobs for the Boys? Men, Masculinity and Non-Traditional Occupations." *Gender, Work, and Organization* 9 (April):204–226.

Croteau, David, and William Haynes. 2006. *The Business of the Media: Corporate Media and the Public Interest.* 2nd ed. Thousand Oaks, CA: Pine Forge Press.

————, and ————. 2014. *Media/Society: Industries, Images, and Audiences.* 5th ed. Los Angeles: Sage.

Croucher, Sheila L. 2004. *Globalization and Belonging: The Politics of Identity in a Changing World.* Lanham, MD: Rowman and Littlefield.

Crouse, Kelly. 1999. "Sociology of the *Titanic.*" *Teaching Sociology Listserv.* May 24.

Crowe, Jerry, and Valli Herman. 2005. "NBA Lists Fashion Do's and Don'ts." *Los Angeles Times,* October 19, pp. A1, A23.

Cuff, E. C., W. W. Sharrock, and D. W. Francis, eds. 1990. *Perspectives in Sociology.* 3rd ed. Boston: Unwin Hyman.

Currie, Elliot. 1985. *Confronting Crime: An American Challenge.* New York: Pantheon.

————. 1998. *Crime and Punishment in America.* New York: Metropolis Books.

Curry, Timothy Jon. 1993. "A Little Pain Never Hurt Anyone: Athletic Career Socialization and the Normalization of Sports Injury." *Symbolic Interaction* 26 (Fall):273–290.

Cushing-Daniels, Brenda, and Sheila R. Zedlewski. 2008. "Tax and Spending Policy and Economic Mobility." Washington, DC: Economic Mobility Project. Also accessible at www.economic-mobility.org/reports_and_research/literature_reviews?id=0004.

D

Dade, Corey. 2012. "Battle Over Voter ID Laws Intensify." June 2. Accessible at www.wbur.org/npr/154152507/battles-over-voter-id-laws-intensify.

Dahl, Robert A. 1961. *Who Governs?* New Haven, CT: Yale University Press.

Dahrendorf, Ralf. 1958. "Toward a Theory of Social Conflict." *Journal of Conflict Resolution* 2 (June):170–183.

————. 1959. *Class and Class Conflict in Industrial Sociology.* Stanford, CA: Stanford University Press.

Daley, Suzanne. 2013. "Danes Rethink a Welfare State Ample to a Fault." *New York Times,* April 12, pp. 1, 13.

Dalla, Rochelle L., and Wendy C. Gamble. 2001. "Teenage Mothering and the Navajo Reservation: An Examination of Intergovernmental Perceptions and Beliefs." *American Indian Culture and Research Journal* 25 (1):1–19.

Daniel, G. Reginald. 2006. *Race and Multiraciality in Brazil and the United States: Converging Paths?* University Park: Pennsylvania State University Press.

Danziger, Sandra K. 2010. "The Decline of Cash Welfare and Implications for Social Policy and Poverty." *Annual Review of Sociology* 36:523–545.

Darlin, Damon. 2006. "It's O.K to Fall Behind the Technology Curve." *New York Times,* December 30, p. B6.

Darwin, Charles. 1859. *On the Origin of Species.* London: John Murray.

David, Gary. 2004. "Scholarship on Arab Americans Distorted Past 9/11." *Al Jadid* (Winter–Spring):26–27.

————. 2008. "Arab Americans." Pp. 84–87, vol. 1, in *Encyclopedia of Race, Ethnicity, and Society,* edited by Richard T. Schaefer. Thousand Oaks, CA: Sage.

Davidson, Paul. 2012. "More U.S. Service Jobs Go Overseas." *USA Today,* December 7, p. B1.

————. 2013. "Low-paid Workers March for Fairness." *USA Today,* August 29, p. A1.

Davies, Christie. 1989. "Goffman's Concept of the Total Institution: Criticisms and Revisions." *Human Studies* 12 (June):77–95.

Davis, Darren W., and Brian D. Silver. 2003. "Stereotype Threat and Race of Interviewer Knowledge." *American Journal of Political Science* 47 (January):33–45.

Davis, Gerald. 2003. *America's Corporate Banks Are Separated by Just Four Handshakes.* Accessed March 7 (www.bus.umich.edu/research/davis.html).

————. 2004. "American Cronyism: How Executive Networks Inflated the Corporate Bubble." *Contexts* (Summer):34–40.

Davis, Kingsley. 1947. "A Final Note on a Case of Extreme Isolation." *American Journal of Sociology* 52 (March):432–437.

————, and Wilbert E. Moore. 1945. "Some Principles of Stratification." *American Sociological Review* 10 (April):242–249.

Davis, Martha F. 2010. "Abortion Access in the Global Marketplace." *North Carolina Law Review* 88:1657–1685.

Davis, Paul K., and Kim Cragin, eds. 2009. *Social Science for Counterterrorism: Putting the Pieces Together.* Santa Monica, CA: RAND.

De Anda, Roberto M. 2004. *Chicanas and Chicanos in Contemporary Society.* 2nd ed. Lanham, MD: Rowman and Littlefield.

Death Penalty Information Center. 2014. "Number of Executions by State and Region Since 1976." Updated December 18, 2013. Accessed December 20 at http://www.deathpenaltyinfo.org/number-executions-state-and-region-1976.

Deegan, Mary Jo, ed. 1991. *Women in Sociology: A Bio-Biographical Sourcebook.* Westport, CT: Greenwood.

————. 2003. "Textbooks, the History of Sociology, and the Sociological Stock of Knowledge." *Sociological Theory* 21 (November):298–305.

Deflem, Mathieu. 2005. "'Wild Beasts without Nationality': The Uncertain Origins of Interpol, 1898–1910." Pp. 275–285 in *Handbook of Transnational Crime and Justice,* edited by Philip Rerchel. Thousand Oaks, CA: Sage.

Deibert, Ronald J., John Palfrey, Rafal Rohozinski, and Jonathan Zittrain. 2008. *Access Denied: The Practice and Policy of Global Internet Filtering.* Cambridge, MA: MIT Press.

Delaney, Kevin J. 2005. "Big Mother Is Watching." *Wall Street Journal,* November 26, pp. A1, A6.

Della Porta, Donatella, and Sidney Tarrow, eds. 2005. *Transnational Protest and Global Activism.* Lanham, MD: Rowman and Littlefield.

DellaPergola, Sergio. 2012. "Jewish Population of the World." Accessible at www.jewishvirtual-library.org.

DeNavas-Walt, Carmen, Bernadette D. Proctor, and Jessica C. Smith. 2011. *Income, Poverty, and Health Insurance Coverage in the United States: 2010.* Washington, DC: U.S. Government Printing Office.

————. 2013. *Income, Poverty, and Health Insurance Coverage in the United States: 2012.* Washington, DC: U.S. Government Printing Office.

Denny, Charlotte. 2004. "Migration Myths Hold No Fears." *Guardian Weekly,* February 26, p. 12.

Denny, Kathleen E. 2011. "Gender in Context, Content, and Approach: Contemporary Gender Measures in Girl Scout and Boy Scout Handbooks." *Gender and Society* 25 (February): 27–47.

Denzin, Norman K. 2004. "Postmodernism." Pp. 581–583 in *Encyclopedia of Social Theory,* edited by George Ritzer. Thousand Oaks, CA: Sage.

DeParle, Jason. 2009. "The 'W' Word, Re-Engaged." *New York Times,* February 8, Week in Review, p. 1.

Department of Health and Human Services. 2013. "TANF: Total Number of Families." Accessed December 27 at http://www.acf.hhs.gov/sites/default/files/main/2013_family_tan.pdf.

————. 2014. "AFCARS, Report." Accessed January 16 (www.acf.hhs.gov/programs/cb/stats_research/afcars/tar/report20.htm).

Department of Homeland Security. 2010. *Haiti Social Media: Disaster Monitoring Initiative.* January 21. Washington, DC: U.S. Department of Homeland Security.

Department of Justice. 2000. *The Civil Liberties Act of 1988: Redress for Japanese Americans.* Accessed June 29 (www.usdoj.gov/crt/ora/main.html).

————. 2008. "Hate Crime Statistics, 2007." Accessible at www.Fbi.gov/ucr/ucr.htm.

————. 2013. "Crime in the United States, 2013." Accessed December 7, 2013 (www.fbi.gov/about-us/cjis/ucr/crime-in-the-u.s/2013/crime-in-the-u.s.-2013).

Department of Labor. 2013a. "Wage and Hour Department." Accessible at www.dol.gov/whd.

Department of State. 2013. "Tier Placements." Accessed December 13, 2013 (www.state.gov/j/tip/rls/tiprpt/2013/index.htm).

Desai, Rani A., Suchitra Krishnan-Sarin, Dana Cavallo, and Marc N. Potenza. 2010. "Video-Gaming among High School Students: Health Correlates, Gender Differences, and Problematic Gaming." *Pediatrics* 126 (November 15):1414–1424.

Deutsch, Francine M. 2007. "Undoing Gender." *Gender and Society* 21 (February):106–127.

Devitt, James. 1999. *Framing Gender on the Campaign Trail: Women's Executive Leadership and the Press*. New York: Women's Leadership Conference.

Dewan, Shaila. 2013. "New, but Not for Sale." *New York Times,* December 5, pp. B1, B9.

Dickler, Jessica. 2011. "Dig Deep to Buy Titanic Visit." *Chicago Tribune,* June 3, p. 25.

Dickson, Martin. 2013. "Lunch with the FT Muhammad Yunnus: Micro-financial Times." *Financial Times,* October 27, p. 3.

Diefenbach, Donald L., and Mark D. West. 2007. "Television and Attitudes toward Mental Health Issues: Cultivation Analysis and the Third Person Effect." *Journal of Community Psychology* 35 (2):181–195.

Dimrock, Michael, Carroll Doherty, and Rob Suls. 2013. "Uncertainty over Court's Voting Rights Decision, Public Divided over Same-Sex Marriage Rulings." July 1. Accessible at http://www.peoplepress.org.

Dobbin, Frank, and Jiwook Jung. 2010. "Corporate Board Gender Diversity and Stock Performance: The Competence Gap on Institutional Investor Bias?" *North Carolina Law Review* 89.

Dodds, Klaus. 2000. *Geopolitics in a Changing World*. Harlow, UK: Pearson Education.

Domeij, David, and Paul Klein. 2013. "Should Day Care Be Subsidized?" *Review of Economic Studies* 80 (2):568–595.

Domhoff, G. William. 1978. *Who Really Rules? New Haven and Community Power Reexamined*. New Brunswick, NJ: Transaction.

———. 2014. *Who Rules America? The Triumph of the Corporate Rich*. 7th ed. New York: McGraw-Hill.

Domi, Tanya L. 2013. "Women in Combat: Policy Catches up with Reality." *New York Times,* February 8.

Dominick, Joseph R. 2009. *The Dynamics of Mass Communication: Media in the Digital Age*. 10th ed. New York: McGraw-Hill.

Donadio, Rachel. 2012. "'Dear Friends': Pope Takes to Twitter, with an Assist." *New York Times,* December 13, p. A8.

Doress, Irwin, and Jack Nusan Porter. 1977. *Kids in Cults: Why They Join, Why They Stay, Why They Leave*. Brookline, MA: Reconciliation Associates.

Dougherty, Kevin, and Floyd M. Hammack. 1992. "Education Organization." Pp. 535–541 in *Encyclopedia of Sociology,* vol. 2, edited by Edgar F. Borgatta and Marie L. Borgatta. New York: Macmillan.

Downey, Liam, and Brian Hawkins. 2008. "Race, Income, and Environmental Inequality in the United States." *Sociological Perspectives* 50 (4):759–781.

Dube, Arindrajit. 2013a. "The Minimum We Can Do." *New York Times,* December 1 (Section S), p. 5.

———. 2013b. "Minimum Wages and Aggregate Job Growth: Causal Effect or Statistical Artifact?" October 4. Accessible at http://arindube.files.wordpress.com/2013/10/dube_minwagejobgrowth.pdf.

DuBois, W. E. B. [1899] 1995. *The Philadelphia Negro: A Social Study*. Philadelphia: University of Pennsylvania Press.

———. [1900] 1969. "To the Nations of the World." Pp. 19–23 in *An ABC of Color,* edited by W. E. B. DuBois. New York: International Publishers.

———. [1903] 1961. *The Souls of Black Folks: Essays and Sketches*. New York: Fawcett.

———. [1903] 2003. *The Negro Church*. Walnut Creek, CA: AltaMira Press.

———. [1909] 1970. *The Negro American Family*. Atlanta University. Reprinted 1970. Cambridge, MA: MIT Press.

———. [1935] 1962. *Black Reconstruction in America 1860–1880*. New York: Athenaeum.

———. [1940] 1968. *Dusk of Dawn*. New York: Harcourt, Brace. Reprint. New York: Schocken Books.

Duggan, Maeve. 2012. "Politics." November 14. Accessible at http://www.pewinternet.org/Commentary/2012/November/Pew-Internet-Politics.aspx.

Duhigg, Charles, and Keith Bradsher. 2012. "How U.S. Lost Out on iPhone Work." *New York Times,* January 22, p. A1.

Dukić, Vanja, Hedibert F. Lopes, and Nicholas G. Polson. 2011. "Tracking Flu Epidemics Using Google Flu Trends and Particle Learning." Accessible at http://faculty.chicagobooth.edu/nicholas .polson/research/papers/Track.pdf.

Dundas, Susan, and Miriam Kaufman. 2000. "The Toronto Lesbian Family Study." *Journal of Homosexuality* 40 (20):65–79.

Duneier, Mitchell. 1994a. "On the Job, but Behind the Scenes." *Chicago Tribune,* December 26, pp. 1, 24.

———. 1994b. "Battling for Control." *Chicago Tribune,* December 28, pp. 1, 8.

Dunlap, Riley E. 2010. "At 40, Environmental Movement Endures with Less Consensus." April 22. Accessed April 27 (www.gallup.com/poll/127487/Environmental-Movement-Endures-Less-Consensus.aspx?version=print).

———, and Angela G. Mertig. 1991. "The Evolution of the U.S. Environmental Movement from 1970 to 1990: An Overview." *Society of National Resources* 4 (July–September):209–218.

Dunne, Gillian A. 2000. "Opting into Motherhood: Lesbians Blurring the Boundaries and Transforming the Meaning of Parenthood and Kinship." *Gender and Society* 14 (February):11–35.

Durden, T. Elizabeth, and Robert A. Hummer. 2006. "Access to Healthcare among Working-Aged Hispanic Adults in the United States." *Social Science Quarterly* 87 (December):1319–1343.

Durex. 2007. "The Face of Global Sex 2007—First Sex: An Opportunity of a Lifetime." Accessible at http://www.durexnetwork.org/SiteCollectionDocuments/Research%20%20Face%20of%20Global%20Sex%202007.pdf.

Durkheim, Émile. [1893] 1933. *Division of Labor in Society*. Translated by George Simpson. Reprint. New York: Free Press.

———. [1895] 1964. *The Rules of Sociological Method*. Translated by Sarah A. Solovay and John H. Mueller. Reprint. New York: Free Press.

———. [1897] 1951. *Suicide*. Translated by John A. Spaulding and George Simpson. Reprint. New York: Free Press.

———. [1912] 2001. *The Elementary Forms of Religious Life*. A new translation by Carol Cosman. New York: Oxford University Press.

Dwyer, Tim. 2010. *Media Convergence*. New York: McGraw-Hill.

Dyrbye, Liselotte, N. Tait, D. Shanafelt, Charles M. Balch, Daniel Satele, and Julie Freischlag. 2011. "Relationship Between Work-Home Conflicts and Burnout Among American Surgeons." *Archives of Surgery* 146 (February):211–217.

Dzidzienyo, Anani. 1987. "Brazil." In *International Handbook on Race and Race Relations,* edited by Jay A. Sigler. New York: Greenwood Press.

E

Ebaugh, Helen Rose Fuchs. 1988. *Becoming an Ex: The Process of Role Exit*. Chicago: University of Chicago Press.

Eby, Lillian T., Charleen P. Maher, and Marcus M. Butts. 2010. "The Intersection of Work and Family Life: The Role of Affect." *Annual Review of Psychology* 61:599–622.

Eckenwiler, Mark. 1995. "In the Eyes of the Law." *Internet World* (August):74, 76–77.

Economic Mobility Project. 2009. *Findings from a National Survey and Focus Groups on Economic Mobility*. Washington, DC: Pew Charitable Trusts.

The Economist. 2005b. "We Are Tous Québécois." (January 8):39.

———. 2010c. "The Dark Side." (September 11):15.

———. 2011c. "Digging for Victory." (September 24):60.

———. 2012. "Digital Diplomacy: Virtual Relations." (September 22):69.

———. 2012u. "Retail in Developing Countries: Selling Sisters." (November 29). Accessed February 26, 2013 at www.economist.com/blogs/schumpeter/2012/11/retail-developing-countries.

———. 2013a. "Romania: The Nanny State." (August 17):51–52.

———. 2013b. "A Giant Cage." (April 6):S1–S16.

———. 2013c. "Little Peepers Everywhere." (July 21):23–24.

———. 2013d. "Raising the Floor." (December 16):36.

———. 2013e. "Game, Sex and Match." (September 7):61–62.

———. 2013f. "Here, There and Everywhere." (January 19):S1–S20.

Ehrenreich, Barbara. 2001. *Nickel and Dimed: On (Not) Getting By in America.* New York: Metropolitan.

———. 2009. "Is It Now a Crime to Be Poor?" *New York Times,* August 2.

Ehrlich, Paul R. and Katherine Ellison. 2002. "A Looming Threat We Won't Face." *Los Angeles Times,* January 20, p. M6.

Eitzen, D. Stanley. 2009. *Fair and Foul: Beyond the Myths and Paradoxes of Sport.* 4th ed. Lanham, MD: Rowman and Littlefield.

El Nasser, Haya, and Paul Overberg. 2011. "Recession Reshapes Life in the USA." *USA Today,* September 12, p. 3A.

Elgan, Mike. 2011. "How to Pop Your Internet 'Filter Bubble.'" *Computer World* (May 7). Accessed November 11 (www.computerworld.com/s/article/9216484/Elgan_How_to_pop_your_Internet_filter_bubble).

Ellison, Brandy. 2008. "Tracking." Pp. 301–304, vol. 2, in *Encyclopedia of Race, Ethnicity, and Society,* edited by Richard T. Schaefer. Thousand Oaks, CA: Sage.

Ellison, Jesse. 2008. "A New Grip on Life." *Newsweek* 152 (December 15):64.

Ellison, Nicole B., Jeffrey T. Hancock, and Catalina L. Toma. 2012. "Profile as Promise: A Framework for Conceptualizing the Veracity of Self Presentation in Online Dating Profiles." *New Media and Society,* 14 (February):45–62.

Ellison, Nicole, Rebecca Heino, and Jennifer Gibbs. 2006. "Managing Impressions Online; Self-Presentation Processes in the Online Dating Environment." *Journal of Computer-Mediated Communication* 11 (2):415–441.

Ellison, Ralph. 1952. *Invisible Man.* New York: Random House.

Ely, Robin J. 1995. "The Power of Demography: Women's Social Construction of Gender Identity at Work." *Academy of Management Journal* 38 (3):589–634.

Engels, Friedrich [1884] 1959. "The Origin of the Family, Private Property, and the State." Pp. 392–394, excerpted in *Marx and Engels: Basic Writings on Politics and Philosophy,* edited by Lewis Feuer. Garden City, NY: Anchor Books.

Ennis, Sharon R., Merarys Rios-Vargas, and Nora G. Albert. 2011. *The Hispanic Population: 2010.* 2010 Census Brief BR-04. Washington, DC: U.S. Government Printing Office.

Entine, Jon, and Martha Nichols. 1996. "Blowing the Whistle on Meaningless 'Good Intentions.'" *Chicago Tribune,* June 20, sec. 1, p. 21.

Environmental Protection Agency. 2012. Global Greenhouse Gas Data, Figure 3 Total Greenhouse Gas Emissions by Region, from Global Anthropogenic Emissions of Non-CO_2 Greenhouse Gases 1990-2020, EPA Report 430-R-06-003. June 2006. www.epa.gov/climatechange/emissions/globalghg.html.

Environmental Protection Agency. 2012. Global Greenhouse Gas Data. Accessible at http://epa.gov/climatechange/emissions/globalghg.html.

Epstein, Cynthia Fuchs. 1999. "The Major Myth of the Women's Movement." *Dissent* (Fall):83–111.

Epstein, Robert. 2009. "The Truth about Online Dating." *Scientific American* (Special Edition).

Erikson, Kai. 1966. *Wayward Puritans: A Study in the Sociology of Deviance.* New York: Wiley.

Esbenshade, Jill. 2008. "Giving Up Against the Global Economy: New Developments in the Anti-Sweatshops Movement." *Critical Sociology* 34 (3):453–470.

Etaugh, Claire. 2003. "Witches, Mothers and Others: Females in Children's Books." *Hilltopics* (Winter):10–13.

Etzioni, Amitai. 1964. *Modern Organization.* Englewood Cliffs, NJ: Prentice Hall.

———. 1965. *Political Unification.* New York: Holt, Rinehart and Winston.

European Metalworkers' Federation. 2010. "What Is Precious Work?" Accessed March 1, 2011 (www.emf-fem.org).

European PWN. 2012. "Women on Boards: The Inside Story on Norway's 40% Target." Accessed February 22 (www.europeanpwn.net/index.php?article_id=150).

Evergeti, Venetia, and Elisabetta Zontini. 2006. "Introduction: Some Critical Reflections on Social Capital, Migration and Transnational Families." *Ethnic and Racial Studies* 29 (November):1025–1039.

F

Fairtrade Foundation. 2010. "Retail Products." Accessed Jan. 5 (www.fairtrade.org.uk/products/retail_products/default.aspx).

Fallows, Deborah. 2006. *Pew Internet Project Data.* Washington, DC: Pew Internet and American Life Project.

Farley, Melissa, and Victor Malarek. 2008. "The Myth of the Victimless Crime." *New York Times,* March 12, p. A27.

Farr, Grant M. 1999. *Modern Iran.* New York: McGraw-Hill.

Farrell, Amy, and Jack McDevitt. 2010. "Identifying and Measuring Racial Profiling by the Police." *Sociology Compass* 4:77–88.

Feagin, Joe R. 1989. *Minority Group Issues in Higher Education: Learning from Qualitative Research.* Norman: Center for Research on Minority Education, University of Oklahoma.

———, Harnán Vera, and Nikitah Imani. 1996. *The Agony of Education: Black Students at White Colleges and Universities.* New York: Routledge.

Featherman, David L., and Robert M. Hauser. 1978. *Opportunity and Change.* New York: Aeodus.

Federal Bureau of Investigation. 2012. "Crime in the United States 2011." Accessible at http://www.fbi.gov/about-us/cjis/ucr/crime-in-the-u.s/2012/crime-in-the-u.s.-2012.

———. 2013. "2012 Hate Crime Statistics." Accessed December 20 at http://www.fbi.gov/about-us/cjis/ucr/hate-crime/2012.

Felson, David, and Akis Kalaitzidis. 2005. "A Historical Overview of Transnational Crime." Pp. 3–19 in *Handbook of Transnational Crime and Justice,* edited by Philip Reichel. Thousand Oaks, CA: Sage.

Ferber, Abby L., and Michael S. Kimmel. 2008. "The Gendered Face of Terrorism." *Sociology Compass* 2:870–887.

Ferree, Myra Marx, and David A. Merrill. 2000. "Hot Movements, Cold Cognition: Thinking about Social Movements in Gendered Frames." *Contemporary Society* 29 (May):454–462.

Feuer, Lewis S. 1989. *Marx and Engels: Basic Writings on Politics and Philosophy.* New York: Anchor Books.

Fields, Jason. 2004. "America's Families and Living Arrangements: 2003." *Current Population Reports,* ser. P-20, no. 553. Washington, DC: U.S. Government Printing Office.

Fieser, Ezra. 2009. "What Price for Good Coffee?" *Time,* October 5, pp. 61–62.

Fiji TV. 2012. Home Page. Accessed January 10 (www.fijitv.com.fj).

File, Thom. 2013. "The Diversifying Electorate-Voting Rates by Race and Hispanic Origin in 2012 (and Other Recent Elections)." Current Population Survey P20-568. Accessible at http://www.census.gov.

Fine, Gary C. 1987. *With the Boys: Little League Baseball and Preadolescent Culture.* Chicago: University of Chicago Press.

———. 2008. " Robbers Cave." Pp. 1163–1164, vol. 3, in *Encyclopedia of Race, Ethnicity, and Society,* edited by Richard T. Schaefer. Thousand Oaks, CA: Sage.

Finkel, Steven E., and James B. Rule. 1987. "Relative Deprivation and Related Psychological Theories of Civil Violence: A Critical Review." *Research in Social Movements* 9:47–69.

Fiola, Jan. 2008. "Brazil." Pp. 200–204, vol. 2, in *Encyclopedia of Race, Ethnicity, and Society,* edited by Richard T. Schaefer. Thousand Oaks, CA: Sage.

Fiss, Peer C., and Paul M. Hirsch. 2005. "The Discourse of Globalization: Framing of an Emerging Concept." *American Sociological Review* (February):29–52.

Fitzgerald, Kathleen J. 2008. "White Privilege." Pp. 1403–1405, vol. 3, in *Encyclopedia of Race, Ethnicity, and Society,* edited by Richard T. Schaefer. Thousand Oaks, CA: Sage.

Fjellman, Stephen M. 1992. *Vinyl Leaves: Walt Disney World and America.* Boulder, CO: Westview Press.

Flacks, Richard. 1971. *Youth and Social Change.* Chicago: Markham.

Fletcher, Connie. 1995. "On the Line: Women Cops Speak Out." *Chicago Tribune Magazine,* February 19, pp. 14–19.

Flores, Glenn, M. Abreu, C. P. Barone, R. Bachur, and H. Lin. 2012. "Errors of Medical Interpretation and Their Potential Clinical Consequences: A Comparison of Professional versus Ad Hoc versus No Interpreters." *Annals of Emergency Medicine* 60 (5):545–553.

Florida, Richard. 2011. "Why Crime Is Down in America's Cities." *The Atlantic* (July). Accessible at www.theatlantic.com.

Fonseca, Felicia. 2008. "Dine College on Quest to Rename Navajo Cancer Terms." *News from Indian Country* 22 (January 7):11.

Forbes. 2012. "Leaderboard: Billionaire Box Scores." 189 (March 26):34.

Forte, Maximilian. 2010. "HTS' Other Handlers." May 20. Accessible at http://zeroanthropology.net.

Foucault, Michel. 1978. *The History of Sexuality.* Vol. 1, An Introduction. New York: Vintage.

Fowler, Geoffrey A. 2013. "Woman Leads Prayer at Mormon Event." *Wall Street Journal,* April 8, p. A3.

Fox, Porter. 2014. "The End of Snow?" *New York Times,* February 9 (Section SR), pp. 1, 6.

Francis, David. 2010. "Homeschoolers Seek Asylum in US." *Christian Science Monitor,* March 8, p. 12.

Frandsen, Ronald J., Dave Naglich, Gene A. Lasuver, and Allina D. Lee. 2013. *Background Checks for Firearm Transfers, 2010— Statistical Tables.* February 2013. NCJ 238226. Washington, DC: Bureau of Justice Statistics.

Franke, Richard Herbert, and James D. Kaul. 1978. "The Hawthorne Experiments: First Statistical Interpretation." *American Sociological Review* 43 (October):623–643.

Franklin, John Hope, and Evelyn Brooks Higginbotham. 2011. *From Slavery to Freedom.* 9th ed. New York: McGraw-Hill.

Freese, Jeremy. 2008. "Genetics and the Social Science Explanation of Individual Outcomes." *American Journal of Sociology* 114 (Suppl.): 51–535.

Freidson, Eliot. 1970. *Profession of Medicine.* New York: Dodd, Mead.

French, Howard W. 2004. "China's Textbooks Twist and Omit History." *New York Times,* December 6, p. A10.

Freudenburg, William R. 2005. "Seeing Science, Courting Conclusions: Reexamining the Intersection of Science, Corporate Cash, and the Law." *Sociological Forum* 20 (March):3–33.

Freundlich, Madelyn, and Joy Kim Lieberthal. 2000. "The Gathering of the First Generation of Adult Korean Adoptees: Adoptees' Perceptions of International Adoption." Accessible at www.adoptioninstitute.org/proed/korfindings.html.

Frey, Benedikt, and Michael Osborne. 2013. "The Future of Employment: How Susceptible Are Jobs to Computerisation?" September 17, 2013. Working paper accessible at http://www.oxfordmartin.ox.ac.uk/downloads/academic/The_Future_of_Employment.pdf.

Frey, William H. 2011. *A Demographic Tipping Point among America's Three-Year-Olds.* February 7. Accessible at http://www.brookings.edu/opinions/2011/0207_population_frey.aspx?p=1.

Fridlund, Alan J., Paul Erkman, and Harriet Oster. 1987. "Facial Expressions of Emotion; Review of Literature 1970–1983." Pp. 143–224 in *Nonverbal Behavior and Communication,* 2nd ed., edited by Aron W. Seigman and Stanley Feldstein. Hillsdale, NJ: Erlbaum.

Friedman, Louis. 2010. "NASA's Down-to-Earth Problems." *Star-Telegram* (Fort Worth), March 28. Accessible at http://www.star-telegram.com/2010/03/28/2072608/friedman-nasas-down-to-earth-problem.html.

Friedman, Richard A. 2012. "In Gun Debate, a Misguided Focus on Mental Illness." *New York Times,* December 18, p. D6.

Friends of the Congo. 2011. "Coltan: What You Should Know." Accessed May 21 (www.friendsofthecongo.org/new/coltan.php).

Fudge, Judy, and Rosemary Owens, eds. 2006. *Precarious Work, Women, and the New Economy: The Challenge to Legal Norms.* Oxford, UK: Hart.

Fuentes-Nieva, Ricardo, and Nicholas Galasso. 2014. *Working for the Few: Political Capture and Economic Inequality.* Accessible at http://www.oxfam.org/en/policy/working-for-the-few-economic-inequality.

Fukase, Atsuko, and Kana Inagaki. 2012. "Japan Insider Penalty: $600." *Wall Street Journal,* March 22, p. C2.

Furstenberg, Frank F. 2007. "The Making of the Black Family: Race and Class in Qualitative Studies in the Twentieth Century." *Annual Review of Sociology* 33:429–448.

———, and Andrew Cherlin. 1991. *Divided Families: What Happens to Children When Parents Part.* Cambridge, MA: Harvard University Press.

G

Gailey, Robert. 2007. "As History Repeats Itself, Unexpected Developments Move Us Forward." *Journal of Rehabilitation Research and Development* 44 (4):vii–xiv.

Galbraith, John Kenneth. 1977. *The Age of Uncertainty.* Boston: Houghton Mifflin.

Galea, Sandro, Melissa Tracy, Katherine J. Hoggatt, Charles DiMaggio, and Adam Karpati. 2011. "Estimated Deaths Attributed to Social Factors in the United States." *American Journal of Public Health* 101 (August):1456–1465.

Gallagher, Kevin P. 2009. "Economic Globalization and the Environment." *Annual Review of Environmental Resources* 34:279–304.

Gallup. 2011a. *Religion.* Accessed March 27 (www.gallup.com).

———. 2012. "Party Affiliation." Accessed March 8 (www.gallup.com/poll/15370/Party-Affiliation.aspx).

Gallup Opinion Index. 1978. "Religion in America, 1977–1978." 145 (January).

Gans, Herbert J. 1995. *The War against the Poor: The Underclass and Antipoverty Policy.* New York: Basic Books.

Garamone, Jim. 1999. "The Challenge." American Forces Press Service. January 12, 1999. Accessed January 24, 2014 at http://www.defense.gov/specials/basic/.

Garcia-Moreno, Claudia, Henrica A. F. M. Jansen, Mary Ellsberg, Lori Heise, and Charlotte Watts. 2005. *WHO Multi-Country Study on Women's Health and Domestic Violence against Women.* Geneva, Switzerland: WHO.

Garfinkel, Harold. 1956. "Conditions of Successful Degradation Ceremonies." *American Journal of Sociology* 61 (March):420–424.

Garner, Roberta. 1996. *Contemporary Movements and Ideologies.* New York: McGraw-Hill.

———. 1999. "Virtual Social Movements." Presented at Zaldfest: A conference in honor of Mayer Zald. September 17, Ann Arbor, MI.

Garrett-Peters, Raymond. 2009. "'If I Don't Have to Work Anymore, Who Am I?': Job Loss and Collaborative Self-Concept Repair." *Journal of Contemporary Ethnography* 38 (5):547–583.

Gasparro, Annie, and Julie Jargon. 2012. "McDonald's to Go Vegetarian India." *Wall Street Journal,* September 5, p. B7.

Gates, Gary J. 2012. "LGBT VOTE 2012." Los Angeles: The Williams Institute. Accessible at www.law.ucla.edu/williamsinstitute.

Gaudin, Sharon. 2009. "Facebook Has Whopper of a Problem with Burger King Campaign." *Computerworld,* January 15.

Gay, Lesbian and Straight Education Network. 2012. "About GLSEN." Accessed March 1 (www.glsen.org).

Gecas, Viktor. 2004. "Socialization, Sociology of." Pp. 14525–14530 in *International Encyclopedia of the Social and Behavioral Sciences,* edited by Neil J. Smelser and Paul B. Baltes. Cambridge, MA: Elsevier.

Gelles, David. 2011. "It's All About the Algorithm." *Financial Times* (July 30).

General Social Survey. 2012. "GSS General Social Survey." Accessed January 25 (www3.norc.org/GSS+Website).

Gentile, Carmen. 2009. "Student Fights Record of 'Cyberbullying.'" *New York Times,* February 8, p. 20.

Gentleman, Amelia. 2006. "Bollywood Captivated by the Call Centre Culture." *Guardian Weekly,* June 2, p. 17.

Gerth, H. H., and C. Wright Mills. 1958. *From Max Weber: Essays in Sociology.* New York: Galaxy.

Gertner, Jon. 2005. "Our Ratings, Ourselves." *New York Times Magazine,* April 10, pp. 34–41, 56, 58, 64–65.

Gibbs, Jennifer L., Nicole B. Ellison, and Chih-Hui Lai. 2011. "First Comes Love, Then Comes Google: An Investigation of Uncertainty Reduction Strategies and Self-Disclosure in Online Dating." *Communication Research* 38. Accessible at https://www.msu.edu/~nellison/GibbsEllisonLai_2011_FirstComesLove.pdf.

Gibbs, Nancy. 2009. "What Women Want Now." *Time* 174 (16):24–33.

Giddens, Anthony. 1991. *Modernity and Self-Identity: Self and Society in the Late Modern Age.* Cambridge, UK: Polity.

Giddings, Paul J. 2008. *Ida: A Sword among Lions.* New York: Amistad.

Gill, Adrian A. 2011. "Dubai on Empty." *Vanity Fair* (April). Accessible at http://www.vanityfair.com/culture/features/2011/04/dubai-201104.

Gilley, Brian Joseph. 2006. *Becoming Two-Spirit: Gay Identity and Social Acceptance in Indian Country.* Lincoln: University of Nebraska Press.

Gillum, Jack. 2011. "How USA Today Analyzed Border Crime Trends." *USA Today,* July 16, p. 7A.

Giordano, Peggy C. 2003. "Relationships in Adolescence." Pp. 257–281 in *Annual Review of Sociology, 2003,* edited by Karen S. Cook and John Hagan. Palo Alto, CA: Annual Reviews.

Girl Scouts of the USA. 2001. *Junior Girl Scout Badge Book.* New York: Girl Scouts of the United States of America.

Giroux, Henry A. 1988. *Schooling and the Struggle for Public Life: Critical Pedagogy in the Modern Age.* Minneapolis: University of Minnesota Press.

Gitlin, Todd. 2002. *Media Unlimited: How the Torrent of Images and Sounds Overwhelms Our Lives.* New York: Henry Holt.

Glazer, Sarah. 2013. "Plagiarism and Cheating: Are They Becoming More Acceptable to the Internet Age?" *CQ Researcher* 23 (January 4).

Glazer, Susan. 2010. "Evaluating Microfinance." *EQ Global Research* 4 (April).

Goering, Laurie. 2008b. "Outsourced to India: Stress." *Chicago Tribune,* April 20, pp. 1, 18.

Goffman, Erving. 1959. *The Presentation of Self in Everyday Life.* New York: Doubleday.

———. 1961. *Asylums: Essays on the Social Situation of Mental Patients and Other Inmates.* Garden City, NY: Doubleday.

———. 1963. *Stigma: Notes on Management of Spoiled Identity.* Englewood Cliffs, NJ: Prentice Hall.

Gold, Rachel Benson, and Elizabeth Nash. 2012. "Troubling Trend: More States Hostile to Abortion Rights as Middle Ground Shrinks." *Guttmacher Policy Review* 15 (Winter):14–19

Goldman, David. 2012. "Are Landlines Doomed?" CNN Money. April 10. Accessed April 11 (http://money.cnn.com/2012/04/10/technology/att-verizon-landlines/index.htm).

Gomez, Alan, Jack Gillum, and Kevin Johnson. 2011. "On U.S. Side, Cities Are Havens from Drug Wars." *USA Today,* July 15, pp. 1A, 6A–7A.

Goode, Erica, and Jack Healy. 2013. "Focus on Mental Health Laws to Curb Violence Is Unfair, Some Say." *New York Times,* February 1, p. A13.

Gorney, Cynthia. 2014. "Far from Home." *National Geographic* (February):7–95.

Gottfredson, Michael, and Travis Hirschi. 1990. *A General Theory of Crime.* Palo Alto, CA: Stanford University Press.

Gough, Margaret, and Alexandra Killewald. 2011. "Unemployment in Families: The Case of Housework." *Journal of Marriage and Family* 73 (October):1085–1100.

Gould, Elise. 2007. "The Health-Finance Debate Reaches a Fever Pitch." *Chronicle of Higher Education,* April 13, pp. B14, B15.

Gould, Larry A. 2002. "Indigenous People Policing Indigenous People: The Potential Psychological and Cultural Costs." *Social Science Journal* 39:171–188.

Government Accountability Office. 2003. "Women's Earnings: Work Patterns Partially Explain Difference between Men's and Women's Earnings." Washington, DC: U.S. Government. Printing Office.

Grady, Sarah, Stacy Bielick, and Susan Aud. 2010. *Trends in the Use of School Choice: 1993 to 2010.* Washington, DC: U.S. Government Printing Office.

Graells-Garrido, Eduardo, Mounia Lalmas, and Daniele Quercia. 2013. "Data Portraits: Connecting People of Opposing Views." Submitted November 19. Accessed December 1 at http://arxiv.org/abs/1311.4658.

Gramsci, Antonio. 1929. *Selections from the Prison Notebooks.* Edited and translated by Quintin Hoare and Geoffrey Nowell Smith. London: Lawrence and Wishort.

Grattet, Ryken. 2011. "Societal Reactions to Deviance." *Annual Review of Sociology* 37:185–204.

Grazian, David. 2010. *Mix It Up: Popular Culture, Mass Media, and Society.* New York: Norton.

Greeley, Andrew M. 1989. "Protestant and Catholic: Is the Analogical Imagination Extinct?" *American Sociological Review* 54 (August):485–502.

Greenhouse, Steven. 2008a. "Unions Look for New Life in the World of Obama." *New York Times,* December 29, p. B6.

———. 2008b. "Millions of Jobs of a Different Collar." *New York Times,* March 26.

———. 2009. "In America, Labor Has an Unusually Long Fuse." *New York Times,* April 5, Week in Review News, p. 3.

———. 2013. "On Register's Other Side, Little Money to Spend." *New York Times,* November 29, pp. B1, B4.

Gregor, Alison. 2013. "A NORC, Up Close and Personal." *New York Times,* May 5, p. 8.

Gregory, Katherine. 2007. "Drawing a Virtual Gun?" Pp. 98–111 in *Open Fire: Understanding Global Gun Cultures,* edited by Charles Fruehling Springwood. New York: Berg.

Gross, Lynne Schaefer. 2013. *Electronic Media: An Introduction.* 11th ed. New York: McGraw-Hill.

Groza, Victor, Daniela F. Ileana, and Ivor Irwin. 1999. *A Peacock or a Crow: Stories, Interviews, and Commentaries on Romanian Adoptions.* Euclid, OH: Williams Custom Publishing.

Guest, Robert. 2011. "Tribes Still Matter." *The Economist* (January 22):17–18.

Guo, Guang, Michael E. Roettger, and Tianji Cai. 2008. "The Integration of Genetic Propensities into Social-Control Models of Delinquency and Violence among Male Youths." *American Sociological Review* 73 (August):543–568.

Gurbuz, Mustafa, and Gulsum Gurbuz-Kucuksari. 2009. "Between Sacred Codes and Secular Consumer Society: The Practice of Headscarf Adoption among American College Girls." *Journal of Muslim Minority Affairs* 29 (September):387–399.

Gutiérrez, Gustavo. 1990. "Theology and the Social Sciences." Pp. 214–225 in *Liberation Theology at the Crossroads: Democracy or Revolution?* edited by Paul E. Sigmund. New York: Oxford University Press.

Guttmacher Institute. 2008. *Facts on Induced Abortion Worldwide.* New York: Guttmacher.

———. 2014. "More State Abortion Restrictions Were Enacted in 2011–2013 than in the Entire Previous Decade." January 2. Accessed at http://www.guttmacher.org/media/inthenews/2014/01/02/index.html?utm_source=feedburner&utm_medium=feed&utm_campaign=Feed%3A+Guttmacher+(New+from+the+Guttmacher+Institute).

H

Haas, Steven A., David R. Schaefer, and Olga Kornienko. 2010. "Health and the Structure of Adolescent Social Networks." *Journal of Health and Social Behavior* 5 (4):424–439.

Hacker, Andrew. 1964. "Power to Do What?" Pp. 134–146 in *The New Sociology,* edited by Irving Louis Horowitz. New York: Oxford University Press.

Hacker, Helen Mayer. 1951. "Women as a Minority Group." *Social Forces* 30 (October): 60–69.

———. 1974. "Women as a Minority Group, Twenty Years Later." Pp. 124–134 in *Who Discriminates against Women?* edited by Florence Denmark. Beverly Hills, CA: Sage.

Hall, Jeremiah. 2013. "Charities Latch onto 'Crowdsourcing.'" *Christian Science Monitor Weekly* (November 25):33–34.

Hallinan, Maureen T. 1997. "The Sociological Study of Social Change." *American Sociological Review* 62 (February):1–11.

Halualani, Rona Tamiko. 2002. *In the Name of Hawaiians: Native Identities and Cultural Politics.* Minneapolis: University of Minnesota Press.

Hamm, Steve. 2007. "Children of the Web." *BusinessWeek,* July 2, pp. 50–56, 58.

Haq, Husna. 2011. "How Marriage Is Faring." *Christian Science Monitor,* February 14, p. 21.

Harlow, Harry F. 1971. *Learning to Love.* New York: Ballantine.

Harman, Donna. 2009. "Dubai's Glitz Lost in Grim Life." *Christian Science Monitor,* May 3, p. 8.

Harmon, Katherine. 2011. "How Obesity Spreads in Social Networks." May 5. Accessible at http://www.scientificamerican.com/article.cfm?id=social-spread-obesity.

Harrington, Michael. 1980. "The New Class and the Left." Pp. 123–138 in *The New Class,* edited by B. Bruce Briggs. Brunswick, NJ: Transaction.

Harrisinteractive. 2008. "Cell Phone Usage Continues to Increase." Accessed January 13 (www.harrisinteractive.com).

Haub, Carl. 2010. "2010 World Population Data Sheet." Washington, DC: Population Reference Bureau.

———, and Toshiko Kaneda. 2013. *World Population Data Sheet 2013*. Accessible at http://www.prb.org/Publications/Datasheets/2013/2013-world-population-data-sheet.aspx.

Hauser, Orlee. 2011. "'We Rule the Base Because We're Few': 'Lone Girls' in Israel's Military." *Journal of Contemporary Ethnography* 40 (6):623–651.

Haviland, William A., Harald E. L. Prins, Dana Walrath, and Bunny McBride. 2008. *Cultural Anthropology—The Human Challenge.* 12th ed. Belmont, CA: Wadsworth.

Hawdon, James, and John Ryan. 2011. "Social Relations that Generate and Sustain Solidarity after a Mass Tragedy." *Social Forces* 89 (4):1383–1384.

Hay, Andrew. 2009. "Spain's New Middle Classes Slip into Poverty." *Reuters.* April 8. Accessed May 11, 2011 (http://uk.reuters.com/article/email/ioUKTRE537029200904).

Hayden, H. Thomas. 2004. "What Happened at Abu Ghraib." Accessed August 7 (www.military.com).

Health Cost Institute. 2013. "The Impact of the Mental Health Parity and Addiction Equity Act on Inpatient Admissions." February. Issue Brief #5. Accessed May 15 at http://www.healthcostinstitute.org/files/HCCI-Mental-Health-Parity-Issue-Brief.pdf.

Heckert, Druann, and Amy Best. 1997. "Ugly Duckling to Swan: Labeling Theory and the Stigmatization of Red Hair." *Symbolic Interaction* 20 (4):365–384.

Hedley, R. Alan. 1992. "Industrialization in Less Developed Countries." Pp. 914–920, vol. 2, in *Encyclopedia of Sociology,* edited by Edgar F. Borgatta and Marie L. Borgatta. New York: Macmillan.

Heilman, Madeline E. 2001. "Description and Prescription: How Gender Stereotypes Prevent Women's Ascent up the Organizational Ladder." *Journal of Social Issues* 57 (4):657–674.

Heisig, Jan Paul. 2011. "Who Does More Housework: Rich or Poor? A Comparison of 33 Countries." *American Sociological Review* 76 (1):74–99.

Hellmich, Nanci. 2001. "TV's Reality: No Vast American Waistlines." *USA Today,* October 8, p. D7.

Hendershott, Ann. 2002. *The Politics of Deviance.* San Francisco: Encounter Books.

Hengeveld, Rob. 2012. *Wasted World: How Our Consumption Challenges the Planet.* Chicago: University of Chicago Press.

Hernandez, Elaine M., and Christopher Uggen. 2012. "Institutions, Politics, and Mental Health Parity." *Society and Mental Health* 2 (3):154–171.

Hertz, Rosanna. 2006. *Single by Chance. Mothers by Choice.* New York: Oxford University Press.

Hewlett, Sylvia Ann, and Carolyn Buck Luce. 2005. "Off-Ramps and On-Ramps: Keeping Talented Women on the Road to Success." *Harvard Business Review* (March):43–53.

Higgins, Chris A., Linda E. Duxbury, and Sean T. Lyons. 2010. "Coping with Overload in Stress: Men and Women in Dual-Earner Families." *Journal of Marriage and Family* 72 (August):847–859.

Hill, Michael R., and Susan Hoecker-Drysdale, eds. 2001. *Harriet Martineau: Theoretical and Methodological Perspectives.* New York: Routledge.

Hillsman, Sally T. 2013. "Gun Violence: Lifting the Shackles on Federal Firearms Research." *Footnotes* (January):2, 4.

Hira, Ron. 2008. "An Overview of the Offshoring of U.S. Jobs." Pp. 14–15 in Marlene A. Lee and Mark Mather. "U.S. Labor Force Trends." *Population Bulletin* 63 (June).

Hirschi, Travis. 1969. *Causes of Delinquency.* Berkeley: University of California Press.

Hirst, Paul, and Grahame Thompson. 1996. *Globalization in Question: The International Economy and the Possibilities of Governance.* Cambridge, UK: Polity Press.

Hitlin, Steven, and Jane Allyn Piliavin. 2004. "Values: Reviving a Dormant Concept." Pp. 359–393 in *Annual Review of Sociology, 2004,* edited by Karen S. Cook and John Hagan. Palo Alto, CA: Annual Reviews.

Hixson, Lindsay, Bradford B. Hepler, and Myoung Ouk Kim. 2012. *Islander Population: 2010.* May 2012. C2010BR-12. Washington, DC: U.S. Government Printing Office.

Hochschild, Arlie Russell. 1990. "The Second Shift: Employed Women Are Putting in Another Day of Work at Home." *Utne Reader* 38 (March –April):66–73.

———. 2005. *The Commercialization of Intimate Life: Notes from Home and Work.* Berkeley: University of California Press.

———, with Anne Machung. 2012. *The Second Shift: Working Parents and the Revolution at Home.* Revised with a new Afterword. New York: Penguin.

Hoeffel, Elizabeth M., Sonya Rastogi, Myoung Ouk Kim, and Hasan Shahid. 2012. *The Asian Population: 2010.* C2101BR-11. Washington, DC: U.S. Government Printing Office.

Holden, Constance. 1980. "Identical Twins Reared Apart." *Science* 207 (March 21): 1323–1328.

———. 1987. "The Genetics of Personality." *Science* 257 (August 7):598–601.

Hollingshead, August B. 1975. *Elmtown's Youth and Elmtown Revisited.* New York: Wiley.

Holmes, Mary. 2009. "Commuter Couples and Distance Relationships: Living Apart Together." Sloan Work and Family Research Network. Accessible at http://wfnetwork.bc.edu/encyclopedia_entry.php?id=15551&area=all.

Homans, George C. 1979. "Nature versus Nurture: A False Dichotomy." *Contemporary Sociology* 8 (May):345–348.

Home School Legal Defense Association. 2005. "State Laws" and "Academic Statistics on Homeschooling." Accessed May 12 (www.hslda.org).

Hondagneu-Sotelo, Pierrette, ed. 2003. *Gender and U.S. Immigration: Contemporary Trends.* Berkeley: University of California Press.

hooks, bell. 1994. *Feminist Theory: From Margin to Center.* 2nd ed. Boston: South End Press.

Hopper, Nate, and Jen Oritz. 2012. "The Appalling Frequency of the Shooting Spree." *New York* (July 30):7.

Horgan, John. 1993. "Eugenics Revisited." *Scientific American* 268 (June):122–128, 130–133.

Horkheimer, Max, and Theodore Adorno. [1944] 2002. *Dialectic of Enlightenment.* Palo Alto, CA: Stanford University Press.

Horowitz, Helen Lefkowitz. 1987. *Campus Life.* Chicago: University of Chicago Press.

Horwitz, Allan V. 2002. *Creating Mental Illness.* Chicago: University of Chicago Press.

Hosokawa, William K. 1969. *Nisei: The Quiet Americans.* New York: Morrow.

Houle, Jason N. 2013. "Disparities in Debt: Parents' Socioeconomic Resources and Young Adult Student Loan Debt." *Sociology of Education* 20 (10):1–17.

Houser, Trevor, Shashank Mohamad, and Robert Heilmayer. 2009. *A Green Global Recovery? Assessing U.S. Economic Stimulus and the Prospects for International Coordination.* Washington, DC: World Resources Institute of Peterson Institute for International Economics.

Howard, Judith A. 1999. "Border Crossings between Women's Studies and Sociology." *Contemporary Sociology* 28 (September): 525–528.

Howard, Michael C. 1989. *Contemporary Cultural Anthropology.* 3rd ed. Glenview, IL: Scott, Foresman.

Howard, Russell D., and Reid L. Sawyer. 2003. *Terrorism and Counterterrorism: Understanding the New Security Environment.* Guilford, CT: McGraw-Hill/Dushkin.

Huang, Gary. 1988. "Daily Addressing Ritual: A Cross-Cultural Study." Presented at the annual meeting of the American Sociological Association, Atlanta.

Hughes, Everett. 1945. "Dilemmas and Contradictions of Status." *American Journal of Sociology* 50 (March):353–359.

Human Genome Project. 2012. "Human Genome Project Information." Accessed April 4 (www.ornl.gov/sci/techresources/Human_Genome/home.shtml).

Human Rights Campaign. 2014. "Marriage Center: Marriage Recognition." As of January 2014. Accessible at http://www.hrc.org/campaigns/marriage-center.

Humes, Karen R., Nicholas A. Jones, and Roberto R. Ramirez. 2011. *Overview of Race and Hispanic Origin: 2010.* 2010 Census Brief

BR-02. Accessible at http://www.census.gov/prod/cen2010/briefs/c2010br-02.pdf.

Hunt, Darnell. 1997. *Screening the Los Angeles "Riots": Race, Seeing, and Resistance.* New York: Cambridge University Press.

Hunter, Herbert M., ed. 2000. *The Sociology of Oliver C. Cox: New Perspectives: Research in Race and Ethnic Relations,* vol. 2. Stamford, CT: JAI Press.

Hunter, James Davison. 1991. *Culture Wars: The Struggle to Define America.* New York: Basic Books.

Huntington, Samuel P. 1993. "The Clash of Civilizations?" *Foreign Affairs* 72 (Summer):22–49.

Hur, Song-Woo. 2011. "Mapping South Korean Women's Movements During and After Democratization: Shifting Identities." *East Asian Social Movements,* edited by J. Broadbent and V. Brockman.

Hurn, Christopher J. 1985. *The Limits and Possibilities of Schooling.* 2nd ed. Boston: Allyn and Bacon.

Hussar, William J., and Tabitha M. Bailey. 2011. *Projections of Education Statistics to 2019.* Washington, DC: National Center for Education Statistics.

———, and ———. 2013. *Projection of Education Statistics to 2021.* Washington, DC: U.S. Government Printing Office. Accessible at http://nces.ed.gov/programs/projections/projections2021/.

Hyde, Janet Shibley. 2005. "The Gender Similarities Hypothesis." *American Psychologist* 60 (6):581–592.

I

Igo, Sarah E. 2007. *The Average American: Surveys, Citizens, and the Making of a Mass Public.* Cambridge, MA: Harvard University Press.

Immervoll, Herwig, and David Barber. 2005. *Can Parents Afford to Work? Childcare Costs, Tax-Benefit Policies and Work Incentives.* Paris: Organisation for Economic Co-Operation and Development.

Inglehart, Ronald, and Wayne E. Baker. 2000. "Modernization, Cultural Change, and the Persistence of Traditional Values." *American Sociological Review* 65 (February):19–51.

Institute for Economics and Peace. 2014. "Global Peace Index 2013." June 11, 2013. Accessed January 26, 2014 (www.visionofhumanity.org/gpi/results/world-map.php).

Interbrand. 2013. "Best Global Brands 2013." Accessible at http://www.interbrand.com/en/best-global-brands/2013/Best-Global-Brands-2013.aspx.

Interface Group Report (Virginia Tech) 2007. *Presidential Internal Review.* Blacksburg, Virginia Polytechnic Institute and State University.

International Gay and Lesbian Human Rights Commission. 2010. Home Page. Accessed February 11 (www.iglhrc.org).

International Institute for Democracy and Electoral Assistance. 2014. "Voter Turnout Database—Custom Query." Accessed January 26 (http://www.idea.int/vt/viewdata.cfm#).

International Monetary Fund. 2000. *World Economic Outlook: Asset Prices and the Business Cycle.* Washington, DC: International Monetary Fund.

International Telecommunication Union. 2012. Global Technology Development Figures. October 11. Accessed November 14, 2013 at http://www.itu.int/net/pressoffice/press_releases/2012/70.aspx#.UoUJgKW50pE.

International Trade Union Confederation. 2009. "Davos: World Unions Call for Action against Corporate Grand Theft." Accessed January 31 at www.ituc-csi.org/spip.php?article2736.

Internet Crime Complaint Center. 2012. *The 2011 Internet Crime Report.* Washington, DC: The National White Collar Crime Center. Accessible at www.ic3.gov/media/annualreport/2011_IC3Report.pdf.

Internet World Stats. 2014. "Usage and Population Statistics" and "Internet World Users by Language." Updated on March 28. Accessed March 29 (www.internetworldstats.com).

Inter-Parliamentary Union. 2014. *Women in National Parliaments.* November 1, 2013. Accessed January 26, 2014 (www.ipu.org).

Ironside, Virginia. 2011. "Romania's Orphanages: Locking the Past Away." *The Independent* (UK) (November 29). Accessed September 25, 2012 at http://www.independent.co.uk/life-style/health-and-families/features/romanias-orphanages-locking-the-past-away-6269173.html.

Isaacs, Julia B. 2007b. *Economic Mobility of Men and Women.* Washington, DC: Economic Mobility Project.

———, Isabel V. Sawhill, and Ron Haskins. 2008. *Getting Ahead or Losing Ground: Economic Mobility in America.* Washington, DC: Pew Charitable Trusts.

ITOPF. 2006. "Statistics: International Tanker Owners Pollution Federation Limited." Accessed May 2 (www.itopf.com/stats.html).

J

Jackson, Philip W. 1968. *Life in Classrooms.* New York: Holt.

Jacobs, Andres. 2010. "As China's Economy Grows, Pollution Worsens Despite New Efforts to Control It." *New York Times,* July 29, p. A4.

Jacobs, Tom. 2009. "Hot Men of the Links." *Miller-McCune* (May–June):79.

Jacobsen, Linda A., Mark Mather, and Genevieve Dupuis. 2012. "Household Change in the United States." *Population Bulletin* 67 (September).

Jaffee, Daniel. 2012. "Weak Coffee: Certification and Co-Optation in the Fair Trade Movement." *Social Problems* 59 (1):94–116.

Jain, Saranga, and Kathleen Kurz. 2007. *New Insights on Preventing Child Marriage: A Global Analysis of Factors and Programs.* Washington, DC: International Center for Research on Women.

Jäntti, Markus. 2009. "Mobility in the United States in Comparative Perspectives." *Focus* 26 (Fall).

Japan Aisaika Organization. 2012. "Aisaika Organization Prospectus." Accessed January 15 (www.aisaika.org/en/prospectus.html).

Jasper, James M. 1997. *The Art of Moral Protest: Culture, Biography, and Creativity in Social Movements.* Chicago: University of Chicago Press.

Jayson, Sharon. 2009. "Holding Up the Value of Marriage." *USA Today,* February 18, pp. D1, D2.

———. 2013. "The End of 'Online Dating.'" *USA Today,* February 14, pp. 1A, 2A.

Jenkins, Henry. 2006. *Convergence Culture: Where Old and New Media Collide.* New York: New York University Press.

Jensen, Gary F. 2005. "Social Organization Theory." In *Encyclopedia of Criminology,* edited by Richard A. Wright and J. Mitchell Miller. Chicago: Fitzrog Dearborn.

Jervis, Rick. 2008. "New Orleans Homicides up 30% over 2006 Level." *USA Today,* January 3, p. 3A.

Jesella, Kara. 2008. "Blogging's Glass Ceiling." *New York Times,* July 27, Style section, pp. 1, 2.

Joas, Hans, and Wolfgang Knöbl. 2009. *Social Theory: Twenty Introductory Lectures.* Cambridge: Cambridge University Press.

John, Robert. 2012. "The Native American Family." Pp. 361–410 in *Ethnic Families in America: Patterns and Variations.* 5th ed., edited by Roosevelt Wright, Jr., Charles H. Mindel, Thanh Van Tran, and Robert W. Halsenstein. Upper Saddle River, NJ: Pearson.

Johnson, Benton. 1975. *Functionalism in Modern Sociology: Understanding Talcott Parsons.* Morristown, NJ: General Learning.

Johnson, Bobbie. 2010. "Privacy No Longer a Social Norm, Says Facebook Founder." January 10. Accessed December 2, 2013 at http://www.theguardian.com/technology/2010/jan/11/facebook-privacy.

Johnson, Ian. 2012. "A Promise to Tackle China's Problems, but Few Hints of a Shift in Path." *New York Times,* November 16, p. A19.

Jones, Jeffrey. 2013. "Americans Still Divided on Energy-Environment Trade-Off." April 10, 2013. Accessible at http://www.gallup.com/poll/161729/americans-divided-energy-environment-trade-off.aspx.

Jones-Puthoff, Alexa. 2013. *Is the U.S. Population Getting Older and More Diverse?* June 14. Accessible at http://www.census.gov/newsroom/cspan/pop_diverse/.

Jordan, Mary. 2007. "The New Face of Global Mormonism." *Washington Post National Weekly Edition* (November 26):20–21.

Jost, Kenneth. 2008. "Women in Politics." *CQ Researcher* 18 (March 21).

Julian, Tiffany, and Robert Kominski. 2011. *Education and Synthetic Work-Life Earnings Estimates.* ACS-14. Washington, DC: U.S. Government Printing Office.

K

Kahn, Joseph. 2006. "Where's Mao? Chinese Revise History Books." *New York Times,* September 1, pp. A1, A6.

Kalleberg, Arne L. 2009. "Precarious Work, Insecure Workers: Employment Relations in Transition." *American Sociological Review* 74 (February):1–22.

———. 2012. "The Social Contract in an Era of Precarious Work." *Pathways* (Fall):3–6.

Kambayashi, Takehiko. 2008. "Japanese Men Shout the Oft-Unsaid 'I love you.'" *Christian Science Monitor,* February 13.

Kamenetz, Anya. 2006. *Generation Debt.* New York: Riverhead.

Kang, K. Connie. 1996. "Filipinos Happy with Life in U.S. but Lack United Voice." *Los Angeles Times,* January 26, pp. A1, A20.

Karides, Marina. 2010. "Theorizing the Rise of Microenterprise Development in Caribbean Context." *Journal of World-Systems Research* 16 (2):192–216.

Katovich, Michael A. 1987. Correspondence. June 1.

Katz, Michael. 1971. *Class, Bureaucracy, and the Schools: The Illusion of Educational Change in America.* New York: Praeger.

Kaufman, Sarah. 2006. "The Criminalization of New Orleanians in Katrina's Wake." Accessed April 4 (www.ssrc.org).

Kavada, Anastasia. 2005. "Exploring the Role of the Interest in the 'Movement for Alternative Globalization': The Case of the Paris 2003 European Social Forum." *Westminster Papers in Communication and Culture* 2 (1):72–95.

Keenan, Jillian. 2013. "Legalize Polygamy! No. I Am Not Kidding." April 15. Accessible at http://www.slate.com/articles/double_x/doublex/2013/04/legalize_polygamy_marriage_equality_for_all.html.

Keeter, Scott, and Courtney Kennedy. 2006. "The Cell Phone Challenge to Survey Research." Washington, DC: Pew Research Center.

Kelleher, Jennifer Sinco. 2011. "23 Arrested for Refusing to Leave Iolani Palace." *News from Indian Country,* November, p. 5.

Kellerman, Arthur L., Frederick P. Rivara, Norman B. Rushforth, Joyce G. Banton, Donald T. Reay, Jerry T. Francisco, Ana B. Locci, Janice Prodzinski, Bela B. Hackman, and Grant Somes. 1993. "Gun Ownership as a Risk Factor for Homicide in the Home." *New England Journal of Medicine* 329:1084–1091.

Kelly, Thomas. 2012. "Thomas Kelly on the Nyinba People of Nepal." Accessible at http://www.annenbergspaceforphotography.org/the-shot-blog/thomas-kelly-nyinba-people-nepal.

Kelly, Timothy A. 2009. *Healing the Broken Mind: Transforming America's Failed Mental Health System.* New York: New York University Press.

Kennickell, Arthur B. 2009. *Ponds and Streams: Wealth and Income in the U.S., 1989 to 2007.* Washington, DC: Federal Reserve Board.

Kennicott, Philip. 2011. "Review: 9/11 Memorial in New York." Accessed August 26 (www.washingtonpost.com).

Kenny, Charles. 2009. "Revolution in a Box." *Foreign Policy* (November):68–74.

Kentor, Jeffrey, and Yong Suk Jang. 2004. "Yes, There Is a (Growing) Transnational Business Community." *International Sociology* 19 (September):355–368.

Kerbo, Harold R. 2006. *World Poverty: The Roots of Global Inequality and the World System.* New York: McGraw-Hill.

———. 2012. *Social Stratification and Inequality.* 8th ed. New York: McGraw-Hill.

Kesmodel, David, and Danny Yadron. 2010. "E-Cigarettes Spark New Smoking War." *Wall Street Journal,* August 25, pp. A1, A12.

Kessler, Ronald C., Emil F. Coccaro, Maurizio Fava, Savina Jaeger, Robert Jin, and Ellen Walters. 2006. "The Prevalence and Correlates of DSM-IV Intermittent Explosive Disorder in the National Comorbidity Survey Replication." *Archives of General Psychiatry* 63 (June):669–678.

Khan, Shamus. 2013. "We Are Not All in This Together." *New York Times,* December 15 (Section SR), p. 4.

Kidder, Jeffrey L. 2012. "Parkour, the Affective Appropriation of Urban Space, and the Real/Virtual Dialectic." *City and Community* 11 (September):229–253.

Killian, Caitlin. 2003. "The Other Side of the Veil: North Africa Women in France Respond to the Headscarf Affair." *Gender and Society* (August 17):576–590.

Kim, Hyun Sik. 2011. "Consequences of Parental Divorce for Child Development." *American Sociological Review* 76 (3):487–511.

Kim, Kwang Chung. 1999. *Koreans in the Hood: Conflict with African Americans.* Baltimore: Johns Hopkins University Press.

Kimmel, Michael S. 2006. "A War against Boys?" *Dissent* (Fall):65–70.

———. 2008. *The Gendered Society.* 3rd ed. New York: State University of New York at Stony Brook.

King, Gary. 2011. "Ensuring the Data-Rich Future of the Social Sciences." *Science* (February 11):719–721.

King, Leslie. 1998. "France Needs Children: Pronatalism, Nationalism, and Women's Equity." *Sociological Quarterly* 39 (Winter):33–52.

King, Meredith L. 2007. *Immigrants in the U.S. Health Care System.* Washington, DC: Center for American Progress.

Kingsbury, Alex. 2008. "Q and A: Sudhir Venkatesh." *US News and World Report,* January 21, p. 14.

Kinsey, Alfred C., Wardell B. Pomeroy, and Clyde E. Martin. 1948. *Sexual Behavior in the Human Male.* Philadelphia: Saunders.

———, ———, and Paul H. Gebhard. 1953. *Sexual Behavior in the Human Female.* Philadelphia: Saunders.

Kiser, Edgar. 1992. "War." Pp. 2243–2247 in *Encyclopedia of Sociology,* edited by Edgar F. Borgatta and Marie L. Borgatta. New York: Macmillan.

Kitchener, Richard F. 1991. "Jean Piaget: The Unknown Sociologist." *British Journal of Sociology* 42 (September):421–442.

Klass, Perri. 2003. "This Side of Medicine." P. 319 in *This Side of Doctoring Reflection for Women in Medicine,* edited by Eliza Lo Chin. New York: Oxford University Press.

Klein, Lloyd. 1994. "We're Going to Disney World: Consumers Credit and the Consumption of Social Experience." *Free Inquiry in Creative Sociology* 22 (November):117–124.

Klein, Naomi. 1999. *No Logo: Money, Marketing, and the Growing Anti-Corporate Movement.* New York: Picador (St. Martin's Press).

Kleiner, Art. 2003. "Are You In with the In Crowd?" *Harvard Business Review* 81 (July):86–92.

Kleinknecht, William. 1996. *The New Ethnic Mobs: The Changing Face of Organized Crime in America.* New York: Free Press.

Klinenberg, Eric. 2012. *Going Solo: The Extraordinary Rise and Surprising Appeal of Living Alone.* New York: Penguin Press.

Knudsen, Morten. 2010. "Surprised by Method—Functional Method and System Theory." *Forum: Qualitative Social Research* 11 (September): article 12.

Kochhar, Rakesh. 2006. "Growth in the Foreign-Born Workforce and Employment of the Native Born." Washington, DC: Pew Hispanic Center.

———, Richard Fry, and Paul Taylor. 2011. "Twenty-to-One: Wealth Gaps Rise to Record Highs between Whites, Blacks and Hispanics." July 26. Accessible at http://www.pewsocialtrends.org/files/2011/07/SDT-Wealth-Report_7-26-11_FINAL.pdf.

Kohut, Andrew, et al. 2005. *American Character Gets Mixed Reviews: 16-Nation Pew Global Attitudes Survey.* Washington, DC: Pew Global Project Attitudes.

———, et al. 2007. *Global Unease with Major World Powers: Rising Environmental Concern in 47-Nation Survey.* Washington, DC: Pew Global Project Attitudes.

Kokmen, Leyla. 2008. "Environmental Justice for All." *Utne Reader* (March–April):42–46.

Koppel, Nathan, and Ashby Jones. 2013. "Firms Balk at Gay Weddings." *Wall Street Journal,* October 2, p. A3.

Korean Women's Association United. 2010. "Republic of Korea: Critical Issues on the Seventh Periodical Report on the Convention on the Elimination of All Forms of Discrimination against Women." November 10. Accessed March 27, 2010 (www2.ohchr.org/English/bodies/cedaw/docs/ngos/Korean_Womens_Association_United(PSWG).pdf).

Kornblum, Janet. 2007. "Meet the 'Tech-No's': People Who Reject Plugging into the Highly Wired World." *USA Today,* January 11, pp. A1, A2.

Kottak, Conrad. 2011. *Anthropology: Appreciating Human Diversity.* 14th ed. New York: McGraw-Hill.

Krane, Jim. 2009. *Dubai: The Story of the World's City.* London: Atlantic Books.

———. 2010. "To Spend or Not to Spend." Interviewed on Al Jazeera television, March 26. Accessed April 20 (http://english.aljazeera .net/ programmes/countingthecost/ 2010/03/201032510494187263.html).

Kratz, Corinne A., and Iman Karp. 1993. "Wonder and Worth: Disney Museums in World Showcase." *Museum Anthropology* 17 (3):32–42.

Kraybill, Donald. 2001. *The Riddle of Amish Culture.* Rev. ed. Baltimore: Johns Hopkins University Press.

Kreider, Rose M. 2010. "Increase in Opposite-Sex Cohabiting Couples from 2009 to 2010 in the Annual Social and Economic Supplement (AEFC) to the Current Population Survey (CPS)." Working Paper. Washington, DC: U.S. Bureau of the Census.

———. 2011. "Contexts of Racial Socialization: Are Transracial Adoptive Families More Like Multiracial or White Monoracial Families?" March 1. Accessible at www.census.gov.

———, and Renee Ellis. 2011. "Living Arrangements of Children: 2009." *Current Population Reports,* ser. P70, no. 126. Washington, DC: U.S. Government Printing Office.

Kriesberg, Louis. 1992. "Peace." Pp. 1432–1436 in *Encyclopedia of Sociology,* edited by Edgar F. Borgatta and Marie L. Borgatta. New York: Macmillan.

Kristof, Nicholas D. 1998. "As Asian Economies Shrink, Women Are Squeezed Out." *New York Times,* June 11, pp. A1, A12.

Kronstadt, Jessica, and Melissa Favreault. 2008. "Families and Economic Mobility." Washington, DC: Economic Mobility Project. Also accessible at www.economicmobility. org/reports_and_research/literature_reviews? id=0004.

Krysan, Maria, Reynolds Farley, and Mick P. Couper. 2008. "In the Eye of the Beholder." *DuBois Review* 5 (1):5–26.

Kunzig, Robert. 2011. "Seven Billion." *National Geographic* (January):40–69.

Kwong, Jo. 2005. "Globalization's Effects on the Environment." *Society* 42 (January–February): 21–28.

L

Ladner, Joyce. 1973. *The Death of White Sociology.* New York: Random Books.

Landtman, Gunnar. [1938] 1968. *The Origin of Inequality of the Social Class.* New York: Greenwood (original edition 1938, Chicago: University of Chicago Press).

Lasswell, Harold D. 1936. *Politics: Who Gets What, When, How.* New York: McGraw-Hill.

Lau, Yvonne M. 2006. "Re-Visioning Filipino American Communities: Evolving Identities, Issues, and Organizations." Pp. 141–153 in *The New Chicago,* edited by John Koval et al. Philadelphia: Temple University Press.

Lauer, Robert H. 1982. *Perspectives on Social Change.* 3rd ed. Boston: Allyn and Bacon.

Laumann, Edward O., John H. Gagnon, and Robert T. Michael. 1994a. "A Political History of the National Sex Survey of Adults." *Family Planning Perspectives* 26 (February):34–38.

———, ———, ———, and Stuart Michaels. 1994b. *The Social Organization of Sexuality: Sexual Practices in the United States.* Chicago: University of Chicago Press.

Lavrakas, Paul J., Charles D. Shuttles, Charlotte Steel, and Howard Fienberg. 2007. "The State of Surveying Cell Phone Numbers in the United States: 2007 and Beyond." *Public Opinion Quarterly* 71 (5):840–854.

Lawson, Sandra. 2008. *Girls Count.* New York: Goldman Sachs.

Lazarsfeld, Paul, Bernard Beretson, and H. Gaudet. 1948. *The People's Choice.* New York: Columbia University Press.

———, and Robert K. Merton. 1948. "Mass Communication, Popular Taste, and Organized Social Action." Pp. 95–118 in *The Communication of Ideas,* edited by Lymon Bryson. New York: Harper and Brothers.

Lazer, David, Ryan Kennedy, Gary King, and Alessandro Vespignani. 2014. "The Parable of Google Flu: Traps in Big Data Analysis." *Science* 343 (March 14):1203–1205.

Leavell, Hugh R., and E. Gurney Clark. 1965. *Preventive Medicine for the Doctor in His Community: An Epidemiologic Approach.* 3rd ed. New York: McGraw-Hill.

Ledgerwood, Joanna, ed. 2013. *The New Microfinance Handbook: A Financial Market Perspective.* Washington, DC: World Bank.

Lee, Alfred McClung. 1983. *Terrorism in Northern Ireland.* Bayside, NY: General Hall.

Lee, Ji Hyun. 2013. "Modern Lessons from Arranged Marriages." *New York Times,* January 18. Accessible at http://www. nytimes.com/2013/01/20/fashion/weddings/ parental-involvement-can-help-in-choosing-marriage-partners-experts-say.html? pagewanted=all.

Lee, Suevon. 2013. "Five Federal Policies on Guns You've Never Heard Of." January 7. Accessed February 25 at http://www.propublica.org.

Lengermann, Patricia Madoo, and Jill Niebrugge-Brantley. 1998. *The Women Founders: Sociology and Social Theory, 1830–1930.* Boston: McGraw-Hill.

Lenski, Gerhard. 1966. *Power and Privilege: A Theory of Social Stratification.* New York: McGraw-Hill.

Leonhardt, David. 2004. "As Wealthy Fill Top Colleges Concerns Grow over Fairness." *New York Times,* April 22, pp. A1, A12.

Levine, Nancy. 1988. *The Dynamics of Polyandry: Kinship, Domesticity, and Population on the Tibetan Border.* Chicago: University of Chicago Press.

Levinson, Daniel J. 1978. *The Seasons of a Man's Life.* With Charlotte N. Darrow et al. New York: Knopf.

———. 1996. *The Seasons of a Woman's Life.* With Judy D. Levinson. New York: Knopf.

Levitt, Peggy, and B. Nadya Jaworsky. 2007. "Transnational Migration Studies: Past Developments and Future Trends." *Annual Review of Sociology* 33:129–156.

Levitt, Steven D., and Stephen J. Dubner. 2006. *Freakonomics: A Rogue Economist Explores the Hidden Side of Everything.* Revised and expanded edition. New York: Morrow.

———, and Sudhir Venkatesh. 2000. "An Economic Analysis of a Drug-Selling Gang's Finances." *Quarterly Journal of Economics* (August):775–789.

Lewin, Tamar. 2011. "College Graduates' Debt Grew, Yet Again, in 2010." *New York Times,* November 3, p. A20.

Li, Jennifer S., Tracie A. Barnett, Elizabeth Goodman, Richard C. Wasserman, and Alex R. Kemper. 2013. "Approaches to the Prevention and Management of Childhood Obesity: The Role of Social Networks and the Use of Social Media and Related Electronic Technologies: A Scientific Statement from the American Heart Association." *Circulation* 127:260–267.

Lichtblau, Eric. 2009. "Telecom Companies Win Dismissal of Wiretap Suits." *New York Times,* June 4, p. A14.

Light, Donald W. 2004. "Dreams of Success: A New History of the American Health Care System." *Journal of Health and Social Behavior* 45 (Extra issue):1–24.

Lindner, Eileen W. 2012. *Yearbook of American and Canadian Churches, 2012.* Nashville: Abingdon Press.

Linn, Susan, and Alvin F. Poussaint. 1999. "Watching Television: What Are Children Learning about Race and Ethnicity?" *Child Care Information Exchange* 128 (July): 50–52.

Lino, Mark. 2013. *Expenditures on Children by Families, 2012.* Washington, DC: U.S. Department of Agriculture, Center for Nutrition Policy and Promotion.

Lio, Shoon, Scott Melzer, and Ellen Reese. 2008. "Constructing Threat and Appropriating 'Civil Rights': Rhetorical Strategies of Gun Rights and English Only Leaders." *Symbolic Interaction* 31 (1):5–31.

Lipka, Sara. 2009. "Do Crime Statistics Keep Students Safe?" *Chronicle of Higher Education* 55 (January 30):A15–A17.

Lipson, Karen. 1994. "'Nell' Not Alone in the Wilds." *Los Angeles Times,* December 19, pp. F1, F6.

Liptak, Adam. 2006. "The Ads Discriminate, but Does the Web?" *New York Times,* March 5, p. 16.

———. 2008. "From One Footnote, a Debate over the Tangles of Law, Science and Money." *New York Times,* November 25, p. A13.

Liska, Allen E., and Steven F. Messner. 1999. *Perspectives on Crime and Deviance.* 3rd ed. Upper Saddle River, NJ: Prentice Hall.

Living Goods. 2013. "A Scalable Model for Massive Impact." Accessed May 15 at http://livinggoods.org/what-we-do/micro-franchise-business-model/.

Livingstone, Sonia. 2004. "The Challenge of Changing Audiences." *European Journal of Communication* 19 (March):75–86.

Llana, Sara Miller, and Whitney Eulich. 2013. "Women at War, Worldwide." *Christian Science Monitor Weekly* (February 4):18–20.

Lo Sasso, Anthony T., Michael R. Richards, Chiu-Fang Chou, and Susan E. Gerber. 2011. "The $16,819 Pay Gap for Newly Trained Physicians: The Unexplained Trend of Men Earning More Than Women." *Health Affairs* 30 (February):193–201.

Loeb, Susanna, Bruce Fuller, Sharon Lynn Kagan, and Bidemi Carrol. 2004. "Child Care in Poor Communities: Early Learning Effects of Type, Quality, and Stability." *Child Development* 75 (January–February):47–65.

Loecke, Janet. 2014. "Minimum Wage by State." *USA Today,* February 11, p. 4A.

Lofland, Lyn H. 1975. "The 'Thereness' of Women: A Selective Review of Urban Sociology." Pp. 144–170 in *Another Voice,* edited by M. Millman and R. M. Kanter. New York: Anchor/Doubleday.

Lofquist, Daphne. 2011. *Same-Sex Couple Households.* ACSBR/10-03. Washington, DC: U.S. Government Printing Office.

Logan, John R., Richard D. Alba, and Werquan Zhang. 2002. "Immigrant Enclaves and Ethnic Communities in New York and Los Angeles." *American Sociological Review* 67 (April):299–322.

———, and Brian Stults. 2011. "The Persistence of Segregation in the Metropolis: New Findings from the 2010 Census." Census Brief prepared for Project US2010. http://www.s4.brown.edu/us2010.

Long, Sharon K., and Paul B. Masi. 2009. *Access to and Affordability of Care in Massachusetts as of Fall 2008: Geographic and Racial/Ethnic Differences.* Washington, DC: Urban Institute.

Longhofer, Wesley, and Evan Schofer. 2010. "National and Global Origins of Environmental Association." *American Sociological Review* 75 (4):505–533.

Lopez, Mark Hugo. 2011. *The Latino Electorate in 2010: More Voters, More Non-Voters.* Washington, DC: Pew Hispanic Center.

Lorber, Judith. 2005. *Breaking the Bowls: Degendering and Feminist Change.* New York: Norton.

Loughran, Thomas A., Holly Nguyen, Alex R. Piquero, and Jeffrey Fagan. 2013. "The Returns to Criminal Capital." *American Sociological Review* 78 (6):925–948.

Ludwig, Jens, and Isabel Sawhill. 2007. *Success by Ten: Interviewing Early, Often, and Efficiently in the Education of Young Children.* Washington, DC: Brookings Institution.

Lukacs, Georg. 1923. *History and Class Consciousness.* London: Merlin.

Lundquist, Jennifer Hickes. 2006. "Choosing Single Motherhood." *Contexts* 5 (Fall):64–67.

Luster, Tom, Kelly Rhoades, and Bruce Haas. 1989. "The Relation between Parental Values and Parenting Behavior: A Test of the Kohn Hypothesis." *Journal of Marriage and the Family* 51 (February):139–147.

Luttinger, Nina, and Gregory Dicum. 2006. *The Coffee Book: Anatomy of an Industry from Crop to the Last Drop.* Revised and updated. New York: New Press.

Lyall, Sarah. 2002. "For Europeans, Love, Yes; Marriage, Maybe." *New York Times,* March 24, pp. 1–8.

Lynn, Barry C. 2003. "Trading with a Low-Wage Tiger." *American Prospect* 14 (February):10–12.

M

MacDorman, Marian F., and T. J. Mathews. 2009. "Behind International Rankings of Infant Mortality: How the United States Compares with Europe." *NCHS Date Brief* (No. 23, November).

MacFarquhar, Neil. 2008. "Resolute or Fearful, Many Muslims Turn to Home Schooling." *New York Times,* March 26, p. A1.

Machalek, Richard, and Michael W. Martin. 2010. "Evolution, Biology and Society: A Conversation for the 21st-Century Sociology Classroom." *Teaching Sociology* 38 (1):35–45.

Mack, Mick G. 2003. "Does Exercise Status Influence the Impressions Formed by College Students?" *College Student Journal* 37 (December).

Mack, Raymond W., and Calvin P. Bradford. 1979. *Transforming America: Patterns of Social Change.* 2nd ed. New York: Random House.

Madden, Mary, Amanda Lenhart, Sandra Cortesi, Urs Gasser, Maeve Duggan, Aaron Smith, and Meredith Beaton. 2013. "Teens, Social Media, and Privacy." May 21. Accessible at http://pewinternet.org/Reports/2013/Teens-Social-Media-And-Privacy.aspx.

Magga, Ole Henrik. 2006. "Diversity in Sami Terminology for Reindeer, Snow, and Ice." *International Social Science Journal* 58 (March):25–34.

Magnier, Mark. 2004. "China Clamps Down on Web News Discussion." *Los Angeles Times,* February 26, p. A4.

Malcolm X, with Alex Haley. [1964] 1999. *The Autobiography of Malcolm X.* Revised with Epilogue by Alex Haley and Afterword by Ossie Davis. New York: One World, Ballantine Books.

Males, Mike, and Meda Chesney-Lind. 2010. "The Myth of Mean Girls." *New York Times,* April 2, p. A21.

Malhotra, Neil, and Yotam Margalit. 2009. "State of the Nation: Anti-Semitism and the Economic Crisis." *Boston Review* (May–June). Accessible at http://bostonreview.net/BR34.3/malhotra_margalit.php.

Marable, Manning. 2011. *Malcolm X: A Life of Reinvention.* New York: Viking.

Margolis, Mac. 2009. "The Land of Less Contrast: How Brazil Reined in Inequality." *Newsweek,* November 28.

Marquis, Julie, and Dan Morain. 1999. "A Tortuous Path for the Mentally Ill." *Los Angeles Times,* November 21, pp. A1, A22, A23.

Martin, Dominique, Jean-Luc Metzger, and Philippe Pierre. 2006. "The Sociology of Globalization: Theoretical and Methodological Reflections." *International Sociology* 21 (July):499–521.

Martin, Joyce A., Brady E. Hamilton, Paul D. Sutton, Stephanie J. Ventura, Fay Menacker, Sharon Kirmeyer, and T. J. Mathews. 2009. "Births: Final Data for 2006." *National Vital Statistics Reports* 57 (January 7).

Martin, Karin A. 2009. "Normalizing Heterosexuality: Mothers' Assumptions, Talk, and Strategies with Young Children." *American Sociological Review* 74 (April):190–207.

Martin, Marvin. 1996. "Sociology Adapting to Changes." *Chicago Tribune,* July 21, sec. 18, p. 20.

Martin, Susan E. 1994. "Outsider within the Station House: The Impact of Race and Gender on Black Women Politics." *Social Problems* 41 (August):383–400.

Martin, Susan F. 2013. "Environmental Change and Migration: What We Know." *Policy Brief of the Migration Policy Institute.* Accessible at http://lawprofessors.typepad.com/files/migration-environmentalchange.pdf.

Martineau, Harriet. [1837] 1962. *Society in America.* Edited, abridged, with an introductory essay by Seymour Martin Lipset. Reprint. Garden City, NY: Doubleday.

———. [1838] 1989. *How to Observe Morals and Manners.* Philadelphia: Leal and Blanchard. Sesquentennial edition, edited by M. R. Hill, Transaction Books.

Marubbio, M. Elise. 2006. *Killing the Indian Maiden: Images of Native American Women in Film.* Lexington: University Press of Kentucky.

Marx, Earl. 2009. "How Will Fair Fare?" *Christian Science Monitor,* April 19, pp. 30–31.

Marx, Karl. [1844] 1964. "Contribution to the Critique of Hegel's Philosophy of Right." In *On Religion,* Karl Marx and Friedrich Engels. New York: Schocker Books.

———, and Friedrich Engels. [1847] 1955. *Selected Work in Two Volumes.* Reprint. Moscow: Foreign Languages Publishing House.

Maryanski, Alexandra R. 2004. "Evolutionary Theory." Pp. 257–263 in *Encyclopedia of Social Theory,* edited by George Ritzer. Thousand Oaks, CA: Sage.

Massey, Douglas S. 2007. *Categorically Unequal: The American Stratification System.* New York: Russell Sage Foundation.

———, and Nancy A. Denton. 1993. *American Apartheid: Segregation and the Making of the Underclass.* Cambridge, MA: Harvard University Press.

———, and Margarita Mooney. 2007. "The Effects of America's Three Affirmative Action Programs on Academic Performance." *Social Problems* 54 (1):99–117.

Masuda, Takahiko, Phoebe C. Ellsworth, Batja Mesquita, Janxin Leu, Shigehito Tanida, and Ellen Van de Veerdonk. 2008. "Attitudes and Social Cognition: Placing the Face in Context: Cultural Differences in the Perception of Facial Emotion." *Journal of Personality and Social Psychology* 94 (3):365–381.

Masud-Piloto, Felix. 2008. "Cuban Americans." Pp. 357–359, vol. 1, in *Encyclopedia of Race, Ethnicity, and Society,* edited by Richard T. Schaefer. Thousand Oaks, CA: Sage.

Mattoni, Alice. 2012. *Media Practices and Protest Politics: How Precarious Workers Mobilise.* Farnham, United Kingdom: Ashgate.

Mazumder, Bhashkar. 2008. *Upward Intergenerational Economic Mobility in the United States.* Washington, DC: Economic Mobility Project.

McCarthy, Justin. 2014. "Same-Sex Marriage Support Reaches New High at 55%." Accessed May 21 at www.gallup.com.

McCormack, Mark. 2010. "Changing Masculinities in Youth Cultures." *Qualitative Sociology* 33:111–115.

McFarland, Andrew S. 2007. "Neopluralism." *Annual Review of Political Science* 10:45–66.

McGirk, Tim. 2009. "Postcard: Dubai." *Time,* October 19, p. 6.

McGuire, Thomas G., and Jeanne Miranda. 2008. "New Evidence Regarding Racial and Ethnic Disparities in Mental Health: Policy Implications." *Health Affairs* 27 (2):393–403.

McGurty, Eileen Maura. 2000. "Warren County, NC, and the Emergence of the Environmental Justice Movement: Unlikely Coalitions and Shared Meanings in Local Collective Action." *Society and Natural Resources* 13:373–387.

McIntosh, Peggy. 1988. "White Privilege and Male Privilege: A Personal Account of Coming to See Correspondence through Work and Women's Studies." Working Paper No. 189, Wellesley College Center for Research on Women, Wellesley, MA.

McKinlay, John B., and Sonja M. McKinlay. 1977. "The Questionable Contribution of Medical Measures to the Decline of Mortality in the United States in the Twentieth Century." *Milbank Memorial Fund Quarterly* 55 (Summer):405–428.

McLanahan, Sara, and Christine Percheski. 2008. "Family Structure and the Reproduction of Inequalities." *Annual Review of Sociology* 38:257–276.

McLane, Daisann. 2013. "Getting Off on the Wrong Foot." *National Geographic Traveler* (January):28.

McLuhan, Marshall. 1964. *Understanding Media: The Extensions of Man.* New York: New American Library.

———. 1967. *The Medium Is the Message: An Inventory of Effects.* New York: Bantam Books.

McNeil, Donald G., Jr. 2002. "W.H.O. Moves to Make AIDS Drugs More Accessible to Poor Worldwide." *New York Times,* August 23, p. D7.

———. 2004. "When Real Food Isn't an Option." *New York Times,* September 3, pp. A1, A5.

Mead, George H. 1934. In *Mind, Self and Society,* edited by Charles W. Morris. Chicago: University of Chicago Press.

———. 1964a. In *On Social Psychology,* edited by Anselm Strauss. Chicago: University of Chicago Press.

———. 1964b. "The Genesis of the Self and Social Control." Pp. 267–293 in *Selected Writings: George Herbert Mead,* edited by Andrew J. Reck. Indianapolis: Bobbs-Merrill.

Mead, Margaret. [1935] 2001. *Sex and Temperament in Three Primitive Societies.* New York: Perennial, HarperCollins.

Mehl, Matthias R., Simine Vazire, Nairán Ramírez-Esparza, Richard B. Slatcher, and James W. Pennebaker. 2007. "Are Women Really More Talkative than Men?" *Science* 317 (July 6):82.

Mendez, Jennifer Bickman. 1998. "Of Mops and Maids: Contradictions and Continuities in Bureaucratized Domestic Work." *Social Problems* 45 (February):114–135.

Merton, Robert. 1948. "The Bearing of Empirical Research upon the Development of Social Theory." *American Sociological Review* 13 (October):505–515.

———. 1968. *Social Theory and Social Structure.* New York Free Press.

———, and Alice S. Kitt. 1950. "Contributions to the Theory of Reference Group Behavior." Pp. 40–105 in *Continuities in Social Research: Studies in the Scope and Methods of the American Soldier,* edited by Robert K. Merton and Paul L. Lazarsfeld. New York: Free Press.

Messner, Michael A. 2002. "Gender Equity in College Sports: 6 Views." *Chronicle of Higher Education* 49 (December 6):B9–B10.

Meston, Cindy M., and David M. Buss. 2007. "Why Humanoids Have Sex." *Archives of Sexual Behavior* 36 (August).

Michals, Jennifer M. 2003. "The Price We Pay to Get Richer: A Look at Student Indebtedness." Unpublished M.A. paper, DePaul University, Chicago, IL.

Michels, Robert. 1915. *Political Parties.* Glencoe, IL: Free Press (reprinted 1949).

Microfinance Information Exchange. 2014. "MIX Market." Accessed January 26 (www.themix.org).

Milgram, Stanley. 1963. "Behavioral Study of Obedience." *Journal of Abnormal and Social Psychology* 67 (October):371–378.

———. 1975. *Obedience to Authority: An Experimental View.* New York: Harper and Row.

Miller, David L. 2014. *Introduction to Collective Behavior and Collective Action.* 3rd ed. Long Grove, IL: Waveland Press.

———, and JoAnne DeRoven Darlington. 2002. "Fearing for the Safety of Others: Disasters and the Small World Problem." Paper presented at Midwest Sociological Society, Milwaukee, WI.

Miller, Jacqueline W., Timothy S. Naimi, Robert D. Brewer, and Sherry Everett Jones. 2007. "Binge Drinking and Associated Health Risk Behaviors among High School Students." *Pediatrics* 119 (January):76–85.

Miller, Laura. 2008. "The Rise of the Superclass." Accessed in *Salon* May 2 (www.salon.com/books/review/2008/03/14/superclass/print.html).

Miller, Reuben. 1988. "The Literature of Terrorism." *Terrorism* 11 (1):63–87.

Mills, C. Wright. [1959] 2000a. *The Sociological Imagination.* 40th anniversary edition. New Afterword by Todd Gitlin. New York: Oxford University Press.

———. [1956] 2000b. *The Power Elite.* New edition. Afterword by Alan Wolfe. New York: Oxford University Press.

Miner, Horace. 1956. "Body Ritual among the Nacirema." *American Anthropologist* 58 (June): 503–507.

Mizruchi, Mark S. 1996. "What Do Interlocks Do? An Analysis, Critique, and Assessment of Research on Interlocking Directorates." Pp. 271–298 in *Annual Review of Sociology, 1996,* edited by John Hagan and Karen Cook. Palo Alto, CA: Annual Reviews.

Moaveni, Azadeh. 2005a. *Lipstick Jihad. A Memoir of Growing Up Iranian in America and American in Iran.* New York: Public Affairs.

———. 2005b. "Fast Times in Tehran." *Time* (June 12):38–42.

———. 2007. "The Unbearable Chic-ness of Jihad." *Time* (April 10).

———. 2009. *Honeymoon in Tehran: Two Years of Love and Danger in Iran.* New York: Random House.

Moeller, Susan D. 1999. *Compassion Fatigue.* London: Routledge.

———, Elia Powers, and Jessica Roberts. 2012. "The World Unplugged and 24 Hours without Media: Media Literacy to Develop Self-Awareness Regarding Media." *Comunicar* 20 (39):45–52.

Mohai, Paul, David Pellow, and J. Timmons Roberts. 2009. "Environmental Justice." *Annual Review of Environmental Research* 34:405–430.

———, and Robin Saha. 2007. "Racial Inequality in the Distribution of Hazardous Waste: A National-Level Reassessment." *Social Problems* 54 (3):343–370.

Mol, A. J. 2010. "Ecological Modernization as a Social Theory of Environmental Reform." Pp. 63–71 in *The International Handbook of Environmental Sociology,* 2nd ed., edited by Michael R. Redcraft and Graham Woodgate. Cheltenham, UK: Edward Elgar.

———, and D. A. Sonnenfeld, eds. 2000. *Ecological Modernization around the World.* Portland, OR: Frank Cass.

———, ———, and G. Spaargaren, eds. 2009. *The Ecological Modernization Reader.* London: Routledge.

Monaghan, Peter. 1993. "Sociologist Jailed Because He 'Wouldn't Snitch' Ponders the

Way Research Ought to Be Done." *Chronicle of Higher Education* 40 (September 1):A8, A9.

Monahan, Torin. 2011. "Surveillance as Cultural Practice." *The Sociological Quarterly* 52:495–508.

Moncarz, Roger J., Michael G. Wolf, and Benjamin Wright. 2008. "Service-Providing Occupations, Offshoring, and the Labor Market." *Monthly Labor Review* (December): 71–86.

Montgomery, Marilyn J., and Gwendolyn T. Sorell. 1997. "Differences in Love Attitudes across Family Life Stages." *Family Relations* 46:55–61.

Moore, Jina. 2013. "'Extreme Poverty' Cut by Half." *Christian Science Monitor Weekly* (January 7):30.

Moore, Malcolm. 2012. "China's New Leader Xi, Jinping Warns Communist Party Forces 'Severe Challenges.'" *Telegraph* (London) (November 15). Accessed at www.telegrapj.co.ul.

Moore, Mignon, and Michael Stambolis-Ruhstorfer. 2013. "LGBT Sexuality and Families at the Start of the Twenty-First Century." *Annual Review of Sociology* 39:491–507.

Moore, Molly. 2006. "Romance, but Not Marriage." *Washington Post National Weekly Edition,* November 27, p. 18.

Moore, Wilbert E. 1967. *Order and Change: Essays in Comparative Sociology.* New York: Wiley.

Morin, Rich, and Seth Motel. 2013. "After a Highly Partisan Election Year, Survey Finds Less Group Conflict." January 10. Accessible at www.pewsocialtrends.org.

Morris, Aldon. 2000. "Reflections on Social Movement Theory: Criticisms and Proposals." *Contemporary Sociology* 29 (May):445–454.

Morrison, Denton E. 1971. "Some Notes toward Theory on Relative Deprivation, Social Movements, and Social Change." *American Behavioral Scientist* 14 (May–June):675–690.

Morse, Arthur D. 1967. *While Six Million Died: A Chronicle of American Apathy.* New York: Ace.

Moskos, Peter. 2008. *Cop in the Hood: My Year Policing Baltimore's Eastern District.* Princeton, NJ: Princeton University Press.

Mosley, J., and E. Thomson. 1995. Pp. 148–165 in *Fatherhood: Contemporary Theory, Research and Social Policy,* edited by W. Marsiglo. Thousand Oaks, CA: Sage.

Motel, Seth, and Eileen Patten. 2012. *The 10 Largest Hispanic Origin Groups: Characteristics, Rankings, and Top Counties.* Washington, DC: Pew Hispanic Center.

Mueller, G. O. 2001. "Transnational Crime: Definitions and Concepts." Pp. 13–21 in *Combating Transnational Crime: Concepts, Activities, and Responses,* edited by P. Williams and D. Vlassis. London: Franklin Cass.

Mulrine, Anna. 2012. "Up in Arms." *Christian Science Monitor Weekly* (July 2): 26–32.

Murdock, George P. 1945. "The Common Denominator of Cultures." Pp. 123–142 in *The Science of Man in the World Crisis,* edited by Ralph Linton. New York: Columbia University Press.

———. 1949. *Social Structure.* New York: Macmillan.

———. 1957. "World Ethnographic Sample." *American Anthropologist* 59 (August):664–687.

Murphy, Dean E. 1997. "A Victim of Sweden's Pursuit of Perfection." *Los Angeles Times,* September 2, pp. A1, A8.

Murray, Velma McBride, Amanda Willert, and Diane P. Stephens. 2001. "The Half-Full Glass: Resilient African American Single Mothers and Their Children." *Family Focus* (June):F4–F5.

Myers, Dowell, and John Pitkin. 2011. *Assimilation Tomorrow: How America's Immigrants Will Integrate by 2030.* Washington, DC: Centers for American Progress.

Myers, Steven Lee, and Nicholas Kulish. 2013. "Growing Clamor about Inequities of Climate Crisis." *New York Times,* November 17, pp. 1, 12.

Myre, Greg. 2013. "Women in Combat: 5 Key Questions." January 24. Accessed March 3 at http://m.npr.org/story/170161752.

N

NAACP. 2008. *Out of Focus—Out of Sync Take 4.* Baltimore: NAACP.

NACCRRA (National Association of Child Care Resource and Referral Agencies). 2010. "Parents and the High Cost of Child Care: 2010 Update." Accessible at http://www.naccrra.org/docs/Cost_Report_073010-final.pdf.

Nakao, Keiko, and Judith Treas. 1994. "Updating Occupational Prestige and Socioeconomic Scores: How the New Measures Measure Up." *Sociological Methodology* 24:1–72.

Nash, Manning. 1962. "Race and the Ideology of Race." *Current Anthropology* 3 (June):285–288.

National Advisory Commission on Criminal Justice. 1976. *Organized Crime.* Washington, DC: U.S. Government Printing Office.

National Alliance for Caregiving. 2009. *Caregiving in the U.S.: Executive Summary.* Washington, DC: NAC and AARP.

National Alliance on Mental Illness. 2008. "What Is Mental Illness?" Accessed May 24, 2011 at www.nami.org.

National Alliance to End Homelessness. 2014. "Cost of Homelessness." Accessed April 14 at http://www.endhomelessness.org/pages/cost_of_homelessness.

National Center for Education Statistics. 2009. *Homeschooled Students.* Accessed May 31 (http://nces.ed.gov/programs/coe/2009/section1/indicator06.asp).

———. 2011a. *Average Undergraduate Tuition and Fees.* Accessed March 29 (http://nces.ed.gov/ programs/digest/d09/tables/dt09_335.asp).

———. 2012. *Digest of Education Statistics, 2011.* Washington, DC: NCCES.

———. 2013. "Fast Facts." Accessible at http://nces.ed.gov/fastfacts/.

National Center for Health Statistics. 2013. *Health, United States, 2012: With Special Feature on Emergency Care.* Accessible at http://www.cdc.gov/nchs/data/hus/hus12.pdf#018.

National Center on Addiction and Substance Abuse at Columbia University. 2007. *Wasting the Best and the Brightest: Substance Abuse at America's Colleges and Universities.* New York: NCASA at Columbia University.

National Conference of State Legislatures. 2013. *Voter Identification Requirements.* Accessed August 6, 2013 at http://www.ncsl.org/legislatures-elections/elections/voter-id.aspx.

National Education Association. 2012. "Rankings and Estimates. Rankings of the States 2012 and Estimates of School Statistics 2013." Accessed January 25, 2014 at http://www.nea.org/assets/img/content/NEA_Rankings_And_Estimates-2013_(2).pdf.

National Employment Law Project. 2013. "Living Wage and Minimum Wage." Accessed December 19 at http://www.nelp.org/index.php/content/content_issues/category/living_wage_and_minimum_wage/.

National Geographic. 2005. *Atlas of the World.* 8th ed. Washington, DC: National Geographic.

National Institute of Justice. 2005. *Sexual Assault on Campus: What Colleges and Universities Are Doing about It.* Washington, DC: National In-stitute of Justice.

National Institute on Aging. 1999. *Early Retirement in the United States.* Washington, DC: U.S. Government Printing Office.

National Oceanic and Atmospheric Administration. 2014. "Climate Information." Accessed February 2, 2014 at http://www.ncdc.noaa.gov/climate-information.

National Organization for Men Against Sexism. 2012. Home Page. Accessed February 22 (www.nomas.org).

National Public Radio. 2013. "Impossible Choice Faces America's First 'Climate Refugees.'" May 18. Accessible at www.wbur.org.

Navarro, Mireya. 2005. "When You Contain Multitudes." *New York Times,* April 24, pp. 1, 2.

Needham, Paul. 2011. "9/11 Memorial Review: At Ground Zero, Staying Above Ground Matters." September 9. Accessible at www.huffingtonpost.com.

Negroni, Lirio K. 2012. "The Puerto Rican American Family." Pp. 129–147 in *Ethnic Families in America: Patterns and Variations.* 5th ed., edited by Roosevelt Wright, Jr., Charles H. Mindel, Thanh Van Tran, and Robert W. Halsenstein. Upper Saddle River, NJ: Pearson.

Nelson, Emily. 2004. "Goodbye, 'Friends'; Hello, New Reality." *Wall Street Journal,* February 9, pp. B6, B10.

Neuman, Lawrence W. 2009. *Understanding Research.* Boston: Allyn and Bacon.

Neumark, David. 2007. *Minimum Wage Effects in the Post-Welfare Reform Era.* Washington, DC: The Employment Policies Institute.

Neves, Barbara Barbosa. 2013. "Social Capital and Internet Use: The Irrelevant, the Bad, and the Good." *Sociology Compass* 7/8:599–611.

New Unionism Network. 2011. "State of the Unions." Accessed February 10, 2011 at http://www.newunionism.net/State_of_the_Unions.htm.

New York Times. 2007. "University Officials Accused of Hiding Campus Homicide." June 24, p. 19.

———. 2008. "Law and Order." January 6, pp. 10–11.

Newman, Katherine S. 2012. *The Accordion Family: Boomerang Kids, Anxious Parents, and the Private Toll of Global Competition.* Boston: Beacon Press.

Newman, William M. 1973. *American Pluralism: A Study of Minority Groups and Social Theory.* New York: Harper and Row.

Newport, Frank. 2010b. *In U.S., Increasing Number Have No Religious Identity.* Accessed March 28, 2011 (www.gallup.com).

———. 2011a. "For First Time, Majority of Americans Favor Legal Gay Marriage." Accessed February 27, 2012 (www.gallup.com/poll/147662/First-Time-Majority-Americans-Favor-Legal-Gay-Marriage.aspx?version=print).

———. 2012a. "In U.S., 46% Hold Creationist View of Human Origins." June 1. Accessible at http://www.gallup.com/poll/155003/Hold-Creationist-View-Human-Origins.aspx.

———. 2012b. "Americans Want Federal Gov't Out of State Marijuana Laws." December 10. Accessible at www.gallup.com.

Newsday. 1997. "Japan Sterilized 16,000 Women." September 18, p. A19.

NICHD. 2007. "Children Who Complete Intensive Early Childhood Program Show Gains in Adulthood: Greater College Attendance, Lower Crime and Depression." Accessed January 7, 2008 (www.nichd.nih.gov/news.releases/early_interventions_082107.cfm).

Nielsen Company. 2010. "Most Super Bowl Viewers Tune in for the Commercials Nielsen Says." Accessed February 11 at http://www.nielsen.com/us/en/insights/press-room/2010/most_super_bowl_vieqwers.html.

Nielsen, Joyce McCarl, Glenda Walden, and Charlotte A. Kunkel. 2000. "Gendered Heteronormativity: Empirical Illustrations in Everyday Life." *Sociological Quarterly* 41 (2):283–296.

Niemi, Richard G., and Michael J. Hanmer. 2010. "Voter Turnout among College Students: New Data and a Rethinking of Traditional Theories." *Social Science Quarterly* 91 (June):301–323.

Niesse, Mark. 2008. "Hawaiian Sovereignty Seekers Take Over Historic Iolani Palace in Honolulu." *News from Indian Country* (May 12):3.

———. 2011. "Native Hawaiian Self-Government May Be Set Up by State." *News from Indian Country* (March):3.

Niezen, Ronald. 2005. "Digital Identity: The Construction of Virtual Selfhood in the Indigenous Peoples' Movement." *Comparative Studies in Society and History* 47 (3):532–551.

Nixon, Darren. 2009. "'I Can't Put a Smiley Face On': Working-Class Masculinity, Emotional Labor and Service Work in the 'New Economy.'" *Gender, Work and Organization* 16 (3):300–322.

Nocera, Joe. 2012. "Guns and Mental Illness." *New York Times,* December 29, p. A17.

Nolan, Patrick D. 2004. "Ecological-Evolutionary Theory: A Reanalysis and Reassessment of Lenski's Theory for the 21st Century." *Sociological Theory* 22 (June):328–337.

———, and Gerhard Lenski. 2009. *Human Societies: An Introduction to Macrosociology.* 11th ed. Boulder, CO: Paradigm.

Noonan, Rita K. 1995. "Women against the State: Political Opportunities and Collective Action Frames in Chile's Transition to Democracy." *Sociological Forum* 10:81–111.

Nordhaus, Ted, and Michael Shellenberger. 2007. *Break Through: From the Death of Environmentalism to the Politics of Possibility.* Boston: Houghton Mifflin.

NORML. 2013. "State Laws." Accessed June 1 (http://norml.org/laws).

Norris, Poppa, and Ronald Inglehart. 2004. *Sacred and Secular: Religion and Politics Worldwide.* Cambridge: Cambridge University Press.

Norris, Tina, Paula L. Vines, and Elizabeth M. Hoeffel. 2012. *The American Indian and Alaska Native Population: 2010.* C2010BR-10. Accessible at http://www.census.gov.

North Carolina Department of Environmental and Natural Resources. 2008. "Warren County PCB Landfill Fact Sheet." Accessed April 9 (www.wastenotnc.org/WarrenCo_Fact_Sheet.htm).

Northam, Jack. 2014. "As Overseas Costs Rise, More U.S. Companies Are 'Reshoring.'" January 27. Accessed January 28, 2014 at www.wbur.org.

O

O'Brien, Daniel Tumminelli, Robert J. Sampson, and Christopher Winship. 2013. *Econometrics in the Age of Big Data: Measuring and Assessing 'Brooklyn Windows' Using Administrative Records.* Cambridge, MA: Radcliffe Institute for Advanced Study, Harvard University.

O'Donnell, Mike. 1992. *A New Introduction to Sociology.* Walton-on-Thames, UK: Thomas Nelson and Sons.

Office for National Statistics. 2013. "Female Male Occupation." Accessed March 3 at www.ons.gov.uk.

Office of Family Assistance. 2014. "Healthy Marriage & Responsible Fatherhood." Accessible at http://www.acf.hhs.gov/programs/ofa/programs/healthy-marriage.

Office of Immigration Statistics. 2013. *2012 Yearbook of Immigration Statistics.* Accessible at http://www.dhs.gov/yearbook-immigration-statistics.

Office of the United States Trade Representative. 2012. "Benefits of Trade." Accessed January 29 (www.ustr.gov/about-us/benefits-trade).

Ogas, Ogi, and Sai Gaddam. 2011. *A Billion Wicked Thoughts: What the World's Largest Experiment Reveals about Human Desire.* New York: Dutton.

Ogburn, William F. 1922. *Social Change with Respect to Culture and Original Nature.* New York: Huebsch (reprinted 1966, New York: Dell).

———, and Clark Tibbits. 1934. "The Family and Its Functions." Pp. 661–708 in *Recent Social Trends in the United States,* edited by Research Committee on Social Trends. New York: McGraw-Hill.

O'Harrow, Jr., Robert. 2005. "Mining Personal Data." *Washington Post National Weekly Edition,* February 6, pp. 8–10.

Okano, Kaori, and Motonori Tsuchiya. 1999. *Education in Contemporary Japan: Inequality and Diversity.* Cambridge: Cambridge University Press.

Oliver, Melvin L., and Thomas M. Shapiro. 2006. *Black Wealth/White Wealth: New Perspectives on Racial Inequality.* 2nd ed. New York: Routledge.

Omi, Michael, and Howard Winant. 1994. *Racial Formation in the United States.* 2nd ed. New York: Routledge.

Onishi, Norimitso. 2003. "Divorce in South Korea: Striking a New Attitude." *New York Times,* September 21, p. 19.

Orfield, Gary, John Kucsera, and Genevieve Siegel-Hawley. 2012. "E Pluribus . . . Separation: Deepening Double Segregation for More Students." September 19. Accessible at http://civilrightsproject.ucla.edu/research/k-12-education/integration-and-diversity/mlk-national/e-pluribus. . .separation-deepening-double-segregation-for-more-students.

Organisation for Economic Co-Operation and Development. 2008. *Growing Unequal? Income Distribution and Poverty in OECD Countries.* Geneva: OECD.

———. 2009b. "Green at Fifteen? How 15-Year-Olds Perform in Environmental Sciences and Geosciences in PISA 2006." PISA, OECD Publishing. Accessible at http://dx.doi.org/10.1787/9789264063600-en.

———. 2012b. "Gender Equality and Social Institutions in Afghanistan." Accessed February 22 (http://genderindex.org/country/Afghanistan).

———. 2012c. "Education at a Glance 2011: OECD Indicators." Accessible at www.oecd-ilibrary.org/education/education-at-a-glance-2011/how-many-students-finish-tertiary-education_eaf-2011-7-en.

———. 2013a. "Dataset: Income Distribution and Poverty." Accessed February 20 at http://stats.occd.org.

———. 2013b. "Aid Statistics." Table 1. Updated December 23, 2013 at http://www.oecd.org/dac/stats/statisticsonresourceflowstodeveloping countries.htm.

Ormond, James. 2005. "The McDonaldization of Football." Accessed January 23, 2006 (http://courses.essex.ac.uk/sc/sc111).

Ortman, Jennifer, and Hyon B. Shin. 2011. "Language Projections: 2010 to 2020." Presented at the American Sociological Association.

Ortulay, Barbara. 2013. "Pew: Love Is in the Air and on the Web." Associated Press, October 21, 2013. Accessible at www.pewinternet.org/Media-Mentions/2013.

Orum, Anthony M., and John G. Dale. 2009. *Political Sociology: Power and Participation in the Modern World.* 5th ed. New York: Oxford University Press.

Orwell, George. 1949. *Nineteen Eighty-Four.* London: Secker and Warburg.

Ostling, Richard N., and Joan K. Ostling. 2000. *Mormon America: The Power and the Promise.* San Francisco: HarperCollins.

Outside the Classroom. 2009. "College Students Spend More Time Drinking than Studying." Accessed March 11 (www.outsidetheclassroom.com).

Oxford Poverty and Human Development Initiative. 2012. "Multidimensional Poverty Index." Accessed January 30 (www.ophi.org.uk).

P

Pace, Richard. 1993. "First-Time Televiewing in Amazonia: Television Acculturation in Gurupa, Brazil. *Ethnology* 32:187–205.

———. 1998. "The Struggle for Amazon Town." Boulder, CO: Lynne Rienner.

Padilla, Efren N. 2008. "Filipino Americans." Pp. 493–497 in vol. 1, *Encyclopedia of Race, Ethnicity, and Society,* edited by Richard T. Schaefer. Thousand Oaks, CA: Sage.

Page, Charles H. 1946. "Bureaucracy's Other Face." *Social Forces* 25 (October):89–94.

Page, Susan. 2012. "Attitudes toward Gays Changing Fast, Poll Finds." *USA Today,* December 6, pp. 1A, 2A.

Pager, Devah. 2007. *Marked: Race, Crime, and Funding Work in an Era of Mass Incarceration.* Chicago: University of Chicago Press.

———, Bruce Western, and Bart Bonikowski. 2009. "Discrimination in a Low-Wage Labor Market: A Field Experiment." *American Sociological Review* 74 (October):777–799.

Pampel, Fred C., Patrick M. Krueger, and Justin T. Denney. 2010. "Socioeconomic Disparities in Health Behaviors." *Annual Review of Sociology* 36:349–370.

Pariser, Ei. 2011a. *The Filter Bubble. What the Internet is Hiding from You.* New York: Penguin Press.

———. 2011b. "In Our Own Little Internet Bubbles." *Guardian Weekly,* June 24, p. 32.

Park, Robert E. 1922. *The Immigrant Press and Its Control.* New York: Harper.

Parker, Ashley. 2010. "Where Parties Look for an Audience." *New York Times,* October 30.

Parker-Pope, Tara. 2012. "America's Drinking Binge." January 11. Accessed January 18 (http://well.blogs.nytimes.com/2012/01/11/Americas-drinking-binge).

Parsons, Talcott. 1951. *The Social System.* New York: Free Press.

———. 1966. *Societies: Evolutionary and Comparative Perspectives.* Englewood Cliffs, NJ: Prentice Hall.

———. 1975. "The Sick Role and the Role of the Physician Reconsidered." *Milbank Medical Fund Quarterly Health and Society* 53 (Summer):257–278.

———, and Robert Bales. 1955. *Family: Socialization and Interaction Process.* Glencoe, IL: Free Press.

Passel, Jeffrey S., D'Vera Cohn, and Ana Gonzalez-Barrera. 2013. *Population Decline of Unauthorized Immigrants Stalls, May Have Reverse.* September 23. Accessible at http://www.pewresearch.org/hispanic.

Passero, Kathy. 2002. "Global Travel Expert Roger Axtell Explains Why." *Biography* (July):70–73, 97–98.

Patel, Reena. 2010. *Working the Night Shift: Women in India's Call Center Industry.* Stanford CA: Stanford University Press.

Patterson, Thomas E. 2005. "Young Voters and the 2004 Election." Cambridge, MA: Vanishing Voter Project, Harvard University.

Pattillo-McCoy, Mary. 1999. *Black Picket Fences: Privilege and Peril among the Black Middle Class.* Chicago: University of Chicago Press.

Paul, Brad. 2014. "Dating Questions for Successful Relationships." Accessed January 18, 2014 at http:/www.solotopia.com/dating-questions.

Paulson, Amanda. 2013. "*Roe v. Wade* at 40: Six Questions about the State of Abortion Rights Today." *Christian Science Monitor* (January 22). Accessible at www.csmonitor.com.

Pavlik, John V. 2013. "Trends in New Media Research: A Critical Review of Recent Scholarship." *Sociology Compass* 7 (1):1–12.

Pear, Robert. 1997. "Now, the Archenemies Need Each Other." *New York Times,* June 22, sec. 4, pp. 1, 4.

———. 2009. "Congress Relaxes Rules on Suits over Pay Inequity." *New York Times,* January 28, p. A14.

Pellow, David N., and Hollie Nyseth Brehm. 2013. "An Environmental Sociology for the Twenty-First Century." *Annual Review of Sociology* 39:229–250.

Pennington, Bill. 2008. "College Athletic Scholarships: Expectations Lose Out to Reality." *New York Times,* March 10, pp. A1, A15.

Peralta, Eyder. 2011. "Who Are the 1 Percent? Gallup Finds They're a Lot Like the 99 Percent." December 5. Accessed December 12 (www.wbur.org/npr/143143332/who-are-the-1-percent-gallup-finds-theyre-a-lot-like-the-99-percent).

Pescosolido, Bernice A. 2013. "The Public Stigma of Mental Illness: What Do We Think; What Do We Know; What Can We Prove?" *Journal of Health and Social Behavior* 54 (1):1–21.

Peter, Laurence J., and Raymond Hull. 1969. *The Peter Principle.* New York: Morrow.

Petersen, John L. 2009. "How 'Wild Cards' May Reshape Our Future." *Futurist* (May–June): 19–20.

Peterson, Kristina. 2013. "Minimum-Wage Maneuvering Begins." *Wall Street Journal,* February 14, p. A9.

Petrášová, Alexandra. 2006. *Social Protection in the European Union.* Brussels: European Union.

Pew Forum on Religion and Public Life. 2008. *U.S. Religious Landscape Survey.* Washington, DC: Author.

Pew Global Attitudes Project. 2007. *Global Unease with Major World Powers.* Washington, DC: Pew Global.

Pew Hispanic Center. 2011. "The Mexican-American Boom: Births Overtake Immigration." Washington, DC: Pew Hispanic Center.

Pew Internet Project. 2009. "Demographics of Internet Users." Accessed February 4 (www.pewinternet.org/trends/User_Demo_Jan_2009.htm).

Pew Internet and American Life Project. 2012. Social Media and Political Engagement. October 10. Accessible at http://www.pewinternet.org/~/media//Files/Reports/2012/PIP_SocialMediaAndPoliticalEngagement_PDF.pdf.

Pew Research Center. 2010. "Glenn Beck, Christians and Mormons." Accessed October 4, 2010 at http://pewresearch.org/pubs/1717/glenn-beck-christians-mormons.

———. 2012b. "Fewer, Poorer, Gloomier: The Lost Decade of the Middle Class." August 22. Accessible at http://www.pewsocialtrends.org/files/2012/08/pew-social-trends-lost-decade-of-the-middle-class.pdf.

Pew Research Center Global Attitudes Project. 2012. "Social Networking Popular across Globe: Accessed Arab Publics Most Likely to Express Political Views Online." Accessible at http://www.pewglobal.org/files/2012/12/Pew-Global-Attitudes-Project-Technology-Report-FINAL-December-12-2012.pdf.

Pew Social and Demographic Trends. 2011. "Twenty-to-One: Wealth Caps Rise to Record Highs Between Whites, Black and Hispanics." Washington, DC: Pew Research Center.

Pfeifer, Mark. 2008. "Vietnamese Americans." Pp. 1365–1368, vol. 3, in *Encyclopedia of Race, Ethnicity, and Society,* edited by Richard T. Schaefer. Thousand Oaks, CA: Sage.

Phelan, Jo C., Bruce G. Lint, and Parisha Tehranifar. 2010. "Social Conditions as Fundamental Causes of Health Inequalities: Theory, Evidence, and Policy Implications." *Journal of Health and Social Behavior* 51 (5):528–540.

Phillips, Susan A. 1999. *Wallbangin': Graffiti and Gangs in L.A.* Chicago: University of Chicago Press.

Piaget, Jean. 1954. *Construction of Reality in the Child.* Translated by Margaret Cook. New York: Basic Books.

Picca, Leslie Houts, and Joe R. Feagin. 2007. *Two-Faced Racism: Whites in Backstage and Frontstage.* New York: Routledge.

Pickert, Kate. 2009. "Getting Well While You Shop." *Time,* June 22, pp. 68–70.

———. 2012. "Doing Good by Texting." *Time* (August 27):27.

Pilkington, Ed. 2010. "Right to Bear Arms Upheld." *The Guardian Weekly* (February 7):8.

Pincus, Fred L. 2003. *Reverse Discrimination: Dismantling the Myth.* Boulder, CO: Lynne Rienner.

———. 2008. "Reverse Discrimination." Pp. 1159–1161, vol. 3, in *Encyclopedia of Race, Ethnicity, and Society,* edited by Richard T. Schaefer. Thousand Oaks, CA: Sage.

Pinderhughes, Dianne. 1987. *Race and Ethnicity in Chicago Politics: A Reexamination of Pluralist Theory.* Urbana: University of Illinois Press.

Pinderhughes, Raquel. 2008. "Green Collar Jobs." Accessed June 29 (www.urbanhabitat.org/node/528).

Piturro, Marlene. 2012. "NORCs: Some of the Best Retirement Communities Occur Naturally." May 30. Accessed November 14, 2013 at www.nextavenue.org/article/2012-05/norcs-some-best-retirement-communities-occur-naturally.

Piven, Frances Fox, and Richard A. Cloward. 1996. "Welfare Reform and the New Class War." Pp. 72–86 in *Myths about the Powerless: Contesting Social Inequalities,* edited by M. Brinton Lykes, Ali Banuazizi, Ramsay Liem, and Michael Morris. Philadelphia: Temple University Press.

Plomin, Robert. 1989. "Determinants of Behavior." *American Psychologist* 44 (February): 105–111.

Plüss, Caroline. 2005. "Constructing Globalized Ethnicity." *International Sociology* 20 (June):201–224.

Poder, Thomas C. 2011. "What Is Really Social Capital? A Critical Review." *American Sociologist* 42:341–367.

Pogash, Carol. 2008. "Poor Students in High School Suffer Stigma from Lunch Aid." *New York Times,* March 1, pp. A1, A14.

Polletta, Francesca, and James M. Jasper. 2001. "Collective Identity and Social Movements." Pp. 283–305 in *Annual Review of Sociology, 2001,* edited by Karen S. Cook and Leslie Hogan. Palo Alto, CA: Annual Reviews.

Population Reference Bureau. 1996. "Speaking Graphically." *Population Today* 24 (June/July).

Porter, Eduardo. 2013. "In the War on Poverty, a Dogged Adversary." *New York Times,* December 16, pp. B1, B3.

Portes, Alejandro, Cristina Escobar, and Renelinda Arana. 2008. "Bridging the Gap: Transnational and Ethnic Organizations in the Political Incorporation of Immigrants in the United States." *Ethnic and Racial Studies* 31 (September 6):1056–1090.

Powell, Brian, Catherine Bolzendahl, Claudia Geist, and Lola Carr Steelman. 2010. *Counted Out. Same-Sex Relationships and Americans' Definitions of Family.* New York: Russell Sage Foundation.

Powell, Gary N. 2010. *Women and Men in Management.* 4th ed. Thousand Oaks, CA: Sage.

Preston, Jennifer. 2011. "Facebook Page for Jesus with Highly Active Fans." *New York Times,* September 5, p. B3.

———, and Brian Stelter. 2011. "Cellphone Cameras Become World's Eyes and Ears on Protests across the Middle East." *New York Times,* February 19, p. A7.

Price, Tom. 2013. "Big Data and Privacy." *CQ Researcher* 23 (October 25):909–932. Accessible at http://library.cqpress.com.ezproxy1.lib.depaul.edu/cqresearcher/.

Prince, Martin, Vikram Patel, Shekhar Saxena, Mario Maj, Johanna Maselko, Michael Phillips, and Atif Rahman. 2007. "No Health without Mental Health." *The Lancet* 370 (September 8):859–877.

Pryor, John H., Kevin Egan, Laura Palucki Blake, Sylvia Hurtado, Jennifer Berdan, Matthew H. Case, and Linda DeAngelo. 2013. *The American Freshman: National Norms for Fall 2012.* Los Angeles: Higher Education Research Institute, UCLA.

———, Sylvia Hurtado, Victor B. Saenz, José Luis Santos, and William S. Korn. 2007. *The American Freshman: Forty Year Trends.* Los Angeles: Higher Education Research Institute, UCLA.

Purser, Gretchen. 2013. "Precarious Work." *Contexts* 12 (4):74–76.

Q

Quadagno, Jill. 2011. *Aging and the Life Course: An Introduction to Social Gerontology.* 5th ed. New York: McGraw-Hill.

Quillian, Lincoln. 2006. "New Approaches to Understanding Racial Prejudice and Discrimination." *Annual Review of Sociology* 32:299–328.

Quinney, Richard. 1970. *The Social Reality of Crime.* Boston: Little, Brown.

———. 1974. *Criminal Justice in America.* Boston: Little, Brown.

———. 1979. *Criminology.* 2nd ed. Boston: Little, Brown.

———. 1980. *Class, State and Crime.* 2nd ed. New York: Longman.

Quinnipiac University. 2013. "Americans Back Women in Combat 3-1, but Less for Draft." Release Detail February 7. Accessed March 3 at www.quinnipiac.edu.

Quiñones-Hinojosa, Alfredo with Mim Eichler Rivas. 2011. *Becoming Dr. Q: My Journey from Migrant Farm Worker to Brain Surgeon.* Berkeley: University of California Press.

R

Rainie, Lee. 2005. *Sports Fantasy Leagues Online.* Washington, DC: Pew Internet and American Life Project.

Rajan, Gita, and Shailja Sharma. 2006. *New Cosmopolitanisms: South Asians in the US.* Stanford, CA: Stanford University Press.

Ramet, Sabrina. 1991. *Social Currents in Eastern Europe: The Source and Meaning of the Great Transformation.* Durham, NC: Duke University Press.

Ramos, Jorge. 2010. *A Country for All.* New York: Vintage Books.

Ramstad, Evan. 2011. "Studying Too Much Is a New No-No in Upwardly Mobile South Korea." *Wall Street Journal,* October 6, p. A1.

RAND. 2010. "Retail Medical Clinics Perform Well Relative to Other Medical Settings." *RAND Review* (Winter 2009–2010). Accessed January 25 (www.rand.org/publications/randreview/issues/winter2009/news.html#medclinics).

Randolph, Tracey H., and Mellisa Holtzman. 2010. "The Role of Heritage Camps in Identity Development Among Korean Transnational Adoptees: A Relational Dialectics Approach." *Adoption Quarterly* 13:75–91.

Rangaswamy, Padma. 2005. "Asian Indians in Chicago." In *The New Chicago,* edited by John Koval et al. Philadelphia: Temple University Press.

Rasmussen Reports. 2013. "59% Believe Voter ID Laws Do Not Discriminate." Accessed December 30 at http://www.rasmussenreports.com/public_content/politics/general_politics/september_2013/59_believe_voter_id_laws_do_not_discriminate.

Ratnesar, Romesh. 2011. "The Menace Within." *Stanford Magazine* (July/August). Accessible at www.stanfordalumni.org.

Rawlinson, Linnie, and Nick Hunt. 2009. "Jackson Dies, Almost Takes Internet with Him." Accessed July 1 (www.cnn.com/2009/TECH/06/26/michael.jackson.internet/).

Reinharz, Shulamit. 1992. *Feminist Methods in Social Research.* New York: Oxford University Press.

Reitzes, Donald C., and Elizabeth J. Mutran. 2006. "Lingering Identities in Retirement." *Sociological Quarterly* 47:333–359.

Religion News Service. 2003. "New U.S. Guidelines on Prayer in Schools Get Mixed Reaction." *Los Angeles Times,* February 15, p. B24.

Revkin, Andrew C. 2007. "Wealth and Poverty, Drought and Flood: Report from Four Fronts in the War on Warming." *New York Times,* April 3, pp. D4–D5.

Ridgeway, Cecilia L. 2011. *Framed by Gender: How Gender Inequality Persists in the Modern World.* New York: Oxford University Press.

Riding, Alan. 1998. "Why 'Titanic' Conquered the World." *New York Times,* April 26, sec. 2, pp. 1, 28, 29.

———. 2005. "Unesco Adopts New Plan against Cultural Invasion." *New York Times,* October 21, p. B3.

Rieker, Patricia R., and Chloe E. Bird. 2000. "Sociological Explanations of Gender Differences in Mental and Physical Health." Pp. 98–113 in *Handbook of Medical Sociology,* edited by Chloe Bird, Peter Conrad, and Allan Fremont. New York: Prentice Hall.

Rifkin, Jeremy. 1995. *The End of Work; The Decline of the Global Labor Force and the Dawn of the Post-Market Era.* New York: Tarcher/Putnam.

Riley, Matilda White, Robert L. Kahn, and Anne Foner. 1994a. *Age and Structural Lag.* New York: Wiley InterScience.

———, Robert L. Kahn, and Anne Foner, in association with Karin A. Mock. 1994b. "Introduction: The Mismatch between People and Structures." Pp. 1–36 in *Age and Structural Lag,* edited by Matilda White Riley, Robert L. Kahn, and Anne Foner. New York: Wiley InterScience.

Ripley, Amanda. 2011. "Teacher, Leave Those Kids Alone." *Time,* December 5, pp. 46–49.

Ritzer, George. 2007. "A 'New' Global Age, but Are There New Perspectives on It?" Pp. 361–370 in *Frontiers of Globalization Research,* edited by Ino Rossi. New York: Springer.

———. 2010. *Enchanting a Disenchanted World: Revolutionizing the Means of Consumption.* 3rd ed. Thousand Oaks, CA: Pine Forge Press.

———. 2013. *The McDonaldization of Society,* 20th Anniversary Edition. Thousand Oaks CA: Sage.

Robertson, Roland. 1988. "The Sociological Significance of Culture: Some General Considerations." *Theory, Culture, and Society* 5 (February):3–23.

Robinson, Kristopher, and Edward M. Crenshaw. 2010. "Reevaluating the Global Digital Divide: Socio-Demographic and Conflict Barriers to the Internet Revolution." *Sociological Inquiry* 80 (February):34–62

Robnett, Belinda, and Cynthia Feliciano. 2011. "Patterns of Racial-Ethnic Exclusion by Internet Daters." *Social Forces* 89 (March):807–828.

Rodman, George. 2011. *Mass Media in a Changing World.* 3rd ed. New York: McGraw-Hill.

Rodriquez, Laura, and Donald Gatlin. 2014. "New Studies Offer Estimates of LGBT Population and Married Same-Sex Couples." Accessed September 29 at http://williamsinstitute.law.ucla.edu.

Rogan, Eugene. 2009. "Sand, Sea and Shopping." *Guardian Weekly,* October 16, pp. 38–39.

Rootes, Christopher. 2007. "Environmental Movements." Pp. 608–640 in *The Blackwell Companion to Social Movements,* edited by David A. Snow, Sarah A. Sovle, and Hanspeter Kriesi. Malden, MA: Blackwell.

Rose, Arnold. 1951. *The Roots of Prejudice.* Paris: UNESCO.

Rose, Peter I., Myron Glazer, and Penina Migdal Glazer. 1979. "In Controlled Environments: Four Cases of Intense Resocialization." Pp. 320–338 in *Socialization and the Life Cycle,* edited by Peter I. Rose. New York: St. Martin's Press.

Rosen, Eva, and Sudhir Alladi Venkatesh. 2008. "A Perversion of Choice: Sex Work Offers Just Enough in Chicago's Urban Ghetto." *Journal of Contemporary Ethnography* (August):417–441.

Rosenberg, Douglas H. 1991. "Capitalism." Pp. 33–34 in *Encyclopedic Dictionary of Sociology,* 4th ed., edited by Dushkin Publishing Group. Guilford, CT: Dushkin.

Rosenberg, Tina. 2012. "The 'Avon Ladies' of Africa." *New York Times,* October 14, Week in Review, p. 9.

Rosenbloom, Stephanie. 2011. "Love, Lies, and What They Learned." *New York Times,* November 13, pp. ST1, ST8.

Rosenfeld, Jake. 2010. "Little Labor." *Pathways* (Summer):4–6.

———, and Meredith Klegkamp. 2012. "Organized Labor and Racial Wage Inequality in the United States." *American Journal of Sociology* 117 (March):1460–1502.

Rosenfeld, Michael J., and Reuben J. Thomas. 2012. "Searching for a Mate: The Rise of the Internet as a Social Intermediary." *American Sociological Review* 77 (4):523–547.

Rosenthal, Robert, and Lenore Jacobson. 1968. *Pygmalion in the Classroom.* New York: Holt.

———. 1992. *Pygmalion in the Classroom: Teacher Expectations and Pupils' Intellectual Development.* Newly expanded edition. Bancyfelin, UK: Crown House.

Rossi, Alice S. 1968. "Transition to Parenthood." *Journal of Marriage and the Family* 30 (February): 26–39.

———. 1984. "Gender and Parenthood." *American Sociological Review* 49 (February):1–19.

Rossi, Peter H. 1987. "No Good Applied Social Research Goes Unpunished." *Society* 25 (November–December):73–79.

Rossides, Daniel W. 1997. *Social Stratification: The Interplay of Class, Race, and Gender.* 2nd ed. Upper Saddle River, NJ: Prentice Hall.

Roszak, Theodore. 1969. *The Making of a Counterculture.* Garden City, NY: Doubleday.

Roter, Debra L., Judith A. Hall, and Yutaka Aoki. 2002. "Physician Gender Effects in Medical Communications: A Meta-analytic Review." *Journal of the American Medical Association* 288 (August 14):756–764.

Rothkopf, David. 2008. *Superclass: The Global Power Elite and the World They Are Making.* New York: Farrar, Straus and Giroux.

Rowe, Aimee Carrillo, Sheena Malhotra, and Kimberlee Pérez. 2013. *Answer the Call: Virtual Migration in Indian Call Centers.* Minneapolis: University of Minnesota Press.

Rubin, Alissa J. 2003. "Pat-Down on the Way to Prayer." *Los Angeles Times,* November 25, pp. A1, A5.

———, and Sam Dagher. 2009. "Election Quotas for Iraqi Women Are Weakened, Provoking Anger as Vote Nears." *New York Times,* January 14, p. A13.

Rudel, Thomas K., J. Timmons Roberts, and Jo Ann Carmin. 2011. "Political Economy of the Environment." *Annual Review of Sociology* 37:221–238.

Ruiz, Rebecca. 2010. "Care for the Caregivers." *The American Prospect* (October):A17–A20.

Ryan, Camille. 2013. *Language Use in the United States.* ACS-22. Washington, DC: U.S. Government Printing Office.

Ryan, William. 1976. *Blaming the Victim.* Rev. ed. New York: Random House.

S

Saad, Lydia. 2004. "Divorce Doesn't Last." *Gallup Poll Tuesday Briefing.* March 30. Accessible at www.gallup.com.

———. 2011. "Americans Decry Power of Lobbyists, Corporations, Banks, Feds." April 11. Accessible at http://www.gallup.com/poll/147026/Americans-Decry-Power-Lobbyists-Corporations-Banks-Feds.aspx.

———. 2012. "In U.S., Half of Women Prefer a Job Outside the Home." September 7. Accessible at www.gallup.com.

———. 2013. "Majority of Americans Still Support *Roe v. Wade* Decision." January 22. www.gallup.com.

———. 2013b. "Americans' Concerns about Global Warming on the Rise." April 8. Accessible at http://www.gallup.com/poll/161645/americans-concerns-global-warming-rise.aspx?version=print.

———. 2013. *More Americans still prioritize economy over environment.* Washington, DC: Gallup Poll.

Sachs, Jeffrey D. 2005. *The End of Poverty: Economic Possibilities for Our Time.* New York: Penguin.

Sacks, Peter. 2007. *Tearing Down the Gates: Confronting the Class Divide in American Education.* Berkeley: University of California Press.

Saez, Emmanuel. 2013. "Striking It Richer: The Evolution of Top Incomes in the United States." Updated with 2012 preliminary estimates. September 3. Accessible at http://Elsa.berkeley.edu/~Saez/.

Saguy, Abigail, and Rene Almeling. 2008. "Fat in the Fire? Science, the News Media, and the 'Obesity Epidemic.'" *Sociological Forum* 23 (March):53–83.

Said, Edward W. 2001. "The Clash of Ignorance." *Nation,* October 22.

Sale, Kirkpatrick. 1996. *Rebels against the Future: The Luddites and Their War on the Industrial Revolution* (with a new preface by the author). Reading, MA: Addison-Wesley.

Salem, Richard, and Stanislaus Grabarek. 1986. "Sociology B.A.s in a Corporate Setting: How Can They Get There and of What Value Are They?" *Teaching Sociology* 14 (October):273–275.

Sampson, Robert. 2011. *Great American City: Chicago and the Enduring Neighborhood Effect.* Chicago: University of Chicago Press.

———, and W. Byron Graves. 1989. "Community Structure and Crime: Testing Social-Disorganization Theory." *American Journal of Sociology* 94 (January):774–802.

Samuelson, Paul A., and William D. Nordhaus. 2010. *Economics.* 19th ed. New York: McGraw-Hill.

Sandefur, Rebecca L. 2008. "Access to Civil Justice and Race, Class, and Gender Inequality." *Annual Review of Sociology* 34:339–358.

Sanders, Edmund. 2004. "Coming of Age in Iraq." *Los Angeles Times,* August 14, pp. A1, A5.

Sanderson, Stephen K., Seth A. Abrutyn, and Kristopher R. Proctor. 2011. "Testing the Protestant Ethic Thesis with Quantitative Historical Data: A Research Note." *Social Forces* 89 (March):905–912.

Santos, José Alcides Figueiredo. 2006. "Class Effects on Racial Inequality in Brazil." *Dados* 2:1–35.

Sanua, Marianne R. 2007. "AJC and Intermarriage: The Complexities of Jewish Continuity, 1960–2006." Pp. 3–32 in *American Jewish Yearbook 2007,* edited by David Singer and Lawrence Grossman. New York: American Jewish Committee.

Sapir, Edward. 1929. "The State of Linguistics as a Science." *Language* 5 (4):207–214.

Sassen, Saskia. 2005. "New Global Classes: Implications for Politics." Pp. 143–170 in *The New Egalitarianism,* edited by Anthony Giddens and Patrick Diamond. Cambridge: Polity.

Satel, Sally. 2013. "Why the Fuss over the D.S.M.-5?" *New York Times,* May 12, Week in the News, p. 5.

Sawhill, Isabel, and Ron Haskins. 2009. "If You Can Make It Here . . ." *Washington Post National Weekly Edition,* November 9, p. 27.

———, and John E. Morton. 2007. *Economic Mobility: Is the American Dream Alive and Well?* Washington, DC: Economic Mobility Project, Pew Charitable Trusts.

———, Scott Winship, and Kerry Searle Grannis. 2012. *Pathways to the Middle Class: Balancing Personal and Public Responsibilities.* Washington, DC: Brookings.

Sayer, Liana C., Suzanne M. Bianchi, and John P. Robinson. 2004. "Are Parents Investing Less in Children? Trends in Mothers' and Fathers' Time with Children." *American Journal of Sociology* 110 (July):1–43.

Scarce, Rik. 2005. "A Law to Protect Scholars." *Chronicle of Higher Education,* August 12, p. 324.

Schaefer, Peter. 2008. "Digital Divide." Pp. 388–389, vol. 1, in *Encyclopedia of Race, Ethnicity, and Society in the United States,* edited by Richard T. Schaefer. Thousand Oaks, CA: Sage.

Schaefer, Richard T. 2008b. "'Power' and 'Power Elite.'" In *Encyclopedia of Social Problems,* edited by Vincent Parrillo. Thousand Oaks, CA: Sage.

———. 2012. *Racial and Ethnic Groups.* 13th ed. Upper Saddle River, NJ: Pearson.

———. 2014. *Racial and Ethnic Groups in the United States.* 14th ed. Upper Saddle River, NJ: Prentice Hall.

———, and William Zellner. 2011. *Extraordinary Groups.* 9th ed. New York: Worth.

Scharfenberg, David. 2013. "Big Data Comes to Boston's Neighborhoods." Accessed at http://www.wbur.org/2013/07/03/big-data-boston.

Scharnberg, Kirsten. 2007. "Black Market for Midwives Defies Bans." *Chicago Tribune,* November 25, pp. 1, 10.

Scheid, Teresa L. 2013. "A Decade of Critique: Notable Books in the Sociology of Mental Health." *Contemporary Sociology* 42 (2):177–183.

Scherer, Michael. 2011. "Introduction: Taking It to the Streets." Pp. 5–12 in *Occupy: What Is Occupy?* New York: Time Books.

———. 2013. "The Next Gun Fight." *Time* (January 20):25–41.

Scherer, Ron. 2010a. "A Long Struggle to Find Jobs." *Christian Science Monitor,* January 31, pp. 18–19.

———. 2010b. "For Jobless, Online Friends Can Be Lifelines." *Christian Science Monitor,* March 25, p. 21.

———. 2010c. "Jim Bunning Delays Vote; Unemployed Face First Week Without Check." *Christian Science Monitor* (March 2).

Schlesinger, Traci. 2011. "The Failure of Race-Neutral Policies: How Mandatory Terms and Sentencing Enhancements Contribute to Mass Racialized Incarceration." *Crime & Delinquency* 57 (January):56–81.

Schmeeckle, Maria. 2007. "Gender Dynamics in Stepfamilies: Adult Stepchildren's Views." *Journal of Marriage and Family* 69 (February):174–189.

———, Roseann Giarrusso, Du Feng, and Vern L. Bengtson. 2006. "What Makes Someone Family? Adult Children's Perceptions of Current and Former Stepparents." *Journal of Marriage and Family* 68 (August):595–610.

Schnaiberg, Allan. 1994. *Environment and Society: The Enduring Conflict.* New York: St. Martin's Press.

Schneider, Christopher. 2008. "Sexuality." Pp. 847–848 in *Encyclopedia of Social Problems,* edited by Vincent Parrillo. Los Angeles: Sage.

Schneider, Friedrich. 2010. "Dues and Don'ts." *The Economist* (August 14):62.

Schnittker, Jason, Jeremy Freese, and Brian Powell. 2003. "Who Are Feminists and What Do They Believe? The Role of Generations." *American Sociologist Review* 68 (August): 607–622.

Schram, Sanford F., Ruhard C. Fording, Joe Soss, and Linda Houser. 2009. "Deciding to Discipline: Race, Choice and Punishment at the Frontlines of Welfare Reform." *American Sociological Review* 74 (June):398–422.

Schulman, Gary I. 1974. "Race, Sex, and Violence: A Laboratory Test of the Sexual Threat of the Black Male Hypothesis." *American Journal of Sociology* 79 (March):1260–1272.

Schur, Edwin M. 1965. *Crimes without Victims: Deviant Behavior and Public Policy.* Englewood Cliffs, NJ: Prentice Hall.

———. 1968. *Law and Society: A Sociological View.* New York: Random House.

———. 1985. "'Crimes without Victims': A 20-Year Reassessment." Paper presented at the annual meeting of the Society for the Study of Social Problems.

Schwartz, Howard D., ed. 1994. *Dominant Issues in Medical Sociology.* 3rd ed. New York: McGraw-Hill.

Schwartz, Shalom H., and Anat Bardi. 2001. "Value Hierarchies across Cultures: Taking a Similarities Perspective." *Journal of Cross-Cultural Perspective* 32 (May):268–290.

Scott, Alan. 1990. *Ideology and the New Social Movements.* London: Unwin Hyman.

Scott, Gregory. 2001. "Broken Windows behind Bars: Eradicating Prison Gangs through Ecological Hardening and Symbolic Cleansing." *Corrections Management Quarterly* 5 (Winter):23–36.

Scott, W. Richard, and Gerald F. Davis. 2007. *Organizations and Organizing: Rational, Natural and Open Systems Perspectives.* New York: Pearson.

Scoville, David. 2010. "Disneyland Deconstructed: Postmodernism Revealed." April 16. Accessible at http://davidscoville.blogspot.com/2010/04/Disneyland-deconstructed-postmodernism.html.

Seccombe, Karen. 2011. *So You Think I Drive a Cadillac?* Boston: Allyn and Bacon.

Security on Campus. 2008. "Complying with the Jeanne Clery Act." Accessed January 13 (www.securityoncampus.org/crimestats/index.html).

Sedgwick, Eve Kosofsky. 1990. *Epistemology of the Closet.* Berkeley: University of California Press.

Sefiha, Ophir. 2012. "Bad Sports: Explaining Sport Related Deviance." *Sociology Compass* 6:949–961.

Segal, Nancy L. 2012. *Born Together—Reared Apart. O Brother, Who Art Thou.* Cambridge, MA: Harvard University Press.

Seidman, Steven. 1994. "Heterosexism in America: Prejudice against Gay Men and Lesbians." Pp. 578–593 in *Introduction to Social Problems,* edited by Craig Calhoun and George Ritzer. New York: McGraw-Hill.

Sellers, Frances Stead. 2004. "Voter Globalization." *Washington Post National Weekly Edition,* November 29, p. 22.

Selod, Saher Farooq. 2008a. "Muslim Americans." Pp. 920–923, vol. 2, in *Encyclopedia of Race, Ethnicity, and Society,* edited by Richard T. Schaefer. Thousand Oaks, CA: Sage.

———. 2008b. "Veil." Pp. 1359–1360, vol. 3, in *Encyclopedia of Race, Ethnicity, and Society,* edited by Richard T. Schaefer. Thousand Oaks, CA: Sage.

Sengupta, Somini. 2009. "An Empire for Poor Working Women, Guided by a Gandhian Approach." *New York Times,* March 7, p. A6.

Sernau, Scott. 2001. *Worlds Apart: Social Inequalities in a New Century.* Thousand Oaks, CA: Pine Forge Press.

Settersten, Richard, and Barbara Ray. 2011. *Not Quite Adults: Why 20-Somethings Are Choosing a Slower Path to Adulthood, and Why It's Good for Everyone.* New York: Bantam.

Shachtman, Tom. 2006. *Rumspringa: To Be or Not to Be Amish.* New York: North Point Press.

Shane, Scott. 2010. "Wars Fought and Wars Googled." *New York Times,* June 27, pp. PWK1–5.

Shapiro, Joseph P. 1993. *No Pity: People with Disabilities Forging a New Civil Rights Movement.* New York: Times Books.

Shapiro, Thomas M., Tatjana Meschede, and Laura Sullivan. 2010. "The Racial Wealth Gap Increases Fourfold." Research and Policy Brief, Institute on Assets and Social Policy, Brandeis University.

Shapley, Dan. 2010. "4 Dirty Secrets of the Exxon Valdez Oil Spill." Accessed May 3 (www.thedailygreen.com).

Sharma, Hari M., and Gerard C. Bodeker. 1998. "Alternative Medicine." Pp. 228–229 in *Britannica Book of the Year 1998.* Chicago: Encyclopaedia Britannica.

Sharp, Ansel M., Charles A. Register, and Paul W. Grimes. 2013. *Economics of Social Issues.* 20th ed. New York: McGraw Hill.

Shaw, Clifford R., and Henry D. McKay. 1942. *Juvenile Delinquency and Urban Areas.* Chicago: University of Chicago Press.

Shea, Andrea. 2013. "Facebook Envy: How the Social Work Affects Our Self-Esteem." February 20. Accessed at www.wbur.org.

Sheehan, Charles. 2005. "Poor Seniors Take On Plans of Condo Giant." *Chicago Tribune,* March 22, pp. 1, 9.

Sherman, Arloc. 2007. *Income Inequality Hits Record Levels, New CBO Data Show.* Washington, DC: Center on Budget and Policy Priorities.

Sherman, Jennifer, and Elizabeth Harris. 2012. "Social Class and Parenting: Classic Debates and New Understandings." *Sociology Compass* 6:60–71.

Shogren, Elizabeth. 1994. "Treatment against Their Will." *Los Angeles Times,* August 18, pp. A1, A14–A15.

Short, Kathleen. 2012. *The Research Supplemental: Poverty Measure 2011.* Current Population Reports. P60-244. Washington, DC: U.S. Government Printing Office.

Shostak, Arthur B. 2002. "Clinical Sociology and the Art of Peace Promotion: Earning a World without War." Pp. 325–345 in *Using Sociology: An Introduction from the Applied and Clinical Perspectives,* edited by Roger A. Straus. Lanham, MD: Rowman and Littlefield.

Sieber, Renée E., Daniel Spitzberg, Hannah Muffatt, Kristen Brewer, Blanka Füleki, and Naomi Arbit. 2006. *Influencing Climate Change Policy: Environmental Non-Governmental Organizations (ENGOs) Using Virtual and Physical Activism.* Montreal: McGill University.

Silva, Jennifer M. 2012. "Constructing Adulthood in an Age of Uncertainty." *American Sociological Review* 77 (4):505–522.

Silver, Ira. 1996. "Role Transitions, Objects, and Identity." *Symbolic Interaction* 10 (1):1–20.

Silverman, Rachel Emma. 2009. "As Jobs Grow Scarce, Commuter Marriages Rise." Accessed March 31, 2010 (http://blogs.wsj.com/juggle/2009/01/16/as-jobs-grow-scarce-commuter-marriages-rise/).

———. 2013. "Tracking Sensors Invade the Workplace." *Wall Street Journal,* March 7, pp. B1, B2.

Silverstein, Ken. 2010. "Shopping for Sweat: The Human Cost of a Two-Dollar T-shirt." *Harpers* 320 (January):36–44.

Simpson, Sally S. 2013. "White-collar Crime: A Review of Recent Developments and Promising Directions for Future Research." *Annual Review of Sociology* 39:309–331.

Skocpol, Theda, and Vanessa Williamson. 2012. *The Tea Party and the Remaking of Republican Conservatism.* New York: Oxford University Press.

Slack, Jennifer Daryl, and J. Macgregor Wise. 2007. *Culture + Technology.* New York: Peter Lang.

Slaughter, Chuck. 2011. "Taking the 'Avon' Way to Reach 'The Last Mile.'" October 31. Accessed February 26, 2013 at http://www.huffingtonpost.com/chuck-slaughter/taking-the-avon-way-to re_b_1067840.html.

Slavin, Barbara. 2007. "Child Marriage Rife in Nations Getting U.S. Aid." *USA Today,* July 17, p. 6A.

Slavin, Robert E., and A. Cheung. 2003. *Effective Reading Programs for English Language Learners: A Best-Evidence Synthesis.* Baltimore: Johns Hopkins University, Center for Research on the Education of Students Placed at Risk.

Sloan, Allan. 2009. "What's Still Wrong with Wall Street." *Time,* November 9, pp. 24–29.

Sloop, John M. 2009. "Queer: Approaches to Communication." Pp. 90–100 in *21st Century Communication,* edited by Bill Eadie. Thousand Oaks, CA: Sage.

Slug-Lines.com. 2011. "A Unique Commuter Solution." Accessed November 10, 2011. (www.slug-lines.com).

Smart, Barry. 1990. "Modernity, Postmodernity, and the Present." Pp. 14–30 in *Theories of Modernity and Postmodernity,* edited by Bryan S. Turner. Newbury Park, CA: Sage.

Smelser, Neil. 1963. *The Sociology of Economic Life.* Englewood Cliffs, NJ: Prentice Hall.

Smith, Aaron. 2009. *The Internet's Role in Campaign 2000.* Washington, DC: Pew Internet and American Life Project.

———. 2012. *Real Time Charitable Giving.* Washington, DC: Pew Research Center's Internet and American Life Project. Accessible at www.pewinternet.org/Reports/2012/MobileGiving.aspx.

———, and Maeve Duggan. 2012. "Presidential Campaign Donations in the Digital Age." October 25. Accessible at http://www.pewinternet.org/Reports/2012/Election-2012-Donations/Key-Findings/Presidential-Campaign-Donations-in-the-Digital-Age.aspx.

———, and ———. 2013. "Online Dating & Relationships." October 21, 2013. Accessible at http://www.pewinternet.org/Reports/2013/Online-Dating/Summary-of-Findings.aspx.

Smith, Christian. 1991. *The Emergence of Liberation Theology: Radical Religion and Social Movement Theory.* Chicago: University of Chicago Press.

———. 2007. "Getting a Life: The Challenge of Emerging Adulthood." *Books and Culture: A Christian Review* (November–December).

———. 2008. "Future Directions of the Sociology of Religion." *Social Forces* 86 (June):1564–1589.

Smith, Craig S. 2006. "Romania's Orphans Face Widespread Abuse, Group Says." *New York Times,* May 10, p. A3.

Smith, Dan. 1999. *The State of the World Atlas.* 6th ed. London: Penguin.

Smith, Lawrence C. 2011. *The World in 2050: Four Forces Shaping Civilizations Northern Future.* New York: A Plume Book.

Smith, Tom W. 2003. *Coming of Age in 21st Century America: Public Attitudes toward the Importance and Timing of Transition to Adulthood.* Chicago: National Opinion Research Center.

———. 2009. *Religious Change around the World.* Chicago: NORC/University of Chicago.

Snyder, Thomas D. 1996. *Digest of Education Statistics 1996.* Washington, DC: U.S. Government Printing Office.

Somaskanda, Sumi. 2012. "European Pensions Targeted." *USA Today,* September 20, p. 2B.

Somavia, Juan. 2008. "The ILO at 90 Working for Social Justice." *World of Work* 64 (December):4–5.

Sorokin, Pitirim A. [1927] 1959. *Social and Cultural Mobility.* New York: Free Press.

Southern Poverty Law Center. 2010. "Active 'Patriot' Groups in the United States in 2009." Accessed November 5 (www.splcenter.org/patriot).

———. 2013. "Patriot Movement." Accessible at http://www.splcenter.org/get-informed/intelligence-files/ideology/patriot-movememnt.

Spalter-Roth, Roberta, Nicole Van Vooren, and Mary S. Senter. 2013. "Using the Bachelor's and Beyond Project to Help Launch Students in Careers." Accessed November 1 at www.asanet.org/documents/research/docs/B%26BLaunchingCareers.pptx.

Spar, Debora. 2001. *Ruling the Waves: Cycles of Discovery, Chaos, and Wealth from the Compass to the Internet.* New York: Harcourt.

Spencer, Nancy. 2008. "Title IX." Pp. 1308–1310, vol. 3, in *Encyclopedia of Race, Ethnicity, and Society,* edited by Richard T. Schaefer. Thousand Oaks, CA: Sage.

Spitzer, Steven. 1975. "Toward a Marxian Theory of Deviance." *Social Problems* 22 (June):641–651.

Sprague, Joey. 2005. *Feminist Methodologies for Critical Research: Bridging Differences.* Lanham, MD: AltaMira Press.

Stacey, Judith. 2011. *Unhitched.* New York: New York University Press.

Stansell, Christine. 2011. *The Feminist Promise: 1792 to the Present.* New York: The Modern Library.

Stark, Rodney. 2004. *Exploring the Religious Life.* Baltimore: Johns Hopkins University Press.

———. 2005. *The Rise of Mormonism,* edited by Reid L. Neilson. New York: Columbia University Press.

———, and William Sims Bainbridge. 1979. "Of Churches, Sects, and Cults: Preliminary Concepts for a Theory of Religious Movements." *Journal for the Scientific Study of Religion* 18 (June):117–131.

———, and ———. 1985. *The Future of Religion.* Berkeley: University of California Press.

Staton, Ron. 2004. "Still Fighting for National Hawaiian Recognition." *Asian Week,* January 22, p. 8.

Steffen, Alex, ed. 2008. *World Changing: A User's Guide for the 21st Century.* New York: Harry N. Abrams.

Stein, Leonard I. 1967. "The Doctor-Nurse Game." *Archives of General Psychology* 16:699–703.

Stevick, Richard A. 2007. *Growing Up Amish: The Teenage Years.* Baltimore: Johns Hopkins University Press.

Stockard, Janice E. 2002. *Marriage in Culture.* Belmont, CA: Thomson Wadsworth.

Stolberg, Sheryl Gay. 2008. "Richest Nations Pledge to Halve Greenhouse Gas." *New York Times,* July 9, pp. A1, A13.

Stray, Jonathan. 2012. "Are We Stuck in Filter Bubbles? Here Are Five Potential Paths Out." July 12. Accessed December 1 at http://www.niemanlab.org/2012/07/are-we-stuck-in-filter-bubbles-here-are-five-potential-paths-out/.

Suárez, Zulema E., and Rose M. Perez. 2012. "The Cuban American Family." Pp. 112–128 in *Ethnic Families in America: Patterns and Variations.* 5th ed., edited by Roosevelt Wright, Jr., Charles H. Mindel, Thanh Van Tran, and Robert W. Halsenstein. Upper Saddle River, NJ: Pearson.

Subramaniam, Mangala. 2006. *The Power of Women's Organization: Gender, Caste, and Class in India.* Lanham, MD: Lexington Books.

Suh, Doowon. 2011. "Institutionalizing Social Movements: The Dual Strategy of the Korean Women's Movement." *Sociological Quarterly* 52:442–471.

Suitor, J. Jill, Staci A. Minyard, and Rebecca S. Carter. 2001. "'Did You See What I Saw?' Gender Differences in Perceptions of Avenues to Prestige among Adolescents." *Sociological Inquiry* 71 (Fall):437–454.

Sullivan, Harry Stack. [1953] 1968. *The Interpersonal Theory of Psychiatry.* Edited by Helen Swick Perry and Mary Ladd Gawel. New York: Norton.

Sullivan, Kevin. 2006. "Bridging the Digital Divide." *Washington Post National Weekly Edition* 25 (July 17):11–12.

Sum, Andrew, Paul Harrington, and Ishwar Khatiwada. 2006. *The Impact of New Immigrants on Young Native-Born Workers, 2000–2005.* Washington, DC: Center for Immigration Studies.

Sumner, William G. 1906. *Folkways.* New York: Ginn.

Sunstein, Cass. 2002. *Republic.com.* Rutgers, NJ: Princeton University Press.

Survival International. 2012. "Brazilian Indians." Accessed January 12 (www.survivalinternational.org/tribes/Brazilian).

SustainAbility. 2006. *Brazil—Country of Diversities and Inequalities.* London: SustainAbility.

Sutch, Richard, and Susan B. Carter. 2006. *Historical Statutes of US: Earliest Time to the Present.* Cambridge: Cambridge University Press.

Sutherland, Edwin H. 1937. *The Professional Thief.* Chicago: University of Chicago Press.

———. 1940. "White-Collar Criminality." *American Sociological Review* 5 (February):1–11.

———. 1949. *White Collar Crime.* New York: Dryden.

———. 1983. *White Collar Crime: The Uncut Version.* New Haven, CT: Yale University Press.

———, Donald R. Cressey, and David F. Luckenbill. 1992. *Principles of Criminology.* 11th ed. New York: Rowman and Littlefield.

Swanson, Emily. 2013. "Poll: Few Identify as Feminists, but Most Believe in Equality of Sexes." *Huffington Post,* April 15. Accessible at www.huffingtonpost.com.

Swartz, Jon. 2012. "Google's Personalized Search Charges Set Off Uproar." *USA Today,* January 12, p. B1.

Swatos, William H., Jr., ed. 1998. *Encyclopedia of Religion and Society.* Lanham, MD: AltaMira.

Sweet, Kimberly. 2001. "Sex Sells a Second Time." *Chicago Journal* 93 (April):12–13.

Swidler, Ann. 1986. "Culture in Action: Symbols and Strategies." *American Sociological Review* 51 (April):273–286.

Szabo, Liz. 2013. "Mental Illness Takes Fall in Gun Laws." *USA Today,* March 12, p. 7D.

Szasz, Andrew. 2007. *Shopping Our Way to Safety: How We Changed from Protecting the Environment to Protecting Ourselves.* Minneapolis: University of Minnesota Press.

Szasz, Thomas. 2010. *The Myth of Mental Illness: Foundations of a Theory of Personal Conduct.* 50th Anniversary Edition. New York: Harper Perennial.

T

Tabuchi, Hiroko. 2013. "Desperate Hunt for Day Care." *New York Times,* February 27, pp. A4, A9.

Tachibana, Judy. 1990. "Model Minority Myth Presents Unrepresentative Portrait of Asian Americans, Many Educators Say." *Black Issues in Higher Education* 6 (March 1):1, 11.

Takei, Isao, and Arthur Sakamoto. 2011. "Poverty Among Asian Americans in the 21st Century." *Sociological Perspectives* 54 (Summer):251–276.

Tanielian, Terri. 2009. "Assessing Combat Exposure and Post-Traumatic Stress Disorder in Troops and Estimating the Costs to Society." Testimony presented before the House Veterans' Affairs Committee, Subcommittee on Disability Assistance and Memorial Affairs (March 24).

Tannen, Deborah. 1990. *You Just Don't Understand: Women and Men in Conversation.* New York: Ballantine.

Tatchell, Jo. 2009. *A Diamond in the Desert: Behind the Scenes in the World's Richest City.* London: Hodder and Stoughton.

Taylor, Rob. 2013. "Australian Court Rejects Same-Sex Marriage." *Wall Street Journal,* December 13, p. A14.

Taylor, Verta. 1999. "Gender and Social Movements: Gender Processes in Women's Self-Help Movements." *Gender and Society* 13:8–33.

———. 2004. "Social Movements and Gender." Pp. 14348–14352 in *International Encyclopedia of the Social and Behavioral Sciences,* edited by Neil J. Smelser and Paul B. Baltes. New York: Elsevier.

———, Leila J. Rupp, and Nancy Whittier. 2009. *Feminist Frontiers.* 8th ed. New York: McGraw-Hill.

Teaching Tolerance. 2012. "LGBT Content Access Denied." Accessed March 29 (www.tollerance.org/blog/lgbt-content-access-denied).

Tedeschi, Bob. 2006. "Those Born to Shop Can Now Use Cellphones." *New York Times,* January 2.

Telles, Edward E. 2004. *Race in America: The Significance of Skin Color in Brazil.* Princeton, NJ: Princeton University Press.

Teranishi, Robert T. 2010. *Asians in the Ivory Tower: Dilemmas of Racial Inequity in American Higher Education.* New York: Teachers College Press.

Themed Entertainment Association. 2012. *Global Attractions Attendance Report 2011.* Burbank, CA: TEA.

Thomas, Gordon, and Max Morgan Witts. 1974. *Voyage of the Damned.* Greenwich, CT: Fawcett Crest.

Thomas Jr., Landon. 2011. "Money Troubles Take Personal Toll in Greece." *New York Times,* May 16, pp. A1, A2. Accessible at www.nytimes.com/2011/05/16/business/global/16drachma.html?pagewanted=all.

Thomas, R. Murray. 2003. "New Frontiers in Cheating." In *Encyclopaedia Britannica 2003 Book of the Year.* Chicago: Encyclopaedia Britannica.

Thomas, William I. 1923. *The Unadjusted Girl.* Boston: Little, Brown.

Thomasrobb.com. 2007. "WhitePride TV." Accessed May 7 (http://thomasrobb.com).

Thompson, Tony. 2005. "Romanians Are Being Paid to Play Computer Games for Westerners." *Guardian Weekly,* March 25, p. 17.

Threadcraft, Shatema. 2008. "Welfare Queen." In *Encyclopedia of Race, Ethnicity and Society,* edited by Richard T. Schaefer. Thousand Oaks, CA: Sage.

Thurow, Lester. 1984. "The Disappearance of the Middle Class." *New York Times,* February 5, sec. 5, p. 2.

Tibbles, Kevin. 2007. "Web Sites Encourage Eating Disorders." *Today,* February 18. Accessed May 7 (www.msabc.msn.com).

Tierney, William G. and Karri A. Holley. 2008. "Intelligent Design and the Attack on Scientific Inquiry." *Cultural Studies Critical Methodologies* 8 (February):39–49.

Tigay, Chanan. 2011. "Women and Sports." *CQ Researcher* 21 (March 25).

Tilly, Charles. 1964. *The Vendée.* Cambridge, MA: Harvard University Press.

———. 1980. "The Old New Social History and the New Old Social History." October. Center for Research on Social Organization Working Paper No. 218. Accessed December 1, 2013 at http://deepblue.lib.umich.edu/bitstream/handle/2027.42/50992/218.pdf?sequence=1.

———. 1993. *Popular Contention in Great Britain 1758–1834.* Cambridge, MA: Harvard University Press.

———. 2003. *The Politics of Collective Violence.* New York: Cambridge University Press.

———. 2004. *Social Movements, 1768–2004.* Boulder, CO: Paradigm.

———. 2007. "Trust Networks in Transnational Migration." *Sociological Forum* 22 (March): 3–24.

Tilly, Chris. 1991. "Reasons for the Continuing Growth of Part-time Employment." *Monthly Labor Review* (March):10–18.

Timmerman, Kelsey. 2009. *Where Am I Wearing?* Hoboken NJ: Wiley.

———. 2013. "Follow the Label: The Odyssey of Our Food and Clothing." *Christian Science Monitor Weekly* (July 22):27–29.

Toensing, Gale Country. 2009. "Akaka Bill Gets Obama Approval." *Indian Country Today* (August 19):1, 2.

Toffler, Alvin. 1970. *Future Shock.* New York: Bantam Books.

———. 1980. *The Third Wave.* New York: Bantam Books.

Toma, Catalina L., and Jeffrey T. Hancock. 2010. "Looks and Lies: The Role of Physical Attractiveness in Online Dating Self-Presentation and Deception." *Community Research* 37 (3):335–351.

———, ———, and Nicole B. Ellison. 2008. "Separating Fact from Fiction: An Examination of Deceptive Self-Presentation in Online Dating Profiles." *Personality and Social Psychology Bulletin* 34:1023–1036.

Tönnies, Ferdinand. [1887] 1988. *Community and Society.* Rutgers, NJ: Transaction.

Toossi, Mitra. 2009. "Employment Outlook: 2008–2018." *Monthly Labor Review* (November):30–51.

———. 2012. "Labor Force Projections to 2020: A More Slowly Growing Labor Force." *Monthly Labor Review* (January):43–64.

Toppo, Greg. 2011. "The Search for a New Way to Test Schoolkids." *USA Today,* March 18, p. A4.

Torres, Lourdes. 2008. "Puerto Rican Americans" and "Puerto Rico." Pp. 1082–1089, vol. 3, in *Encyclopedia of Race, Ethnicity, and Society,* edited by Richard T. Schaefer. Thousand Oaks, CA: Sage.

Torrey, E. Fuller. 2013. "Fifty Years of Failing America's Mentally Ill." *Wall Street Journal,* February 5, p. A15.

Touraine, Alain. 1974. *The Academic System in American Society.* New York: McGraw-Hill.

Transactional Records Access Clearinghouse. 2009. "TRAC Monthly Bulletins by Topic, September 2009." Accessed February 11, 2010 (www.trac.syr.edu/tracreports/bulletins/white_collar_crime/monthly_sep09/fil).

Trimble, Charles. 2008. "Itheska: Notes from Mixed Blood Country." *Indian Country Today* (May 7):5.

Trimble, Lindsey B., and Julie A. Kmec. 2011. "The Role of Social Networks in Getting a Job." *Sociology Compass* 5 (2):165–178.

Trotter III, Robert T., and Juan Antonio Chavira. 1997. *Curanderismo: Mexican American Folk Healing.* Athens: University of Georgia Press.

Trottman, Melanie, and Kris Maher. 2013. "Organized Labor Loses Members." *Wall Street Journal,* January 24, p. A6.

Truman, Jennifer, Lynn Langton, and Michael Planty. 2013. *Criminal Victimization, 2012.* NCJ243389. October 2013. Accessed at www.bjs.gov.

Trumbull, Mark. 2006. "America's Younger Workers Losing Ground on Income." *Christian Science Monitor,* February 27.

Tuan, Mia, and Jiannbin Lee Shiao. 2011. *Choosing Ethnicity, Negotiating Race: Korean Adoptees in America.* New York: Russell Sage Foundation.

Tuchman, Gaye. 1992. "Feminist Theory." Pp. 695–704 in *Encyclopedia of Sociology,* vol. 2, edited by Edgar F. Borgatta and Marie L. Borgatta. New York: Macmillan.

Tucker, Robert C. (ed.) 1978. *The Marx-Engels Reader.* 2nd ed. New York: Norton.

Ture, Kwame, and Charles Hamilton. 1992. *Black Power: The Politics of Liberation.* With new Afterword by authors. New York: Vintage Books.

Turkle, Sherry. 2004. "How Computers Change the Way We Think." *Chronicle of Higher Education* 50 (January 30):B26–B28.

———. 2011. *Alone Together: Why We Expect More from Technology and Less from Each Other.* New York: Basic Books.

Turner, Bryan S., ed. 1990. *Theories of Modernity and Postmodernity.* Newbury Park, CA: Sage.

Turner, C. F, L. Ku, S. M. Rogers, L. D. Lindberg, H. Pleck, and F. L. Sonenstein. 1998. "Adolescent Sexual Behavior, Drug Use, and Violence: Increased Reporting with Computer Survey Technology." *Science* 280 (May 8):867–873.

U

Uggen, Christopher. 2012. "The Crime Wave that Wasn't." *Pathways* (Fall):13–18.

UNAIDS. 2013. *AIDS by the Numbers.* November 20, 2013. Accessible at http://www.unaids.org/en/media/unaids/contentassets/images/infographics/2013/20131120aids bythenumbers01/20131120_aidsbythe numbers_en.pdf.

UNICEF. 2009. *Progress for Children: A Report Card on Child Protection.* September. Vienna: UNICEF.

———. 2010. "Child Marriage." Accessed January 15 (www.unicef.org/progressfprchildren/2007n6/index_41848.htm?q=printme).

United Nations. 2005. *The Millennium Development Goals Report.* Washington, DC: United Nations.

———. 2009. *International Migration Report 2006: A Global Assessment.* New York: United Nations, Economic and Social Affairs.

———. 2013. "Number of International Migrants Rises above 232 Million, UN Reports." September 11. United Nations News Centre. Accessible at www.un.org.

United Nations Development Programme. 1995. *Human Development Report 1995.* New York: Oxford University Press.

———. 2000. *Poverty Report 2000: Overcoming Human Poverty.* Washington, DC: UNDP.

———. 2009. *Overcoming Barriers: Human Mobility and Development.* New York: Palgrave Macmillan.

United Nations Economic and Social Council. 2010. "Review of the Implementation of the Beijing Declaration." New York: Economic and Social Council.

United Nations Office on Drugs and Crime. 2010. *The Globalization of Crime: A Transnational Organized Crime Threat Assessment.* New York: UNODO.

United Nations Population Division. 2013a. "World Abortion Policies." Accessed January 15, 2014 at http://www.un.org/en/development/desa/population/publications/policy/world-abortion-policies-2013.shtml.

———. 2013. *Median Age at First Marriage.* Geneva: Department of Economic and Social Affairs.

United Nations Statistics Division. 2009. *Demographic Yearbook 2007.* Accessed April 1, 2010 (http://unstats.un.org/unsd/ demographic/products/dyb/dyb2.htm).

———. 2013. *Demographic Yearbook 2013.* New York: United Nations.

United States Copyright Office. 2012. *Annual Report of the Register of Copyrights.* Accessible at http://www.copyright.gov/reports/annual/2011/ar2011.pdf.

United States Patent and Trademark Office. 2012. *Patenting by Organizations, 2012.* Accessible at http://www.uspto.gov/web/offices/ac/ido/oeip/taf/topo_12.pdf.

University of Michigan. 2003. *Information on Admissions Lawsuits.* Accessed August 8 (www.umich.edu/urel/admissions).

Urban Dictionary. 2012. "Urban Amish." Accessed March 29 (www.urbandictionary.com/define.php?term=urban+20amish).

U.S. English. 2012. "Making English the Official Language." Accessed January 12 (www.us-english.org/inc/).

U.S. Surgeon General. 1999. *Surgeon General's Report on Mental Health.* Washington, DC: U.S. Government Printing Office.

V

Vaidhyanathan, Siva. 2008. "Generational Myth: Not All Young People Are Tech-Savvy." *Chronicle of Higher Education,* September 19, pp. B7–B9.

Vamosi, Robert, Mary Monahan, and Rachel Kim. 2010. *2010 Identity Fraud Survey Report.* Pleasanton, CA: Javelin Strategy.

van den Berghe, Pierre L. 1978. *Race and Racism: A Comparative Perspective.* 2nd ed. New York: Wiley.

van Dijk, Jan, John van Kesteren, and Paul Smit. 2007. *Criminal Victimisation* [sic] *in International Perspective.* Tilburg, Netherlands: United Nations Office on Drugs and Crime. Accessible at http://www.uncri.it/services/library_documentation/publications/icvs/publicatons/ICVS2004_05report.pdf.

Van Gennep, Arnold. [1909] 1960. *The Rites of Passage.* Translated by Monika B. Vizedom and Gabrielle L. Caffee. Chicago: University of Chicago Press.

van Vucht Tijssen, Lieteke. 1990. "Women between Modernity and Postmodernity." Pp. 147–163 in *Theories of Modernity and Postmodernity,* edited by Bryan S. Turner. London: Sage.

VandenBrook, Tom. 2013. "Army Leaders Warned about Issues with Human Terrain System." September 23. Accessible at http://www.armytimes.com/article/20130923/NEWS/3092230032/.

Vasagar, Jeeran. 2005. "'At Last Rwanda Is Known for Something Positive." *Guardian Weekly,* July 22, p. 18.

Vaughan, R. M. 2007. "Cairo's Man Show." *Utne Reader* (March–April):94–95.

Veblen, Thorstein. [1899] 1964. *Theory of the Leisure Class.* New York: Macmillan. New York: Penguin.

———. 1919. *The Vested Interests and the State of the Industrial Arts.* New York: Huebsch.

Venkatesh, Sudhir Alladi. 2006. *Off the Books: The Underground Economy of the Urban Poor.* Cambridge, MA: Harvard University Press.

———. 2008. *Gang Leader for a Day: A Rogue Sociologist Takes to the Streets.* New York: Penguin Press.

Vernon, Glenn. 1962. *Sociology and Religion.* New York: McGraw-Hill.

Vespa, Jonathan, Jamie M. Lewis, and Rose M. Kreider. 2013. "America's Families and Living Arrangements 2012." August 2013. Accessible at http://www.census.gov/prod/2013pubs/p20-570.pdf.

Vigdor, Jacob L. 2011. "Comparing Immigrant Assimilation in North American and Europe." May 2011. Accessible at www.manhattan-institute.org/cgl-bin/apMI/print.cgi.

Violence Policy Center. 2012. *Gun Deaths Outpace Motor Vehicle Deaths in 10 States in 2009.* Washington, DC: VPC.

Viramontes, Helena Maria. 2007. "Loyalty Spoken Here." *Los Angeles Times,* September 23, p. R7.

Visser, Jelle. 2006. "Union Membership Statistics in 24 Countries." *Monthly Labor Review* (January):38–49.

Volti, Rudi. 2010. *Society and Technological Change.* 6th ed. New York: Worth Publishers.

W

Wages for Housework Campaign. 1999. *Wages for Housework Campaign.* Circular. Los Angeles.

Wagley, Charles, and Marvin Harris. 1958. *Minorities in the New World: Six Case Studies.* New York: Columbia University Press.

Waitzkin, Howard. 1986. *The Second Sickness: Contradictions of Capitalist Health Care.* Chicago: University of Chicago Press.

Walder, Andrew. G. 2009. "Political Sociology and Social Movements." *Annual Review of Sociology* 35:393–412.

———, and Giang Hoang Nguyen. 2008. "Ownership, Organization, and Income Inequality: Market Transition in Rural Vietnam." *American Sociological Review* 73 (April):251–269.

Waldman, Amy. 2004a. "India Takes Economic Spotlight, and Critics Are Unkind." *New York Times,* March 7, p. 3.

———. 2004b. "Low-Tech or High, Jobs Are Scarce in India's Boon." *New York Times,* May 6, p. A3.

———. 2004c. "What India's Upset Vote Reveals: The High Tech Is Skin Deep." *New York Times,* May 15, p. A5.

Walker, Edward. 2010. "Activism Industry-Driven." *Contexts* (Spring):43–49.

Wallace, Ruth A., and Alison Wolf. 1980. *Contemporary Sociological Theory.* Englewood Cliffs, NJ: Prentice Hall.

Wallerstein, Immanuel. 1974. *The Modern World System.* New York: Academic Press.

———. 1979a. *Capitalist World Economy.* Cambridge: Cambridge University Press.

———. 1979b. *The End of the World as We Know It: Social Science for the Twenty-First Century.* Minneapolis: University of Minnesota Press.

———. 2000. *The Essential Wallerstein.* New York: New Press.

———. 2012. "Reflections on an Intellectual Adventure." *Contemporary Sociology* 41 (1):6–12.

Wallis, Claudia. 2005. "A Snapshot of Teen Sex." *Time,* February 7, p. 58.

———. 2008. "How to Make Great Teachers." *Time* 171 (February 25):28–34.

Walsh, Anthony. 2000. "Behavior Genetics and Anomie/Strain Theory." *Criminology* (November):1075–1107.

Wang, Esther. 2013. "As Wal-Mart Swallows China's Economy, Workers Fight Back." April 23. Accessed November 16 at http://prospect.org/article/wal-mart-swallows-chinas-economy-workers-fight-back.

Wang, Wendy. 2012. "The Rise of Intermarriage: Rates, Characteristics Vary by Race and Gender." Washington, DC: Pew Social and Demographic Trends.

Warrell, Helen. 2013. "Cost of Malnutrition to Global Economy Put at $125bn by 2030." *Financial Times* (May 28):3.

Wattenberg, Martin P. 2008. *Is Voting for Young People?* New York: Pearson Longman.

Weber, Max. [1904] 1949. *Methodology of the Social Sciences.* Translated by Edward A. Shils and Henry A. Finch. Glencoe, IL: Free Press.

———. [1904] 2011. *The Protestant Ethic and the Spirit Capitalism.* The Revised 1920 Edition. Translation by Stephen Kalberg. New York: Oxford University Press.

———. [1913–1922] 1947. *The Theory of Social and Economic Organization.* Translated by A. Henderson and T. Parsons. New York: Free Press.

———. [1916] 1958. *The Religion of India: The Sociology of Hinduism and Buddhism.* New York: Free Press.

Wechsler, Henry, J. E. Lee, M. Kuo, M. Seibring, T. F. Nelson, and H. Lee. 2002. "Trends in College Binge Drinking during a Period of Increased Prevention Efforts: Findings from Four Harvard School of Public Health College Alcohol Surveys: 1993–2001." *Journal of American College Health* 50 (5):203–217.

———, Mark Seibring, I- Chao Liu, and Marilyn Ahl. 2004. "Colleges Respond to Student Binge Drinking: Reducing Student Demand or Limiting Access." *Journal of American College Health* 52 (4):159–168.

Weeks, John R. 2012. *Population: An Introduction to Concepts and Issues.* 11th ed. Belmont, CA: Cengage.

Weinberg, Daniel H. 2004. *Evidence from Census 2000 About Earnings by Detailed Occupation for Men and Women.* CENSR-15. Washington, DC: U.S. Government Printing Office.

———. 2007. "Earnings by Gender: Evidence from Census 2000." *Monthly Labor Review* (July–August):26–34.

Weinraub, Bernard. 2004. "UPN Show Is Called Insensitive to Amish." *New York Times,* March 4, pp. B1, B8.

Weitz, Rose. 2009. *The Sociology of Health, Illness, and Heath Care.* 5th ed. Belmont, CA: Cengage.

Welch, William M. 2011. "More Hawaii Residents Identify as Mixed Race." *USA Today,* February 28.

Wells-Barnett, Ida B. 1970. *Crusade for Justice: The Autobiography of Ida B. Wells.* Edited by Alfreda M. Duster. Chicago: University of Chicago Press.

Wentling, Tre, Elroi Windsor, Kristin Schilt, and Betsy Lucal. 2008. "Teaching Transgender." *Teaching Sociology* 36 (January):49–57.

Wesolowski, Amy, Nathan Eagle, Andrew J. Tatem, David L. Smith, Abdisalam M. Noor, Robert W. Snow, and Caroline O. Buckee. 2012. "Quantifying the Impact of Human Mobility on Malaria." *Science* (October 12):267–270.

Wessel, David. 2011. "Untangling the Long-Term-Unemployment Crisis." *Wall Street Journal,* October 20, p. A6.

———. 2012. "Race's Roles in Economic Fate." *Wall Street Journal,* September 20, p. A6.

———, and Stephanie Banchero. 2012. "Education Slowdown Threatens U.S." *Wall Street Journal,* April 26, p. A1.

West, Candace, and Don H. Zimmerman. 1987. "Doing Gender." *Gender and Society* 1 (June):125–151.

Westergaard-Nielsen, Niels. 2008. *Low-Wage Work in Denmark.* New York: Russell Sage Foundation.

Western, Bruce, and Jake Rosenfeld. 2011. "Unions, Norms, and the Rise in U.S. Wage Inequality." *American Sociological Review* 70 (4):513–537.

White House. 2013. "Fact Sheet: The President's Plan to Reward Work by Raising the Minimum Wage." February 13. Accessed February 20 at www.whitehouse.gov.

Whitlock, Craig. 2005. "The Internet as Bully Pulpit." *Washington Post National Weekly Edition* 22 (August 22):9.

Whittaker, Stephanie. 2006. "Who Would You Prefer to Work For?" *Gazette* (Montreal), November 4, p. 1.

Whyte, William Foote. 1981. *Street Corner Society: Social Structure of an Italian Slum.* 3rd ed. Chicago: University of Chicago Press.

Wildsmith, Elizabeth, Nicole R. Steward-Streng, and Jennifer Manlove. 2011. "Childbearing Outside of Marriage: Estimates and Trends in the United States." *Child Trends Research Brief* #2011-29. Accessible at www.childtrends.org.

Wilford, John Noble. 1997. "New Clues Show Where People Made the Great Leap to Agriculture." *New York Times,* November 18, pp. B9, B12.

Wilgoren, Jodi. 2005. "In Kansas, Darwinism Goes on Trial Once More." *New York Times,* May 6, p. A14.

Wilkes, Rima, and John Iceland. 2004. "Hypersegregation in the Twenty-First Century." *Demography* 41 (February):23–36.

Wilkins, Amy C. 2012. "Becoming Black Women: Intimate Stories and Intersectional Identities." *Social Psychological Quarterly* 75 (2):173–196.

Wilkinson, Tracy. 2011. "Cuba: Now Open for Business." *Chicago Tribune,* August 15, p. 14.

Williams, Carol J. 1995. "Taking an Eager Step Back." *Los Angeles Times,* June 3, pp. A1, A14.

Williams, David R., and Chiquita Collins. 2004. "Reparations." *American Behavioral Scientist* 47 (March):977–1000.

Williams, J. Allen, Christopher Podeschi, Nathan Palmer, Philip Schwadel, and Deanna Meyler. 2012. "The Human-Environment Dialog in Award-winning Children's Picture Books." *Sociological Inquiry* 82 (February): 145–159.

Williams, Robin M., Jr. 1970. *American Society.* 3rd ed. New York: Knopf.

———, with John P. Dean and Edward A. Suchman. 1964. *Strangers Next Door: Ethnic Relations in American Communities.* Englewood Cliffs, NJ: Prentice Hall.

Wills, Jeremiah B., and Barbara J. Risman. 2006. "The Visibility of Feminist Thought in Family Studies." *Journal of Marriage and Family* 68 (August):690–700.

Wilson, Edward O. 1975. *Sociobiology: The New Synthesis.* Cambridge, MA: Harvard University Press.

———. 1978. *On Human Nature.* Cambridge, MA: Harvard University Press.

———. 2000. *Sociobiology: The New Synthesis.* Cambridge, MA: Belknap Press, Harvard University Press.

Wilson, James Q. 2011. "Hard Times, Fewer Crimes." *Wall Street Journal,* May 28, pp. C1–C2.

Wilson, John. 1973. *Introduction to Social Movements.* New York: Basic Books.

Wilson, William Julius. 1996. *When Work Disappears: The World of the New Urban Poor.* New York: Knopf.

———. 1999. *The Bridge over the Racial Divide: Rising Inequality and Coalition Politics.* Berkeley: University of California Press.

———. 2009. *More Than Just Race: Being Black and Poor in the Inner City.* New York: Norton.

———. 2012a. *The Declining Significance of Race: Blacks and Changing American Institutions.* 3rd ed. Chicago: University of Chicago Press.

———. 2012b. *The Truly Disadvantaged: The Inner City, the Underclass and Public Policy.* 2nd ed. Chicago: University of Chicago Press.

———, J. M. Quane, and B. H. Rankin. 2004. "Underclass." In *International Encyclopedia of Social and Behavioral Sciences.* New York: Elsevier.

———, and Richard P. Taub. 2006. *There Goes the Neighborhood: Racial, Ethnic, and Class Tensions in Four Chicago Neighborhoods and Their Meaning for America.* New York: Alfred A. Knopf.

Winant, Howard B. 1994. *Racial Conditions: Politics, Theory, Comparisons.* Minneapolis: University of Minnesota Press.

———. 2006. "Race and Racism: Towards a Global Future." *Ethnic and Racial Studies* 29 (September):986–1003.

Winickoff, Jonathan P., Joan Friebely, Susanne E. Tanski, Cheryl Sherrod, George E. Matt, Melbourne F. Hovell, and Robert C. McMillen. 2009. "Beliefs about the Health Effects of 'Thirdhand' Smoke and Home Smoking Bans." *Pediatrics* 123 (January):74–79.

Winkler, Adam. 2009. "Heller's Catch-22." *UCLA Law Review* 56 (June).

Winter, J. Allen. 2008. "Symbolic Ethnicity." Pp. 1288–1290, vol. 3, in *Encyclopedia of Race, Ethnicity, and Society,* edited by Richard T. Schaefer. Thousand Oaks, CA: Sage.

Wirth, Louis. 1931. "Clinical Sociology." *American Journal of Sociology* 37 (July):49–60.

Wolf, Naomi. 1992. *The Beauty Myth: How Images of Beauty Are Used against Women.* New York: Anchor Books.

Wolfe, Alan. 2008. "Pew in the Pews." *Chronicle of Higher Education,* March 21, pp. B5–B6.

Women's Sports Foundation. 2011. *Title IX.* Accessed March 29 (http://www.womens sportsfoundation.org/Issues-And-Research/ Title-IX.aspx).

Wong, Morrison G. 2006. "Chinese Americans." Pp. 110–145 in *Asian Americans: Contemporary Trends and Issues,* 2nd ed., edited by Pyong Gap Min. Thousand Oaks, CA: Sage.

Wood, Daniel B. 2012. "How Serious Crime Fell in US." *Christian Science Monitor* (January 16):18.

Woon, Lee Kang. 2005. "Socialization of Transracially Adopted Korean Americans: A Self Analysis." *Human Architecture: Journal of the Sociology of Self-Knowledge* 3 (Spring):79–84.

Working Women's Forum. 2012. Home Page. Accessed March 27 (www.workingwomens forum.org).

World Association of Girl Guides and Girl Scouts. 2011. "Our World." Accessed November 10 (www.wagggs.org/en/world).

World Bank. 2011. *Development Indicators 2011.* Washington, DC: World Bank.

———. 2012a. *World Development Indicators 2012.* Washington, DC: World Bank.

———. 2012b. *Gender Equality and Development.* Washington, DC: World Bank

———. 2013. "World Indicators 2013." Accessible online data at http://wdi.worldbank.org/tables.

World Development Forum. 1990. "The Danger of Television." 8 (July 15):4.

World Health Organization. 2009. "Biotechnology (GM Foods)." Accessed May 11 (www.who.int/foodsafety/biotech/en/).

———. 2010. "Suicide Prevention." Accessed October 31 (http://www.who.int/mental_health/prevention/en/).

World Stats. 2014. "Internet World Stats." Accessed February 11, 2014 at http://www.internetworldstats.com.

World Unplugged. 2013. "One World Unplugged. 'Comparison Charts.'" Accessible at http://theworldunplugged.wordpress.com/about/comparison-charts-of-reactions/.

Worth, Robert F. 2008. "As Taboos Ease, Saudi Girl Group Dares to Rock." New York Times, November 24, pp. A1, A9.

Wortham, Robert A. 2008. "DuBois, William Edward Burghardt." Pp. 423–427, vol. 1, in Encyclopedia of Race, Ethnicity, and Society, edited by Richard T. Schaefer. Thousand Oaks CA: Sage.

Wray, Matt, Matthew Miller, Jill Gurvey, Joanna Carroll, and Ichiro Kawachi. 2008. "Leaving Las Vegas: Exposure to Las Vegas and Risk of Suicide." Social Science and Medicine 67:1882–1888.

———, Cynthia Colen, and Bernice Pescosolido. 2011. "The Sociology of Suicide." Annual Review of Sociology 37:505–528.

Wright II, Earl. 2012. "Why, Where, and How to Infuse the Atlanta Sociological Laboratory into the Sociology Curriculum." Teaching Sociology 40 (43):257–270.

Wright, Charles R. 1986. Mass Communication: A Sociological Perspective. 3rd ed. New York: Random House.

Wright, Eric R., William P. Gronfein, and Timothy J. Owens. 2000. "Deinstitutionalization, Social Rejection, and the Self-Esteem of Former Mental Patients." Journal of Health and Social Behavior (March).

Wright, Erik O. 2011. "The Classical Marxist Theory of the History of Capitalism's Future." October 3. Accessed January 20, 2012 (www.ssc.wisc.edu/~wright/621-2011/lecture%208%202011%20--%20Classical%20Theory%20of%20Capitalisms%20future.pdf).

———, David Hachen, Cynthia Costello, and Joey Sprague. 1982. "The American Class Structure." American Sociological Review 47 (December):709–726.

Wyatt, Edward. 2009. "No Smooth Ride on TV Networks' Road to Diversity." New York Times, March 18, pp. 1, 5.

Y

Yemma, John. 2013. "Teaching the Freedom to Believe." Christian Science Monitor (June 17):5.

Yinger, J. Milton. 1970. The Scientific Study of Religion. New York: Macmillan.

York, Richard, Eugene A. Rosa, and Thomas Dietz. 2010. "Ecological Modernization Theory: Theoretical and Empirical Challenges." Pp. 77–90 in The International Handbook and Environmental Sociology, 2nd ed., edited by Michael R. Redclift and Graham Woodgate. Cheltenham, UK: Edward Elgar.

Young, Kevin, ed. 2004. Sporting Bodies, Damaged Selves. New York: Elsevier.

Yourish, Karen, and Larry Buchanan. 2013. "State Gun Laws Enacted in Year Since Newtown." New York Times, December 11, p. A20.

Yunus, Muhammad. 2010. Building Social Business. New York: Perseus.

Z

Zakaria, Fareed. 2012. "Incarceration Nation." Time, April 2, p. 18.

Zarembo, Alan. 2004a. "A Theater of Inquiry and Evil." Los Angeles Times, July 15, pp. A1, A24, A25.

Zeitzen, Miriam Koktvedgaard. 2008. Polygamy: A Cross-Cultural Analysis. Oxford, UK: Berg.

Zellner, William M. 1995. Counter Cultures: A Sociological Analysis. New York: St. Martin's Press.

Zernike, Kate. 2002. "With Student Cheating on the Rise, More Colleges Are Turning to Honor Codes." New York Times, November 2, p. A10.

Zhang, Xiaodan. 2009. "Trade Unions under the Modernization of Paternalists Rule in China." Journal of Labor and Society 12 (June):193–218.

Zi, Jui-Chung Allen. 2007. The Kids Are OK: Divorce and Children's Behavior Problems. Santa Monica, CA: RAND.

Zia, Helen. 2000. Asian American Dreams: The Emergence of an American People. New York: Farrar, Straus & Giroux.

Zimbardo, Philip G. 1972. "Pathology of Imprisonment." Society 9 (April):4, 6, 8.

———. 2004. "Power Turns Good Soldiers into 'Bad Apples.'" Boston Globe, May 9. Also accessible at www.prisonexp.org.

———. 2007. The Lucifer Effect: Understanding How Good People Turn Evil. New York: Random House.

———. 2007a. "Revisiting the Stanford Prison Experiment: A Lesson in the Power of the Situation." Chronicle of Higher Education 53 (March 20):B6, B7.

———, Craig Haney, W. Curtis Banks, and David Jaffe. 1974. "The Psychology of Imprisonments: Privation, Power, and Pathology." In Doing unto Others: Joining, Molding, Conforming, Helping, and Loving, edited by Zick Rubin. Englewood Cliffs, NJ: Prentice Hall.

———, Robert L. Johnson, and Vivian McCann Hamilton. 2009. Psychology: Core Concepts. 6th ed. Upper Saddle River, NJ: Pearson.

———, Ann L. Weber, and Robert Johnson. 2003. Psychology: Core Concepts. 4th ed. Boston: Allyn and Bacon.

Zimmerman, Seth. 2008a. "Globalization and Economic Mobility." Washington, DC: Economic Mobility Project. Also accessible at www.economic-mobility.org/reports_and_research/literature_reviews?id=0004.

———. 2008b. Labor Market Institutions and Economic Mobility. Washington, DC: Pew Charitable Trusts.

Zipp, Yvonne. 2009. "Courts Divided on Police Use of GPS Tracking." Christian Science Monitor, May 15.

Zirin, Dave. 2008. "Calling Sports Sociology off the Bench." Contexts (Summer):28–31.

Zittrain, Jonathan, and John Palfrey. 2008. "Reluctant Gatekeepers: Corporate Ethics on a Filtered Internet." Pp. 103–122 in Access Denied, edited by Ronald Deibert, John Palfrey, Rafal Rohozinski, and Jonathan Zittrain. Cambridge, MA: MIT Press.

Zogby. 2010. "Zogby Interactive: 54% Support Ethnic & Religious Profiling; 71% Favor Full-Body Scans." February 4. Accessed July 2, 2011 (http://www.zogby.com/news/2010/02/04/zogby-interactive-54-support-ethnic-religious-profiling-71-favor-full-body-scans/).

Zola, Irving K. 1972. "Medicine as an Institution of Social Control." Sociological Review 20 (November):487–504.

———. 1983. Socio-Medical Inquiries. Philadelphia: Temple University Press.

Zweigenhaft, Richard L., and G. William Domhoff. 2006. Diversity in the Power Elite: How It Happened, Why It Matters. 2nd ed. New York: Rowman and Littlefield.

PHOTO CREDITS

ABOUT THE AUTHORS: Page v: (top) Image courtesy of Sandra L. Schaefer, (bottom) Image courtesy of Robert S. Feldman.

FRONTMATTER: Page vii: (left) Robert Churchill/Getty Images, (right) AmmentorpDK/iStock/Getty Images; p. vii: (left) Exotica.im/Getty Images, (right) OJO Images Ltd/Alamy; p. ix: (top) ferrantraite/Getty Images, (bottom) Flash Parker/Getty Images; p. x: (top) XiXinXing/Getty Images, (center) Peathegee Inc/Getty Images, (bottom) UpperCut Images/Getty Images; p. xi: (left) Catherine Yeulet/Getty Images, (right) OJO Images Ltd/Alamy; p. xii: (top) Ray Pfortner/Peter Arnold/Getty Images, (bottom) GoGo Images Corporation/Alamy; p. xiii: (left) Martin Harvey/Getty Images, (right) Stephane Victor/Getty Images; p. xiv (left) Laura Arsie/Cultura Travel/Getty Images, (right) Asanka Brendon Ratnayake/Getty Images; p. xv: (top) © Ingram Publishing RF, (bottom) © Don Hammond/Design Pics RF; p. xvi: © Resort/PhotoDisc/Getty Images RF; p. xvii © Peathegee Inc/Blend Images/Corbis; p. xxiii: © Mike Kemp/Blend Images/Corbis.

CHAPTER 1: Page 1: Robert Churchill/Getty Images; p. 2: Comstock/PunchStock; p. 4: James Marshall/The Image Works; p. 5: Justin Sullivan/Getty Images; p. 8: Nicholas Pitt/Getty Images; p. 9: Spencer Arnold/Hulton Archive/Getty Images; p. 10: Altrendo/Getty Images; p. 11 (top left): French Photographer/The London Art Archive/Alamy; p. 11 (top center): Keystone Pictures USA/Alamy; p. 11 (top right): © Alfredo Dagli Orti/The Art Archive/Corbis; p. 11 (top right): CSU Archives/Everett Collection/Alamy; p. 12: © Jane Addams Hull-House Photographic Collection, JAMC_0000_0042_0064, University of Illinois at Chicago Library, Special Collections; p. 16: © Earl & Nazima Kowall/Encyclopedia/Corbis; p. 17: Elmer Martinez/AFP/Getty Images; p. 18: Science Source; p. 19: David Hiller/Photodisc/Getty Images; p. 22: Science Photo Library/Alamy; p. 23: AP Images/Eugene Tanner; p. 28: Christopher Robbins/Image Source.

CHAPTER 2: Page 30: AmmentorpDK/iStock/Getty Images; p. 31: Blend Images/Alamy; p. 34 (bottom left): Jason Lindsey/Alamy; p. 34 (top left): © Graham Bell/Cardinal/Corbis; p. 36: The McGraw-Hill Companies, Inc.; p. 37: Muskopf Photography, LLC/Alamy; p. 38 (top left): © Tom Grill/Corbis; p. 38 (bottom left): Martin Novak/Alamy; p. 41: David Gould/Photographer's Choice RF/SuperStock; p. 42: Carnegie Mellon University; p. 44 (top center): AP Images/Meegan M. Reid/Kitsap Sun; p. 44 (top right): Rudi Von Briel/PhotoEdit; p. 50: © Royalty-Free/Corbis; p. 50 (bottom left): John Gaps III/AP Images; p. 52: Chris Jackson/Getty Images; p. 55: Christopher Robbins/Image Source.

CHAPTER 3: Page 57: Exotica.im/Getty Images; p. 58: Jake Lyell/Alamy; p. 59: Photo by Gillian Bolsover. www.bolsoverphotos.com; p. 61: Andres Rodriguez/Alamy; p. 65: Oneida Indian Nation; p. 66: Carmen K. Sisson; p. 68: Juice Images/Alamy; p. 73: Frank Zeller/AFP/Getty Images; p. 74: Ariel Skelley/Blend Images/Alamy; p. 78: Christine Pemberton/The Image Works; p. 79: Ty Cacek/Redux; p. 80: EdBockStock/Alamy; p. 85: Christopher Robbins/Image Source.

CHAPTER 4: Page 87: OJO Images Ltd/Alamy; p. 88: Radius Images/Alamy; p. 90: Thomas Coex/AFP/Getty Images; p. 91: TongRo Image Stock/Jupiterimages; p. 92: Dennis MacDonald/AGE Fotostock; p. 95: JUPITERIMAGES/BananaStock/Alamy; p. 96: © Blue Jean Images/Corbis; p. 100: Wavebreak Media Ltd/Alamy; p. 101: Michel Renaudeau/AGE Fotostock; p. 102: Jake Lyell/Alamy; p. 103: © Eric AUDRAS/Onoky/Corbis; p. 105: The McGraw-Hill Companies, Inc.; p. 106: Paul Chesley/Stone/Getty Images; p. 107: Bubbles Photolibrary/Alamy; p. 110: Courtesy, Communicare, Perth, Australia; p. 114: Christopher Robbins/Image Source.

CHAPTER 5: Page 116: ferrantraite/Getty Images; p. 117: Tim Robbins/Mint Images Limited/Alamy; p. 118: Clement Mok/Photodisc/Getty Images; p. 119: Lew Robertson/Brand X Pictures/Getty Images; p. 120: ZUMA Press, Inc./Alamy; p. 121: Marc Romanelli/Blend Images LLC; p. 122: AP Images/Fernando Vergara; p. 125: Pat Tuson/Alamy; p. 126 (top left): Stan Honda/AFP/Getty Images; p. 126 (bottom left): Monty Brinton/CBS/Getty Images; p. 129: Sean Locke/The Agency Collection/Getty Images; p. 132: Dinodia Photo/Photos of India/Alamy; p. 133: Brand X Pictures/Punchstock; p. 134: Mark Evans/E+/Getty Images; p. 135: Digital Vision RF/Punchstock; p. 139: Kevin Peterson/Photodisc/Getty Images; p. 140: Mike Goldwater/Alamy; p. 142: Courtesy of Peter Schaefer; p. 146: Aaron Roeth Photography; p. 149: Christopher Robbins/Image Source.

CHAPTER 6: Page 151: Flash Parker/Getty Images; p. 152: © davidgoldmanphoto/Image Source/Corbis; p. 154: AP Images/Osservatore Romano; p. 155 (bottom right): Columbia Pictures/Photofest; p. 155 (top right): Andres Rodriguez/Alamy; p. 156 (top left): Dirck Halstead/The LIFE Images Collection/Getty Images; p. 156 (top center): Vince Bucci/Getty Images; p. 156 (top right): AP Images/Rex Features; p. 156 (top right): AP Images/Tim Clary; p. 156 (top right): Ferdaus Shamim/WireImage/Getty Images; p. 158: Design Pics Inc/Alamy; p. 161: Kami/arabianEye; p. 162: Jill Braaten/The McGraw-Hill Education; p. 172: Noel Vasquez/Getty Images Entertainment/Getty Images; p. 173: Noah Flanigan; p. 174 (top left): Maxime Bessieres/Alamy; p. 174 (bottom left): Caters News Agency; p. 175: Everett Collection; p. 178: Christopher Robbins/Image Source.

CHAPTER 7: Page 180: XiXinXing/Getty Images; p. 181: Comstock/PictureQuest; p. 182: Koichi Kamoshida/Getty Images Sport/Getty Images; p. 183: Steven Lawton/FilmMagic/Getty Images; p. 184 (top left): © Lehtikuva/Jussi Nukari; p. 184 (top right): John Smierciak/Chicago Tribune/Getty Images; p. 185: David McLain/Aurora Photos; p. 186 (bottom left): Brand X Pictures/PunchStock; p. 186 (bottom left): D. Hurst/Alamy; p. 188: Stockbyte/Punchstock; p. 189 (top right): Frank and Helena/Cultura/Riser/Getty Images; p. 189 (bottom right): Don Mason/Blend Images LLC; p. 191: © David Pollack/Corbis; p. 195: Digital Vision; p. 196: Courtesy, Mrs. Alexandra Milgram. © 1965 by Stanley Milgram. From the film OBEDIENCE, distributed by Penn State, Media Sales; p. 197 (top right): Comstock Images/Punchstock; p. 197 (top right): The McGraw Hill Companies; p. 202: Comstock/SuperStock; p. 203: Fotosearch; p. 205: Clement Mok/Photodisc/Getty Images; p. 209: Kathryn Thorpe Klassen/Alamy; p. 214: Christopher Robbins/Image Source.

CHAPTER 8: Page 216: Peathegee Inc/Getty Images; p. 217: Steve Debenport/Getty Images; p. 222: The New York Times/Redux; p. 224 (top left): SAUL LOEB/AFP/Getty Images; p. 224 (top right): © Christina Simons/Encyclopedia/Corbis; p. 225: AP Images/Seth Perlman; p. 226 (top left): © Gopal Chitrakar/Reuters/Corbis; p. 226 (bottom left): Jose Luis Pelaez Inc/Blend Images RF/Photolibrary; p. 228: The History Channel/Photofest; p. 232: Comstock/SuperStock; p. 238: The McGraw-Hill Companies, Inc.; p. 241: image100/PictureQuest; p. 242: Emory Kristof/National Geographic Creative; p. 245 (top right): Eclipse Studios/McGraw-Hill Education; p. 245 (bottom right): Stockbyte/Getty images; p. 246: Bloomberg/Getty Images; p. 252: Christopher Robbins/Image Source.

CHAPTER 9: Page 254: UpperCut Images/Getty Images; p. 255: Andersen Ross/Blend Images/Getty Images; p. 256: Jim West/Alamy Live News; p. 258: UpperCut Images/Glow Images; p. 261 (top right): Juanmonino/Getty Images; p. 261 (top right): © Motofish Images/Corbis; p. 261 (bottom right): Kevin C. Cox/Getty Images; p. 262: Yellow Dog Productions/The Image Bank/Getty Images; p. 264: Rob Daly/OJO Images/AGE Fotostock; p. 265: Enigma/Alamy; p. 266: Library of Congress Prints and Photographs Division Washington, DC 20540 USA[LC-USF33- 020522-M2 [P&P]]; p. 271: Tony Savino/The Image Works; p. 273: Gaizka Iroz/AFP/Getty Images; p. 274: Barbara Penoyar/Getty Images RF; p. 279: Rubberball; p. 280: Bram Belloni/Hollandse Hoogte/Redux Pictures; p. 282: New Line Cinema/PhotoFest; p. 284: George Rose/Getty Images Entertainment/Getty Images; p. 286 (top left): Sacramento, CA 95821; p. 286 (bottom left): MCT/Tribune News Service/Getty Images; p. 287 (top right): Rachel Morton/Impact/HIP/The Image Works; p. 287 (bottom right): David L. Moore - OR/Alamy; p. 291: Robert Nickelsberg/Getty Images; p. 294: Christopher Robbins/Image Source.

CHAPTER 10: Page 296: Catherine Yeulet/Getty Images; p. 297: BananaStock/Jupiterimages; p. 298: Dylan Ellis/Corbis/Glow Images, Inc.; p. 299: Monashee Frantz/OJO Images/AGE fotostock; p. 300 (top left): AP Images/Eric Jamison; p. 300 (center): Picture provided by Harrison G. Pope Jr. adapted from THE ADONIS COMPLEX by Harrison G. Pope, Jr., Katherine Phillips, Roberto Olivardia. The Free Press, © 2000; p. 301: © Gideon Mendel/Encyclopedia/Corbis; p. 302: AP Images/Rex Features; p. 304: STR/EPA/Newscom; p. 305: Emile Wamsteker/Bloomberg/Getty Images; p. 307: Inti St Clair/Digital Vision/Getty Images; p. 310: Golden Pixels LLC/Alamy; p. 313: George Doyle/Getty Images; p. 316: Sergey Komarov-Kohl/Alamy; p. 322: Christopher Robbins/Image Source.

NAME INDEX

Note: Page numbers in *italics* indicate material in illustrations and their captions; page numbers followed by *f* indicate figures; page numbers followed by *t* indicate tables. All names of persons mentioned or cited as references, as well as all organizations or publications cited, are found in this index.

A

Aaronson, Daniel, 248
ABC Television, 492
Abercrombie, Nicholas, 229
Aberle, David F., 128
Abraham (Biblical figure), 476*t*, 477
Abreu, M., 80
Abrutyn, Seth A., 480
ACLU, 267, 339
Acosta, R. Vivian, 23–24
Adam (Biblical figure), 477
Adams, Tyrene L., 155
Addams, Jane, *12*, 12–13, 22, 25, 50, 306
Adler, Freda, 192, 192*t*
Adler, Patricia A., 41, 42, 45
Adler, Peter, 41, 42, 45
Adorno, Theodor, 60
Agence France-Presse, 161
Ahmed, Karuna Chanana, 464
Alain, Michel, 422
Alba, Richard D., 281, 288
Albert, Nora G., 257*t*, 285*f*
Alderman, Liz, 436
Ali, Muhammad, 156*t*
Ali, Syed, 436
Allen, Bem P., 196
Allen, Greg, 350
Alliance for Board Diversity, 313
Allport, Gordon W., 271, 272
Almeling, Rene, 160
Alon, Sigal, 400
Alvord, Lori Arviso, 371
Alwin, Duane F., 517
Alzheimer's Association, 368
Ambani, Mukesh, *457*
American Academy of Cosmetic Surgery, 183
American Academy of Pediatrics, 102
American Community Survey, 37, 263*f*
American Jewish Committee, 287
American Lung Association, 383
American Psychiatric Association (APA), 376
American Psychological Association (APA), 349
American Sociological Association (ASA), 6*t*, 49
Anatale, Alex, 163
Andersen, Margaret, 306
Anderson, Elijah, 20
Anderson, Gretchen, 107

Anderson, John Ward, 464
Andrews, Lori, 175
Angier, Natalie, *300*
Angwin, Julia, 174, 175
Aniston, Jennifer, 156*t*
Ansell, Amy E., 262
Anthony, Susan B., 315
Anti-Defamation League, 287
APA (American Psychiatric Association), 376
APA (American Psychological Association), 349
Arab American Institute, 285*f*
Arana, Renelinda, 443
Arbit, Naomi, 386
Archer, Patrick, 224
Aristotle, 7
Armer, J. Michael, 460
ASA (American Sociological Association), 6*t*, 49
Ash, Timothy Gordon, 463
Ashe, Arthur, 120
Asi, Maryam, 257*t*
Aslanian, Sasha, 90
Association of Theological Schools, 482
Atchley, Robert C., 108–109, 112
Aud, Susan, 411
Aunio, Anna-Lisa, 443
Azumi, Koya, 132

B

Babad, Elisha Y., 403
Bachur, R., 80
Bacon Lovers' Talk, 164
Bagby, Ihsam, 479
Bagilhole, Barbara, 301
Bahri, Aaniya, 152, *152*
Bailey, Tabitha M., 301, 410*f*
Bainbridge, William Sims, 488, 490
Bajaj, Vikas, 528
Baker, Dean, 466
Baker, Peter, 319
Baker, Therese L., 45
Baker, Wayne E., 460
Bale, Christian, 156*t*
Bales, Robert, 304, 305
Banchero, Stephanie, 398
Banton, Joyce G., 210
Barber, David, 111
Barber, Jake, 358, *358*
Bardi, Anat, 70
Barker, Kristin K., 359
Barnes, Patricia, 373*f*
Barnes, Taylor, 504
Barnett, W. Steven, 111
Barone, C. P., 80
Barra, Mary, *246*
Barrett, David B., 477
Barrino, Fantasia, 341
Barton, Bernadette, 349
Baudrillard, Jean, 142, 143, 156
Bauerlein, Monika, 432
Bauman, Kurt J., 237
Bazar, Emily, 238

BBC News, 26
Beagan, Brenda, 362
Bearman, Peter S., 127
Beaton, Meredith, 102
Beaulieu, Daniel, 257*t*
Beauvoir, Simone de, 315
Becker, Howard S., 190, 192*t*, 362, 363, 363*t*, 402
Beckley, Robert E., 491*t*
Beddoes, Zanny Milton, 464
Beisel, Nicola, 306
Belkin, Douglas, 175
Bell, Daniel, 141, 143, 203
Bell, Wendell, 459
Beller, Emily, 246
Benedict XVI (Pope), *154*
Benford, Robert D., 420
Bengtson, Vern L., 342
Berdan, Jennifer, 69*f*, 407, 476
Beretson, Bernard, 169
Bergen, Raquel Kennedy, 192
Berger, Peter, 118, 129
Berman, Paul, 70
Bernhardt, Annette, 248
Bernstein, Mary, 352
Berry, Halle, 156*t*
Bessen-Cassino, Yasemin, 248
Best, Amy, 183
Best, Joel, 182
Bhagat, Chetan, 78
Bhandare, Sharda, *528*
Bialik, Carol, 103
Bianchi, Suzanne M., 314, 330, 345
Biddlecom, Ann, 347, 348
Bielby, Denise D., 161
Bielick, Stacy, 411
Bilbao-Osorio, Beññat, 163
Billboard, 172
Billitteri, Thomas J., 235
bin Laden, Osama, 133
Bird, Chloe E., 368
Bishaw, Aleyayehu, 241
Bitler, Marianne, 467
Black, Donald, 67, 187, 198
Blake, Laura Palucki, 69*f*, 407, 476
Blank, Rebecca M., 223, 239
Blau, Peter M., 244
Blauner, Robert, 270
Blum, Rachel, 499, *499*
Blumer, Herbert, 118, 420
Boase, Jeffery, 164
Bodeker, Gerard C., 373
Bogart, Humphrey, 156
Boje, David M., 143
Bolzendahl, Catherine, 351
Bonaparte, Napoleon, 8
Bonikowski, Bart, 263
Bonilla-Silva, Eduardo, 259, 262
Bono, 156*t*
Bonus, Rick, *282*
Borges, Luisa, 31, *31*
Borjas, George S., 289
Bottomore, Tom, 430
Bourdieu, Pierre, 13, 14, 64, 164

Bout, Viktor, 520
Bowles, Samuel, 100, 397, 401, 406
Bowman, Thomas, 303
Boy Scouts of America, 44
Bradford, Calvin P., 128
Bradsher, Keith, 526
Brady, Jim, 209
Brady Campaign, 209
Brandchannel.com, 155
Brannigan, Augustine, 143
Bray, James H., 331
Brehm, Hollie Nyseth, 380, 381, 382
Breines, Winifred, 306, 316
Brennan Center, 267
Brewer, Benjamin D., 456
Brewer, Kristen, 386
Brewer, Rose M., 192
Brewis, Alexandra, 200
Brint, Steven, 403
Britannica Online, 467*t*, 488
Brown, David K., 400
Brown, Geoff, 211
Brown, Patricia Leigh, 349
Brown, Robert McAfee, 481
Browne, Irene, 307
Brubaker, Bill, 204
Brulle, Robert, 386
Brunson, Blake, *338*
Buchanan, Larry, 211
Buchmann, Claudia, 402
Buckee, Caroline O., 173
Buckingham, David, 156
Budig, Michelle J., 314
Bullard, Robert D., 243, 382
Burawoy, Michael, 22
Bureau of Consular Affairs, 339
Bureau of Labor Statistics, 103, 279, 312, 312*t*, 312*f*, 428*t*, 482, 524, 525*f*
Bureau of the Census, 5, 35*f*, 110, 111, 219*f*, 234*f*, 247*t*, 259*f*, 274, 284, 285, 312*f*, 314, 327*f*, 334, 335*f*, 337*f*, 339, 341, 345*f*, 347, 368, 398, 405, 428*t*, 510, 517*f*
Bures, Frank, 441
Burger, Jerry M., 197
Burger King, 164
Burns, Melinda, 240
Bush, George H. W., 156*t*
Bush, George W., 156*t*, 223, 347, 413, *520*
Buss, David M., 41, 41*t*
Butler, Daniel Allen, 242
Butts, Marcus M., 315
Byrd-Bredbenner, Carol, *300*
Byrnes, Liam, 419, *419*

C

Cai, Tianji, 62
Calhoun, Craig, 425, 426, 443
Calvin, John, 480
Cameron, Deborah, 307

Campo-Flores, Arian, 227
Caplan, Ronald L., 361
Caplow, Theodore, 510
Carbon Trust, 385
Carey, Anne R., 156, 158
Carey, Mariah, 259
Carlton-Ford, Steve, 510
Carmin, Jo Ann, 388
Carolan, Megan E., 111
Carpenter, Linda Jean, 23–24
Carr, Nicholas, 173
Carrol, Bidemi, 110
Carroll, Diahann, 156*t*
Carroll, Joanna, 8
Carroll, Joseph, 82
Carter, Rebecca S., 102*t*
Carter, Susan B., 428*t*
Case, Matthew H., 69*f*, 407, 476
Castells, Manuel, 159, 163, 172, 386, 425
Castro, Fidel, 286
Cauchon, Dennis, 466
Cavallo, Dana, 164
Cayne, James C., 197
CBS News, 197
Center for Communitiy Initiatives, 22
Centers for Disease Control and Prevention, 345*f*, 367, 368, 408
Centers for Medicare and Medicaid Services, 370*f*
Chalfant, H. Paul, 491*t*
Chambliss, William, 190, 192*t*
Chan, Sewell, 155
Chase-Dunn, Christopher, 455, 456, 459
Chavira, Juan Antonio, 367
Chen, Paul, 255, *255*
Cherlin, Andrew J., 326, 331, 341, 342, 345, 347
Chesney-Lind, Meda, 192, 192*t*, 208
Cheung, A., 81
Chiasson, Alana, 362
Child Welfare Information, 338
Chin, Kolin, 203
Cho, John, *282*
Chronic Poverty Research Centre, 453*f*
Chu, Kathy, 504
Chubb, Catherine, 311
Chung, Esther K., 197
Clark, Burton, 409
Clark, Candace, 363
Clark, E. Gurney, 359
Clarke, Adele E., 439
Clayton, Mark, 413
Clemmitt, Marcia, 492
Clifford, Stephanie, 155
Clinard, Marshall B., 188
Clinton, Bill, 156*t*, 520
Clinton, Hillary, 156*t*
Cloward, Richard A., 467
Clymer, Adam, 517
Coates, Rodney, 262

Patterson, Thomas E., 517
Pattillo-McCoy, Mary, 99
Paulson, Amanda, 317
Pavlik, John V., 161
Pear, Robert, 127, 314
Pellow, David N., 380, 381, 382
Pelosi, Nancy, *516*
Penn, Kal (Kalpen Modi), *282*
Pennebaker, James W., 7
Peralta, Eyder, 223
Percheski, Christine, 401
Pérez, Kimberlee, 78
Perez, Rose M., 337
Pescosolido, Bernice A., 8, 375
Peter, Laurence J., 134
Petersen, John L., 440
Peterson, Kristina, 249
Petrášová, Alexandra, 468
Pew Forum on Religion and
     Public Life, 491
Pew Global Attitudes
     Project, 388
Pew Hispanic Center, 285
Pew Internet and American Life
     Project, 166*f*
Pew Internet Project, 164
Pew Research Center, 235, 490
Pew Research Center Global
     Attitudes Project, 171*f*
Pew Social and Demographic
     Trends, 235
Pfeifer, Mark, 283
Phelan, Jo C., 366
Phillips, Michael, 374
Phillips, Susan A., 187
Piaget, Jean, 96, 97, 97*t*, 98
Picasso, Pablo, 73
Picca, Leslie Houts, 265
Pickert, Kate, 372
Pierre, Philippe, 75
Piestewa, Lori, 510
Piliavin, Jane Allyn, 70
Pilkington, Ed., 210
Pinderhughes, Dianne, 521
Pinderhughes, Raquel, 386
Piquero, Alex R., 189
Pitkin, John, 275
Pitt, Brad, 156*t*
Piturro, Marlene, 110
Piven, Frances Fox, 467
Planty, Michael, 207*f*
Plomin, Robert, 92
Plüss, Caroline, 443
Poder, Thomas C., 13
Podeschi, Christopher, 45
Pogash, Carol, 402
Poitier, Sidney, 156*t*
Polletta, Francesca, 423
Polson, Nicholas G., 46
Pomeroy, Wardell B., 51
Population Reference
     Bureau, 327
Porter, Caroline, 175
Porter, Eduardo, 241
Porter, Jack Nusan, 488
Portes, Alejandro, 443
Portman, Natalie, 156*t*
Potenza, Marc N., 164
Potter, Louisa, 311
Poussaint, Alvin F., 99
Powell, Brian, 316, 351
Powell-Griner, Eve, 373*f*
Preston, Jennifer, 159, 479
Price, Tom, 176

Prince, Martin, 374
Prins, Harald E. L., 65, 326
Proctor, Bernadette D., 38*f*,
     234, 234*f*, 237, 239, 241*t*,
     263*f*, 264, 278, 280, 285,
     336, 367*f*
Proctor, Kristopher R., 480
Prodzinski, Janice, 210
Pryor, John H., 69*f*, 387,
     407, 476
Purser, Gretchen, 239
Pythagoras, 7

Q

Quadagno, Jill, 109
Quane, J. M., 241
Quillian, Lincoln, 262
Quinney, Richard, 191, 192*t*
Quinnipiac University, 303

R

Rahman, Atif, 374
Rainie, Lee, 164
Rajan, Gita, 443
Ramet, Sabrina, 420
Ramirez, Roberto R., 257*t*,
     259, 259*f*
Ramírez-Esparza, Nairán, 7
Ramstad, Evan, 69
RAND, 372
Randolph, Tracey H., 340
Rangaswamy, Padma, 282
Rankin, B. H., 241
Rasmussen Reports, 267
Rastogi, Sonya, 257*t*, 281*f*
Rawlinson, Linnie, 154
Ray, Barbara, 106
Reagan, Ronald, 145, 156*t*, 209,
     283, 508
Reay, Donald T., 210
Redfoo, *172*
Reese, Ellen, 210
Register, Charles A., 23–24
Reinharz, Shulamit, 45, 50
Reitzes, Donald C., 109
Religion News Service, 493
Revkin, Andrew C., 385
Rhoades, Kelly, 336
Richards, Keith, 156*t*
Ridgeway, Cecilia L., 306
Riding, Alan, 152, 242
Rieker, Patricia R., 368
Rifkin, Jeremy, 432
Riley, Matilda White, 432
Riley, Richard, 408
Rios-Vargas, Merarys, 257*t*, 285*f*
Ripley, Amanda, 69
Risman, Barbara J., 331
Ritzer, George, 73, 74, 75,
     372, 439
Rivara, Frederick P., 210
Roberts, J. Timmons, 382, 388
Roberts, Julia, 156*t*
Robinson, John P., 314, 330
Robinson, Kristopher, 152
Rodman, George, 156
Rodriguez, Alex, *182*
Rodriguez, Laura, 351
Rodriguez-Soto, Isa, 200
Roettger, Michael E., 62
Rogan, Eugene, 436

Romney, Mitt, 489
Roosevelt, Franklin D., 508
Rootes, Christopher, 386
Rosa, Eugene, 382
Rose, Arnold, 270
Rose, Peter I., 107
Rosen, Eva, 188
Rosenberg, Douglas H., 501
Rosenfeld, Jake, 144, 145
Rosenthal, Robert, 402–403
Rossi, Alice S., 338
Rossi, Peter H., 51
Rossides, Daniel W.,
     221–222, 230
Roszak, Theodore, 79
Rothkopf, David, 520
Rothkoph, Amy C., 197
Rowe, Aimee Carrillo, 78
Rubel, Maximilien, 430
Rubin, Alissa J., 518
Rudel, Thomas K., 388
Ruiz, Rebecca, 111
Rule, James B., 422
Rupp, Leila J., 331
Rushforth, Norman B., 210
Rutherford, Stuart, 527
Ruthven, Orlanda, 527
Ryan, Addison, 474, *474*
Ryan, Camille, 80, 81*f*
Ryan, John, 124
Ryan, William, 242

S

Saad, Lydia, 300, 317, 345, 383
Sachs, Jeffrey D., 454
Sacks, Peter, 400
Saenz, Victor B., 69*f*, 387, 407
Saguy, Abigail, 160
Saha, Robin, 382
Said, Edward W., 70
Sakamoto, Arthur, 280
Sale, Kirkpatrick, 432
Sampson, Robert, 190, 241
Sampson, Robert J., 46
Samuelson, Paul A., 234
Sandefur, Rebecca L., 192
Sanders, Edmund, 101
Sanderson, Stephen K., 480
Sanger, Margaret, 420
Santos, José Alcides
     Figueiredo, 463
Santos, José Luis, 69*f*, 387, 407
Sanua, Marianne R., 287
Sapir, Edward, 65
Sassen, Saskia, 289
Satel, Sally, 376
Sawhill, Isabel V., 110, 244,
     245, 246
Sawyer, Reid L., 413
Saxena, Shekhar, 374
Sayer, Liana C., 314, 330
Scarce, Rik, 49
Schaefer, Peter, 152
Schaefer, Richard T., 11*f*, 36*f*,
     38*f*, 43*t*, 82, 101, 119*f*, 128,
     156*t*, 185, 186*t*, 205*t*, 259*f*,
     264, 274*f*, 290*f*, 315*f*, 319*f*,
     428*t*, 458*f*, 476*t*, 482, 490,
     507, 520
Scharfenberg, David, 46
Scharnberg, Kirsten, 361
Scheid, Teresa L., 376

Scherer, Michael, 211, 223
Scherer, Ron, 127, 466
Schilt, Kristin, 349
Schlesinger, Traci, 192
Schmeeckle, Maria, 342
Schnaiberg, Allan, 381
Schneider, Christopher, 348
Schneider, Friedrich, 504
Schnittker, Jason, 316
Schofer, Evan, 388
Schram, Sanford F., 467
Schulman, Gary I., 196
Schur, Edwin M., 199, 202
Schwadel, Philip, 45
Schwartz, Howard D., 363
Schwartz, Shalom, 70
Scopes, John T., 492
Scott, Alan, 423
Scott, Gregory, 17
Scott, W. Richard, 136
Scoville, David, 143
Searle, Kerry, 246
Seccombe, Karen, 466
Sefiha, Ophir, 23–24
Segal, Nancy L., 92
Segura, Jeri, 449, *449*
Seidman, Steven, 299
Sellers, Frances Stead, 443
Selod, Saher Farooq, 479
Sengupta, Somini, 239
Sernau, Scott, 75, 246, 507
Settersten, Richard, 106
Shachtman, Tom, 101
Shahid, Hasan, 257*t*, 281*f*
Shane, Scott, 154
Shapiro, Thomas M., 235, 246
Shapley, Dan, 384
Sharma, Hari M., 373
Sharma, Shailja, 443
Sharp, Ansel M., 23–24
Sharrock, W. W., 228
Shaw, Clifford R., 189, 190, 192*t*
Shea, Andrea, 227
Sheehan, Charles, 110
Shellenberger, Michael, 385
Shepard, Matthew, 409
Sherman, Arloc, 235
Sherman, Jennifer, 336
Sherrod, Cheryl, 191
Shiao, Jianbin Lee, 340
Shim, Janet K., 439
Shin, Hyon B., 81
Shogren, Elizabeth, 377
Short, Kathleen, 239
Shostak, Arthur B., 512
Siddhartha, Gautama (Buddha),
     476*t*, 477
Sieber, Renée E., 386
Siegel-Hawley, Genevieve, 399
Silva, Jennifer M., 106
Silver, Ira, 122
Silverman, Rachel Emma,
     176, 341
Simpson, Sally S., 204
Sims-Bowles, Denise, 465
Siyawati, 527
Skocpol, Theda, 224
SkyBlu, *172*
Slack, Jennifer Daryl, 432
Slatcher, Richard B., 7
Slavin, Barbara, 61
Slavin, Robert E., 81
Sloan, Allan, 234
Sloop, John M., 160

Slug-Lines.com, 18
Smart, Barry, 143
Smelser, Neil, 501
Smit, Paul, 208
Smith, Aaron, 102, 516
Smith, Adam, 501, 502
Smith, Christian, 106, 474, 481
Smith, Craig S., 90
Smith, Dan, 511
Smith, David L., 173
Smith, Jessica C., 38*f*, 234, 234*f*,
     237, 239, 241*t*, 263*f*, 264,
     278, 280, 285, 336, 367*f*
Smith, Joseph, 489
Smith, Lawrence C., 385, 442
Smith, Stephen A., 155
Smith, Tom W., 106, 486*f*
Snow, Robert W., 173
Snowden, Edward, 173, 176
Snyder, Thomas D., 432
Somaskanda, Sumi, 466
Somavia, Juan, 239
Somes, Grant, 210
Sonnenfeld, D. A., 381
Sorell, Gwendolyn T., 107
Sorokin, Pitirim A., 243
Soss, Joe, 467
Sotomayor, Sonia, *286*
Southern Poverty Law Center,
     79, 261
Spain, Daphne, 345
Spargaren, G., 381
Spears, Britney, 156*t*
Spencer, Herbert, 9, 11–12, 14
Spitzberg, Daniel, 386
Spitzer, Steven, 191
Sprague, Joey, 228
Springsteen, Bruce, 156*t*
Squires, James H., 111
St. Rose, Andresse, 402
Stacey, Judith, 348
Staggenborg, Suzanne, 443
Stambolis-Ruhstorfer,
     Michael, 351
Stang, Janine, 362
Stansell, Christine, 316
Stanton, Elizabeth Cady, 315
Stark, Rodney, 474, 488, 490
Steelman, Lola Carr, 351
Steffen, Alex, 425–426
Stein, Leonard I., 371
Stelter, Brian, 159
Stephens, Diane P., 331
Stevick, Richard A., 101
Steward-Streng,
     Nicole R., 326
Stewart, Martha, 204
Stohr, Oskar, 91–92
Stolberg, Sheryl Gay, 388
Stone, Lucy, 401
Storry, Raymond, 311
Stovel, Katherine, 127
Strauss, Anselm, 362
Stults, Brian, 275*t*
Suárez, Zulema E., 337
Subramaniam, Mangala, 424
Suchman, Edward A., 398
Suh, Doowon, 424
Suitor, J. Jill, 102*t*
Sullivan, Harry Stack, 95
Sullivan, Kevin, 103
Sullivan, Laura, 235
Suls, Rob, 352
Sum, Andrew, 289

SUBJECT INDEX

boundary maintenance, 185
Bourdieu, Pierre, 13
bourgeoisie, 225, 228, 305
Boy Scouts of America, 44, *44*
BP (British Petroleum), 458*f*
Brady Campaign to Prevent Gun
  Violence, 210
Brady Handgun Violence
  Prevention Act of 1994, 209
brain drain, 361
"brand casting," *155,* 156
brand loyalty, 172
brass ceiling, 302
Brazil, 52*f,* 335*f,* 451*f*
  economy of, 501*f*
  elimination of rain forest,
    380–381
  growth of middle class in, 464
  income distribution in, 462*f*
  same-sex marriage in, 351
  skin color groupings in, 258
  stratification in, 463, *463*
  television use in Amazon,
    172, *173*
  voter turnout in, 515*f*
Breaking Bad (TV series), 161
British Airways, 503
British Empire, 455
British Petroleum (BP), 458*f*
"bromance," 303
Brown v. Board of Education
  (1950), 399
Buddhism, 476*t,* 477, 487
Bulgaria, 451*f*
bureaucracies, 132–134, 134*t,*
  136, 405–406
  alienation in, *132,* 133
  bureaucratization process,
    134–135, 137
  division of labor in, 132–133,
    134*t,* 147, 405
  hierarchy of authority in, 133,
    134*t,* 406, 523
  as ideal types, 10, 132–134,
    134*t,* 136
  impersonality of, 133, 134*t,*
    406, *406*
  oligarchies, 135
  organizational culture and,
    135–136
  qualifications for employment
    in, 134, 134*t,* 406
  written rules and regulations in,
    133, 134*t,* 406
bureaucratization
  process of, 134–135, 137
  of schools, 399, 405–406, *406,*
    413–414
Bureau of Indian Affairs
  (BIA), 280
Bureau of Justice Statistics, 207
Bureau of the Census, 80
Burger King, 164
Burj Khalifa (Dubai), 435
Burkina Faso, 62*f,* 451*f*
burnout, from teaching, 407
Burundi, 451*f,* 503

C

California, 81, 82
call center subcultures, 78, *78*
Cambodia, 451*f,* 515*f*
Cameroon, 451*f*
campaign finance system, 161

Canada, 52*f,* 144*f,* 157*f,* 335*f,* 451*f*
  assimilation in, 275
  college graduation rates, 395*t*
  economy of, 501*f*
  environmentalism in, 388*f*
  foreign aid per capita, 454*f*
  income distribution in, 462*f*
  infant mortality rates in, 362*f*
  poverty rate in, 240*t*
  religious participation in, 486*f*
  same-sex marriage in, 351
  social spending in, 466
  temporary workforce, 525*f*
  voter turnout, 515*f*
  women in combat, 303
  women in government, 518*f*
capital, 13
capitalism, 225, 228
  as economic system, 500–503,
    502, 504*t,* 505
  globalization of, *502,* 502–503
  need for skilled labor force, 401
  role of Protestant ethic in, 11*f,*
    479–480, *480*
  trend toward giant
    corporations, 522
career criminals, 203
careers in sociology
  in business sector, 31, 117,
    152, 297
  college recruiting, 255
  community organizing, 419
  community services, 217
  counseling, 88, 325, 474, 499
  environmental analysis, 358
  journalism, 2
  with Peace Corps, 58
  teaching, 181, 394, 449
caregiving, *107,* 108, 112
Carnegie Mellon University, *42*
castes *(varnas),* 221, 230
cattle (zebu), 16, *16,* 60
causal logic, 35–36, 36*f*
cause-and-effect relationships,
  35–36, 36*f*
CCI (Center for Community
  Initiatives), 22, *22*
CDC (Centers for Disease
  Control), 210
celibacy, 128
cell phones, *102,* 102–103, *437*
  demographics of, 171, 171*f*
  in less-developed countries,
    440, 440–441
  public health use of, 173
censorship, 438–439
Center for Community Initiatives
  (CCI), 22, *22*
Centers for Disease Control
  (CDC), 210
Central African Republic, 62*f,*
  362*f,* 451*f*
Central Americans, 285*f,* 286
Central Intelligence Agency
  (CIA), 133, 350
Chad, 451*f*
charismatic authority, 508, *508,* 513
charismatic figures, 422, *508*
Chicago Coalition for the
  Homeless, 51
child care
  male v. female involvement in,
    330, 331
  social policy, *110,* 110–112
  women's employment and, 314

childless marriage, 347–348, 353
child pornography, 205
child-rearing patterns,
  338–342, 343
  adoption, 338–339, 340
  dual-income families, 331, 339,
    339, 341, 343
  parenthood and grandparent-
    hood, 338, *338*
  single-parent families, 337*f,* 341
  stepfamilies, 341–342
children. *See also* adolescents
  adoption of, 338–339, 340, 343
  "boomerang children," 336
  child care, *110,* 110–112, 314,
    330, 331
  child pornography, 205
  cognitive theory of develop-
    ment, 97
  development of self, 94–95, 95*t*
  female stereotypes in books
    for, 300
  in foster care, 339
  illness and social class, 366
  impact of divorce on, 346, 353
  impact of isolation on,
    89–90, 93
  lack of health insurance,
    366, 367*f*
  marriage with adults, 61, 62*f*
  neglected, *90,* 90–91
  parental involvement with,
    330, 331
  socialization of, 67, 95,
    100, 351
  use of TV as babysitter, 155
Chile, 311*f,* 451*f,* 458*f*
China, People's Republic of, 70*f,*
  362*f,* 451*f,* 458*f*
  Communist Party, 134–135,
    146, 509
  cultural practices in, *59*
  cyber-police of, 159
  economy of, 501*f*
  female infanticide in, 465
  Great Leap Forward, 396
  greenhouse gas emissions
    in, 384
  growth of middle class in, 464
  industrialization in, 500
  Internet censorship by, 439
  labor unions in, 146
  language education in, 82
  movement out of poverty, 464
  offshoring to, 526
  as oligarchy, 509
  respect for elderly in, 119–120
  revisionist history in, 396
  as socialist society, 503
  women in combat, 303
  women in government, 518*f*
China National Petroleum, 458*f*
Chinatowns, 281
Chinese Americans, 281, 281*f,* 516
Chinese Exclusion Act of 1882, 281
Chinese immigrants, 203, 271
chiropractors, 361
Christianity, 476, 476*t*
  "born again" experience,
    486–487
  fundamentalism in, 485,
    491–492
  gender issues in, 481
Christian Science Church,
  482, 490

Chrysler Corporation, 524
Church of Jesus Christ of Latter
  Day Saints (LDS). *See*
  Mormon Church
CIA (Central Intelligence
  Agency), 133, 350
cigarette smoking, 75–76, 182,
  191, 368
cities
  air pollution in, 383
  employment prospects in,
    464, *464*
  ethnic neighborhoods of, 276,
    281, 288
  segregation index for, 274, 275*t*
  urban poverty, 240, 241
civil disobedience, 279
Civil Liberties Act of 1988, 283
civil rights, gun ownership as
  issue of, 210
Civil Rights Act of 1964, 266, *266*
civil rights movement, 279
Civil Union Act of 1998, 348
civil unrest, 208
"clash of civilizations," 70, 72
class, defined, 225–226
class consciousness, 225, 226–227
classical theory of formal organizations, 135, 137
class warfare, 223–224, *224*
Clean Air Act, 386
Clean Water Act, 386
climate change, 43, 45, *383,*
  384–385, 389
clinical sociology, 24, 26
Clinton Global Initiative, 520
cliques, 409
closed stratification systems, 243
CMC (computer-mediated communication), 425, 427
CMHC (Community Mental
  Health Centers) Act of
  1963, 376–377
coal-fired power generation, 385
coalitions, *126,* 126–127
coal miners, *225*
codes of ethics, 2, 31, 48, 49–50, 53
cognitive theory of development, 97
cohabitation, 326, 346–347, 353
collective consciousness,
  315–316, 320
collective identities, 423
colleges and universities
  anticipatory socialization to, 106
  bias-related incidents on,
    260–261
  campus security, 197
  college recruiting as career, 255
  Gallaudet University
    protests, *423*
  graduation rates, 395*f*
  preferential admission to, 266
  profit motives of, 400
  student subcultures, 409–410,
    410*f, 410,* 414
  Title IX mandates, 402,
    411–413
  tuition costs, 400, 401*f*
college students
  interest in environment, 387,
    388*f*
  student subcultures, 409–410,
    410*f, 410,* 414
  values and goals of, 69, 69*f*

collegiate subculture, 409, 414
Colombia, 451*f*
Colombian immigrants, 203
colonialism, legacy of, 455*f,*
  455–456, *456,* 461
color-blind racism, 261–262,
  262, 268
"color line," 259
coltan (columbite-tantalite), *502,*
  502–503
Columbine High School shootings
  (1999), 125, 159, 208
Columbo (TV series), 161
Commission on Opportunity in
  Athletics, 413
common sense, 6–7
communication. *See also* language
  computer-mediated, 425, 427
  "crosstalk," 307
  facilitated by Internet, 172
  nonverbal, 19, 66, *66,* 71
communications technologies. *See
  also* cell phones; Internet
  cultural diffusion and, 75, 76
  digital divide, 162
  globalization of social move-
    ments and, 424–427, *425*
  increased political participation
    and, 521
  use in developing nations, *102,*
    102–103, 441
communism, 503, 504*t*
Communist League, 10
Communist Manifesto, The (Marx
  & Engels), 10, 11, 11*f,*
  25, 133
Communist Party, 134–135, 146,
  225, 509
community-based mental health
  care, 377
community-based
  organizations, 126
Community Mental Health
  Centers (CMHC) Act of
  1963, 376–377
community organizing, 419
community service, 217
companionship, 330
comparative function of reference
  groups, 126
comparative perspective, on
  global inequality, 462*f,*
  462–465
competition, 100
computer-mediated communication (CMC), 425, 427
computer-mediated
  instruction, 406
computer technology
  Internet. *See* Internet
  social change and, 437,
    438*t,* 444
Comte, Auguste, 8
conclusions, in research, 33*f,*
  37–38, *38*
concrete operational stage of
  development, 97
confidentiality, 49
conflict of interest, 50, *50,* 53
conflict perspective, 17–18,
  20*t,* 21
  on bilingualism, 81–82
  on bureaucratization of educa-
    tion, 406, 414
  on child care costs, 111

deviance—*Cont.*
  sexual behaviors as, 303
  social construction of,
    191, 192*t*
  social disorganization theory
    of, 189, *189*, 192*t*
  sociological perspectives on,
    184–192, 192*t*, 193
  sociological research on, 13
  stigma of, 183, *183*, 193, 204
  symbols of, 183
  technology and, 184
Devoted Husband Organization
  (Japan), 118
*Diagnostic and Statistical Manual
  of Mental Disorders
  (DSM)*, 376
dictatorships, 509, *509*, 513
differential association theory,
  189, 192*t*
differential justice, 191
differentiation, in social
  change, 429
diffusion, cultural, *73*, 73–76, *74*
digital divide, 162
digital surveillance, 173–176
direct-selling networks, 455
dirt eating (*pica*), 452
disability, 120, 205, 205*f*,
  222, 241*t*
discovery, 73, 76
discrimination. *See also* prejudice;
  racism
  assimilation and, 275
  against Blacks at White
    universities, 410
  cumulative disadvantage of, 245
  discriminatory behavior,
    262–264, 263*f*,
    268, 271
  educational, 401
  institutional. *See* institutional
    discrimination
  by labor unions, 144
  against lower class, 227
  "reverse discrimination," 412
  against same-sex couples,
    351, 352
  sex discrimination,
    309–310, 314
disenchantment phase of
  retirement, 109
District of Columbia v. Heller
  (2008), 209
divine right to rule, 508–509
division of labor
  in bureaucracies, 132–133,
    134*t*, 147, 405
  housework, gender inequality
    in, 311, 311*f*, 314–315
Division of Labor in Society, The
  (Durkheim), 11, 11*f*, 138
divorce, 344–346, 348. *See also*
  family(ies); marriage
  factors associated with,
    345–346
  impact on children, 346, 353
  resocialization in stepfamilies
    and, 341–342
  statistical trends in, 345,
    345*f*, 353
"doctor-nurse game," *371*,
  371–372
Doctors Without Borders, 512
"doing gender," 298, 307

DOMA (Defense of Marriage
  Act) of 1996, 352
Domhoff, G. William, 519*f*, 520
dominant culture, 77–78
dominant groups
  functions of racism for, 270
  hate crimes committed by, 205
  men as, 305
  privileges of, 264–265, *265*
  stereotypes created by, 261
dominant ideology, 71, 72
  conflict perspective on, *228*,
    228–229
  cultural differences, *161*,
    161–162
  forced obedience to, 81
  reality constructed by, 160–161
Dominican Republic, 62*f*, 451*f*
Dongria Kondh people (India), *420*
Do the Right Thing (film), 283
double consciousness, 12
downsizing, 523–524, 529
Dr. Phil (TV series), 169
dramaturgical approach, 19,
  96, 512
"drapetomania," 363
dress codes, symbolism in, 19
Driving While Black (DWB), 191
drugs
  campaigns against marijuana,
    191, *191*
  drug trade, 188, 286
drum circle, *126*
*DSM (Diagnostic and Statistical
  Manual of Mental
  Disorders)*, 376
dual-income families, 331, 339,
  339, 341, 343
Dubai, *435*, 435–436, 441, 444
DuBois, W. E. B., 11*f*, 11–12
Dunne-Za tribe, 280
Durkheim, Émile
  on deviance, 185–186, 192*t*
  mechanical and organic soli-
    darity, 138,
    143–144, 147
  on religion, 475–476, 483, 487
  theory of suicide, 7–8, 11*f*, 50
  views of, 9, 11*f*
DWB (Driving While Black), 191
dysfunctions, 17
  illness viewed as, 359–360
  of immigration, 289
  of informal economy, 504
  of liberation theology, 481
  marital, divorce and, 346
  of media advertising, 157–158
  narcotizing effect, 158
  Peter principle, 134
  of racial prejudice, 270
  of religious loyalties, 479
  written rules and
    regulations, 133

E

Earth Day, 386, 388, 389
earthquake in Haiti (2010), 165,
  339
East Timor, 451*f*
eBay, 159
Ebony magazine, 156*t*
ecclesiae, 487, 490, 491*t*, 494
ecological modernization,
  381–382

economics, 4, 5
economic systems, 500–505, 501*f*
  capitalism. *See* capitalism
  global, 455*f*, 455–456,
    460*t*, 461
  Industrial Revolution and, 500,
    501, 505
  informal economy, 504,
    505, 527
  socialism, 503–504, 504*t*, 505
economy. *See also* economic
  systems
  child care costs, 111
  childlessness and, 348
  effect of technological
    advances on, 229
  effect on retirement, 108,
    109, *109*
  family as economic unit,
    330–331
  "global economy," 163, 441
  government and. *See*
    government
  informal economy, 504,
    505, 527
  resistance to social change and,
    431, 433
  social policy: microfinancing,
    526–528, *527, 528*
  of U.S., change in, 522–529
  war as stimulus to, 510
Economy and Society (Weber), 11*f*
ecotourism, *384*
Ecuador, 451*f*
education, 330, 393–417. *See also*
  colleges and universities;
  high school(s); school(s)
  as agent of change, 397–398,
    398*f*, 404
  available on Internet, 406, 414
  bilingual education, 80–82, 81*f*,
    394, 397
  bureaucratization of, 406,
    413, 414
  completion of, 106
  conflict perspective on,
    128–129, 399–401, 404
  credentialism in, 399–400
  culture transmitted by, 396, *396*
  discrimination in, 401
  effect of global recession on, 5
  effects on income levels, 33,
    35*f*, 38, 264
  familismo and, 337, 343
  feminist perspective on,
    401–402, 404
  formal, 128, 395*f*, 395–396
  functionalist perspective on,
    396, 396–398, 399, 404
  hidden curriculum in, 399
  homeschooling, 410–411, 414
  integrative function of,
    396–397
  interactionist perspective on,
    402–403, 404
  labeling in classroom, 402
  of middle class, 222
  of minorities, 398*f*, 399
  public health education, 449
  sexism in, 401
  social control and, 397, *397*
  social mobility and, 245
  social policy: Title IX, 411–413
  sociological perspectives on,
    394–404, 395*f*, 403*t*

status bestowed by,
    400–401, 401*f*
  of women, 401–402
Education Act of 1972, 402,
    411–413
egalitarian families, 329, *329*,
    330, 333, *341*
egocasting, 165
Egypt, 161, 284, 384, 451*f*
elderly persons
  age as ascribed status, 119–120
  health and illness in, 368, 369
  retirement and, 108–110,
    109, 112
  romantic relationships
    among, 107
elections. *See also* political
    participation
  institutional discrimination in,
    267, *267*
  voting. *See* voting
electronic church, 491
electronic cigarettes, 75–76
Electronic Communications
    Privacy Act of 1986, 175,
    438–439
electronic media, 153
Elementary and Secondary
    Education Act (ESEA) of
    1965, 82
*Elementary Forms of Religious
    Life* (Durkheim), 11*f*
elite models of power relations,
    518–520, 522
  Domhoff's model, 519*f*, 520
  Mills's model, 518–520, 519*f*
"Elmtown" study of schools, 409
El Salvador, 208, 451*f*
emotion, 422
employment
  ascribed statuses and, 121
  based on technical qualifica-
    tions, 134, 134*t*
  green-collar jobs, 386, 388
  in industrial societies, 141
  job status of teaching, 409
  middle class and, 223
  at minimum wage, 237
  opportunities for, 127, 246,
    464, *464*
  part-time or temporary, 145,
    524–525, 525*f*
  precarious work, 238–239
  preferential policies in, 266
  professional occupations,
    399–400
  racial discrimination in, 263,
    265, 271
  rising occupational require-
    ments, 400
  role of networking in, 127
  in service industries, 281
  social policy: minimum wage
    laws, 247*t*, 247–249
  top reasons for leaving,
    315, 315*f*
  of women, 246, 311*f*, 314–315,
    315*f*
Endangered Species Act, 386
endogamy, 335
England. *See* Great Britain
Engle v. Vitale (1962), 492
English language, 64–65, 74
English-only rules, 266
Enron scandal, 519

environment (environmental
    issues)
  air pollution, 383, 389
  climate change, *383*,
    384–385, 389
  coltan mining in Congo, *502*,
    502–503
  conflict perspective on, *380*,
    380–381, 381*f*, 385, 389
  ecological modernization
    approach to, 381–382
  ecotourism, *384*
  effects of neglect and isolation,
    89–91, 93
  environmental justice move-
    ment, 382, *382*, 389
  human ecology, 380, 380*t*, 389
  impact of globalization, 385–
    386, 389
  social policy: environmental-
    ism, 386–388, 387*f*,
    388*f*, 389
  sociological perspectives on,
    379–389
  water pollution, *383*,
    383–384, 389
  world systems analysis of, 380,
    380, 385–386
environmental analysis, 358
environmentalism
  as new social movement, 423
  social policy on, 386–388,
    387*f*, 388*f*, 389
  values associated with, 69, 69*f*
environmental justice movement,
    22, 24, 382, *382*, 389
Environmental Protection Agency
    (EPA), 386
environmental refugees, 385–386
environmental sociology, 22,
    24, 26
EPA (Environmental Protection
    Agency), 386
Episcopal Church, 488
equilibrium model, of society, 429
Eritrea, 62*f*, 451*f*, 452
ESEA (Elementary and Secondary
    Education Act) of 1965, 82
established sect, 488
estate system of stratification,
    221, 224, 230
esteem, 232
Estonia, 451*f*
ethics
  codes of ethics, 48, 49–50
  confidentiality, 49
  conflict of interest, 50, *50*, 53
  individual privacy, 47
  Protestant ethic, 11*f*,
    479–480, *480*
  of sociological research, 31,
    48–53
  value neutrality, 50–51, 52, 53
Ethiopia, 57*f*, 451*f*
ethnic groups, 69, 70*f*, 256, 335
ethnicity, 260, *260*, 268. *See also
    specific ethnic groups*
  campus subcultures and,
    410, 410*f*
  employment opportunity
    and, 127
  experience of retirement
    and, 109
  hate crimes based on, 205, 205*f*
  health and, 366–367, 369

heredity, 91–92, 93
heritage camps, 340
heterosexuality, 67
hidden curriculum, 399
hierarchy of authority
  in bureaucracies, 133, 134*t*, 406, 523
  in medical establishment, 370–371
  in Roman Catholic Church, 133
high school(s). *See also* adolescents
  free lunches in, 402
  gender differences in, 301
  popularity in, 101–102, 102*t*, 104
  romantic relationships in, 127
  sex-education classes, 397, *397*
  student subcultures in, 409–410, 410*f, 410*, 414
Hill-Burton Act of 1946, 373
Hinduism, 16, *16*, 60, 476*t*, 477
hip-hop, *73*
Hispanics. *See* Latinos/Hispanics
history, 4, 5
HIV/AIDS. *See* AIDS
Ho Chi Minh City Stock Exchange, 503–504
holistic (wholistic) medicine, 372–373
Holocaust, 196, 273, 287
home-based businesses, 527–528, *528*
Homeland (TV series), 161
homelessness, 51
homeschooling, 410–411, 414
homework strategies, 471
homicide, 208, 279, 408
homogamy, 335
homophobia, 299
homosexuality. *See also* queer theory
  American Psychiatric Association on, 348–349
  fear of and prejudice against, 299
  gay marriage, 348, 350–352, 352*f*, 353
  labeled as mental illness, 363, 376
  media presentation of, 160
  Nazi genocide and, 273
  relationships, 326, 339, *349*, 349–350, 350*f*, 353
  sports and, 23
  terminology of, 349
Honduras, 208, 451*f*
honeymoon phase of retirement, 108
Hong Kong, 74, 451*f*
Hopi tribe, 510
horizontal mobility, 243, 250
horticultural societies, 140, 141*t*
House of Representatives, U.S., 516
housework, 311, 311*f*, 314–315
housing issues, 46, 264
Hull House, 12, 22
human behavior
  audience behavior, 169–170
  cultural transmission of, 187, 189, 192*t*
  differential association theory of, 189, 192*t*

effects of biology on, 61–63, 184–185
  gender roles. *See* gender roles
  inborn drives and, 96
  incivility, 184
  inequality as determinant of, 452
  labeled as mental illness, 363
  norms for, 66–68
human ecology, 380, 380*t*, 389, 429
human relations approach, 135–136
human sexuality, 348–350. *See also* homosexuality; sexual behavior
  adolescent sexual networks, 127
  celibacy, 128
  gender roles and, 303
  heterosexuality as social norm, 67
  homophobia, 299
  Internet and, 165
  labeling and, 303, *348*, 348–349
  median age of first sex, 52*f*
  same-sex relationships, *349*, 349–350, 350*f*, 353
  sex-education classes, 397, *397*
  sex in advertising, *52*
  social norms for sexual behavior, 303
  social policy: gay marriage, 350–352, 352*f*, 353
  sociological research on, 51–52, *52*
  sports and, 23
  study of, 18, 51, 52
  surveys about, 41, 41*t*
human trafficking, 220, 220*t*
Hungary, 451*f*, 525*f*
hunting-and-gathering societies, 140, *140*, 141*t*
Hurricane Katrina (2005), 5–6
  social inequality and, 25
  victims of, poverty and, 242–243
Hutterites, 488
hyperconsumerism, 142, *155*, 156–158, 157*f*
hyper-local media, 161
hypertension, 367
hypotheses
  formulating, 33*f*, 34–36, *36*, 38, 39
  support for, 37–38, 38*f*

I

Iceland, 346, 351
Ice Road Truckers (TV series), *228*
ID (intelligent design), 492, 494
"ideal minorities," 13, 281
ideal types
  bureaucracies, 10, 132–134, 134*t*, 136
  socialist economic systems, 503
identity theft, 174, 204
illegal abortions, 319
illegal immigration
  culture lag and, 443
  immigrants as slaves, 220
  to U.S. from Mexico, 290–291, *291*

IMDb (Internet Movie Database), 155, 156*t*
immigrants
  assimilation of, 275
  bilingualism, 82, 394, 397
  Chinese, 203, 271
  in organized crime, 203
  religions of, 478, *478*, 479
  socializing children of, 397
  treatment of, in Dubai, 436
immigration
  following September 11, 2001, 512–513
  global, social policy on, 288–291, 290*f*
  illegal, 220, 290–291, *291*, 443
  sociological perspectives on, 289, 290, 292
Immigration Act of 1965, 282, 283
Immigration Reform and Control Act of 1986, 290
impersonality
  of bureaucracies, 133, 134*t*, 406, *406*
  of in-store health clinics, 372, *372*
impression management, 96, *96*
incest taboo, 335
inclusion, 429
income. *See also* poverty; wealth
  disparity in family incomes, 224
  distribution of, 222, 234*f*, 234–235, 235*f*, 462, 462*f*, 465
  educational level and, 33, 35*f*, 38, 264
  family and, 224, 336–337
  gross national income, 450, 451*f*
  household income, 234*f*, 234–235, 235*f*, 236
  increase in, divorce and, 345
  intergenerational mobility based on, 244, 244*f*
  lifetime earnings, 398, 398*f*
  national, per capita, 451*f*
  patterns in United States, 218, 219*t*
  role in social class, 234*f*, 234–235, 235*f*
  from teaching, 407, 407*f*
income inequality
  due to discrimination, 263, 263*f*
  due to globalization, 235
  gender gap, 313–314
  household income, 224
independent variables, 34, 35, 36*f*
index crimes, 206*t*, 206–207, 211
India, 52*f*, 70*f*, 335*f*, 451*f*, 515*f*
  call center subculture in, 78, *78*
  caste system in, 16, *16*
  child marriage rates, 62*f*
  Dongria Kondh people, *420*
  economy of, 501*f*
  emigration of physicians from, 361
  female infanticide in, 465
  greenhouse gas emissions in, 384
  growth of middle class in, 464
  Hinduism, 16, *16*, 60, 476*t*, 477
  immigrants from, 281–282

infant mortality rates in, 362*f*
microfinancing in, 527, *528*
movement out of poverty, 464
open displays of social inequality in, *457*
partitioning of, 273
religious clashes in, 479
television use in, 172
women in government, 518*f*
women's social movements in, 424
Indian Gambling Regulatory Act of 1988, 280
Indian reservations, *34*, 280
Indonesia, 443, 451*f*
industrialized nations
  child care in, 111
  consumer technologies in, 436–437
  as core nations, 455, 455*f*
  deindustrialization, 523–524, *524*
  economies of, 504
  greenhouse gas emissions in, 384
  labor unions in, 458
  loss of physicians to, 361
  social and economic inequality in, 229
  social mobility in, 462, 464, 468, 469
  social spending in, 466
  sociocultural evolution and, 141, 141*t*
  spirituality in, 485
  world consumption by, 381
Industrial Revolution, 141, 452
  economic systems and, 500, 501, 505
  resistance to technology during, 432
industrial societies, 141, 500. *See also* industrialized nations
industry, decline of, 145
inequality
  in computer technology, 437, 438*t*
  in health care, 361–362, 362*f*
  in income. *See* income inequality
  racial or ethnic. *See* racial and ethnic inequality
  social, 25, 26, 229, 400, *457*
  worldwide. *See* global inequality
infant mortality rates, 22, *22*, 361–362, 362*f*, 366
infants, 97, 99, 465
influence, 507
informal economy, 504, 505, 527
informal norms, 67, 68*t*, 72
informal social control, 184, 197, 201
in-groups, 125, 130, 256
innovation, 73, 76, 186*t*, 187
innovators, 13, 186*t*, 187, 188
insanity. *See* mental illness
institutional discrimination, 265–266, *266*, 268
  slavery and, 279
  social institutions, 129
  in voting, 267, *267*
  against women, 310, 320
institutionalization of health care, 370–371, 378

in-store health clinics, 372, *372*
instrumentality, 304–305
integrative function
  of education, 396–397
  of religion, *478*, 478–479, 483
intelligence tests, 92
intelligent design (ID), 492, 494
interactionist perspective, 18–19, 20*t*, 21
  on charismatic authority, 508
  on child care, 111
  cultural transmission theory, 187, 189
  on culture, 79*t*
  on deviance, 187, 189–190, 192*t*, 193
  dramaturgical approach in, 19
  on education, 402–403, 403*t*, 404, 493
  on environmental ills, 385
  on family, 331, 332*t*, 333
  on gay marriage, 351
  on gender stratification, 307, 307*t*, 308
  on gun control issue, 210
  on health, 362, 363*t*
  on language, 78
  on mass media, 164–166, *165*, 166*f*, 167*t*, 168, 175
  on microfinancing, 527–528
  on Milgram experiment, 196
  on minimum wage, 248
  on postindustrial societies, 143
  on racial and ethnic inequality, 270, 272, 272*t*, 276
  on religion, 479, *480*, 481, 482*t*, 483
  on religion in schools, 493
  on religious ritual, 486
  on self, 94–96, 97*t*
  on single-parent families, 341
  social disorganization theory, 189, *189*, 192*t*
  on social institutions, 129, 130, 130*t*
  on sports, 23–24
  on stratification, *226*, 226–227, 229*t*, 230
  on transnationals, 442
  on U.S. workforce, 523
  on women in combat, 302
interest groups, 158, 159–160
intergenerational mobility, 243–244, 244*f*, 245
  based on income, 244, 244*f*
  in industrialized nations, 462, 464
intergroup relations, 272–276, *273*, 274*f*
  amalgamation, 274, 276
  assimilation, 275, 276
  genocide, 196, 272–273, *273*, 287
  pluralism, 275–276, *520*
  segregation, 273–274, 275*t*, 276
  spectrum of, 273, 274*f*
international adoptions, 339
international crime rates, 208
International Criminal Police Organization (Interpol), 205–206
International Monetary Fund, 456
International Women Count Network, 233

Internet, 74, 165, 172
adolescent use of, 102
availability of education on, 406, 414
censorship of, 439
cyberattacks, 513
demographics of use, 166, 166f
education available on, 406, 414
electronic church on, 491
gender differences in use of, 164
lack of gatekeeping, 159
medical information on, 371
online courtship, 334
online gaming, 163, 164
online social movements, 425
use by transnationals, 441–442
websites and blogs, 161
Internet hosts, 437
Internet Movie Database (IMDb), 155, 156t
Interpol (International Criminal Police Organization), 205–206
interracial marriage, 68, 259, 274, *334*, 335
interviews, 41, 47
intragenerational mobility, 244, *245*
introvert, 178
intuitors, 178
invention, 73
Invisible Man (Ellison), 278
involuntary retirement, 109
Iran, 70f, 329, 434–435, 479, 518f
Iraq, 68, 196, 451f, 479, 510–511
Iraq War, 510
Ireland, 451f
college graduation rates, 395t
foreign aid per capita, 454f
gender inequality in house-work, 311f
religious participation in, 486f
Irish Americans, 203, 260, 288
Iron Chef (TV series), 161
iron law of oligarchy, 135, 137, 145
"Isabelle," 89–90
"Is Feminism Dead?" *(Time),* 316
Islam, 476, 476t, 477
"color blindness" of, 486
as ecclesia in Saudi Arabia, 487
fundamentalism in, 434–435, 485
Qur'an (Koran), 284, 476, *516*
Shia or Sunni Muslims, 479
isolation, impact of, 89–91, 93
"Isabelle," 89–90
primate studies of, 91, 93
Romanian orphans, *90,* 90–91, 93
on transnationals, 443
Israel, 303, 451f, 479
Issei, 283
Italian Americans, 203, 260, 288
Italy, 157f, 451f, 501f, 515f
antiabortion activism in, 318
environmentalism in, 388f
pattern of family life in, 344–345

J

Jamaica, 451f, 462f
Japan, 144f, 157f, 362f, 395t, 451f
American television in, 161
child care in, 111

"cram schools" in, 69, *402*
cuisine of, 73
economy of, 501f
education in, 399
environmentalism in, 388f
foreign aid per capita, 454f
greenhouse gas emissions in, 384
health practices in, *359*
marriage in, 118
temporary workforce, 525f
women-only subway cars, *304*
Japanese Americans, 271, 281f, 283
Jehovah's Witnesses, 488
Jewish Americans, 203, 260, 286–287, *287,* 292
Jews
Hebrew language, *287*
Holocaust, 196, 273, 287, 479
refused asylum by U.S., 289
Jim Crow laws, 279
job security, 238
Jordan, 451f, 518f
journalism, careers in, 2
Judaism, 476t, 477, *477, 485*
judgers, 178
Justice Department, U.S., 502

K

kava kava, 373
Kazakhstan, 451f
Kenya, 70f, 451f, 465
Kinsey Report, 51
kinship, 328, 337
Kitzmiller v. Dove Area School District (2005), 492
Kiwai Papuan people, 227
Koran (Qur'an), 284, 476, *516*
Korean Americans, 281f, 283
Korean War, 283
Korean Women's Association United (KWAU), 424
Kota rite, 105
Kraft Foods, 164
Ku Klux Klan, 261, 279
Kurds, 284
Kuwait, 518f
KWAU (Korean Women's Association United), 424
Kyoto Protocol (1997), 384–385
Kyrgyzstan, 451f

L

labeling
in classroom, 402
of homosexuality as mental illness, 363, 376
human sexuality and, 303, *348,* 348–349
of Latino children, 285
of poor people as deviants, 242
of slaves as diseased, 363
stigma of mental illness, 375, *375,* 377
labeling theory
of deviance, 190–191, 192, 192t, 193, 362–363
of health, 362–363, 363t, 364
of mental illness, 376
power to apply labels, 202–203

of racial and ethnic inequality, *271,* 271–272, 272t, 276
of sexual behavior, 348–349
labor force
in developing countries, 458
migrant laborers, 436, 441, 442f
participation of women in, 311–313, 312t, 312f
labor unions
decline in membership, 144f, 144–145
emergence of, 225
in industrialized nations, 458
labor relations arbitration, 117
scientific management and, 135
social policy on, 144f, 144–146, 147
Labour Party (G. Britain), 146
laissez-faire principle, 501, 503
language. *See also specific languages*
argot, 77–78
of Central and South America, 286
nonverbal communication, 19, 66, *66,* 71
role in culture, 64–66, 71
social policy: bilingualism, 80–82, 83
written and spoken, 64–65, *65*
Laos, 451f, 503
Las Vegas, suicide in, 8
latent functions, 16, 396, *396,* 404, 478
Latin America, 161, 317, 456, 480–481
Latinos/Hispanics, *286*
bilingualism and, 80–81
Central and South Americans, 285f, 286
contact hypothesis and, 272
Cuban Americans, 105, 285f, 286
cultural health practices, 367
differential justice for, 191
education of, 398f, 399
as ethnic group, 260
families of, 336, 337, 337f
health and illness among, 366–367
immigration protests by, 291
labeling of children, 285
lifetime earnings of, 398f
mental health care and, 377, 378
Mexican Americans. *See* Mexican Americans
population statistics, 284, 285, 285f
Puerto Ricans, 285, 285f, *286*
racial inequality and, 284–286, 285f, 292
single-parent families, 341
social mobility of, 246
tradition of male domination among, 306, 307
Latvia, 451f
law(s), 67, 187. *See also specific laws*
antitrust legislation, 502
attempts at marriage legislation, 347, 348
citizen right to privacy and, 438–439

definition of rape, 192
Jim Crow laws, 279
labor unions and, 145, 146
liberalization of divorce laws, 345
rational-legal authority of, 507
restrictive abortion laws, 318–319
social control by, 198–200, 199f, 201
social policy: minimum wage laws, 247t, 247–249
unpopular, 199
voter ID laws, 267, *267*
law enforcement, 121
LDS. *See* Mormon Church
LDs (learning disorders), 411
League of Arab States, 284
learning disorders (LDs), 411
learning style, 149, 150
Lebanon, 284, 451f, 479
Lenski, Gerhard
sociocultural evolution approach of, 140–144, 147
view of stratification, 229
lesbian relationships, 326, *349,* 349–350, 350f, 353
adoption and, 339
marriage, 348, 350–352, 352f, 353
Lesotho, 451f
LGBT persons, 350, 351, 352
liberal-labor coalition, 520
liberal views, education and, 398
liberation theology, 480–481, 483
Liberia, 451f
Libya, 451f
life chances, *242,* 242–243, 250
life course, 105–106, *106*
role transitions throughout, 107–110
socialization process. *See* socialization
life course approach, 105
life expectancy, 361
Lithuania, 451f
living wage, 249, 250
LMFAO, *172*
lobbying groups, *520*
looking-glass self, 94, 97t, 98
Los Angeles riots (1992), 170
Los Angeles Times, 154
love relationship, 335, 343
lower class, 222
discrimination against, 227
families of, 336
lower-middle class, 222
Luddites, 432, 433
Lutheran Church, 487, 488
Luxembourg, 453
lynching campaigns, 279

M

Macedonia, 451f
machismo, 337
macro-level analysis, 34
macrosociology, 13, 169
macro view
of audience, 169, 170
of ecological modernization, 381
of religion, 478–482
of sociocultural evolution, 144
Madagascar, 326, 451f

Magnolia Project, 22, *22*
Maid in Manhattan (film), 243
malaria, 173, 373
Malawi, 62f, 451f
Malaysia, 52f, 451f, 458f
Malcolm X, 120
Mali, 62f, 451f
malnourishment, 454
manifest functions, 16, 396, 404, 477–478
man-made disasters
Deepwater Horizon oil spill (2010), 384
Exxon *Valdez* oil spill (1989), *50,* 383–384
marijuana, 191, *191,* 199, 199f
marital rape, 192, 349
market research, 31
marriage, 333–343. *See also* divorce; family(ies)
age at first marriage, 334, 335f
among racial or ethnic groups, 335
arranged marriages, 334, 335
attempts at marriage legislation, 347, 348
childless, 347–348, 353
between children and adults, 61, 62f
couples living apart, 339, *339,* 341
couples therapy, 325
courtship, 334, 335, 335f
effect of global recession of 2008 on, 5
interracial, 68, 259, 274, *334,* 335
Jewish-Gentile, 287
love relationship and, 335, 343
mate selection, 335, 343
in minority groups, 256
social policy: gay marriage, 350–352, 352f, 353
statistical trends in, 345, 345f
Martineau, Harriet, 8–9, *9*
Marx, Karl, 10–11, *11f*
development of sociology and, 430
on representative democracy, 518, 519
view of stratification, 224–225, *225,* 230
Marxist theory, *17,* 17–18
class theory of racism, 270–271
dominant ideology, 71
on future of capitalism, 480
of labor unions, 145
of relative deprivation, 421
on religion and inequality, 481–482
of social change, 430
masculinity, 301, 303
Massachusetts, 351
mass media, 151–179
as agent of socialization, *102,* 102–103, 104, *154,* 154–155
audience for, 168–170
conflict perspective on, 158–162, 168, 174
consumption promoted by, *155,* 156–158, 157f, 164
cultural issues, *161,* 161–162
demographics of media penetration, 171f, 171–172

preoperational stage of development, 97

preparatory stage of self, 94, 95t

preretirement, 108

Presbyterian Church, 478

preschool programs, 110

preservation of order, 128

prestige, occupational, 232, 233t, 236, 243

prestige symbols, 183

primary groups, 124, 125t, 130

primate studies of isolation, 91, 93

print media, 153

PRISM operation (NSA), 173, 176

prisons
  Abu Ghraib, 196, 510–511
  in Finland v. U.S., *184*
  mock prison experiment, 511
  prison gangs, 17
  as total institution, 106–107

privacy
  as global issue, 438–439, 444
  individual, ethics of, 47
  media monitoring and, 159
  personal, invasion of, 68
  social policy on right to, 173–176

problem solving, 531, 532

pro-choice groups, 316

product placement, *155,* 156

profane realm, 476, 483, 492

professional crime, 203

profitability of crime, 188

profiteering in microfinancing, 527, 528

Project Head Start, 397

proletariat, 10, 225, *225,* 228, 305

pro-life groups, 316, 317

property crimes, 206, 207, 208

prostitution (sex work), 202, 349

protective function of family, 329

protest(s)
  civil disobedience, 279
  by deaf students, *423*
  by illegal immigrants, 291
  against institutional discrimination, 266
  for minimum wage, 249
  by Native Americans, *224*

Protestant Ethic and the Spirit of Capitalism, The (Weber), 11f, 479–480

Protestant Reformation, 480, 488

psychological approaches to self, 96–97, 97t, 98

psychology, 4, 5

public health advocates, 211

public health education, 449

public opinion
  about war, 510
  on environmentalism, 386–387, 387f, 388
  on minimum wage, 248–249
  opinion polls, 36–37

public sociology. *See* applied sociology

public speaking, 416, 417

Puerto Ricans, 285, 285f, *286*

Puerto Rico, 285, 451f

pure (basic) sociology, 24, 26

Puritans, 185

Pygmalion in the Classroom (Rosenthal & Jacobson), 402

Q

Quakers, 271

qualitative research, 41–42

quantitative research, 41, 42

Québec, 82

queer theory, 18, 21
  on heterosexual norm, 67
  media presentation of homosexuality, 160
  research methodology of, 46, 47
  of sports, 23–24
  view of gay marriage, 351

questionnaires, 41, 47

questions, careful wording of, 41, 46

quinceañera, 105

quota systems, 313, 463, 518

Qur'an (Koran), 284, 476, *516*

R

race. *See also* African Americans; racial and ethnic inequality
  as ascribed status, 119, 120
  campus subcultures and, 410, 410f
  cultural assumptions regarding, 99
  employment opportunity and, 127
  environmental hazards and, 382
  experience of retirement and, 109
  fear of diversity, 289
  hate crimes based on, 205, 205f
  health and, 366–367, 369
  ignored by television, 160
  lifetime earnings and, 398, 398f
  in matrix of domination, 306f, 306–307
  multiple identities, 259
  people of Central and South America, 286
  poverty and, 241, 241t
  racial discrimination in hiring, 263, 265
  role in social mobility, 245–246
  social class as proxy for, 262
  social construction of, 258–259, 259f, 268
  social institutions and, 129
  social position and, 222
  sociological imagination and, 25, 26
  transracial adoption, 340
  in U.S. politics, 516, *516,* 522
  wealth and, 235, 236

racial and ethnic inequality, 254–295. *See also* ethnicity; race; *specific ethnicities*
  conflict perspective on, 270–271, 276, 399
  functionalist perspective on, 270, 276
  interactionist perspective on, 270, 272, 276
  labeling perspective on, *271,* 271–272, 276
  minority groups, 256, 257t
  prejudice and discrimination, 260–268
  social policy: global immigration, 288–291, 290f

spectrum of intergroup relations. *See* intergroup relations
  in United States, 259f, 277–292, 278f
  White privilege, 264–265, *265*

racial differences
  in families, 336–337, 337f
  in perceptions, 170
  in voter turnout, 516

racial formation, 258, 261

racial groups, 69, 70f, 256, 258, 335

racial myths, 270

racial neutrality principle, 262, 268

racial profiling, 271–272, 276
  of African Americans, 190–191, 271, *271*
  of Arab Americans, 272, 284
  of illegal immigrants to U.S., 290

racism, 261. *See also* discrimination; prejudice
  color-blind, 261–262, *262,* 268
  exploitation theory of, 270–271
  in medical establishment, 366–367
  in Mormon Church, 489

rain forest, destruction of, 380–381

random sample, 36

rape, 192, 207, 349

rational-legal authority, 507, 513

reading strategies, 85, 86

rebellion, 186t, 187

Recognition of Customary Marriages Act of 1998, 348

recruitment, 350, 422

Red Crescent, 512

Red Cross, 512

reference groups, 125–126, *126,* 130

relationship marketing, 164–165, 165f

relative deprivation approach, 421–422, 426

relative poverty, 239

reliability, ensuring, 37, 39

religion, 473–497. *See also* specific religions and churches
  as agent of socialization, 103–104
  of Arab Americans, 284, 285f
  case study of, 495
  components of, 484–487, 487t, 494
  conflict perspective on, 481–482, 483
  culture lag and, 432
  denominations, 487–488, 489, 490, 494
  Durkheim on, 475–476, 483, 487
  ecclesiae, 487, 490, 494
  electronic church, 491
  feminist perspective on, 482, 483
  forms of organization, 487–491, 491t
  functionalist perspective on, *478,* 478–479, 483
  fundamentalist. *See* fundamentalism, religious
  hate crimes based on, 205, 205f
  homeschooling and, 411

impact on society, 475–476
  integrative function of, *478,* 478–479, 483
  interactionist perspective on, 479, *480,* 481, 483
  liberation theology, 480–481, 483
  marketing techniques of, 74
  new religious movements (cults), 488, 490, 494
  norms of religious faiths, 476, 485–486
  in schools, 491–493, *493,* 494
  sects, 488, 491t, 494
  secularization process, 474
  social change and, 479–481
  social control and, 481–482
  as social institution, 127
  social policy: religion in schools, 491–493, *493*
  social support function of, 479, *480,* 481
  sociological imagination and, 26
  sociological perspectives on, 477–482, 482t, 483
  sociological research on, 9, 11
  as source of conflict, 70
  Weberian thesis of, 479–480, *480,* 483
  world religions, 476t, 476–477, 483

religious beliefs, 484–485, 487t, 494

religious experience, 486–487, 487t, 494

religious fundamentalism. *See* fundamentalism, religious

religious ritual, *485,* 485–486, 486f, 487t, 494

remarriage, 345, 345f

remittances, 282, 289

reorientation phase of retirement, 109

reparations, 283

replacement of personnel, 128

representative democracy, 509–510

reproductive function of family, 329

Republican Party, 169

research designs, 31, 40–48. *See also* sociological research; *specific experiments/studies*
  developments in methodology, 45–46
  elements of, 40–45
  ethnography, 42, *42,* 45t, 47, 96
  experiments, 43, 45t
  online research, 46–48
  surveys, 40–42, 41t, 45t
  use of existing sources, 43, 43t, 45, 45t

researcher bias, 50

researcher role, 196

research methodology, 45–46

reshoring, 526

resistance to social change, 431–432, 433

resistance to technology, 80, 432, 433

resocialization, 106–107, 112, 113, 341–342

resource allocation, 128
  control over resources, 228

differential access to, 224
  surplus resources, inequality and, 229

resource mobilization approach, 422, *423,* 425t, 426

retirement, 108–110, 112
  NORCs, 109–110
  phases of, 108–109, *109*

retreatism, 186t, 187

"reverse discrimination," 412

review of literature, 33f, 33–34, *34,* 35f, 38

reward(s)
  differential, in stratified systems, 227–228
  for instrumental skills, 305, *305*
  as sanction, 67
  social inequality and, 229

riots, 170, 275

rites of passage
  Kota rite, 105
  retirement, 108–110
  in socialization process, 103–104, 105

ritualism, 186t, 187

Roe v. Wade (1973), 316, 317

role conflict, 121, 123

role exit, 121–122, *122,* 123

role-playing, 95

role strain, 121, 123

role taking, 95

role transitions, 107–110
  adjusting to retirement, 108–110
  sandwich generation, *107,* 108, 112

Rolling Stone (magazine), 156t

Roman Catholic Church, *154,* 432, 488
  fundamentalism in, 485
  hierarchy of authority in, 133
  immigrants in, 282, 478, *478*
  liberation theology and, 480–481
  women as nonordained pastors, 482

Romania, 451f

Romanian orphans, neglect of, *90,* 90–91, 93

romantic relationships, 107, 127

Roma people ("Gypsies"), 273, *273*

Roommate.com, 264

Royal Dutch Shell, 458f

rules and regulations
  in bureaucracies, 133, 134t, 406
  personnel policies, 134

rum springa, 101, *101*

rural areas, poverty in, 240

Russia, 70f, 335f, 451f
  economy of, 501f
  greenhouse gas emissions in, 384
  growth of middle class in, 464
  religious participation in, 486f

Russian immigrants, 203

Russian language, 65

Rwanda, 163, 451f, 503, 518, 518f

S

sabotage, 432

sacred realm, 475–476, 483, 492

Sami people, 65

sample selection, 36–37, 39
sanctions, 195
    for inappropriate behavior, 185
    for violation of social norms,
        67–68, 68*t*, 72, 195,
        485–486
sandwich generation, *107,*
    108, 112
sa pamilya, 282
Sapir-Whorf hypothesis, 65, 71
Saudi Arabia, 451*f*, 465, *485,*
    486, 487
Scalpel and the Silver Bear, The
    (Alvord & Van Pelt), 371
scheduled castes, 221
school(s). *See also* education
    as agent of socialization,
        100, 104
    "apartheid schools," 399
    bureaucratization of, 399,
        405–406, *406,* 413–414
    "cram schools," 69, *402*
    as formal organizations,
        405–414
    high schools. *See* high
        school(s)
    homeschooling, 410–411, 414
    preschool programs, 110
    religion in, 491–493, *493,* 494
    roles of teachers in, 407, 407*f,*
        409, 414
    segregation in, 399
    shootings in. *See* shootings
    sociological perspectives of,
        100, 408, 493
    student subcultures in,
        409–410, 410*f, 410,* 414
    teacher-expectancy effect in,
        402–403, 404
    tracking, 400
    unequal public financing
        of, 129
    violence in, 407, 408
school choice programs, 406, 414
scientific management
    approach, 135
scientific method, 31, 32–39
    case study of, 54
    data collection and analysis,
        36–37, 38
    defining problem in, 33, 38
    developing conclusions in,
        37–38
    effective research using, 32–33
    formulating hypotheses, 34–36,
        36, 38, 39
    review of literature, 33–34, *34,*
        35*f,* 38
    summary of, 38, 39
    testing hypotheses, 398
SCLC (Southern Christian
    Leadership
    Conference), 279
SEC (Securities and Exchange
    Commission), 132
secession, 273
secondary analysis, 43, 43*t,* 45,
    45*t,* 47
secondary groups, 125, 125*t,*
    125, 130
Second Sex, The (Beauvoir),
    315–316
"second shift," 314–315, 320
sects, religious, 488, 491*t,* 494
secularization, 474

Securities and Exchange
    Commission (SEC), 132
segmented audience, 169
segregation, 266, *266,* 273–274,
    274*f,* 275*t,* 276
segregation index, 274, 275*t*
self, 93–98
    Freud's theory of, 97
    looking-glass self, 94, 97*t,* 98
    Mead's stages of, 94–95,
        95*t,* 98
    Mead's theory of, 95, 97*t,* 98
    presentation of, 96, *96*
    psychological approaches to,
        96–97, 97*t,* 98
    sociological approaches to,
        94–96, 98
self-evaluation
    critical thinking, 295
    decision making, 497
    goal setting, 56
    memory improvement, 115
    note-taking, 215
    personality type, 179
    problem solving, 532
    public speaking, 417
    reading habits, 86
    receptive learning style, 150
    role of reference groups in, 126
    stress management, 392
    study skills, 447, 472
    test-taking, 356
    time management, 253
    writing strategically, 323
"self-help," 370
self-identity
    multiracial, 259, 261
    role exit and, 122
    role of perceptions in, 94
self-image, 89, 132
self-injury, 45
self-interest, 139, 271
semiperiphery nations, 455, 455*f*
Senate, U.S., 52, 516
Seneca Falls Convention
    (1848), 315
Senegal, 451*f*
sensorimotor stage of develop-
    ment, 97
sensors, 178
September 11, 2001 attacks
    antiterrorist actions following,
        512–513
    awareness of identity theft fol-
        lowing, 204
    bureaucratic failure to
        prevent, 133
    culture war and, 70
    economic decline following, 25
    immigration procedures fol-
        lowing, 291
    increased security
        following, 198
    Internet gatekeeping and, 159
    national security concerns fol-
        lowing, 206
    racial profiling following, 272
    role of mass media follow-
        ing, 154
    USA Patriot Act of 2001 and,
        175
Serbia, 451*f*
serial monogamy, 327
service industries, 281, 301
SES (socioeconomic status), 234

settlement house movement, *12,*
    12–13
Seventh-Day Adventists, 488
sex-education classes, 397, *397*
sexism, 309–310, 320
    in education, 401
    in medicine, 368
    in Mormon Church, 489
sex trafficking, 349
sexual behavior
    labeling theory of, 348–349
    prostitution, 349
    regulation of, as purpose of
        family, 329–330
    social acceptance of, 353
    social norms for, 303
sexual harassment, 121, 302
Sexual Politics (Millett), 315–316
sex work (prostitution), 349
Shakers, 128, 482
Shiite Muslims, 479
shootings
    Aurora, Colo. theater shootings
        (2012), 208
    Columbine High School
        shootings (1999), 125,
        159, 208
    Newtown, Conn. shootings
        (2012), 183, 209,
        374–375
    Virginia Tech shootings (2007),
        124, 159, 197
Shopping Our Way to Safety
    (Szasz), 387
Shoshit, Setkari, Kashtakari,
    Kamgar, Mukti Sangharsh
    (SSKKMS), 424
Shout Your Love from the Middle
    of a Cabbage Patch
    Day, 118
sickle-cell anemia, 366, 373
sick role, 359–360
Sierra Leone, 62*f,* 451*f*
Silent Warriors, *66*
Singapore, 82, *185,* 451*f*
single fathers, 341
singlehood, 347, 353
single mothers, 331, 339, 341, 343
single-parent families, 240, 326,
    337*f,* 341, 343
Sinopec, 458*f*
skin color, 258, 265, 271
Skype, 165
slave reparations, 279
slavery, 270
    economic motivation for, 271
    history of, 279
    slaves labeled as diseased, 363
    as stratification system, 220,
        220*t,* 230
    as transnational crime, 205
Slovakia, 451*f*
Slovenia, 451*f*
"slugging," 18
small-group behavior, 134,
    135–136
SNAP (Supplemental Nutrition
    Assistance Program), 239
snowball (convenience) sample, 36
social capital, 13, 164
social change, 418–444
    attitudinal shifts during, 262
    clinical sociology and, 24
    conflict perspective on,
        429–430, *430,* 433

costs of, 242
education as agent of, 397–398,
    398*f,* 404
evolutionary theory of, 429, 433
functionalist perspective on,
    429, 433
global. *See* global social
    change
moving beyond models of,
    434–435
religion and, 479–481
resistance to, 431–432, 433
social movements, 419–427
theories of, 428–430, 430*t*
in United States, 427–428, 428*t*
social characteristics of audi-
    ence, 170
social class, 221–224
    class warfare, 223–224, *224*
    differences in, 336, 400
    health and, 365–366, 367*f,* 369
    in matrix of domination, 306*f,*
        306–307
    measuring objectively, 232,
        233*t,* 236
    middle class, 222–223, *223*
    multiple measures of, 231,
        233–234
    of parents, 330–331
    as proxy for race, 262
    role of income and wealth,
        234*f,* 234–235, 235*f*
    stratification by, 231–236
    struggle between, 17–18
    upper and lower classes,
        222, *222*
    of women, 232–233, 236
    working class, 223
social construction
    of deviance, 191, 192*t*
    of gender, 297–308
    of health and illness, 359, 364
    of race, 258–259, 259*f,* 268
social control, 184, 194–201
    agents of. *See* agents of social
        control
    conformity and obedience,
        195–197, *196,*
        200–201, 399
    education and, 397, *397*
    formal and informal, 184,
        197–198, 198*f*
    in *Gemeinschaft,* 138–139
    of gender roles, 304
    in *Gesellschaft,* 139
    of health or illness, 359
    laws, 198–200, 199*f,* 201
    medicine as, 360–361
    Milgram experiment in, 195–
        197, *196,* 200–201
    norms and, 194–198, 200, 397
    power to exercise, 199
    religion and, 481–482
    in Singapore, *185*
    social policy: gun control,
        208–211, *209*
social disorganization theory, 189,
    189, 192*t*
social epidemiology, 365,
    366*f,* 369
social indicators of moderniza-
    tion, 460
social inequality
    in Argentina, *430*
    in Brazil, 463, *463*

credentialism and, 400
in industrialized nations, 229
open displays of, *457*
sociological imagination and,
    25, 26
social institutions, 127–129, 130*t*
    conflict perspective on,
        128–129, 130
    functionalist perspective on,
        128, 130, 130*t*
    interactionist perspective on,
        129, 130, 130*t*
social interaction(s), 117–123
    groups. *See* groups
    as key to development of self,
        117–123
    social reality and, 118–119
    social structure and. *See* social
        structure
    study of. *See* interactionist
        perspective
socialism, 503–504, 504*t*
social isolation, 8
socialization
    agents of. *See* agents of
        socialization
    anticipatory, 106–107, 112
    of children, 67, 95, 100,
        340, 351
    to dominant standards, 195
    to gender roles, 298, 299, 300*t,*
        308, 397
    impact of isolation on,
        89–91, 93
    influence of heredity on,
        91–92, 93
    nature v. nurture debate, 89
    parenthood and, 338
    as purpose of family, 329
    role of, 88–93
    role of primary groups in, 124
    role transitions and, 107–110
    self and, 93–98
    to social norms, 67
    social policy: child care, *110,*
        110–112
    as source of conformity, 200
    through formal education, 395*f,*
        395–396
    throughout life course,
        105–112
social meaning, 119, 261
social media
    case study of, 177
    religion on, 479
    use by Occupy Wall Street, 238
    use in research, 152
social mobility, 243–246, 250
    in developing nations, 464,
        464, 468, 469
    gender differences in, 246, *246,*
        464–465, 468–469
    impact of education on, 245
    importance to poor, 243
    in industrialized nations, 462,
        464, 468, 469
    occupational mobility,
        244–245, *245*
    open v. closed stratification
        systems, 243
    role of race and ethnicity,
        245–246
    traditional v. new, 423
    types of, 233*t,* 243–244, 244*f*
    in United States, 244–246, *245*

Applications of Major Theoretical Approaches

Sociology and Your Life provides comprehensive coverage of the major sociological perspectives. This summary table includes a sample of the topics in the text that have been explored using the major approaches. "M" indicates the module and the numbers in parentheses indicate the pertinent chapters.

FUNCTIONALIST PERSPECTIVE

- M2 Defined and explained (1)
- M34 Adoption (11)
- M22 Anomie theory of deviance (7)
- M10 Bilingualism (3)
- M41 Bureaucratization of schools (13)
- M2 Cow worship in India (1)
- M8 M40 Culture (3, 13)
- M25 Davis and Moore's view of stratification (8)
- M8 Dominant ideology (3)
- M22 Durkheim's view of deviance (7)
- M29 Dysfunctions of racism (9)
- M7 Ethnocentrism (3)
- M33 Family (11)
- M17 Formal organizations (5)
- M29 Functions of racism (9)
- M27 Gans's functions of poverty (8)
- M35 Gay marriage (11)
- M31 Gender stratification (10)
- M30 Global immigration (9)
- M36 Health and illness (12)
- M39 Human ecology (12)
- M16 In-groups and out-groups (5)
- M47 Integrative function of religion (16)
- M21 Internet privacy (6)
- M19 Media and social norms (6)
- M19 Media and socialization (6)
- M19 Media and status conferral (6)
- M21 Media concentration (6)
- M19 Media promotion of consumption (6)
- M45 Modernization theory (15)
- M45 Multinational corporations (15)
- M19 Narcotizing effect of the media (6)
- M28 Racial prejudice and discrimination (9)

- M47 Religion as a source of social support (16)
- M40 M43 Social change (13, 14)
- M23 M40 Social control (7, 13)
- M16 Social institutions (5)
- M47 Socialization function of religion (16)
- M13 M40 Socialization in schools (4, 13)
- M3 Sports (1)
- M10 Subcultures (3)
- M44 Transnationals (14)

CONFLICT PERSPECTIVE

- M2 Defined and explained (1)
- M32 Abortion (10)
- M36 Access to health care (12)
- M43 Access to technology (14)
- M10 Bilingualism (3)
- M41 Bureaucratization of schools (13)
- M49 Capitalism (17)
- M46 Corporate welfare (15)
- M40 Correspondence principle (13)
- M40 Credentialism (13)
- M8 Culture (3)
- M14 Day care funding (4)
- M22 Deviance (7)
- M15 Disability as a master status (5)
- M8 M19 M25 Dominant ideology (3, 6, 8)
- M52 Downsizing (17)
- M51 Elite model of the U.S. power structure (17)
- M39 Environmental issues (12)
- M39 Environmentalism (12)
- M29 Exploitation theory of discrimination (9)
- M33 Family (11)
- M35 Gay marriage (11)
- M40 Gender equity in education (13)
- M31 Gender stratification (10)
- M30 Global immigration (9)
- M24 Gun control (7)
- M40 Hidden curriculum (13)
- M17 Iron Law of Oligarchy (5)
- M18 Labor Unions (5)
- M26 Marx's view of stratification (8)
- M31 Matrix of domination (10)
- M21 Media concentration (6)
- M19 Media gatekeeping (6)

- M19 Media stereotypes (6)
- M36 Medicalization of society (12)
- M52 Microfinancing (17)
- M27 Minimum wage laws (8)
- M30 Model minority (9)
- M45 Multinational corporations (15)
- M27 Poverty (8)
- M21 Privacy and technology (6)
- M37 Racism and health (12)
- M47 Religion and social control (16)
- M41 School violence (13)
- M43 Social change (14)
- M23 Social control (7)
- M16 Social institutions (5)
- M13 Socialization in schools (4)
- M3 Sports (1)
- M10 Subcultures (3)
- M40 Tracking (13)
- M44 Transnationals (14)
- M24 Victimless crimes (7)
- M24 White-collar crime (7)
- M31 Women in combat (10)
- M45 World systems analysis (15)

INTERACTIONIST PERSPECTIVE

- M2 Defined and explained (1)
- M34 Adoption (11)
- M50 Charismatic authority (17)
- M2 Commuter behavior (1)
- M25 Conspicuous consumption (8)
- M29 Contact hypothesis (9)
- M8 Culture (3)
- M14 Day care funding (4)
- M22 Differential association (7)
- M12 M50 Dramaturgical approach (4, 17)
- M19 Electronic communication (6)
- M33 Family relationships (11)
- M35 Gay marriage (11)
- M31 Gender stratification (10)
- M36 Health and illness (12)
- M17 Human relations approach (5)
- M51 Microfinancing (17)
- M27 Minimum wage laws (8)
- M23 Obedience (7)
- M12 Presentation of the self (4)
- M22 Routine activities theory (7)
- M22 Social disorganization theory (7)
- M16 Social institutions (5)
- M3 Sports (1)
- M15 Tattoos and social reality (5)

- M40 Teacher-expectancy effect (13)
- M44 Transnationals (14)
- M43 Vested interests in NASA's Constellation Project (14)
- M31 Women in combat (10)

FEMINIST PERSPECTIVE

- M2 Defined and explained (1)
- M14 Day care funding (4)
- M22 Deviance (7)
- M8 Dominant ideology (3)
- M33 Family (11)
- M40 Gender gap in education (13)
- M31 Gender stratification (10)
- M8 Language (3)
- M31 Matrix of domination (10)
- M19 Media stereotypes (6)
- M52 Microfinancing (17)
- M20 Pornography (6)
- M22 Rape (7)
- M47 Religion and socialization (16)
- M5 Research methodology (2)
- M3 Sports (1)
- M24 Victimless crimes (7)
- M32 Women's movement (10)

LABELING THEORY

- M22 Defined and explained (7)
- M15 Disabilities and labeling (5)
- M36 Health and illness (12)
- M35 Human sexuality (11)
- M38 Mental Illness (12)
- M29 Profiling at airports (9)
- M22 Racial profiling (7)
- M22 Societal reaction approach (7)
- M40 Teacher-expectancy effect (13)
- M24 Victimless crimes (7)

QUEER THEORY

- M2 Defined and explained (1)
- M35 Gay marriage (11)
- M19 Homosexuality in the mass media (6)
- M35 LGBT households (11)
- M5 Research methodology (2)
- M3 Sports (1)